# TREDGOLD'S
# MENTAL RETARDATION

*Tredgold's*

# *Mental Retardation*

## TWELFTH EDITION

Edited by

## MICHAEL CRAFT

M.D., F.R.C.P., F.R.C.PSYCH.,
M.R.A.N.Z.C.P., D.P.M.

*Consultant Psychiatrist,*
*Bryn-y-Neuadd Hospital,*
*Llanfairfechan, Wales*

with

eighteen contributors

Foreword by

## KENNETH RAWNSLEY

M.B., CH.B.,
F.R.C.P., F.R.C.PSYCH., D.P.M.

*Professor of Psychological Medicine,*
*Welsh National School of Medicine, Cardiff*

LONDON
## BAILLIÈRE TINDALL

A Baillière Tindall book published by
Cassell Ltd,
35 Red Lion Square, London WC1R 4SG

and at Sydney, Auckland, Toronto, Johannesburg

an affiliate of
Macmillan Publishing Co. Inc.
New York

First edition (A. F. Tredgold) 1908
Eighth edition 1952
Ninth edition (R. F. Tredgold and K. Soddy) 1956
Eleventh edition 1970
Twelfth edition (M. J. Craft) 1979

ISBN 0 7020 0684 X

Set in monotype Imprint by Santype International Ltd., Salisbury, Wilts
Reproduced, printed and bound in Great Britain by
Fakenham Press Limited, Fakenham, Norfolk

**British Library Cataloguing in Publication Data**

Tredgold's mental retardation.   12th ed.
  1. Mental deficiency
  I. Tredgold, Alfred Frank   II. Craft, Michael
  III. Mental retardation
  616.8′588    RC570

ISBN 0–7020–0684–X

# LIST
# OF CONTRIBUTORS

ROBERT ANDREWS, Ph.D., has a background as a teacher, guidance officer and researcher. Since 1962 he has engaged in research and teaching at the University of Queensland, Australia and for the last 15 years at the Schonell Educational Research Centre, where he is presently Acting Director and Reader in Special Education. One of his major research interests is in the areas of service delivery for handicapped children, adolescents and adults. He is a member of the National Advisory Council for the Handicapped and the Australian Schools Commission, and is Deputy Chairman of the Queensland Advisory Council for Special Education.

ROBYN BENCE, B.S.T. (Hons.), Postgrad. Dip. Spec. Ed., has been Principal of the Autistic Children's Centre in Brisbane, Australia, for the past six years. She graduated with a degree in Speech Therapy and then obtained a Diploma in Special Education. Mrs Bence is particularly interested in the diagnosis and treatment of the very young autistic child.

PAUL BERRY, Ph.D., has specialized in psychological and educational research in the mildly, moderately, severely and profoundly intellectually handicapped. He began his career as a teacher in 1970 and in 1975 he was appointed a research fellow at the Hester Adrian Research Centre, Manchester University, where his main concern was language and communication research among handicapped children. Since that time he has been a Senior Lecturer in Special Education at the Schonell Educational Research Centre, University of Queensland, Australia, where one of his principal interests is in the evaluation of services for all handicapped people.

GORDON BLAND, B.Sc. (Econ.), Ph.D., entered teaching after war service. After experimenting with classes of mentally handicapped children in normal schools, he became Head of Brockhall Hospital School, near Blackburn, Lancs, in 1959. He graduated in 1964 in sociology at London University. He obtained his doctorate from the University of Bath in 1970 with a thesis on the Sociology of Education. He has developed Further Education for mentally handicapped adults in hospital and in the community.

ANN CRAFT, B.Sc. (Econ.), C.Q.S.W., is a graduate of the University College of Swansea. She obtained her social work qualification in 1973. From 1973–75 she carried out research into mentally abnormal offenders and their fate. She and her husband, Michael, were then awarded a two-year research grant to study marriage among the mentally and multiply handicapped, and to investigate the field of health and sex education for the handicapped.

MICHAEL CRAFT, M.D., F.R.C.P., F.R.C. Psych., M.R.A.N.Z.C.P., D.P.M., graduated in neurology at Edinburgh University, and studied psychiatry at the Maudsley Hospital, London. He has worked in mental handicap throughout Wales for some years.

He evolved guardianship systems for long-stay patients with local authority social service departments, and a forensic psychiatric service with probation officers. He has been visiting professor in several Universities in North America, and has recently been teaching at the Royal Brisbane Hospital, Australia.

CLIFF CUNNINGHAM, B.Sc., taught for six years, specializing in educational technology and slow-learning children. He graduated in psychology at London University and began researching into mental handicap at the Hester Adrian Research Centre, Manchester University, in 1969. His particular areas of interest are education, parent training and counselling, and the early development and stimulation of handicapped children.

LARRY O. GOSTIN, B.A., J.D., has a juris-doctorate from Duke University, Durham, North Carolina. He was called to the New York Bar in 1974 and to the Bar of the Council of Europe in 1977. In 1974–75 he was a Fulbright Fellow at Oxford University and in 1978–79 Visiting Professor of Law, McMaster University, Hamilton, Ontario. He is currently Legal Director of MIND (The National Association for Mental Health of Great Britain) and is the Western European and United Kingdom editor of the *International Journal of Law and Psychiatry*. He has written widely and is the author of the definitive work on the Mental Health Act of England and Wales (*A Human Condition*, 2 vols.).

CYRIL GREENLAND, M.Sc., is Professor, School of Social Work, and an Associate in the Faculty of Medicine, Department of Psychiatry, McMaster University, Hamilton, Ontario. He is a graduate of the London School of Economics, London University, and of the University of Wales. After completing the Mental Health course in 1948 Professor Greenland was on the social staff of the Crichton Royal Hospital, Dumfries, Scotland for ten years. He emigrated to Canada in 1959 and served as Director of Social Work, Ontario Hospital, Whitby; Social Work Advisor, Ministry of Health, Ontario; and

Research Scientist, Clarke Institute of Psychiatry; he was appointed to his present post in 1970.

PETER HARPER, D.M., F.R.C.P., trained in medicine at Oxford University and at St. Thomas's Hospital, London. After developing his interest in genetics at Oxford, he trained in medical genetics in Liverpool and at the Johns Hopkins School of Medicine, Baltimore, before returning to Britain to develop medical genetics at the Welsh National School of Medicine, Cardiff, where he is currently Reader and Consultant in Medical Genetics. His main research interests are in inherited neurological disorders, particularly muscular dystrophies and Huntington's chorea, and in preventive aspects of inherited metabolic disease.

PETER MITTLER, M.A., Ph.D., M.Ed., is Director of the Hester Adrian Research Centre for the study of learning processes in the mentally handicapped, and Professor of Special Education, Manchester University. Since 1975 he has been Chairman of the National Development Group for the Mentally Handicapped, which advises the Secretary of State for Social Services on mental handicap policy and its implementation. He has edited *Psychological Assessment of Mental and Physical Handicaps; Assessment for Learning in the Mentally Handicapped; Research to Practice in Mental Retardation* (3 vols.,); *Advances in Mental Handicap Research*, with James Hogg. His particular interests include language acquisition and teaching, and evaluation of service delivery assessments.

DESMOND POND, M.D., F.R.C.P., F.R.C. Psych., D.P.M., did most of his work on epilepsy and brain-damaged children while Senior Lecturer in the EEG Department of the Institute of Psychiatry and Consultant to the Children's Department at the Maudsley Hospital, London. In the 1950s, years before such things became generally accepted, he and Dr (now Professor Sir Denis) Hill ran a family ward for epileptic patients with psychological difficulties, and he collaborated closely with the late Mr Murray Falconer in the early studies of temporal lobectomy. Professor Pond holds the Chair of Psychiatry at the London Hospital and is currently President of the Royal College of Psychiatrists.

JOHN RENDLE-SHORT, M.A., M.D., F.R.C.P., F.R.A.C.P., is currently Professor of Child Health in the University of Queensland, Australia. He studied medicine in the United Kingdom and has made many contributions to paediatrics, including writing a *Synopsis of Children's Diseases* (5th Edition) and a source book for para-medical students, *The Child* (2nd Edition). He pioneered the study of infantile autism in Australia and has written several articles on the subject.

G. ALLAN ROEHER received his training in the social sciences and rehabilitation at the University of British Columbia (B.A., B.S.W.) and at New York University (M.A., Ph.D.). He developed the National Institute on Mental Retardation (Canada) and was its Director until 1976. He is currently Executive Vice-President of the Canadian Association for the Mentally Retarded, which sponsors the Institute. Dr Roeher's work has been focussed on long-range planning and innovative programme development. Internationally, he serves as a Vice-President of the International League of Societies for the Mentally Handicapped and is Vice-President (Administrative) of the American Association on Mental Deficiency. He is also the Chief Consultant to the Caribbean Institute on Mental Retardation which serves some 20 nations in the area.

ALAN RUNDLE, F.R.F.P.S., M.R.C.P., graduated in biochemistry in Sir Hans Krebs's department at Sheffield University, and, after three years spent in research into endocrine involvement in schizophrenia in Bristol, moved to Caterham where he has spent 20 years investigating mental retardation. His early interest in endocrinology still remains, as is shown in a number of publications, but during the last two decades genetics in general and cytogenetics in particular has absorbed much of his energy, resulting in a doctoral thesis on tissue protein studies in Down's syndrome. Since the re-organization of the National Health Service in 1974 he has been committed to the acute services, particularly in endocrine and toxicological investigations, but mental retardation still remains his principal interest.

MALCOLM SAVAGE, B.Sc., M.S.W., was educated at University College, London, at Liverpool University and at McGill University in Canada. After a number of years' experience in community services for families and children, he was appointed Chief Social Worker at the Children's Psychiatric Research Institute in London, Ontario. He later held a similar position for seven years in the Huronia Regional Centre, Canada's oldest institution for the mentally retarded. He is now engaged in a number of small community programmes for the mentally retarded and is director of a community mental health service for the families of emotionally disturbed children.

MORA SKELTON, M.S.W., graduated in social work from the School of Social Work, University of Toronto. She has spent her working life in mental health and mental retardation settings in Toronto, serving as chief Social Worker at the Surrey Place Mental Retardation Centre for the first six years following its foundation. Since 1970 she has been Assistant Executive Director of the Ontario Association for the Mentally Retarded. She is co-author of a book on *The Retarded Child and His Family* and author of a number of articles on mental retardation, published in Canada.

PETER SYLVESTER, M.R.C. Psych., M.R.C. Path., D.C.H., studied medicine at Sheffield University and subsequently worked in clinical paediatrics before joining the mental handicap services at St Lawrence's Hospital, Caterham, where he is a consultant psychiatrist. He has interested himself in neuropathology and growth studies and was awarded the Burden Research Medal and Prize in 1973 for work in mental handicap.

EDWARD WHELAN, Ph.D., obtained his doctorate at Sheffield University in 1968. He subsequently trained as a clinical psychologist and then joined the staff of the Hester Adrian Research Centre, Manchester University, where he is Senior Lecturer and Director of the 'Habilitation Technology Project', a four-year programme supported by the Department of Health and Social Security. In attempting to apply research to practice he has contributed to staff training and assessment and acted as consultant to many organizations, including the DHSS, local authorities, the Employment Service Agency, the BBC and the National Development Group.

# CONTENTS

# FOREWORD

It is perhaps a sign of the times that the new *Tredgold* should devote the first of its six Sections to Administration and the last but one to the Law. In recent years the organization of services for the mentally handicapped and the distribution of roles among various disciplines have changed radically and in changing have been the focus for much critical comment. In Chapter 2 of the first Section Michael Craft grasps the nettle with a thoughtful analysis of the work of the multidisciplinary team and its relation to joint care planning. Indeed one of the striking features of the entire book is the broadly based approach to the subject, which must make the volume attractive to the wide range of personnel concerned.

Doctors in general and psychiatrists in particular have sometimes appeared a trifle anxious about their future participation in the assessment and care of the mentally handicapped with the advent of enthusiastic cadres of psychologists, teachers and social workers. Any doubts they might harbour about the massive and continuing medical contribution to the field must be mitigated by reading Section II of the book with its eight authoritative chapters on clinical matters. Michael Craft has an arresting opening sentence in his chapter on the neurology of mental retardation: 'Nearly one half of the practice of paediatric neurology has to do with mentally retarding causes; much of the rest has to do with febrile brain illnesses or accidents which can have similar sequelae'. One has the feeling reading through the chapters on chromosomal anomalies and primary genetic disorders that diagnosis whether pre- or post-natal is increasingly becoming the basis for a preventive approach of great promise. Sophisticated techniques involving chromosomal or chemical analysis of fetal tissue, cells or exudate together with ultrasonic visualization of the developing embryo provide the data on which clinical decisions may be based. The same issue of prevention keeps on nudging the attention during the chapters on acquired conditions and on the neurocytology of damaging environmental factors. The latter especially with its focus on the effect of protein malnutrition has immense implications if one takes a world-wide perspective.

In Chapter 9 we are reminded that mental handicap provides no immunity to the development of other psychiatric disorders; rather the reverse, and here in particular the psychiatrist may have a key role in assessment and treatment. Chapter 10 on medication and Chapter 11 on the use and abuse of the laboratory provide a bracing and critical perspective.

'The evidence now available from both research and practice strongly suggests that mentally handicapped people are capable of learning to a far greater extent than was previously thought possible.' Thus, early on in his chapter providing an overview of training, education and rehabilitation, Peter Mittler summarizes a generation of painstaking research and action projects which have begun to transform the philosophy of care of the mentally retarded. The importance of this realization in the management of patients of all ages and of all levels of impairment is very great and the chapters making up Section III on psychology and education are concerned both with the theory and with the practice. Crucial in all this is the possibility firstly of making a detailed assessment of the level of development of the patient and of his existing skills and repertoire of social behaviour. Section III underlines the possibilities for exploiting learning potential in a wide variety of settings from home to hospital school and local authority training centre.

The keynote to Section IV on social work and residential care is struck by a sentence in the chapter by Mora Skelton and Cyril Greenland: 'Once the retarded person was seen as a fellow citizen with all the rights of citizenship it became necessary to work towards securing a place in the community for him.' The concepts of normalization and integration, the development of generic social work services, community supports and the education of the general public are among the issues which are dwelt upon. In particular the whole matter of residential care and residential provision and the balance to be struck between this and home care is taken up in other chapters in this Section.

Section V concerned with the Law includes chapters by Larry Gostin on the situation in England and Wales, in Scotland and in the USA. At the present time, the whole question of the rights and privileges of the mentally handicapped, as of other minority groups, is a burning issue and social control through the medium of legislation is very much under review.

The final section is devoted to consideration of selected 'specialized areas' and among these the chapter by Desmond Pond on epilepsy and mental retardation incorporates the significant advances that have been made in recent years, for example, in the field of monitoring plasma levels for anticonvulsants. The last chapter of all on personal relationships and partnerships for the mentally handicapped by Ann and Michael Craft deals *inter alia* with the question of sexual outlets and marriage for the mentally handicapped. The authors speak from a deep and humane concern with the realization of full potential for the mentally handicapped and on the basis of their own pioneering work.

The transformation of *Tredgold* in its new edition is evidence of important advances on several fronts and of a shift in the balance of professional forces operating in the field. The editor has made a bold revision ably supported by his distinguished contributors. The result will appeal to a wide readership.

KENNETH RAWNSLEY
*June 1979*

# PREFACE

During the 1970s the pace of advance in mental retardation has been rapid. This twelfth edition has not only been totally re-written, but much of the emphasis of the book has been changed.

The new edition might well have been published under a new title, but Dr A. F. Tredgold's book, when it first appeared in 1908, was the first major textbook on mental handicap that aimed at promoting compassionate and careful study of the many factors which lie behind any one individual's handicap and need, and this multifactorial and humane approach is as relevant today as it was seventy years ago. Dr Tredgold produced no less than eight editions of his book, the last in 1952. The ninth and subsequent editions were prepared by his son, the late Dr Roger Tredgold, and Dr Kenneth Soddy, following the same approach to the subject as that of Dr Tredgold, senior. This same approach has been faithfully followed in the preparation of this edition. The emergence of the multidisciplinary team reflects such an approach, and this edition is addressed to the graduate members of the team, both medical and non-medical.

The medical contribution to the care of the mentally handicapped was heavily emphasized in the early editions of this book, and rightly so because the medical profession was at that time the profession most concerned with mental defect. Those aspects of the subject which are primarily medical are dealt with in the Clinical Section of this edition where the exciting advances in chromosomal aberrations and genetic misendowments are reviewed. There now seems a real chance of alleviation, if not of replacement treatment, in some genetic misendowments. To the general reader the teasing-out of the relative effects of fetal damage by alcohol and tobacco respectively will be of interest and the new knowledge concerning the transmission of neurogenic viruses, as in Creutzfeldt's disease, may remind him of a science fiction novel. It is important to point out that the Clinical Section contains both description and reference entities for the medical graduate. Short notes and reference to new treatment methods for all known major retardation syndromes are provided for the medical member of the multidisciplinary team. In addition, current chromosomal and genetic research findings are described, in the introductory sections of Chapters 5 and 6 respectively, and these should also be of interest to the M.R.C. Psych. candidate.

Once a diagnosis has been made the contributions of psychologists, educationalists and social workers tend to overshadow the medical component of care; no one, however, should forget the need that exists to treat coincident mental illness in adult life with the very powerful new tranquillizers that are available (Chapters 9 and 10). The value of community care for the mentally handicapped has become increasingly recognized in the last ten years, and this recognition represents a major change in philosophy. Community care can be used successfully for most handicapped people. There has been a steady improvement in public tolerance and a growing realization among professionals that many mentally handicapped people have hitherto been underfunctioning. It is now felt that with continued stimulation and programming, most of them can be taught to care for themselves in the community. This has led to a mushrooming of day-care and residential facilities. Detailed psychological assessments have shown that most humans, especially the handicapped, have untapped abilities. Resourceful teaching, from infancy onwards, can substantially improve the abilities of retarded children; assessment batteries linked to behaviour-shaping techniques can be used to advantage with the retarded of all ages and levels; and imaginative social education enables the handicapped to acquire the skills needed for leading as normal a life as possible. The increased input from the disciplines of psychology and education has had a major impact on the expectations of those who care for the handicapped, and concomitantly on the abilities of the retarded themselves.

With the growing importance of community care, the role of the social worker has increased in significance, both in supporting parents and care staff and in working with handicapped clients. Section IV reflects this. It goes on to remind the reader that the monitoring of residential facilities and the education of those employed to provide services are essential elements in any care system. Hostels which develop the worst characteristics of older institutions are a travesty of community care.

Section v discusses the law relating to mental handicap in Britain and in the United States. The landmark case in American legal history (*Wyatt* v. *Stickney*) is included as an Appendix at the end of the book, for it sets out the minimum standards of care to which retarded citizens are entitled. Although at present used only in the United States, these standards are a pointer to the future and, like the concept of normalization, will surely become a yardstick by which care systems will be measured.

The last part of the book, Section VI, gathers together a series of specialized essays on practical aspects of the care of the handicapped. It ends with a discussion on the most basic of human needs, the need for sympathy, friendship and love. With help, counselling and support, many handicapped people can be aided to a place and a partner of their own.

The intention of this twelfth edition of Tredgold is to describe and evaluate the many challenging advances that have been made in the various disciplines that now offer services to the retarded. The contributors come from three continents, and such is the cross-fertilization of philosophy and practice that the ideas expressed are internationally valid.

I would like to thank all those whose enthusiasm and experience have helped to create this book. It has been a literary multidisciplinary effort as is fitting in a work devoted to a subject which embraces so many disciplines. No longer is the care of the mentally retarded solely the concern of the medical profession. It could well be said that it is the concern of everyone.

Thanks are also due to all the secretaries who deciphered scripts which were often difficult. At the editorial stage thanks go particularly to Mrs Alice Clark, Mrs Margaret Miller and Mrs Anne Williams at Bryn-y-Neuadd Hospital, and to my wife Ann for the many chores of rewriting, organization and advice.

*Tredgold's Mental Retardation* is now designed as a text for multidisciplinary teams concerned with mental handicap. With the preparation of the thirteenth edition in mind, I would appreciate constructive criticism and comments on this edition, and clinical photographs would be particularly welcome.

MICHAEL CRAFT
*June 1979*

# ACKNOWLEDGEMENTS

The editor and publishers gratefully acknowledge permission to reproduce illustrations as follows: to Mr D. Greaves, Department of Audio-Visual Communications, Institute of Ophthalmology, London for Fig. 6.15; to Dr P. Harper, Welsh National School of Medicine, Cardiff for Figs 6.3, 6.10, 6.16, 6.17, 6.34, 6.35, 6.36, 6.50, 6.52, 7.1 and 7.12; to Dr J. Jancar, Stoke Park Hospital, Stapleton, Bristol for Figs 5.10, 5.11, 5.12, 5.13, 5.14, 5.15, 6.11, 6.12, 6.14, 6.21, 6.22, 6.23, 6.33, 6.38, 6.41, 6.42, 6.44, 7.2, 7.7, 7.10 and 7.11; to *Clinical Genetics*, Copenhagen and Dr J. Jancar for Fig. 6.5; to the *Journal of the Irish Medical Association* and Dr J. Jancar for Fig. 6.27; to the *Journal of Mental Deficiency Research* and Dr J. Jancar for Figs 6.39, 6.43 and 6.46; to the *Postgraduate Medical Journal* and Dr J. Jancar for Fig. 6.26; to Dr B. Kirman, Queen Mary's Hospital for Children, Carshalton for Figs 5.7, 5.8 and 5.9; to Dr F. Kratter, Brockhall Hospital, Langho, Lancashire for Figs 5.4, 6.9, 6.18, 6.19, 6.20, 6.24, 6.25, 6.29, 6.30, 6.31, 6.32, 6.37, 6.40 and 7.6; to Dr A. McDermott, Southmead Hospital, Westbury-on-Trym, Bristol and Dr J. Insley, Infant Development Unit, Queen Elizabeth Medical Centre, Edgbaston, Birmingham for Figs 5.5 and 5.6; to Dr B. Richards, St Lawrence's Hospital, Caterham for Fig. 6.6; to Dr P. E. Sylvester, St Lawrence's Hospital, Caterham for Figs 6.28, 6.45, 6.48, 6.49, 7.3, 7.4, 7.5, 7.8 and 7.9; to Dr D. Wechsler for Fig. 1.1 (from *The Measurement and Appraisal of Human Intelligence*, Williams and Wilkins, 1958).

# I
# ADMINISTRATIVE
# SECTION

# CHAPTER I

# CLASSIFICATION, CRITERIA, EPIDEMIOLOGY AND CAUSATION

## MICHAEL CRAFT

Man needs to organize his knowledge and labelling plays an essential part in this. There are fashions in labelling particularly where the subject rouses strong emotion, as with the mentally and multiply handicapped. Thus labels change from time to time and successive editions of this book have reflected this.

### CLASSIFICATION IN MENTAL DISORDER

Man has always known the difference between those retarded from birth and those temporarily affected by madness. The Bible makes this clear in discussing those temporarily 'possessed by spirits'. In Greek the term *idiot* means a private person, and the term *lunatic* is derived from the Latin word *luna*, or moon, and was applied to those believed to have been affected by the waxing and waning of the moon. In England a statute of Edward I distinguished between those who were 'born fools' and those temporarily mad—principally for guidance in disposition of their property. For the poor in Western Europe care was provided by the Catholic Church and the word *cretin*, a corruption of the French word *chrétien* (Christian) is a reminder of those times. The word *mongol* has a similarly interesting derivation. Mongols were believed by Langdon Down, the first European to describe the condition, to be an ethnic throwback, for until 1944, when Stalin returned the Crimean Tartars to Central Asia, there had been groups of ethnic 'mongols' throughout central Europe, a reminder of previous

conquests. Both cretins and mongols have now been relabelled as sufferers from hypothyroidism and Down's syndrome respectively, although the latter will be found described in this book under its latest label, 21 trisomy.

The terms *idiocy* and *lunacy* have long histories, and, as befits their Greek and Latin origins respectively, give rise to similar words in most European languages today. The eighteenth century French writer Jean Jacques Rousseau introduced the concept of the noble savage, a simple person unsullied by civilization, and by the end of the century the French physician Itard had published a book explaining his attempts to civilize such a noble savage, Victor. It is still not clear whether Victor was autistic, retarded or deprived, but Itard stimulated much nineteenth century work with the mentally disordered.

In France Pinel emphasized the importance of work and occupation for the retarded, Séquin took this one stage back in writing on the need for early education. We shall see these arguments in modern guise in this book; research has shown the importance of starting to educate Down's syndrome subjects in their first year of life (Chapter 13).

In the United States, first Benjamin Rush, and then Howe, underlined the importance of accurate diagnosis and labelling of mentally disordered patients. Rush in particular showed what a substantial part environmental

The author would like to express his thanks to Albert Kushlick and Roger Blunden from whose chapter (see Bibliography) some of the material presented here was obtained; also to Rodney Wilkins, friend and mentor, for help with Chapters 1 and 2.

deprivation could play in either causing retardation in childhood or exacerbating the effect of non-progressive genetic misendowments.

In Victorian England retardation was seen as a medical matter. Later Victorian humanists introduced compulsory education with the Education Act of 1870. Universal education made clear that there were groups unable to profit, and the 1899 Act distinguished defective and epileptic children who had special needs. Contemporaneously the need for refuge and asylum in a system of residential care was reflected by the 1886 Idiots Act which clarified the special residential needs of idiots and imbeciles (as opposed to lunatics provided for under a separate Lunacy Act of 1890). In most languages the term *idiot* has kept its meaning over the centuries, applying to one who needs special care from birth. The widely used term *imbecile* was applied to the less retarded, ambulant persons who nevertheless from birth needed special supervision and occupation. These terms were recently changed with labels given by the 1968 World Health Organization Expert Committee to *profound* (IQ 0–20), *severe* (IQ 20–35) and *moderate* (IQ 35–50) respectively (Table 1.1).

In the nineteenth century there was a worldwide movement towards the provision of asylums for the needy defective as well as the insane, the poor, and the social misfits or inadequates. This arose partly from an attempt to do better than previous generations, partly from a desire to order the unordered and unlabelled, partly from the wish to banish those who offended the sight. The Victorians were good at both ordering the masses and labelling those with needs. In addition to idiots and imbeciles further educational labels were needed for the *educable imbecile* and the *feeble-minded*. In France the latter were called *morons*, and at the turn of the century Alfred Binet devised the first IQ tests to help distinguish between those who could be educated and thus be enabled to become partly self-supporting, and those who could not. In England one-third of the army recruits for the Boer War were found unfit to serve, a great shock to the government

TABLE 1.1

Classification of the mentally handicapped*

| 1968 WHO terms and standard deviations from normal† | IQ | Old terms | Proportion per thousand general population | Other terms | 1959 English Mental Health Act | 1960 Mental Health Act Scotland and elsewhere |
|---|---|---|---|---|---|---|
| Profound<br>Over 5.3 SD | 0–20 | Idiot | 0.5 | Low grade | | |
| Severe<br>4.3–5.3 SD | 20–35 | | | | Severely subnormal | |
| Moderate<br>3.3–4.3 SD | 35–50 | Imbecile | 3.0 | Medium grade | | Mentally defective |
| Mild<br>2.0–3.3 SD | 50–70 or 75 | Feeble-minded or moron | 20–30 | High grade | Subnormal and/or psychopathic | |

\* The World Health Organization terms are used in this book.

† Meeting in 1968 the World Health Organization Expert Committee proposed IQ limits for the different gradations of mental defect, assuming a mean of 100 and a standard deviation of 15 points. It emphasized that IQs were not exact measurements and should not be regarded as sole criteria and that in practice groups overlapped. Both this committee and others subsequently, on International Classification of Disease, opposed the term 'borderline mentally retarded' for the IQ group 68–85 (16 per cent general population) and this has been deleted.

and the ruling classes. As often happens in Britain, a Royal Commission was set up in 1904 to investigate the problem. Many of its recommendations were included in the 1913 Mental Deficiency Act. This advised segregation of 'the feeble-minded' on eugenic grounds, with voluntary and compulsory admission to *colonies*, keeping the sexes apart to reduce the number of their defective progeny with which it was thought the State was having to cope. Fashions had changed again by the time this Act became generally operational in Britain after the First World War. The voluntary provisions for admission to institutions were forgotten and only compulsory provisions were applied from 1918 to 1957. Much grief and suffering resulted from strict application of the rules. For instance, a woman of average intelligence in receipt of unemployment allowance who had an illegitimate child could be certified as a defective, and many were (Craft 1959). By the time fashions had changed again in the 1960s in England, some hundreds of such females had spent many years in colonies before release.

Yet the Victorian systems of labelling and of order were intended to protect the individual defective from exploitation and society from depredation. At the turn of the century Binet's IQ tests apparently showed most convicts and prostitutes to be illiterate and thus feeble-minded, whilst case histories of improvident families such as the Kallikaks and Jukes read like a roll-call of detrimental Darwinian natural selection: 'The feeble-minded are a parasitic predatory class, never capable of self-support or of managing their own affairs. The great majority ultimately become public charges in some form.' As Sarason and Doris (1969) who quoted Fernald above, make clear in their excellent historical discussion on the subject, most countries rapidly followed the English model and established medical asylums for such people under the care of the profession which had taken the earliest and liveliest interest. Within these asylums, colonies or hospitals, conditioning factors were at work. Most were unlocked and placed emphasis on work and self-sufficiency, having a graduated system of rewards and staged release towards licence and freedom. Over a period of three to six years

this reward system often improved the *morally defective*, who later came to be known as *subnormal and psychopathic*, for hospital placement often represented the first ordered educational experience in a disordered childhood. There were legal checks upon the system, as potential patients had to be 'subject to be dealt with' and certifiable as mentally defective whilst the periodic recertifications had to be signed by a magistrate. This still operates in some countries. In the last resort, absconding from under-staffed institutions was relatively easy, and there was a selective staff disinclination to hunt too hard for those who were too aggressive, too difficult or too intelligent. Absconders disappeared within their native slums.

THE USE OF LABELS

Labels, and classifications generally, are used to clarify human thought and possible action. The labelling of one group by another may be the result of reason or action and both have played their part in the nomenclature of the mentally handicapped.

1. *Legal labels* were the first attempt to bring order into confusion, as we have seen, principally to clarify medieval disposition of property. The idiot needed his property under permanent care as he would not have the lucid intervals of the lunatic during which he could think logically for himself. Despite the modern tolerance of the handicapped such labels are still needed and in most countries an initial medico-legal label, authenticated by a registered professional, is required before benefits can be obtained. These legal labels are further discussed later in the book.

2. *Medical labels* or diagnoses can now be made during the first days of life for the profoundly affected and, if disorder is suspected before birth, tests can be made *in utero*. As the next chapters show, this is increasingly a field where intervention or treatment can avoid or reverse otherwise severe retardation. Thus efficient labelling here can lead to highly effective early treatment of metabolic anomalies such as the amino acid disorders.

3. *Educational labelling* depends initially on the medical diagnosis the child has received.

The diagnosis of the infant often has poor predictive value.

4. *Administrative labels*. It is a truism to say that administrators only act when they are provided with a label to serve as authorization. Yet it is important to note that the labelling or classification process is important for government or organization, allowing a particular machinery to operate it is hoped to the advantage of the individual. For example, to be termed *mentally handicapped* once invited permanent residential placement. It now indicates the many community social needs that have to be met. There has arisen a cadre of professionals, social workers, to meet these needs, with their own labels and classifications.

5. *Social labels* reflect community ethos. The 8000-strong American Hutterite biblical community removed the responsibility of Christian baptism from its mentally handicapped. Absolved from this responsibility the handicapped move among the community in a state of permanent childhood, loved and reproved by all, and not required to work or keep a family (Eaton & Weil 1955).

6. *Research classification*. The more accurate the label the more accurate the action possible and expected. Doctor can communicate with teacher, American with Australian. The 'true' Down's syndrome subject with 47 chromosomes can be distinguished from an identical-looking mosaic, genetically with the potential to be a professional but whose expectations might otherwise be geared low. The child with muscular atrophy can be classified as either recoverable or degenerative with implications for appropriate management. For administrators, research may clarify whether Down's syndrome subjects are everywhere living longer, with the important deductions about residential care that follow from this.

## CLASSIFICATIONS IN MENTAL HANDICAP

Whilst it is relatively simple to separate most varieties of mental illness from mental handicap, it is by no means easy to distinguish between the mentally handicapped needing special education during childhood (the mild) and those needing supervision for most of their life (the moderate). Those permanently incapacitated throughout life (the

severe and the profound) are the most obvious.

Early classifications were not much concerned with nuances, for if a person was certified as defective this was a long-term label. The label could be applied to a wide variety of people who misbehaved socially, providing they were 'subject to be dealt with' under the Act. One of six criteria had to be satisfied: these included placement for the person's own safety; being on unemployment benefit; and being convicted by a court. 'Placement for one's own safety' obviously begs the question as to type of care.

### Pathological/subcultural

One of the best-known early classifications was that proposed by Tredgold (1952) in an earlier edition of this book—primary and secondary amentia. By primary he meant constitutional, that is genetic, chromosomal et cetera and by secondary he referred to that damage occurring later to the fetus at childbirth or from infant infection. In timing, he referred to antenatal, natal and postnatal causes. This classification was also used by Lewis (1933) as the basis of his pathological/subcultural dichotomy, and by Penrose (1963) who pointed out that at IQ 38 the two separated neatly, the pathological group being mainly below, the subcultural above this marker. By 1962 Penrose noted an interesting shift in viewpoint over the century. Earlier writers, including Tredgold, thought that genetic factors played the major part in etiology for the milder defective and damaged 'germ plasm' for the severe. Now it is believed that inheritance of recessive genes (such as for phenylketonuria and galactosaemia) and chromosomal anomalies such as Down's syndrome cause most of the severe handicaps, with environmental deprivations playing the major part in causation of milder handicap. Clarke (1969) reminds us that even with the subculture group almost half the contribution to the handicap may be supplied by normal genetic variation.

The classification used in this book follows the above traditions. Pathological (or following Tredgold, primary) causes are discussed first, in Chapter 5 dealing with *chromosomal anomalies* and Chapter 6 on *primary genetic disorders* and their management. Tredgold's original secondary causes are discussed in Chapter 7 on *acquired conditions*, Chapter 8 on *neurological damage* resulting from environmental deprivation, and Chapter 9 on *psychoses in the mentally handicapped*. However, most retardation is not monocausal. There is multiple as well as mental handicap. In the past the major handicap has often been environmental, that is, lack of stimulation, the wrong stimulation, or even negative stimulation due to community ostracism, banishment within sheltered villages, or plain institutionalization. Including protein deprivation, it has been calculated that most of the 100 million mentally handicapped in the world are moderately to severely retarded because of environmental deprivation. The latter part of this book is concerned with methods of improving management and environment so that the potentialities of the individual may best be fulfilled.

## CRITERIA OF MENTAL HANDICAP

Social criteria have always been principal boundary markers for mental handicap, but unfortunately they are also the most vague and most open to chance. Particularly for the mildly and moderately handicapped, elements of total chance may operate, such as the local unemployment level. Many in this category can manage in the community for long periods until an unexpected illness, the demands of children or unemployment causes the collapse of their adjustment.

Some guidelines have been established, especially for the severely handicapped. They depend on three main criteria—low intelligence, low standard of behaviour and low achievement at peer group level.

### Low intelligence

The early enthusiasm for delineating mental handicap by the use of intelligence tests waxed and has now waned. At one time intelligence tests were used by some American States as the principal criterion in assessing mental deficiency. The argument for their use and abuse has raged through many books and the interested reader is referred to Clarke and Clarke (1974) for a general discussion.

The following summary outlines the assets and defects of intelligence tests.

1. Binet's earlier IQ tests depended heavily on education to understand the nature of the questions. Where the deprived had had little or no education, as was the case with many convicts and prostitutes, they scored low. Thus American negroes and Indians were found generally to score low, many being in the defective range, although it was clear that the prowess of many outside the test situation was of a high order. This bias diminished with the development of non-verbal IQ tests and comprehensive education, but remains greatest for those most in need of careful assessment, that is the delinquent retarded adolescent about to have his liberty removed.

2. It has now been shown that growth in intelligence is not steady for everyone, and is particularly variable in the growth spurts in individuals at puberty compared with their age peer groups. In adolescence the stresses of school or work throw up most candidates for the label 'mentally handicapped'.

3. Because of standardization, the same IQ figure does not necessarily have the same significance from test to test. This could be overcome by using standard deviations (see Table 1.1) but this concept is less popular than IQ scores for those working in the assessment field.

4 Even with a well standardized IQ test there will be variations in score from day to day and week to week. This can be between tester and tester, or for testee with variations in health, mood, distractions et cetera. Whilst these considerations may cause differences of a few points each, the result is vitally important if an arbitrary figure of IQ 70 or 75 is set as the demarcation between two very different placements.

### Individual achievements compared with peer group

Since it was in childhood that individuals could be excluded from state schools on grounds of mental deficiency—and still is so in some States in Australia—the criterion of individual achievements compared with peer group deserves a mention. For deprived youngsters this can be a 'catch 22' situation of double indignity, for owing to lack of tuition they fail to meet the criterion which would have allowed them access to tuition.

## Social behaviour

Social behaviour, the vaguest criterion, has always been the most important. Standards of behaviour outlining what is unacceptable will vary between classes in a community as well as between communities, and may apply to some of the mentally ill, sex deviants, the armed forces, the inadequate and the reforming eccentrics. The Soviet Union has been accused of labelling social misfits as both mentally ill and mentally handicapped from time to time to suit the political climate.

Among the most explicit accounts of social misbehaviour as a criterion of mental deficiency was that evolved from the 1913 English Mental Deficiency Act which nowhere discussed low intelligence, but always 'arrested or incomplete development of mind' throughout its various amendments up to repeal in 1959. Consider this comment from the British Medical Association and Magistrates Association in 1947: 'The concept of mind is wider than intellect, and . . . mental defect (that is, deficiency of mind) is not the same thing as intellectual deficiency, although it includes it.' The Board of Control (1954) went further: 'We regard the present definitions as enabling medical practitioners to certify mentally defective patients on the ground that they have characteristics from early youth which make them antisocial, although their intelligence might be quite normal.' In the same year O'Connor and Tizard (1954) showed in a 5 per cent survey of some 12 000 in-patients that the *average* IQ of younger adult feeble-minded defectives in south-east England was just over IQ 70. In England for some years after, about a quarter of institutionalized defectives were between IQ 70 and 100. Earlier editions of this textbook supported this viewpoint strongly. In 1952 Tredgold wrote: 'An arrested development of any process or department of mind, provided it resulted in social incapacity, constituted mental deficiency.' However, fashions in England changed in the 1970s and whilst it remains perfectly legal to treat such patients with an IQ in the average range informally or compulsorily (as psychopathic) in a hospital administratively run for the mentally handicapped, it is now uncommon to find many above IQ 70. Fashions differ in different communities, and some still believe the mental deficiency hospital to be an effective system for treating personality-disordered delinquents.

## THE AMERICAN ASSOCIATION ON MENTAL DEFICIENCY CRITERIA

Social behaviour and other criteria were discussed at length by a widely based committee of experts set up by the American Association on Mental Deficiency to propose definitions. The resulting manual (Heber 1961) started with a statement, and then evolved an interdisciplinary concept of retardation intended to serve as a new basis for interstate statistical comparisons.

'Mental retardation refers to subaverage general intellectual functioning which originates during the developmental period and is associated with impairment in one or more of the following: (1) maturation, (2) learning, and (3) social adjustment.'

The manual defines *subaverage* as more than one standard deviation below the population mean for the age groups concerned; *intellectual functioning* in terms of 'objective tests'; *developmental period* as childhood to 16 years; *maturation* in terms of rate of attainment of self-help skills; *learning ability* as the acquisition of achievements during school years; and *social adjustment* in terms of ability to maintain oneself in adult life in community living, employment and conformity to accepted standards. The manual repeatedly emphasizes mental retardation as a label denoting *current* functioning of the individual, without necessarily auguring permanent arrest. For a comment on the current status of definitions and practice in North America the reader is referred to Chapters 3, 17, 18 and 22.

## EPIDEMIOLOGY

### KUSHLICK'S CRITERIA

Kushlick (1961) and his associates (Kushlick & Cox 1968; Kushlick & Blunden 1974) have carried out important surveys in England

TABLE 1.2

Subjects' IQ 0–50 in age-groups where all are likely to be known

| | Age-group | IQ under 50 per thousand | Down's syndrome per thousand |
|---|---|---|---|
| England and Wales 1926–9 (Lewis 1929) | | | |
| Urban | 7–14 | 3.71 | 0.34 |
| Rural | | 5.61 | NK |
| Baltimore 1936 (Lemkau et al. 1943) | 10–14 | 3.3 | NK |
| Onondaga County 1953 (Onondaga Survey 1955) | 5–17 | 3.6 | NK |
| Rural Sweden 1959 (Akesson 1961) | All ages | 5.8 | 0.03 |
| Middlesex 1960 (Goodman and Tizard 1962) | 7–14 | 3.45 | 1.14 |
| Salford 1961 (Kushlick 1961) | 15–19 | 3.62 | 0.90 |
| Aberdeen 1962 (Birch et al. 1970) | 8–10 | 3.7 | NK |
| Northern Ireland 1962 (Scally and MacKay 1964) | 15–19 | 4.7 | 1.45 |
| Edinburgh 1962–4 (Drillien et al. 1966) | $7\frac{1}{2}$–$14\frac{1}{2}$ | 5.0 | 1.8 |
| Wessex 1963 (Kushlick 1968) | | | |
| County boroughs | 15–19 | 3.54 | 1.15 |
| Counties | 15–19 | 3.84 | 1.18 |
| Camberwell 1967 (Wing 1971) | 5–14 | 3.89 | 0.90 |

Adapted from Kushlick and Blunden (1974).

using IQ 50 as the cut-off point for severe, and IQ 70 for mild, subnormality.

IQ 50 is a useful point, for as Tizard (1958) noted, follow-up studies show only 10 to 20 per cent of those below IQ 50 capable in adult life of becoming economically independent, whereas many of those above IQ 50 are capable of deletion from a mental deficiency register on grounds of no longer needing supervision (Kushlick 1961). In the discussion to follow World Health Organization terms of *severely*, *moderately* and *mildly retarded* are used.

In fact, IQ 50 is a widely recognized cut-off point, and numerous international studies suggest a prevalence for the severely and moderately subnormal (IQ 0–50) of about 3.7/1000 general population (Table 1.2). It will be seen that more recent surveys are very similar in the rates found. Inspection of the results shows that in early surveys less than a quarter, more recently nearer a third, of those under IQ 50 are Down's syndrome subjects, who now tend to live longer. In Kushlick's Wessex survey 10 per cent of these subjects scored over IQ 50, probably being phenotypes and mosaics (see pp. 49–51) rather than true trisomy.

Possession of an IQ under 50 was a severe disadvantage to subjects in all the countries under survey. Tizard's follow-up studies (Tizard 1958) showed 90 per cent to be permanently dependent, and the remaining 10 per cent was likely to contain many, for reasons given earlier in the discussion, who would later score much higher than IQ 50. Earlier surveys in England suggested that most of those under IQ 50 would eventually be admitted to hospital accommodation, but this is no longer true for most developed countries. The social services of many local authorities are developing group homes able to care for most if not all the range of disabilities once cared for only in parallel systems of accommodation under regional or state hospital authorities.

KUSHLICK'S SURVEYS

In their surveys in Salford and Wessex Kushlick and his associates (Kushlick 1961; Kushlick & Cox 1968) used the practical criteria of being continent, ambulant and having severe behaviour disorder to rate the degree of care needed by the handicapped. Continence and ambulance were easy enough to define but behaviour disorder not so, as would be expected. Nevertheless a surprising degree of agreement was obtained on this last criterion from care personnel.

Despite most of the children being incontinent and non-ambulant, throughout childhood the majority were cared for at home. By age group 15–19, 71 per cent of those under IQ 50 had become continent, ambulant, and were without severe behaviour disorder, and this proportion continued to rise with age due both to the higher death rate among the severely physically handicapped, and the tendency for behaviour disorders to improve with the years. Yet Kushlick's early surveys (1961, 1968) showed that of those over 16 an increasing proportion arrived in hospital as the years advanced.

Table 1.3 shows the residential care status of those in the Wessex survey of 1963 per 100 000 general population. Not only are two-thirds of severely subnormal (SSN) adults continent, ambulant and free from behaviour disorder in residential institutions (mainly hospital) but also 86 per cent of the mildly subnormal (MSN) (IQ 50–70). The original survey also showed that among both SSN and MSN the vast majority were able to feed, wash and dress themselves. The results show that hospitals care for a considerable proportion of people who lack serious disability, and the British Government's planning document *Better Services for the Mentally Handicapped* (DHSS 1971) advised that most of these people should be transferred to hostel and other local authority care, hospitals being reserved for physical handicap, behaviour disorder and those needing specialist medical and nursing care. Most of those now admitted are said to have behaviour disorder *at the time of admission.*

## CAUSATION

### CAUSATION OF SEVERE AND MODERATE HANDICAP (IQ 0–50)

Surveys in Western countries (Lemkau et al. 1943; Penrose 1938; Sabagh et al. 1959; Saenger 1960) have shown very clearly that parents of severely and moderately handicapped children come from all social classes, and cases are scattered throughout the general population. The chromosomal anomalies and genetic misendowments contributing to these cases of handicap are described in Chapters 5 and 6. Others are caused by trauma or

TABLE 1.3

Wessex Survey 1963 for social and physical incapacity for children and adults, and place of care (per 100 000 general population)

| Age | Grade | Place of care | Non-ambulant | Ambulant, severe behaviour disorder | Ambulant, no severe behaviour disorder but severely incontinent | Continent, ambulant, no severe behaviour disorder |
|---|---|---|---|---|---|---|
| 0–15 | SSN | Home | 3 | 4 | 2 | 20 |
| | | Residential | 5 | 5 | 3 | 5 |
| | MSN | Home | 1 | 1 | 1 | 7 |
| | | Residential | 0 | 0 | 0 | 1 |
| 16 and over | SSN | Home | 2 | 2 | 1 | 45 |
| | | Residential | 6 | 14 | 6 | 53 |
| | MSN | Home | 1 | 0 | 0 | 69 |
| | | Residential | 2 | 4 | 1 | 45 |

Adapted from Kushlick and Blunden (1974).

infection at birth or thereafter and are described in Chapter 7. Whilst the basic etiological cause, whether chromosomal trisomy, recessive genetic phenylketonuria or birth anoxia, may set restrictions on the total acquisition of ability, the actual rate of achievement will depend on environmental variables such as quality of home care, availability of special education or institutionalization. These aspects are discussed in detail in later sections of the book but it is important to emphasize that considerable secondary retardation can occur with those of IQ 0–50 because of the low expectations of those who care for them or because of poor facilities, common at one time for children in hospital. For example Eaton and Weil's (1955) survey of 51 subnormals in the American Hutterite community, where every individual is entitled as of right to be loved by every other in the 8000 strong community, showed that all adult subnormals had a job of some sort, all managed at least some self-care and none were in hospital. Kibbutz communities show similar results. The incidence of genetic abnormalities in the community gene pool has overall similarities in most communities, but the degree of environmental retardation, or to put it another way, the rate of advance, can be very different given good community care and expert tuition. The problem is highlighted by the difficulty facing the expert in accurately assessing progress in young handicapped (see also Chapter 13. Hence the need to ensure good care of the most handicapped because many will do surprisingly well. For instance Illingworth (1961), Professor of Child Health at Sheffield, followed up 122 infants for whom he had originally made a confident diagnosis of mental subnormality excluding Down's syndrome, hypothyroidism or hydrocephalus, at less than 12 months of age. Thirty died under the age of six, many of these with severe brain pathology. Of 87 of the remainder who could be traced there were six with IQ 100 and over; three with IQ 90–99; nine with IQ 80–89; eight with IQ 70–79; ten with IQ 50–69; and 51 with IQ 0–50. Thus there were 36 with IQ over 50 and 26 were not subnormal at all. In addition the hypothyroid and hydrocephalic subjects would nowadays be treated whilst the Down's subject could respond to special tuition (see

Chapter 13). There are now many studies showing the slowing rate of development resulting from unstimulating environments, and it is important to realize that this may occur in the over-protective home, as well as in an ill-staffed hostel or hospital. The classic Brooklands experiment was carried out by Tizard (1964) who transferred a group of imbecile children from hospital, matched for relevant factors with a group of children who stayed behind in hospital. The transferred group had much play and close verbal and practical stimulation from adults who grew to love them, and improved markedly in verbal IQ compared with the control group. Other research studies have confirmed these findings and emphasized that it is not the number of staff but their deployment which is crucial. The handicapped child at home may actually have fewer adult hours per week than an institutional child but the face-to-face time and its quality will be quite different.

## CAUSATION OF MILD HANDICAP (IQ 50–70)

Clinical studies have shown that whereas for instance Birch et al. (1970) could find clear evidence of central nervous system impairment in all except one of a group of 100 severely mentally handicapped children, only one-third of children with IQ 50–75 had such damage. A pathological study by Crome (1960) showed that 267 out of 272 brains sectioned by him in a hospital for severe and moderately handicapped children had 'definite abnormality'. Most surveys show that the mildly handicapped (IQ 50–70) have only a small proportion showing central nervous system abnormality, and much more importantly that mental handicap in the absence of central nervous system abnormality occurs mainly among the lower social classes. In other words, there is now evidence that it is rare for a child in a higher social class to have an IQ less than 80 unless he has one of the pathological syndromes outlined in the clinical section.

The evidence is compelling. Birch (1970) in the Aberdeen survey showed the incidence of mental handicap among children in the lowest social class to be nearly nine times that in the top two classes. The Scottish Council for Research in Education (1953)

noted that fathers in their top social class had no children scoring less than IQ 86, whilst lowest class fathers had 26 per cent who scored less than IQ 86. Stein and Susser (1963) confirmed this in a sophisticated analysis of referrals to a child health service for 'backwardness'. Not only did schools serving 'aspirant'—higher social class—families refer fewer children for backwardness (8.7/1000) than 'demotic'—of the people—schools for working class areas (25/1000), but at the 11-plus intelligence examination the schools serving the higher social class gave only 0.9 per cent scoring IQ 50–79 whilst 10 per cent of all pupils scored in this range from working class areas. In their area of survey, Salford, education is compulsory and state-provided, and the writers were able to show a gradation between these figures according to district. They also checked private schools to ensure retardates had not been preferentially streamed there. In a further examination of 106 severely retarded children, the seven who came from 'aspirant' families all had clinical abnormalities; of the 50 who came from 'demotic' families 30 were clinically normal.

It is now possible to conclude from the evidence that whilst *moderate* and *severe* mental handicap (IQ 0–50) is due mainly to the chromosomal anomalies, severe rare genetic misendowments and brain damage described in the clinical section, *mild* mental handicap (IQ 50–70) has only a small proportion caused in this way. Most mildly retarded individuals without central nervous system signs, biochemical abnormality or sense deprivation occur among the working classes and it is rare to find a clinically normal retardate under IQ 86 among professional classes.

There are profound implications from this when one comes to consider a general theory of genetic endowment.

## GENETIC ENDOWMENT AND MENTAL HANDICAP

The contribution of dominant and recessive genes and chromosomal anomalies to severe handicap is well known. Indeed there is no known example of chromosomal anomaly increasing potential; all such anomalies reduce mental and physical ability usually to a profound degree. Down's syndrome (21 trisomy) is a perfect example of too many (genetic) cooks spoiling the final human broth.

Some cases of mild mental handicap are caused by single genes of high import, such as with muscular dystrophy, but since the research by Roberts et al. (1938) it has been generally agreed that above IQ 50 the general population assumes a normal distribution in respect of intelligence as for other bodily characteristics (Fig. 1.1). Roberts and his colleagues built upon earlier work to show that large scale IQ tests among children produced results in accord with a normal distribution down to IQ 50. Beyond IQ 50 there can be an *excess* presumably due to pathological variants. They postulated that intelligence above IQ 50 was the result of multiple factors, particularly additive genes. The theory has been widely accepted and supported by subsequent work, although as O'Connor and Tizard (1956) pointed out, IQ tests have been generally framed to fit this theory rather than the other way about.

At about the same time Penrose (1938) showed that relatives of the severely handicapped tended to have normal intelligence but those of the mildly handicapped tended to have low IQs in direct proportion to the closeness of relationship. This could support common environmental—or deprivative—as well as genetic factors among the lower social classes. Later Penrose (1963) reviewed the evidence for the additive genetic theory being supported by closeness of relatives to the mildly subnormal, and stated that this theory depended on random mating in the general population. Research has shown that this does not apply, for like tends to marry like. University graduates marry graduates, unskilled workers other unskilled workers. Apart from intelligence, other human characteristics such as height, believed to be due to additive genes, also tend to be assortative. Assortative mating would tend to exacerbate the tendency for low IQ to occur in lower classes where like also marries like.

It is clear that a theory of multiple genetic causation cannot explain all the IQ differences between individuals. The environmental contribution is also considerable, as Susser and Watson (1962) pointed out, and genetic factors cannot explain the rarity of mild mentally handicapped children among professional classes, as opposed to working class. Applying statistics to a theory of multiple genetic endowment gives a greater number of expected cases than are actually found. In addition there are proportionately more

IQ among children with birth weight less than 3.5 lb (1.6 kg) is less than the mean IQ of those with birth weight above this. Craft (1967) reviewing studies to that date noted that, as with height mentioned earlier,

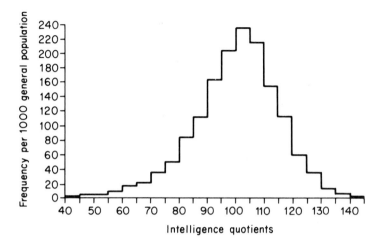

*Fig. 1.1   The normal curve of distribution for many human characteristics including intelligence (from Wechsler 1958).*

mildly handicapped children found among unskilled workers than among skilled workers of similar IQ and one has to hypothesize that children with the same genetic potential rise to a higher level of achievement with the second group than the first, presumably because of the environmental improvement resulting from their parental handling.

Environmental differences are well shown up by the American research studies analysing Army recruits, comparing negroes and whites, and comparing Northern states negroes with those from the South. Klineberg (1940) with many others showed that among this group from a presumably similar genetic pool, Northern negro recruits scored significantly higher on IQ tests than Southern. In a similar way, the Onondaga (1955) survey in New York found a much higher incidence of mental handicap among whites from lower income and poorer districts than whites from better districts. Many surveys have shown the same effects of income, poorer district, unemployment, in their association with prevalence of mental handicap.

Low birth weight is a further factor associated with mild mental handicap. Drillien (1961) showed that among all classes the mean

birth weights of children correlated with maternal shortness which itself correlated with social class. In other words the incidence of 'premature' babies (below 5.5 lb, 2.5 kg) rises from social class I to V as does the incidence of perinatal mortality and of morbidity. There is a concatenation of adverse factors behind the association of low IQ children, with low birth weight, low social class and small women. Among many others, Birch et al. (1970) also found mild subnormality in Scotland associated with poor houses, big families and congestion.

Minimal brain damage has been suggested, notably by Lilienfeld and Pasamanick (1955), as an important component in the association between low IQ and low social class. The idea has generated much work and many reviews (see also Chapters 7 and 8). It is perfectly true that both perinatal morbidity and mortality are greater in the lower social classes than in the higher and that this holds good for most Western countries. Since minimal brain damage is by definition associated with few if any central nervous system signs and little or no demonstrable brain pathology, it is by definition hard to prove or disprove this claim, or to use it for treatment purposes.

## COMMUNICATION DEFECTS AS A CAUSE OF MENTAL HANDICAP

The incidence of blindness, deafness and mutism has always been high among populations of mentally handicapped and it is well known that memory deficits retard the development of children who later show quite normal intelligence. Luria (1963) has pointed out the importance of language to the rate of advancement of achievement in children. In later books he showed that lacks in internal communication arising from lacks in external communication with others, lead to lack in mental activity, understanding and self-help skills. Using monozygotic twins, he taught one to speak faster than the other, and showed how language may speed up the rate of acquisition of skills in children. Other works have related the usage of language to class. For instance, on average a working class family often has a smaller vocabulary, a larger family and reduced verbal contact between adults and children, than a professional family. The latter is likely to have a greater wealth of verbal and written material about the house with which to stimulate the children, and to use schools where classes are smaller and teachers stay longer. The natural development of Luria's teaching and his behavioural approach with its emphasis on early language development and wealth of stimulating material needed to maximize rate of development in those with limited genetic potential, may be followed in Chapters 13 and 15. The authors of these chapters both maximize communication in order to accelerate achievement, with Down's syndrome infants, and with the intellectually retarded respectively.

## ESTIMATIONS OF FUTURE TRENDS IN NUMBERS OF HANDICAPPED

A variety of surveys have suggested that the incidence of moderate and severe mental handicap (IQ 0–50) in the general population lies between 3.3/1000 (Lemkau et al. 1936) and 5.8/1000 (Akesson 1961) (see Table 1.2). High figures, such as the latter, for rural areas probably reflect the findings for those under 14 years, whose subsequent work-holding and community success bore little relation to the early prognoses. Most recent surveys give results between 3.8 and 3.5/1000 for the post-school-age group.

From these surveys over the decades one cannot immediately deduce whether the prevalence is rising or falling. Even if one examines the proportion of Down's syndrome subjects within these surveys deductions are not straightforward. The incidence of Down's syndrome is 1/660 live births and 90 per cent are IQ 0–50 (see p.52). In recent surveys they range between 0.9/1000 (Kushlick 1961) to the 1.8/1000 Edinburgh (Drillien et al. 1966) (see Table 1.2). This evidence and the knowledge that better methods of medical care are now available, underlines the increasing longevity and thus prevalence of the Down's group. Because the total rate of the IQ 0–50 group has not changed much over the years, for example urban 3.71 (Lewis 1929) and 3.45 Middlesex (Goodman and Tizard 1962), 3.54 Wessex (Kushlick and Cox 1968), one could conclude that the proportion of non-Down's syndrome severely handicapped (IQ 0–50) must have fallen. Lewis' figures showed a high incidence among rural children but fell substantially in the 15 to 19 age group, and it seems that he included a number of children who either improved or were mislabelled (Lewis 1929). It is possible that part of the improvement was due to recovery from minor brain damage or infections (ear infections were common in rural areas) or even communication, for his highest rates came from Cardigan, Wales, where Welsh was the first language. At all events age group 15 to 19 probably represents a truer prevalence rate.

More recently Stein and Susser (1971) considered changes in prevalence. They concluded that prevalence was increasing slightly, owing to longevity of Down's syndrome subjects and there was only a slight decrease in incidence of all other types. Kushlick and Cox (1968) agree, analysing mortality rates for a four-and-a-half year period using Wessex data. These suggested an increase in the more able and a static prevalence of the less able (profound) handicapped in the IQ 0–50 group. For the mildly handicapped (IQ 50–70) it is much harder to estimate change, for numbers and incidence depend so much on environmental variables. As Illingworth (1961) and others have found, it is difficult enough to predict the later ability of infants found to be mentally handicapped, although the predictive value of being under IQ 50 for children aged 7 to 14 is fairly good. In contrast the evidence shows that children of IQ 50–70 are responding to a variety of environmental deprivations and many make good social and work adjustments after leaving school. Indeed, where groups of these children have been tested in adult years, they have commonly risen in IQ test results, a sizable proportion being beyond IQ 80 and by no means intellectually handicapped. That they may still have degrees of personality or social handicap has been shown by Gibbens (1963) who found boys from low status homes to be much more likely to be convicted·and institutionalized than those from high status homes. Earlier editions of this book subscribed to the general view that the mildly handicapped tended to produce large families of dull if not problem children and therefore were best placed in segregated colonies. The theory behind this view has now been teased out into component parts and at least where marriage with birth control is concerned, might be thought to have swung full circle to advocacy in Sweden and elsewhere as Chapter 27 reports. Since it is perfectly true that larger families were common among the poor, two surveys of intelligence among 11-year-old Scottish children are relevant (Scottish Council for Research in Education 1949). These surveys were analysed to examine whether national intelligence was being adversely affected by large families born to low status parents. In 1932 87 498 children were found to have a mean test score of 34.5 (S.D. 15.5) compared to a mean of 36.7 (S.D. 16.1) for 70 805 children in 1947. It was felt that this small increase was due principally to improved tuition for low scorers. In other words it was possible to effect an improvement with these Scottish children by improving one of the environmental variables. Other variables such as low birth weight, large families and poor adult language contact may be currently being influenced by better obstetric facilities, falling birth rate, and television respectively.

Kushlick (1961) made an attempt to measure the number of mildly mentally handicapped people produced by the Salford community. He estimated the prevalence for the years 1948 and 1961 and found little difference. In addition the annual figures produced by the Department of Health and Social Security (1976) show a substantial decline in the proportion of mildly mentally handicapped in hospital which has more than halved from the figure of 52 per cent in 1954, and continues to fall. It is probable that this reflects a number of changes, including the increase in facilities for day work for this group in the community, the increase in hostel and boarding-house beds and the pressure on hospitals not to admit 'social problems'. Such figures do not represent the prevalence of the mildly mentally handicapped throughout the whole community. It is likely that the hospital numbers of mildly handicapped will continue to fall as measures to deal with such people by hospitalization fall increasingly out of favour (see Chapter 2). Unfortunately this policy, humane on many counts, leads to a dearth of facilities for the person from an overcrowded, poor home, once scoring IQ 50–70 but now an adult scoring IQ 70–90 in social difficulties in an increasingly automated society which does not need his work (Craft et al. 1975).

## SUMMARY AND CONCLUSIONS

It will be seen from this chapter that there have always been mentally handicapped people in our society. Not only are their handicaps commonly multiple, but so also is the causation. Research means that one can be far more clear as to causation now than in former editions and this is important as a guide to treatment.

The profoundly, severely and moderately handicapped (IQ 0–50) occur at an incidence of 3.45–3.89/1000 general population in most developed countries. Causation is multiple. *Chromosomal anomalies* such as Down's syndrome are responsible for over a third of the severely mentally handicapped; their genetic condition cannot be changed after conception, although modern methods of tuition aid many to reach a higher level of adult achievement than formerly, and many to be independent with supervision. *Genetic anomalies* such as phenylketonuria are increasingly open to treatment. *Neonatal and postnatal damage and infection* are preventable and treatable to a large extent. The effect of these variables is that the total incidence of these (IQ 0–50) is static, although the proportion with Down's syndrome within this group is rising. The proportion is also rising of those who with age are ambulant, continent and without severe behaviour disorder. The obvious deduction is that there is a diminishing proportion in this group who need to be in hospitals.

The mildly handicapped (IQ 50–70) are nine or more times commoner in incidence, and causation is rarely due to the pathological factors responsible for the IQ 0–50 group. The mild group rarely occurs among the higher social classes, and results from predom-inantly environmental and to a lesser degree multiple and additive genetic factors. In under-developed countries the effect of protein malnutrition and other deprivative variables are believed to raise the number of those affected. In developed countries there is evidence that special remedial education pro-grammes decrease the incidence.

The mildly handicapped, IQ 50–70, and others above this intellectual level, whose primary problems are lack of work in an auto-mated society, lack of adequate residence, or lack of controlling social influences and who may be labelled 'behaviourally disordered' are not discussed in this chapter. Some of their particular problems are discussed later—psychiatric problems in Chapter 9 and legal problems in Chapters 20 and 21. The political and economic aspects of planning are beyond the scope of a text such as this.

## BIBLIOGRAPHY

Akesson, H. (1961) *Epidemiology and Genetics of Mental Deficiency in a Southern Swedish Population.* Sweden: University of Uppsala.

Birch, H. G., Richardson, S. A., Baird, D., Horobin, C. & Illsley, R. (1970) *Mental Subnormality in the Community: A Clinical and Epidemiological Study,* Baltimore: Williams & Wilkins.

Board of Control (1954) *Memorandum of Evidence before the Royal Commission on the Law relating to Mental Illness and Mental Deficiency.* London: HMSO.

British Medical Association and Magistrates' Association (1947) *Interpretation of Definitions in the Mental Deficiency Act, 1927.* London: British Medical Association.

Clarke, A. D. B. (1969) *Recent Advances in the Study of Subnormality,* 2nd ed. London: National Association for Mental Health.

Clarke, A. M. & Clarke, A. D. B. (1974) *Mental Deficiency,* 3rd ed. London: Methuen.

Craft, M. J. (1959) Personality disorder and dullness. *Lancet, 1,* 856.

Craft, M. J. (1967) *Patterns of Care for the Subnormal,* Oxford: Pergamon.

Craft, M. J., Elliott, J. R. & Sime, D. A. (eds.) (1975) *Lost Souls: Services for Mentally Abnormal Offenders.* Mental Handicap Papers 7. London: King's Fund Centre.

Crome, L. (1960) The brain and mental retardation. *Br. med. J., 1,* 897–900.

Department of Health and Social Security and Welsh Office (1971) *Better Services for the Mentally Handicapped.* Cmnd. 4683. London: HMSO.

Drillien, C. M. (1961) A longitudinal survey of the growth of prematurely and maturely born children. Part VII. *Archs Dis. Childh., 36,* 233–40.

Drillien, C. M., Jameson, S. & Wilkinson, E. M. (1966) Studies in mental handicap. Part I: Prevalence and distribution by clinical type and severity of defect. *Archs Dis. Childh., 36,* 233–40.

Eaton, J. W. & Weil, R. J. (1955) *Culture and Mental Disorders.* Glencoe, Illinois: Free Press.

Gibbens, T. C. N. (1963) *Psychiatric Studies of Borstal Lads.* Oxford: Oxford University Press.

Goodman, N. & Tizard, J. (1962) Prevalence of imbecility and idiocy among children. *Br. med. J., 1,* 216–19.

Heber, R. (1961) A manual on terminology and classification in mental retardation, 2nd ed. *Am. J. ment. Defic.,* Suppl. No. 64.

Illingworth, R. S. (1961) The predictive value of developmental tests in the first year, with special reference to the diagnosis of mental subnormality. *J. Child Psychol. Psychiat., 2,* 210–15.

Klineberg, O. (1940) *Negro Intelligence and Selective Migration.* New York: Columbia University Press.

Kushlick, A. (1961) Subnormality in Salford. In: Susser, M. W. & Kushlick, A. (eds.), *A Report on the Mental Health Services in the City of Salford for the Year 1960.* Salford: Salford Health Department.

Kushlick, A. & Blunden, R. (1974) The epidemiology of mental subnormality. In: Clarke, A. M. & Clarke, A. D. B. (eds.), *Mental Deficiency,* 3rd ed. London: Methuen.

Kushlick, A. & Cox, G. (1968) Planning services for the subnormal in Wessex. In: Wing, J. K. & Bransby, B. R. (eds.), *Psychiatric Case Registers.* DHSS Statistical Report Series, No. 8. London: HMSO.

Lemkau, P., Tietze, C. & Cooper, M. (1943) Mental-hygiene problems in an urban district. Fourth Paper. *Ment. Hyg. Concord, 27.* 279–95.

Lewis, E. O. (1929) *The Report of the Mental Deficiency Committee being a Joint Committee of the Board of Education and Board of Control: Part IV—Report on an Investigation into the Incidence of Mental Deficiency in Six Areas, 1925-27.* London: HMSO.

Lewis, E. O. (1933) Types of mental deficiency and their social significance. *J. ment. Sci., 79,* 298–304.

Lilienfeld, A. M. & Pasamanick, B. (1955) Association of maternal and fetal factors with development of mental deficiency. Relationship to maternal age, birth order, previous reproductive loss and degree of mental deficiency. *Am. J. ment. Defic., 60,* 557–69.

Luria, A. R. (1963) *The Mentally Retarded Child.* Oxford: Pergamon.

O'Connor, N. & Tizard, J. (1954) A survey of patients in twelve mental deficiency institutions. *Br. med. J., 1,* 16–18.

O'Connor, N. & Tizard, J. (1956) *The Social Problem of Mental Deficiency.* Oxford: Pergamon.

*Onondaga County Survey* (1955) A special census of suspected referred mental retardation. *Community Ment. Hlth Res.* New York State Dept. of Mental Hygiene Report.

Penrose, L. S. (1938) A clinical and genetic study of 1280 cases of mental defect (Colchester Survey). *Spec. Rep. Ser. med. Res. Coun.,* No. 229. London: HMSO.

Penrose, L. S. (1962) Biological aspects. *Proc. Lond. Conf. scient. Stud. ment. Defic., 1,* 11–18.

Penrose, L. S. (1963) *The Biology of Mental Defect,* 3rd ed. London: Sidgwick & Jackson.

Roberts, J. A. F., Norman, R. M. & Griffiths, R. (1938) Studies on a child population: IV. The form of the lower end of the frequency distribution of Stanford Binet intelligence quotients and the fall of low intelligence quotients with advancing age. *Ann. Eugen., 8,* 319–36.

Sabagh, G., Dingman, H. F., Tarjan, G. & Wright, S. W. (1959) Social class and ethnic status of patients admitted to a state hospital for the retarded. *Pacific Sociol. Rev., 2,* 76–80.

Saenger, G. S. (1960) *Factors Influencing the Institutionalization of Mentally Retarded Individuals in New York City.* Report to the New York Interdepartmental Health Resources Board.

Sarason, S. B. & Doris, J. (1969) *Psychological Problems in Mental Deficiency,* 4th ed. New York: Harper & Row.

Scally, B. G. & Mackay, D. N. (1964) Mental subnormality and its prevalence in Northern Ireland. *Acta psychiat. Scand., 40,* 203–11.

*Scottish Council for Research in Education* (1949) *The Trend of Scottish Intelligence.* London: University of London Press.

*Scottish Council for Research in Education* (1953) *Social Implications of the 1947 Scottish Mental Survey, XXXV.* London: University of London Press.

Stein, Z. & Susser, M. (1963) The social distribution of mental retardation. *Am. J. ment. Defic., 67,* 811–21.

Stein, Z. & Susser, M. (1971) Changes over time in the incidence and prevalence of mental retardation. In: Helimuth, J. (ed.), *Exceptional Infants; vol. 2, Studies in Abnormalities.* New York: Brunner/Mazel Inc.

Susser, M. W. & Watson, W. (1962) *Sociology in Medicine.* Oxford: Oxford University Press.

Tizard, J. (1958) Longitudinal and follow-up studies. In: Clarke, A. M. and Clarke, A. D. B. (eds.) *Mental Deficiency: The Changing Outlook,* 1st ed. London: Methuen.

Tizard, J. (1964) *Community Services for the Mentally Handicapped.* Oxford: Oxford University Press.

Tredgold, A. F. (1952) *Mental Deficiency,* 8th ed. London: Baillière, Tindall.

Wechsler, D. (1958) *The measurement and Appraisal of Human Intelligence.* Baltimore: Williams and Wilkins.

Wing, L. (1971) Severely retarded children in a London area: prevalence and provision of services. *J. psychol. med. 1,* 405–15.

*World Health Organization* (1968) *Organization of Services for the Mentally Retarded.* 15th Report of the WHO Expert Committee on Mental Health. *Tech. Rep. Ser. Wld Hlth Org.,* 392.

# CHAPTER 2

# THE MULTIDISCIPLINARY TEAM AND FORWARD PLANNING

## MICHAEL CRAFT

Although there is much lip-service paid to the concept of a multidisciplinary team, it is more commonly talked about than successfully put into practice.

Like many ideas concerning democracy the concept requires good leaders and good organization to be effective. In theory different groups of qualified professionals need to assess the needs of handicapped individuals at important points in life progress. Both leaders and members of the team will vary according to the priorities at issue. For example the pregnant woman with a rhesus incompatible fetus will expect her obstetrician to lead a team at the time of birth which will include nursing, ancillary and pathological staff. The obstetrician will also be responsible for records at this point.

If the exchange transfusion of blood which is planned does not successfully avoid brain damage to the infant, then a different multidisciplinary team will be responsible for care. Despite advances rhesus incompatibility still caused the death of 34 infants in the United Kingdom in 1977 and many more were permanently damaged.

The paediatrician is likely to lead, and his secretary to record, the team's decisions on care for a brain-damaged infant. Breathing, feeding and the mobility problems of a spastic child are likely to engage the attentions of a team of doctors, nurses and physiotherapists during the child's infancy.

Often the first, and a major, task facing the multidisciplinary team is to break the news to parents that their newly born or young infant is mentally handicapped. The manner of the presentation of this information

and the follow-up, has far-reaching consequences. Chapter 13 indicates the advantages of involving parents in early stimulation of handicapped infants; this can be a therapy both to the child in terms of future development and to the parents as a positive way to reduce their feelings of helplessness and desperation. Chapter 23 describes in detail the counselling of parents in the initial stages of diagnosis (and shock) so that they can start the process of optimal stimulation of their child. The majority of parents of handicapped infants feel that they did not receive sufficient or accurate information on these points during the early period after the disclosure. The well-organized multidisciplinary team has a major part to play during this vital period, especially if parents are going to enter into intervention programmes as soon as possible.

For the child who is brain damaged, early and skilled educational advice is important, as although the damage is dome, brain damage at birth is non-progressive and the brain has alternative learning pathways which can be brought into use. The needs here are therefore different from those of a progressive disability with genetic programming for advance, such as Huntington's chorea with risk of death in adolescence. Parents of the non-progressive brain-damaged child need advice from the team psychologist on learning methods and ways in which they can help their child in learning acquisition such as speech and motor

The author is grateful to Dr. G. B. Simon, Director, National Development Group, for the many discussions which preceded the writing of this chapter.

skills. Whoever leads the team at this point needs to allot responsibility for action and follow-up based on team decisions.

At different stages, needs change and *ad hoc* teams can best be assembled to meet the needs of the moment. Educational needs in childhood give way to work needs in adolescence; unfortunately the families of handicapped people are prone to break up, so that possibly social work, residential needs, further training, even psychiatric advice without or within hospital may be required.

At each point in time there is either a clear leader (for example, headmaster at school) or one should be appointed. The leader has important duties:

1. To record agreements.
2. To note who is responsible for the implementation of team decisions.
3. To clarify dates at which progress is to be monitored (if at all).
4. To give a clear summary of the position to mother, subject—and the team! This avoids confusion, overlap between team members and the waste of second opinions sought by an uncomprehending or despairing mother.

## RESPONSIBILITY IN THE MULTIDISCIPLINARY TEAM

It is self-evident that the members of the team should take a pride in their work as well as enjoy it. Their *official responsibility* should be to ensure that their standards are the best that can be obtained. *Interpersonal responsibility* should acknowledge that ideals represent perfection and few team members are saints; some fill in the gap between ideals and actuality by means of alcohol, nicotine, sex or psychiatric illness. Where private lives do not hinder professional competence, they have a right to be private; but one part of official responsibility in a team is to recognize when team members need help, and to arrange that help is available.

Much argument has recently raged as to *legal responsibilities*. This problem should be clear enough in most Western countries. All Western states allot responsibility of patients in a hospital bed to a hospital consultant, who leads the hospital team which assesses needs. Within the community this responsi-bility is taken by the person responsible for the care system, the headmaster within school, psychiatrist for a course of out-patient treatment, hostel warden for hostel residents, psychologist for assessment and behaviour modification procedures. A professional is expected at law to make an assessment, to embark on such manoeuvres as seem warranted and lie within his competence, to avoid negligence, to terminate care when targets have been achieved (or are no longer possible) *and to record so.* An action for negligence is only likely to succeed if someone can be shown to have practised substantially below the standards expected by his profession *and that the recipient has suffered damage as a result.* An essential part of judgement will be on records kept. This point is laboured since personal experience is that many multi-disciplinary teams lack records, and are often seriously negligent in noting their decisions, actions and who is responsible for next steps forward. This discussion on legal responsi-bility should clarify responsibilities in a team, where members might like to think they are equal, but in practice they are not. Someone will be expected at a court of enquiry or investigation to have accepted responsibility.

The multidisciplinary team will experience pressure upon it from both community and hospital-based services. In many ways it is an unenviable position for deficiencies are highlighted, while smooth functioning goes unremarked, yet it is a position which a team is far better able to cope with than a lone professional. The team has a responsibility to the community, the base hospital, the employing authority, and last, but by no means least, the *raison d'être* of the whole system, the client/patient. What happens when a patient is referred from the community and the hospital or residential unit staff feel they do not have the necessary security or resources to deal with him? Several options might be appropriate:

1. Convincing nursing and administrative colleagues of the need for re-arrangement of services to provide what is needed. For instance one hospital ward could be designated as 'locked' on a temporary or permanent basis, with patients who do not need this being transferred out.

2. Obtaining a second opinion. The local general psychiatric hospital may still give this service. The consultant may ask the Department of Health and Social Security for permission to transfer to the locked special hospitals of Rampton and Moss Side.

3. If the patient has committed an offence which is serious enough, an arrest may be made for remand or prison centre, for further enquiries or re-arrangements to be made.

4. A better staffed hospital in the region (usual population 2–5 000 000) may be prevailed upon to accept the patient.

5. The area authority should be informed, in detail, and if necessary on more than one occasion, of the needs to be met. Area staff would be expected to investigate how far these could be met from current resources, or to report the deficiencies to the regional health authority. Such appeals would weigh heavily in any subsequent inquiry as to whether the team 'had made every effort to secure treatment, as was commensurate with the situation.'

6. Appeals to members of parliament, newspapers, radio or television can be viewed with disapproval if not first cleared with the employing authority. One medical superintendent in New England made a famous television film later denounced by his employing authority. His subsequent permanent vacation to Bermuda was said to be enhanced only by the royalties from the resultant best-seller.

Whichever profession has the major responsibility for the care of a difficult client/patient it is essential that a record of decisions and the reasons for these is kept, and that the next senior link in the hierarchy is fully briefed.

Whilst records, letters and team decisions are important, meetings are crucial and should be attended by all who carry responsibility. Most professionals are prepared to carry their share of responsibility; a few are not. What is the team to do when faced with a key member who is always late, or often absent, or who sabotages each meeting, claiming perhaps that he is acting 'in the best interests of the patient?' The team may try to do without this person, but if so, his persistent lateness or absence should be recorded, in case the team's decisions may later be ques-

tioned. At other times a second opinion at a different level of the hierarchy may be needed. The occasional consultant may be so self-righteous that he can only function with a few adulatory colleagues. The occasional chief nurse may be so fearful, or his union so militant that his hospital needs an enquiry. The occasional social worker may be so full of client-centred concepts of illness, that he cannot function in a hospital-based team, or alongside hospital-orientated colleagues.

*Decision-making*

As a guide to team work, there are at least three basic assessments to be made. First is the *anatomic diagnosis* and the resultant treatment. Where the brain damage is non-progressive there may be little medical input needed, but for many genetic misendowments continuing medication is advisable, such as diets and drugs in phenylketonuria.

A second decision for the team is an estimation of the *present level of functioning* and following from this the gaps in achievement which need attention. Many handicapped people advance faster in one area such as self-help skills than another such as communication. A concerted effort in language tuition may be needed.

A third decision is the assessment of *current and future residential need*. Children ought to be at home, and most can be taught sufficient self-help skills to be able to maintain themselves in sheltered accommodation (see Chapter 18). In adolescence and early life, the skills of a social worker may be much needed to obtain home relief for tension, or a residential placement for further education.

To meet the needs of children, the multidisciplinary team will come together on an *ad hoc* or temporary basis. For the needs of adolescents and adults, a more permanent team with longer term planning is required. The team will need access to a residential assessment unit. Research shows that a parent population of 200 000 provides sufficient mental handicap problems for a team of convenient size to meet at frequent intervals. The residential and day care needs for this population have been estimated with considerable accuracy (see Table 2.1), updated by Craft and Wilkins (1978).

TABLE 2.1

Planning figures for services for the mentally handicapped compared with existing provision

| Type of service | Places for children (age 0–15) | | | Places for adults (age 16 + ) | | |
|---|---|---|---|---|---|---|
| | Required | | Provided | Required | | Provided |
| | Per 100 000 total population | Total England and Wales 1969 | Total England and Wales 1969 | Per 100 000 total population | Total England and Wales 1969 | Total England and Wales 1969 |
| Day care or education for children under five | 8 | 3900 | 500* | — | — | — |
| Education for children of school age: | | | | | | |
| In the community | | | | | | |
| (i) for children with severe mental handicap living in the community | 56 | 27 400 | 23 400 | — | — | — |
| (ii) for children coming by day from hospital | 6 | 2900 | | — | — | — |
| In hospitals | | | | | | |
| (iii) for in-patients | 7 | 3400 | 4600 | — | — | — |
| (iv) for day patients | 6 | 2900 | 200 | — | — | — |
| Occupation and training for adults: | | | | | | |
| In the community | | | | | | |
| (i) for adults living in the community | — | — | — | 130 | 63 700 | 24 500 |
| (ii) for adults coming by day from hospital | — | — | — | 20 | 9800 | 100 |
| In hospitals | | | | | | |
| (iii) for in-patients | — | — | — | 35 | 17 200 | 30 000* |
| (iv) for day patients | — | — | — | 10 | 4900 | 200* |
| Residential care in the community (including short-stay) | | | | | | |
| (i) in local authority, voluntary or privately owned residential homes | 10 | 4900 | 1800 | 60 | 29 400 | 4300 |
| (ii) foster homes, lodgings, etc. | 2 | 1000 | 100 | 15 | 7400 | 550 |
| Hospital treatment: | | | | | | |
| (i) for in-patients | 13 | 6400 | 7400† | 55 | 27 000 | 52 100† |
| (ii) for day patients | 6 | 2900 | 200* | 10 | 4900 | 500* |

* Estimated.
† NHS beds allocated to mental handicap.

From DHSS (1971).

The short and medium term residential beds in hospitals and hostels needed by a team for a population of 200 000 are 50 child (under 15) and 260 adult (15+) beds for all degrees of mental handicap. Using Kushlick's analysis, over half the children and less than a quarter of the adults need intensive care on a one-to-one staffing basis, but how the mix is organized will be up to the team. Currently in the UK most intensive care needs are met by mental handicap hospital beds, but there is a current move toward small residential units for this group; understandably such units find it easiest to care for the least handicapped who by definition have least need of residential care.

DISTRICT FORWARD PLANNING

### Joint planning

It is very important that the team contributes to planning in such a way that its decisions are accepted by the organizations which control the funds. If the team already consists of the local professionals labelled as experts in the field, it is very likely that they themselves would be nominated by the various statutory bodies in charge of planning. Thus in the UK, the area health authority for hospitals; social service department for homes; educational authority for residential schools; and local voluntary bodies for charity complexes, all need to have a say. Without joint planning wasteful overlap is common, chaos possible. It is also essential for the chairman to keep his members to targets which are practical for the handicapped rather than ideals which may be wish-fulfilment by parents who sit on voluntary bodies.

### The target population

Chapter 1 in this book gives the epidemiological guidelines for assessment of population needs in an area under survey. More detailed ways to achieve this end are to enumerate the actual people who are receiving services to date in the area, or those who need them. The latter can be culled from waiting lists and registers. A review such as this is likely to show up shortfalls in service provision and outline areas of forward need. Whilst actual case registers are time-consuming, listing of names and comparison with neighbouring district lists allows avoidance of duplication. An extra help is a simple letter or questionnaire sent to names on a list to check they are living and needing further care. Recently three Welsh housing authorities cut their waiting lists by half by such measures, although to their chagrin their government grant was reduced in proportion!

### Monitoring

Continuous listing of names, or similar case registry, allows an annual or periodic check on usage of services. Commonly used by social workers, such monitoring also allows holiday residential needs to be planned, day work places to be allocated and planned, and bed needs forecast. This procedure is in the nature of local research. An example is an annual check with neonatal departments. Some English counties have reported a halving in the rate of production of Down's syndrome babies over recent years, presumably the result of refinements of obstetric intervention. The implications for later residential needs are clear, for such subjects have to date accounted for one third of the residential needs among the severely mentally handicapped.

### Organizational priorities

*Primary care* is obviously the first priority need. The family doctor at the health clinic may be the first professional consulted by the mother in her quest for help, therefore every general practitioner in the area needs to know where he can get assistance for the mother of a handicapped child. In many places there is a specialist nurse or health visitor attached to each family practice with the statutory duty to visit all newly born infants and give advice to the mothers of the handicapped. If they are also attached to the specialist paediatric clinic at the local hospital then continuity of care will be assured. They may also benefit from occasional seminars, visits and discussions on an area or regional basis. In the same way specialist psychiatric nurses are becoming available for the mentally disordered, including the behaviourally disturbed adult handicapped. Similarly social workers may be attached to a large practice.

*The multidisciplinary team* for the mentally handicapped may be based in the paediatric clinic for the child, or the out-patient clinic of the district general hospital for the adult. In each case the important thing is not so much where the team meets, but that it is seen to have a regular meeting place so that professionals including nurses, relatives and others know where to seek help. Some teams prefer to meet at regular intervals in the adult training centre, sheltered workshop or hostel. In this way on-going assessment and problems of clients can be regularly reviewed together with the staff worries which are often as important. Some clinics consist only of staff interviews, with requests for expert guidance.

*Voluntary services, employment agencies and housing authorities* have contributions to make in the mental handicap field and need expert advice on how they might best be deployed. Voluntary bodies often have a great deal of enthusiasm and a good deal of dedication, but need professional estimation of realistic goals. Employment niches have always been difficult to achieve for the mentally handicapped and with increasing automation in Western countries are likely to become yet more difficult. The guidance of the team will be needed to ensure an adequate progression from special school to adult training centre and thence to sheltered workshop and possibly open employment. Sheltered housing is a critical area for forward planning. It is rare to find in mental handicap services the range of housing such as is now frequently provided for the elderly, yet this parallel is close. A small proportion of each needs intensive care, that is, nursing or personal care on a one-to-one basis; a large proportion can look after immediate personal needs in bedsitting rooms, but need some supervision. The biggest group can live independently or in partnership, needing only day occupation and easy access to social work services.

## Priorities in childhood

Bringing up a mentally handicapped child is fraught with hazards and it is now known that a greater proportion of families raising handicapped children end in divorce than do families with normal children. Mothers of handicapped children need continuous counselling and guidance from the birth onwards, not only in educational targets but also in methods of handling and the type of self-care targets feasible with their particular child. An early priority for the team will therefore be regular assessments for the children within their area of practice so that at least mothers will have a forum in which to air their difficulties.

A further priority is short-term day or residential relief in case of need. There are many ways in which this can be provided, most depending on local facilities. Voluntary bodies may be able to help, together with local churches, in providing playgroups and baby-sitting services; mental handicap hospitals and hostels usually set aside a number of short-term care beds; short-term fostering is another possibility.

The need for hospital care for children under 14 is decreasing fast, indeed some believe that no child under 14 should be in a mental handicap hospital at all. At all events for those in hospital much can be done by way of visiting, holidays, and help for the family when their child returns home.

## Priorities in adult needs

By the time the mentally handicapped person reaches adult age, his needs will be more circumscribed. However, holiday care, evening or weekend leisure pursuits, further education and social visits are all likely to be areas of continuing need. The team may be able to make a contribution in association with voluntary societies and redeployment of government services at present under-used.

Eventually planning will be needed for alternative homes when parents die, or can no longer look after their son or daughter. Throughout the Western world there has been a great upsurge of interest recently in alternative residential possibilities for the mentally handicapped. In some areas enthusiasm is for small group homes, in others religious units, in others it is a commune with a degree of mysticism. There is plenty of room for people to enter the field with panache and enthusiasm to help the handicapped. Whilst some organizations need advice, and others careful inspection to ascertain motivation, the fact remains that Western communities commonly have a good deal of under-deployed residential accommodation, and people able and willing to give help. Queen Victoria observed with feeling that females in our society have a distressing tendency to live considerably longer than their husbands. Many women, having lost married partners somewhat older than themselves, have empty houses and empty lives which with help and counselling they might be aided to fill. Any local residential scheme needs a good deal of organization and professional expertise to become successful, but this is an area of priority which will provide work to be done for many years ahead. Elsewhere in this book there is discussion of improvements in the quality of residential care, and methods of enriching the lives of the handicapped (see Chapters 18 and 19).

Due to the overlap of agencies, and the multiplication of services interested in the mentally and physically handicapped, parents are often unclear about where to go for various needs. The production of a local index or guide to services by the team is a very valuable resource. The index should include agencies with their addresses and telephone numbers and a brief description of the services they can offer. Such an index needs regular, if not annual, updating.

*Links with the community*

Much can be done by a coordination of local facilities and agencies. Among local services which can be persuaded to help are: Boy Scout and Girl Guide groups; job creation schemes; local church groups; community leisure and recreation centres; education units of all kinds; charity organizations. Any one of these might feel their services under-used, or be looking for fresh outlets for local energy.

MENTAL HANDICAP SERVICES
FOR THE FUTURE

The concept of a multidisciplinary team is hardly a panacea for current problems in the mental handicap field, but it is one way of bringing expert help and advice to the affected, and of proposing and implementing improvements in a democratic society. If people do work together in planning and action, what will this mean for the shape of services in the future? It is possible to make some forecasts using data from England and Wales that have become available since the 1971 forecast, *Better Services for the Mentally Handicapped* (DHSS 1971, and Table 2.1).

In planning a range of special services for mentally handicapped people it is important for each planning team to be aware of the different types of service required and to form an estimate of the numbers of likely users. For instance, there is a good deal of information on the prevalence of severe mental handicap in Western societies, whereas the prevalence of mild mental handicap is not known with accuracy and to some extent its identification is dependent upon employment opportunities and the presence of special services for the mentally handicapped. In general, countries with high birth rates are likely to have high birth incidence but low childhood prevalence rates for mental handicap. With increasing development of a society, however, the better prospect for survival of cases of severe mental handicap will increase their prevalence, and the urbanization and sophistication of a developing society will pose greater problems for the mildly mentally handicapped. However, the development of services for the mentally handicapped is frequently not seen as a high priority in the medical, social or political sense. This is largely due to the lack of recognition of the developmental potential of the mentally handicapped and to the failure to appreciate the prospects for reducing the numbers of dependent mentally handicapped people by the provision of a comprehensive range of services. Such a range should contain a number of clearly identifiable elements.

*Prevention and early detection services*

The prospects are that with a general improvement in social conditions and medical services there are likely to be fewer mentally handicapped people who require special services. The availability of good family planning services, genetic advisory services, improved antenatal and postnatal care and immunization programmes are significant factors in reducing the incidence of severe mental handicap. Regular screening and developmental assessment, particularly of children at special risk, will improve the early detection of mental handicap. Amniocentesis is the recent procedure whereby amniotic fluid is extracted from the sac surrounding the fetus and examined for cells and for protein. Four per cent of fetuses are chromosomal anomalies (although most are miscarried) whose cells can be detected (see pp. 68–70). In addition, detection of abnormal proteins allows spina bifida to be diagnosed and therapeutic abortion offered (see p. 119).

### Comprehensive assessment and re-assessment

Comprehensive assessment is a coordinated and multiprofessional procedure which takes account of social, educational, medical and psychological aspects and should lead to the development of a plan to meet the individual's needs. A comprehensive assessment service is of course necessary for all handicapped children.

Periodic re-assessment should take place at particular times of stress such as at school-leaving age and in the early post-school years. It will also, of course, take place whenever considered necessary by any change in the circumstances.

### Special education

As a general principle no child, however handicapped, should be excluded from the educational system. Countries developing educational programmes should include mentally handicapped children within them from the beginning. In general handicapped children should not be placed in special schools if their needs can be met in ordinary schools. However, some of the more severely handicapped children, often with major emotional and physical handicaps, may need to be provided for in special schools. Many mentally handicapped children require specific programmes with clear objectives and periods of intensive help, often on a one-to-one basis.

### Community support services

Local social services and other agencies should provide coordinated advice, support and practical help for the mentally handicapped person and his family. This may need to be supplemented by residential accommodation from time to time and by day services for adults.

### Day care for adults

In times of good employment most school leavers who are mentally handicapped can go directly into some form of open or sheltered employment. The more severely handicapped need some form of permanent day care which provides sheltered work or occupation together with further education and social training geared to develop the individual's maximum potential. Mildly mentally handicapped people should be acceptable in government training rehabilitation schemes whilst the more severely handicapped will require special day centres. These might be from 20 to 100 places in size depending on the area served. The working day should reflect that of normal industry as far as possible but it is important that the centres can provide for small groups of people with different needs and every attempt should be made to secure integration with industrial, social and other community facilities (see Chapter 16).

### Residential accommodation

In general mentally handicapped people should be enabled to live with their own families. Where this is not possible they should live as close as possible to their home area and for children the first choice would be a foster home. The needs of adults may be met by small group homes or hostels. This accommodation should be domestic in character and the aim should be to provide small living groups of up to about six for children and 12 for adults. Adults and children should be provided for separately and the children should go daily to school and the adults to their employment or day centre.

### Hospital medical services

Generally mentally handicapped people will use the medical services available to the community. Some special hospital services may need to be provided for those mentally handicapped people with physical disabilities and behaviour disorders which require considerable medical and nursing care. Yet again such special hospital accommodation should be domestic in character, provide for small group care, serve local communities and provide day facilities, and there should be separate provision for children and for adults.

The range of services outlined above requires contributions from a number of agencies including health, social services, education and employment and the recognition by these agencies of the contribution they have to make is probably best achieved by the formulation of a national policy which remits to each agency, after discussion, a clear responsibility for providing certain elements of the service. In England, the provision of services at local level is principally the responsibility of the health authority and the local authority, the latter including the social services department and the education authority. In order to plan coordinated services for certain groups such as the elderly, the mentally ill and the mentally handicapped the health authority and the local authority have established joint consultative committees and many of these joint committees have now established joint care planning teams for mental handicap whose function is to draw up a coordinated set of plans following the general guidelines of the government's White Paper, *Better Services for the Mentally Handicapped* (DHSS 1971), for the area for which they are responsible. These planning teams should review existing resources and formulate some idea of the local need for services, taking account both of their own knowledge of the numbers receiving and requiring services and of the quantitative planning guidelines in the White Paper. Of course, it is not sufficient to plan only for special schools, day services for adults and residential accommodation. In addition an organic element must be added to what is otherwise a collection of isolated facilities provided by different agencies. Formerly this depended on the presence of a strong leader in the clinical team, now it is the *raison d'être* of the multidisciplinary team comprising members with equal professional status.

A substantial contribution to this concept has occurred in England since 1975 as a result of the booklets and activities of the National Development Group. Many of their recommendations have been used in this chapter, and they will be referred to again in later chapters (see Part III, Psychology and Education).

Where countries have no agreed national plan for the development and provision of services for the mentally handicapped a working group at national level should consider drawing up recommendations for service development. The WHO technical report, *Organization of Services for the Mentally Retarded* (WHO 1968), might form a useful discussion document and the working group might include representatives from the major government agencies involved—social security, education, health and employment—the principal professions involved—the social services, education, medicine, nursing, psychology—and the representatives of parents or voluntary organizations. The functions of such a committee would be to develop general policies for the development of services, to advise on good service practice and to encourage and promote research and the application of its findings. Generally services for the mentally handicapped are best provided from existing social, educational, medical and vocational services making use of joint planning committees to assist with the problems of coordination. Provision of services in this way avoids the segregating concept of a special service for the mentally handicapped and allows them to benefit from developments in the individual specialist services. It may also be useful to develop one or more 'model services'. These may be located in areas with good professional and academic resources. The model service should serve a defined catchment area of perhaps half a million people. This should make it possible for basic epidemiological data to be collected and evaluated which may give an indication for national needs. It could allow also for a range of services to be developed which would form both a sophisticated base for assessing and meeting the needs of the handicapped people but would also constitute a staff training and development base of national benefit.

## PROGRESS TOWARDS SOME POLICY TARGETS IN ENGLAND

Table 2.2 records the position in 1977 comparing it with the White Paper estimates (DHSS 1971). There has been an annual in-

TABLE 2.2

Number of places provided in 1969 and 1977,
and White Paper targets*

| Type of service | Places provided 1969 | Places provided 1977 | White Paper targets 1991 |
|---|---|---|---|
| Local authority residential care | | | |
| Children | 1800 | 2100 | 4900 |
| Adults | 4300 | 11 300 | 29 400 |
| Adult training centres | 24 600 | 37 600 | 73 500 |
| Hospitals | 59 500 | 52 700 | 33 400 |

* From DHSS (1971).

crease of 2 per cent and 13 per cent respectively in children and adult residential places and 6 per cent in local authority day places. To reach White Paper targets by 1991 growth rates of 6 per cent and 7 per cent would have to be sustained in local authority children and adult residential provision and 4 per cent growth in local authority day places. If local authorities are broadly able to continue the rate of growth achieved to date then they should be able to reach the White Paper targets by the early 1990s.

## CONCLUSIONS

The idea of the multidisciplinary team and its joint care planning is a challenging concept for professionals working in a catchment area. It is more difficult to carry through than the earlier simplistic system whereby a powerful leader issued orders which were obeyed without question. This was usually a clinician, wearing a medical halo, which in this age of powerful drugs still fits well on many doctoral brows. However the needs of a mentally handicapped person usually become more educational, occupational and social in nature as the years advance, and the clinical priority decreases in importance.

The advantages to the recipients of a well-run multidisciplinary service are obvious. Parents can be supported and they know where to turn to for relief and advice. Referrals from one professional to another are expedited, records of progress can cover all areas of life and are not duplicated, a high standard of delivery of care can be maintained.

There are also profound personal advantages in the multidisciplinary approach. Shared responsibility leads to decreased stress for the isolated and often lonely professional; it leads to shared enjoyment with joint meetings which are often social as well as professional; it can lead to the stimulation of a minor research project; it brings professionals into contact with lay volunteers.

It may need a new brand and generation of professionals to develop the concept to the full, but recent graduates are increasingly keen to evolve a system of care which makes use of all their expertise.

## BIBLIOGRAPHY

Craft, M. & Wilkins, R. (1978) Residential needs in hospital and the community for mentally handicapped people. *Br. J. psychiat.*, *132*, 450–54.

Department of Health and Social Security and Welsh Office (1971) *Better Services for the Mentally Handicapped.* Cmnd. 4683. London: HMSO.

World Health Organization (1968) *Organization of Services for the Mentally Retarded.* 15th Report of WHO Expert Committee on Mental Health. *Tech. Rep. Ser. Wld Hlth Org.*, 392.

# CHAPTER 3

# ORGANIZING SERVICES FOR MENTALLY RETARDED PERSONS: A NORTH AMERICAN VIEW

## G. ALLAN ROEHER

Although they differ in many ways, both Canada and the United States followed the world-wide trend of institutionalizing the handicapped in the nineteenth century, and current needs are complicated by attachment of present resources to past buildings. Yet nowhere has the pace of change been greater. The rate of hospital discharge has been fast, and the total number of institutionalized patients has dropped, aided partly by natural wealth available for alternative homes, partly by parental pressure against new admissions and professional response to court requirements for discharge. Whilst provinces and states set differing standards throughout the North American continent, the rights of handicapped people have now been enshrined in federal law, notably Section 504 of the US 1973 Vocational Rehabilitation Act, and in the recent court case of *Wyatt* v. *Stickney* (see Chapter 22, and Appendix, p. 372). Parental groups, affiliated to the National Association for Retarded Citizens in the USA, and the Association for the Mentally Retarded in Canada, have spoken out to ensure these rights operate locally. Whilst almost all agree that there is a place for hospitals treating the multiply handicapped, the concept of small homely neighbourhood units has evolved for the vast majority, visited by members of the multidisciplinary team on a community basis.

## THE PRESENT SITUATION IN THE UNITED STATES

Both in Canada and the United States services have developed unevenly, with some excellent systems evolving in some big towns, while in some rural areas the handicapped remain relatively unserviced. The US Department of Health, Education and Welfare (HEW) currently estimates some six million citizens are mentally retarded, 95 per cent being mildly and 5 per cent being severely handicapped. In 1974 it was estimated that some nine billion US dollars, including $1.9 billion for state institutions, were deployed on direct costs of treatment and the result of economic losses. The federal support of $1.5 billion is an important boost to predominantly state financed programmes, for it is contingent on state improvements in care, protection and rights to treatment.

The 'present' really starts in 1963 when, as a result of President Kennedy's enthusiastic lead, massive federal funds became available. These helped state governments, private voluntary organizations and the universities to expand educational, vocational and community programmes, provide personal pensions and supplementary benefits and promote research into causation respectively. The federal lead was intended to aid community support and the development of alternative homes. In 1971 President Nixon established as a national goal the return to community living of one-third of the mentally retarded persons living in institutions.

Statistics tell one side of the story. Whereas in 1963 there were 176 500 retardates in the state mental handicap institutions, and this actually advanced to 193 200 in 1967, it fell steadily thereafter. There were 181 000 in 1971, 168 300 in 1975 with further declines in subsequent years. Unfortunately, there has been a concomitant rise in re-admissions just as in the mental illness field, although it has not been so great. Re-admissions in 1963 were 12 per cent of all admissions (total 15 150) compared with 27 per cent for 1971 of a total of 15 370, and an estimated 28 per cent in 1974. Some 67 per cent of new admissions were between the ages of 3 and 21, the years at which it might be supposed that the retarded are most susceptible to community education and community support measures. That figure is a measure of how far we have yet to go. In fact, in 1974 the primary reasons given for re-admissions were lack of community services and follow-up, failure to adjust to community living, and rejection by the community, although in another survey 85 per cent of former institution residents stated that they much preferred living in local community group residences.

The American courts have greatly aided both this return to the community and the prevention of further institutional placements by laying down strict requirements and safeguards for admissions (see Chapter 22). As a result, in some states, there has been a wholesale discharge of inmates from institutions and the growth of many nursing home and private-for-profit units of poor standard, some of which are so large that in effect residents merely move from one institution to another without gain in programme or privacy. It was once said that the excellent state institutions compared to the worst were 'islands of excellence surrounded by oceans of inadequacy' but there is no reason why this analogy should not also describe community group homes. The problem becomes how to aid the least effective homes to develop better programmes, and how best to use the considerable funding available. In fact, almost every type of service needed for the handi-

capped can be funded wholly or partly by federal funds. Over one hundred federal programmes operated by eleven major departments and agencies are currently in operation.*

Cost evaluation of these programmes and residential units is in its infancy. Conley's (1973) review reported a range of findings from the community approach costing less than institutions to about the same.

Federal funding is unique in being influenced (but not determined) by the President's Committee on Mental Retardation. This is a standing committee appointed by the President to coordinate interests without jurisdictional power and has been particularly effective in determining the direction of government leads. Unfortunately it is difficult to ensure that these federal guidelines are translated to effective action at local level. Just as in other big countries, local community services are commonly fragmented and unclear. The discharged resident may become lost among various agencies and levels of local government, whereas in the institution the superintendent had clearcut responsibility. The individual efforts of federal agencies, according to the General Audit Office, are often not well coordinated, resulting in a wastage of funding. In fact the basic problem at all levels of government is that the agencies which have parallel responsibility commonly do not control all the funds necessary to develop the adequate comprehensive community-based care systems which were intended. Nor do they have sufficient responsibility to monitor or regulate standards of community care. No unified national strategy or management system exists either to implement a comprehensive service or to coordinate the plethora of efforts made by the many major federal departments and programmes involved in the field. This is despite numerous offices, task forces and committees

* The main federal department is HEW, other influential bodies are the American Association of Mental Deficiency (representing workers in general); the Council for Exceptional Children (primarily serving special education workers); the Association of University Affiliated Programs (staff of the university affiliated centres); the National Association of Coordinators of State Programs for the Mentally Retarded; and the National Association for Retarded Citizens (the primary citizen-orientated action group).

set up to coordinate the considerable array of programmes. It is hoped that the recent initiative by President Carter to consolidate with HEW the variety of sub-divisions concerned (for example, the Developmental Disabilities Office, and the President's Committee on Mental Retardation) will be effective at federal level.

## THE PRESENT SITUATION IN CANADA

Although Canada is larger in land area than the United States, the population of 23 million is approximately one tenth and is mainly concentrated along the border. The division of power and responsibility between federal and provincial governments is similar to the United States, except that in education the US Federal Government has a direct role, which is not the case in Canada. US federal agencies are far more effective in determining programme direction, although in both countries in 1978 the federal governments contributed half the funds to the state/province of the cost of human services.

Canada has nothing similar to the President's Committee on Mental Retardation, for the Canadian Association for the Mentally Retarded (CAMR) is a non-governmental advocacy body. CAMR is a federation of ten provincial and 370 local organizations with approximately 30 000 members, in contrast with the US National Association for Retarded Citizens which has about 150 000 members in 50 states, and 1800 local units. The Canadian Association plays a significant role in influencing national programmes, partly because of the more passive role of Canadian federal government agencies, and also because it serves as a major link between professional interests and the consumer citizen movement. This is achieved in part through the National Institute on Mental Retardation which is operated by CAMR.

Canadian law makes it very difficult, if not impossible, to resort to legal action and use of the courts, as has been done successfully within the United States. A major impetus to progress in the field has been the prestige and influence of the late President Kennedy and members of his family, and the support of subsequent presidents and major congressional leaders.

No such parallel situation has occurred in Canada. Another difference is that general human services are provided in a more universal and less complex manner in Canada. Medical and hospital care is a universal, comprehensive (provincial government-operated, federal government-supported) service. The United States has a series of medical care programmes but not a universal scheme. Education is the complete responsibility of provincial education departments; federal support for social services, vocational rehabilitation and supplementary income is less complex. These distinctions have had a significant influence on the roles performed by voluntary agencies. Voluntary non-profit organizations function more in partnership with governments at the national level* (though at the local levels the pattern within each of the two countries is similar). There are also fewer proprietary private-for-profit operations, except perhaps in Quebec.

Pressure in Canada for improving the situation for its mentally retarded citizens seems to have lagged somewhat behind that of the United States (for example NARC was established in 1953; CAMR in 1958). This may be due, in part, to Canadian health and social services developing more along the European pattern (universal coverage, less categorical and fragmented) and, in part, to demography—a more dispersed population. A third reason is the more passive role of the federal agencies in specific programmes. Long-range planning and programme stimulation at the national level have depended largely on the citizen movement (CAMR), described in more detail under the section on the CAMR 'Plan for the 1970s' (p. 32). How do the two countries now compare in provision of services? In general, the answer appears to be—about the same.

---

* Examples: 1. The human blood supply service—one of the finest in the world—is operated by the Canadian Red Cross Blood Donor Service, but funded by government.

2. The CAMR developed a Plan (for the 1960s) for a nation-wide series of Demonstration and Research Projects, which included the establishment of university-affiliated mental retardation centres and other programmes. In the United States such developments were stimulated through federal government agencies.

One comparative measure could be with respect to the relative growth and change in the use of institutional facilities. Statistics Canada reports the residential population to be 19 172 in 1971, and 18 950 in 1976. In relative terms, this is almost identical to the United States, although the definitions of what constitutes institutionalization may vary among states and provinces†. Since the general population of Canada increased by over one million (to 23 million) between 1971 and 1974 (latest figures available), the proportionate decrease is more significant.

Although all jurisdictions in Canada are, to a greater or lesser degree, committed to reductions in institutional populations, there is not the same factor of pressure from federal authorities, so this country has not had to resort so much to the use of intermediate care facilities—which are not staffed or prepared for this role—in order to meet the letter of the law to reduce institution populations. The provision of community living arrangements has largely been in the hands of the voluntary sector, with government funding, as opposed to the use of proprietary boarding and nursing homes, and there has been less reason, therefore, for (and probably a minimum of) 'dumping'. Community placements are apt to be delayed until the proper support services are available.

The past seven years have seen a remarkable growth in numbers of group homes with less than 12 residents—Ontario had 12 in 1970, and more than 120 in 1977. There is a similar or greater increase in most other parts of the country in group homes, sheltered work, pre-school and day programmes and day-care developments. Most of those living in their homes, or in the community, received some sort of service with varying degrees of adequacy. Yet the continuing demand for admissions and re-admissions, and the slow decline in institutional populations, are a telling reminder that the community services in existence are as yet an uncertain alternative.

It is, therefore, not surprising that opinion among parents and workers in the field ranges from convictions that if community services were truly adequate there would be no need for institutions (of any size), to those who believe institutions will always be needed. There are many projects or programmes in both countries which claim to achieve comprehensiveness of services, but most are partial efforts and lack the conditions necessary to represent adequate models. Thus both sides have evidence to support their position.

## THE FUTURE

### FORWARD-LOOKING CONCEPTS AND DEVELOPMENTS IN SERVICE DELIVERY

Five criteria are becoming the accepted guidelines for future progressive programme patterns:

1. The developmental principle. A belief in the capability of a mentally handicapped person to grow and develop, given an optimal, appropriate and enriched environment.

2. The matter of right. The belief that the handicapped person is worthy of all the dignity and rights granted to non-handicapped citizens.*

3. The dignity of risk. The concept of learning through risk-taking and avoiding over-protection.

4. The principle of normalization. Making available to mentally retarded persons patterns and conditions of everyday life which are as close as possible to norms and patterns of the mainstream of society.

5. The use of generic environments and services, where possible.

A number of exemplary programmes are under way incorporating these concepts. Some will be referred to later. The plan which

---

† The national data show an increase in institutionalization in the Province of Ontario from 1971 to 1976 (7377 to 7969). In contrast, a story in the Toronto *Globe and Mail*, of September 2, 1977, quotes a spokesman from the Ministry of Community and Social Services, that institution populations declined over 36 per cent since 1972. This is likely to be due, in part, to a transfer of persons to community services, but also to the shifting of residents from older overcrowded 'Hospital Schools' to new or remodelled smaller institutions—now renamed 'Regional Resource Centres'.

* 'No reject' in education legislation is being implemented in the US (P.L. 94–142). The law's implication is that severely/profoundly retarded children can no longer be denied their share of education funds because they are considered to be unable to benefit.

will be described incorporates the features of the other developments. It is chosen because of its nation-wide character and experimental features. It is probably also replicable in many other countries.

## THE CAMR PLAN FOR THE 1970S

In 1969, CAMR, as part of a consortium (CELDIC, Commission on Emotional and Learning Disorders in Children) of national organizations serving disadvantaged persons, published the results of a three-year study entitled *One Million Children*, which pointed out that this many children required special attention to achieve their potential. Moreover, the problem was less that of inadequate resources, but more a need for better utilization of existing resources. In the same year CAMR conducted a 'Needs and Resources' survey, which revealed that the cost of meeting just the needs of mentally retarded persons through the addition of special facilities and programmes would be too costly for the public and government to provide.

It was concluded that in future greater emphasis should be placed on using *existing* community services, rather than expanding segregated and special facilities. Existing special services should phase down the direct service function and operate more as preparatory and support resources to generic programmes. Examination of existing generic and/or special service delivery systems revealed that current health, education and social service programmes are fragmented and isolated from each other. Despite this, they function reasonably well for 'normal' consumers who can obtain the individual specific needs from time to time. The system does not function well, however, for handicapped persons whose needs are complex, multi-problem and who cannot either comprehend the complexity of the system, utilize or manipulate it to meet their continuing and changing needs in the same way that normal citizens can. The challenge was to develop a plan which could realize rational, effective and cost-beneficial human service delivery systems, capable of providing a wide range of options within the system.

CAMR is the only national consumer-oriented entity in the country, the one which

has assumed responsibility for long-range programme planning and development. At the request of its membership, CAMR developed what has become known as the 'Plan for the 1970s'. The Plan has as its objective a local–regional service delivery system, which is:

1. *Community-based*—with as many services as possible provided close to the home of the handicapped person.
2. *Comprehensive*—all types of needs are met.
3. *Continuous*—available as needed throughout the life of the individual.
4. *Systemic*—all the service activity will function in a coordinated way.
5. *High quality*—consistent with the expectations implied in the concepts of normalization and integration in an optimal way, with generic services and mode of living.
6. *Dignified and rightful*—treating retarded persons as any other citizens.

## COMPONENTS OF CHANGE

While many will concede that problems exist and that change is needed, resistance to actual change will be the major obstacle to overcome. Inevitably, each will take the position that it is the others who should change. Change of this nature and magnitude is unlikely to come from within professions, governments and agencies now in the field. The primary change agent will ultimately be the citizens at large.

If concerned citizens are to bring about far-reaching change, however, they will need extensive technical and professional leadership and guidance. This partnership between citizens and professional workers is illustrated in Canada by CAMR and the National Institute on Mental Retardation (NIMR) which it sponsors. NIMR was developed to offer this expertise. Under the aegis of CAMR, it serves as the national technical and professional resource body to governments, institutions of learning, and public and private organizations.

NIMR was developed on the basis of the following concepts and strategies:

1. Changes in attitudes toward research, training and service programme activities, and toward retarded people themselves, continue only as long as there are dynamic, well-informed and organized citizen-action groups. Given appropriate leadership and technical–professional support, consumer movements have the potential to create major changes in public and professional opinion and behaviour.

2. It is essential that a sound and extensive technical foundation evolves in parallel with service programme developments and the involvement of the public. Such technical and service developments, combining public and private agency support and blending research, technical–professional and general citizen involvement, will together result in better programmes for the client and will accelerate the problem-solving process.

3. A stronger link is needed than has yet existed between theory and practice. The scientist and the teacher still do not communicate effectively with the practitioner; the worker in the field and the parent in the community need ways of channelling their concerns to the problem-solver or researcher.

NIMR is thus experimental, a national effort to bridge the theory–practice gap. It has enabled specialists on the one hand and citizens on the other to bring their respective powers to bear on either local problems or national issues affecting retarded people and those close to them. The Institute strives continually to increase the quality and quantity of community programmes, through collecting, analysing and converting relevant data into service delivery systems.

After extensive study, NIMR proposed a long-term national goal for a more advanced kind of service delivery, and in September 1971, CAMR adopted this as its major 'Plan for the 1970s'—the development of comprehensive community services for the developmentally handicapped across Canada. This project, generally called 'ComServ' (Comprehensive Community Services System) was to take top priority in the concerns of CAMR and of NIMR. It is an ambitious plan which will require supreme effort, extensive financial and human resources, and deep commitment. ComServ clearly cannot succeed without active involvement of the citizen action movement. At the same time, the consumer organization needs the support of technical and professional resources if it is to be effective.

## COMSERV—PRINCIPLES AND ORGANIZATION

As postulated by the CELDIC study, there is growing acceptance of the belief that enough funds are being expended and that sufficient resources exist to meet the needs of the handicapped, but that fragmentation, duplication, lack of coordination and maladaptation of resources contribute to an illusion of shortages. Neither central nor local governmental and other agencies have developed mechanisms for overcoming the problem. ComServ is intended to provide the needed mechanism. The following are essential elements of the scheme.

### Regional planning

Fundamental to the ComServ plan is a regional approach to service delivery. Regional here refers to areas *within* provinces (or states) designated for delivery of health, education and social services. Regional service systems offer advantages over local service systems in that they permit greater specialization of services, counter excessive parochialism, provide greater cost efficiency through economies of scale, better utilization of expertise, and have greater impact on other agencies and governments. Regional service systems also offer advantages over centralized (provincial/state) services in that they permit closer client–family ties, have a greater sensitivity to local conditions and needs and make for increased citizen identification with services.

It appears that for preliminary planning purposes a population of at least 200 000 persons is needed for a ComServ region. Deviations from this figure should be specifically justified and the dangers inherent in low or high-population regions carefully safeguarded against. Certain rural regional areas may not, for these reasons, be viable settings.

Regions should be planned to coincide with, and take advantage of, existing geo-demographic service patterns and be defined and subdivided by boundaries which are co-terminous with those of established health, education and welfare areas.

## Service delivery

Services are delivered and administered as close to the local community as possible, for better consumer-orientation, maintenance of family ties, use of existing community resources and ultimately less expensive service delivery. Service delivery at the local level is governed by community boards. This strengthens consumer involvement and orientation, increases community support and understanding of the objectives of the service and makes services more responsive to community needs.

Wherever possible, existing community boards should be encouraged to broaden their responsibility to incorporate the delivery of services for handicapped people. If it is necessary to establish new local or regional boards, these boards should be encouraged to become more generic in time by taking responsibility for some services for non-handicapped people.

Not all the services a region needs to become 'comprehensive' should be exclusively for retarded or handicapped persons. They can be provided by *generic* service agencies, such as general hospitals, schools, community recreation centres, social services agencies, et cetera. Ideally, most services to handicapped persons should be provided by the same agencies that are used by the general public. It is also a fact, however, that for many reasons retarded persons have been denied access to these services, and if not turned away, they may find the staff lacking in the necessary knowledge to be helpful.

## Types of service

The quantity and variety of services included in a comprehensive system are much greater than previously expected. They fall into logical groups or subsystems of the total service system.

*The family resource services subsystem.* A range of services are provided which help to make it possible for retarded persons to live in the community with their own families or in adoptive, foster and group homes. The goal is to ensure that the handicapped member does not cause more stress than the family/residence can tolerate. Family resource services include (in typical order of usage, not importance) genetic counselling and testing; assessment and diagnosis; individual and family counselling; information resources; lending library (reading material, toys); financial subsidy (for specialists, equipment); crisis assistance and respite care; provision of domestic help; in-home parent/child training; recreation; and transportation.

It is important to remember that these services must be *available* (located in the area) and also *accessible* (do not exclude people due to age, type of disability, family income, et cetera). This means in many cases going into the home, rather than having the families come to the service agency. The challenge is to ensure that every family can receive, at the right time, the type and the amount of service necessary to keep the handicapped person in his own environment.

*The child development subsystem.* This subsystem includes developmental programmes for pre-school-age children; elementary and secondary school education, and post-school programmes. It is also necessary to have available a number of special units or programmes to provide *behaviour shaping* in special circumstances (hyperactivity, destructiveness, extreme withdrawal and other major behaviour problems). A variety of behaviour shaping and behaviour management techniques may be used. Multi-handicapped and severely retarded children often require physiotherapy, speech therapy and other therapies in order to overcome their physical and other limitations. These highly specialized services should be as much as possible built into existing community-based children's services (day care, nurseries, schools and so on).

*The vocational services subsystem.* Vocational services provide a continuum of vocational work choices and supports to meet the specific needs of each individual, and to challenge each individual to move on to higher levels of independence and productivity. This wide range of vocational options includes sheltered work; sheltered industry; training-on-the-job; work stations in commerce and industry; trades training and employment; part-time employment; full-time employment; self-employment; and other options yet to be identified. It also includes a range of activities which *support* the efforts of both the employers and employees, such as vocational training; vocational exploration; vocational evaluation; work adjustment training; personal adjustment training; skill training; placement; follow-up; on-site orientation; job stabilization; re-training; and other services yet to be identified.

*The residential services subsystem.* Residential services are concerned with *where* retarded persons live and what happens to them in addition to receiving shelter. Residences tend to be the most expensive and difficult services to obtain and operate. Therefore, it is logical to give non-residential services first priority, particularly family resource services. Where a family home exists why create another? However, despite family services, there will always be some children and adults who for one reason or another cannot live with their family in a home of their own. The second level of priority in residential services is housing choices that closely approximate the home. These include *family home substitutes* such as adoption, which provides all the physical, social and emotional advantages of family life; foster families, when adoption is impossible or the residential need is temporary; emergency homes, for crisis and other short-term situations; boarding homes or group homes, for adults, with supervision included; drop-in supervision, to ensure individuals in boarding homes, group homes, apartments, et cetera, are not in difficulty.

A third group of residential options are designed to meet *special needs*. They provide the needed back-up which allows the other less restricted options to remain flexible. For example, child development homes can prepare a child for family life at home or in a foster home. These options require some trained staff and provide supervision 24 hours a day. The range can include the following: child development residence—to provide special in-home training, extra supervision,

medical care, and to avoid having children live in even less normative circumstances; adolescent development residence—needed because families and foster homes will tolerate problems presented by children but not by teenagers and young adults; supervised group residence and apartments—for persons over 18 years who require daily assistance; intensive programming residence—a short-term residence specializing in extensive behaviour modification and training; and intensive medical treatment residence—for the small number of persons requiring around the clock medical supervision and treatment.

*The protective services subsystem.* One of the main reasons for using residential institutions and special residences of all kinds, is to ensure the retarded person is safe from physical harm and social misadventure, such as becoming pregnant, breaking the law, losing property, committing vagrancy, being lonely, et cetera. The 'residential' means of protecting the individual is used because other ways of protection are not available or do not work. As the movement to integrate handicapped persons gains momentum, a range of services is coming into existence which service planners are learning to combine and modify so that they protect people and property. Protective services include: legal guardianship; property management (plenary and partial); trusteeship and representative payee; protective service 'workers' (paid staff employed to follow up handicapped persons); corporate advocates (such as associations for the mentally retarded and other voluntary organizations that are prepared to act on behalf of handicapped persons); legal aid (free legal advice and representation should always be available to retarded persons because they are usually too poor to afford a lawyer); and the ombudsman (where these are established). Citizen advocacy is another innovative approach in which a competent person voluntarily agrees to represent a handicapped person's interests (either personal, material or both) as if they were his or her own. Citizen advocacy programmes have proved to be highly effective in protecting handicapped persons from all manner of harm and abuse, at very modest cost to the community.

*Central support services.* Obviously, a service delivery system, which may include dozens of service units and hundreds of staff scattered over a large geographical region and serving a large population, will require a solid organizational structure and sound administration. The central services subsystem will hold the entire system together and help it to function efficiently and effectively. It includes administration (senior staff), fiscal control, staff development, evaluation, research and public education.

### Governance and funding of ComServ

The ComServ plan requires that part of the state or provincial government's mandate for service delivery must be delegated to some structure which is closer to the people requiring the service, together with enough power to bring both qualitative and quantitative changes in programmes. Mechanisms to safeguard local service autonomy must be considered as well.

In the envisioned scheme, central government retains the comprehensive long-term planning function for the state or province as a whole. It has responsibility for establishing global policies, priorities and implemental strategies, and for certain general regulations and standards for services which must be set and enforced within all sub-areas or regions. Central government also retains the mandate and resources to arrange for manpower development and training, to obtain appropriate consultation and programme support for regional services, to provide the major share of operating funds (matching other sources, et cetera), to arrange for impartial external evaluation of the services it funds, and to provide or obtain applied research.

In order to carry out its mandate, the provincial/state government delegates certain functions to approved regional service systems with appropriate governing bodies (known as directorates). These 'directing' bodies may be for special services or for general services. They are composed of representatives from agencies, voluntary associations, interested professional and public leaders, local and central government, and so on. The directorate has full-time paid staff and is given specific powers to carry out its mission effectively.

The functions of the regional service system directing body (or directorate) are: to see that needed services are provided and coordinated in the region, to conduct long-term planning on a regional basis for comprehensive services, to evolve regional implemental strategies, to determine regional policies and set regional priorities, to develop local funding sources and allocate funds, and to employ and direct staff to carry out these functions.

The regional body also needs to be responsible for control and/or direct administration of the services and to have the authority to exercise regulatory powers, to review grant requests, to control the (operating and capital) funds made available from central government, to have the right to purchase services for the client and allocate funds, to contract for provision of services with or without exchange of funds, to control a significant share of governing seats on the directorate, to stimulate voluntary coordination, and to obtain from voluntary and governmental bodies funds beyond those granted from central government.

Regional bodies which have no real authority and work only on a voluntary coordination basis (while this may be useful at times) are not able to develop and manage a full and effective coordinated comprehensive service system.

A regional authority could be quite workable without a legislated mandate of all these powers but would need at least the power of grant review, some control of the granted funds, the ability to purchase and/or contract for provision of services, and to facilitate coordination on a voluntary basis. A regional authority should also have power to administer services directly but this should be used only when economies of scale demand regional rather than local services.

### Implemental strategy for ComServ

Immediate large-scale development of ComServ is not feasible for four reasons:

1. It would not be possible to reorient all existing services at the same time.

2. While much is known about the general character that such comprehensive services ought to embody, more has yet to be learned

about the best ways to organize and implement them.

3. There is simply not enough money for immediate total implementation, even if the 'change force' existed. Although ComServ is geared to use already existing monies, it will require additional funds and these are unlikely to be generated all at once on the necessary scale.

4. Experience has shown that relatively few people fully appreciate the possible complexity of the ComServ system, nor do most realize the extent to which service systems can normalize the lives of most retarded persons.

These considerations influenced NIMR to recommend that implementation of ComServ services must be a gradual and careful process. It recommended the establishment of a limited number of experimental and demonstration (E & D) ComServ projects which will develop and test methods of organizing and delivering community service in various settings and types of regions. NIMR recommended that (at most) one suitable area be selected as an E & D region in each of several Canadian provinces.

Previous experience with demonstrations in other places indicates that they frequently fail if strong direction, guidance and quality control are not instituted at the beginning and sustained throughout. If a project does fail, there may be increased resistance to future innovations. It is crucially important, therefore, that as many E & D ComServ projects as possible be successful. The ultimate test of success will be whether the project can actually influence long-term and large-scale service policy by convincing the public and its decision-makers to institute comprehensive systems across the nation.

In order to help assure such quality, twelve criteria have been evolved for selecting and approving any project before it is designated as an E & D ComServ project. These criteria mean that projects will not be selected primarily because new services are needed in some region or because a region is more deprived and more in need of service than most others. What must be shown is that any new services that are needed fit into a general overall plan for developing a comprehensive service system for the region, that the region is suitable

in other important ways as an E & D ComServ region, and that the preconditions to a successful demonstration exist.

The twelve criteria that have been set down for selecting an E & D project fall into those determining the suitability of a region for an E & D project and those determining the suitability of the programme. The six criteria for regional suitability include sufficient population size to justify a wide range of services; accessibility of a region to transportation routes; availability of professional resources in the region such as might be found in an institution of higher learning; community receptivity to the project; strength of existing consumer and related organizations within the region; and prospects of local and long-term funding. The six criteria for programme suitability include a plan to offer a wide range of services; evidence of strong project direction; commitment to the demonstration role; willingness of regional personnel to accept consultation; applicability of the demonstration lesson to other areas of the country; and adoption of some specific research mission.

*Personnel needs*

The development in the ComServ regions, and indeed nation-wide, of a knowledgeable and able leadership, as well as of a supportive attitude base, are critical to the success of the ComServ programme. There is an acute shortage of both staff and volunteers who are trained and experienced in modern change agencies and organizational system approaches in the field of mental retardation. Existing training programmes in colleges and universities are being supplemented by short-term training for large numbers of people.

All these workers will need to be trained for new roles and responsibilities. Many jobs now done only by professionals will be performed more effectively by less specialized frontline workers—volunteers and staff—while professionals must have more time to develop services to meet special and changed needs. In this way, there will be considerable savings of manpower and also development of human talents. The training thrust extends to preparing new leadership in the human service programme planning and implementation areas, emphasizing the dynamics of change within and between service organizations and systems.

A National Manpower Model (see Bibliography) has been proposed by CAMR, and will be implemented in stages.

## PROGRESS TO DATE

The research, concept formulation, development of materials, launching of training programmes and orientation of the Canadian constituency has absorbed much of the time and effort to date. The principal document, *Plan and Guidelines for Comprehensive Community Service*, is in the field and proposals for Com-Serv are being received. Two projects are under way in Lethbridge, Alberta and in the region of Sept-Iles, Quebec. The findings from these experiments are proving of great assistance in planning projects in other parts of the country, where similar programmes are now evolving. The prediction based on progress so far is that in the 1980s communities will be developing complete community alternatives to institutional care. As a result institutions will depopulate and fade from the scene. The other major emphasis in the next decade will be on primary and secondary prevention of the problem.

The regional authority aspect of the Com-Serv Plan is the most difficult to implement because it requires changes in existing government approaches. The subsystems proposals are, however, gaining wide acceptance.

While ComServ is the only nation-wide plan of its kind, some provincial/state governments are formulating similar approaches. At the state level, California some years ago introduced a Regional Centre approach, with only partial success. Pennsylvania, under its office of Mental Retardation, has successfully pioneered some of the subsystems outlined in the ComServ system, as have various states and provinces. Two successful ComServ-type regional projects are: ENCOR (Eastern Nebraska Community Office of Retardation) which has pioneered in testing the ComServ-type model; MacComb-Oakland Regional Center (bordering Detroit, Michigan), a county-wide programme. MacComb-Oakland has not been able to overcome certain institu-

tional components as has ENCOR, but its residential placement programme demonstrates that a total community approach is possible.

At the national level, the (US) National Institute on Mental Health (NIMH), after supporting first improved institutional care in the 1950s, then the concept of Regional Centres (smaller resource-oriented institutions), has recently announced a new initiative aimed at developing 'Comprehensive Community Support Systems' via the vehicle of the 'Community Support Program' (CSP). Much forward-looking legislation is being proposed and/or enacted at both state/provincial and federal levels including laws forbidding discrimination in education and care (US) and a proposed Canadian Government Social Services Act (SSA). The latter was very progressive, favouring *priority* attention to the needs of the handicapped and a full range of services (as outlined under the Com-Serv subsystems). Such laws clearly reveal the value and influence of nation-wide long-range action programmes, such as the CAMR 'Plan for the 1970s'. Even though the SSA has not been passed, it clearly suggests acceptance of the changing trends in service programming for the handicapped by both government and the membership of consumer groups.

## PROSPECTS AND POTENTIAL

There are signs that the once dynamic parent movement which declined in influence and effectiveness as professionals and governments took over, once again has a key role to serve as change agents. In British Columbia, Canada, a group of parents developed a plan to rehabilitate 200 mentally retarded citizens from an institution, and won government support for it. The result is the establishment of a regional coordinating agency called Living Independently For Equality (LIFE). Its purpose is to guide and monitor the development of alternative living arrangements and to demonstrate that institutions should and can be replaced. The (parent) leader developed the competence needed to undertake such a venture from the training she received from the ComServ thrust. In the neighbouring province, Alberta, the government is already sponsoring an E & D ComServ project. It has also developed the 'Feasible Placement Concept' whereby funds being spent to maintain a resident in an institution are transferred with the person to finance the provision of suitable support services when he/she is returned to community living.

One other measure of progress since the parents first organized to operate some day classes on their own, is the 'People First' movement which is just beginning to develop. 'People First' are local groups of mentally retarded persons organizing themselves as a self-help and consumer-demand movement.

The systems, knowledge and methods are known and most of the necessary resources are potentially available. With consumer competence in systems organization and with parent–professional partnership action, the one-hundred-year legacy of institutionalization *can* become *past* history.

BIBLIOGRAPHY

American Psychological Association (1977) NIMH eyes new support systems: seeking the missing rungs in the service ladder. *APA Monitor*, *8*, 7.

Commission on Emotional and Learning Disorders in Children (CELDIC) (1970) *One Million Children: A National Study of Canadian Children with Emotional and Learning Disorders.* Canadian Association for the Mentally Retarded, Canadian Council on Children and Youth, Canadian Education Association, Canadian Mental Health Association, Canadian Rehabilitation Council for the Disabled, Canadian Welfare Council, Dr. Barnado's, Toronto.

Comptroller General of the United States (1977) *Returning the Mentally Disabled to the Community: Government Needs To Do More.* US General Accounting Office, Washington, D.C. HRD–76–156.

Conley, R. W. (1973) *The Economics of Mental Retardation.* Baltimore: Johns Hopkins University Press.

National Health and Welfare Department (1977) *The Proposed Social Services Act* (pamphlet). Ottawa.

National Institute on Mental Retardation (1972) *Guidelines for the preparation of proposals for the establishment of comprehensive community services (ComServ) experimental and demonstration (E & D) projects for persons with developmental handicap.* Downsview, Canada.

National Institute on Mental Retardation (1972) *A National Mental Retardation Manpower Model.* Downsview, Canada.

National Institute on Mental Retardation (1977) *Orientation Manual on Mental Retardation*, revised ed. Downsview, Canada.

President's Committee on Mental Retardation (1977) *Mental Retardation Past and Present.* Washington, D.C.

Roeher, G. A. (1976) ComServ Canada *and* Public and professionals. In: Kugel, R. B. (ed.), *Changing Patterns in Residential Services for the Mentally Retarded*, revised ed. Wahington, D.C.: President's Committee on Mental Retardation.

Roeher, G. A. (1977) International models for research utilization: national institutes on mental retardation. In: Mittler, P. (ed.), *Research to practice in mental Retardation*, vol. 1. Baltimore: University Park Press.

Statistics Canada (1972 and 1977) *Preliminary Mental Health Statistics.* Ottawa.

University of Wisconsin-Madison (Fall 1977) The Happiness Factor, *WAISMAN Center Interactions.*

# II
# CLINICAL
# SECTION

CHAPTER 4

# THE NEUROLOGY
# OF MENTAL RETARDATION

## MICHAEL CRAFT

Nearly one half of the practice of paediatric neurology has to do with mentally retarding causes; much of the rest has to do with febrile brain illnesses or accidents which can have similar sequelae. For both groups the diagnostic and treatment possibilities have much improved over recent years, as is illustrated by the following instances of research into diagnosis in mental handicap. Penrose (1938) in the then best researched group of in-patient defectives found diagnosis possible in only one-third of 1280 cases. In 1959 Heber in a similarly researched group found 15.5 per cent known, and 84.5 per cent unknown, causes (Heber 1961). In 1971 Holmes and his colleagues obtained the results shown in Table 4.1 with a similar group of 1378 in-patients (Holmes et al. 1972).

Advances in diagnosis and treatment continue, and are the special concern of this book. Chapters 5, 6 and 7 describe those syndromes for which world (predominantly Anglo-American) literature either gives more than 40 examples where all are retarded such as Down's syndrome, or conditions such as muscular dystrophy where over one hundred cases have been described and at least one-third are retarded. Intending diagnosticians are referred to Table 4.2 where common causes of the principal features of mental retardation are listed.

Since the medical graduate or near graduate is expected to have worked out his own methods of neurological and/or psychological assessment they are not further described here, but can be well revised from *Harrison's Principles of Internal Medicine* or *The Practice of Pediatric Neurology* (see Bibliography, p. 48).

TABLE 4.1

Causation of retardation

| | IQ < 50 | IQ > 50 | % of population surveyed |
|---|---|---|---|
| Chromosomal anomalies [Ch. 5] | 247 | 10 | 18.7 |
| Primary genetic disorders [Ch. 6] Metabolic and endocrine diseases | 38 | 5 | 3.1 |
| Progressive diseases of the nervous system | 5 | 7 | 0.9 |
| Central nervous system abnormalities | 49 | 16 | 4.7 |
| Multiple congenital deformities | 64 | 16 | 5.8 |
| Neurocutaneous diseases | 4 | 0 | 0.3 |
| Acquired conditions [Ch. 7 and Ch. 8] | 278 | 79 | 25.9 |
| Psychoses [Ch. 9] Not known Not retarded | 392 | 168 | 40.6 |

For ease of comparison, the diagnosed groups may be totalled as 59.4 per cent.

From Holmes et al. (1972).

In the *diagnosis* of mental retardation a good family history is essential, since so many syndromes are genetically endowed, and other affected family members may lead to a diagnosis. *Examination* shows the principal features of the abnormality; Tables 4.2, 4.3 and 4.4 list these features with their common causes. Syndromes listed in Table 4.2 which cause retardation are described in Chapters

5 and 6, with supporting features for diagnosis, laboratory tests and recent references to treatment. Methods for cytogenetic study for chromosomal abnormality, which are always indicated where the IQ is less than half the average, are described in Chapter 5. Metabolic abnormalities are described in Chapter 6. Finally, one abnormal test result is not conclusive: typing errors and artefacts have been known to occur!

In *treatment*, clearly the potentialities are limited for chromosomal anomalies, whose abnormalities were set at conception. There are many more treatment possibilities for genetically-endowed abnormalities of metabolism whose ill effects often become manifest in the first year or two of life, and recent advances in replacement therapies are indicated under the appropriate syndrome.

For *acquired* syndromes (Chapter 7), new antibiotic treatments have become available for infections of the brain.

TABLE 4.2

Principal feature diagnostic table

Principal features are listed under (1) the head, (2) the central nervous system, and (3) the body. If the principal feature is, for example, macrocephaly or enlarged head, common causes when it occurs with retardation will be found in the section that follows. An asterisk designates a syndrome not described in this book, either because (1) less than 40 cases of retardation associated with this syndrome have so far been described in world literature, or (2) it is common but less than one-third of those afflicted are mentally retarded out of over 100 cases reported in the literature.

For those syndromes marked with an asterisk, i.e. not described in this book, the reader is referred to the following texts after which Tables 4.2–4.4 are modified: M. W. Wintrobe et al., *Harrison's Principles of Internal Medicine*, 7th ed. (New York, McGraw Hill, 1974); K. F. Swaiman and F. S. Wright, eds., *The Practice of Pediatric Neurology* (St. Louis, Mosby, 1975); D. W. Smith, *Recognizable Patterns of Human Malformation* (Philadelphia, W. B. Saunders, 1970).

Syndromes listed in Table 4.2 are described in the following chapters: Chapter 5, Chromosomal Anomalies, e.g. 21 trisomy (Down's); Chapter 6, Genetic Disorders, in alphabetical order; Chapter 7, Acquired Conditions, e.g. brain damage, infections, drugs.

## HEAD

SHAPE

*Craniosynostosis* (premature closure of cranial sutures), common in:
Apert
Carpenter
Chotzen
Crouzon (familial)
Pfeiffer
Sporadic

*Craniosynostosis*, sometimes in:
Drug-induced anomaly
Oculomandibulodyscephaly
Vitamin D deficiency

SIZE

*Macrocephaly* (large head), common in:
Achondroplasia*
Cerebral gigantism*
Gangliosidosis
Hydrocephalus (aqueductal)
Hydrocephalus (X-linked)
MPS I & II (Hurler & Hunter)

*Macrocephaly*, sometimes in:
18 trisomy (Edwards)
Basal cell nevus* (*see* Xeroderma)

*Microcephaly* (small head), common in:
5p- (Cri-du-chat)
13 trisomy (Patau)
18q- (long arm deletion)
Cornelia de Lange
Cytomegalus infection
Dwarf (bird-headed)
Microcephaly (Cockayne)*
Microcephaly (X-linked)
Phenylketonuria
Rubella
Xeroderma
X-ray irradiation of fetus

*Microcephaly*, sometimes in:
18 trisomy (Edwards)
Carpenter

Fanconi*
Incontinentia pigmenti
Muscular dystrophy
XXXXY

FOREHEAD

*Hypertelorism* (high forehead), common in:
Apert

*Hypertelorism*, sometimes in:
5p- (Cri-du-chat)
13 trisomy
18q- long arm deletion
Craniocleidodysostosis*
Crouzon (familial)
Ichthyosis (Sjögren–Larsson)
MPS II (Hunter)
Vitamin D deficiency
XXXXX
XXXXY

*Prominent forehead bossing*, common in:
Crouzon (familial
Dwarf (Russell)
Gangliosidosis (late)
Oculomandibulodyscephaly
Rubinstein Taybi syndrome

FACE

*Cleft lip and/or cleft palate*, common in:
13 trisomy (Patau)
Lip fistula–Cleft lip*
Mohr*
Oral-facial-digital

*Cleft lip/palate*, sometimes in:
5p- (Cri-du-chat)
18 trisomy (Edwards)
Oculodentodigital*

'*Flat face*', common in:
21 trisomy (Down)
Achondroplasia*
Apert
Carpenter
Larsen*
XXXXX
XXXXY

'*Flat' face*, sometimes in:
13 trisomy (Patau)
Cleidocranial dysostosis*
Crouzon (familial)

'*Loutish' face*
Cerebral gigantism*
Gangliosidosis (late in MPS I, II & III)
Hypothyroidism
MPS IV (Morquio's syndrome, early)

Scheie*
Vitamin D deficiency

'*Wide' face*, common in:
Apert
Carpenter
Crouzon (familial)

'*Wide face*', sometimes in:
Cerebral gigantism*
Cleidocranial dysostosis*
Laurence–Moon–Biedl

*Receding chin*, common in:
5p- (Cri-du-chat)
18 trisomy (Edwards)
21q- (long arm deletion)*
Cornelia de Lange
Drug-induced anomalies
Dwarf (bird-headed)
Dwarf (Russell)
Mandibulofacial dysostosis
Oculomandibulodyscephaly
Progeria*
XO (Turner)

*Receding chin*, sometimes in:
13 trisomy (Patau)
Rubinstein–Taybi
Turner-like (Noonan)

EARS

*Malformed*, common in:
13 trisomy (Patau)
18 trisomy (Edwards)
18q- (long arm deletion)
21q- (long arm deletion)*
21 trisomy (Down)
Drug-induced anomalies
Dwarf (bird-headed)
Mandibulofacial dysostosis
Rubinstein–Taybi
XO (Turner) prominent
XXXXY

*Malformed*, sometimes in:
5p- (Cri-du-chat)
Carpenter
Fanconi*
Prader–Willi
Vitamin D deficiency

EYES

*Nystagmus* (slow deviation of eyes to periphery, quick return to centre), common in:
21 trisomy (Down)
Fanconi*
Laurence–Moon–Biedl

Table 4.2 continued

Microcephaly (Cockayne)*
Oculomandibulodyscephaly

*Prominent inner eye fold, epicanthic*, common in:
5p- (Cri-du-chat)
21 trisomy (Down)
Familial anomaly in general population*
Rubinstein–Taybi syndrome
Vitamin D deficiency
XO (Turner)
XXXXX
XXXXY

*Prominent inner eye fold*, sometimes in:
18 trisomy (Edwards)
18q- (long arm deletion)

*Slanted eyes*, common in:
5p- (Cri-du-chat), up or down
21 trisomy (Down), up
Apert, down
Mandibulofacial dysostosis, down
Rubinstein–Taybi, down
XXXXX, up
XXXXY, up

*Squint*, common in:
5p- (Cri-du-chat)
18 trisomy (Edwards)
Apert
Glioma (supratentorial)
Incontinentia pigmenti
Prader–Willi
Rubinstein–Taybi
XO (Turner)
XXXXY

*Squint*, sometimes in:
21 trisomy (Down)
Cornelia de Lange
Dwarf (bird-headed)
Fanconi*
Laurence–Moon–Biedl
Oculomandibulodyscephaly
Vitamin D deficiency

## CENTRAL NERVOUS SYSTEM

ATAXIA, common in:
Brain tumours
Cerebellar agenesis
Drug overdosage
Hallervorden–Spatz
Hereditary ataxias
Huntington's chorea
Hydrocephalus
Lead poisoning
Sphingomyelin lipidosis (Niemann–Pick)
Subacute sclerosing panencephalitis

*Ataxia*, sometimes in:
Argininosuccinic aciduria
Hartnup disease
Hypoglycaemia
Sulphatide lipidosis

DEAFNESS, common in:
13 trisomy (Patau)
18q- (long arm deletion)
Apert
Cornelia de Lange
Friedreich
Huntington's chorea
Mandibulofacial dysostosis
Microcephaly
Mohr*
MPS I & II (Hurler & Hunter)
MPS IV (Morquio)
Oto-palato-digital*
Rubella
Toxoplasmosis

*Deafness*, sometimes in:
Cleidocranial dysostosis*
Craniofacial dysostosis
Crouzon (familial)
Fanconi*
Hepatolenticular degeneration (Wilson's disease)
Laurence–Moon–Biedl
Noonan (Turner-like)
Progeria*
XO (Turner)

EPILEPSY, common in:
Argininosuccinic aciduria
Citrullinaemia*
Gangliosidoses 1 & 2
Glycogenoses
Hyperammonaemia 1 & 2*
Idiopathic hypoglycaemia of infancy*
Maple syrup urine disease
Menkes
Methionine malabsorption*
Phenylketonuria
Sturge–Weber
Tuberous sclerosis

*Epilepsy*, sometimes in:
13 trisomy (Patau)
21q- (long arm deletion)*
Ichthyosis (Sjögren–Larsson)
Neurofibromatosis

HYPERTONICITY (spasticity), common in:
18 trisomy (Edwards)
21q- (long arm deletion)*
Cornelia de Lange
Ichthyosis (Sjögren–Larsson)

Menkes
Neuronal lipidoses

*Hypertonicity*, sometimes in:
  13 trisomy (Patau)
  Hydrocephalus (X-linked)
  Incontinentia pigmenti
  Sturge–Weber

HYPOTONICITY (flaccidity), common in:
  18q- (long arm deletion)
  21 trisomy (Down)
  Gangliosidosis (late)
  Prader–Willi
  Sphingomyelin lipidosis

*Hypotonicity*, sometimes in:
  5p- (Cri-du-chat)
  13 trisomy (Patau)
  Myotonic dystrophy
  Vitamin D deficiency

## BODY

ABNORMAL SKIN PIGMENTATION, common in:
  Basal cell nevus* (*see* Xeroderma)
  Fanconi (general increase)*
  Hypohidrotic ectodermal dysplasia (diminished pigment)*
  Incontinentia pigmenti (spidery pigment)
  Neurofibromatosis (café-au-lait spots)
  Tuberous sclerosis
  Xeroderma pigmentosum
  XO (Turner)

*Abnormal skin pigmentation*, sometimes in:
  Ataxia-telangiectasia (altered skin or hair pigmentation) (café-au-lait spots)*
  Dwarf (Russell) (café-au-lait spots)

ABNORMAL HAIR, common in:
  18 trisomy (Edwards) (excess)
  Cornelia de Lange (excess)
  Homocystinuria (sparse)
  Incontinentia pigmenti (sparse)
  Leprechaunism (excess)*
  MPS I, II & III (excess)
  Menkes (sparse and wiry)
  Microcephaly (Cockayne) (sparse)*
  Myotonic dystrophy (sparse)
  Oculomandibulodyscephaly (sparse)
  Progeria (sparse)*

### TABLE 4.3

Progressive retardation in childhood†

| | |
|---|---|
| *Under 2* | Cerebroside lipidosis |
| | Cretinism (hypothyroidism) |
| | Fructose intolerance* |
| | Galactosaemia |
| | Globoid cell dystrophy (Krabbe) |
| | Glycogenosis |
| | GM1 gangliosidosis |
| | GM2 gangliosidosis (Tay–Sachs) |
| | Hypoglycaemia of varied etiology* |
| | Menkes (steely) hair disease |
| | Methylmalonic aciduria* |
| | Mucopolysaccharidosis, types I and II (Hurler and Hunter) |
| | Pyridoxine deficiency* |
| | Sphingomyelin infantile lipidosis (Niemann–Pick) |
| *Aged 2–5* | GM2 gangliosidosis (juvenile) |
| | Hepatolenticular degeneration (Wilson's disease) |
| | Hypothyroidism |
| | Mucopolysaccharidosis, type III (Sanfilippo) |
| | Sphingomyelin lipidosis (Niemann–Pick child form) |
| | Sulphatide lipidosis |
| *Over 5* | Hallervorden–Spatz (iron storage disease) |
| | Hepatolenticular degeneration (Wilson's disease) |
| | Huntington's chorea |
| | Multiple sclerosis* |
| | Neurofibromatosis |
| | Sphingomyelin lipidosis (Niemann–Pick) |
| | Subacute inclusion body encephalitis (slow virus diseases) |
| | Tuberous sclerosis |

† For progressive retardation in adult life, see Table 9.3 (p. 154).
* Not described in this book.

TABLE 4.4

Abnormal movements

| Movement | Speed | Location | Direction | Stereotype | Rhythmicity | Interval |
|---|---|---|---|---|---|---|
| Athetosis | Slow | Most frequently in distal limbs | (writhing) and hyperextension | Common; continuous movement in extremities | Not rhythmic | Continuous, amplitude increased by excitement |
| Ballismus | Rapid | Shoulder, hip, trunk, face, chest | Hurling, flinging, throwing, kicking, circumducting | Constant location; movements vary | Not rhythmic | 0.5–120 seconds |
| Chorea | Rapid | Generalized; may be unilateral | Also facial grimacing; flexion and extension | None; movements generally dance from joint to joint | Not rhythmic | 0.5–5 seconds |
| Dystonia | Rapid, slow; very slow relaxation | Trunk, head, extremities | Any, often twisting | Common; because of location of movements | Irregular | Irregular |
| Myoclonus | Very rapid | Localized or generalized | Any | Stereotyped, twitching | Irregular | 0.5–5 seconds |
| Tic | Rapid | Usually facial, shoulder, neck | Rotational, away from midline | Stereotyped | Irregular | 1 second to minutes |
| Tremor | Variable | Usually localized, often in hand | Complex or simple | Extreme stereotype | Very rhythmic; may be irregular | 0.1–1 second |

Adapted from Swaiman and Wright (1975).

BIBLIOGRAPHY

Heber, R. (1961) Manual on Terminology and Classification in Mental Retardation, 2nd ed. *Am. J. ment. Defic. Suppl.*, No 64.
Holmes, L. B., Moser, H. W., Halldorsson, S., Mack, C., Pant, S. & Matzilevich, B. (1972) *Mental Retardation: An Atlas of Diseases with Associated Physical Abnormalities*. New York and London: MacMillan [extensive illustration of mental retardation syndromes].
Penrose, L. (1972) *Biology of Mental Defect*, 4th ed. London: Sidgwick & Jackson.
Smith, D. W. (1970) *Recognizable Patterns of Human Malformation*. Philadelphia: Saunders.
Swaiman, K. F. & Wright, F. S. (1975) *The Practice of Pediatric Neurology*. St. Louis: Mosby.
Wintrobe, M. W., Thorn, G. W., Adams, R. D., Braunwald, E., Isselbacher, K. J. & Petersdorf, R. G. (eds.) (1974) *Harrison's Principles of Internal Medicine*, 7th ed. New York: McGraw Hill.

# CHAPTER 5

# CHROMOSOMAL ANOMALIES

## MICHAEL CRAFT

Considerable advances in the understanding of chromosomal abnormalities have occurred in the last ten years. Advance itself was not possible before techniques for the accurate identification of chromosomes became available in 1956 thus allowing the first reports of autosome (body) anomalies by LeJeune and her associates in 1959 (see Bibliography, p. 54). Descriptions of sex chromosomal abnormalities followed soon after. Since then the newer band-staining methods have allowed autosomes to be more clearly distinguished one from another, and to show when they have lost constituent parts of arms and so on.

A practitioner who wishes to have chromosomal analysis performed on his patient, should therefore consult his laboratory as to the specimens they need and the techniques they employ. For instance, for the relatively simple inspection of a buccal smear for Barr bodies to demonstrate nuclear sex, they would probably only require a fresh buccal smear, and a supporting fresh blood slide for double confirmation of their findings. For the more detailed analysis of an autosome abnormality, they are more likely to require a fresh specimen of human tissue which might conveniently be taken at the laboratory, whilst not all laboratories have the trained personnel or material available to do the newer chromosome band-staining techniques with quinacrine fluorescence and other methods (see also Chapter 11).

The early descriptions allocated chromosomes in order of size, the biggest being 1 and the smallest autosome being 23. Because the gradations of size are small, and for ease of staining, they have more recently been grouped according to their distinguishing marks (see Fig. 5.1 for illustrative karyotype of Turner's syndrome XO (45 chromosomes) and Fig. 5.15 for XXYY anomaly).

Down's syndrome is the most common autosome abnormality at 1 in 660 live births and is a trisomy in group D—or in order of size, chromosome 21. The trisomy may be complete or secondly, mosaic, meaning that only a proportion of cells throughout the body have trisomy. A third reason for an individual to look like a Down's syndrome (the technical term is phenocopy) is if he has translocation. This means that at one stage in fetal cell division important genetic material from another chromosome became attached to one of the D group chromosomes, that is one of the pair of chromosomes at the 21st position. Technically this is called unbalanced (that is, only one of chromosome 21 D group) translocation, causing a Down's syndrome phenocopy (similar physical and mental make-up). The importance of this third cause, is that such people may have all or few stigmata. Some have become university graduates. Single or multiple characteristics of Down's syndrome are common in the general population, and some may well be translocations.

A person with a mosaic, with normal 21 trisomy cells has a aneuploid (abnormal) cell line and a euploid (normal) cell line and can also have all the clinical characteristics of Down's syndrome or only some of the features. The greater or lesser degree probably represents the amount of developmental abnormality corresponding to the greater or smaller amount of the additional genetic coding available. The abnormal cell line usually occurs at the second or later cell division of the infant, and if it continues in strict proportion in the developing cell mass, would

Familial tendencies to non-disjunction do occur. Occasionally patients are reported with both trisomy such as D-21, and XXY in the same individual. Other families may have one

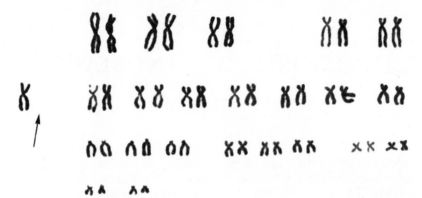

*Fig. 5.1    Karyotype of XO (45 chromosomes) (Turner's syndrome).*

eventually comprise half, a quarter or less, of the total cell material. However sometimes the developing abnormal cells appear to be 'squeezed out' by more normal cells, so an infant looking unmistakably like a Down's syndrome at birth, at two years may be less abnormal and more easily taken for a normal child.

A fourth type of phenocopy may also occur. These are individuals presenting, or copying, most of the abnormalities of, say, Down's syndrome, but having no chromosomal abnormality on karyotyping. It is presumed that such people have a translocation of chromosomal segment so small as to be undemonstrable by current methods of investigation. Alternative explanations are that such a person is a mosaic, abnormal cells happening not to be present in the biopsy material removed, or the phenocopy arises from a mutant gene acting upon susceptible target organs. Such people are still phenocopies, that is they have similar physical characteristics and appearances, yet are all produced by different causative factors. Thus two Down's syndrome children from different families present in the same ward, may look more alike than two twins. Yet one could be a trisomy, the other due to translocation, mosaicism or action of a mutant gene. The discussion has concerned Down's syndrome but the same principles underlie all other chromosomal anomalies.

kind of aneuploidy (abnormal cell line) such as 21 trisomy in one sibling, with another such as Turner's syndrome in a different offspring. It has been clearly shown that the relatives of a person with aneuploidy are at greater risk of having a second occurrence than the general population. Thus the sibling of a sporadic trisomy has double the risk of producing a trisomy child than a person in the general population, that is 1 in 300 compared with one in 660.

Isochromes and ring chromosomes are the results of mis-divisions or breaks in chromosome division. An isochrome is formed at meiosis when the chromosome divides across the short rather than the long axis, that is at a right angle to the usual. The resulting chromosome will have two long or two short arms and therefore be 'unbalanced' compared with a normal chromosome in the amount of genetic material now contained within it. When this occurs with the long arm of a D group autosome the child resulting can have many features of the 13 trisomy condition.

When breaks occur in two arms of one chromosome and union occurs by the broken end of each small part joining together to form a ring, this is inactive and there is net loss of the broken-off genetic material. The result with a D chromosome is that the subjects have a D deletion syndrome, for example 13q-. The clinical features of this 13q-can be quite variable. The presence of a ring still means there is a deletion syndrome.

Where isochromosomes of the X chromosome occur the typical features of Turner's syndrome are seen when the isochromosome lacks both short arms.

A balanced carrier is an individual who looks and is entirely normal, yet has an abnormal chromosomal pattern. In such individuals the total amount of chromosomal material is clearly normal but abnormally arranged. For example a translocation of material from the D to the G group may result in a probability of trisomy in the offspring because one germ cell will contain more material than another. Just as in biochemical investigations so in chromosomal, increasing frequency of investigation is yielding a variety of abnormalities often not correlated with the clinical disorder affecting the patient. This may represent another type of 'normal variation' to be expected in the animal world. Sometimes an abnormal child shows a chromosomal abnormality, later shown to be widespread in his family, all others being normal. The abnormal finding represents 'normal variation', another cause now having to be sought for the abnormality in the child.

## Dermatoglyphics

Dermatoglyphics is the study of hand, foot and finger prints which are under such strict genetic control that each is individual to the person concerned. Dermal ridges in the hands and the feet are formed by sweat gland openings, and are present in all primates. In humans they are determined by the fourth intrauterine month, and whilst identical twins are similar, no two have exactly the same structure. Early uterine maldevelopment can upset the formation of ridges and patterns, but no single gene disorder has an effect. However, the chromosomal anomalies do have a direct effect. Down's syndrome causes a specific alteration in the number of ridges, whilst in mosaics there is change proportional to the degree of mosaicism in the individual. Methods of classification have been evolved by Penrose (1963) and Loesch (1974).

It has been suggested that between 5 and 10 per cent of conceived fetuses have chromosomal abnormalities of which between 80 and 90 per cent spontaneously miscarry. It has now been established that one in every 200 newborn infants is in fact a chromosomal abnormality. Dermatoglyphs can play a part in the elucidation of some of these.

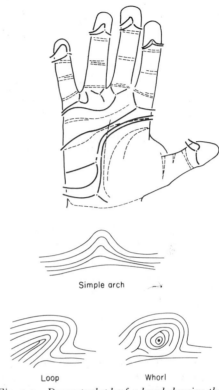

Simple arch

Loop       Whorl

*Fig. 5.2 Dermatoglyph of a hand showing the pattern on the finger tips and the main lines across the palm which are indicated by thick lines. The radii are where three lines meet. Palm and finger creases are shown by dotted lines.*

*Basic patterns.* There are three basic patterns: the arch, the loop and the whorl, which differ in the ways in which three lines may meet (see Fig. 5.2). A simple arch consists of a continuous curving line and lacks the third line or radius. A loop has an extra line, or radius, and may point to the ulnar or radial side of the body. Whorls have two extra radii, and may be concentric or double loop. Distribution varies between populations and between chromosomal abnormalities. The abnormalities are counted for the three main areas of the hand, the thenar area at the base of the thumb, the hypothenar or ulnar side of the bottom of the hand, and the four interdigital areas between the fingers and thumb. In the same way the areas of the foot can be counted.

In addition the skin creases on the palm are different between chromosomal anomalies and the normal. For instance Down's syndrome usually has one crease across the palm, called the simian crease, which also occurs in 5 per cent of the normal population. Only if this occurs in association with a single crease on the little finger, a distal axial triradius in the palm and the loops on all fingers, is it characteristic of 21 trisomy.

## BIBLIOGRAPHY

Loesch, D. (1974) Dermatoglyphic characteristics of 21 trisomy mosaicism in relation to the fully developed syndrome and normality. *J. ment. Defic. Res.*, *18*, 209–69.

Penrose, L. S. (1963) Finger-prints, palms and chromosomes. *Nature*, *197*, 933–38.

The account that follows describes autosomal anomalies in order of frequency, then proceeds with the sex chromosomes.

TABLE 5.1

Order of frequency (as described in text)

| Autosomes | 21 trisomy | 1 : 660 |
|---|---|---|
| | 18 trisomy | 1 : 3500 |
| | 13 trisomy | 1 : 7600 |
| | 5 deletion | 1 : 50 000 |
| *Sex chromosomes* | XYY | 1 : 1400 |
| | XXY | 1 : 1400 |
| | XXX | 1 : 1600 |
| | XO | 1 : 3300 |
| | XXXY | 1 : 23 000 |

Prevalence of chromosomal anomalies is 4 per cent of all fetuses of which 90 per cent abort. Among newborn it is 1 in 200, half being autosomal, half being sex anomalies.

## CHROMOSOME 21 TRISOMY
(47 XX + 21, G.1 Trisomy, Down's syndrome, mongolism)

Brachycephaly, facial stigmata, long life.

*History.* First reported by Langdon Down in 1866,

LeJeune et al. (1959) first identified the extra chromosome in the 21 position.

*Frequency.* Responsible for one third of all those under IQ 50; males equal to females, frequency about 1 in 660 overall (Ratcliffe et al. 1970) but 1 in 1050 in mothers aged 15–19 rising to 1 in 50 children for mothers aged 45 and over.

*Clinical features. Head and face*: brachycephaly (overall cranial capacity is decreased by shortness in all dimensions). The face is characteristic with upwardly and outward slanting eyes, simplified ears, a mouth often open with the tongue horizontally fissured, and a small nose. The eyes have Brushfield spots which are a collection of white patches on the edge of the iris (70 per cent) and poor development of the iris itself (about 50 per cent). The tongue is commonly protruded in infants due to maxillary hypoplasia and a narrow palate resulting in too little space for the tongue. There may be a third fontanelle in the newborn.

*Thorax*: Half have congenital heart lesions, mainly ventricular; less often atrioventricular canal defect, atrial septal defect and patent ductus occur. A short thick neck but no webbing is seen; the nipples are often small.

*Abdomen*: Umbilical herniae are common. Genitalia are usually underdeveloped; the male is usually sterile, females not so. Half of the affected female's children are affected (Down's).

*Limbs*: Hands and feet are short and broad and characteristically there is a wide space between the thumb and second digit together with the great toe and second digit. Hypotonia is usual so all joints are often hyper-retractile. The fifth finger is usually small with two clefts instead of the normal three.

*Dermatoglyphics*: A simple simian palm, with one transverse crease, a palmar distal axial triradius and ten ulnar or radial loops on fourth and fifth fingers is diagnostic. The skin generally is dry and often cyanotic with scanty hair follicles everywhere. Palmprints and sole-prints have been intensively used in comparing 21 trisomy with mosaics and parents. Mosaics, and parents of mosaics, occupy an intermediate position between 21 trisomy and normal controls. For a detailed discussion of the latest system of classification, see Loesch (1974).

*Height and weight*: Usually short and small. Hypothyroidism is common (see p. 91).

*CNS*: There have been many studies of intellectual ability. Most subjects are below IQ 50; the 10 per cent of Down's syndromes who are above IQ 50 are often mosaics, that is the non-disjunction has occurred at the second or later stage of the embryonic stage of development so that only one half or one quarter of all cells are then the 21 trisomy anomaly. Subjects usually have marked hypotonia. Coordination is poor, a cerebellar deficit may be noted, there is often tremor. Final personality development may be immature and emotional tantrums during childhood frequent, but with adult

been reported, subjects are noted for a deteriorating intellectual performance from middle age on. However, the steady if slow neurological development means that educational programmes which began

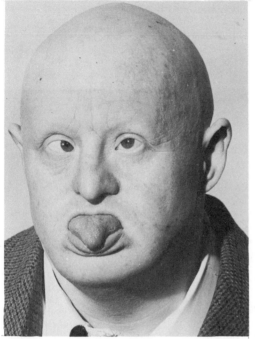

Fig. 5.3 Trisomy 21 showing epicanthic folds of eyes, striated tongue, and the common squint and baldness.

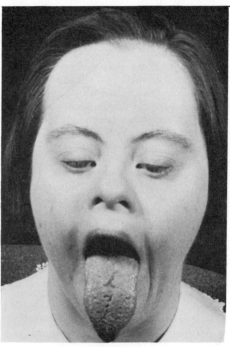

Fig. 5.4 Trisomy 21 showing epicanthic folds and striated tongue (Dr Kratter).

years most are noted for a happy, amiable and tractable disposition, conscientious at work and undemanding at home. Degrees of deafness used to be common, probably due to untreated upper respiratory infections.

Morbid anatomy. The brain is simple, under weight, but without consistent severe anomaly. In a pathological study of 2421 subject (Fabia and Drolette 1970) 29 per cent were born with heart defects, 3 per cent had duodenal obstruction, and in this series of autopsies 1 per cent had had leukemia. There is some evidence that 21 trisomy subjects are immunodeficient, Lopez (1974) found lowered IgE immunoglobulin, but this is still disputed.

Treatment and outcome. With surgery for the 29 to 50 per cent who have cardiac anomaly and antibiotic treatment of the common respiratory diseases, long life is frequent, many now living over 60. The earlier series (Lilienfeld 1969) giving 30 per cent dying during the first year of life and 50 per cent by five years old are probably out of date. Genetic programming for early senile plaques has

from six months of age have been attended with significant success in terms of childhood achievements. (See Chapter 13.)

Genetics. 95 per cent of phenotypes have chromosome 21 anomaly, the rest are mosaics in various studies or due to translocation (see pp. 49–50).

Diagnosis. The fully developed clinical picture is characteristic, although epicanthic folds can be seen in 20 per cent of normal people and upward slant of the eyes is also seen in 14 per cent of normals. Hypothyroidism is common in Down's syndrome subjects, but cretins do not have the characteristic palms and feet.

Counselling. The birth of a Down's syndrome baby is an upsetting experience for most parents. It has recently been shown (British Medical Journal 1977) that mothers (and animals) who fail to see their children frequently in the first days of life may fail to develop 'bonding' or maternal love. It is therefore important for mothers of Down's syndrome children to see them soon, so as not to exacerbate any feelings of rejection that may occur. Thereafter encouragement and counselling of both parents alone and together should be the responsibility of a skilled person (see Chapter 22) who may be asked about remedial needs (see Chapter 13), education (Chapter 14) and independent living (Chapter 18) and so on. Much medical care is required for the many complications common in Down's syndrome.

Genetic counselling should be available at the regional clinic. Enough has already been said in this chapter to point out that whilst at any maternal age most Down's syndrome babies are G.1 (21) trisomy, an inherited translocation is more common among young mothers, accounting for 9 per cent of those born to mothers under 30. Of these translocations, 25 per cent are transmitted, 75 per cent sporadic, which means that a quarter of the 9 per cent (or 2 per cent overall) are inherited.

Thus chromosomal analysis of young mothers with trisomy babies is particularly important. In the translocation group, that from D to G (from 14 to 21) is the most common. In addition some 1.5 per cent of institutionalized Down's syndrome persons are mosaics, and since such people are more intelligent than complete trisomies, this figure may be higher for community phenotypes. The dull young mother with a phenotypic Down's child could be a G trisomy mosaic herself with few stigmata. Without detailed chromosomal analysis she may be accused of 'family non-disjunction'.

In summary, it seems better to karyotype all mothers under 30 with Down's syndrome babies; the risk of a second Down's syndrome child may thus be estimated with some accuracy.

## BIBLIOGRAPHY

British Medical Journal (1977) Helping mothers to love their babies. *Br. med. J.*, *2*, 595.

Fabia, J. & Drolette, M. (1970) Malformations and leukemia in children with Down's syndrome. *Pediatrics*, *45*, 60–70.

LeJeune, J., Gauthier, M. & Turpin, R. (1959) Etudes des chromosomes somatiques de neuf enfants mongoliens. *C.R. Acad. Sci. (Paris)*, *248*, 1721–22.

Lilienfeld, A. M. (1969) *Epidemiology of Mongolism.* Baltimore: Johns Hopkins University Press.

Loesch, D. (1974) Dermatoglyphic characteristics of 21 trisomy mosaicism in relation to the fully developed syndrome and normality. *J. ment. Defic. Res.*, *18*, 209–69.

Lopez, V. (1974) Serum IgE concentration in trisomy 21. *J. ment. Defic. Res. 18*, 111–14.

Ratcliffe, S. G., Stewart, A. L., Melville, M. M. & Jacobs, P. A. (1970) Chromosomes studies on 3500 newborn male infants. *Lancet*, *1*, 121–22.

## CHROMOSOME 18 TRISOMY
(47 XX + 18, E trisomy, Edwards' syndrome)

Face has small eyes, mouth, ears; childhood death.

*History.* Reported by Edwards et al. (1960).

*Numbers and frequency.* Some 200 reported. Frequency 1 in 3500 live births in North America, survival at birth 1 male to 3 females.

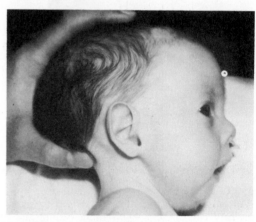

*Fig. 5.5   Trisomy 18 (Edwards' syndrome) showing typical head profile (Dr McDermott and Dr Insley).*

*Clinical features.* Microcephaly rare, but a pronounced occiput and a long skull are present in all. Hypertelorism, epicanthic folds, narrow fissures, ptosis of eyes and small chin are usual. Microphthalmos noted in one third (Taylor 1968), cataracts and opacities of cornea are common, with small maldeveloped ears. Cleft palate was present in 3 out of 27. A short neck is common.

*Heart:* One report gave 99 per cent as having congenital abnormality, mainly ventricular septal defect, or patent ductus.

*Abdomen:* Undescended testicles are usual. Inguinal hernia is common.

*Limbs:* The hands are distinctive in that they swing to the ulnar side and the second and fifth fingers are often curved, whilst other fingers have a flexion deformity. The thumb is unduly mobile and the nails poorly developed. Fused fingers are common but the commonest foot deformity is a rocker-bottom, valgus deformity. Flexion contractures develop.

*Weight:* Usually small, short and slow.

*CNS:* All have been markedly retarded, with hypertonia of muscles and frequent epilepsy. Deafness is common. A child who could be taught to walk was so uncommon it has been recorded (Abbie 1976).

*Dermatoglyphics*: Characteristic six to ten low arches, high axial triradius, this occurs in only 0.1 per cent of normals.

*Morbid anatomy.* A quarter have non-specific brain abnormalities such as hydrocephalus, absent occipital lobes, poorly developed cerebellum. Thirteen out of sixteen infants had cerebral agenesis in one study by Terplan et al. (1970). One half of the infants had congenital heart defects, other defects included renal anomalies and hernias. Intestinal maldevelopment is common.

*Treatment and outcome.* Taylor's (1968) review reports one study of 153 infants where a 71-day life was the mean; and another study where one half survived beyond two months and only one subject for ten years.

*Diagnosis.* Cleft lip and microphthalmos are also features of trisomy 13.

*Genetics.* The stigmata most often occur in those with E trisomy, as in Down's syndrome, but a few are mosaics, and again the phenotype may occur among those without clear chromosomal abnormality and is presumed due to an abnormal recessive gene. Again as in Down's, double trisomy occurs, with a presumed predisposition to aneuploidy. Unbalanced translocation is rare and parents can be reassured that this sporadic event occurs in only 1 in 3500 births, so recurrence is negligible.

BIBLIOGRAPHY

Abbie, M. (1976) Unusual development of motor skills in a child with trisomy 18. *Devl. Med. Child Neurol.*, *18*, 85–9.
Edwards, J. H., Harnden, D. G., Cameron, A. H., Crosse, V. M. & Wolff, O. H. (1960) A new trisomic syndrome. *Lancet*, *1*, 787–90.
Taylor, A. I. (1968) Autosomal trisomy syndromes: a detailed study of 27 cases of Edwards' syndrome and 27 of Patau's syndrome. *J. med. Genet.*, *5*, 227–52. [the best review]
Terplan, K. L., Lopez, E. C. & Robinson, H. B. (1970) Histologic structural anomalies in the brain in trisomy 18 syndrome. *Am. J. Dis. Child.*, *119*, 228–35.

CHROMOSOME 13 TRISOMY
(47 XX + 13, D.1 trisomy,
13–15 trisomy, Patau's syndrome)

Microcephaly, severe facial defects, infantile death.

*History.* Described by Patau et al. (1960).

*Numbers and frequency.* Over 200 described, but it is one of the least common trisomies at 1 in 7600 live births, males–females equal.

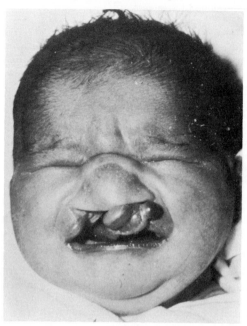

*Fig. 5.6    Trisomy 13 (Patau's syndrome) (Dr McDermott and Dr Insley).*

*Clinical features. Head*: Most are microcephalic with severe abnormalities of face, cleft lip, hypertelorism and small chin. Some have absent or small eyes with cataracts and iris defects. Most have simple or small ears. Half have cleft palate as well as cleft lip. Shortness of neck is common.

*Heart*: 88 per cent have congenital defects—ventricular septal defect and patent ductus are common, rotation less common.

*Abdomen*: Hernias are frequent, as are undescended testicles.

*Limbs*: Polydactyly and crooked fingers are common, with long nails. Some have fused fingers or toes.

*Weight*: Most are small and short.

*CNS*: All reported are severely retarded with marked hypertonia, and myoclonic spasms. Many are deaf.

*Dermatoglyphics*: 25 per cent have more than three arches in finger patterns, 81 per cent a high triradius, 58 per cent simian crease.

*Morbid anatomy.* Capillary haemangiomas of the skin are found. The cortex is usually abnormal in formation, and gyri are poorly developed. The cerebellum is often small and infantile. Heart defects are frequent with patent ductus reported in half of one series. Renal anomalies are also present, half the females have had abnormal uteri, the eye may be replaced by cartilage, those deaf may have undeveloped inner ears.

*Treatment and outcome.* Magenis et al. (1968) showed that only half of 221 patients lived beyond one month, over half the remainder died before three months, and only 5 per cent survived beyond three years of age.

*Diagnosis.* Some of the features are found in the Gruber syndrome but these often have an encephalocele, hypertelorism, cleft palate and lip, and are found in the 4p- syndrome, chromosome four anomaly; males with blindness due to X-linkage may also be retarded but have a normal karyotype.

*Genetics.* As with other trisomic conditions, most patients indeed have trisomy, but phenotypes also occur when the chromosome analysis shows balanced and unbalanced D group translocation when the stigmata are usually complete. Mosaics (normal/13 trisomy) occur with fewer signs. Parents can be told that the incidence is 1 in 7000, recurrence rate is 1 in 3500. If the patient has no unbalanced translocation, parental examination is necessary. If a 'normal' parent shows a balanced translocation, the recurrence rate of affected fetuses is high enough to warrant amniocentesis (see p. 124).

### BIBLIOGRAPHY

Magenis, R. E., Hecht, F. & Milham, S. (1968) Trisomy 13 (D1) syndrome: studies on parental age, sex ratio and survival. *J. Pediat., 73*, 222–28.

Patau, K., Smith, D. W., Therman, E., Inhorn, S. L. & Wagner, H. P. (1960) Multiple congenital anomaly caused by an extra autosome. *Lancet, 1,* 790–93.

## CHROMOSOME 5—deletion of short arm
### (in a female 46 XX 5p-, Cri du chat)

Cat cry, microcephaly, antimongoloid eyes, prolonged life.

*History.* Described by LeJeune and her associates (1963).

*Numbers and frequency.* Of 744 patients IQ less than 35, 1 per cent affected (Breg et al. 1970), more girls than boys, frequency 1 per 50 000 live births (Niebuhr 1971).

*Clinical features.* The head is microcephalic, a round small face with high forehead, markedly alert eyes slanted down and epicanthic, nose small and beaked, small chin, often receding; eye defects are common (such as squint, defects of iris); ears simple and set low.

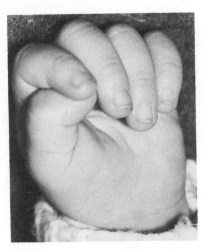

*Fig. 5.7    5p-(cri du chat syndrome) showing fisted hand (Dr Kirman).*

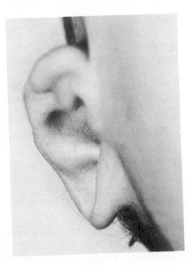

*Fig. 5.8    5p-(cri du chat syndrome) showing abnormal ear (Dr Kirman).*

*Catlike cry*: This is distinctive, and like facial features best recognized in early infancy. It is curiously high in note and wailing like a cat, said to be due to a weak epiglottis which flops over a very narrow larynx during in-breathing, causing the strange mewing note. The vocal chords fail to meet properly and during the early years of life the voice is high pitched. Like the facial features, the voice improves with age.

*Limbs*: Most reported to have short hands and feet with occasional club foot and other deformities.

*Heart*: 50 per cent congenital anomalies, mainly ventricular septal defect or patent ductus.

*CNS*: All reported have been severely retarded,

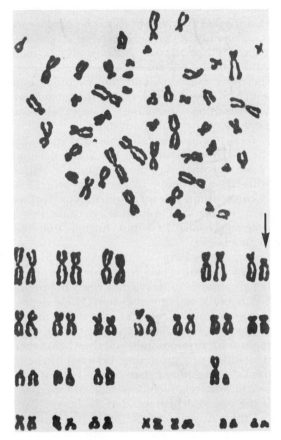

*Fig. 5.9   5p-(cri du chat syndrome) showing partial deletion of chromosome no. 5 (Dr Kirman).*

average IQ less than 20 (Niebuhr 1971). Speech is slow and walking delayed due to hypertonia. Epilepsy is uncommon. Niebuhr found IQ 58 the highest in his series.

*Dermatoglyphics*: Distal axial triradius and increased whorls.

*Morbid anatomy*. Some have congenital cardiac defects but the few brains examined have shown dilated ventricles with some atrophy.

*Treatment and outcome*. Compatible with adult life.

*Diagnosis*. The cry is distinctive in infancy but otherwise the small round face and hypertelorism are similar to other syndromes.

*Genetics*. Rare and sporadic, parents can be advised of non-repetition.

BIBLIOGRAPHY

Breg, W. R., Steele, M. W., Miller, O. J., Warburton, D., deCapoa, A. & Allerdice, P. W. (1970) The Cri du Chat syndrome in adolescents and adults: clinical findings in 13 older patients with partial deletion of the short arm of chromosome No. 5 (5p-). *J. Pediat.*, 77, 782–91.

Lejeune, J., Lafourcade, J., Berger, R., Vialette, J., Boeswillwand, M., Seringe, P. & Turpin, R. (1963) Trois cas de délétion partielle du bras court d'un chromosome r. *C.R. Acad. Sci. (D) (Paris)*, 257, 3098–3102.

Niebuhr, E. (1971) The Cat Cry syndrome (5p-) in adolescents and adults. *J. ment. Defic. Res.*, 15, 277–91.

## CHROMOSOME 18—partial deletion of long arm
### (46 XX or XY 18q-, Group E)

Microcephaly, flat face, simple ears, fair lifespan.

*History*. Reported by deGrouchy et al. (1964).

*Numbers and frequency*. Some 40 patients.

*Clinical features. Head and face*: Most are microcephalic, with deep set eyes, flattened maxillae and central face, normal forehead, downward slanting angles of mouth. Eyes are usually normal. Simple external ears occur with a narrow external canal.

*Abdomen*: There are underdeveloped genitalia, male and female, with labia and penis small, and undescended testes.

*Limbs*: Long with extra dimples present over the major joints.

*Weight*: Birth weight only slightly below normal on average.

*CNS*: All reported severely retarded with marked infantile hypotonia. In one series most had nystagmus.

*Morbid anatomy*. 40 per cent have congenital heart lesions.

*Treatment and outcome*. Apart from heart defect, life expectancy to childhood.

*Diagnosis*. Mid-face underdevelopment is the characteristic feature. Microcephaly and genital underdevelopment are also found in the sex anomalies.

BIBLIOGRAPHY

deGrouchy, J., Royer, P., Salmon, C. & Lamy, M. (1964) Délétion partielle des bras longs du chromosome 18. *Path. Biol., Paris*, 12, 579–82.

## SEX CHROMOSOMAL ANOMALIES

With the development in 1956 of techniques which enabled the number of chromosomes to be counted, both autosomal trisomy for Down's syndrome and sex chromosome trisomy XXY for Klinefelter's syndrome could be established. Shortly after, the common Turner's syndrome with its stigmata was associated with the missing X chromosome and the hunt was on for rarer anomalies.

It was in 1949 that Barr and Bertram noticed a difference in the division stage between male and female cells. First in animals then in humans it was shown that female cells had a dense mass of chromatin in the nuclei of somatic cells. An extension of this test allowed the nuclear sex of human cells to be shown. Scraping the inside of a human mouth, and spreading the cells from the buccal mucosa from this onto a slide which is then stained allows the presence or absence of this dense sex chromatin mass to be shown. This distinguishes the female from the male, or rather shows whether the individual has more than one X chromosome.

With the appropriate staining method the normal XX human female has this densely staining chromatin mass along the inner surface of most of her buccal mucosal nuclei. The normal human XY male with only one X chromosome does not have this. However within 1 to 2 per cent of his cells there are darkly staining masses that can be mistaken for what are now called 'Barr bodies'.

Together with the buccal smear, it is usual to send a blood smear to the laboratory for confirmation. The reason for this is that in the mature human female some 5 per cent of her mature polymorphonuclear cells have a drumstick projection from the nucleus, but this is difficult to distinguish from other nuclear structures. The buccal smear slide, with its supporting blood slide, are useful methods of checking nuclear sex. The number of Barr bodies to a cell is always one less than the number of X chromosomes. Thus the normal male has none, the normal female one, the XXY male has one and an XXX female two Barr bodies to each nucleus. The Barr bodies have no relationship to the number of Y chromosomes.

It is the Y chromosome which determines the sexual phenotype of the infant, with a few exceptions the result of abnormal circulation of sex hormones. The result of this is that the XO Turner subject is a phenotypical female, and the XXY Klinefelter's syndrome although having two XXs is still a male. Although the one may have a Barr body and the other not, it is still the Y chromosome which determines the sex of the gonad, and the resulting production of sex hormones establishes the male body-type.

As with autosomal chromosomal anomalies, the sex chromosomes can also suffer deletions of genetic material. For instance a patient who has a deletion of the long arm of an X chromosome has many phenotypic features of a Turner XO condition. Because this is excessively rare it is not further described in this book.

Arguments have recently been put forward to describe why one X chromosome in the female appears to stain a dark mass to produce a Barr body and one does not. These depend upon autoradiographic studies with titrated thymidine which is taken into the DNA of replicating chromosomes and shows that there is a difference in timing between them. It has been suggested that one X chromosome is late and relatively inactive and that this is the one which is the Barr body.

Other dyes such as quinacrine mustard effectively stain the Y chromosome fluorescent in cell division preparation. Thus normal male cells can show a fluorescent Y and XYY individuals two fluorescent bodies in each cell. This procedure and the Barr body procedure can be used in conjunction with one another. There are difficulties, for chromosomes 3 and 13 take up quinacrine to some extent but it is not usually too difficult to differentiate between the different chromosomes in a well-prepared slide. One final variable is that the nature of the human material is important, Y bodies in fibroblasts stain in some 90 per cent of cells, whereas in white cells the same stain is far less taken up.

The reader may well wonder why if one X chromosome is relatively inactive there are such manifest differences between the sex chromosomal anomalies. For instance both the XO Turner's syndrome and the XXY Klinefelter's syndrome can have individuals with intelligence in the average range, some may even go to college, but individuals with XXXXY usually have an intelligence in the IQ 20–50 range. It has been suggested that the inactive X chromosome carries loci needing to be present in duplicate for normal function to proceed. Thus the normal XX female and XY male have these in duplicate and can develop (because the Y chromosome also carries these loci on part of its substance) but the XO has not, and the XXY has these in triplicate. The more X chromosomes the more the confusion of genetic messages. Such explanations are not entirely satisfying but present a growth point for further research.

In exactly the same way as with autosomal trisomy (see pp. 49–51), phenotypes of the sex chromosome anomalies may occur. The best known of these is with XO Turner's syndrome where the phenocopy is called Noonan's syndrome. This may occur in male or female and does not have the sexual agenesis; it is described in Chapter 6 (p. 103). It is presumed due to a mutant gene acting on sensitive target organs and is relatively common. Mosaics for Turner's syndrome have also been reported, including normal-XO, XO-XXX; XO-XX-XXX. As might be expected the degree of phenotype in general depends on the proportion of abnormal cell lines, though this is not conclusive. Shortness of height is usual with those reported. In addition isochromosomes of both the long arm and the short arm together with long arm deletions and ring chromosomes have been reported. Such people have the normal number of chromosomes, but structurally abnormal X chromosomes. Some have sufficient Turner's stigmata to diagnose XO Turner's syndrome, some Noonan's syndrome. The buccal smear shows Barr bodies which may be larger than normal.

## XYY 47 SYNDROME

Most over 190 cm tall, normal lifespan.

*History.* Recent studies suggest that the XYY syndrome is not necessarily associated with mental retardation as such, although since the first individuals to be described were found in retardation institutions the association between the two arose (Craft 1978).

*Numbers and frequency.* Numerous examples to date. Frequency among live births said to be 1 in 1400.

*Clinical features.* Now believed to have no distinguishing physical features.
   *Weight*: Now believed to be normal. There is an excess of these individuals above 190 cm in height.
   *CNS*: Most reported dull normal, although many in retardation hospitals.

*Morbid anatomy.* Nil.

*Treatment and outcome.* Compatible with normal life and health. Recent comprehensive reviews suggest that the presence of the extra Y chromosome induces an immaturity in development of personality and intellect; this is associated with an increased number who develop adolescent behavioural upsets and sexual overactivity which may lead to convictions.

BIBLIOGRAPHY

Craft, M. J. (1978) The current status of the XYY and XXY syndromes. *Int. J. Law & Psychiatry*, *1*, 319–24.
Hunter, H. (1977) XYY males: some clinical and psychiatric aspects deriving from a survey of 1811 males in hospitals for the mentally handicapped. *Br. J. Psychiatry*, *131*, 468–77.

## XXY 47 SYNDROME
(Klinefelter's syndrome)

Male feminization, scratch voice, normal lifespan.

*History.* Reported by Klinefelter et al. (1942) as a distinctive clinical syndrome manifest at adolescence.

*Numbers and frequency.* Males, approximately 1 to 1400 total live births (Ratcliffe et al. 1970).

*Clinical features. Head and face*: Diminished facial hair, otherwise normal. High pitched voice.
   *Thorax*: 25 per cent have bilateral breast enlargement with pronounced mammary glands.
   *Abdomen*: 90 per cent have a small penis, all have small testes.
   *Limbs*: Minor anomalies only, such as deviation of the fifth finger.
   *Weight*: Usually normal.
   *CNS*: Surveys of mental retardation institutions have shown that frequency of such individuals in these populations is three times greater than normal,

but the majority of subjects in the community are near-average in intelligence. The personality has been described as tendentious, argumentative and querulous. There is said to be a high incidence of personality abnormalities and divorce.

*Dermatoglyphics*: Average ridge count low.

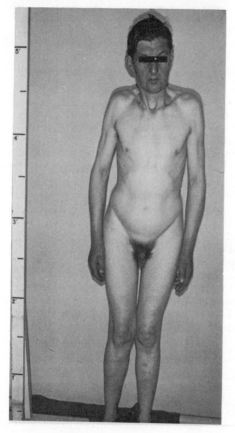

*Fig. 5.10  XXY (Klinefelter's syndrome) showing absent facial hair and scant pubic hair (Dr Jancar).*

**Morbid anatomy.** The testes are hypoplastic.

**Treatment and outcome.** Compatible with normal health, but there is an excess incidence of diabetes mellitus, need for psychiatric treatment for personality upsets, and convictions (Craft 1978).

**Diagnosis.** This syndrome can be differentiated from those with XXXY and XXXXY syndromes, also from normal adolescence with adolescent gynaecomastia and undescended testicles.

**Phenotypes.** As with other chromosomal abnormalities, there are persons with all or most of the stigmata and no chromosomal abnormality, presumably the result of an abnormal gene.

BIBLIOGRAPHY

Craft, M. J. (1978) The current status of the XYY and XXY syndromes. *Int. J. Law & Psychiatry*, *1*, 319–24.
Ratcliffe, S. G., Stewart, A. L., Melville, M. M. & Jacobs, P. A. (1970) Chromosomes studies on 3500 newborn male infants. *Lancet*, *1*, 121–22.

## XXX 47, XXXX 48 AND XXXXX 49
### SYNDROMES

*History.* Carr et al. (1961) described the first two females.

*Numbers and frequency.* Many such patients have now been described, almost all the results of surveys among in-patient mental retardates, so the exact association with degree of retardation is uncertain. The frequency of XXX among the general population is 1 per 1600 births.

*Clinical features.* The XXX syndrome has been wrongly called the superfemale syndrome. It is the most common, and whilst many subjects are underdeveloped, with menstrual disorder, with scanty or absent menses and breast development, others show normal physical and mental development, even bearing children. It is possible that only the abnormal have been reported, and more common normal subjects are unreported, as has happened with the XYY syndrome.

*Features of the multiple X syndrome*: Reports suggest that the greater the number of X chromosomes, the greater the physical and mental disability. Hypertelorism and microcephaly have been reported commonly with the XXXX and XXXXX subjects, many are kyphotic.

*Thorax*: A short neck and infantile breasts have been reported.

*Abdomen*: Irregular menstruation is common.

*Limbs*: Short phalanges and skew deviation of the fifth finger are usual.

*Weight*: Low at birth.

*CNS*: Because surveys have concentrated on retardation institutions, most have been severely retarded, few are in the borderline range.

*Treatment and outcome.* These syndromes appear to be compatible with normal life, and one XXX case had two children. One of these was normal, the other had chromosome 21 anomaly. Antenatal diagnosis is possible (Muellerheubach et al. 1977).

*Diagnosis.* From other causes of microcephaly and hypertelorism.

BIBLIOGRAPHY

Carr, D. H., Barr, M. L. & Plunkett, E. R. (1961) An XXXX sex chromosome complex in two mentally defective females. *Can. med. Ass. J., 84,* 131–7.
Muellerheubach, E., Garver, K. L. & Ciocco, A. M. (1977) Prenatal diagnosis of trisomy X, its implications for genetic counselling. *Am. J. Obstet. Gynec., 127,* 211–12.

## XO 45 SYNDROME
### (Turner's syndrome)

Genital infantilism, neck webbing, normal lifespan.

*History.* First described by Turner in 1938.

*Numbers and frequency.* 97 per cent of 45X conceptions are said to die *in utero* (Hecht and Macfarlane 1969). Frequency of 1 in 3300 live births.

*Clinical features. Head and face*: Girls with Turner's syndrome often look alike with sad, somewhat pinched expressions, small chins and with a small nose. A few have hypertelorism, epicanthus and ptosis. Squint and corneal opacities occur. Ears are often large. 50 per cent have webbed neck.
    *Heart*: 35 per cent have coarctation of aorta.
    *Chest and abdomen*: Wide-spaced small nipples and protuberant abdomen.
    *Limbs*: A small opposed fifth finger, hypoplastic nails in the newborn, and oedema are common in hands and feet.
    *Weight*: Subjects are short, and small at birth.
    *CNS*: Intelligence may be dull normal or better. One recent report found only 2 out of 25 subjects to be subnormal (Nielson 1973). Hearing loss is common.
    *Dermatoglyphics*: 25 per cent have distal axial triradius.

*Morbid anatomy.* There is gonadal dysgenesis. Feminization and menarche do not occur and in place of normal gonads there is a mass of collagen without true Graafian follicles present. Heart defects and renal defects are common in those born live whilst severe defects of heart and kidneys are most common among spontaneous abortions.

*Treatment and prognosis.* Dependant upon anomalies as above. Otherwise compatible with a reasonable life, intelligence and good health.

*Diagnosis.* The absence of secondary sexual characteristics is characteristic. Where hypertelorism and epicanthic folds occur Apert's syndrome has to be distinguished.

Neck webbing and short stature are features of chromosome 18 (see p. 57). Short neck and epican-

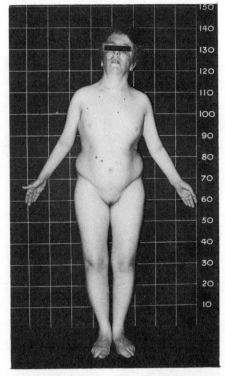

*Fig. 5.11 XO (Turner's syndrome) showing lack of pubic hair and breast development (Dr Jancar).*

thic folds are also features of Down's syndrome, Noonan's syndrome (Turner-like) occurs in both sexes, has 46 chromosomes and does not cause sexual infantilism. This is a phenocopy of Turner's syndrome, believed due to an autosomal dominant gene and depending on the subject's sex is usually called Noonan XX or Noonan XY. At 1 to 1000 general population it is more common than XO Turner's.

BIBLIOGRAPHY

Goldberg, M. B., Scully, A. L., Solomon, I. L. & Steinbach, H. L. (1968) Gonadal dysgenesis in phenotypic female subjects. A review of 87 cases, with cytogenetic studies in 53. *Am. J. Med., 45,* 529–43. [the best review]
Hecht, F. & Macfarlane, J. P. (1969) Mosaicism in Turner's syndrome reflects the lethality of XO. *Lancet, 2,* 1197–8.
Nielson, J. (1973) Mental retardation in Turner's syndrome. *J. ment. Defic. Res., 17,* 227–30.

## XXXY (48) AND XXXXY (49) SYNDROMES

Excess feminization.

Both 48 and 49 chromosome individuals as above have been described. As might be expected, whilst those reported have small penis and testes, and decreased pubic hair, the greater the number of X chromosomes the greater the disorder. The frequency is less than with Klinefelter's. One in 23 000 born males was found to be XXXY, and some 25 have been described. The frequency of XXXXY syndromes does not appear less frequent, as more than 70 subjects have been described.

*Clinical features.* Most of the clinical features are similar to Klinefelter's but accentuated.

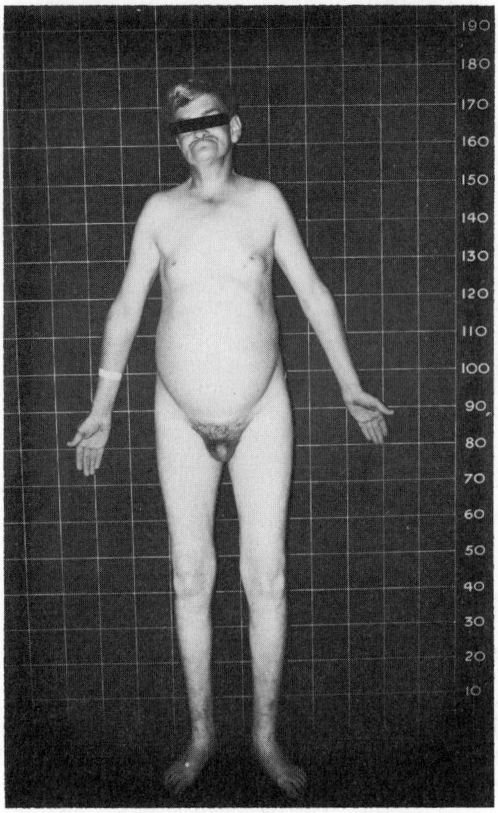

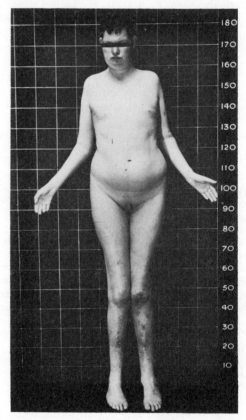

Fig. *5.12*    *XXXY syndrome showing feminization (Dr Jancar).*

Fig. *5.13*    *XXXXY syndrome showing feminization (Dr Jancar).*

## XXYY (48) SYNDROME

Feminized males.

*History.* Muldal and Ockey first described this syndrome (1960).

*Numbers and frequency.* Nearly 100 individuals described.

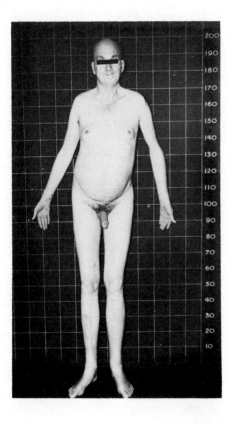

*Clinical features.* Neck webbing reported.
  *Thorax*: Most patients have gynaecomastia.
  *Abdomen*: Phallus normal, testes usually small.
  *Limbs*: Of normal size.
  *Weight*: Excessive fat deposition.
  *CNS*: All described as being mentally retarded, possibly due to having been selectively found among mental retardation institutions.

*Morbid anatomy.* Excessive hyalinization of testes.

*Treatment and outcome*: Compatible with normal length of life.

*Diagnosis.* Many features are in common with Klinefelter's syndrome (XXY) but the latter have increased height compared with XXYY individuals.

### BIBLIOGRAPHY

Muldal, S. & Ockey, C. H. (1960) The 'double male': a new chromosome constitution in Klinefelter's syndrome. *Lancet*, 2, 492–3.
Parker, C. E., Mavalwala, J., Melnyk, J. & Fish, C. H. (1970) The 48 XXYY syndrome. *Am. J. Med.*, 48, 777–81.

*Fig. 5.14   XXYY syndrome showing feminization (Dr Jancar).*

*Fig. 5.15   Karyotype of XXYY syndrome showing 48 chromosomes (same patient as Fig. 5.14) (Dr Jancar).*

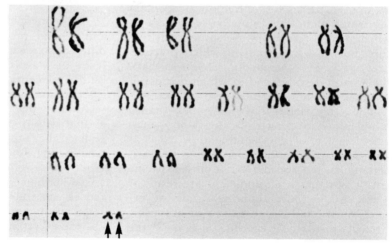

# CHAPTER 6

# PRIMARY GENETIC DISORDERS AND THEIR MANAGEMENT

## MICHAEL CRAFT AND PETER HARPER

Genetic factors are of major importance in almost all forms of mental retardation, but it is only in a minority of cases that one can identify a specific disorder with a recognizable genetic basis. Increasing understanding at a clinical, genetic and biochemical level has steadily enlarged the number of disorders in this group and enabled a specific cause to be given in many instances that would previously have been termed 'non-specific' mental retardation.

In some of these disorders the existence of a unique clinical syndrome is clear, but the genetic basis appears slight or obscure; in a small but important number a recognizable abnormality of chromosome morphology can be found. In the majority there is no visible chromosome defect, but the condition can be attributed to the action of a major gene whose pattern of transmission follows Mendelian inheritance.

It is this last group which is emphasized in this chapter. Not only does it contain numerous clinically distinctive disorders in which mental retardation is a prominent feature, but it is the group in which practical preventive and therapeutic measures have their greatest scope, and in which our depth of understanding is greatest.

The recognition that Mendelian inheritance is operating in a particular form of mental retardation is of considerable theoretical as well as practical importance, for it makes it certain that the disorder is not only a specific entity, but that it is ultimately the result of a unique biochemical abnormality, almost certainly in the primary structure of a specific protein coded by a specific portion of the

genetic material. Study can then be directed towards identifying the complex chain of events connecting this basic defect with the end result of the clinical and pathological features. The degree to which this understanding has been achieved varies greatly from condition to condition, and it is possible to recognize a number of stages, summarized below:

1. Identification of a specific clinical syndrome.
2. Recognition of a specific mode of Mendelian inheritance.
3. Discovery of an underlying metabolic abnormality.
4. Identification of the specific enzyme or other protein that is absent or defective.
5. Identification of the precise nature of the change in the nucleic acid of the particular gene.
6. Replacement of the defective gene product.

The mucopolysaccharidoses (gargoylism and others) provide an illustration of the different stages and of how rapidly our knowledge may evolve. Stage 1 was represented by the recognition of a clinical syndrome of 'gargoylism' and was taken further by the realization that individual clinical entities existed within this group. In stage 2 it was realized that not only was Mendelian inheritance acting, but that one form (type II, the Hunter syndrome) followed X-linked recessive inheritance while the others were inherited in an autosomal recessive manner. In stage 3 characteristic changes in mucopolysaccharide excretion were identified, along with the storage of partly degraded mucopolysaccharide molecules in the tissues, while in stage 4, only recently achieved, specific deficiencies of individual lysosomal enzymes were identified, corresponding in general with the clinical and biochemical groups already defined. Although stage 5 has not been reached, our existing knowledge already allows accurate preventive measures such as genetic counselling, carrier detection and prenatal diagnosis, while attempts are in progress to realize stage 6 with the use of implants of cultured cells from elsewhere, which may allow construction of the missing enzyme within the affected person.

## THE BASIS OF MENDELIAN INHERITANCE

The majority of primary genetic disorders causing mental retardation have not had all six stages of elucidation, and indeed the grounds for a genetic basis of some of the specific disorders considered later in this chapter are tenuous, but the rapid changes for some disorders provide a challenge both for improving the level of understanding of others, and in identifying new entities whose existence is at present not clearly defined.

The mode of inheritance can help in other ways than simply identifying a disorder as Mendelian. It is a remarkable fact that almost all the disorders for which a clear biochemical basis has been identified show recessive inheritance, and that most of these have proved to be enzymatic defects. This arises from two factors: firstly our understanding of non-enzymatic proteins of cells under direct genetic control is poor in comparison with our knowledge of specific enzymatic processes; secondly the great majority of enzymes can be reduced to a level of well under half the original amount or activity without harmful result, so that the heterozygote for an enzymatic disorder, where enzyme activity is generally around half the normal level, will be clinically normal. By definition therefore such disorders will be recessively inherited; the heterozygous carriers will show minimal or no abnormalities, and may require special investigations for their identification. The metabolic basis of the numerous dominantly inherited disorders is one of the major challenges of medical genetics, for at present few of them are understood even in the most general

terms. The few dominantly inherited enzyme defects known, such as the porphyrias, are related to pathways which are unusually critical and sensitive in their regulation. Some others are thought to result from mutations in structural molecules of cell membranes and other components, yet others to specific failures of regulatory processes in development, but in most instances we simply do not know.

### TABLE 6.1

X-linked disorders associated with mental retardation

| |
|---|
| Non-specific X-linked mental retardation (Renpenning's syndrome) |
| Cerebral sclerosis with adrenal insufficiency* |
| Diffuse cerebral sclerosis (Pelizaeus-Merzbacher type) |
| X-linked hydrocephalus with aqueduct stenosis |
| Pseudohypoparathyroidism (Albright's hereditary osteodystrophy)* |
| Lesch–Nyhan syndrome |
| Incontinentia pigmenti |
| Oculocerebrorenal syndrome (Lowe)* |
| Mucopolysaccharidosis, type II (Hunter syndrome) |
| Menkes 'kinky hair' syndrome |
| Muscular dystrophy, Duchenne type |
| Norrie's disease |
| Hyperammonia (ornithine transcarbamylase deficiency type)* |

* Not described in this book.
Based on McKusick (1975).

The specific chromosomes on which are located the genes controlling the various Mendelian forms of mental retardation have for the most part not been identified, but in the case of the X chromosome the pattern of inheritance itself provides this information. There are in fact numerous X-linked disorders accompanied by mental retardation, and some are listed in Table 6.1. Of particular interest is the existence of a clinically non-specific form of mental retardation following a clearly X-linked pattern in families (Renpenning's syndrome), and it is likely that a number of isolated cases of mental retardation in males which cannot clearly be separated from those with polygenic or environmental causes are in fact due to this or other X-linked genes, and may account in part for the well-documented excess of males with mental retardation.

Mapping of autosomal genes is still fragmentary, but is rapidly increasing. The original approach of studying families with the disease in relation to a variety of genetic markers has been extended by the development of cell hybridisation techniques and new methods of chromosome staining, so that many genes can now be accurately localized. In some instances this can be used as a predictive test in genetic counselling and prenatal diagnosis, as is the case for the linkage between myotonic dystrophy and the secretor locus (Harper 1973).

## INBORN ERRORS OF METABOLISM

Although documentation of dominantly inherited abnormalities has in most cases not passed the descriptive stage in terms of clinical recognition and pathology, a wide variety of different types of metabolic defect has now been identified in recessively inherited disorders, allowing a classification within the broad framework of the term 'inborn error of metabolism'. Table 6.2 summarizes the main groups, which are rapidly becoming subdivided as knowledge increases. At present the disorders causing mental retardation fall principally into groups 1 and 2, probably because the normal processes of groups 3 and 4 as occurring in the brain are very little understood.

Although this classification provides a useful framework for the consideration of inborn errors of metabolism, many disorders either overlap or do not accurately fit a specific group. Phenylketonuria, one of the most extensively studied of inborn errors, may be used as an example. The most important clinical finding in untreated phenylketonuria is mental retardation, but pathological studies (Crome 1971) have shown no macroscopic or microscopic features which are diagnostic of phenylketonuria, reduction in brain weight being the most constant finding. A raised blood phenylalanine has itself been shown to have toxic effects in animals, inhibiting a number of key brain enzymes (Weber et al. 1970) and reducing myelin formation (Agrawal et al. 1971). However there is also accumulation of a number of metabolites of phenylalanine and deficiency of other substances normally derived from tyrosine, and it remains possible that the cerebral changes

TABLE 6.2

Inborn errors of metabolism

1. Classical 'Garrodian' inborn error with specific block in a metabolic pathway causing
   a. accumulation of precursors, eg phenylketonuria;
   b. deficiency of products, eg adrenogenital syndrome due to 21-hydroxylase defect, with cortisol deficiency.
2. Storage diseases, due to specific lysosomal enzyme defects, eg mucopolysaccharidoses, Tay–Sachs disease.
3. Defects of membrane transport processes, eg cystinuria, Hartnup disease.
4. Defects of specific non-enzymic proteins, eg haemoglobinopathies.

in phenylketonuria may be related to deficiency of these factors as well as to phenylalanine accumulation.

Phenylketonuria illustrates another cardinal feature of inborn errors of metabolism, that of genetic heterogeneity. Although the great majority of patients have a deficiency of phenylalanine hydroxylase as the brain defect, (Fig. 6.1) cases have been described in which the enzymatic abnormality has been either of phenylalanine transaminase or dihydropteridine reductase. In addition transient and partial deficiencies of phenylalanine hydroxylase itself have been described, producing the various hyperphenylalaninaemic syndromes that require distinction from classical phenylketonuria.

Genetic heterogeneity has proved to be an almost universal feature of those inherited disorders whose metabolic basis is well understood, and is likely to be responsible for much of the clinical variation seen in the many conditions for which we do not yet understand the metabolic basis. There is a fundamental difference between heterogeneity produced by alleles at the same genetic locus, where the biochemical defect is likely to be the same, and heterogeneity due to genes at different loci, which implies that the types are both biochemically and genetically distinct, even though producing a similar clinical picture.

The second group of inborn errors of metabolism which makes a major contribution to the genetic causes of mental retardation is the group of storage diseases. This group is characterized by the defective breakdown of macromolecules such as glycoproteins, mucopolysaccharides and complex lipids, which accumulate within neural and other

marises some of the approaches used, which vary from the well-established to some that are still entirely experimental.

Where a specific product is missing the

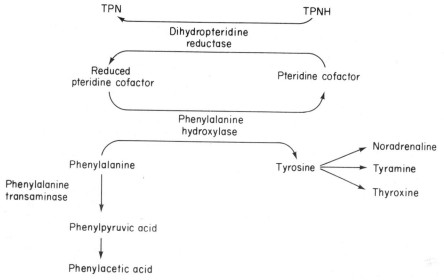

*Fig. 6.1   Metabolic pathways affected in phenylketonuria.*

cells, with slowly progressive deterioration in function as a result. The nature of the stored material can be identified both histochemically and by more specific biochemical studies, and electron microscopy shows the accumulated substances to be located in the lysosomes. Specific deficiencies of a variety of lysosomal enzymes are now recognized as the primary cause, and a major factor in our understanding of this group has been the discovery that the entire group of lysosomal enzymes is expressed in generalized cells such as the cultured skin fibroblast, the white blood cell and the cultured amniotic cell. This has not only made diagnosis feasible without the need for taking samples of cerebral tissue, but has allowed techniques of prenatal diagnosis and carrier detection to be evolved and to play a major role in prevention of these disorders.

THERAPY

Although the possibility for treatment of most genetic forms of mental retardation remains slim, it is becoming feasible in a growing number, providing added importance for their accurate and early diagnosis. Table 6.3 sum-

logical aim is to attempt to replace it, a task which is frequently difficult even when the product is known and available. One of the simplest and most satisfactory examples of this approach is thyroxine therapy for congenital hypothyroidism; here the product is readily available, can be taken orally, and has a therapeutic effect on cerebral development related directly to the age at which treatment is started.

Where the clinical features of the disease are due to accumulation of an intermediate product, dietary treatment may allow this to be avoided. Phenylketonuria again provides an excellent example, with phenylalanine restriction allowing near normal blood phenylalanine levels and brain development. The use of a low protein diet in organic acid disorders such as methylmalonic aciduria is a similar, though less successful example, as is the avoidance of milk products in galactosaemia.

In those disorders with a defined enzymatic basis it may be possible to increase enzyme activity by the use of suitable cofactors. The use of vitamin B6 (pyridoxine) and vitamin B12 in the responsive forms of homocystinuria and methylmalonic aciduria respectively provides examples of this approach. It

TABLE 6.3

Approaches to therapy in genetic causes of mental retardation

| Approach | Example |
| --- | --- |
| 1. Replacement of deficient product | Thyroxine in congenital hypothyroidism |
| 2. Avoidance of harmful or excessive product | Low phenylalanine diet in phenylketonuria |
| 3. Stimulation of enzyme activity by cofactor | Pyridoxine in homocystinuria |
| 4. Direct administration of deficient enzyme | Experimental at present (lysosomal disorders) |
| 5. Replacement of enzyme-producing cells | Marrow or thymic transplant in immune deficiencies (experimental trials of fibroblast implants in mucopolysaccharidoses) |
| 6. Correction or replacement of defective genetic material | Various experimental 'genetic engineering' approaches |

is important to realize in this respect that a small amount of extra enzyme activity may produce a dramatic clinical effect, and that the aim need not be to restore a normal level of enzyme activity. Direct replacement of deficient enzymes has so far been much less satisfactory owing to rapid breakdown and failure to reach the main site of action, even when administered by injection and when encapsulated in various particulate forms. This approach has been used particularly for the lysosomal enzyme deficiencies, particularly the lipidoses and mucopolysaccharidoses, in which it is hoped that the enzyme will reach the appropriate site by direct ingestion by the lysosomes. So far, however, the effects have not proved sufficiently satisfactory for this approach to be used in clinical practice.

A somewhat different approach to enzyme replacement has been the use of living tissue to provide enzymatic activity. Although the use of marrow and thymic transplants in certain immune deficiencies provides a precedent for this, the field of mental retardation is less encouraging. Trials are in progress to evaluate the use of implanted normal fibroblasts in patients with mucopolysaccharidoses, but careful objective and long-term assessment of results will be essential before this can be regarded as therapy rather than experiment.

It is likely that even more fundamental approaches to therapy will be undertaken in the near future, with the possibility of replacement of the actual genetic material itself rather than the enzymic product. New techniques of cell hybridization and gene transfer, along with the identification and isolation of small segments of DNA by use of restriction enzymes, are all making this a practical possibility for the next few years rather than for the distant future. This rapid development gives extra importance for the identification of specific genetic disorders within the residue of non-specific mental retardation.

PREVENTIVE MEASURES

It has been calculated that on average all of us carry one harmful gene and three lethal ones, the latter expressing themselves in spontaneous abortions and miscarriages. The harmful gene is only harmful if the owner mates with a partner possessing the same harmful gene, for if recessive on Mendelian laws one quarter of their offspring will be affected. For a common syndrome such as phenylketonuria where 1 in 50 of the population are carriers, there are still only 1 in 10 000 live births affected, excluding rare new mutations. Abortion or sterilization of homozygotes would therefore make little difference to the gene pool. However genetic counselling can help. Over 50 per cent of referrals to such a clinic are concerned with causes of possible mental retardation.

In those disorders where the harmful effects on brain development are largely postnatal, the role of preventive measures is principally to enhance the effectiveness of treatment. The mass screening of newborns for phenylketonuria is an excellent example of this, ensuring that treatment is applied before significant irreversible brain damage has occurred. Unfortunately we do not know the relevant factors in many disorders, while in others where we do, such as the lipidoses, severe brain damage may have already occurred in prenatal life. In such situations preventive measures

feasible for a number of the lysosomal enzyme deficiencies, and an excellent example of its application is provided by the lipidosis, Tay–Sachs disease, where population screening of

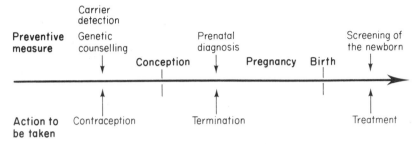

Fig. 6.2 *Preventive measures in inherited disease.*

are aimed principally at preventing the conception of an individual at high risk of being affected, or at terminating a pregnancy which can be shown to be abnormal.

In Figure 6.2 the main available preventive measures are summarized, seen against the time scale of development. It is clear that measures designed to prevent conception of an affected individual such as genetic counselling and tests of carrier detection, will only be effective if undertaken before a pregnancy occurs, and preferably before an affected child has already been born into the family. Genetic counselling is discussed in various chapters; it is essential that other tests are considered in the light of this and of the overall estimate of risk that genetic counselling produces.

Carrier detection is particularly valuable in those disorders showing X-linked recessive inheritance, such as the Hunter syndrome, Duchenne dystrophy and the Lesch–Nyhan syndrome. Unfortunately this is also the group where results are most variable owing to the variability of X chromosome inactivation in the carrier females, and in most X-linked disorders there is a proportion of carriers that are difficult, even impossible to distinguish from normal unless tests can be carried out on cloning (asexual reproduction) from single cells.

Carrier detection in autosomal recessive disorders is of less general importance except for the small number where the gene is at high frequency, for it is only here that the risks of a known carrier marrying another carrier become appreciable, in the absence of consanguinity. Identification of carriers is

Ashkenazi Jewish communities in America has allowed identification of those married couples where both members are carriers and thus at risk of having an affected child. The availability of prenatal diagnosis increases the efficacy of this approach.

Autosomal dominant disorders of late onset or variable severity provide another group in which carrier detection is of considerable importance. Asymptomatic individuals with myotonic dystrophy may require electromyography or slit-lamp examination for lens opacities, while skull X-ray or computerised axial tomography of the parents of a child with tuberous sclerosis may show the case to be a transmitted one rather than a new mutation.

Even when pre-conceptual measures have failed to prevent conception of a high-risk pregnancy, intrauterine diagnosis may make it possible to offer selective termination of an affected pregnancy. The technique of amniocentesis is the principal approach used at present, though the development of ultrasound, and of methods of fetal blood sampling, promise to extend greatly the range of disorders for which prenatal diagnosis is possible. Although some disorders can be diagnosed from study of the amniotic fluid itself (for example, organic acidurias, some mucopolysaccharidoses), most intrauterine diagnoses are dependent on the use of cultured amniotic cells. Table 6.4 lists some of the genetic causes of mental retardation for which prenatal diagnosis is feasible.

The possibility of prenatal diagnosis is not limited to those disorders for which a specific biochemical basis has been found. For

TABLE 6.4

Prenatal diagnosis in metabolic causes of mental retardation

| Lipidoses | Mucopolysaccharidoses and related disorders | Carbohydrate disorders |
|---|---|---|
| Gaucher's disease | | Galactosaemia |
| Generalized (GMI) gangliosidosis | MPSI (Hurler) | Glycogen storage disease type II |
| | MPSII (Hunter) | |
| Tay–Sachs disease | MPSIIIA and B (Sanfilippo) | Amino acid and related disorders |
| Sandhoff's disease* | MPSVI (Maroteaux–Lamy)* | Maple syrup urine disease |
| Metachromatic leukodystrophy | 'I' cell disease | Methylmalonic aciduria* |
| Krabbe's globoid cell leukodystrophy | Fucosidosis* | Propioniaciduria* |
| | Mannosidosis* | Homocystinuria |
| Niemann–Pick disease | | Citrullinaemia* |
| Refsum's disease* | | Argininosuccinic aciduria |

* Not described in this book.

chromosomal defects, discussed fully else-where, the karyotype of cultured amniotic cells allows uterine detection, while structural defects accompanied by open lesions (that is, spina bifida), notably neural tube defects, can now be detected by the elevation of alpha-fetoprotein that occurs in the amniotic fluid as a consequence of leakage from fetal tissues. It is now feasible also to detect directly those disorders showing obvious limb abnormali-ties, such as the acrocephalysyndactyly group, by means of a fine flexible amnioscope, though this procedure still carries a high risk of in-ducing abortion.

Although most of the conditions discussed individually in the latter part of this chapter are Mendelian in inheritance a substantial number are clearly not. However, it is impor-tant to recognize that the fact that most cases of a disorder are sporadic does not disprove Mendelian inheritance. Thus in those dominantly inherited diseases preventing reproduction there will be new mutations and thus sporadic cases will appear. This is so in Apert's syndrome, where dominant inheri-tance was suspected on grounds of increased paternal age and the Mendelian nature of related defects, but where direct transmission of the disease was only shown subsequently. A similar situation may prove to be the case for other disorders, such as the Goldenhaar and Sturge–Weber syndromes, where familial cases are exceptional, but at present it is im-possible to exclude the action of environmen-tal factors in development. Goldenhaar is not, but Sturge–Weber commonly is, associated

with retardation.

In the future it is certain that the list of specific genetic disorders producing mental retardation will increase greatly, partly as a result of the recognition of new disorders within the overall population of the mentally retarded, partly as the result of heterogeneity being discovered within specific disorders now considered as a single entity. Although a proportion of patients will inevitably remain for whom no specific factors can be found, it is probably true to say that the rate of progress in treatment and prevention of men-tal retardation will depend directly on the rate at which specific factors, both genetic and environmental, can be identified.

BIBLIOGRAPHY

Agrawal, H. C., Bone, A. H. & Davison, A. N. (1971) Hyperphenylalaninaemia and the develop-ing brain. In: Bickel, H., Hudson, F. P. & Woolf, L. I. (eds.), Phenylketonuria and Some Other Inborn Errors of Aminoacid Metabolism. Stuttgart: Georg Thieme Verlag.

Crome, L. (1971) The morbid anatomy of phenylke-tonuria. In: Bickel, H., Hudson, F. P. & Woolf, L. I. (eds.), Phenylketonuria and Some Other In-born Errors of Aminoacid Metabolism. Stuttgart: Georg Thieme Verlag.

Harper, P. S. (1973) Pre-symptomatic detection and genetic counselling in myotonic dystrophy. Clin. Genet., 4, 134–40.

Weber, G., Glazer, R. I. & Ross, R. A. (1970) Regulation of human and rat brain metabolism: inhibitory action of phenylalanine and phenylpyr-uvate on glycolysis, protein, lipid, DNA and RNA metabolism. In: Weber, G. (ed.), *Advances in Enzyme Regulation*, vol. 8. Oxford: Pergamon Press.

SOURCES OF INFORMATION ON GENETIC CAUSES OF MENTAL RETARDATION

McKusick, V. A. (1975) *Mendelian Inheritance in Man*, 4th ed. Baltimore: Johns Hopkins University Press. [an accurate, detailed and regularly updated compendium of information on genetic disorders and an invaluable source of references]

Penrose, L. S. (1972) *Biology of Mental Defect*, 4th ed. London: Sidgwick & Jackson. [still the outstanding contribution to the subject written from the viewpoint of the worker in mental handicap]

Pratt, R. T. C. (1968) *The Genetics of Neurological Disorders*. Oxford: Oxford University Press.

Slater, E. & Cowie, V. (1975) *The Genetics of Mental Disorders*. Oxford: Oxford University Press.

Stanbury, J. B., Wyngaarden, J. B. & Fredrickson, D. S. (eds.) (1972) *The Metabolic Basis of Inherited Disease*, 3rd ed. New York: McGraw Hill. [the most comprehensive source of detailed information on inborn errors of metabolism]

## ARGININOSUCCINIC ACIDURIA

Friable hair, hepatomegaly, ataxia, fits, infant death.

*History.* First described by Allan et al. (1958).

*Numbers and frequency.* Some 40 patients described.

*Genetics.* Autosomal recessive, therefore males and females. Heterozygotes also have reduced argininosuccine in red blood cells. Prenatal diagnosis feasible on amniotic fluid cells.

*Clinical features.* Scanty, thin, friable hair in all parts, microscopically showing many transverse fractures, arginine being an essential constituent of hair. Marked enlargement of the liver. There seem to be two types. In the first there is relatively normal development during the first year, with rapid deterioration in the second and third; in the second type there is 'failure to thrive' following birth with poor feeding, hepatomegaly, abdominal distension and CNS deterioration with epilepsy. This milder type may have few hair abnormalities and reach adult life. It may result from usage of alternative metabolic pathways, or less susceptible target organs.

*CNS:* All patients are markedly retarded, many have epilepsy and some have cerebellar ataxia. Most die within a few days of birth, after milk ingestion.

*Treatment and outcome.* The missing enzyme acts in the Krebs-Hemseleit cycle of ammonia detoxication, thus there is a marked rise in blood ammonia level after protein ingestion. On reduced protein intake improvement is reported and life prolonged to adulthood. Adequate arginine is needed to restore the hair to normal (Brenton et al. 1974).

*Morbid anatomy.* Brain shows widespread oedema and spongiform change (Crome & France 1971).

*Diagnosis.* Argininosuccinic acid is raised in the red cells, plasma, CNS and urine.

BIBLIOGRAPHY

Allan, J. D., Cusworth, D. C., Dent, C. E. & Wilson, V. K. (1958) A disease, probably hereditary, characterized by severe mental deficiency and a constant gross abnormality of amino acid metabolism. *Lancet*, 1, 182–7.

Brenton, D. P., Cusworth, D. C., Hartley, S., Lumley, S. & Kuzemko, J. A. (1974) Argininosuccinic aciduria: clinical, metabolic, and dietary study. *J. ment. Defic. Res.*, 18, 1–7.

Crome, L. & France, N. E. (1971) The pathological findings in argininosuccinic aciduria. *J. ment. Defic. Res.*, 15, 266–70.

## ASPARTYLGLUCOSAMINURIA (AGU)

Coarsened face, 'failure to thrive', skeletal change, childhood deterioration.

*History.* Described by Jenner and Pollitt (1967).

*Numbers.* Over 100 now reported.

*Genetics.* Autosomal recessive. Heterozygous carriers can be assayed by using skin fibroblasts (Autio 1974).

*Clinical features.* Believed due to defective production and activity of N aspartyl-6-glucosaminidase (AADGase). Like mannosidosis there is a gargoyle-like face, progressive psychomotor retardation with a 'failure to thrive' and diffuse skeletal changes. There is an excess of glycoprotein residues in the urine, and intracellular storage of the same.

*Further testing.* Urine shows excess glycoprotein.

*Treatment and outcome.* The results of treatment are quite variable (see Autio et al. 1974).

BIBLIOGRAPHY

Autio, S. (1972) Aspartylglycosaminuria: analysis of 34 patients. *J. ment. Defic. Res.*, Monograph No. 1.

Autio, S., Aula, P. & Manto, U. (1974) Cultured skin fibroblasts in disorders of glycoprotein catabolism and cell disease. *Devl Med. Child Neurol.,* *16*, 376–8.

Jenner, F. A. & Pollitt, R. J. (1967) Large quantities of AADG in the urine of mentally retarded siblings. *Biochem. J., 103*, 48.

## CEREBROSIDE LIPIDOSIS
### (Gaucher's disease)

'Failure to thrive', hepatosplenomegaly, spasticity, fair lifespan.

*History.* Described by Gaucher in 1882.

*Morbid anatomy.* Typically the lymph nodes, liver, spleen and bone marrow develop the Gaucher cell, which is large and whose cytoplasm shows a picture like crumpled paper from accumulation of lipid. The CNS shows progressive cellular fall-out.

*Further investigations.* There is a deficiency of the glucocerebroside-cleaving enzyme B glucosidase which can be demonstrated in white blood cells and skin fibroblasts. The serum acid phosphatase is high, and forms a useful preliminary test.

*Treatment.* Severe cases die in infancy, milder types may survive to adult life. Splenectomy has been helpful; replacement of glucocerebrosidase has been

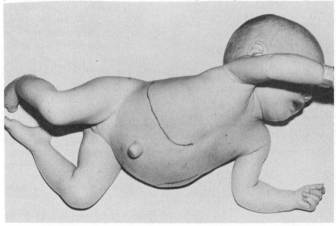

*Fig. 6.3    Cerebroside lipidosis showing hepatosplenomegaly and spasticity (Dr Harper).*

*Numbers and frequency.* Over 1000 patients of all types of Gaucher's disease reported (Fredrickson & Sloan 1972). There are at least three types, the abdominal, the cerebral and infantile forms, whose separation depends on main site of deposition of glucocerebroside in sensitive target-organs; the adult abdominal form commonly shows hypersplenism without neurological features.

*Genetics.* Autosomal recessive, thus male and female, with particularly high incidence in Jewish populations. The different clinical forms all have the same enzymatic defect; since each 'breeds true' within a family there are probably several alleles at the same locus. Prenatal diagnosis is feasible using cultured amniotic fluid cells. There is a deficient action of glucocerebrosidase.

*Clinical features.* A normal infant develops hepatomegaly and splenomegaly in the first few months with deterioration of mental function in the cerebral type. In this type there is hypertonicity, squint and deterioration of the cranial nerves with difficulty in swallowing.

attempted (Brady et al. 1974) with equivocal results.

*Diagnosis.* Niemann-Pick's disease shows CNS deterioration with hepatosplenomegaly but the infant is hypotonic and has a macular cherry-red spot. The mucopolysaccharidoses show characteristic long X-ray changes.

BIBLIOGRAPHY

Brady, R. O., Pentchev, P. G., Gal, A. E., Hibberd, S. R. & Dekeban, A. S. (1974) Replacement therapy with purified glucocerebrosidase in Gaucher's disease. *New Engl. J. Med., 291,* 989–93.

Fredrickson, D. S. & Sloan, H. R. (1972) Glucosyl ceramide lipidoses: Gaucher's disease. In: Stanbury, J. B., Wyngaarden, J. B. & Fredrickson, D. S. (eds.), *The Metabolic Basis of Inherited Disease,* 3rd ed. New York: McGraw-Hill.

Sengers, R. C. A., Lamers, K. J. B., Bakkeren, J. A. J., Schretlen, E. D. & Trijbels, J. M. F. (1975) Infantile Gaucher's disease: glucocerebroside deficiency in peripheral blood leucocytes and cultivated fibroblasts. *Neuropädiatrie, 6,* 377–82.

## CONGENITAL BLINDNESS

A variety of syndromes exist in which congenital blindness may be associated with mental retardation. Some of these are clearly environmental in origin (for example, rubella syndrome), in some the etiology is unknown, while others follow Mendelian inheritance. The usual defect may be the result of numerous ocular abnormalities, and some of the major syndromes considered to be genetic in origin are considered below.

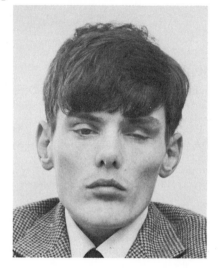

*Fig. 6.4   Congenital blindness with mild retardation.*

### NORRIE'S DISEASE (Pseudoglioma)

Blindness, mild retardation, deafness.

*History.* Described by Norrie in 1927.

*Numbers and frequency.* Between one and two hundred patients reported.

*Clinical features. Eyes:* There is little if any vision from birth. White vascularised masses behind clear lenses appear at birth or shortly afterwards and the globes become shrunken.
   *Other features:* Short fingers have been reported in two families, deafness is fairly common but is mild and responds to appliances.
   *CNS:* In a series of 35, 20 were mentally retarded, 9 severely so (Warburg 1968). Warburg showed that the retinal abnormalities were primary, and other features appeared to be secondary, including possibly environmental retardation, emotional instability, violence, but not the hearing loss said to be due to cochlear degeneration.

*Morbid anatomy.* Absence of rods, cones in the retina.

*Further testing.* No biochemical abnormality yet found.

*Treatment and outcome.* Hearing aids are the most effective help, apart from environmental stimulation.

*Diagnosis.* From retrolental fibroplasia, retinoblastoma and glaucoma (Abbassi 1968).

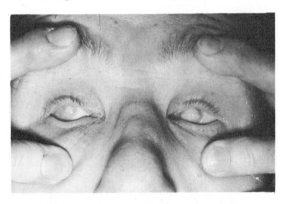

*Fig. 6.5   Congenital blindness in Norrie's disease (Dr Jancar).*

### BIBLIOGRAPHY

Anophthalmos: Joseph, R. (1975) A pedigree of anophthalmos. *Br. J. Ophthal., 41*, 541–3.
Congenital glaucoma: Abbassi, R., Lowe, C. U. & Calcagno, P. L. (1968) Oculo-cerebro-renal syndrome: a review. *Am. J. Dis. Child., 115,* 145–68.
Norrie's disease: Warburg, M. (1968) Norrie's disease. *J. ment. Defic. Res., 12,* 247–51.

### OTHER CONDITIONS

Cyclops (one central forehead eye), ethmocephaly (rudimentary eyes and a central nasal proboscis) and cebocephaly (as before but proboscis is at side) are found with multiple anomalies among stillbirths.

### MICROPHTHALMOS

This heterogeneous condition is commonly associated with mental retardation and the causes are well reviewed by Warburg (1971).

### BIBLIOGRAPHY

Warburg, M. (1971) The heterogeneity of microphthalmia in the mentally retarded. *Birth Defects, Original Articles Series 7,* 3, 136–54.

## CORNELIA DE LANGE SYNDROME
(Amsterdam dwarf)

Microcephaly, abnormal face and limbs.

*History.* Described by Cornelia de Lange as the Amsterdam dwarf in 1933. Now reported from most countries.

*Numbers and frequency.* One to 40 000 (Berg et al. 1970).

*Genetics.* Most cases are sporadic, but affected siblings have been reported. The empiric recurrence rate is not over 5 per cent. Early reports of a chromosomal abnormality have not been confirmed.

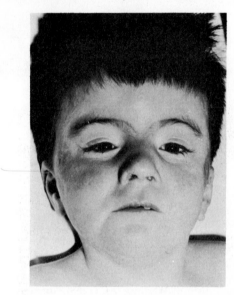

*Fig. 6.6　Cornelia de Lange syndrome showing microcephaly, low set eyes and abnormal face (Dr Barry Richards).*

*Clinical features.* Microcephaly and excess facial hair may be noted at birth with a downward outward slanting of eyes and mouth. There may be eye anomalies such as ptosis, nystagmus and microphthalmia; the ears are often small. The palate is often narrow with irregular teeth. The genitals are underdeveloped both for males and females.

Characteristically the limbs are highly abnormal with small hands and feet, inability to fully extend each limb, and gross anomalies of hands or feet consisting of absent digits or any variety of syndactyly and clinodactyly. Birth weight is usually low and height below the third percentile.

*CNS:* All patients are reported retarded, often severely so. Some have epilepsy, others are spastic. The deep tendon reflexes are usually excessive.

*Morbid anatomy.* Congenital heart defects are common, as are abnormalities of the brain of very varied extent.

*Further investigations.* The limb X-rays may be highly abnormal with various defects of bone.

*Treatment and outcome.* This depends on the degree of abnormality. If there are gross defects of the mouth and palate, aspiration pneumonia is common.

*Diagnosis.* From other causes of microcephaly and dwarfism, and from the Rubinstein–Taybi syndrome (see pp. 108–9).

BIBLIOGRAPHY

Beck, B. (1976) Epidemiology of Cornelia de Lange's syndrome. *Acta paediat., Stockh.*, 65, 631–8.
Berg, J. M., McCreary, B. D., Ridler, M. A. C. & Smith, G. F. (1970) *The de Lange Syndrome*, p. 127. Oxford: Pergamon Press.
McArthur, R. G. & Edwards, J. H. (1967) de Lange syndrome: report of 20 cases. *Can. med. Ass. J.* 96, 1185–98.

## CRANIOSYNOSTOSIS SYNDROMES
(Apert's, Chotzen's, Pfeiffer's and Carpenter's)

Tower skull, fused digits, polydactyly.

*History.* In 1901 Carpenter first reported two sisters with *acrocephaly* (Tower skull) but Apert described the most common variant in 1906. A number of other syndromes with acrocephaly and syndactyly have since been reported by different authors, most of which appear to be constant within families and to represent distinct genetic syndromes. Acrocephaly may occur as an isolated abnormality, or with fusion of digits (acrocephalysyndactyly), or with extra digits in addition to fusion (acrocephaly polysyndactyly).

*Genetics.* Most types of acrocephalysyndactyly are presumed to be autosomal dominant, and being autosomal occur equally among men and women. With 'true' Apert's (type I) there is often severe mental handicap, and therefore lack of reproduction, so it is assumed that many cases are fresh mutants. Increased paternal age in isolated cases has been documented. With the milder types there have been a number of instances of passage from parent to child along classical dominant Mendelian lines. Carpenter's syndrome is likely to be an autosomal recessive as it has been reported in siblings but not transmitted from one generation to the next.

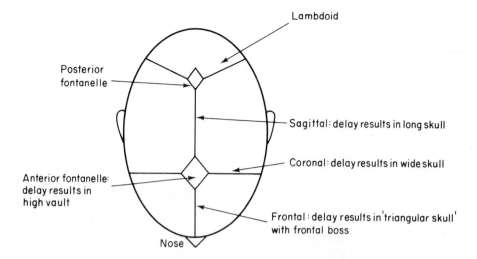

Fig. 6.7    Effects of premature closure of cranial sutures.

*Classification.* For full details of the classification of this group of diseases see the reviews of Temtamy and McKusick (1969) and McKusick (1968). The main forms to be considered are as follows:

Group A. Acrocephalysyndactyly

Apert's syndrome (type I). A milder form (type II) has been distinguished, but may be part of the same disorder.

Chotzen's syndrome (type III). Here both syndactyly and the cranial abnormality are partial.

Pfeiffer's syndrome (type VI). The digital abnormalities, particularly of the thumb, are specific. There are large thumbs and great toes, only two digits may have syndactyly and intellectual ability is average or borderline.

Group B. Acrocephaly with minor syndactyly (Carpenter's syndrome)

Group C. Acrocephaly without limb abnormalities

## GROUP A. ACROCEPHALYSYNDACTYLY

### Types I and II (Apert's syndrome)

*Clinical features.* In 1906 Apert described the high wide forehead and flattened occiput with the apex at the anterior fontanelle which is characteristic of acrocephaly. The mid-face bones are poorly developed causing apparent prominence of nose and chin and eyes which are normal in size. The face is often asymmetrical and the eyes are wide apart, protuberant and have a downward slant. Apert's syndrome of types I and II is the most severe and most common, many hundreds of cases being reported.

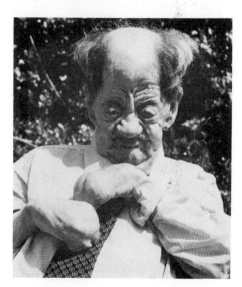

Fig. 6.8    *Craniosynostosis type I (Apert) showing tower skull, poor mid-face bone development, protuberant eyes and syndactyly of fingers.*

The palate is usually high and may be cleft; the teeth are often irregular. In type I all digits in hand and foot are fused by skin, and sometimes the bone, cartilage and nails are also fused. In the milder type II some fingers and toes are separate. There is often limitation of movement of any separate digits and of the elbow and shoulder. The upper arm may be limited in size.

*CNS:* Because of common premature closure of

cranial sutures there is often an increase in intra-cranial pressure with dilated ventricles and atrophy of brain tissue. Craniectomy has been used to relieve pressure, and intelligence is then potentially normal. Older patients in institutions have not had surgery and are moderately or severely retarded. Peripheral CNS signs are usually minimal.

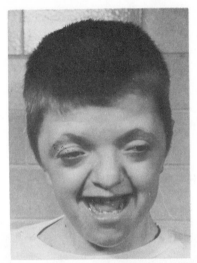

*Fig. 6.9   Craniosynostosis type I (Apert) showing tower skull and wide space between eyes (Dr Kratter).*

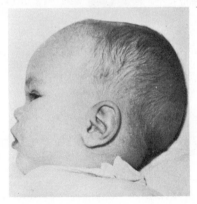

*Fig. 6.10   Early craniostenosis showing bulging of anterior fontanelle (Dr Harper).*

*Morbid anatomy.* Recent series of post-mortems show many congenital cardiac defects. Some brains showed hydrocephalus and atrophy.

*Further investigations.* The variability in premature synostosis may cause a lopsided skull on X-ray, with markings of the convolutions and bossing at the bregma from bulging of the anterior fontanelle. X-rays of hands and feet may show skeletal synostosis of digits, whose terminal members may be spade-shaped.

*Treatment and outcome.* Craniectomy is recommended, together with repair where possible for syndactyly of hands.

### Type III (Chotzen's)

*Clinical features.* This has milder features of acrocephaly and only soft tissue syndactyly. The forehead is wide and flat and the eyes are far apart with pronounced nose and chin as before. Ptosis is common and the teeth are poorly developed.

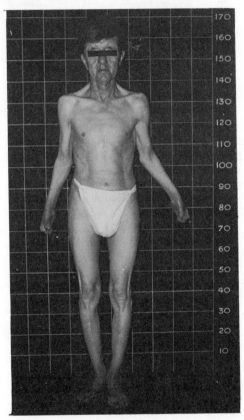

*Fig. 6.11   Craniosynostosis type III (Chotzen) showing milder features; subject was dull normal (Dr Jancar).*

Syndactyly of fingers extends only to the soft tissues and thus might better be called webbing.

*CNS:* Intelligence may be average or borderline. In some families the inheritance from parent to child makes clear the autosomal dominant inheritance.

*Treatment and outcome.* Craniectomy is recommended, but the webbing of hands and feet is rarely severe enough to require surgery.

*Type VI (Pfeiffer's)*

*Clinical features.* Here the high skull of acrocephaly is present, together with wide eyes which protrude and prominent chin as before. As in other examples the teeth are poorly developed with a high palate. The main features are spade-shaped thumb and great toe which have marked deviation medially. Syndactyly is least common, affecting soft tissues only. There is occasionally decreased movement of elbows.

*CNS*: No systemic abnormalities. Intelligence appears to be average or borderline.

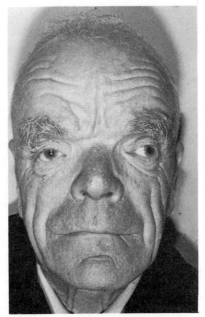

*Fig. 6.12   Craniosynostosis type VI (Pfeiffer);
subject was dull normal (Dr Jancar).*

GROUP B. ACROCEPHALY WITH
MINOR SYNDACTYLY
(Carpenter's)

*Clinical features.* Carpenter's syndrome has a high tall skull with early widespread cranial synostoses causing relative microcephaly and diminution of intelligence. The face is flat but there is underdevelopment of the chin in this variety. There may be epicanthic folds and corneal opacities. All reported examples have hypogenitalism, polydactyly of feet and soft tissue syndactyly, often of third and fourth fingers of the hand.

*CNS*: Mentally handicapped, no systemic signs.

*Further investigations.* Skull X-rays show premature fusion of the sutures. There is polydactyly in the foot.

*Treatment and outcome.* Craniectomy is indicated, also the removal of unnecessary digits.

*Diagnosis*

The features of the various types are distinctive and the prognosis in accordance with degree of intracranial pressure and severity. Skull and limb X-rays aid in differential diagnosis between the subtypes. The Laurence-Moon-Biedl syndrome has polydactyly but also has retinal abnormalities.

Types IV and V of the syndrome are extremely rare and associated with severe internal malformations usually with early death.

BIBLIOGRAPHY

Blank, C. E. (1960) Apert's syndrome (a type of acrocephalosyndactyly): observations on a British series of 39 cases. *Ann. hum. Genet.*, *24*, 151–64.
McKusick, V. A. (1968) *Mendelian Inheritance in Man*, 2nd ed. Baltimore: Johns Hopkins University Press.
Temtamy, S. & McKusick, V. A. (1969) Synopsis of hand malformations with particular emphasis on genetic factors. In: Berzoma, D. (ed.), *Clinical Delineation of Birth Defects*, vol. 3. New York: National Foundation.

GROUP C. ACROCEPHALY, OR SYNOSTOSES
WITHOUT POLYDACTYLY OR SYNDACTYLY
(Familial craniosynostosis, Crouzon's disease)

*History.* Described by Crouzon in 1912.

*Numbers and frequency.* Between one and two hundred patients reported.

*Genetics.* Autosomal dominant.

*Clinical features.* This is a reproducible set of synostoses of face and head, and is variable in severity and site, as might be expected from an autosomal dominant which has to be passed from parent to child. Where many sutures close early, the result may be one variety of microcephaly with a pointed anterior fontanelle, but others have a wide flattened forehead, are broad from ear to ear, with resulting low set ears, and widely spaced protruding eyes with a downward and outward slant. Alternatively, the facial bones may be undeveloped, the nose bridge flat, and underdevelopment of the mid-part of the face may give a flat face, with close-set eyes and a protruding chin. If the eyes are markedly protruding, or as is common there is a squint, convergence or fixation is difficult. There may be hearing loss due to malformation of the external auditory canal. The palate is usually high with irregular teeth.

*CNS*: Normal intelligence for most, about a third are moderately retarded.

*Further investigations.* Marked convolutional markings on skull X-ray with small orbital fossa and poorly developed facial bones.

*Fig. 6.13  Craniosynostosis (familial or Crouzon):
mild acrocephaly without limb abnormalities.*

*Treatment and outcome.* Craniectomy has been used with success, but many patients have developed with normal intelligence without such treatment.

*Diagnosis.* The varieties of acrocephaly, hypertelorism and microcephaly need to be distinguished. Chotzen's (type III) is similarly dominant as is Crouzon's; it is the type of facial structure which is different, and inherited from parent to child.

BIBLIOGRAPHY

Neuhauser, G., Kaveggio, E. G. & Opitz, J. M. (1976) Studies of malformation syndromes of man. *Eur. J. Paediat.*, *123*, 15–28.

## DWARFISM

Three major classes can be recognized among the numerous causes of dwarfism.

1. Primary dysplasias of bone, generally associated with disproportionate dwarfism. In most such dysplasias intelligence is normal.
2. Endocrine disorders, in particular deficiency of growth hormone and in hypothyroidism.
3. Low birth weight dwarfism, in which a primary failure of somatic growth is part of a variety of syndromes, some chromosomal, some genetic (such as Cornelia de Lange syndrome), others environmental or nutritional and poorly understood. Mental retardation is a frequent accompaniment of many of these conditions.

Table 4.2 (see pp. 44–47) summarizes some of the conditions (excluding chromosomal disorders) in which dwarfism, microcephaly and mental retardation are frequently associated.

### RUSSELL'S DWARF (Silver's syndrome)
Small size.

*History.* Silver and his associates (1953) and Russell (1954) described children with particular features of dwarfism.

*Numbers and frequency.* Almost a hundred cases reported, although the genetics are unclear.

*Genetics.* Siblings have been reported as affected, but most cases appear sporadic, and thus not hereditary.

*Clinical features.* Even *in utero*, dwarfism has been demonstrated, and the infant at birth is underweight with a peculiar triangular face. The mouth is small, the lips are thin and point downwards and outwards. Some have scoliosis, and males usually have cryptorchidism. The fifth fingers are often small and point medially (clinodactyly). There may be syndactyly between the second and third toes, some have café-au-lait spots. In one series one third were sexually precocious in development. Development of limbs is often asymmetrical.
*CNS*: It has been suggested that one third are retarded.

*Further investigation.* One third have raised urinary gonadotropins, not always associated with sexual precocity.

*Diagnosis.* From hypervitaminosis D and other causes of dwarfism.

BIBLIOGRAPHY

Russell, A. (1954) A syndrome of 'intra uterine' dwarfism recognizable at birth with cranio-facial dysostosis, disproportionately short arms and other anomalies (5 examples). *Proc. R. Soc. Med.*, *47*, 1040–44.
Silver, H. K. (1964) Asymmetry, short stature and variations in sexual development. *Am. J. Dis. Child.*, *107*, 494–515.

Silver, H. K., Kiyasu, W., George, J. & Deamer, W. C. (1953) Syndrome of congenital hemihypertrophy, shortness of stature and elevated urinary gonadotropins. *Pediatrics*, *12*, 368–76.

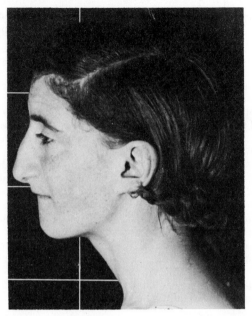

*Fig. 6.14   Dwarfism (Seckel's syndrome) : mild subnormality (Dr Jancar).*

## BIRD-HEADED DWARFISM (Seckel's syndrome)

Small size, normal lifespan.

*History.* By Seckel (1960).

*Numbers and frequency.* Uncertain, a number of reports quote different groupings of signs so that it is uncertain whether different syndromes are involved.

*Genetics.* Probably autosomal recessive (see Frijns and van den Berg 1976).

*Clinical features.* Microcephaly is the main feature with a pronounced nose but small chin and forehead. The palate is narrow and high with hypoplastic molar area and absent teeth. The ears are small and simple. Numerous skeletal anomalies affecting curvature of the fingers, syndactyly of the toes, and dislocations of various joints have been reported.

Hypogonadism is common with cryptorchidism.

Height and weight at birth are low and remain so.

*CNS*: Most were retarded with intelligence up to IQ 80.

*Morbid anatomy.* The brain is underdeveloped.

*Further investigation.* The bones are immature in chronological age, no specific abnormalities have been identified.

*Treatment and outcome.* Compatible with normal expectation.

*Diagnosis.* From other types of dwarfism and microcephaly.

### BIBLIOGRAPHY

Frijns, J. P. & van den Berg, H. E. H. (1976) Bird-headed dwarfism. *Acta paediat. belg.*, *29*, 121–22.

Lambotte, C., Dony, G. & Bonnet, F. (1976) Seckel syndrome: bird-headed dwarfism. *Acta paediat. belg.*, *29*, 79–82.

Seckel, H. P. G. (1960) *Bird-headed Dwarfs*. Basel: S. Karger; Springfield, Ill.: Charles Thomas.

## GALACTOSAEMIA

'Failure to thrive', hepatosplenomegaly, rapid deterioration in infancy.

*History.* Described by von Reuss in 1908.

*Numbers and frequency.* Estimated one in 70 000 live births (Schwartz et al. 1961). One in 30 000 live births in the United Kingdom (Lee 1972).

*Genetics.* Autosomal recessive, two related variants (see diagnosis). It is one of the more important and preventable inborn errors. The classical form is due to lack of galactose-1-phosphate uridyl transferase with inability to break down galactose-1-phosphate. Prenatal diagnosis using amniotic fluid cells is feasible but of questionable value.

*Clinical features. Head and face*: There is a 'failure to thrive' during the first few weeks of life, with the development of cataracts. Fatal overwhelming septicaemia is frequent in the neonatal period.

*Abdomen*: All develop enlargement of the liver, and about one third ascites and splenomegaly. There is jaundice in about half during the first few weeks of life, anaemia, and occasional thrombosis from sepsis of the feet.

*CNS*: Lethargy and hypotonia common. Epilepsy rare, progressive mental retardation.

*Morbid anatomy.* In affected infants the liver cells show damage repair, which in older patients develops into a picture like cirrhosis.

*Further investigations.* There is increased serum and urine galactose with the red blood cells showing increased galactose-1-phosphate, but specific assay for transferase activity should be done on all suspected cases. The serum glucose level may later drop with signs of hypoglycaemia. As a result of later kidney damage, there may be proteinuria.

*Treatment.* This consists of removal of dietary galactose as a result of which there should be improvement and recovery although the cataracts may not totally regress and may need needling. If diagnosis is late there is a high death rate, and some continue with mental retardation. In a follow-up of 60 affected children Lee (1972) found 16 per cent with residual visual difficulty, mainly cataracts, a marked shift towards dullness, 25 per cent had speech impairment. In some areas screening of all infants is performed using testing of urine for galactose, or enzyme assay on cord blast.

*Diagnosis.* Rubella shows cataracts and enlargement of the spleen and liver, but the urine is clear and serum galactose normal. In galactokinase deficiency galactose also accumulates but cataract is the only abnormality and mental retardation does not occur. Of the other related genetic abnormalities the Duarte variety appears to be without symptoms or signs of illness although the homozygotes have a moderate reduction in levels of transferase activity and red blood cell galactose-1-phosphate is increased as in classical galactosaemia. The heterozygotes also show no clinical features of the illness. A Negro homozygous variant has also been described with ability to metabolize galactose via an alternative metabolic pathway (Segal et al. 1965).

BIBLIOGRAPHY

Donnell, G. N., Bergren, W. R. & Cleland, R. S. (1960) Galactosemia. *Pediat. Clins N. Am.*, 7, 315–32.
Lee, D. H. (1972) Psychological aspects of galactosemia. *J. ment. Defic. Res.*, 16, 173–91.
Schwartz, V., Wells, A. R., Holzel, A. & Komrower, G. M. (1961) A study of the genetics of galactosemia. *Ann. hum. Genet.*, 25, 179–88.
Segal, S., Blair, A. & Roth, H. (1965) The metabolism of galactose by patients with congenital galactosemia. *Am. J. Med.*, 38, 62–70.

## GM1 GANGLIOSIDOSIS
### (Late infantile systemic lipidosis, familial lipidosis)

Hepatosplenomegaly, hirsutism, spasticity.

*History.* Described by Norman and his associates (1959) as a variant of Tay–Sachs disease with lipid-laden histiocytes in the liver and spleen.

*Numbers and frequency.* Nearly 50 cases reported.

*Genetics.* Autosomal recessive, apparently deficient activity of beta-galactosidase demonstrable in white blood cells, and fibroblasts. This can be detected antenatally (Kleijer et al. 1976) and in heterozygotes.

*Clinical features. Head and face*: There are coarse features similar to mucopolysaccharidosis with prominent brow and excess hair on the forehead. The tongue is enlarged and gums hypertrophied.
    *Eyes*: Cherry-red macular spots have been noted in half the patients reported.
    *Chest and abdomen*: There is hepatosplenomegaly.
    *Limbs*: Broad hands with deflexion deformities of the fingers.
    *CNS*: There is 'failure to thrive' with hyperactive deep reflexes, and more rapid deterioration and retardation in the second and subsequent years. Convulsions occur, and blindness, deafness and rigidity advance.

*Morbid anatomy.* Lipid-laden histiocytes in the spleen, liver and kidney.

*Further investigation.* The brain has about ten times average GM1 ganglioside. The enzyme defect, deficient beta-galactosidase can be demonstrated in the internal organs, white blood cells and fibroblasts. Urine level of mucopolysaccharide is often raised.

*Treatment.* Death in the early years of childhood. No successful treatment reported.

*Diagnosis.* Mucopolysaccharidosis I (Hurler's) has corneal opacities and increased urinary polysaccharides. Tay–Sachs disease has a cherry-red spot in the macula but not such coarse features.

BIBLIOGRAPHY

Kleijer, W. J., Veer, E. V. & Niermeiji, M. F. (1976) Rapid prenatal diagnosis of GM1 gangliosidosis using microchemical methods. *Hum. Genet.*, 33, 299–305.
Norman, R. M., Urich, H., Tingey, A. H. & Goodbody, R. A. (1959) Tay–Sachs disease with visceral involvement and its relationship to Niemann–Pick's disease. *J. Path. Bact.*, 78, 409–21.

## GM2 GANGLIOSIDOSIS
### (Tay–Sachs disease)

'Failure to thrive', enlarging head, CNS deterioration.

*History.* Described by Tay in 1881 and Sachs in 1887.

*Numbers and frequency.* Among North American Jews 1 in 6000 (Myrianthopoulos and Aronson 1966). There are three GM2 disorders; Tay–Sachs, Sandhoff and Bernheimer–Sentelberger; and two GM1 disorders, the Norman–Landing and Derry, each having distinctive enzyme specific defects, type of ganglioside and laboratory tests. GM2 disorders most severely affect the brain (reviewed by Volk and Schneck 1975).

*Genetics.* Autosomal recessive, about 1 in 30 Ashkenazi Jews of Eastern Europe are heterozygous. Heterozygote and prenatal diagnosis is possible (Schneck et al. 1970, and Lane et al. 1976), and screening for heterozygotes in high risk populations has been undertaken. The disorder is now known to be due to deficient activity of the lysosomal enzyme hexosaminidase A which results in an excess up to tenfold of ganglioside deposition in all tissues.

*Clinical features. Head and face*: Initially normal, the head enlarges in children over two years of age due to the depositions. A cherry-red macular spot develops from three months of age onwards because of retinal degeneration. It is fully developed by one year, and thereafter vision fades and optic atrophy develops.
   *CNS*: There is 'failure to thrive' after six months of age with a loss of previous skills, overactivity to sound with excessive auditory reflex, excessive drooling and convulsions. The muscles are hypotonic, but after two years spasticity and rigidity supervene with hyperactive reflexes.

*Morbid anatomy.* The enlarged brain is due to oedema, white matter gliosis and distortion of nerve cell cytoplasm, due to lipid accumulation.

*Further investigation.* The nerve cells show GM2 ganglioside deposition. There are no special findings other than gliosis in the white matter.

*Treatment.* Gradually progressive with death usually at four years of age due to pneumonia. No successful treatments yet reported.

*Diagnosis.* The cherry-red macular spot may also be present in GM1 gangliosidosis and Niemann–Pick disease which has a similar mode of development.

BIBLIOGRAPHY

Lane, A. B., Skikne, M. I. & Jenkins, T. (1976) Prenatal diagnosis of Tay–Sachs disease. *S. Afr. med. J.*, *50*, 1553–5.

Myrianthopoulos, N. C. & Aronson, S. M. (1966) Population dynamics of Tay–Sachs disease. I. Reproductive fitness and selection. *Am. J. hum. Genet.*, *18*, 313–27.

Pampiglione, G., Privett, G. & Harden, A. (1974) Tay–Sachs disease. Neurophysiological studies in 20 children. *Devl Med. Child Neurol.*, *16*, 201–8.

Schneck, L., Friedland, J., Valenti, C., Adachi, M., Amsterdam, D. & Volk, B. W. (1970) Prenatal diagnosis of Tay–Sachs disease. *Lancet*, *1*, 582–4.

Volk, B. W. & Schneck, L. (eds.) (1975) *The Gangliosidoses*, pp. 1–277. London: Plenum Press.

### GLOBOID CELL LEUKODYSTROPHY
### (Krabbe's disease)

'Failure to thrive', fits, CNS deterioration.

*History.* Described by Krabbe in 1916.

*Numbers and frequency.* Estimated as 2 per 100 000 births in Sweden (Hagberg et al. 1969). Over 100 cases reported.

*Genetics.* Autosomal recessive. Prenatal diagnosis possible (Harzer et al. 1976).

*Clinical features.* The characteristic feature is the abnormal extensor posture. There is a 'failure to thrive' after the first few weeks of life. From four to six months the child becomes irritable and develops tonic spasms with periods of fever, after six months developing rapid motor deterioration with marked extensor (opisthotonic) spasm, head back, flexed arms and extended legs. There is epilepsy, excessive salivation, with probable pneumonia, and in the second year of life patients become unresponsive and decerebrate.

*Morbid anatomy.* Atrophy of the brain due to disappearance of the white matter. The visible cells show galactocerebroside.

*Further investigation.* The enzyme galactocerebroside beta-galactosidase is absent in the brain, liver, spleen and white blood cells. The CSF protein is over 100 mg per cent.

*Treatment.* Rapid progression to death within an average of 1.2 years in a series of 32 (Hagberg et al. 1969). Treatment results are as yet inconclusive. Synthetic stimulants are not yet successful.

*Diagnosis.* From other causes of 'failure to thrive' such as spongy degeneration of the CNS (Alexander's disease) and Tay–Sachs disease. The latter has the macular cherry-red spot, and diminished hexosaminidase A in the serum.

BIBLIOGRAPHY

Besley, G. T. N. & Bain, A. D. (1976) Krabbe's globoid cell leucodystrophy. *J. med. Genet.*, *13*, 195–9.

Dunn, H. G., Dolman, C. C., Farrell, D. F., Tischler, B., Hasinoff, C. & Woolf, L. I. (1976) Krabbe's leukodystrophy without globoid cells. *Neurology*, *26*, 1035–41.

Hagberg, B., Kollberg, H., Sourander, P. & Akesson, H. O. (1969) Infantile globoid cell leucodystrophy (Krabbe's disease). A clinical and genetic study of 32 Swedish cases, 1953–1967. *Neuropädiatrie*, *1*, 74–88.

Harzer, K., Benz, H. U., Knorr-Gartner, H., Jonatha, W. D. & Knorr, K. (1976) Prenatale Diagnose der Globoidzell Leukodystrophie. *Dt. med. Wschr.*, *101*, 821–4.

## GLYCOGENOSIS, TYPES I–VI

The essential building block of normal muscle and tissue glycogen is glucose. There are a number of enzymes necessary to build up glucose derived from the gut into bodily depots of glycogen, and other enzymes for deconversion at times such as exercise when the body needs more glucose. The various types of glycogenosis represent specific enzymic deficits, all resulting in deficiencies of glucose (and thus hypoglycaemia) and excess storage of glycogen in the tissues (and thus visceral enlargement). Only type II produces significant mental retardation.

### GLYCOGENOSIS, TYPE II (Pompe's disease)

'Failure to thrive', muscle hypotonia.

*History.* Described by Pompe in 1932.

*Numbers and frequency.* Between one and two hundred patients now described.

*Genetics.* Autosomal recessive (Sidbury 1967). Prenatal diagnosis achieved. Heterozygous state also assayed by acid maltase in lymphocytes (Hirschhorn et al. 1969).

*Clinical features. Face and mouth*: the tongue protrudes markedly.
   *Chest and abdomen*: Enlarged heart and liver.
   *CNS*: Muscles are markedly hypotonic with progressive weakness and later atrophy. There is a 'failure to thrive' with mental deterioration, loss of reflexes and finally paralysis of musculature.

*Morbid anatomy.* The muscle fibres are replaced by glycogen deposits and the heart is enormously

### TABLE 6.5

Glycogenosis, types I–VI

| Type | Enzyme lack | Symptoms | Mental retardation |
|---|---|---|---|
| I | Glucose 6 phosphatase (von Gierke) | Hypoglycaemia, even to hemiplegia; fits, FT* | Rare |
| II | Acid maltase (Pompe) | FT, hepatosplenomegaly | Common and progressive |
| III | Amylo 1–6 glucosidase (Forbes) | FT, hepatosplenomegaly | Rare |
| IV | Amylo 1–4 1–6 transglucosidase | FT, hypotonia | No |
| V | Myophosphorylase | FT, muscle atrophy | No |
| VI | Hepatophosphorylase | FT, hepatosplenomegaly | No |

* FT: failure to thrive as infant.

enlarged with the muscle fibres also thickened by glycogen deposits.

*Further investigation.* All organs show increased glycogen deposition due to deficient activity of the enzyme acid maltase. The EMG is abnormal as is the ECG whilst the chest X-ray shows a large globular heart.

*Treatment.* Epinephrine has been effective (Swaiman & Wright 1975, but see their discussion concerning difficulties pp. 444–6). Most deaths are between one and four years with pneumonia and heart failure. There is a late onset variant of acid maltase deficiency occurring at two years of age or even later with clinical features suggestive of a limb-girdle muscular dystrophy; this may be misdiagnosed unless muscle biopsy is done.

*Diagnosis.* The hypotonia, protruding tongue and drooling also occur in hypothyroidism and Down's syndrome. If muscular features are pronounced muscular dystrophy may be suspected.

BIBLIOGRAPHY

Hirschhorn, K., Nadler, H. L., Waithe, W. I.,

Brown, B. I. & Hirschhorn, R. (1969) Pompe's disease: detection of heterozygotes by lymphocyte stimulation. *Science*, *166*, 1632–3.

Sidbury, J. B. (1967) The genetics of glycogen storage diseases. *Prog. med. Genet.*, *5*, 32–58.

Swaiman, K. F. & Wright, F. S. (eds.) (1975) *The Practice of Pediatric Neurology*. St. Louis: Mosby.

## HALLERVORDEN-SPATZ SYNDROME

Parkinsonian features.

*History.* First described in 1922.

*Numbers and frequency.* A rare but familial syndrome.

*Genetics.* Autosomal recessive.

*Clinical picture.* There is an accumulation of pigmented material containing iron in the basal ganglia of the brain resulting in brownish discolouration. The result is an abnormality in muscle tone and movement with choreoathetosis in late childhood or adolescence with finally cerebellar ataxia, myoclonus and an adult picture similar to Parkinsonism with slurred speech and retardation.

*Further investigation.* Serum iron and transferrin are normal. Hepatolenticular degeneration has no Kayser–Fleischer corneal rings and deficient serum ceruloplasmin. There are no specific laboratory tests.

*Treatment and outcome.* Death is usually ten years after onset. Chelating agents have been ineffective. L-dopa is effective symptomatically (Richardson and Adams 1974).

### BIBLIOGRAPHY

Richardson, E. P. and Adams, R. D. (1974) Degenerative diseases of the nervous system. In: Wintrobe, M. W., Thorn, G. W., Adams, R. D., Braunwald, E., Isselbacher, K. J. & Petersdorf, R. G. (eds.), *Harrison's Principles of Internal Medicine*, 7th ed. New York: McGraw Hill.

## HARTNUP DISEASE

Pellagra rash, ataxic episodes, instability of emotion.

*History.* Described by Baron et al. (1956).

*Numbers and frequency.* 1 in 20 000 (Massachusetts survey, Levy et al. 1972), over 50 patients reported.

*Genetics.* Autosomal recessive. Heterozygous state not yet detectable. The enzyme defect results in the inability to prevent loss of monoamino monocarboxylic acids across the renal tubules, and intestinal mucosa. The result is a massive loss of all amino acids resulting in pellagra.

*Clinical features.* There is a pellagra type rash after exposure to sunlight, coincident attacks of cerebellar ataxia, and mental changes with variable retardation, and emotional instability, depending on degree of protein intake, with dementia in later life. Some 20 per cent of children are said to show steady retardation.

*Further investigation.* The diagnosis is established by the pattern of urine amino acids, measured by paper or iron exchange chromatography.

*Treatment.* Oral nicotinamide (50 to 200 mg per day) is effective together with a high protein diet (Jepson 1972).

### BIBLIOGRAPHY

Baron, D. N., Dent, C. E., Harris, H., Hart, E. W. & Jepson, J. B. (1956) Hereditary pellagra-like skin rash with temporary cerebellar ataxia, constant renal amino aciduria, and other bizarre biochemical features. *Lancet*, *2*, 421.

Jepson, J. B. (1972) Hartnup disease. In: Stanbury, J. B., Wyngaarden, J. B. & Fredrickson, D. S. (eds.), *The Metabolic Basis of Inherited Disease*, 3rd ed. New York: McGraw Hill.

Levy, H. L., Madigan, P. M. & Shih, V. E. (1972) Massachusetts Metabolic Disorders Screening Program. 1. Technics and results of urine screening. *Pediatrics*, *49*, 6, 825–36.

## HEPATOLENTICULAR DEGENERATION
(Wilson's disease)

Liver, basal ganglia or kidney failure

*History.* Described by Kinnier Wilson in 1912 in a classic monograph, 'Progressive lenticular degeneration'.

*Numbers and frequency.* One in 200 of the population are heterozygous, one in 200 000 homozygous (Cartwright 1974).

*Genetics.* Autosomal recessive trait, for deficiency of serum ceruloplasmin. The precise enzymatic defect remains unknown.

*Clinical features.* The disease is due to a copper accumulation mainly in the liver. When the liver reaches values of 500–2000 mg/g dry weight, after several years, the liver cells die and copper is released to the serum and deposited elsewhere, in particular in the basal ganglia and cornea where the rusty brown ring is called the Kayser-Fleischer ring. The accumulation in the kidneys damages the proximal renal tubules.

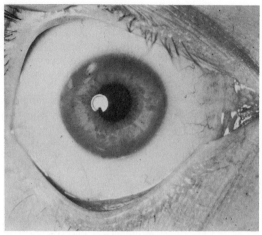

*Fig. 6.15   Hepatolenticular degeneration (Wilson's disease) showing Kayser–Fleischer ring (Mr Desmond Greaves).*

The serum protein ceruloplasmin is deficient. It is normally responsible for binding about 95 per cent of the copper in the serum. Five per cent is carried by albumin, and this fraction is increased in Wilson's disease. It is easily dissociated by the kidneys and therefore causes damage here. The total result is an overall decrease in serum copper.

The disease is manifest between the ages of 6 and 20, occasionally as late as over 40 years of age. The presentation is very variable, depending on the organ most damaged at first. Thus mental retardation, kidney, anaemic or liver failure are possible presentations. Usually the liver first gives rise to symptoms, with a clinical picture resembling chronic active hepatitis.

*Treatment.* Two types are effective. Potassium sulphate 20 mg three times daily prevents the absorption of copper by rendering it insoluble in the diet. The treatment is usually given for up to 12 months and no side effects have been observed.

The copper-chelating agent D-penicillamine causes mobilization of copper from the tissues and therefore its excretion. 500 mg is given orally three times daily for the subject's lifetime. Sensitivity does occur. Treatment can be very effective and compatible with normal life (Cartwright 1974).

*Diagnosis.* Kayser-Fleischer rings, cirrhosis of the liver, basal ganglia disease are a distinctive triad. For diagnosis the serum copper should be less than 80 mg per 100 ml, the serum ceruloplasmin less than 20 mg per 100 ml, and a urinary excretion of over 100 mg of copper in 24 hours is expected.

## BIBLIOGRAPHY

Bearn, A. G. (1972) Wilson's disease. In: Stanbury, J. B., Wyngaarden, J. B. & Fredrickson, D. S. (eds.), *The Metabolic Basis of Inherited Disease*, 3rd ed. New York: McGraw Hill.

Cartwright, G. (1974) Hepatolenticular degeneration (Wilson's disease). In: Wintrobe, M. W., Thorn, G. W., Adams, R. D., Braunwald, E., Isselbacher, K. J. & Petersdorf, R. G. (eds.), *Harrison's Principles of Internal Medicine*, 7th ed. New York: McGraw Hill.

## HEREDITARY ATAXIAS

The hereditary ataxias are a heterogeneous and poorly delineated group of genetic disorders generally associated with normal intelligence. Apart from Friedreich's ataxia there are other rare recessively inherited ataxias in which mental retardation may occur, including ataxia telangiectasia (Boder and Sedgewick 1958), Refsum syndrome (Steinberg et al. 1967), and Hallervorden-Spatz syndrome (see Table 4.2).

### FRIEDREICH'S ATAXIA

*History.* Described by Friedreich in 1863.

*Numbers and frequency.* Many hundreds.

*Genetics.* Both autosomal dominant and autosomal recessive have been described, the recessive being the more common. Thus there are probably a number of syndromes with different genetic origin. A metabolic defect involving pyruvate oxidation has been reported.

*Clinical features.* Classically a posterior column degeneration of the spinal cord with absent tendon reflexes in the legs, resulting foot deformity (pes cavus) and later nystagmus, kyphoscoliosis and cerebellar ataxia.

*Thorax and abdomen*: Up to 90 per cent of patients develop scoliosis and kyphosis with consequent displacement of the internal organs.

*CNS*: Some analyses suggest that mental retardation is no more common than in the general population. Others find an increased incidence of mental retardation, particularly among those who develop CNS signs when young, even as young as 7 years of age. The ataxia first affects legs and then arms, with muscles becoming soft and then atrophic. Leg tendon reflexes become absent and the plantars extensor. Posterior column sensory loss develops early, then nystagmus and gross ataxia.

*Morbid anatomy.* Gross deterioration of the posterior columns, cerebellar spinal tracts and posterior and anterior spinocerebellar tracts.

*Treatment and outcome.* Those affected in early childhood become severely retarded and bedridden in their early teens, but most persons with this common disease are not affected until their thirties (Greenfield 1954) with death ten years later. The variable duration, which may last up to 24 years, has been suggested as due to the different genetic inheritance. 75 per cent die from cardiac dysfunction and heart failure. The recent research on pyruvate retarded metabolism offers only hope, not treatment (Kark et al. 1974).

*Diagnosis.* X-linked and autosomal recessive disorders are also associated with ataxia (see later); each differs in the severity of the component of the CNS most affected. Friedreich's has mainly posterior column loss, the X-linked recessive disorders have predominantly cerebellar ataxia, the inborn errors of metabolism described above have distinctive biochemical findings.

BIBLIOGRAPHY

Boder, E. & Sedgewick, R. P. (1958) A familial syndrome of progressive cerebellar ataxia, oculocutaneous telangectasia and frequent pulmonary infection. *Pediatrics, 21*, 526–54.
Greenfield, J. G. (1954) *The Spinocerebellar Degenerations.* Springfield, Illinois: Charles Thomas.
Kark, R. A. P., Blass, J. P. & Engel, W. K. (1974) Pyruvate oxidation in neuromuscular diseases. *Neurology, Minneap., 24*, 964–71.
Steinberg, O., Mire, C. E., Avigon, J., Fules, H. M., Eldjarn, L., Try, K., Stokke, O. & Refsum, S. (1967) Studies on the metabolic error in Refsum's disease. *J. clin. Invest., 46*, 313–22.

OTHER PROGRESSIVE HEREDITARY ATAXIAS

There are several syndromes in this group which appear in particular families and have not yet been fully evaluated.

*Type 1 (Pelizaeus–Merzbacher)*

*History.* Described by Pelizaeus (1885), and later Merzbacher.

*Numbers.* Over 100.

*Genetics.* Autosomal recessive and X-linked recessive inheritance have been cited, but there is probably more than one interrelated syndrome.

*Clinical features.* Normal at birth, thereafter nystagmus, ataxia and spasticity. Extensor plantars, increased deep reflexes, intention tremors and hearing loss develop over the infant months with severe spasticity in legs and arms causing immobility by three to six years of age. Dementias, seizures and final swallowing difficulty precede death. There are gross deformities.

*Morbid anatomy.* Widespread loss of myelin.

*Treatment and outcome.* Most die by the age of six.

*Type 2 (Marinesco–Sjögren)*

*History.* Marinesco et al. (1931), and later Sjögren (1950) described a new syndrome.

*Numbers.* Some 50 reported.

*Genetics.* Autosomal recessive.

*Clinical features.* Slow development during infancy of microcephaly, bilateral cataracts, dwarfism, mental retardation and cerebellar ataxia which are fully developed by the age of five. Most learn to walk and may be able to speak and feed themselves, but some develop considerable spinal deformities needing surgery (Hensinger and McEwan 1976). The tendon reflexes are variable and muscle weakness may be a feature. Sensation is normal.

*Morbid anatomy.* Cerebellar atrophy is the main feature on post-mortem.

*Treatment and outcome.* Symptomatic removal of cataracts is effective, otherwise symptomatic drug treatment.

BIBLIOGRAPHY

*Type 1*
Pelizaeus, F. (1885) Über eine eigenthümliche Form spastischer Lähmung mit Cerebralerscheinungen auf hereditärer Grundlage (multiple Sklerose). *Arch. Psychiat. Nervenkrankh., 16*, 698–710.
*Type 2*
Hensinger, R. N. & McEwan, D. (1976) Spinal deformity associated with hereditable neurological conditions. *J. Bone Jt Surg., 58A*, 13–24.
Marinesco, G., Dragonesco, St. & Vasiliu, D. (1931) Nouvelle maladie familiale caractérisée par une cataracte congénitale et un arrêt du développement somato-neuro-psychique. *Encéphale, 26*, 97–109.

Neuhauser, G., Wiffler, C. & Opitz, J. M. (1976) Familial spastic paraplegia with distal muscle wasting in the old order Amish. *Clin. Genet.*, 9, 315–23.

Sjögren, T. (1950) Hereditary congenital spinocerebellar ataxia accompanied by congenital cataract and oligophrenia. *Confinia neurol.*, 10, 293–308.

Whyte, M. P. & Dekaban, A. S. (1976) Familial cerebellar degeneration. *Devl Med. Child Neurol.*, 18, 373–80.

Zee, D. S., Cogan, D. G., Robinson, D. A. & Engel, W. K. (1976) Ocular motor abnormalities in hereditary cerebellar ataxia. *Brain*, 99, 207–34.

## HISTIDINAEMIA

'Failure to thrive' but little else.

*History*. Reported from surveys in mental handicap hospitals as an enzyme defect associated with retardation and speech defect.

*Numbers and frequency*. One in 14 190 of live births (Massachusetts survey, Levy et al. 1972).

*Genetics*. Autosomal recessive. Enzyme deficiency histidine A-deaminase (histidase) resulting in increased histidine in blood and urine, increased excretion of the imidazolepyruvate group, high blood and urine alanine. Histidase is detectable in epithelial cells but not fibroblasts; prenatal diagnosis is not feasible.

*Clinical features*. There is a 'failure to thrive' without distinguishing features as to any particular system affected other than speech. Since the original surveys took place in mental handicap hospitals, it is uncertain how far the association with speech is general or specific to histidinaemia. The results of mass screening of newborns suggest that the majority of affected individuals are entirely normal, and the need for treatment is not proven.

CNS: Later surveys have shown that about a third of the affected individuals are said to be retarded (La Du 1972). Epilepsy and cerebellar ataxia are reported for some 20 per cent of reported cases.

*Further investigation*. Urine amino acid chromatography shows increased histidine and alanine content. Increased imidazolepyruvatic acid will give a positive ferric chloride test (green or green blue) to the urine. Urocanic acid is absent in urine and sweat; skin biopsy shows absent histidase activity.

*Treatment*. Reduction of protein intake in the diet has been recommended (La Du 1972). Histidine is an amino acid essential for growth, so the attempt to keep to less than 6 mg/100 ml is difficult (Holmgren et al. 1974).

BIBLIOGRAPHY

Holmgren, G., Hambraeus, L. & Le Chateau, P. (1974) Histidinemia and 'normohistidinemic histidinuria'. *Acta paediat., Stockh.*, 63, 220.

La Du, B. N. (1972) Histidinemia. In: Stanbury, J. B., Wyngaarden, J. B. & Fredrickson, D. S. (eds.), *The Metabolic Basis of Inherited Disease*, 3rd ed. New York: McGraw Hill.

Levy, H. L., Madigan, P. M. & Shih, V. E. (1972) Massachusetts Metabolic Disorders Screening Program. 1. Technics and results of urine screening. *Pediatrics*, 49, 6, 825–37.

Sabater, J., Ferre, M., Puliol, M. & Maya, A. (1976) Histidinuria: a renal and intestinal histidine transport deficiency found in two mentally retarded children. *Clin. Genet.*, 9, 117–24.

## HOMOCYSTINURIA

Dislocated lens, malar flush, osteoporosis, infarcts.

*History*. Described by Field et al. (1962) and Gerritsen et al. (1962).

*Numbers and frequency*. One in 20 000 to 40 000 live births. 100 cases reported.

*Genetics*. An autosomal recessive trait. Most of those affected have a reduced or absent cystathionine synthetase, an enzyme in the pathway converting methionine to cystine which can be detected in cultured skin fibroblasts. Heterozygotes (parents) have a decreased activity of this enzyme, only shown up in the decreased clearance of plasma methionine on heavy loading. Pyridoxine can be effective in treatment, but since not all those affected respond to pyridoxine, the precise mechanism of the chemical derangement is unclear. A small number of patients have different enzymatic defects, and since prenatal diagnosis of the classical type is feasible it is important to establish an enzymatic diagnosis.

*Clinical features*. Only 50 to 60 per cent of patients develop the pronounced features of dislocated lens in the eye, malar flush, osteoporosis, infarcts and mental retardation. While infants are normal at birth, there is 'failure to thrive' some months after birth. The disease is slower in onset than in maple syrup disease. The limbs are long and slender, the joints are stiff, the palate narrow and the mouth and teeth crowded. There is a marked thrombotic tendency.

*Treatment and outcome.* Not all homozygotes are sufferers; for the affected, pyridoxine (250–500 mg per day) is variably effective (Kang et al. 1970). A diet low in methionine (20–40 mg per kg body weight per day) supplemented by L-cystine has also been tried with improvement.

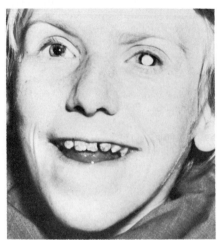

*Fig. 6.16   Homocystinuria : one lens has prolapsed (Dr Harper).*

*Diagnosis.* From Marfan's syndrome but this has no malar flush, joint stiffness, retardation, or positive urinary nitroprusside test for homocystine.

BIBLIOGRAPHY

Field, C. H. B., Carson, N. A. J., Cusworth, D. C., Dent, C. E. & Neill, D. W. (1962) Homocystinuria: a new disorder of metabolism. (Abstract) *Tenth Int. Congr. Pediat., Lisbon*, p. 274.

Gerritsen, T., Vaughan, J. G. & Waisman, H. A. (1962) The identification of homocystine in the urine. *Biochem. biophys. Res. Commun.*, *2*, 493–6.

Kang, E. S., Byers, R. K. & Gerald, P. S. (1970) Homocystinuria: response to pyridoxine. *Neurology, Minneap.*, *20*, 503–7.

HUNTINGTON'S CHOREA
(see Table 4.4)

*History.* Described by Huntington in 1872.

*Numbers and frequency.* Many hundreds described, incidence between 0.2 and 17.4 per 100 000 general population, greatest in Tasmania (Myrianthopoulos 1966), and in some other regions where the gene has been introduced into a small, rapidly expanding founder population.

*Genetics.* Although inherited as a regular autosomal dominant trait, the late and variable age of onset causes severe problems in the effective genetic counselling of family members at risk. No predictive test currently exists that will allow recognition of those destined to develop and transmit the disease; although there are a number under review (BMJ 1978). New mutations are exceedingly rare.

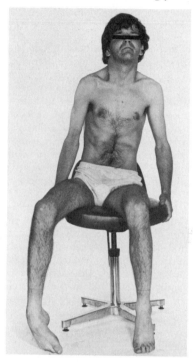

*Fig. 6.17   Juvenile Huntington's chorea developed at age 10, mild mental handicap, death at age 24 (Dr Harper).*

*Clinical features.* There is progressive dementia, ataxia, slurred speech, flat expression of the face, deterioration of behaviour and personality. Later there are increasing adventitial movements of limbs, tongue and facial muscles. The relative importance of chorea and dementia varies greatly, as does the age at onset.

*CNS*: Huntington's chorea in children affects 1 to 2 per cent of cases according to locality, although the mean age is 35. In childhood behaviour disturbances are early, and mental retardation is frequent; there is a rigidity of musculature, and examination reveals ataxia, increased or normal tendon reflexes and a variable plantar response. Epilepsy is early, but choreic movements are late. Most childhood cases are paternally transmitted, for reasons not understood.

*Morbid anatomy.* There is a loss of cells first in the caudate nucleus and putamen, and later throughout the cerebral cortex.

*Investigations.* Pneumoencephalography and computerized axial tomography may show increased size of the lateral ventricles due to cerebral atrophy and in particular may show caudate nucleus atrophy. Recent studies show that there are low levels of the neurotransmitter GABA and related enzyme glutamic acid decarboxylase in these areas, giving hope for replacement therapy in the future.

*Treatment and outcome.* Duration is said to be from fifteen years in adults, and in children some eight years. No long-term effective treatment is possible; tetra benazine and related drugs may help control chorea, while in some rigid cases L-dopa is useful but the disease is relentless. Suicide occurred in 8 per cent of men and 7 per cent of women (Myrianthopoulos 1966). General inanition causing secondary infections is the usual cause of death. The implications for children and other relatives must be carefully considered and acted upon.

*Diagnosis.* Hepatolenticular degeneration has similar features but has the Kayser-Fleischer ring, and serum tests. Drug-induced dyskinesias may be difficult to distinguish. The neuronal lipidoses have a specific histology and biochemical changes. A careful and persistent search almost always reveals a positive family history, and in the absence of this the diagnosis should only be made after most careful consideration.

BIBLIOGRAPHY

Barbeau, A., Chase, T. N. & Paulson, G. W. (1973) *Huntington's Chorea, 1872–1972.* New York: Raven Press.
British Medical Journal (1978) Predictive tests in Huntington's chorea. *Br. med. J.*, *1*, 528–9.
Myrianthopoulos, N. C. (1966) Huntington's chorea. *J. med. Genet.*, *3*, 298–314. [the best review]

HYDROCEPHALIC SYNDROMES

AQUEDUCTAL STENOSIS

*History.* Detailed by Bickers and Adams (1949).

*Numbers.* Over 100 reported.

*Genetics.* It is of interest that Elvidge (1966) found stenosis of the aqueduct in 30 per cent of a series of 44 infants with hydrocephalus; more recently Shellshear and Emery (1976) found gliosis to be responsible for 29 out of 30 hydrocephalics. An X-linked recessive mutant gene causing stenosis of the aqueduct has been identified by Edwards et

al. (1961) but has associated specific features and accounts only for a minority of cases, the remainder having a low risk of recurrence.

*Clinical features.* The infant presents with gross enlargement of the head either *in utero* or at birth. In the few that live after birth, the hydrocephalus is liable to increase with gross mental retardation. There are long-tract signs, proptosed and divergent eyes, and associated abnormalities. In those that develop in the first months of life, shunts are possible.

*Treatment and outcome.* Ventriculo-atrial shunts have been effective (Elvidge 1966).

*Morbid anatomy.* In the X-linked syndrome, the aqueduct is narrowed at the level of the fourth nerve.

BIBLIOGRAPHY

Bickers, D. S. & Adams, R. D. (1949) Hereditary stenosis of the aqueduct of Sylvius as a cause of congenital hydrocephalus. *Brain*, *72*, 246–62.
Edwards, J. H., Norman, R. M. & Roberts, J. M. (1961) Sex-linked hydrocephalus: report of a family of 15 affected members. *Archs Dis. Childh.*, *36*, 481–5.
Elvidge, A. R. (1966) Treatment of obstructive lesions of the aqueduct of Sylvius and the fourth ventricle by interventriculostomy. *J. Neurosurg.*, *24*, 11–23.
Shannon, M. W. & Nadler, H. L. (1968) X-linked hydrocephalus. *J. med. Genet.*, *5*, 326–8.
Shellshear, I. & Emery, J. L. (1976) Gliosis and aqueductal formation in the aqueduct of Sylvius. *Devl Med. Child Neurol.*, *18*, Supp. 37, 22–28.
[For a very comprehensive review of hydrocephalus, treatment and outcome, see *Devl Med. Child Neurol.* (1976) *18*, Supp. 37, 1–172.]

DANDY-WALKER SYNDROME

*History.* Dandy in 1921 and Walker (1944) first described the syndrome and later suggested the shunt, which has transformed the outlook.

*Numbers and frequency.* Not known.

*Genetics.* Other members of the family rarely affected.

*Clinical features.* There is said to be a failure of development of the foramina of Luschka and Magendie in the roof of the fourth ventricle, a membrane across the aqueduct, or an abnormality of the cerebellum with cleft formation and a posterior medullary sac. Either way, the fourth ventricle becomes an enlarged cyst and expands up, down and sideways.

The head enlargement is sometimes noticeable at birth, but some infants normal at birth develop steady deterioration in the first few months. The occiput is pronounced, and transillumination of the head of the infant is possible, due to the eggshell-like cranial bones and excess fluid within.

*CNS*: There is gross psychomotor retardation in the absence of treatment, a cracked-pot sound on gently knocking the occiput, and delayed development of the use of the limbs, with increased deep tendon reflexes. Long-tract signs may be pronounced, but the cerebellum is affected later if at all.

*Morbid anatomy.* In extreme cases the dilated ventricles occupy the greater part of the skull cavity. *Tests*: The dilatation of the fourth ventricle may be so large as to extend into the cervical canal, where it can be shown by pneumoencephalography. The insertion of the tentorium into the skull may be shown to be high, on skull X-ray.

*Treatment and outcome.* Walker (1944) has shown that a ventriculo-atrial shunt can be highly successful. This has to be supervised carefully over the first few years of life, as with growth of the child there may be slippage of the tube. Puri and Eckstein (1976) reviewed 347 children with hydrocephalus treated by Holter valve, following them for 6 to 18 years: 37 died post-operatively, 170 revision operations were needed, 81 patients died (aged 4 days to 13 years), in 38 due to valve complications.

BIBLIOGRAPHY

D'Agostino, A. N., Kernohan, J. W. & Brown, J. R. (1963) The Dandy-Walker syndrome. *J. Neuropath. exp. Neurol.,* 22, 450–70.
Puri, P. & Eckstein, H. B. (1976) Results of treatment of hydrocephalus by Holter valves, a 6 to 18 year follow-up. *Devl Med. Child Neurol., 18,* Supp. 37, 169.
Walker, A. E. (1944) A case of congenital atresia of the foramina of Luschka and Magendie: surgical cure. *J. Neuropath. exp. Neurol., 3,* 368–73.

## HYDRANENCEPHALUS

*History.* This term is now applied to children whose skull cavity is replaced almost entirely by fluid, yet whose head circumference is not as large as classical hydrocephalus with a skull circumference over 60 cm and no excess CSF pressure.

*Numbers and frequency.* Not known.

*Clinical features.* Following a normal infant at birth, there is 'failure to thrive' and increasing cranial circumference. The sutures remain separated, there is difficulty in gaze, nystagmus, squint, screaming with the 'cracked-pot' sound on percussing the skull. Transillumination becomes apparent by six months. The fundi are pale. There is no increase in CSF pressure and sight is retained better than in classical hydrocephalus.

*CNS*: Gross retardation.

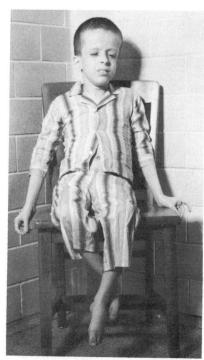

*Fig. 6.18  Hydranencephalus showing enlarged skull, mild retardation (Dr Kratter).*

*Morbid anatomy.* A thin layer of cortical matter surrounds an accumulation of ventricular fluid. Due to gross distortion, original abnormalities causing the hydrocephalus may be impossible to assess accurately.

*Further investigation.* The electroencephalogram shows a classical absence of activity, the pneumoencephalogram shows the skull cavity almost entirely filling with air. In the absence of increased pressure, some children are able to function, even to become literate, with brain weight less than 10 per cent of that expected for age.

*Treatment and outcome.* Affected infants may be still-born, others die in early infancy, but with modern by-pass operations normal potential can be achieved.

BIBLIOGRAPHY

Hill, K., Cogan, D. C. & Dodge, P. R. (1961) Ocular signs associated with hydranencephaly. *Am. J. Ophthal.*, 51, 267–75.

## HYPOTHYROIDISM

'Failure to thrive' in infancy, progressive retardation in adults.

*History.* One of the best known causes of mental retardation.

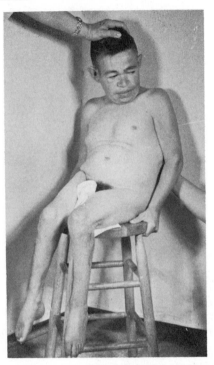

*Fig. 6.19   Hypothyroidism (cretinism) : untreated case in remote area (Dr Kratter).*

*Numbers.* Congenital hypothyroidism (cretinism) occurs around 1 in 4–6000 births in most European and American populations; cases of juvenile onset are somewhat less common. Endemic areas, such as Nepal, Andes, Rockies, New Guinea, are mountainous areas deficient in iodine where over 5 per cent of the adolescent population have Grade 1 (visible) goitre, and 30 per cent (palpable) goitre (White 1977). It has been estimated that worldwide there are 200 million people affected by goitre, hypothyroidism or cretinism (BMJ 1978).

*Clinical features.* There are a number of methods of causation varying from maternal ingestion of antithyroid medication during pregnancy, to iodine deficient soil leading to endemic cretinism. Familial goitrous forms may result from specific defects of thyroxine synthesis syndrome. The different causes result in similar clinical features of *hypothyroidism*, although the presence or absence of a *goitre* depends specifically on iodine non-availability. Hypothyroidism in adults is also termed myxoedema.

*Head and face*: The affected infant develops puffiness of the eyelids, a thick tongue which appears larger than the mouth, and drools. The anterior fontanelle remains open late. Older children and adults develop coarseness of the face with a hoarse voice and thickening of the neck and supra-

*Fig. 6.20    Hypothyroidism in adult (myxoedema) (Dr Kratter).*

clavicular fossae. Constipation and feeding problems are common neonatal features. Pulse rate is slow and the heart is often enlarged, as is the abdomen with development of umbilical herniae.

*Limbs*: The skin appears dry and scaly and the hands appear broad with shortened fingers. There is a doughy, indurated feel to the subcutaneous tissue. The hair is brittle and may be sparse. If there is no treatment, delay in sexual maturation occurs.

*CNS*: There is hypotonia, weakness and diminished reflexes, with untreated patients becoming moderately to severely retarded. White (1977) describes 31 children with a variety of 'nervous endemic cretinism' common in developing areas, in which the main features are goitrous children with severe retardation, deafness and spastic paraplegia, without marked hypothyroidism. The degree of mental retardation is directly related to age at start of treatment.

*Further investigation.* The thyroid function tests are diagnostic with serum thyroxine reduced and T.S.H. greatly elevated. X-rays may show a delay in bone age. However if the target organs are highly sensitive to thyroxine, clinical signs of hypothyroidism may occur with low normal biochemical tests.

*Treatment.* Treatment with L-thyroxine (0.2–0.3 mg daily) results in improvement of the signs; completeness of recovery depends on severity and age at treatment. Dosage is dependent on degree of clinical improvement. Large goitres may need to be removed surgically. Development of radioimmunoassays for thyroid hormones on small blood samples has given the possibility of newborn screening to detect those cases not obvious clinically. Endemic goitre and cretinism occur where the daily intake of iodine is below 50 µg; iodine supplement abolishes these and reduces the incidence of toxic nodular goitre and carcinoma (BMJ 1978).

*Diagnosis.* In Down's syndrome there may be coexistent hypothyroidism, otherwise the horizontally striated tongue, distinctive hands and eyes should clarify the diagnosis, together with an abnormal thyroid test. Mucopolysaccharidosis results in corneal opacities and increased glycosaminoglycan in the urine. See Tables 4.3 (p. 47) and 9.3 (p. 154) for differential diagnosis of progressive retardation in children and adults respectively.

BIBLIOGRAPHY

British Medical Journal (1978) Iodine and the thyroid. *Br. med. J., 2,* 1566.
Klein, A. H., Foley, T. P., Sarsen, P. R., Agustin, A. V. & Hopwood, N. J. (1976) Neonatal thyroid function in congenital hypothyroidism. *J. Pediat., 89,* 545–9.
Stanbury, J. B. (1972) Familial goiter. In: Stanbury, J. B., Wyngaarden, J. B. & Fredrickson, D. S. (eds), *The Metabolic Basis of Inherited Disease,* 3rd ed. New York: McGraw Hill.
White, N. J. (1977) Nervous endemic cretinism in Eastern Nepal. *Devl Med. Child Neurol., 19,* 208–12.
Wilkins, L. (1965) *The Diagnosis and Treatment of Endocrine Disorders in Childhood and Adolescence.* 3rd ed. Springfield, Ill.: Charles Thomas.

## ICHTHYOSIS
### (with spasticity and mental retardation)
### (Sjögren–Larsson)

Skin hyperkeratosis, spasticity.

*History.* Reported by Sjögren and Larsson (1957) from an isolated population of Northern Sweden.

*Numbers.* Over 50.

*Genetics.* Autosomal recessive.

*Clinical features.* Although first reported in Sweden it is now known to occur throughout the world. There is ichthyosis of the trunk, extremities and neck, particularly in the underarm and popliteal fossae. The palms are hyperkeratotic. There are

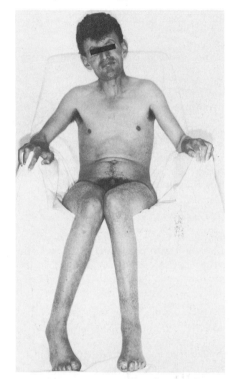

Fig. 6.21 *Ichthyosis with spasticity (Sjögren–Larsson) (Dr Jancar).*

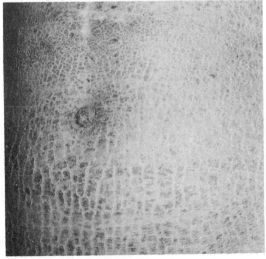

Fig. 6.22 *Ichthyotic skin, dry and scaly (Dr Jancar).*

variations in different parts of the world as to the dryness of skin and ichthyosis, but most of those affected have difficulty in sweating. The hair is usually unaffected although may be thin. Nails are normal. There may be macular degeneration of the retina in about a quarter of the cases. Dwarfism is frequent.

*CNS*: Most are severely retarded with spastic legs and hyperactive deep reflexes. Some are epileptic.

*Further investigation.* No biochemical abnormalities reported.

*Treatment.* This is symptomatic. Life expectation is near-normal.

*Diagnosis.* To be distinguished from Refsum's syndrome in which there is behaviour disorder, low-average intelligence, peripheral neuropathy, and retinal degeneration. Phytanic acid excess in serum confirms Refsum's syndrome.

BIBLIOGRAPHY

Sjögren, T. & Larsson, R. (1957) Oligophrenia in combination with congenital ichthyosis and spastic disorders: a clinical and genetic study. *Acta psychiat. Scand.*, *32* (Suppl. 113), 1–112.

## INCONTINENTIA PIGMENTI
(Bloch–Sulzberger syndrome)

Skin bullae, eye abnormalities, spasticity.

*History.* Described by Bloch in 1926 and Sulzberger in 1927.

*Numbers and frequency.* Over 300 patients described.

*Genetics.* Almost all females, so probably an X-linked dominant, lethal in the male.

*Clinical features.* The infant is normal at birth, but develops pruritic bullae in the first few months which develop into pustules. These are variable in extent, eventually being replaced by fibrotic and hyperkeratotic areas which are the second stage of the abnormality. Once the crusts have gone, the third stage of dermal fibrosis occurs, all three taking a variable time, up to several years. There is a degree of fading, with atrophic areas as the result in adolescence. The teeth are irregular, the nails poorly developed, microcephaly may occur with variable eye abnormalities affecting up to a third of patients. These vary from corneal opacities, cataracts and squints to masses in the posterior chamber.

*CNS*: In one review one-third had retardation, microcephaly, spastic paresis and epilepsy.

*Morbid anatomy.* The bullae contain eosinophilic extravasations and the skin has increased histamine content. Hyperkeratosis distinguishes the second stage, whilst the epidermis is atrophied in the third.

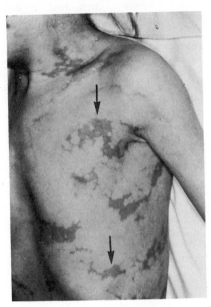

Fig. 6.23    *Incontinentia pigmenti showing skin bullae (Dr Jancar).*

*Further investigation.* Eosinophilia, affecting up to 50 per cent of white blood cells, is the cardinal feature.

*Treatment and outcome.* Supportive measures are indicated, and a favourable outcome is probable. By adolescence bullae are few, and it is the atrophic skin which needs life-long care.

BIBLIOGRAPHY

Asboe-Hansen, G. (1968) Incontinentia pigmenti: bullous keratogenous and pigmentary dermatitis with blood eosinophilia in newborn girls. *Cutis*, *4*, 1341–4.
Carney, R. G. & Carney, E. G. (1970) Incontinentia pigmenti. *Archs Derm.*, *102*, 157–62.

## LAURENCE–MOON–BIEDL SYNDROME

Cataracts, optic atrophy, hypogonadism, polydactyly.

*History.* Described by Laurence and Moon in 1866.

*Numbers and frequency.* 273 patients reviewed by Bell (1958), frequency not known.

*Genetics.* Autosomal recessive, both sexes affected.

*Clinical features.* Some have hypertelorism but the

*Diagnosis.* In the Alstrom syndrome retinitis pigmentosa, obesity and diabetes are associated with nerve deafness. Some of the skeletal features are also found in Carpenter's syndrome but this lacks retinal dystrophy and the facial features are acrocephalic.

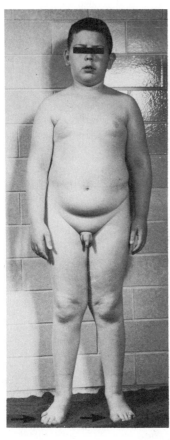

*Fig. 6.24 Laurence–Moon–Biedl syndrome showing retinitis, polydactyly (12 toes), hypogonadism and obesity (Dr Kratter).*

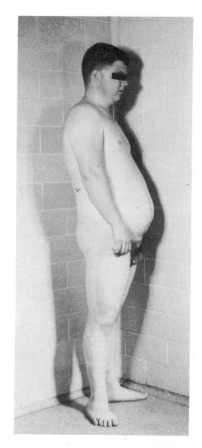

*Fig. 6.25 Laurence–Moon–Biedl syndrome showing polydactyly (extra little finger) and hypogonadism (Dr Kratter).*

most common features are retinal degeneration with macula involvement, optic atrophy, cataracts, hypogonadism and digit abnormalities. Polydactyly of feet or hands is common and may include each limb. Obesity is usual and present mainly on the trunk.

*CNS*: Most patients are mentally retarded, usually of mild degree.

*Further investigation.* Urinary gonadotropins are diminished.

*Treatment and outcome.* Compatible with average length of life. No specific treatment indicated.

BIBLIOGRAPHY

Bell, J. (1958) The Laurence–Moon syndrome. *The Treasury of Human Inheritance*, vol. 5, part 3, pp. 51–69. Cambridge: Cambridge University Press.

Koepp, P. (1975) Laurence–Moon–Biedl syndrome associated with diabetes insipidus neurohormonalis. *Eur. J. Paediatrics, 121,* 59–62.

Moini, A. R., Emamy, H. & Asadian, A. (1975) The Laurence–Moon–Biedl syndrome. *Clin. Pediat., 14,* 9, 812–15.

## LESCH–NYHAN SYNDROME
### (hyperuricaemia with choreoathetosis)

Torsion spasms and self-mutilation.

*History.* Described by Lesch and Nyhan (1964).

*Numbers.* 150 patients described.

*Genetics.* X-linked recessive. Prenatal diagnosis achieved (Demars et al. 1969). There is deficient activity of the enzyme hypoxanthine guanine phosphoribosyl transferase (HGPRT). It is easiest to consider this as a rare sub-type of gout in which the target organs in the basal ganglia are unduly sensitive to hyperuricaemia, resulting in choreoathetosis. Gout itself consists of hyperuricaemia (due to hereditary endowment when it starts young; environmental overindulgence when it starts later; or due to kidney and other organ failures) acting mainly on joints as sensitive target organs, to a lesser extent the CNS (Wyngaarden & Kelly 1976).

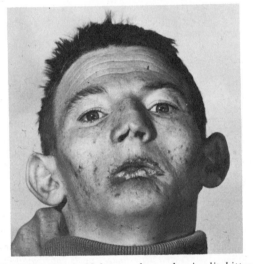

*Fig. 6.26    Lesch–Nyhan syndrome showing lip bitten by patient (Dr Jancar).*

*Clinical features. Head and face:* The face is normal, but in severe cases lip-biting in early childhood causes scarring and loss of tissue. There may be gouty tophi containing uric acid on the tips of ears.
   *Trunk and limbs:* The ends of fingers may be bitten and there may be gouty arthritis of the joints.
   *CNS:* Most reported patients have been severely retarded but the less affected can show symptoms in adolescence or adult life with torsion spasm, spastic paresis and developing athetosis, with involuntary movements of limbs and trunk. The deep reflexes are hyperactive and the plantars are extensor. There may be speech difficulties. There are two striking features of the disease, the compulsion to self-mutilation, and the torsion spasms particularly of neck muscles.

*Further investigation.* There is a deficiency of HGPRT in the brain, liver, red blood cells and amniotic cells, hence prenatal diagnosis. The urinary uric acid is raised, also its ratio to creatinine. The blood uric acid is also usually raised. Gouty tophi may be seen and there may be urinary stones containing uric acid. The syndrome seems the most severe of a range of rare genetically endowed deficiencies of the enzyme, which in adults may result in gout, with milder or even absent neurological abnormalities.

*Treatment.* Allopurinol is effective in lowering blood uric acid by blocking its synthesis, but has not been proved to help the behavioural abnormalities. Adenine addition to the diet may be useful (van der Zee et al. 1970).

*Diagnosis.* Other causes of chorea and involuntary movement do not have the biochemical abnormality or the clinical features of gout.

BIBLIOGRAPHY

Demars, R., Santo, G. & Felix, J. S. (1969) Lesch–Nyhan mutation. *Science, 164,* 1303–5.
Lesch, M. & Nyhan, W. L. (1964) A familial disorder of uric acid metabolism and central nervous system function. *Am. J. Med., 36,* 561–70.
Seegmiller, J. E. (1976) Lesch–Nyhan syndrome and its variants. *Archs hum. Genet., 6,* 75–163.
van der Zee, S. P. M., Lommen, E. J. P., Trijbels, J. M. F. & Schretlen, E. D. A. M. (1970) The influence of adenine on the clinical features and purine metabolism in the Lesch–Nyhan syndrome. *Acta paediat., Stockh., 59,* 259–64.
Wyngaarden, J. B. & Kelley, W. N. (1976) *Gout and Hyperuricemia.* New York: Grune & Stratton.

## MANDIBULOFACIAL DYSOSTOSIS
### (Treacher Collins syndrome)

Antimongol slanting eyes, sunken facial centre, small ears.

*History.* Described by Berry in 1889 as having downward and outward slanting eyes, cleft lip, notched eyelids. Many other authors, in particular Treacher Collins in 1900, describe variants.

*Numbers and frequency.* Over 200 so far reported (Rogers 1964).

*Genetics.* Autosomal dominant. The expression of the gene varies greatly within a family, so a mildly affected parent may have a severely affected child.

*Clinical features.* The eyes slant downwards and outwards and there is underdevelopment of the malar and zygoma areas so that the child has a pinched-in look in the centre of its face. The eyes may have colobomata and the normal nose and mouth appear large. About half of affected patients have underdeveloped ears, which may be entirely absent leaving a simple hole for the external auditory meatus. The teeth are irregular and crowded, and with some a cleft lip course.

*CNS*: Most are of average intelligence but a substantial number are retarded. The external ear anomalies may be associated with inner ear anomalies causing deafness.

*Further investigation.* Skull X-rays show underdevelopment of the central skull bones of maxilla, the zygoma, mandible, middle ear bones.

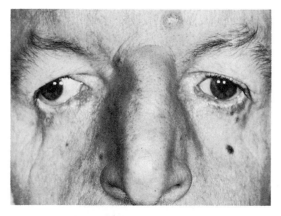

*Fig. 6.27    Mandibulofacial dysostosis in adult (Dr Jancar).*

*Treatment and outcome.* Any hearing loss should be remedied, cosmetic surgery has been used with effect.

*Diagnosis.* The Goldenhaar syndrome shows occasional association with mental retardation but has specific physical abnormalities including conjunctival dermoid tumours. A variety of genetic syndromes cause abnormalities of the ears and eyes which must be distinguished from this syndrome. See also Oculomandibulodyscephaly (p. 103).

BIBLIOGRAPHY

Rogers, B. O. (1964) Berry–Treacher Collins syndrome: a review of 200 cases. *Br. J. plast. Surg.*, *17*, 109–37.

## MAPLE SYRUP URINE DISEASE

'Failure to thrive', fits, CNS signs, urinary smell.

*History.* Described in detail by Wada et al. (1963).

*Numbers and frequency.* Between one in 100 000 and one in 250 000 live births.

*Genetics.* Autosomal recessive. An enzyme, or enzyme group, is deficient in the leucine group transamination cycle.

*Clinical features.* In treated cases appearance is normal, in untreated cases there are no specific physical features other than those due to the generalized neurological damage in mental retardation. Whilst normal at birth, within a few days there is 'failure to thrive', lethargy, poor feeding, convulsions, hypotonia alternating with hypertonicity and the characteristic urinary odour of maple syrup.

*Further tests.* The urine is positive with ferric chloride (grey with green tinge) and dinitrophenylhydrazine for ketoacids. Raised levels of leucine, isoleucine and valine are found in the plasma. The enzymic defect in white cells can be demonstrated in white cells and cultured fibroblasts.

*Treatment and outcome.* The principles of treatment are similar to those of phenylketonuria. A diet of restricted amino acids has to be started early before onset of permanent nerve cell damage. This is both difficult and expensive and there have been few reports of encouraging results. It is not clear whether the body tolerates a more generous diet in later life (*Can. med. Ass. J.* 1976).

*Diagnosis.* In maple syrup disease the enzymes oxidizing all three amino acids to their ketoacid substrate are missing or reduced and it is postulated that this is due to a single abnormal autosomal Mendelian recessive gene. What is not explained is that whilst there are up to one hundred patients described with maple syrup disease, there has also been the occasional patient with only hypervalinaemia and isovaleric acidemia. It is possible that more than one enzyme is involved. The full mechanism of neurological damage has also not been worked out but it is believed that the ketoacid derivatives of leucine and valine reduce the effect of L-glutamic dehydrogenase in the brain.

BIBLIOGRAPHY

Committee for Improvement of Hereditary Disease Management (1976) Management of maple syrup urine disease in Canada. *Can. med. Ass. J.*, *115*, 1005–10.

Dancis, J. & Levitz, M. (1972) Abnormalities of branched-chain amino acid metabolism. In: Stanbury, J. B., Wyngaarden, J. B. & Fredrickson, D. S. (eds.), *The Metabolic Basis of Inherited Disease*, 3rd ed. New York: McGraw Hill.

Wada, Y., Taka, K., Minagawa, A., Yoshida, T., Morikawa, T. & Okamura, T. (1963) Idiopathic hypervalinemia: probably a new entity of inborn error of valine metabolism. *Tohoku J. exp. Med.*, *81*, 46.

## MENKES SYNDROME
(kinky-hair disease, steel-hair syndrome)

'Failure to thrive', weight loss, deterioration.

*History.* Described by Menkes et al. (1962).

*Numbers.* Some 50 cases described and in Victoria, Australia, 1 in 35 000 live births are said to be affected (Gordon 1974).

*Genetics.* X-linked recessive, therefore males only. A homologous X-linked gene has been described in the mouse. Both in man and mouse the disorder is due to a defect in copper metabolism. Prenatal diagnosis is likely to become feasible.

*Clinical features. Head and face*: A high-arched palate and micrognathia are reported. The hair is thin, kinky and has a wiry feel to it like steel wool. All parts of the body have the same abnormality and the hair fades in colour during infancy so that it may become quite white, stiff and lustreless. There is a 'failure to thrive' with epilepsy, myoclonus and development of spasticity, nystagmus and retardation. By the age of three weight starts to decrease and retardation is profound with little spontaneous movement. Death follows.

*Morbid anatomy.* The hair shows fractures and is variable in size. Microscopically it can be seen to be twisted around its long axis. There is atrophy of the brain.

*Investigation.* Biochemical studies (O'Brien and Sampson 1966) show low brain docosohexaenoic acid on biopsy, but more recently low serum copper and ceruloplasmin are held to be diagnostic with an inability to absorb copper from the intestine (Dekaban et al. 1976).

*Treatment and outcome.* Intravenous copper has been used, but the degree of success is unclear (Gordon 1974; Garnica et al. 1977).

*Diagnosis.* Twisty curly hair is common in the population, but kinky hair has a particular look and feel, apart from specific associated abnormalities. The arginino-succinic aciduria has abnormal hair but also has the abnormal metabolite in the urine.

BIBLIOGRAPHY

Dekaban, A. S., Aamodt, R., Rumble, F., Johnston, G. S. & O'Reilly, S. (1976) Kinky hair disease: study of copper metabolism with use of 67 CU. *Archs Neurol., Chicago, 32*, 672–5.

Garnica, A. D., Frias, J. L. & Rennert, O. M. (1977) Menkes kinky-hair syndrome, is it a treatable disorder? *Clin. Genet., 11*, 154–61.

Gordon, N. (1974) Menkes kinky hair (steely-hair) syndrome. *Devl Med. Child Neurol., 16*, 827.

Menkes, J., Alter, M., Steigleder, G. K., Weakley, D. R. & Sung, J. H. (1962) A sex-linked recessive disorder with retardation of growth, peculiar hair and focal cerebral and cerebellar degeneration. *Pediatrics, 29*, 764–9.

O'Brien, J. S. & Sampson, E. L. (1966) Kinky hair disease. II. Biochemical studies. *J. Neuropath. exp. Neurol., 25*, 523–30.

## MICROCEPHALY
(Pure, recessive and X-linked)

*History.* Recognized very early.

*Numbers.* Hundreds described.

*Genetics.* In some families it occurs among males and females, behaving like an autosomal recessive, with others it affects only males, yet elsewhere it is sporadic, and may be a new mutation (see Kloepfer et al. 1964; van den Bosch 1959; Böök et al. 1953; Paine 1960). It can be due to severe infections or drug influences *in utero* (see p. 117).

*Clinical features.* The forehead recedes rapidly and the cranial capacity is less than 80 per cent of normal. There may be excess scalp folds of skin, but the eyes, trunk and limbs are often unaffected. The diagnostic feature is the discrepant size of near-normal face and small receding forehead and skull.

*CNS*: Gross retardation, often spastic legs and arms.

*Further tests.* Skull X-rays show normal vault and sutures and no signs of pressure.

*Treatment and outcome.* Many live long. No specific treatment.

*Diagnosis.* There are many causes of microcephaly (see Table 4.2) for which a good history is essential.

BIBLIOGRAPHY

Böök, J. A., Schut, J. W. & Reed, S. C. (1953) A clinical and genetic study of microcephaly. *Am. J. ment. Defic.*, *57*, 637–60.

Kloepfer, H. W., Platou, R. V. & Hansche, W. J. (1964) Manifestations of a recessive gene for microcephaly in a population isolate. *J. Genet. Hum.*, *13*, 52–9.

Paine, R. S. (1960) Evaluation of familial biochemically-determined retardation in children, with special reference to aminoaciduria. *New Engl. J. Med.*, *262*, 658–65.

van den Bosch, J. (1959) Microcephaly in the Netherlands: a clinical and genetical study. *Ann. hum. Genet.*, *23*, 91–116.

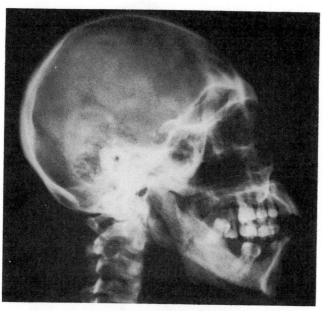

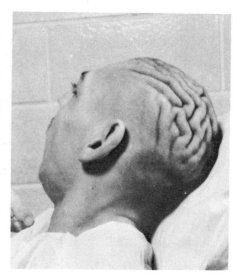

*Fig. 6.29   Microcephaly showing scalp folds (Dr Kratter).*

*Fig. 6.28   X-ray of microcephaly (Dr Sylvester).*

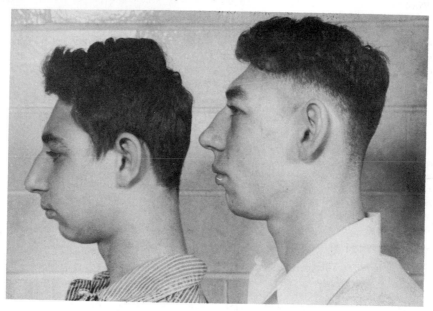

*Fig. 6.30   Microcephaly in twins (Dr Kratter).*

## MUCOPOLYSACCHARIDOSES

Coarse facial features, hepatosplenomegaly, other features according to type.

Clinical, genetic and biochemical classification (see Table 6.4, p. 70) allows recognition of at least seven varieties of mucopolysaccharidosis, in addition to allied disorders such as mucolipidoses. All

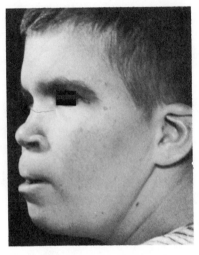

Fig. 6.31    *MPS type IH (Hurler) showing facial coarsening (Dr Kratter).*

are inherited as autosomal recessive disorders except for type II (Hunter syndrome) which is X-linked and confined to males. Each type results from a specific deficiency of one of the lysosomal enzymes involved in breakdown of mucopolysaccharides, though in some cases different enzyme defects cause an identical clinical picture (type IIIA and B) while in others different clinical syndromes (IH and IS) share the same enzyme defect. Type IS (Scheie) is associated with normal intelligence, the enzyme defect not affecting the target organ of the brain.

Common features of those forms showing mental retardation are coarse facial features ('gargoyle-like'), characteristic bony X-ray changes, hepatosplenomegaly and evidence of mucopolysaccharide accumulation in tissues. Prenatal diagnosis is feasible using cultured amniotic cells. Treatment has been attempted using plasma infusions and fibroblast implants, but remains experimental.

### HURLER SYNDROME (type IH)

Affected children are normal at birth, but show slowed development, hepatosplenomegaly, corneal clouding, with progressive facial coarsening, dwarfing, joint contractures and frequent deafness. Increased urinary mucopolysaccharides and X-ray

changes in spine (beaking of lumbar vertebrae), skull (J-shaped sella) and hands (short carpal bones) will confirm the diagnosis of a mucopolysaccharidosis. Presence of corneal clouding will exclude type II and of mental retardation type VI. In type III physical abnormalities are generally less marked.

Progressive downhill course is usual with severe mental impairment and death by the age of ten.

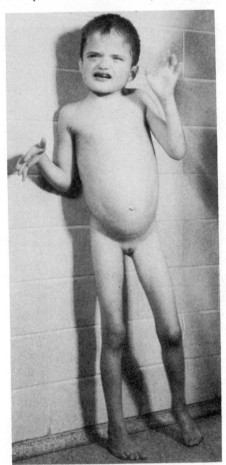

Fig. 6.32    *MPS type II (Hunter) showing deterioration (Dr Kratter).*

### HUNTER SYNDROME (type II) (males only)

Physical abnormalities appear later than in Hurler syndrome, with more benign course and moderate to minimal mental retardation. Absence of corneal clouding distinguishes this type from types I and VI. Survival is common into adult life, but cardiac involvement is commonly fatal. The X-linked inheritance puts asymptomatic female relatives at risk of having affected sons. Carrier detection remains difficult and it is wise for pregnancies of female relatives to be monitored by fetal sexing and specific biochemical studies.

## SANFILIPPO SYNDROME (type IIIA and B)

Types A and B are phenotypes (clinically indistinguishable) with a different enzyme subtype responsible for each. Physical abnormalities are slight in comparison with other forms, but progressive mental deterioration commonly requires hospitalization. Hepatosplenomegaly, mildly suspicious facial and X-ray changes and increased mucopolysacchar-

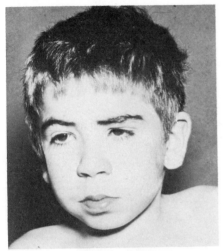

*Fig. 6.33   MPS type III (Sanfilippo) showing facial characteristics (Dr Harper).*

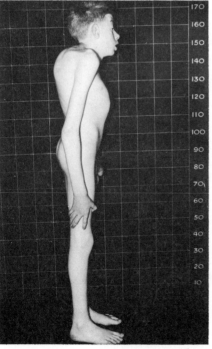

*Fig. 6.34   MPS type IV (Morquio) (Dr Jancar).*

ide excretion suggest the diagnosis. Corneal clouding is absent.

## MORQUIO'S SYNDROME (type IV)

Here the variation affects the visceral organs severely, but the mental impairment is slighter.

## 'I' CELL DISEASE (mucolipidosis type I)

This rare disorder is not a mucopolysaccharidosis but a phenocopy which presents from early infancy, with similar features, cloudy cornea and severe mental retardation. Patients with clinical features of mucopolysaccharidosis but no mucopolysacchariduria should be suspected of having this or related disorders.

## MUSCULAR DYSTROPHY
### (Duchenne type)

Progressive muscular weakness.

*History.* First described by Duchenne in 1868.

*Numbers and frequency.* 1 in 3500 live male births in most European populations, making it much the commonest childhood muscular dystrophy.

*Genetics.* X-linked recessive and thus practically confined to males, though very rare instances of a closely similar disorder in girls have been recorded. Heterozygous female carriers may show minor degrees of muscle weakness. About one-third of cases are the result of new mutations. Detection of the majority of carrier females is feasible from slight elevation of serum creatinephosphokinase (CPK); but performance and interpretation of the test requires great caution and an experienced laboratory, as well as consideration of the full genetic data, if serious errors are to be avoided. Serum CPK is greatly raised in affected males.

*Clinical features.* Affected children are normal at birth. Most present with motor delay or waddling gait at two to four years, with signs of proximal weakness at hip and shoulder girdles and pseudohypertrophy of calf muscles. Many children are mentally normal, but there is clear evidence of a downward shift of IQ overall (Dubowitz 1965) and some are seriously mentally retarded, with this as the presenting feature. Progressive muscle weakness results in death usually between 15 and 25 years of age. Confirmation of the diagnosis can be obtained by serum CPK, electromyography and muscle biopsy (only worthwhile if facilities exist for expert preparation and interpretation). The late onset X-linked (Becker) form of muscular dystrophy is a distinct disorder following a more benign course and rarely associated with mental deterioration. Particular care must be taken to distinguish this and other dystrophies from the Duchenne type in view of the different prognosis and in some cases inheritance.

*Treatment and prevention.* No specific treatment exists, but families require much support. Accurate assessment of mental capacity is important in view of the eventually severe physical disability. All close female relatives should be carefully checked for carrier status. Fetal sexing for pregnancies of carriers, with termination of male pregnancies, is feasible, but there is no prenatal diagnosis at present.

BIBLIOGRAPHY

Dubowitz, V. (1965) Intellectual impairment in muscular dystrophy. *Archs Dis. Childh.*, *40*, 296–301.

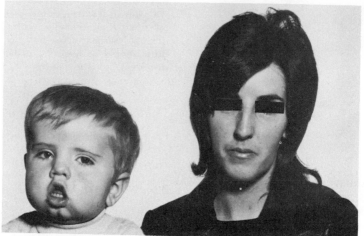

*Fig. 6.35    Myotonic dystrophy showing affected child and affected mother (Dr Harper).*

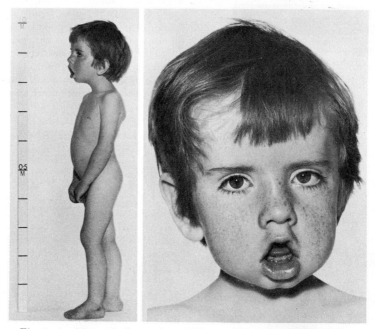

*Fig. 6.36    Myotonic dystrophy: child aged 6 showing drooling mouth, mild mental handicap (with speech defect which increased retardation) (Dr Harper).*

## MYOTONIC DYSTROPHY
(dystrophia myotonica, Steinert's disease)

Progressive muscular weakness.

*History.* First described by Batten and Gibb, and by Steinert in 1909. Childhood type recognized by Vanier (1960).

*Numbers and frequency.* Probably around 1 in 10–15 000 births.

*Genetics.* Autosomal dominant, with both sexes equally affected, but with extreme variability in severity, mode of presentation and age at onset. Almost invariably maternally transmitted in severe childhood cases. Linked to secretor and Lutheran blood group loci, but precise chromosome uncertain.

*Clinical features.* In adult life most patients present with muscle weakness, stiffness, cataract or related symptoms. Characteristic signs include facial weakness, ptosis, distal limb weakness, with myotonia of grip and on percussion of the thenar muscles. Cataract and testicular atrophy are frequent. Most asymptomatic gene carriers can be detected by slit-lamp search for lens opacities and electromyography. Many affected adults show mild to moderate mental deterioration with marked lethargy and somnolence. Affected children are frequently mentally retarded and may have no muscle symptoms. Myotonia may be slight and in infancy absent, but this frequently overlooked condition has a characteristic facial appearance from jaw weakness and facial diplegia (Harper 1975). No definite biochemical defect is known; serum creatine phosphokinase is generally normal.

*Treatment and prevention.* Cataract may require surgery. General anaesthesia should be undertaken with care because of increased sensitivity to normal doses of many agents. Careful family study usually shows other affected members, with 50 per cent risk to offspring. Linkage with the secretor locus can be used in some families to predict affected individuals prenatally (Harper 1973).

BIBLIOGRAPHY

Harper, P. S. (1973) Presymptomatic detection and genetic counselling in myotonic dystrophy. *Clin. Genet., 4,* 134–40.
Harper, P. S. (1975) Congenital myotonic dystrophy in Britain. *Archs Dis. Childh., 50,* 505–13, 514–21.
Vanier, T. (1960) Dystrophia myotonica in childhood. *Br. med. J., 2,* 1284–8.

## NEUROFIBROMATOSIS
(von Recklinghausen's disease)

Skin tumours, café-au-lait spots.

*History.* Reported in 1882 by von Recklinghausen.

*Numbers and frequency.* Said to be 1 in 3000 live births (Crowe et al. 1956).

*Genetics.* Autosomal dominant.

*Clinical features.* The infant may present at birth with pale or light brown patches on the trunk; or facial skin café-au-lait spots, which are diagnostic. Both increase steadily during childhood and adolescence and are quite distinctive. Axillary freckles are said to be pathognomonic and do not occur outside neurofibromatosis. Skin tumours occur in adolescence, consisting of firm nodules of a few millimetres in size. These may be pedunculated, flat, initially red but later flesh coloured. On pressure these may subside under the skin forming a kind of buttonhole. These tumours may run to many thousand in a severely affected person. They may affect the eye socket. They are painless.
   *CNS*: About a third are mentally retarded, and some develop gliomas of the cranial nerves affecting function. They are common upon the auditory nerve causing deafness.

*Morbid anatomy.* The tumours are due to elongated connective tissue cells but the café-au-lait patches are due to accumulation in the malpighian cells of melanosomes. Intracranial tumours interfere with brain function and may develop into glioblastomata.

*Treatment and outcome.* Little treatment is effective apart from removal of tumours, if unsightly or malignant.

*Diagnosis.* In general a child with more than six café-au-lait spots is likely to develop this disease. It has to be distinguished from Albright's syndrome of fibrous hyperplasia, but this also has bone cysts and normal intelligence.

BIBLIOGRAPHY

Crowe, F. W., Schull, W. J. & Neel, J. V. (1956) *A Clinical, Pathological and Genetic Study of Multiple Neurofibromatosis.* Springfield, Ill.: Charles Thomas.
Fienman, N. L. & Yakovac, W. C. (1970) Neurofibromatosis in childhood. *J. Pediat., 76,* 339–46.

## NEURONAL LIPIDOSES WITHOUT SPHINGOLIPIDS
(juvenile amaurotic idiocy, ceroid-lipofuscinoses)

Failure of vision, CNS degeneration.

*History.* Described for ages: infancy by Biel-schowsky (1913); childhood by Batten (1903), Spielmeyer (1905) and Vogt (1909); adulthood by Kufs (1925).

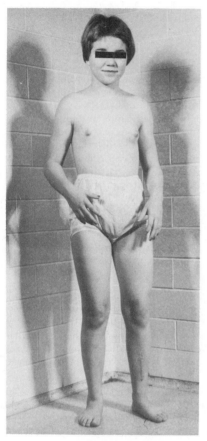

*Fig. 6.37    Neuronal lipidosis: adolescent variety (Dr Kratter).*

*Genetics.* Autosomal recessive. There is lipid accumulation in cells without sphingolipid accumulation possibly due to deficiency in the peroxidase enzyme group.

*Clinical features.* CNS: Eye degeneration is among the first abnormalities, with central vision impairment, narrowing of the retinal vessels and optic disc pallor. Next peripheral vision deteriorates with yellow pigmented areas in the retinal periphery. Later there is optic atrophy with thin arteries and

finally the abnormality covers the entire retina. Dementia advances quickly in younger patients, more slowly in older patients, and in Sjögren's (1931) series emotional instability was the main feature of oncoming dementia. Later there is spasticity, extensor plantars, with deep tendon jerks, and cerebellar ataxia. Epilepsy has been noted.

*Morbid anatomy.* The grey matter is thin with reduced cells and atrophy.

*Further investigation.* Lipid accumulation with vacuoles may be seen in white blood cells. Ganglion cells in the rectum may also show characteristic lipid accumulation.

*Treatment.* The age of death is variable as the many investigators have noted and vitamin E has been successfully used to delay deterioration (Nelson 1974). Anti-epileptic, dopaminergic and other symptomatic drugs are needed.

*Diagnosis.* From Tay–Sachs disease, GM1 gangliosidosis, Niemann–Pick disease and other lipid accumulations. Diagnosis depends on the laboratory analysis but brain biopsy is less preferable than rectal biopsy of ganglion cells (Nelson 1974).

BIBLIOGRAPHY

Batten, F. E. (1903) Cerebral degeneration with symmetrical changes in the maculae in two members of a family. *Trans. ophthal. Soc. U.K.,* *23*, 386–90.
Bielschowsky, M. (1913) Uber spätinfantiler familiärer amaurotischer Idiotie mit Kleinhirnsymptomen. *Dt. Z. NervHeilk.,* *50*, 7–29.
Kufs, H. (1925) Uber einer Spätform der amaurotischen Idiotie und ihren heredofamiliären Grundlagen. *Z. ges. Neurol. Psychiat.,* *95*, 169–88.
Malone, M. J. (1976) The cerebral lipidoses. *Pediat. Clins N. Am.,* *23*, 303–26.
Motulsky, A. G. (1976) Current concepts in genetics: the genetic hyperlipidemias. *New Engl. J. Med.,* *294*, 823–7.
Nelson, J. S. (1974) Rectal biopsy in the diagnosis of paediatric neurological disorders. *Devl Med. Child Neurol.,* *16*, 830–1.
Sjögren, T. (1931) Die juvenile amaurotische Idiotie. *Hereditas,* *14*, 197–426.
Spielmeyer, W. (1905) Weitere Mitteilung über eine besondere Form von familiärer amaurotischer Idiotie. *Neurol. Zbl.,* *24*, 1131–2.
Swaiman, K. F. & Wright, F. S. (eds.) (1975) *The Practice of Pediatric Neurology.* St. Louis: Mosby. [a good review]
Vogt, H. (1909) Familiärer amaurotischer Idiotie, histologische und histopathologische Studien. *Arch. Kinderheilk.,* *51*, 1–35.

## NOONAN'S SYNDROME
### (Turner-like syndrome)

Tower forehead, eye signs, webbed neck.

*History.* Described by Noonan and Ehmke (1963). A phenocopy (similar features) for Turner's syndrome, occurring in both males and females as mental retardation, skeletal abnormalities, webbing of neck, short stature and ptosis, without chromosomal abnormality.

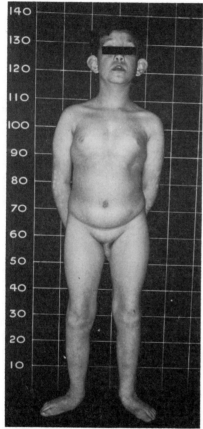

*Fig. 6.38   Noonan's syndrome (Turner-like syndrome) showing neck webbing, hypertelorism and ptosis (Dr Jancar).*

*Numbers and frequency.* Over one hundred males and as many females reported. Said to occur at 1 in 1000 general population (see Turner's syndrome, p. 61).

*Genetics.* Although some families with an autosomal dominant inheritance have been described, abnormalities among relatives may be mild or minimal, and many cases are isolated. No visible chromosome abnormality has been found even with modern band staining techniques.

*Clinical features.* Hypertelorism, ptosis and slanted eyes are common. Some have a webbed neck, others a deformity of the lower sternum. The murmur and right ventricular hypertrophy of pulmonary stenosis may be found. Genital underdevelopment with cryptorchidism in the males is common. There may be scoliosis and kyphosis. Females may also be underdeveloped sexually with delayed puberty.

*CNS*: Most patients have been reported retarded.

*Morbid anatomy.* A variety of congenital cardiac abnormalities have been reported, the most common being pulmonary stenosis.

*Investigations.* Chromosome studies will exclude Turner (XO) syndrome. No biochemical abnormalities have been found.

*Treatment and outcome.* Compatible with good life expectation.

*Diagnosis.* Turner's syndrome is differentiated by the chromosomal typing, and only occurs in females, who are usually dull normal rather than severely retarded, and have gross sexual immaturity.

BIBLIOGRAPHY

Noonan, J. A. & Ehmke, D. A. (1963) Associated noncardiac malformations in children with congenital heart disease. *J. Pediat.*, *63*, 468–70.

## OCULOMANDIBULODYSCEPHALY
### (Hallermann–Streiff syndrome)

Large skull vertex, small face.

*History.* Described by Hallermann in 1948 and Streiff in 1950.

*Numbers and frequency.* Nearly a hundred described.

*Genetics.* Uncertain, but affected siblings have been described. Siblings and monozygotic twins have been affected occasionally but most cases are isolated.

*Clinical features. Head and face*: The cranial sutures and both fontanelles remain open, in one case for 20 years (Falls and Schull 1960). As a result the forehead and sides of the skull appear prominent although the circumference is almost average, all enlargement taking place upwards. The facial bones appear hypoplastic and the nose is small and beaked. The mouth and chin are hypoplastic and receding.

*Ears*: Low set. *Hair*: Thin and sparse. *Eyes*: Often small and with cataracts (90 per cent). Nystagmus and squint are common. *Mouth*: Small;

teeth early, often some are absent; the joints may be stiff.

*Abdomen*: Small penis and testes in males. *Skin*: Over face may be thin with many visible blood vessels.

*CNS*: There is no excess CSF pressure, and only a third or possibly less, are retarded (Suzuki et al. 1970).

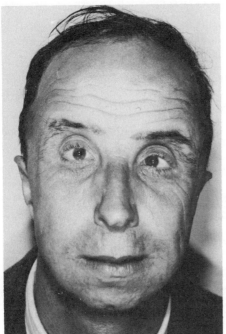

*Fig. 6.39   Oculomandibulodyscephaly (Hallermann–Streiff syndrome) showing large skull vertex, small face and small beaked nose (Dr Jancar).*

*Morbid anatomy.* Occasionally absent testes.

*Treatment.* No specific treatment.

*Further tests.* X-rays show wide sutures and hypoplastic face and mandible. No abnormal sera.

*Diagnosis.* To be distinguished from Cockayne's dwarfism with light-sensitive skin, from Treacher Collins where ear anomalies are more extreme, and from craniocleidodysostosis where mental deficit is uncommon.

BIBLIOGRAPHY

Falls, H. F. & Schull, W. J. (1960) Hallermann–Streiff syndrome. *Archs Ophthal. (Chicago)*, *63*, 409–20.
Suzuki, Y., Fujü, T. & Fukuyama, Y. (1970) Hallermann–Streiff syndrome. *Devl Med. Child Neurol.*, *12*, 496–506.

## ORAL-FACIAL-DIGITAL SYNDROME
### (Papillon syndrome)

Skull vertex appears large, face and mouth grossly abnormal.

*History.* Described by Papillon-Leage and Psaume (1954).

*Numbers and frequency.* Almost a hundred are reported.

*Genetics.* Almost always female, therefore probably a dominant X-linked trait lethal for males, or possibly sex-limited autosomal dominant.

*Clinical features.* Characteristically there is a midline cleft of the upper lip with large nasal bridge and medial canthi displaced laterally. The forehead is prominent and the mid-face appears flattened. The mouth is highly abnormal with lateral incisors often absent, the tip of the tongue split into two or three parts, and pronounced frenulum, a cleft palate and split soft palate with bands and clefts to the side of the mouth. The fingers and toes may show syndactyly, polydactyly or clinodactyly.

*CNS*: Mild subnormality affects up to one half of the series reported (Gorlin and Psaume 1962).

*Morbid anatomy.* Tongue may show haemartomata.

*Further investigation.* The skull X-ray may show a poorly developed mandible and irregularities of the bones of the hands and feet.

*Diagnosis.* This syndrome is distinctive, although the Mohr syndrome has a bifid nasal tip, bifid great toe and hearing loss. This occurs in males as well as females.

BIBLIOGRAPHY

Dodge, J. A. & Kemohan, D. C. (1967) Oral-facial-digital syndrome. *Archs Dis. Childh.*, *42*, 214–19.
Gorlin, R. J. & Psaume, J. (1962) Orodigitofacial dysostosis—a new syndrome. A study of 22 cases. *J. Pediat.*, *61*, 520–30.
Papillon-Leage, Mme & Psaume, J. (1954) Une malformation héréditaire de la muqueuse buccale, brides et freins anormaux: généralities. *Revue Stomat. Chir. maxillofac.*, *55*, 209–27.

### PHENYLKETONURIA (PKU)

'Failure to thrive', fits.

*History.* In 1934 Fölling first described defective patients who excreted phenylpyruvic acid, whilst in 1953 Jervis showed this was due to an inability to metabolize phenylalanine.

*Numbers and frequency.* Commonly around 1 in 14 000 births, but in the United Kingdom varies from 1 in 5000 (Ireland) to less than 1 in 20 000 (SE England). Particularly common in some Gypsy groups.

*Genetics.* Autosomal recessive. Heterozygotes are clinically normal, but can be detected by phenylalanine loading tests. The reasons for the high gene frequency are uncertain; evidence as to reproductive advantage of heterozygotes is conflicting. Most classical cases result from deficiency of the liver enzyme phenylalanine hydroxylase responsible for conversion of phenylalanine to tyrosine. Partial or transient deficiency of this enzyme may produce hyperphenylalaninaemic states detected by screening but without clinical effects. Rare cases result from deficiency of related enzymes (for example, phenylalanine transaminase; dihydropteridine reductase). Heterozygous carriers can usually be identified by being given a high phenylalanine protein diet, which causes a temporarily raised plasma phenylalanine (Westwood and Raine 1975).

*Clinical features.* Often normal, especially with the treated.
*Head and face*: Half the untreated become microcephalic. A light colour of the skin, hair and iris is developed.
*Thorax and abdomen*: Eczema occurs in about a third of those untreated.
*Hair*: This is lighter than other members of the family.
*CNS*: Untreated individuals rarely develop beyond an IQ of 20. They may learn to walk but only a quarter are able to talk. Epilepsy is common.

*Diagnosis.* All infants in Britain and in many other countries are screened in the postnatal period, using a microbiological (Guthrie) or biochemical phenylalanine estimation on capillary blood. Before starting treatment, confirmation of the diagnosis is required by finding a blood phenylalanine greater than 20 mg/dl, and the presence of phenylpyruvic acid and its metabolites in the urine. In symptomatic children suspected of being affected, a positive ferric chloride or phenistix test, followed by urine chromatography, are useful preliminary tests. In tyrosinaemia, a raised phenylalanine may occur but is accompanied by much increased tyrosine. The diet has to be controlled with much care for it is easy to cause neurological damage with variation in diet even up to 7–10 years old. Despite this, a minimum of phenylalanine is essential for the diet, thus proper control is difficult. Too little phenylalanine leads to weight loss, eczema, feeding difficulties and poor

development, too much leads to mental retardation, microcephaly and growth retardation. With successful treatment affected individuals are now beginning to reproduce. While the risk of phenylketonuria in the offspring is small, affected females may have brain-damaged children as a result of transplacental passage of phenylalanine, and will require strict dietary control in pregnancy. Similar cases have

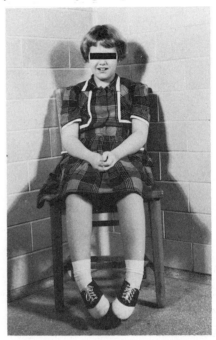

*Fig. 6.40   Phenylketonuria (partially treated) (Dr Kratter).*

resulted from reproduction by the rare untreated women who are only mildly retarded.

*Treatment.* A synthetic phenylalanine diet with sufficient added phenylalanine to supply nutritional requirements allows normal or near normal physical and mental development, if started before the age of two months and well controlled by regular blood phenylalanine measurement. Although dietary control in later childhood need not be so strict there is no general agreement as to when it should be stopped.

BIBLIOGRAPHY

Brown, E. S. & Warner, R. (1976) Mental development of phenylketonuric children on or off diet after age of six. *Psychol. Med.*, 6, 287–96.
Knox, W. E. (1972) Phenylketonuria. In: Stanbury, J. B., Wyngaarden, J. B. & Fredrickson, D. S. (eds.), *The Metabolic Basis of Inherited Disease*, 3rd ed. New York: McGraw Hill.

Westwood, A. & Raine, D. N. (1975) Heterozygote detection in phenylketonuria. *J. med. Genet.*, *12*, 327–33.

Woolf, L. I., McBean, M. S., Woolf, F. M. & Cahalane, S. F. (1975) Phenylketonuria as a balanced polymorphism: the nature of the heterozygote advantage. *Ann. hum. Genet.*, *38*, 4, 461–9.

## PIERRE ROBIN SYNDROME

Small mouth and mandible, small or fused digits.

*History.* Described by Pierre Robin between 1923 and 1934. Probably the result of a number of syndromes, all characterized by small development of the mouth and mandible, with mental retardation as an accompanying feature in some cases.

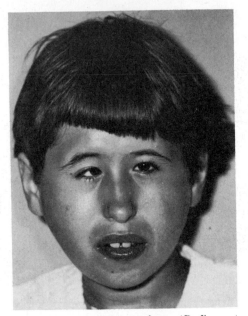

*Fig. 6.41    Pierre Robin syndrome (Dr Jancar).*

*Numbers and frequency.* Nearly 200 patients reported.

*Genetics.* Most cases sporadic, but inheritance will depend on the specific cause.

*Clinical features.* A small receding chin is noted at birth, one third also have eye abnormalities including glaucoma. The ears are low. A markedly underdeveloped mandible allows the tongue to fall back with consequent difficulty in breathing and feeding. Some have a high arched palate. Others have syndactyly, short digits and clubfoot.

*CNS*: Retardation is very variable ranging from all to few, with different series (Sacrez et al. 1967).

*Morbid anatomy.* Heart defects are common.

*Treatment and outcome.* Respiratory and feeding difficulties are the urgent problem in infancy and much nursing and care may have to be done with the infant on its side. Tracheotomy has been needed, also gastrostomy to feed the infant. In some the chin develops to normality, others will need cleft palate operation.

*Diagnosis.* Micrognathia is a feature of the 18 trisomy syndrome and may be one of the features of microcephalus.

### BIBLIOGRAPHY

Sacrez, R., Francfort, J. J., Gigonnet, J. M., Beauvais, P. & Boll, G. (1967) A propos de la débilité intellectuelle et d'anomalies associées à la triade symptomatique du syndrome de Pierre Robin. *Ann. Pediat.*, *14*, 28–33.

Smith, J. L. & Stowe, F. R. (1961) The Pierre Robin syndrome: a review of 39 cases. *Pediatrics*, *27*, 128–33.

## PRADER–LABHART–WILLI SYNDROME
### (Adiposo-hypogenitalism)

Obesity, genital underdevelopment.

*History.* Described by Prader, Labhart and Willi in 1956.

*Numbers and frequency.* Between one and two hundred cases reported. Being poorly defined, it is probably overdiagnosed at present.

*Genetics.* Reported principally in males, the type of inheritance is uncertain. The name designates that form described by Prader, Labhart and Willi, probably recessive in causation. The adiposogenitalis syndrome is a looser term covering a variety of states such as Frohlichs in which fatness and genital underdevelopment are combined, usually with normal intelligence.

*Clinical features. Head and face*: Excessive fat, open mouth, thick saliva and extreme dental caries are reported. *Genitals*: Males have small penis and undescended testicles; females small external genitalia, and amenorrhoea.
   *Chest and trunk*: Grossly obese. *Limbs*: The hands and feet appear small, below lines of fat, the skin is thick.
   *Height and weight*: Height slightly below average in childhood; overeating leads to overweight in adult life.

*CNS*: Muscular hypotonia, delayed milestones, poor speech, broad walking and amiable disposition are reported. Most are moderately retarded.

*Morbid anatomy.* There have been few autopsies and the only real abnormality is testicular atrophy.

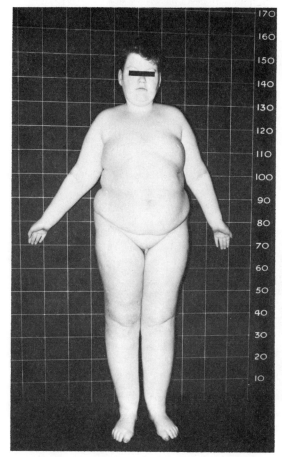

*Fig. 6.42   Prader–Willi syndrome showing obesity and hypogonadism (Dr Jancar).*

*Further investigation.* Some have mild diabetes which responds to insulin and tolbutamide; there is little else positive (Sareen et al. 1975).

*Treatment.* Antidiabetic agents for the diabetes, diet for obesity. Life duration is good, but limited by the obesity.

*Diagnosis.* The Laurence–Moon–Biedl syndrome shows similar features but has polydactyly and retinal degeneration.

BIBLIOGRAPHY

Dunn, H. G. (1968) The Prader–Labhart–Willi syn-

drome: review of the literature and report of nine cases. *Acta paediat., Stockh.*, Supp. *186*, 1–38.

Prader, A., Labhart, A. & Willi, H. (1956) Ein Syndrom von Adipositas, Kleinwuchs, Kryptorchimus und Oligophrenie nach myatonieartigem

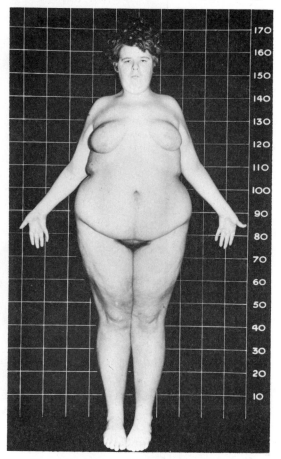

*Fig. 6.43   Prader–Willi syndrome in female (Dr Jancar).*

Zustand im Neugeborenenalter. *Schweiz. med. Wschr.*, *86*, 1260–61.

Sareen, C., Ruvalcaba, R. H. A. & Kelley, V. C. (1975) Some aspects of carbohydrate metabolism in Prader–Willi syndrome. *J. ment. Defic. Res.*, *19*, 113–20.

## RENPENNING'S SYNDROME

No signs.

*History.* Described by Renpenning (1962) and by Davison (1973).

*Genetics.* Believed to be an X-linked cause of non-specific retardation in families. Some writers ascribe to this some of the statistical excess of retardates among males over females.

genes. *Br. J. Psychiat.*, Spec. Pub. No. 8.

Renpenning, H., Gerrard, J. W., Zaleski, W. A. & Tabata, T. (1962) Familial sex-linked mental retardation. *Can. med. Ass. J.*, 87, 954–6.

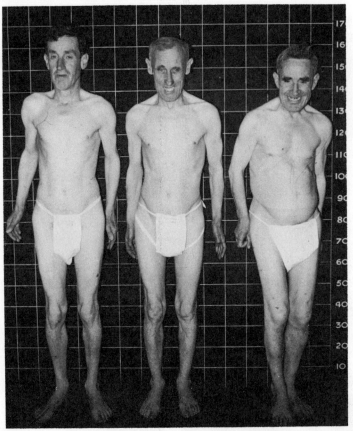

*Fig. 6.44   Renpenning's syndrome (X-linked mental handicap)*
*(Dr Jancar).*

*Clinical features.* Non-specific in nature, thus has no characteristic physical signs, other than a degree of mild mental retardation. In any family where a characteristic pattern of X-linkage can be identified it is important that potential female carriers are advised about the risk to their male offspring.

*Morbid anatomy.* No specific features reported.

*Further investigation.* None.

*Treatment and outcome.* None. Compatible with normal life expectation.

## BIBLIOGRAPHY

Davison, B. C. C. (1973) Genetic studies in mental subnormality. Familial idiopathic severe subnormality: the question of a contribution by X-linked

## RUBINSTEIN–TAYBI SYNDROME

Abnormal facies, broad thumbs and toes.

*History.* Described by Rubinstein and Taybi (1963) as having facial abnormality, broad thumbs and toes and retardation.

*Numbers and frequency.* Over 100 patients reported (Rubinstein 1969).

*Genetics.* Usually sporadic, with no evidence of genetic basis.

*Clinical features. Head*: Features are variable, some being microcephalic, others having hypertelorism. The eyes are set normally but have a downward and outward slant, there may be a beaked nose with ptosis, cataracts and squints. The palate is often high and the teeth irregular. The broad thumbs and big toes are most characteristic, but other digits are often broad with flat wide nails. The thumb or great toe may also be deviated

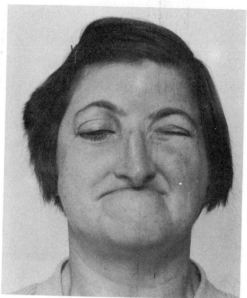

*Fig. 6.45 Rubinstein–Taybi syndrome showing downwards and upwards slanting eyes and ptosis (Dr Sylvester).*

radially. Some patients have excessive dark hair.

*CNS*: All are said to be mentally retarded with epilepsy in one quarter. The tendon reflexes appear to be variable.

*Morbid anatomy.* Defects of the heart have been noted in several autopsies. The corpus callosum has been totally absent in some.

*Further investigation.* Skull X-rays may show delay in closure of the anterior fontanelle. The phalanges are broad. Characteristic dermatoglyphic pattern.

*Treatment and outcome.* Compatible with adult life.

*Diagnosis.* From other causes of combined digital and facial abnormalities.

BIBLIOGRAPHY

Marshall, R. E. & Smith, D. W. (1970) Frontodigital syndrome: a dominantly inherited disorder with normal intelligence. *J. Pediat.*, 77, 129–33.
Naveh, Y. & Friedman, A. (1976) A case of Rubinstein–Taybi. *Clin. Pediat.*, 15, 779–83.
Rubinstein, J. H. & Taybi, H. (1963) Broad thumbs and toes and facial abnormalities. *Am. J. Dis. Child.*, 105, 588–608.

Rubinstein, J. H. (1969) The broad thumb syndrome—progress report 1968. *Birth defects: Original Article Series* 5, No. 2, 25–41. Baltimore: Williams & Wilkins.

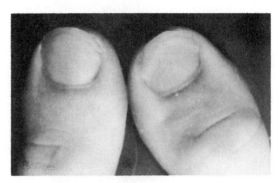

*Fig. 6.46 Rubinstein–Taybi syndrome showing broad thumb (Dr Jancar).*

## SPHINGOMYELIN LIPIDOSIS
(Niemann–Pick disease)

'Failure to thrive', CNS deterioration, splenomegaly.

*History.* Described by Niemann in 1914 and Pick in 1927.

*Numbers and frequency.* Between half and a third are Jewish.

*Genetics.* Autosomal recessive but probably more than one type, most but not all due to lack of enzyme sphingomyelinase. Antenatal diagnosis is feasible.

*Clinical features. Type A*: Rapidly progressive, death usually before two years of age. There is rapid degeneration with hypotonia, splenomegaly, thrombocytopenia, petechiae, a cherry-red macular spot and blindness. The spleen, white blood cells and skin fibroblasts show an absence of spingomyelinase and there is lipid accumulation causing the cytoplasm of affected cells (Niemann–Pick cells) to look large and foaming.

*Type B*: Starts later with enlargement of the liver but the mental state remains normal as does the CNS.

*Type C*: Starts between the ages of two and six; striking CNS changes, with retardation, spasticity and epilepsy, macular degeneration including the cherry-red spot.

*Type D*: Only reported from Nova Scotia, having neonatal jaundice, prominent CNS signs, exaggerated deep tendon reflexes, hypersplenism, retardation and death in adolescence or adult life. In this

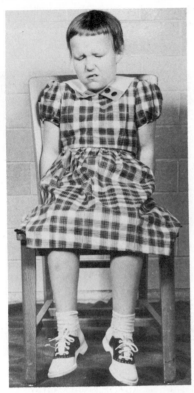

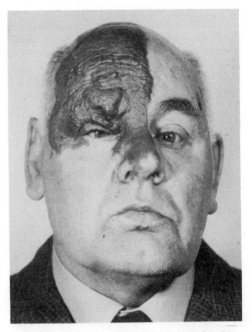

*Fig. 6.48    Sturge–Weber syndrome showing port–wine stain (Dr Sylvester).*

*Fig. 6.47    Sphingomyelin lipidosis showing deterioration.*

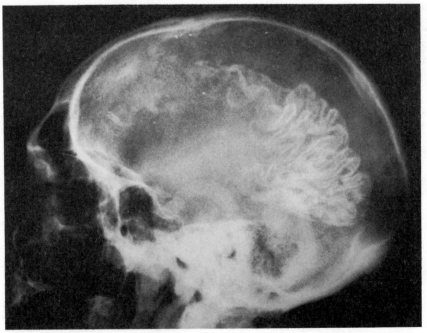

*Fig. 6.49    Sturge–Weber syndrome, X-ray (Dr Sylvester).*

variant the sphingomyelin is increased in the liver but not in the brain.

*Further investigation.* Type A can be differentiated with the specific enzymatic assay.

*Treatment.* No successful treatment yet reported.

BIBLIOGRAPHY

Da Silva, V., Vassella, F., Bischoff, A., Spycher, M., Wiesmann, U. N. & Herschkowitz, N. (1976) Niemann–Pick's disease: clinical biochemical and ultra-structural findings in cases of the infantile form. *J. Neurol.*, *211*, 61–8.

Fredrickson, D. S. & Sloan, H. R. (1972) Sphingo-myelin lipidoses: Niemann–Pick disease. In: Stanbury, J. B., Wyngaarden, J. B. & Fredrick-son, D. S. (eds.), *The Metabolic Basis of Inherited Disease*, 3rd ed. New York: McGraw Hill.

## STURGE–WEBER SYNDROME
### (Port-wine stain)

*History.* Described by Sturge in 1879 and Weber in 1922. The main features are a port-wine stain of the skin over one side of the face, glaucoma on the affected side with spastic hemiparesis and epilepsy.

*Numbers and frequency.* Some hundreds of patients.

*Genetics.* Relatives not affected, not hereditary.

*Clinical features.* The infant presents the port-wine stain over the affected half of the face at birth, usually in one or more of the distributions of the fifth nerve. The colour lessens with adolescence but the skin may become dry. The capillary haem-angioma may also affect the anterior chamber of the eye causing glaucoma. There may be asso-ciated angiomata in the mouth and nose with early eruptions of teeth on the affected side.

CNS: Epilepsy may be frequent, of grand mal type, and associated with status epilepticus. The degree of retardation is very variable, in one series only half were retarded (Peterman et al. 1958).

*Morbid anatomy.* Haemangiomata of skin and the meninges is the main defect. The size of the abnor-mality on the meninges is associated with the degree of retardation and epilepsy. There may be calcifica-tion of the fibrous overgrowth with age. Atrophy of the affected area of the brain follows.

*Further investigation.* There is specific skull X-ray evidence of calcification on the side of the nevus,

the EEG may show decreased amplitude on the side affected with epileptic spike and wave abnor-mality.

*Treatment and outcome.* Removal of intracranial angioma has benefited some with severe epilepsy. Effective anti-epileptic medication is possible.

*Diagnosis.* The extent of the facial nevus is not indicative of the size of that inside the skull. Intra-cranial calcification is also seen in other conditions such as intracranial prenatal infections and tuberous sclerosis.

BIBLIOGRAPHY

Alexander, G. L. & Norman, R. M. (1960) *The Sturge–Weber Syndrome*. Bristol: John Wright & Sons.

Boltshauser, E., Wilson, J. & Hoare, R. D. (1976) Sturge–Weber syndrome with bilateral intra-cranial calcification. *J. Neurol. Neurosurg. Psych-iat.*, *39*, 429–35.

Peterman, A. F., Hayles, A. B., Dockerty, M. B. & Love, J. G. (1958) Sturge–Weber disease: clini-cal study of 35 cases. *J. Am. med. Ass.*, *167*, 2169–76.

## SULPHATIDE LIPIDOSIS
### (metachromatic leukodystrophy)

Late 'failure to thrive', CNS deterioration.

*History.* Described by Witte in 1921.

*Numbers and frequency.* Between 100 and 200 cases described.

*Genetics.* Autosomal recessive. Antenatal diagnosis achieved (Stumpf et al. 1971). Heterozygotes assayed by measuring deficiency of arylsulphatase A activity in fibroblasts. This enzyme is essential to convert sulphatide to cerebroside, and the former accumulates in large metachromatic staining masses.

*Clinical features.* Early development is normal, until in the second or third year when there is difficulty in walking and standing, with later articulation and swallowing defects. The mental deterioration is very slow. In later years the deep reflexes may be diminished or become absent.

Eyes: A steady discolouration of the macula, finally with a red spot like that in Tay–Sachs disease and due to deposition of lipids in retinal cells.

*Morbid anatomy.* The CNS shows extensive loss of myelin and deposition of metachromatic lipids in glial cells and in peripheral nerves.

*Further investigation.* There is deficiency of the enzyme cerebroside sulphatase which consists of two parts: arylsulphatase A which may be assayed, and is an essential element of cerebral lipid metabolism; arylsulphatase B which is deficient in mucopolysaccharidosis type VI. Skin fibroblasts can be used to demonstrate the deficiency.

*Treatment.* Death usually occurs between five and six years of age. A diet low in vitamin A has been used with variable success, on the grounds that it is a cofactor in sulphatide synthesis.

*Diagnosis.* A cerebral space-occupying lesion may have a similar onset and both may have raised CSF protein. A careful history may help to differentiate from brain injury at birth.

BIBLIOGRAPHY

Gustavson, K.-H. & Hagberg, B. (1971) The incidence and genetics of metachromatic leucodystrophy in Northern Sweden. *Acta paediat., Stockh.,* 60, 585–90.

Moser, H. W. (1972) Sulfatide lipidosis: metachromatic leukodystrophy. In: Stanbury, J. B., Wyngaarden, J. B. & Fredrickson, D. S. (eds.), *The Metabolic Basis of Inherited Disease,* 3rd ed. New York: McGraw Hill.

Stumpf, D., Neuwelt, E., Austin, J. & Kohler, P. (1971) Metachromatic leukodystrophy (MLD), X. Immunological studies of the abnormal sulfatase A. *Archs Neurol.,* 25, 427–31.

TUBEROUS SCLEROSIS
(epiloia)

Skin macules, facial butterfly rash, fits.

*Numbers and frequency.* Said to be one in 20 000 to 40 000 live births in USA. The triad of epilepsy, retardation and sebaceous adenoma has long been known.

*Genetics.* Autosomal dominant. Zaremba (1968) calculated one-third, Penrose (1972) one-half of cases to arise by fresh mutations, but parents must be carefully examined before mutation can be accepted.

*Clinical features.* Normal at birth, the infant develops macules of variable size over the trunk, and flesh-coloured nodules on the face and elsewhere by five years of age. The classical butterfly rash of the face is most marked by adolescence when it may be large and indurated. There may be fibromas underneath the nails and up to half may develop retinal nodules. These are small white raised glioses. Less frequent are nodules in the conjunctiva, and cataracts.

*CNS*: In one series one-third were of average intelligence and two-thirds retarded. Most have epilepsy in infancy, which decreases with adolescence. Cerebral astrocytomata are not uncommon (Galant et al. 1976).

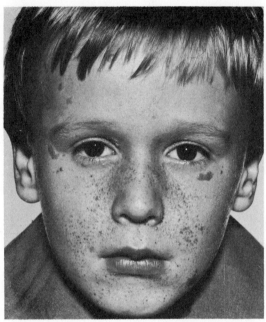

*Fig. 6.50    Tuberous sclerosis (epiloia) showing butterfly rash (Dr Harper).*

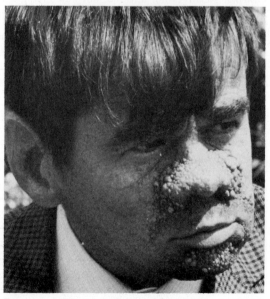

*Fig. 6.51    Tuberous sclerosis showing fully developed facial features.*

*Morbid anatomy.* The brain shows smooth white haemartomata which may be in any part of the brain. In one series rhabdomyomata of the heart caused one-third of the deaths. Kidney haemartomata may be quite large and may interfere in function.

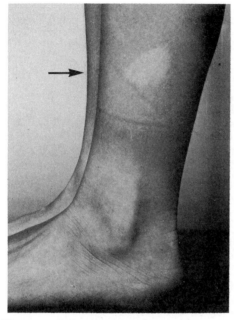

*Fig. 6.52 Tuberous sclerosis showing pigmented patch in leg (Dr Harper).*

*Special investigations.* Skull X-rays often show calcifications in adult life in the basal ganglia, their incidence increases with age. Computerized axial tomography should prove helpful in detecting intracranial lesions. The EEG is usually abnormal and may show specific abnormalities in infancy, such as infantile spasms, macroglobulin level (1 gM) in cases and relatives have been used for genetic counselling (Rundle & Atkin 1976).

*Treatment and outcome.* The degree of retardation is said to vary with the number of abnormalities, as over one-third are of average intelligence and show few abnormalities. Removal of skin lesions may help appearance, internal tumours which are common and which interfere with function may need removal (Galant et al. 1976). Life expectation varies with severity of lesions.

*Diagnosis.* Skull X-ray calcification may be seen in intracranial infections such as herpesvirus, rubella, toxoplasmosis as well as the Sturge–Weber syndrome.

BIBLIOGRAPHY

Galant, S. P., Fowler, G. W., Amin, L., Davis, R. & Fish, C. H. (1976) Immunological status in tuberous sclerosis. *Devl Med. Child Neurol.,* *18*, 503–11.

Pampiglione, G. & Maynahan, E. J. (1976) The tuberous sclerosis syndrome: clinical and EEG studies in 100 children. *J. Neurol. Neurosurg. Psychiat.,* *39*, 666–73.

Paulson, G. W. & Lyle, C. B. (1966) Tuberous sclerosis. *Devl Med. Child Neurol.,* *8*, 571–86.

Penrose, L. S. (1972) *The Biology of Mental Defect,* 4th ed. London: Sidgwick & Jackson.

Rundle, A. T. & Atkin, J. (1976) Serum X2 macroglobulin levels in tuberous sclerosis. *J. ment. Defic. Res.,* *20*, 231–6.

Zaremba, J. (1968) Tuberous sclerosis: a clinical and genetic investigation. *J. ment. Defic. Res.,* *12*, 63–80.

## XERODERMA PIGMENTOSUM

Light sensitivity, microcephaly, CNS signs.

*History.* Reported by Hebra and Kaposi in 1874 as a skin syndrome with freckles, excess sensitivity to light and a subsequent tendency to develop skin cancer. In 1932 de Sanctis and Cacchione described such individuals who also developed microcephaly, severe retardation and gonadal dystrophy.

*Numbers and frequency.* At least 500 described, frequency unknown.

*Genetics.* Autosomal recessive; prenatal diagnosis is possible (Regan et al. 1971) using thymidine incorporation into ultraviolet-exposed amniotic cells. Recognition of the failure of DNA repair following damage by U-V light has led to identification of several distinct types, and further heterogeneity is likely to be shown in the future.

*Clinical features.* What appear to be freckles occur on exposure to light in infancy, and over the years become more pronounced with more sun. They fuse and extend over several centimetres in length and width. The centres atrophy, become white and develop pedunculated growths. In adult life they become cancerous and bleed. Eyes become photophobic, develop excessive tears and the eyelid may atrophy. There may be corneal ulceration. Genitals may be underdeveloped.

CNS: In one study half were severely handicapped, others were microcephalic, spastic and had ataxia (El-Hefnawi et al. 1967).

*Morbid anatomy.* The skin is grossly atrophic.

*Further investigation.* The group of endonuclease enzymes, essential for repair of skin and replication of DNA, are deficient. On exposure to ultraviolet light or introdermal injection of tritiated thymidine there is a lack of DNA synthesis in a skin biopsy.

*Treatment and outcome.* Sunlight exposure is deleterious and thus to be avoided. U-V barrier creams should be used. Cancers should be excised, where feasible.

*Diagnosis.* To be distinguished from the basal cell multiple nevus syndrome, which occurs in people of normal intelligence and does not cause such extensive areas of atrophy of the skin. Xeroderma pigmentosum is the first of a now rapidly growing group of genetic disorders of DNA repair, and it is of interest that mental retardation is a common feature of many of these disorders (for example,

Fanconi's anaemia, ataxia telangiectasia, Cockayne dwarfism).

BIBLIOGRAPHY

El-Hefnawi, H., Gawad, M. S. A. & Rasheed, A. (1967) Neuropsychiatric manifestations in xeroderma pigmentosum. *Gaz. Egypt. Soc. Derm. Vener.*, *2*, 6–22.

Epstein, W. I., Fukuyama, K. & Epstein, J. H. (1969) Early effects of ultraviolet light on DNA synthesis in human skin *in vitro*. *Archs Derm.*, *100*, 84–9.

Holton, J. B. & Ireland, J. T. (eds.) (1975) *Inborn Errors of Skin, Hair and Connective Tissue.* Lancaster: Medical and Technical Publishing Co. [for review of skin anomalies]

Regan, J. D., Setlow, R. B., Kaback, M. M., Howell, R. R., Klein, E. & Burgess, G. (1971) Xeroderma pigmentosum: a rapid sensitive method for prenatal diagnosis. *Science*, *174*, 147–50.

# CHAPTER 7

# ACQUIRED CONDITIONS

## PETER SYLVESTER AND MICHAEL CRAFT

Brain and systemic injury due to physical harm at birth, infection or noxious agents, account for up to a quarter of those who are severely mentally and multiply handicapped. They comprise some of the most frequent causes. With improved antenatal, natal and postnatal care the frequency of their contribution has been declining over the last century. However, they are much more frequent as etiological agents among social class V than among social class I in all developed countries. This morbidity gradient from class V through to class I has remained constant throughout the twentieth century. It appears that severity and frequency of exposure to causal and adverse conditions of child rearing and child care have much to do with the degree of resulting damage.

This chapter deals with causes which are known to occur during three critical phases—the prenatal, perinatal and postnatal periods of fetal and childhood life. Emphasis is placed on preventative as well as therapeutic measures. The important subject of oxygen deprivation (anoxia and hypoxia) is considered under perinatal causes for convenience, but it should be appreciated that it can occur in all three periods of life.

The pattern of causes leading to mental handicap is changing. Diseases which were common several years ago—congenital syphilis, kernicterus and phenylketonuria—are now rare. There is evidence that genetic counselling is beginning to make an impact on the incidence of Down's syndrome. A frequently quoted incidence of 1 per 660 live births has become 1 per 1042 for the London Borough of Croydon from 1974 to 1977. On the other hand, some new conditions are being recognized, notably children who suffer brain damage from violent abuse. In a highly technical world with problems of pollution, risks from harmful intoxicants can be a hidden threat to the health of the developing brain, even well-known poison such as lead is still linked with mental handicap, whilst the association of alcoholism and smoking with retardation is now being verified.

Research, in many countries, has played a highly significant part in determining causes of mental handicap and seeking ways of preventing it. Specific infections have been controlled by better hygienic measures and specific treatment following the discovery of penicillin and development of appropriate vaccines. An era of biochemical exploration and genetic and cytogenetic discovery has made enormous contributions to knowledge and prevention over the past 30 years. This information is now being applied clinically. There have been spurts of interest into causes associated with maternal health, fetal security within the uterus and complications arising at birth. However, a revival of interest in these problems has started. Obstetric prevention of mental handicap still has much to contribute, as pointed out by Rhodes (1973). New techniques of monitoring pregnant women and their fetuses are being discovered and developed. Armed with a large array of new opportunities the obstetrician will be able to increase his level of suspicion as to when difficulties are likely to arise, and to take appropriate counter measures.

## PRENATAL CAUSES

### ADVERSE FACTORS IN MATERNAL ENVIRONMENT

A pregnancy in which the uterus is either too large or too small for the appropriate period of gestation, may indicate either hydramnios or multiple pregnancy or an abnormal-sized fetus from which mental handicap may result. Premature rupture of the membranes carries the risk of infection to the

affecting the development of the fetus are the following:

*Maternal age.* Expectant mothers in the latter half of their reproductive period, that is to say, over the age of 35, run an increased risk of conceiving a child with Down's syndrome. Mothers in the same age group are more prone to bear a child with hydrocephalus, spina bifida or hydranencephaly.

*The thyroid gland.* It is well known that lack

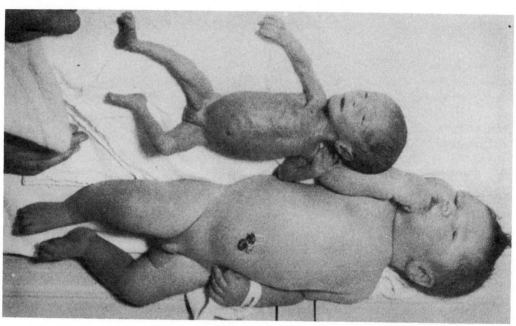

Fig. 7.1 *Small-for-dates baby (top) contrasted with baby born to diabetic mother (Dr Harper).*

contents of the womb. Prolonged or precipitate labour and premature separation of the placenta increase the risk of anoxia and intracranial haemorrhage. Abnormal presentation constitutes a hazard to the child, particularly when the presentation is a breech where manipulative procedures and insufficient time for moulding of the head increase the risk of intracranial bleeding. Infants born by Caesarean section are exposed to increased risks of brain damage from anoxia for a variety of reasons which may include prematurity, prolonged labour, abnormal lie, fetal distress and the risks of anaesthesia.

Among the more important specific factors

of iodine in the diet can cause endemic goitre and that women with this condition are prone to bear children with cretinism. Fortunately this situation is easily prevented by giving small amounts of iodine in deficient diets, thus endemic cretinism is now rare.

Maternal thyrotoxicosis has been linked with congenital defects of the brain (porencephaly) and mental handicap in the offspring. Neonatal hypothyroidism has been reported in thyrotoxic mothers who have received antithyroid drugs during pregnancy.

*Pancreas.* Women with diabetes mellitus run a risk above the average of having mentally handicapped children, especially if they have episodes of acetonuria during pregnancy. Insulin coma therapy used in psychiatry if applied during early pregnancy has been linked with brain damage and mentally handicapped children.

*Drugs.* Drugs may act (1) directly on the fetus causing damage (thalidomide, anticancer drugs), (2) on the placenta (hydroxytryptamine is believed to be vasoconstrictive to placental vessels), and (3) on the uterus (fetal anoxia is thought to result from drugs causing vasoconstriction in the maternal blood supply). Apart from medical prescriptions there is the problem of self-administered medication in pregnancy such as alcohol and cigarettes.

It has been found that the mothers producing infants with congenital abnormalities indulged in a greater variety of drugs including aspirin, antacids, amphetamine, barbiturates, iron, cough mixtures and sulfonamides during early pregnancy, than did those of a control group of mothers who produced infants without malformations. It would not be wise to conclude that the drugs were necessarily the cause of the defects. A disease process may well account for the deformities as might also some idiosyncrasy of fetal tissue to the drugs. Nevertheless, administration of drugs to the pregnant woman is a hazard to be avoided. Their exclusion may make it easier to reveal the true causes of abnormal fetuses. Anaesthesia and analgesia during labour can also affect the fetus. Mild maternal hypoxia or hypertension may result in severe fetal hypoxia. The situation can be aggravated if the fetus is premature and suffers from anoxia or injury.

There are now 1500 substances, many classified as 'drugs' known to be teratogenic. Many of their mechanisms are still uncertain, but some such as aminopterin, warfarin and ethyl alcohol affect the brain and body, others such as thalidomide, the body only. Just as in genetic misendowments, the result of a noxious substance on the developing fetus is probably a complex inter-reaction. Variables include genetic sensitivity, various protective genetic mechanisms or available alternative biochemical pathways for potential toxins, the timing and strength of the toxin, and chance environmental factors which may compound or alleviate the damage such as intercurrent infection. Anticonvulsants, particularly phenytoin and phenobarbitone, have been incriminated as causes of microcephaly, congenital heart defects and facial clefts.

*Alcohol.* Although not usually classed as a drug, alcohol has now been shown to affect fetuses when drunk to excess by the pregnant woman (Mulvihill et al. 1976). It also appears to be teratogenic (Chernoff 1975). There have been several papers recently showing that the 'fetal alcohol syndrome' is most common in women drinking the equivalent of over a bottle of wine daily (50 ml alcohol). At this level, Jones et al. (1973) showed that among a series of 23 such babies 4 died, 13 were 'very small' and 6 were malformed, whilst out of a series of 12 such infants Ulleland (1972) found 11 small for dates. In a series by Shruygin (1974) half the children born to 'alcoholic' mothers were mentally retarded.

The 'fetal alcohol syndrome' shows microcephaly, mental retardation, maxillary hypoplasia, with prominent forehead and lower jaw, short palpebral fissures, small eyes and epicanthic folds, squint and unilateral ptosis. They are short and light for dates and the growth potential is poor. There is 'failure to thrive', tremulousness, unresponsiveness to sedation, incoordination and poor motor performance. Congenital heart disease is common, the ears are simple, there is stiffness of some joints and two cases had hirsutism. Some have previously been misdiagnosed as Cornelia de Lange syndrome, trisomy 18, even Noonan's syndrome.

Treatment has to be preventative for further children. Removal of affected infants to foster parents has not prevented subsequent retardation developing. It must be remembered that social alcoholic intake is not damaging, the mother has to be consistent in her alcoholic intake in early pregnancy to affect her fetus, consuming the equivalent of a bottle of wine daily, that is 45 ml absolute alcohol daily (*Br. Med. J.* 1978).

*Cigarette-smoking.* Smoking during pregnancy is linked with an increased risk of abortion; surviving infants are likely to be small and run the risk of increased neonatal mortality.

Mechanisms involved are probably multiple. Vasoconstriction of placental and uterine vessels, interference with respiratory enzymes and an elevated carboxyhaemoglobin (CO) content with reduced oxygen-carrying capacity of the blood may be important factors. The sort of risks that infants face in these circumstances are likely to result in suppressed mental function if they survive.

*Excess vitamin D.* Vitamin D in excess during pregnancy has been identified as causing the 'elfin-face' syndrome. Some 300 examples have been reported (Fraser et al. 1966). The elf-like face is characteristic, affected infants having an upturned nose, low prominent ears, a small chin and wide mouth. Premature closure of the cranial synostoses may give the head a small, neat look. X-rays show transverse bands in the metaphyses, with deposits of calcium in the kidneys, blood vessels and bronchi. Severity of mental retardation seems to be directly proportional to the degree of hypercalcaemia induced by the excess vitamin D. The high infantile blood level of calcium is characteristic, although it tends to decrease with time. Unfortunately, the damage to the sensitive brain tissue will have been effected by this time.

*X-ray.* X-ray irradiation of the unborn child is well known to be associated with microcephaly and mental handicap. Nowadays X-ray departments try to avoid examination of women with early pregnancies, for the seventh to fifteenth weeks of gestation appear to be critical. This period was important in the atomic bomb explosions over Nagasaki and Hiroshima when the incidence of the defects was found to be related to the intensity of the radiation and gestational age of the unborn child.

CONGENITAL DEFECTS OF THE
CENTRAL NERVOUS SYSTEM
LINKED WITH MENTAL HANDICAP

*Congenital hydrocephalus.* The incidence of all cases of hydrocephalus in a Swedish survey was 0.68 per 1000 live births. Hydrocephalus and spina bifida cystica occurred in 0.49 per 1000 live births. The total incidence of spina bifida cystica was 0.72 per 1000 live births

(Hagberg et al. 1963). Since some examples of hydrocephalus are believed genetic in causation, this subject was discussed in Chapter 6 (pp. 88–90).

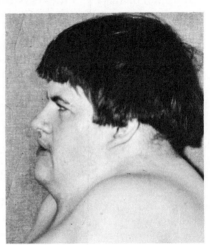

Fig. 7.2    Cranium bifidum with encephalocele
(Dr Jancar).

*Neural tube defects.* Congenital fissurings of the skull and spinal column (craniorachischisis) are linked with incomplete midline fusion of the primary neural tube (dysraphia). Mesodermal as well as ectodermal tissues are involved in the deformity. A variety of anomalies occur ranging from mild *spina bifida* in which the fault is covered by skin and soft tissue, to life-limiting complete rachischisis.

A number of conditions showing different permutations of congenital cleft defects are linked with mentally and physically handicapped children.

Anencephaly is an extreme form which is non-viable but encephaloceles (see also Fig. 7.4) occurring in either frontal, parietal, occipital or occipitocervical regions and spina bifida are the principal deformities. Spina bifida commonly affects the lumbosacral region. Meningoceles and myelomeningoceles are the manifestations. The neural tube defects may be protected by complete closure of the overlying skin. More serious problems arise when the skin is incompletely closed and the meninges and spinal cord defects are exposed, thus increasing the risk of infection. The deformity often results in the protrusion of a sac containing CSF and is then referred to as *cystic spina bifida*.

Spina bifida (lacking mental retardation) tends to show a geographical distribution in the UK being more common in Ireland and Wales than in England.

## CONGENITAL DEFORMITIES OF THE CEREBRAL HEMISPHERES

Other congenital defects affecting the brain

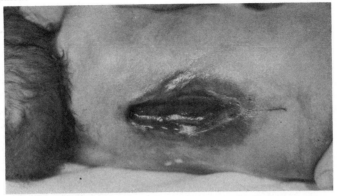

*Fig. 7.3   Spina bifida (Dr Sylvester).*

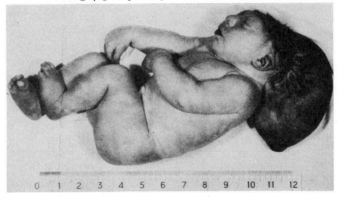

*Fig. 7.4   Stillbirth with anencephaly (Dr Sylvester).*

Diagnosis can be made prenatally firstly by estimating the alphafetoprotein content of the amniotic fluid and maternal blood, and secondly by an ultrasonic scan of the fetus. Anencephaly can be diagnosed in this way, and probably some of the more severe spinal deformities. Postnatally, radiography of the spine assists in assessing the size of the defects.

Treatment can be by surgical repair. Early surgery reduces the risk of infection. Treatment may be needed for complications, such as orthopaedic help for physical deformities, physiotherapy, special education in later life and help with psychological and psychosexual problems as the patient gets older.

Motor deficits may be one sequel, with disturbances of the urethra and sphincters.

are less clearly understood. Whatever the cause may be there are disturbances in the growth and development of the brain which result in mental handicap. The brains of mentally handicapped people are, on the whole, lighter in weight than those of the non-handicapped. Congenital abnormalities contribute to this deficit. Micrencephaly and megalencephaly are two extremes in brain size, but other congenital abnormalities are also important.

*Micrencephaly.* True micrencephaly is a condition in which the cerebral hemispheres are small and the gyral pattern extremely simplified and the weight under 900 g. The cerebellum tends to be normal in size. True micrencephaly is inherited by autosomal recessive means. Other forms of micrencephaly are secondary to brain atrophy following a variety of diseases including pre- and postnatal infections, phenylketonuria and amaurotic family idiocy.

*Megalencephaly.* Megalencephaly is the term usually applied to large brains weighing over 1800 g which are occasionally seen in the mentally handicapped. In some instances the brain is normal in structure but in other instances there is additional pathology such as diffuse glial proliferation, tuberous sclerosis, cerebral lipidosis, degenerative diseases of the white matter or ectopia of grey matter.

*Prosencephaly.* Prosencephaly is a condition in which the telencephalon has not divided and the lateral ventricles are fused into one single ventricle. Minor forms of the deformity are seen. Cyclopia, hypotelorism, absence of the pituitary and aplasia of the nasal bones are additional features. Chromosomal abnormalities including D & E trisomies and deficiency of part of the short arm of chromosome 18, have been described with severe forms.

*Porencephaly.* In porencephaly there is cavitation of the cerebrum. The cavity is lined by ependyma and extends from the lateral ventricles to the surface of the hemisphere. A severe form, schizencephaly, is bilateral. Other malformations such as heterocopias and microgyria frequently border the cavity. Porencephaly is an arrested developmental defect of the pallium, to be distinguished from cavities which occur secondarily to other pathology.

*Arhinencephaly.* Arhinencephaly is a condition in which the olfactory bulbs and tracts have failed to form. The deformity can involve other territories of the rhinencephalon and complete absence of the corpus callosum. Prosencephaly may appear in combination with this condition. Chromosome anomalies particularly the Cri-du-chat syndrome have been associated with arhinencephaly.

*Agenesis of the corpus callosum.* This can be partial or complete. It can occur on its own or in conjunction with other deformities. The corpus callosum starts development from a thick mass in the precommissural area connecting the two hemispheres of the fetal brain. It grows and develops caudally from the genu to form the body and splenium and its formation is usually complete about the eighth month of fetal life.

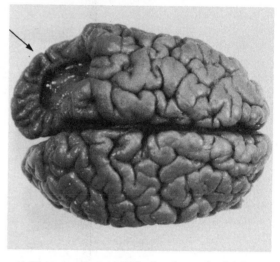

*Fig. 7.5   Porencephaly showing cavitation in occipital lobe (Dr Sylvester).*

*Cortical malformations.* These are due to disturbances in the migration of primitive neuroblasts in the embryo leading to a variety of abnormal gyral patterns. Microgyria or micropolygyria is the commonest. As its name implies there are many minute gyri. Macrogyria or pachygyria is the opposite type of malformation in which there are too few gyri. In extreme examples gyri are absent altogether (agyria or lissencephaly). Lamination of cortical neurones in these conditions is simplified and only four layers can be identified. Micropolygyria can also affect the cerebellum as well as the cerebral cortex.

*Ectopia.* Ectopia refers to masses of grey matter containing neurones, neuroglia, capillaries and blood vessels which are seen in the white matter of the area semiovale adjacent to the caudate nucleus. They can also be found in the cerebellar white matter and the brain stem. They occur in conjunction with other congenital deformities such as megalencephaly. Ectopic grey matter in the cerebellum has been seen in chromosomal defects such as D-trisomy, D-ring chromosomal anomaly and around the lateral ventricles in E-trisomy.

The cause of congenital malformations of the brain is largely undetermined. Some syndromes are obvious at birth (such as microcephaly), others become clear later. There are many factors to be considered including genetic and cytogenetic factors, effects of maternal age and infections and maternal diabetes mellitus. Drugs and anoxia can also be related to deformed brains on occasions.

## INTRAUTERINE INFECTIONS

### Bacterial infections

*Septic meningitis.* The incidence is 0.46 per 1000 live births. Infection may be due to either gram-positive or gram-negative organisms. The prognosis is poor.

*Listeria.* This is a bacterial infection in pregnancy. It can reach the fetus through the placenta or through ascending infection causing choreoamnionitis leading to fetal infection and meningoencephalitis. The diagnosis is difficult because serological tests and cultures are unreliable. Antibiotic treatment may be effective. Prevention is achieved by early diagnosis and treatment of the mother.

*Mycoplasma infection.* There is a high incidence of small-for-dates babies born to expectant mothers carrying this infection. Such small infants run the risk of mental handicap shared by other small-for-dates babies.

*Syphilis.* Congenital syphilis has been known for a long time. It decreased in frequency with the advent of penicillin. Recently it has become more common and seems to be increasing. The incidence is 0.12 to 0.2 per 1000 live births.

Transplacental infection does not apparently occur until the second trimester and depends on the severity and length of the mother's infection and degree of her protective antibodies. This is the reason for the old observation of early fetal deaths, later stillbirths, infected infants and normal infants. If the mother is treated early, results are good. Severely infected infants are premature, wizened and develop a purulent nasal discharge in a week or so. There is thrombo-

cytopenic purpuric rash and mucous condylomata round the mouth and anus. There may be meningitis, osteochondritis and other affections of the bone and cartilages with much pain. Children show retardation, epilepsy, a saddle nose deformity and tooth hypoplasia.

Neurosyphilis with its various manifes-

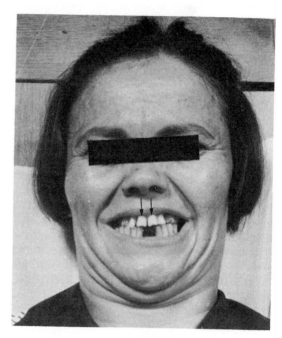

*Fig. 7.6  Congenital syphilis showing abnormal teeth (Dr Kratter).*

tations may begin from late childhood depending on how severe the infection and the antibody production. Other signs of adult syphilis may develop with age. Syphilitic signs of infection may cause widespread fibrosis. Usual blood serology tests are performed with mother or newborn, with darkfield examination for spirochetes using material from umbilical cord, skin or condylomata.

The treatment is intensive penicillin, now needing high dosage, which is still very effective. There may be permanent brain damage even with treatment at birth. The avoidance of infection, and early treatment of expectant mothers, is the best prevention. The diagnosis is from rubella, cytomegalovirus and herpesvirus as well as bacterial sepsis as above.

### Protozoal infections

*Toxoplasmosis.* Toxoplasmosis was first reported by Wolf, Cowen and Paige (1939).

The incidence is said to be 1 per 1000 live births in France (Couvreur & Desmonts 1962). Toxoplasma gondii is a protozoan parasite which is widespread in the environment. The infection is rarely serious in the adult but can cause brain damage in the fetus. As a transplacental infection of the fetus from the infection there may be widespread destruction with granulomata through the body, in all organs, including the brain. Hydrocephalus results from occlusion of the midbrain aqueduct.

The organism can be demonstrated by serology using antibody tests, which show a rising

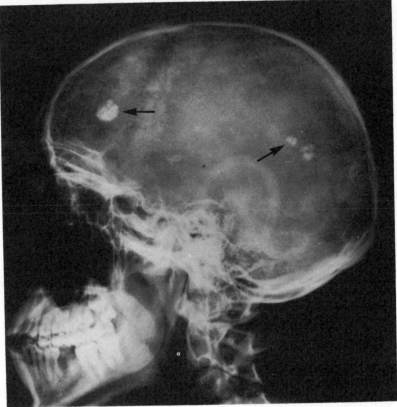

*Fig. 7.7    Toxoplasmosis showing calcified nodules in brain (Dr Jancar).*

the mother there may be early abortion or stillbirth or survival of a damaged infant as in other parental infections. In Couvreur and Desmonts' (1962) review of 300 infants one quarter had microcephaly or hydrocephalus, two thirds had chorioretinitis affecting the macula and elsewhere in the retina. Cataracts, glaucoma, optic atrophy and microphthalmia have been reported. The cause is eating raw or undercooked meat and ingesting faeces of infected cats. The liver and spleen may be enlarged and there may be thrombocytopenia with purpura or jaundice. Epilepsy is common and there may be spasticity, deafness and a variable degree of retardation together with hydrocephalus. Depending on the severity of

titre with active infection. Antibodies persist for many years, which may be of use in diagnosis in later childhood. Cerebral calcification in skull X-rays were present in 32 per cent in a series of 300 patients. Sulphadiazine and pyrimethamine have been recommended for treatment; the latter is a folic acid antagonist.

Prevention concerns the avoidance of undercooked meat; good hygienic measures in dealing with cat faeces; early treatment of infected expectant mothers. Differential diagnosis is from rubella, syphilis, cytomegalovirus and herpesvirus as above. Intracranial calcifications are also present in a variety of conditions such as tuberous sclerosis and herpesvirus.

## Viral infections

*Rubella.* Rubella (German measles) was first outlined by Gregg in 1941. The 1964–65 epidemic in the United States in which 30 000 infants were affected also showed that 15 per cent of mothers infected in the first three

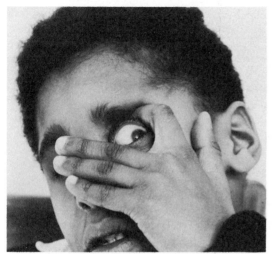

*Fig. 7.8 Rubella child manipulating blind eye to gain maximal light (Dr Sylvester).*

months of pregnancy had spontaneous abortions and some fetuses born live were seriously affected. At the other end of the continuum, many have no defects ascertainable in early infancy. This continuum might be expected from natural variation in the degree of infection, host-resistance and other chance variables. The incidence is 0.25 to 0.3 per 1000 live births.

Cataracts occurred in one-third of a major review of 376 children (Cooper et al. 1969), retinopathy in 147, glaucoma in 12; the cataracts were believed to result from the virus being in the lens. Microphthalmia may also occur. Retinopathy is usually non-progressive.

The liver and spleen are usually enlarged with an increased incidence of indirect inguinal herniae. In the major study above (Cooper et al. 1969) ecchymoses were present in one-quarter due to thrombocytopenia. These are usually gone at ten days of age although the platelet count may continue reduced. The most severely affected are low in weight but weight may be gained later.

In the major review of 376 patients one half had psychomotor retardation varying from slight to gross with quadriplegia. Deafness was found in two-thirds including a fifth in which this was the sole sign. The degree of loss was very variable.

The brain weight was markedly low in severe cases, less so in those near average size. In order of frequency the major congenital abnormalities included the heart and great vessels, giant cell hepatitis, renal damage and fibrosis of the spleen.

The virus has been isolated from all tissues of affected infants. The virus continues to be excreted for some months of early life. Even at three years of age cataracts have yielded rubella virus. In the pregnant woman the quickest and most effective test is the complement fixation test using acute or convalescent serum. There is no antibiotic for rubella virus and in general the more severe the infection the greater the damage to the child. Cardiac, eye and hearing defects should be investigated as soon as possible, with the removal of cataracts when the eyes are of adequate size.

Prevention is now possible using attenuated vaccines. Prenatal diagnosis is now possible (Cederquist et al. 1977). Diagnosis is from toxoplasmosis, syphilis, cytomegalic-inclusion virus, herpes and bacterial infections.

*Cytomegalic-inclusion virus infection.* Between one and three per cent of pregnant mothers excrete cytomegalic virus (Birnbaum et al. 1969). However, urinary excretion of virus by infants is not necessarily associated with signs of infection and many develop normally. Others develop neurologic damage later. The incidence is 0.5 to 1.0 per 1000 live births.

The infant may appear normal at birth or may develop microcephaly then or later. Microphthalmia, optic atrophy and chorioretinitis have been reported. Sinha et al. (1972) found 38 per cent of microcephalics positive on complement fixation in Wisconsin Colony, compared with 7 per cent of control residents. The liver and spleen may be enlarged at birth or later. Inguinal herniae are common. Jaundice may be present with a thrombocytopenic rash. Seriously affected infants are both short and small at birth.

Meningoencephalitis with seizures may occur, although Starr et al. (1970) found that only two out of 26 with viraemia showed definite CNS signs. However, one-third of another series (McCracken et al. 1969) of 18 infected had later retardation with hyperactivity, spasticity and deafness. At autopsy inclusion-bearing cells are found widely throughout the body. Subarachnoid haemorrhages, scattered areas of necrosis and periventricular calcification may be found in the brain. Nephritis and hepatitis are common.

The viral isolation and cytomegalic IgM macroglobulin fluorescent antibody test is positive. However, this latter may not detect non-affected excretors of virus. Cerebral calcification may appear in skull X-rays.

Anti-viral agents are of doubtful value, according to the review by Illis (1975).

Prevention is difficult, active immunization is being explored.

Congenital syphilis and herpesvirus also cause jaundice at birth together with icterus gravis. Skull calcification on X-ray may also be present in toxoplasmosis as well as tuberous sclerosis.

*Laboratory diagnosis of infectious agents* concerns (1) the isolation or identification of infectious agents by culture microscopy, dark ground fluorescence or electron microscopy; (2) the determination of IgM in cord blood; (3) the determination of specific IgM fraction; (4) a persistence of infantile antibody level beyond that normally expected from maternal transmission of antibodies.

### PRENATAL INVESTIGATIONS

*Amniocentesis* is performed during the tenth to fourteenth week of pregnancy to obtain fetal cells for tissue culture, fluid for chemical analysis, and to define the cytogenetic problems or inborn errors of metabolism. It has been possible to diagnose about 20 different conditions of the unborn child in this way. The best known example is Down's syndrome and certain storage diseases of the nervous system. Amniotic fluid can also be used to determine the need for fetal transfusion and to assess the timing of delivery in fetuses with haemolytic disease of the newborn. A raised alphafetoprotein level may indicate anencephaly and spina bifida malformations.

*Ultrasonography (Sonar)* or ultrasonic sound waves of short wavelength have proved valuable in safely outlining the position of the fetus and placenta. Certain structural abnormalities, particularly those of the head and multiple pregnancies, can be defined. Gestational age can be estimated fairly accurately by measuring the biparietal diameter of the fetal head. The measurement correlates well with fetal weight.

*Electrocardiography* of the fetus is now possible and is used to assess the heart rate and observe arrhythmias of fetal heart and therefore define fetal distress at an early stage.

### PERINATAL CAUSES

#### PREMATURITY AND LOW BIRTH WEIGHT

Among the variables 'small for dates', low birth weight, short gestation, precipitate birth and multiple birth, associated with mental retardation, it seems probable that a multifactorial causation is more likely than just one variable.

Prematurity, defined as low birth weight (see pp. 13, 125), has always been known to be associated with high stillbirth, neonatal mortality and morbidity rates. Only recently have many of the variables at issue been disentangled (*Br. med. J.* 1978a). For example, tobacco, alcohol, drug ingestion, perinatal infections and maternal bonding have all now been shown to be individually and independently related to low birth weight, neonatal mortality and mental retardation. They are discussed elsewhere in this chapter. In addition, there is a statistically significant relationship for neonatal mortality and morbidity with mental retardation between social classes in all developed countries, social class V having higher morbidity than social class I (Drillien 1964, p. 13). Other variables are themselves related to social classes. There is a greater consumption of tobacco in social class V than I, perinatal infections and drug ingestion are also related. The variable most clearly associated with mental retardation and neonatal morbidity is low birth weight. In Britain over two-thirds of all deaths in the first week following birth occur with babies of less than 2500 g.

Within 49 430 USA live births, Churchill et al. (1974) found 856 (1.7 per cent) weighing less than 2 kg. Rhodes' (1973) estimate was higher, at 7 per cent of infants weighing less than 2.5 kg; he calculated that 2000 to 3000 infants may ultimately be handicapped annually in England and Wales from this cause. Forty-four (5 per cent) were found to have spastic diplegia and varying degrees of retardation at one year old; seven born by Caesarean section were affected, but none of the 199 believed to have had gestations over 36 weeks. Compared with a control group for variables such as genetic factors, birth trauma, asphyxia, infective factors and prenatal maternal factors, the only significant finding was high haematocrit findings in the spastic, suggestive of intracranial bleeding. So this study, as others, suggests a multifactorial rather than unifactorial causation, remembering that the degree of retardation that subsequently develops in brain-damaged infants owes much to environmental stimulation and nourishment or its absence.

Roughly two out of three infants delivered at 28 weeks are handicapped, whereas only one in three at 32 to 34 weeks is affected. A similar gradient applies to birth weight, 85 per cent of children weighing 950 g or less are seriously damaged. Among those weighing 1300 to 1500 g the incidence is 35 per cent (Lubchenko et al. 1972). Children in the range 1500 to 2500 g are more likely to function as retarded or demonstrate learning disabilities, if they are members of the lower social class than if they are middle class (Douglas 1956).

Part of the answer to alleviating this damage lies in improved antenatal care, and part in the provision of intensive care units. With these, survival rates can be improved to 50 per cent for infants of 750 to 1000 g and 70 per cent for infants of 1001 to 1500 g. Neonatal survival statistics, even more so morbidity statistics, have to be interpreted with care, since so much depends on the type of assessment and the time after birth it is made, but dramatic improvements have occurred. For instance, the incidence of cerebral palsy has been reduced to 0 to 5 per cent, the incidence of serious visual disturbance (usually retrolental fibroplasia) previously 10 to 30 per cent, reduced; and sensorineural deafness, previously affecting 10 per cent has been reduced to 0 to 10 per cent, varying between treatment units (*Br. med. J.* 1978b).

Intensive-care resuscitation units are still uncommon in Britain, and are extremely expensive. Yet the cost per child rescued is less than the cost of caring for lifetime handicap. They may be run on a regional or area basis and depend for their success on effective antenatal care and fetal monitoring, on effective mechanical ventilation and speedy transit for babies in need, and a high ratio of intensively trained staff paying meticulous care to detail. Incipient or established respiratory-distress infants need intubation by those trained in intubating a very small trachea; transpyloric or total intravenous feeding is commonly needed as also is continuous temperature monitoring, and frequent monitoring of blood glucose, bilirubin, electrolytes and antibiotics. Frequent estimations of coagulability, with small fresh-blood transfusions, may be needed, for the jaundiced; others need treatment for sepsis. There are appreciable differences in success rates between individual special-care units which appear to be related to deficiencies in staffing, particularly at night and week-ends.

Improvement in care for low birth weight infants of under 2500 g seems to offer one of the most effective ways of reducing the incidence of cerebral palsy and mental retardation in well-developed countries, and can be cost-effective.

## OXYGEN DEPRIVATION

Under this heading it is necessary to define the terminology in order to avoid confusion. Asphyxia is a condition in which there is a lack of oxygen in respired air resulting in impending or apparent cessation of life. This leads in turn to a reduced oxygen tension in the blood and an elevation of the carbon dioxide content. *Anoxia* results from a complete lack of oxygen in the inspired air whereas in *hypoxia* the alveolar oxygen tension is reduced but not completely absent. *Ischaemia* refers to an arrest of flow of blood to an organ or part of an organ.

In the sphere of mental handicap the most important organ to suffer from deprivation of oxygen is the brain. Anoxia of 4 to 5 minutes is likely to lead to irreversible changes in the brain. Brain damage following successful resuscitation is likely to be due to a combination of two factors, anoxia and circulatory

be adopted. Inadequate amounts of haemoglobin may necessitate blood transfusion. Stagnant circulation may be more difficult to improve; supportive measures such as cardiovascular stimulants and oxygen therapy may

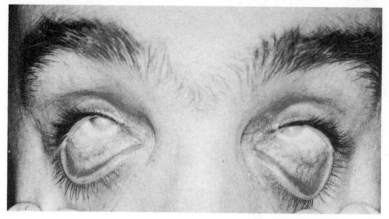

*Fig. 7.9   Retrolental fibroplasia due to excess oxygen at childbirth (Dr Sylvester).*

failure. Parts of the brain particularly susceptible to damage under these circumstances are the cerebral cortex, cerebellum, hippocampi and basal ganglia. Hypoxia, if prolonged, reveals a pattern of selected vulnerability of brain damage. Nerve cells are the most sensitive tissues, then glial cells; microglia and cellular components of blood vessels being the most resistant. The damage is usually greater in the parietal and occipital lobes than in the temporal and frontal regions.

There are four conditions which are important:

1. Reduced oxygen tension in the blood.
2. Inadequate amounts of haemoglobin by which to convey oxygen to the tissues.
3. Stagnation of circulation in the tissues.
4. Histotoxic damage in which the oxygen tension and content of the arterial blood are normal while those in the brain venous blood are raised because of poisons affecting the brain respiratory enzymes resulting in failure to utilize oxygen.

Treatment must be directed towards the specific cause. Where there is a reduced oxygen tension in the blood immediate and efficient resuscitative procedures require to

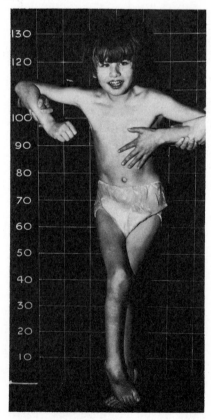

*Fig. 7.10   Cerebral palsy showing scissor-like gait from hypoxia during pregnancy (Dr Jancar).*

help. Histotoxic damage may be remedied by a specific treatment to the cause; for instance in hypoglycaemia correction of the sugar imbalance will help return the situation to normal.

As far as mental handicap is concerned, there are two main aspects of complications. One deals with damage to the brain in general, leading to mental handicap. The second refers to specific areas of brain which may be damaged and lead to motor and sensory deficits, with symptoms of basal ganglia disorder and epilepsy. Symptoms vary according to the permutation of sites of damage.

PERINATAL INFECTIONS

Herpesvirus was shown in 1967 to be able to cause mental retardation and early damage to the CNS. Between 1 in 3500 and 1 in 30 000 infants are said to be infected thus with herpes which is commonly latent in adults. Corneal and retinal damage, cataracts, conjunctivitis and keratitis result from the eye being affected during passage through the mother's genitals. In the review by Nahmias et al. (1970) one third of 98 patients had an enlarged liver, with a further third also jaundiced. Eleven had enlarged spleens. Vesicles are common in the skin, meningoencephalitis is frequent and microcephaly, hydrocephalus, intracranial calcification, choroidoretinitis and microphthalmia may result.

Genital herpesvirus (type 2) is most commonly found in newborns, the oral variety (type 1) being less common. For diagnosis serial increases in type 1 or type 2 antibodies, together with increase in the infant's serum cytomegalus IgM macroglobulin are necessary.

The severely infected infant may die but of those who survive many have serious CNS damage. Recent reports on treatment recommend 5-iodo-2-deoxyuridine (Tuffli & Nahmias 1969) and cytosine arabinoside (Brown & Bower 1975). It may be necessary to consider Caesarean section in women with genital herpes.

TRAUMA

Head injury can result from the following:

1. Excessive moulding of the head due to disproportion between the size of the fetal head to the maternal passages.
2. Precipitate delivery.
3. Prolonged labour.
4. Abnormal presentation.
5. Prematurity and postmaturity.
6. Instrumental delivery.
7. Caesarean section.
8. Toxaemia of pregnancy.
9. Placenta praevia.
10. Excessive coiling of the umbilical cord round the neck.

The type of brain damage may be subdural haemorrhage following rupture of tentorium cerebelli and bleeding from ruptured venous sinuses and also intracerebral haemorrhage occurring in the drainage area of the superior longitudinal sinus and great vein of Galen.

A variety of haemorrhagic and thrombotic features have been demonstrated in the neonate after death. It should not be assumed that such pathology automatically correlates with and explains brain pathology found in later life. Additional considerations are the ways in which anoxia and cardiovascular failure can complicate pathology. Pathological sequelae show a wide diversity of conditions which are thought to follow brain injury at birth. Cortical atrophy (atrophic sclerosis or ulegyria), sclerosis and cavitation of the central white matter, scarring of the basal ganglia (état membré or status marmoratus) and Ammon's horn sclerosis are the principal entities. Clinical complications are those of cerebral palsy, athetosis, mental handicap and epilepsy. All these conditions occur in a variety of permutations and severity according to the site and extent of the injury.

Prevention of birth trauma is achieved by monitoring the fetus with an ultrasonic (sonagraphic) scan and EEG. Fetal size, presentation, placental size and site can be assessed. By these means early signs of fetal distress may be anticipated and detected.

*Cerebral palsy*

Cerebral palsy varies in severity from minimal cerebral dysfunction through diplegia to death. It may arise from severe jaundice, hypoxia, infection or trauma. Because severity and the degree of mental retardation vary, estimates of prevalence also vary, but up to

70 per cent of diplegics are found in the 6 per cent of infants of low birth weight (less than 2500 g) (*Br. med. J.* 1978a and b). Many believe it is eminently preventable (*Br. med. J.* 1978a). Neonatal mortality among infants of low birth weight has declined in the United Kingdom from 155 per 1000 live births in 1953 to 90 per 1000 live births in 1976. With intensive care units (see above) for low birth weight infants it can now be expected that not only mortality among such infants can be decreased, but also morbidity for cerebral palsy. In Sweden this has been achieved with the incidence falling successively and significantly from 2.2 to 1.3 per 1000 live births, due predominantly to decrease in numbers of severely spastic and ataxic diplegias among infants of low birth weight. A similar reduction has been reported from Western Australia, also to significant extent (*Br. med. J.* 1978a).

Prevention depends on avoidance of fetal jaundice (one of the success stories of modern times) dependent on careful antenatal supervision of rhesus negative mothers, fetal monitoring and intensive care of the low birth weight infant.

Treatment of cerebral palsy linked with mental handicap requires long and careful nursing and the application of physiotherapeutic techniques (Bobath & Bobath 1975; Cotton 1975) to retain and develop useful limb movements and prevent skeletal deformities by muscular contractures. Nursing care is particularly important in preventing pressure sores and also chest complications. Groups of cerebral palsied people can often help themselves in a way which other people find difficult to do; a good example of this is the way in which Joey Deacon was able to establish communication with Ernie Roberts in spite of severe dysarthria (Deacon 1974). Tenotomies relieve immobile and deformed joints. Special chairs, walking frames, calipers and shoes are important surgical accessories. Special education (including the Peto Conductive Educational System), speech therapy and habit training help considerably in constructively reshaping the lives of these children.

Epilepsy must be controlled by suitable anticonvulsant therapy. Otherwise medicines on the whole are not helpful, except occasionally drugs such as diazepam which relieve painful muscle spasms. Steriotaxic neurosurgery for cerebral palsy was reported successful by Narabayashi (1962) whilst some patients have been improved by thalamotomy and dentatomy. These procedures aim at restoring balance in the central nervous system (Cornall et al. 1975). Surgical extirpation of serious scarring supported by careful educational training can be helpful in some cases.

The concept of *minimal brain damage* has concerned psychiatrists and neurologists for some years, and the literature upon the subject is extensive. Interested readers are referred to the admirable survey by O'Connor (1975). It is an abused and overused concept. Attempts were made to distinguish between subjects which were supposedly brain damaged, and those supposedly due to multiple causation. Not surprisingly the problem of definition waxed large in the arguments, not least because whatever groups of mentally handicapped individuals are studied, there is likely to be some overlap in the causative factors involved. As explained in this chapter, the actual factors can range from degrees of haemorrhage at birth through anoxia, to maternally ingested drugs, and to disturbance of cerebellar dendritic growth which is particularly susceptible to adverse factors during the first six months of life and can cause all the neurological signs described under this heading (see Chapter 8). The concentration on diagnostic tests in order to discriminate between brain-damaged (supposedly less receptive to education, due to localized damage) and non-brain-damaged (supposedly more receptive and due to multiple causation) overlooks the end point of assessment which is to devise constructive treatment for each individual. Moreover, as is shown in Chapter 13, where handicapped children are mishandled, if not mislabelled, as being non-receptive to stimulation, a secondary handicap of environmental non-stimulation is added to the original handicap of, say, primary hypoxia with brain cell loss. Both can be alleviated by devising alternative remedial education, physiotherapy and parental reinforcement of residual ability.

TOXIC FACTORS

Important poisons affecting the child during

the perinatal period are drugs administered to the mother, including anaesthetics and analgesics. After the birth of a premature baby it is important to avoid administering an atmosphere too rich in oxygen. Retrolental fibroplasia has been known since 1955. The rich oxygen supplied to premature babies prior to that time resulted in retinal capillary proliferation leading eventually to retinal detachment and a mushroom-shaped protrusion of glial tissue behind the lens. Fortunately this is now a rare condition, but long-stay hospitals for the mentally handicapped contain a residue of patients who are blind from this cause.

*Kernicterus* (rhesus incompatibility) has been known for some years to cause damage to affected infants. Eighty-five per cent of the United Kingdom population is positive and 15 per cent negative for the Rhesus blood group. Kernicterus occurs only when a Rhesus-negative woman has a *second* pregnancy which is Rhesus-*positive*, the result of a union with a Rhesus-positive man. A first pregnancy or blood transfusion sensitizes her to a fetus, which after birth has a massive haemolysis. Resultant unconjugated bilirubin circulating in the infantile blood is toxic to the developing CNS and apart from severe jaundice the affected infant (after being normal at birth) becomes lethargic and hypotonic with fever. Opisthotonos develops and severe hypertonicity follows in the first week of life. Many die but survivors develop various defects including severe motor retardation, hypotonia, with development during later infancy of athetosis, hearing loss and growth retardation. At autopsy there is atrophy of the basal ganglia with intense yellow pigmentation if death occurs during the early months. The best treatment is preventive. Nowadays Rh-negative mothers give birth in hospital so that an exchange transfusion may be administered to their children as soon as possible after birth. Intrauterine transfusions for the fetus have also been advocated. Hyperimmune gamma globulin has been used within 72 hours after birth of a Rh-positive child to Rh-negative mothers, to prevent sensitization to antigens affecting later fetuses.

## POSTNATAL CAUSES

### NUTRITIONAL FACTORS
(see also Chapter 8)

School performance of children who had been severely malnourished in infancy was found to be less than that of children in a control sample. Physical growth, immaturity in social behaviour, backwardness in school as well as retardation in growth were reported in studies by Richardson et al. (1973). Protein is the ingredient which is lacking in these children's diets. Extrapolating from animal studies to the human was cautiously undertaken by Dobbing and Sands (1973). There are two possible periods of brain vulnerability; one occurs during the 12 to 18 weeks of fetal life when multiplication of neuroblasts is very active, the other occurs during the main brain growth spurt up to the end of the second year of life. During this period there is growth of glial tissue, establishment of synapses and myelination. Thus there is a period of two and a half years during which a fetus or infant is at risk of serious reduction in the number of brain and glial cells, providing the period of undernutrition is serious and prolonged. Children exposed to undernutrition are also likely to be deprived in other ways, for example socially and emotionally. A Swedish nutrition foundation study found difficulty in isolating nutritional factors per se as entirely responsible for mental impairment (WHO 1974).

Neonatal hypoglycaemia can cause serious brain damage leading to mental handicap and epilepsy. Chance and Bower (1966) pointed out that small-for-dates babies or children who have suffered intrauterine malnutrition are particularly vulnerable to hypoglycaemia. Hypoglycaemia in later life can lead to irreversible brain damage similar to that found in anoxia; areas of cortical necrosis, loss of cells in the Ammon's horn, striatum and cerebellum may be found. Causes include islet cell adenoma, liver disease, pituitary, adrenocortical or hypothalamic lesions. Prediabetes and other forms of carbohydrate disturbance including galactosaemia and fructose intolerance as well as glycogen storage disease can be related to hypoglycaemia.

Unclassified mental retardation is sometimes related to a number of other biochemical problems. Routine urine chromatography and examination of the plasma amino acids may be rewarding. Tryptophan metabolism may be disturbed in children with brain disorders. Clayton (1972) has reviewed the complex stories of these and other metabolic difficulties related to mental handicap in children. Temptingly, she postulates that the unclassified patients of today are likely to become the specific syndromes and metabolic disorders of tomorrow. She invites participation in this fruitful field of investigation.

POSTNATAL INFECTIONS

*Acute pyogenic meningitis.* This results from meningococci, streptococci or pneumococci invading the leptomeninges. They can be blood-borne from a focus in a distant part of the body; follow middle ear infection either by direct spread or secondary to lateral sinus thrombosis; follow open skull fractures or from an open myelomeningocele. Meningitis causes pyrexia, vomiting, convulsions, neck stiffness, opisthotonos and a bulging anterior fontanelle in children under 18 months, due to brain oedema and swelling. This resulting pressure may cause obstruction to the blood supply of brain tissue with extensive death of brain cells and result in cerebral palsy, mental retardation or both.

*Chronic granular meningitis.* This is usually tubercular in developed countries but occasionally results from fungi such as cryptococcus. The onset is insidious, early symptoms including lethargy, loss of appetite, behaviour disturbance and convulsions. After a prodromal period of up to 6 weeks more positive signs of meningeal involvement including neck stiffness and Kernig's sign appear. Choroid tubercles are an important diagnostic sign but diagnosis is by lumbar puncture which reveals a clear to slightly opalescent fluid with 50 to 500 cells most of which are lymphocytes. A fine cobweb of fibrin forms if the fluid is left to stand. A direct film may reveal acid-fast bacilli. Mental handicap and epilepsy used to be common sequelae but both are now rare.

*Encephalitis.* Encephalitis, like meningitis,

may be acute or chronic. These are viral infections of the substance of the brain which may lead to the death of cells in any or all parts of the brain.

*Japanese encephalitis B* has been known since 1871 and *St. Louis encephalitis* since 1933. Clinically both are similar diseases although they are caused by different viruses transmitted by arthropods. Clinically, there is fever, headache, meningeal irritation, limb pains, convulsions, tremors, delirium and coma.

Pathologically there is congestion and oedema of the brain with lymphocytic infiltration of the meninges and perivascular cuffing of blood vessels with lymphocytes and plasma cells. Inclusion bodies are seen in diseased neurones. Damaged nerve cells die. Areas of demyelination are present. Lumbar puncture which reveals a clear to slightly opalescent fluid with 50 to 500 cells most of aphasia, cerebellar ataxia, tremors, mental deterioration and handicap. Whilst there is as yet no specific treatment available, mosquito control is important in preventing the spread of infection. The possibility of a vaccine being developed to offer active immunization is being investigated.

*Disseminated encephalomyelitis following measles* is rare. Hodes and Livingston (1950) found one child in 1200 who developed encephalomyelitis following measles. Ford (1966) distinguished six syndromes, some of which may overlap:

1. Symptoms of diffuse cerebral involvement (meningism, see also SSPE, p. 131).
2. Signs of multiple focal lesions.
3. Signs of single focal cerebral lesions.
4. Cerebellar lesions.
5. Spinal symptoms.
6. Optic neuritis.

The mortality is low but half the survivors show permanent neurological damage including spastic paraplegia and cerebellar ataxia. According to Ford reduction in intelligence occurs in about one-third of the affected children. Epilepsy is another complication. Treatment is by gamma globulin given intramuscularly as soon as signs appear.

*Post-vaccination encephalomyelitis* is a rare complication of vaccination against whooping cough and other childhood infections. Symptoms appear one or two weeks after vaccination and include headache, malaise, vomiting, irritability, drowsiness, coma and fits with possible sequelae of epilepsy, cerebral palsy or mental handicap.

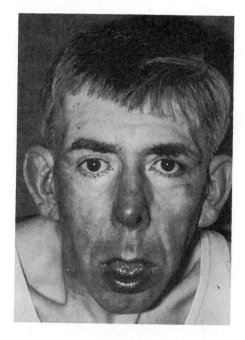

*Fig. 7.11 Postencephalitic Parkinsonism (Dr Jancar).*

*Subacute sclerosing panencephalitis (SSPE).* This is a group of slow-developing virus infections of childhood and adolescence varying in incidence round the world. Jabbour (1975) quotes an incidence of one per 100 000 children, with 400 on the SSPE registry in the United States. Some cases are believed to occur some years after clinical measles and are thought to be due to discrepancy between passive immunity from the mother and active immunity by the child. Others are believed to be due to viruses of the Creutzfeldt type. One famous example occurred some years ago after a corneal transplant from a road accident victim. When the disease developed, brain biopsy showed the pathognomonic intranuclear inclusion bodies present in cells; by chance the brain of the road accident victim had also been preserved; it was examined for the second time and showed the pathognomonic histology. It was deduced that the virus

had been transferred with the corneal transplant some years before (*Br. med. J.* 1978). The signs of SSPE are those of cerebral degenerative diseases or viral encephalitis, according to Jabbour who has studied the 400 cases in the United States. Four stages may be described:

1. One to two months: frontal lobe syndromes, over-affectionate, forgetful, apathetic, irritable, lethargic, speech poor, 'failure to thrive'.
2. One to 12 months: motor stage, epilepsy, choreoathetosis, ataxia, tremors, incoordination. SSPE may arrest in this stage for at least 4 years (Jabbour 1975).
3. Months or many years later: decerebrate rigidity, lessening response, incontinence, infections and death common.
4. Quadriparesis, little or no self-help.

Treatment is on the whole ineffective. Another similar syndrome in New Guinea, called Kuri, has an incubation period of 5 to 20 years. This results from the cannibal practice of eating the brain of a human victim. The disease is decreasing in incidence with the decrease in the practice of cannibalism in that country. The numerous drugs tried are reviewed by Jabbour. Outcome in SSPE is variable and erratic for some children die, others reach a 'plateau'.

## TRAUMA

Mental handicap following head injury is seen from time to time in children and adults. Most causes are due to road traffic accidents. Symptoms and signs include loss of speech, motor and sensory defects, cranial nerve palsies, poor motivation, sphincter disturbances, lack of interest in surroundings, memory defects, psychiatric disorders and epilepsy.

It is difficult to know the precise brain pathology in an individual case. Necropsy studies reveal a variety of lesions. Cerebral contusions, haemorrhages (subdural, subarachnoid and intracerebral) and cerebral oedema are common pathological features following closed head injury. Skull fractures can be either simple or compound and linked with the above features but include extradural haematomata and tearing of cranial nerves as additional complications. Brain tissue can be lost through compound fractures and risks of infection are great. By the time that mental handicap has asserted itself as a sad complication, then treatment in an appropriate centre becomes necessary. Many patients will need full nursing care, physiotherapy, speech and occupational therapy and special education.

*Non-accidental injury to children* by parents has been well documented in most western countries. Martin (1974) estimated that the number of children rendered mentally handicapped by this means was rising in the United States; in Britain the Royal College of Psychiatrists calculated that 18 to 19 children per million population 'could suffer intellectual impairment' each year. In a survey of 140 hospitalized children under 16, between 3 and 11 per cent had received sufficient brain damage to be 'thus rendered mentally handicapped. In 24 per cent (parental) neglect was considered to be a contributory factor in reducing intellectual potential' (Buchanan and Oliver 1977). It is very difficult to come to an exact estimate of the numbers of children made mentally handicapped by battering parents, but recent evidence suggests that it is indeed at least 3 per cent of handicapped children in residential care, and that the proportion could be increasing. For care personnel faced with the taxing situation of parents believed to be battering their children, it is clear they must act on, or seek, the advice of their multidisciplinary team, not least because such parents are likely to be litigious, they are also likely to be young, immature, emotionally unstable, threatening and 'difficult'. Often very fertile, they may have other non-battered children upon whom they dote, the battered child being the 'scapegoat' and therefore as much needed in his absence as in his presence. He can even be re-battered on his afternoon out with initially loving young parents.

## LEAD INTOXICATION

Lead intoxication was first recognized by Frost among children eating lead paint in 1892 in Australia. This is still the commonest cause. Lead is either sucked from painted surfaces or ingested as flakes. Other sources have been car batteries, or contaminated dust or soil in the neighbourhood of lead-using industries. Soft water can also dissolve the metal from lead tanks and pipes. The children most at risk are those with pica (picking habits). Their symptoms can involve the nervous, gastrointestinal, haematological and

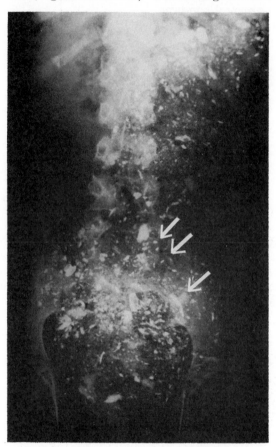

Fig. 7.12    *Abdominal X-ray in pica showing lead in colon from ingested paint (Dr Harper).*

renal systems. They can be constipated, complain of abdominal pain and may vomit. A common feature is microcytic anaemia which fails to respond to iron therapy. Albuminuria and oedema of face indicate renal involvement. Encephalopathy with drowsiness, coma and convulsions with or without fever is the most serious form of intoxication. It can lead to mental handicap in a normal child and cause abnormal behaviour patterns such as hyperactivity in those already handicapped. The diagnosis depends on blood lead estimation. Normal blood levels in children are minimal, above 3.6 mg/dl (0.18 millimoles/litre) is regarded as evidence of toxicity. In the body, ingested lead goes first to the liver and kidneys and to a lesser extent the brain. It is then deposited in bone as lead triphosphate, from which source it can be mobilized back into the soft tissues by alteration of the acid–base metabolism. Eosinophilic hepato-renal cell inclusions and peripheral nerve myelin breakdown occur. A recent US survey showing that the progress of many city-bred children is adversely affected by atmospheric lead from petrol fumes, if verified, may be fuel for political action (Needleman et al. 1979).

MALIGNANT GROWTHS

Brain tumours cause retardation in childhood and are common at 10 per 100 000 children annually. In childhood, leukaemia is the commonest cause of death from cancer, brain tumours are second, at two per 20 000 children per year. Most tumours cause the usual triad of raised intracranial pressure (headache, vomiting and optic disc swelling) after the first three months, with clear signs of local pressure, cranial nerve palsies (especially squints), weakness of limbs from pressure or invasion of the internal capsule. Epilepsy itself in childhood, in the absence of fever, suggests intracranial growths until proved otherwise.

Two types of malignant growth in the brain in childhood cause mental retardation over months or years with few specific features. These are firstly *all* slow-growing tumours in the first two years of life, for the cranial sutures and fontanelles have not united, and an enlarging head, or hydrocephalus due to intermittent CSF obstruction, may be the only signs apart from head-holding, 'failure to thrive', apathy and irritability. The increased pressure is accommodated by the enlarging head. Secondly, *astrocytomas* in the temporal lobe are prone to cause mental retardation in childhood. They are particularly slow to cause signs. Their *average* duration of deterioration before diagnosis is 16 months, and some develop for two years before a dramatic fit, or paralysis, raises suspicion.

In youth, a slow-growing glioma like the oligodendroglioma, may cause steady mental deterioration, for the length of deterioration and growth may be five or more years. The young child may not complain because he cannot vocalize his complaints, but a recent series showed that a considerable minority of dull adolescents and adults were similarly non-vocal. Brain growths are common, and whilst some retardation syndromes such as tuberous sclerosis cause growths, space-occupying lesions such as abscesses and subdural haematoma may also cause childhood deterioration in behaviour and ability.

The diagnosis is by lumbar puncture which shows raised pressure, and protein. Care must be taken not to cause medullary pressure coning if pressure is high. On X-ray there may be parting of the sutures, or shift in mid-line structures. Other investigations now include: air encephalograms which may confirm shift, or show enlarged ventricles; the EEG which may show a focus or dysrhythmia; angiography (the arterial injection of dye) may show displacement of arteries; computerized transaxial tomographic scanning can visualize sequential slices of the brain, showing up the invasive tumours well; in gamma scintography a fast-growing tumour takes up injected radioactive isotopes faster than normal cells; whilst ultra-sonoencephalography uses echo sound to show displacement of the water-containing ventricles. Surgical removal of tumours followed by irradiation now gives at best an average of 60 per cent survival rate for five years (Gomez 1975) but in many more there is an improved quality of life.

BIBLIOGRAPHY

PRENATAL

Birnbaum, G., Lynch, J. I., Margileth, A. M., Lonergan, W. M. & Sever, J. L. (1969) Cytomegalovirus infections in newborn infants. *J. Pediat.*, 75, 789–95.
British Medical Journal (1978) Maternal alcohol consumption and birth weight. *Br. med. J.*, 2, 76–7.
Brocklehurst, G., Sharrad, W. J. W., Forrest, D. & Stark, G. (1976) *Spina bifida for the clinician.* Clinics in Developmental Med. No. 57. London and Philadelphia; Spastics International.
Brown, W. J. & More, M. B. (1963) Congenital syphilis in the United States. *Clin. Pediat.*, 2, 220–22.

Butler, N. R. (1973) Smoking in pregnancy and subsequent child development. *Br. med. J.*, *4*, 573.

Cederquist, L. L., Zervoudakis, I. A., Ewool, L. C., Senterfit, L. B. & Litwin, S. D. (1977) Prenatal diagnosis of congenital rubella. *Br. med. J.*, *1*, 615.

Chernoff, G. F. (1975) A mouse model of the fetal alcohol syndrome. *Teratology*, *11*, 14A.

Christoffel, K. K. & Salafsky (1975) Fetal alcohol syndrome in dizygotic twins. *J. Pediat.*, *87*, 963–7.

Cockburn, W. C. (1969) World aspects of the epidemiology of rubella. *Am. J. Dis. Child.*, *118*, 112–22.

Cooper, L. Z., Ziring, P. R., Ockerse, A. B., Fedun, B. A., Kiely, B. & Krugman, S. (1969) Rubella: clinical manifestations and management. *Am. J. Dis. Child.*, *118*, 18–29.

Couvreur, J. & Desmonts, G. (1962) Congenital and maternal toxoplasmosis: a review of 300 congenital cases. *Devl Med. Child Neurol.*, *4*. 519–30.

Couvreur, J. & Desmonts, G. (1976) Congenital toxoplasmosis in twins. *J. Pediat.*, *89*, 235–40.

Crome, L. & Stern, J. (1972) *Pathology of Mental Defect*, 2nd ed. Edinburgh: Churchill Livingstone.

Feldman, H. A. (1968) Toxoplasmosis. *New Engl. J. Med.*, *279*, 1370–75.

Feldman, R. A. (1969) Cytomegalovirus infection during pregnancy. *Am. J. Dis. Child.*, *117*, 517–21.

Fraser, D., Kidd, B. S. L., Kooh, S. W. & Paunier, L. (1966) A new look at infantile hypercalcemia. *Pediat. Clins N. Am.*, *13*, 503–25.

Hagberg, B., Sjogren, I., Beusch, K. & Hadnios, A. (1963) The incidence of infantile hydrocephalus in Sweden. *Acta paediat., Stockh.*, *52*, 588–94.

Hanson, J. W., Myrianthopoulos, N. C., Sedgewick Harvey, M. C. & Smith, D. W. (1976) Risks to the offspring of women treated with hydantoin anticonvulsants with emphasis on the foetal hydantoin syndrome. *J. Pediat.*, *89*, 662–8.

Harbison, R. D. (ed.) (1975) *Perinatal Addiction*. New York: J. Wiley.

Harrison, J. W. (1976) The foetal hydantoin syndrome. *Devl. Med. Child Neurol.*, *18*, 252.

Illis, L. S. (1975) *Viral Diseases of the Central Nervous System*. London: Baillière Tindall.

Jones, K. L., Smith, D. W., Ulleland, C. N. & Streissguth, P. (1973) Pattern of malformation in offspring of chronic alcoholic mothers. *Lancet*, *1*, 1267.

Korones, S. B. (1976) Congenital rubella: an encapsulated review. *Teratology*, *14*, 111–14.

McCracken, G. H., Shinefield, H. R., Cobb, K., Rausen, A. R., Dische, M. R. & Eichenwald, H. F. (1969) Congenital cytomegalic inclusion disease: a longitudinal study of 20 patients. *Am. J. Dis. Child*, *117*, 522–39.

Mulvihill, J. J., Kilimas, J. T., Stokes, D. C. & Risemberg, H. M. (1976) Fetal alcohol syndrome: seven new cases. *Am. J. Obstet. Gynec.*, *125*, 937–41.

Nelson, M. M. & Forfar, J. O. (1971) Association between drugs administered during pregnancy and congenital abnormalities of the foetus. *Br. med. J.*, *1*, 523.

Rhodes, P. (1973) Obstetric prevention of mental retardation. *Br. med. J.*, *1*, 399–402.

Seip, M. (1976) Growth retardation following massive exposure to phenobarbitone *in utero*. *Acta paediat., Stockh.*, *65*, 617–21.

Shapiro, S., Hartz, S. C., Siskind, V., Mitchell, A. A., Slone, D., Rosenberg, L., Monson, R. R. & Heinonen, O. P. (1976) Anticonvulsants and parental epilepsy in the development of birth defects. *Lancet*, *1*, 272–5.

Shapiro, S., Monson, R. R., Kaufman, D. W., Siskind, V., Heinonen, O. P. & Slone, D. (1976) Perinatal mortality and birthweight in relation to aspirin taken during pregnancy. *Lancet*, *1*, 1375–6.

Shaul, W. L. & Hall, J. G. (1977) Multiple congenital abnormalities associated with oral anticoagulants. *Am. J. Obstet. Gynec.*, *127*, 191–8.

Shruygin, G. I. (1974) Ob osobennosticakh psikhichesgogo razvitica detef ot materie, stradaiushchickh khronich eskrim alkogolizmom. *Pediatriya (USSR)*, *11*, 71–3.

Sinha, S. K., Kaveggia, E. & Gordon, M. C. (1972) The incidence of cytomegalovirus among mentally retarded and microcephalic children in a state institution. *J. ment. Defic. Res.*, *16*, 90–6.

Starling, P. F. (1971) Diagnosis and treatment of syphilis. *New Engl. J. Med.*, *284*, 642–53.

Starr, J. G., Bart, R. D. & Gold, E. (1970) Inapparent congenital cytomegalovirus infection. *New Engl. J. Med.*, *282*, 1075–8.

Streissguth, A. P., Herman, C. S. & Smith, D. W. (1978) Intelligence, behaviour, and dysmorphogenesis in the fetal alcohol syndrome: a report on 20 patients. *J. Pediat.*, *92/3*, 363–7.

Ulleland, C. N. (1972) The offspring of alcoholic mothers. *Ann. N.Y. Acad. Sci.*, *197*, 167.

Willcocks, J. (1977) Nutrition and the foetus. *Proc. Nutr. Soc.*, *36*, 1–7.

Wolf, A., Cowen, D. & Paige, B. (1939) Human toxoplasmosis. *Science*, *89*, 226–7.

Yamazaki, J. N. (1966) A review of the literature on the radiation dosage required to cause manifest central nervous system disturbances 'in utero' and postnatal exposures. *Pediatrics*, *37*, 877–903.

PERINATAL

Bobath, K. & Bobath, B. (1975) *Motor Development in the Different Types of Cerebral Palsy.* London: Heinemann Medical.

British Medical Journal (1978a) Preventing cerebral palsy. *Br. med. J.*, 2, 979.

British Medical Journal (1978b) Caring for babies of very low birth weight. *Br. med. J.*, 2, 1105–6.

Brown, R. S. & Bower, B. D. (1975) Neonatal disseminated herpes simplex virus infection with encephalitis treated with cytosine arabinoside. *Devl Med. Child Neurol.*, 17, 493–516.

Catalano, L. W., Safley, G. H., Museles, M. & Jarzynski, D. J. (1971) Disseminated herpesvirus infection in a newborn infant. *J. Pediat.*, 79, 393–400.

Churchill, J., Masland, R. L., Naylor, A. A. & Ashworth, M. R. (1974) The aetiology of cerebral palsy in pre-term infants. *Devl Med. Child Neurol.*, 16, 143–9.

Cornall, P., Hitchcock, E. & Kirkland, I. S. (1975) Stereotaxic neurosurgery in the management of cerebral palsy. *Devl Med. Child Neurol.*, 17, 279–86.

Cotton, E. (1975) *Conductive Education and Cerebral Palsy.* London: The Spastics Society.

Deacon, J. J. (1974) *Tongue Tied.* Subnormality in the Seventies, No. 8. London: National Society for Mentally Handicapped Children.

Diamond, J. (1966) Kernicterus: revised concept of pathogenesis and management. *Pediatrics*, 38, 539–42.

Douglas, J. W. B. (1956) Mental ability and school achievement of premature children at eight years of age. *Br. med. J.*, 1, 1210.

Drillien, C. M. (1964) *The Growth and Development of the Prematurely Born Infant.* Baltimore: Williams and Wilkins.

Lubchenko, L. O., Delivaria-Papadopolous, M. & Searls, D. (1972) Long-term follow-up of premature infants, II. *J. Pediat.*, 80, 509.

Nahmias, A. J., Alford, C. A. & Korones, S. B. (1970) Infection of the newborn with herpesvirus hominis. *Adv. Pediat.*, 17, 185–226.

Narabayashi, H. (1962) Stereotaxic surgery for athetosis or the spastic state of cerebral palsy. *Confinia neurol.*, 22, 364.

O'Connor, N. (1975) Brain function in mental handicap. In: Kirman, B. & Bicknell, J. (eds.), *Mental Handicap.* Edinburgh: Churchill Livingstone.

Rhodes, P. (1973) Obstetric prevention of mental retardation. *Br. med. J.*, 1, 399–402.

Tobin, J. O'H. (1975) Herpesvirus hominus infection in pregnancy. *Proc. R. Soc. Med.*, 68, 371–4.

Tuffli, G. A. & Nahmias, A. J. (1969) Neonatal herpetic infection: report of two premature infants treated with systemic use of iodoxuridine. *Am. J. Dis. Child.*, 118, 909–14.

Urich, H. (1976) Malformations of the nervous system, perinatal damage and related conditions in early life. In: Blackwood, W. & Corsellis, J. A. N. (eds.), *Greenfield's Neuropathology*, 3rd ed. London: Edward Arnold.


POSTNATAL

British Medical Journal (1978) Creutzfeldt-Jakob under control. *Br. med. J.*, 1, 463–4.

Buchanan, A. & Oliver, J. E. (1977) Abuse and neglect as a cause of mental retardation. *Br. J. Psychiat.*, 131, 458–67.

Chance, G. W. & Bower, B. D. (1966) Hypoglycaemia and temporary hyperglycaemia in infants of low birth weight for maturity. *Archs Dis. Childh.*, 41, 279–85.

Clayton, B. (1972) Clinical biochemistry and unclassified mental retardation. In: Cavanagh, J. B. (ed.), *The Brain in Unclassified Mental Retardation, Study Group 3, I.R.M.M.H.* Edinburgh: Churchill Livingstone.

Dobbing, J. & Sands, J. (1973) The quantitative growth and development of the human brain. *Archs Dis. Childh.*, 48, 757.

Dohremann, G. J., Farwell, J. R. & Flannery, J. T. (1976) Glioblastoma multiform in children. *J. Neurosurg.*, 44, 442–8; *see also* (1976) Ependymomas and ependymoblastomas in children. *J. Neurosurg.*, 45, 237–8.

Ford, F. R. (1966) *Diseases of the Nervous System in Infancy, Childhood and Adolescence*, 5th ed. Springfield, Ill.: Charles Thomas.

Goldberg, A. (1973) Lead poisoning in mental deficiency. In: Clayton, B. (ed.), *Mental Retardation: Environmental Hazards*, Symposia 9, 10 and 11. Sevenoaks, Kent: Butterworths.

Gomez, M. R. (1975) Supratentorial tumors. In: Swaiman, K. F. & Wright, F. S. (eds.), *The Practice of Pediatric Neurology.* St. Louis: Mosby.

Hodes, H. L. & Livingston, S. (1950) Electroencephalographic findings in measles encephalitis. *J. Pediat.*, *36*, 577.

Jabbour, J. T. (1975) Slow virus diseases. In: Swaiman, K. F. & Wright, F. S. (eds.), *The Practice of Pediatric Neurology*. St. Louis: Mosby.

Martin, H. P. (1974) The development of abused children. *Adv. Pediat.*, *21*, 25–73.

Needleman, H. L., Gunnoe, C., Leviton, A., Reed, R., Peresie, H., Maher, C. & Barrett, P. (1979) Deficits in psycholosic and classroom performance of children with elevated dentine lead levels. *New Engl. J. Med.*, *300*, 13, 689–95.

Richardson, S. A., Birch, H. G. & Hertzig, M. E. (1973) Performance of children who were severely malnourished in infancy. *Am. J. ment. Defic.*, *77*, 623–32.

Royal College of Psychiatrists (1976) Evidence presented to the Select Committee on Violence in the Family.

Strick, S. J. (1976) Cerebral trauma. In: Blackwood, W. & Corsellis, J. A. N. (eds.), *Greenfield's Neuropathology*, 3rd ed. London: Edward Arnold.

World Health Organization Chronicle (1974) Malnutrition and mental development. *Wld Hlth Org. Chron.*, *28*, 95–102.

# CHAPTER 8

# THE NEUROCYTOLOGY OF DAMAGING ENVIRONMENTAL FACTORS

## MICHAEL CRAFT

Chapters 5 and 6 dealt with chromosomal and genetic misendowments at conception, whilst in Chapter 7 congenital abnormalities were described, together with syndromes resulting from *gross damage* from poisons, infections, road accidents and parental battering.

This chapter describes research concerned with *nerve cell damage* arising from a variety of environmental factors. Admittedly it is difficult to differentiate between the cell damage described in Chapter 7 as due to lead toxicity, alcohol or smoking and the dietetic and other deprivations described in this chapter. Both chapters could well be regarded as dealing with 'acquired syndromes'. Chapter 7 was concerned with those resulting from *extra* noxious factors such as harmful drugs additionally delivered to a fertilized egg with normal endowed potential. This chapter is concerned with *deprivative* environmental factors such as inadequate protein. A fertilized egg needs adequate protein and other substances if it is to develop normally; inadequacies result in subtle change at cell or functional level.

### PRENATAL FACTORS

The prenatal noxious influence of tobacco and alcohol on the fetus was described in Chapter 7. Among animals steroid hormones given to fetuses and to young rats cause change in proliferation and differentiation of central nervous system cells, whilst Raisman and Field (1973) showed that excess neonatal androgens (such as result from certain drugs) may cause a decrease in number of presynaptic endings on dendritic spines in the preoptic area of rat cortex. Tranquillizers in rats, such as chlorpromazine, or even LSD, during the last stages of pregnancy have been shown to affect the concentrations of serotonin, a neurotransmitter, for up to 80 days in the infant rat hypothalamus, whilst reserpine alters cell proliferation. Reserpine acts in the human by altering neurotransmitter activity, so it is probable that phenothiazines, widely used in depression and schizophrenia, may also affect cell proliferation in the developing brain if given to pregnant women.

### PERINATAL FACTORS

Perinatal interference with the human brain has taught us much because the immature brain is highly plastic. Its plasticity is related to swift learning ability, and surgical removal shows how adaptable it can be. If half the cortex of a human infant is removed to relieve intractable epilepsy after severe birth injury, the child still gains control over four limbs subserved by the removed half cortex, also developing much more than half the intelligence half a cortex might be expected to allow.

Although the number of nerve cells does not greatly change after birth, brain weight

The author wishes to thank Professor A. N. Davison, Department of Neurochemistry, Institute of Neurology, London, for assistance with this chapter.

and size do. There appear to be two peaks in this; firstly a rapid increase in its wet weight at and after birth corresponding to the last phase of neuroblast and glial (brain connective cell) multiplication, peaking at one month lasting to eighteen months of age; secondly an increase in *dry* weight corresponding to later myelinization (fat-containing sheathing of nerve axons) peaking at six months and continuing rapidly for four years and then up to the late teens. The first phase demands much energy and nutrients (for example, protein) for cell biosynthesis. The second phase relies on the metabolic activity of the oligodendrocyte, and undernutrition at this stage interferes with the formation of myelin sheaths.

The most vulnerable period of brain development is thus the first two years after birth and there are numerous dietary and hormonal agents capable of interference. The cerebellum, responsible for limb and muscle coordination, is particularly fast growing and thus susceptible to deprivation immediately after birth. This may be one reason for the clumsiness of movement common among retardates (see minimal brain damage, p. 128). It is possible that reduction in size and aborization of neurones and hence formation of synaptic contacts in this final phase of multiplication in the cerebellum may be crucial, for nerve endings are known to mediate the activity of neurotransmitter agents (Davison 1977). A deficit results in decreased control of muscle coordination. The number of neuroblasts and, to a lesser extent, glial cells is established by birth, and it is unlikely that dietary deprivation affects the number of neurones. Two postnatal developments are crucially affected.

Firstly, the dendritic connections made by one cell to another are constructed during the first two years. Comparing microscopic cortical sections at birth, one and two years, one sees similar numbers of brain cells in each, but successive proliferation of dendritic connections between them. It is rather like watching mustard and cress growing in a transparent container, the number of seeds is the same, but their roots enmesh like dendrites. The dendrites account for the wealth of inter-cell stimulation and thus information available. Environmental deficits such as thyroxine deficiency (causing cretinism), low pro-

tein diets in pregnancy and lactation, and severe alcoholism greatly reduce the rich growth of dendrites. Brain weight and subsequent ability can be permanently decreased. In South Africa Stoch and Smythe (1976) followed groups of malnourished and control children over 15 years. Lowered capacity and smaller head circumference among the former persisted into the teens despite post-infantile environmental improvements. Myelin deficiency in brains of undernourished children and those with the African protein deficiency disease of kwashiorkor have been repeatedly found (Davison 1977). As noted above, brain demyelinization is found both in states of memory loss in presenile dementia and in conduction failure illnesses such as disseminated sclerosis. Checking recovery from this, Hoorweg and Stanfield (1976) in Uganda followed two groups of diet-deprived children, one group later having a better diet than the other. They reached the same conclusion, that chronic early undernutrition particularly for protein, related more closely with subsequent intellectual deficits, than later change or inter-current illnesses which 'might punctuate or terminate' the children. Other studies showed the *average* IQ difference between compared groups to be 18 points, believed due to the *protein* deficit.

Secondly, diet deficits have been recently demonstrated within nerve cells as a result of improvements in histochemical staining and electron microscopy (surveyed by Shute 1974). It seems that the vesicles in the synaptic ultrastructure, responsible for accumulation and release of neurotransmitters, are adversely affected by protein malnutrition resulting in impulses between cells being impaired (Jones and Dyson 1976). Eckhart et al. (1976) have recently shown that presynaptic cholinergic terminals (a specific transmitter system) are particularly susceptible to malnutrition. The cholinergic neurones, thought to be of particular importance in memory and cognition, also go early in presenile dementia (Spillane et al. 1977), whilst in Down's syndrome O'Hara (1972) has recently shown synapses depleted of vesicles and others with primitive coated vesicles. He suggested a deficit in construction of neurotransmitter-containing vesicles. Shute (1974) in one of the best reviews of chemical neurotransmitters, shows that new histochemical staining techniques under the electron microscope can clarify variations in vesicle production at synaptic ultrastructure. Elsewhere, extrapolation of animal experiments to humans poses difficulties. For example 'disruptive early experiences' to young rats using extreme temperatures, and electrical shock do alter adult behaviour permanently with increased startle responses and emotional lability but have doubtful validity for Western children.

## POSTNATAL FACTORS

There are known to be many deprivative environmental factors which can cause long-lasting damage to the developing fetus or child. Most argued of recent years has been the *postnatal* factor of maternal deprivation which has been discussed at length by Rutter (1972) and recently updated by Bowlby (1977). Whilst the association with intellectual delay and personality damage is well proven (Clarke et al. 1958), the association with cellular change in the nervous system is quite unproven, and likely to remain so with current tools of investigation. Attempts to show nerve cell changes in humans causes ethical difficulties, the nature of which the following experiment with kittens will illustrate.

It has been known for years that the squinting child who 'suppresses' visual impulses from the weak eye becomes blind due to non-development or even degeneration of the cortical nerve cells involved. This knowledge is the basis of 'treatment' involved in covering the stronger eye, allowing development of both by alternate usage, and later surgical correction of muscle insertion if then necessary. A similar state has been developed in kittens. Weisel and Hubel (1965) sewed together the eyelids of a newborn kitten for three months. When the eyelids were untied, vision was permanently lost in the affected eye. In adults cats similarly sewn, loss did not occur. Both newborn and adult cats are endowed with the capacity for cells at the visual cortex to respond to patterns of lights such as lines and shapes, but affected newborn lose this capacity, although retinal and geniculate reflexes to light remain. Thus a neurological connection with cortical cells has been made permanently inoperative. A similar cortical correlate has recently been shown in rabbit brains after visual exposure to vertical bands of light and dark. It was possible to demonstrate similar bands with the ophthalmic cortical cells subserving the retinal cells so stimulated.

Armen (1974) described the permanent anatomical changes which can occur, with a boy raised by gazelles from an early age: 'he browsed and ran on all fours with great bounds of up to four metres'. When the boy was chased by French army officers in a jeep they clocked 50 kph without overtaking him and failed to capture him. Armen, who lived with the gazelle herd for some months, found the boy's ankles and thigh muscles centimetres thicker and more powerful than a normal man's, although he appeared to be only 10 years old. He sniffed at everything as gazelles do, he browsed on grass, thorn bushes, roots and flowers, 'his expression open, unlike that of wolf children, with lively eyes'. There are now some 50 documented cases of animal-reared children known, including a gazelle boy found in 1946 in Syria. We do not know of further anatomical changes in Armen's boy because he escaped; the Syrian boy had his ligaments cut by his captors to prevent his escaping 'the better to understand his make-up', which perhaps tells us more about the captors than the boy.

More directly referrable to humans are recent experiments relating activity of areas of the brain to increase in blood supply to the stimulated area. For instance when visual pathways are activated by light, thermocouple measurement shows increased occipital cortex blood flow. When hand muscles are activated there is a similar increase in blood flow to the appropriate areas of the human brain. Whilst it is still not quite known why this occurs, it seems to hold good for all ages of man. As expected hypothermia and barbiturates lead to a differential reduction, whilst epilepsy, hyperthermia, certain drugs such as amphetamine, anxiety states and stress lead to differential increase. By differential is meant a proportional reduction or increase of blood flow to those parts of the brain involved in the activity.

These findings begin to have more significance when taken in conjunction with recent advances in neurocytology described below.

## INFANT MALNUTRITION

Whilst the relevance of animal experiments and the interpretation of field trials among undernourished children is open to dispute, there is no doubt whatsoever that undernourishment is the commonest cause of mental retardation as such, and that as many as 100 million children world-wide may be at risk. Malnutrition is a cause that acts on the fetus perinatally, with the likelihood of difficulty for the child at birth and throughout the longer postnatal period. Although the agent may vary, from alcoholic mothers in California, to malnourished Asian children in Britain and aboriginal children in Queensland or protein malnutrition in Africa, severe malnutrition in the first two years of life can cause permanent mental retardation.

In the USA, Canada and UK amino acid lack in infants has recently been seen in children of vegans, adherents of the yin and yang philosophies, and periodically the zen macrobiotic diet. Here there are ten stages of increasing dietary restriction to be followed, until only cereals are taken. The zen macrobiotic infant food called kokoh can cause severe infant malnutrition (Roberts et al. 1979) resulting in some infants being taken into care. Ideally vegetarian diets should contain a mixture of proteins, say legumes (20 per cent protein) which are short in methionine but good on lysine, and cereal grains (10 per cent protein) which are short on lysine but have adequate methionine (BMJ 1978).

It is probable that the deleterious effects result from imbalance in the essential amino acids. Lack causes a severe reduction in rate of deoxyribonucleic acid (DNA) synthesis, essential for the nuclei produced during multiplication of brain cells. It appears that the cell number is little reduced, it is the delayed DNA synthesis and therefore quantity which is defective (Balazs et al. 1977). The circuitry of the developing brain is affected and there may be permanent imbalance between excitatory and inhibitory neuroses, or in the pattern of synaptic transmission. Similarly gross excess of an amino acid, such as phenylalanine, histidine and methionine has been shown to decrease protein synthesis in the young rat brain, and decrease final weight. The imbalance has also been shown to cause

deficiency in neurotransmitter production, which may be temporary. Thus there is growing neurological evidence to support old observations on differences in behavioural pattern between normal and severely dietarily deprived youngsters, although it is important to note that one cannot extrapolate from these to children deprived of relationship formation in otherwise affluent societies.

This chapter has been primarily concerned with noting the effects upon cells of various deprivations. The effect on the neurotransmitter system can now be shown histologically by visible change in the vesicles at end-plates. The effect of protein *derivatives* on memory or learning has not been shown in this visual way. (See also Shull et al. 1974.)

## DEVELOPMENT OF MEMORY

Memory is believed to contain two parts, a short and a long-term component. Short-term memory is labile, lasts from minutes to an hour, and is easily disrupted by electrical, mechanical or chemical insult. It is thought to rely predominantly on electrical circuitry. Long-term memory is extraordinarily stable, and often lasts the lifetime of the individual. Apart from death, surgical or accidental removal of brain tissue, only the reversal of a previously learned habit obliterates this type of memory. It is believed that long-term memory relies on chemical traces laid down, a deduction from which is that if such substances can be found, it would be possible to transfer knowledge from one individual to another by 'injection' of the substance. Ungar et al. (1972) believe that they have demonstrated this. Others are not convinced, most believing that accumulation of knowledge correlates with neuronal protein synthesis, and citing animal experiments to back their view (Rose and Haywood 1977). Thus rat brain visual cortex cells exposed to light patterns show more neuronal protein synthesis than cells left in the dark. Many of these experiments are indicted because of lack of controls, and because the subjects were animals, but it is significant that most point in the same direction. Currently it is generally believed that learning starts with the activation of brain cells in the appropriate region, by a unique set of stimuli, followed by ribonucleic acid (RNA) synthesis. After some 30 minutes there is increased RNA polymerase activity and within an hour increased production of glycoprotein in the cell with increased weight. It is probable that this is only part of the picture and such changes are merely precursors to others, for instance increased production of neurotransmitters. It is also likely that among the many stimuli which help 'fire' cells to start the learning process, are enhancing agents such as the hormone vasopressin released from the neurohypophysis under certain emotional stimuli. This hormone acts particularly on the midbrain limbic centres and may strengthen memories related to emotion associated with basic reward—avoidance behaviour to do with sex, flight and fight. 'In this way the neurohypophysial system is involved in the consolidation of memory processes which enables the organism to cope adequately with environmental changes' (Davison 1977).

Sleep patterns are also influenced by vasopressin. Rats with genetically-endowed diabetes insipidus (that is, vasopressin absent) are severely memory defective, relieved by vasopressin, and show paradoxical sleep patterns similarly relieved. As expected, there have also been reports, from experiments on rabbits, that neurones in waking animals synthesize more ribosomal RNA than those in sleeping animals. It has also been shown that this synthesis correlates at cellular level between cortical level of activity both with EEG and using observations of light and deep sleep (Guiditta 1977). Indeed 'during paradoxical sleep cerebral protein synthesis may attain levels comparable with waking levels' with decreased synthesis in deep sleep.

## CONCLUSIONS

Despite the many variables involved and the dangers inherent in extrapolating animal experiments to humans, the general trend of recent research has a broad measure of agreement. The development of recent microhistological visualization and assay has made it possible to correlate intracellular changes with a number of external deprivative factors.

Foremost among these is protein malnutrition especially of the essential amino acids. This can occur as part of malnutrition in developed and developing countries, and is particularly important in the first two years of life, when an intracellular pattern indicative of lasting damage may be laid down. Since learning has been shown to be associated with RNA protein synthesis throughout life, it is also likely that other interferences with cellular metabolism and the enhancement of protein synthesis also play a part in non-specific retardation. It seems probable that synthesis of RNA protein depends on intracellular shuttles of amino acids from cytoplasm to nucleus, itself dependent on an effective supply of stimuli and metabolites. These, in turn, are dependent on extracellular variables, much open to interference by factors as diverse as hormones, toxins, and different food metabolites.

Using recent methods, delay in maturation of electrical activity and reflexes in malnourished rats can be shown 12 hours after birth. Where this is associated with additional extracellular variables such as degree of visual and auditory stimuli (which enhance brain blood flow with its metabolites), hormonal dysfunction, availability of glucose, or persistent infection, the inferences for retardation or the reverse are clear. (see also Ingvar & Lassen 1975.)

Elsewhere in this book emphasis is properly placed on the need for a stimulating environment for the infant retardate, and early patterning of training. Whether this is called behaviour reinforcement or educational patterning is less important than the now proven need for parental counselling at birth, and for the handicapped to have continuous training thereafter. Advances in the understanding of intracellular mechanisms in the nervous system—that is, neurocytology—are only likely to aid this hard and continuous work in two ways, so far as can be seen at the time of writing.

The first depends on the possible facilitation of the action of neurotransmitters in the learning process (for a general discussion see Kastin et al. 1977). It will be appreciated from the earlier discussion in this chapter, that neurotransmitter production, end-plate activity and later destruction of substances by enzymes, can only be aided to proceed at normal, that is optimal, level, by supply of all necessary metabolites. It can be sub-optimal, due to famine or deprivation, but cannot be rendered supra-optimal if substances are supplied in excess. Facilitation of basic learning does occur, however, in conditions of emotional stress or susceptibility, for instance fear responses or imprinting probably occur as a result of this. It is probable that speedy learning in times of stress occurs as a result of intracerebral production, possibly in the hypothalamic area, of specific facilitator hormones. Among facilitating substances occurring naturally are the pituitary peptide melanocyte-stimulating hormone, and adrenocorticotrophic hormone. There has been a tremendous amount of work carried out to elucidate their effect, but this is neither complete, nor has this reached the stage whereby normal behaviour shaping or learning of young children can be enhanced. It is a possibility for the future.

The second depends on the possibility of influencing general or specific cell inhibitors within the nervous system (for discussion see Saavedra 1977). The existence of inhibitor enzymes has been known for a long time, but only recently, with the development of microassay methods, has it been possible to investigate their interactions in detail. The development of specific inhibitors, for instance, in the field of the transmethylase enzyme system, would open up exciting possibilities of influencing mental disorder, but again their practical utility in degrees of cellular brain damage is some way off yet.

BIBLIOGRAPHY

Armen, J. C. (1974) *Gazelle-Boy*. London: Bodley Head.

Balazs, R., Patel, A. J. & Lewis, P. D. (1977) Metabolic influences on cell proliferation in the brain. In: Davison, A. N. (ed.), *Biochemical Correlates of Brain Structure and Function*. London: Academic Press.

Bowlby, J. (1977) The making and breaking of affectual bonds: II. Some principles of psychotherapy (the Fiftieth Maudsley Lecture, expanded version). *Br. J. Psychiat.*, *130*, 421–31.

*British Medical Journal* (1978) Exotic diets and the infant. *1*, 804.

Clarke, A. D. B., Clarke, A. M. & Reitman, S. (1958) Cognitive and social changes in the feeble-minded. *Br. J. Psychol.*, *49*, 144–57.

Davison, A. N. (ed.) (1977) *Biochemical Correlates of Brain Structure and Function*. London: Academic Press.

Eckhart, C. D., Barnes, R. M. & Levitsky, D. A. (1976) Regional changes in rat brain choline acetylotransferase and acetylcholinesterase activity resulting from undernutrition imposed during different periods of development. *J. Neurochem.*, *27*, 227–83.

Guiditta, A. (1977) Biochemistry of sleep. In: Davison, A. N. (ed.), *Biochemical Correlates of Brain Structure and Function*. London: Academic Press.

Hoorweg, J. & Stanfield, J. P. (1976) The effects of protein energy malnutrition in early childhood on intellectual and motor abilities in later childhood and adolescence. *Devl. Med. Child Neurol.*, *18*, 330–50.

Ingvar, D. H. & Lassen, N. A. (1975) *Brain Work Coupling of Function, Metabolism and Blood Flow in the Brain*. Copenhagen: Munksgaard.

Jones, D. G. & Dyson, S. E. (1976) Synaptic junctions in undernourished rat brain: an ultrastructural investigation. *Expl Neurol.*, *51*, 529–35.

Kastin, A. J., Miller, L. H., Sandman, C. A., Schally, A. V. & Plotnikoff, N. P. (1977) CNS and pituitary effects of hypothalmic peptides and MSH. In: Youdim, M. B. H., Lovenberg, W., Sharman, D. F. & Lagnado, J. R. (eds.), *Essays in Neurochemistry and Neuropharmacology*, vol. I. Chichester: John Wiley.

O'Hara, P. T. (1972) Electron microscopical study of the brain in Down's syndrome. *Brain*, *95*, 681–4.

Raisman, G. & Field, P. M. (1973) Sexual dimorphism in the neuropil of the preoptic area of the rat and its dependence on neonatal androgens. *Brain Res.*, *54*, 1–29.

Roberts, I. F., West, R. J., Ogilvie, D. & Dillon, M. J (1979) Malnutrition in infants receiving cult diets: a form of child abuse. *Br. med. J.*, *1*, 296–8.

Rose, S. P. R. & Haywood, J. (1977) Experience, learning and brain metabolism. In: Davison, A. N. (ed.), *Biochemical Correlates of Brain Structure and Function.* London: Academic Press.

Rutter, M. (1972) *Maternal Deprivation Reassessed.* Harmondsworth: Penguin.

Saavedra, J. M. (1977) The role of methylating enzymes in brain function. In: Youdim, M. B. H., Lovenberg, W., Sharman, D. F. & Lagnado, J. R. (eds.), *Essays in Neurochemistry and Neuropharmacology*, vol. I. Chichester: John Wiley.

Shull, M. W., Reed, R. B., Valadian, I., Palombo, R., Thorne, H. & Dwyer, J. T. (1977) Velocities of growth in vegetarian preschool children. *Pediatrics, 60,* 410–17.

Shute, C. C. D. (1974) Chemical transmitter systems in the brain. In: Williams, D. (ed.), *Modern Trends in Neurology.* Sevenoaks, Kent: Butterworths.

Spillane, J. A., White, P., Goodhardt, M. J., Flack, R. H. A., Bowen, D. M. & Davison, A. N. (1977) Selective vulnerability of neurones in organic dementia. *Nature, 266,* 558–9.

Stoch, M. B. & Smythe, P. M. (1976) 15 year developmental study on effects of severe undernutrition during infancy on subsequent physical growth and intellectual functioning. *Arch Dis. Childh., 51,* 327–35.

Ungar, G., Desiderio, D. M. & Parr, W. (1972) Isolation, identification and synthesis of a specific behaviour-inducing brain peptide. *Nature, 238,* 198–202.

Weisel, T. V. & Hubel, D. H. (1965) Extent of recovery from the effects of visual deprivation in kittens. *J. Neurophysiol., 28,* 1060–72.

# CHAPTER 9

# THE PSYCHIATRY OF
# MENTAL RETARDATION

## MICHAEL CRAFT

At out-patient clinics children with mental retardation have different needs in diagnosis and treatment from mentally handicapped adults. Two-thirds of the practice of paediatric neurology is concerned with the causes of retardation in children. Those with actual or possible retardation now comprise over half of the out-patients of most paediatricians in the United Kingdom. Paediatric practice in North American or Australian states differs from the UK, for such office practices may deal predominantly with many problems of upbringing often dealt with by the family doctor in the UK. Earlier chapters in this book were mainly concerned with problems of diagnosis and treatment of retardation in children, whilst counselling of parents and their children is covered in the chapters on early education (Chapter 13) and social work (Chapter 17).

Out-patient consultations for the adult mentally retarded differ from those for children in having greater psychiatric content. The out-patient series reported by Craft (1960) and Reid (1972) reflect the interests of their clinics; the one in a teaching hospital, the other in a general hospital practice. It is probable that there would be higher proportions of referrals with mainly social problems, as opposed to psychiatric illness, in local authority clinics.

### Diagnosis at adult mental retardation out-patient clinics

The majority of out-patient consultations for the adult mentally retarded are for behaviour disorders of varying severity. Most of these are minor situational disturbances within the family between persons whose needs and orientations differ, the only difference from the ordinary family being that one member is mentally handicapped. Thus the same principles of diagnosis apply. A physician needs to take a *detailed history* from more than one participant so as to escape bias, and preferably to have a *social report* to gain the feel of the family within its home. Since he will be depending on the social worker to carry through much of his advice, the social worker should also be at the clinic; both physician and social worker need reports on the adult mentally handicapped person's behaviour at the training centre and club, so that they can form an impression of the behaviour level outside the home.

The *psychiatric*, and if necessary *medical examination*, is important to evaluate intellectual and personality assets, but it should always be remembered that the mentally handicapped person is often at his most tense and anxious at out-patients, being the one least able to express himself clearly.

*Further investigations* are rarely necessary for situational disturbances, although the EEG is occasionally useful where epilepsy is indicated, or where a temporal lobe, or generally unstable record, is suspected.

### Court referrals

Sexual offenders against children may be sent to out-patient clinics, labelled 'behaviour disorder', but especially with the adolescent and young adult, their offences are often examples of mental peer 'experimentation'. Sex education and its results are discussed in Chapter 27. Finally, such offences as thieving and arson used to be explained by many (including the earlier editions of this book) as due to mental defect alone. Current thinking explains these behaviours along the lines of learning theory that they are expressions of lack of personality training, or indeed misdirection of personality training, by a single parent, or parents themselves in conflict. The out-patient analysis then resolves itself into considerations of whether it is a case of an isolated offence solely due to chance factors, with an appropriate report to the court; or whether there needs to be home input by way of social work counselling, home teaching, or extra counselling at the training centre; or whether an alternative residential placement is needed. This last by no means necessarily requires a hospital admission, for observations in a residential community assessment unit (or hostel) or even a college of further education for the adolescent handicapped may be alternatives. Major personality distortions, almost always the result of highly destructive or twisted family upbringing or deprivation, are rare among those under IQ 70. The higher up the IQ range the more common are these extreme examples because of the greater percentage of population in the country as a whole. Only a few per cent of the general population score under IQ 70 so that extreme examples of personality distortion are very rare; some 25 per cent of the population score IQ 70–90. The diagnosis and treatment of such extreme personality distortions IQ 70 and above, is described in detail elsewhere (Craft 1967).

## Psychoses and neuroses

A minority of referrals to the adult out-patient clinic are for psychoses and neuroses. Psychoses in the mentally handicapped differ from those in the general population both in quantity and quality of illness. These are therefore dealt with at some length in the pages that immediately follow. Neuroses such as anxiety states, obsessional syndromes, and tension states are more similar in their manifestation in the adult mentally handicapped compared to the normal population, and are therefore not dealt with in detail here. The interested reader is referred to Slater and Roth (1974).

## Progressive retardation in the adult, and dementia

A small number of out-patient and an important section of in-patient referrals to the psychiatrist concern the differential diagnosis of *progressive retardation* in adult mental retardates of any age. This is not the same as *dementia* although it may be loosely termed such by some professional persons who should be more precise. Dementia is the permanent brain syndrome resulting from continuing organic damage to neurones. It is thus a first-stage diagnosis, in which the second stage should be the demonstration of its physiological cause. The differential diagnosis of progressive retardation in the adult mentally handicapped is given in Table 9.3 (see page 154); it must never be forgotten that an important cause of apathy, listlessness and deteriorated behaviour in the adult mentally handicapped, as with the normal population, is poor living conditions associated with lack of stimulation. Among those endowed with normal IQ it has been described as institutional 'dementia', or 'institutional neurosis' and used to be demonstrable in the larger institutions for the 'normal' blind.

## Mental illness in the handicapped

Mental illness in the handicapped is poorly dealt with in current Anglo-American textbooks of psychiatry, one dismissing this area in a paragraph, another saying 'There is much research to be done.' Even in texts on mental handicap help is meagre, and in previous editions of this book, interest dwelt on the psychopath. Only Penrose, who lived in a mental handicap hospital and 'loved fools' as J. B. S. Haldane feelingfully observes, is constructive with data and treatment culled from the 1938 Colchester survey: 'Mental illness, whether in the form of epilepsy, neurosis, psychopath or psychosis, is a very important contributory factor in the selection of cases for hospital treatment ... high grade cases (IQ 38–69) admitted to hospitals are only a very small sample of all those of comparable ability in the general population . . . (admitted) . . . because they are mentally ill . . . most mental disturbances tend to reduce efficiency on intelligence tests' (Penrose 1938). Such comments are as true today as yester-year.

## THE INCIDENCE OF MENTAL ILLNESS

As stated elsewhere, the incidence of mental illness as of other clinical signs, will vary among the mentally handicapped according to the population under survey. There are four differing populations:

1. *The socially inadequate or incompetent scoring IQ 70–95+* forwarded by courts and other agencies because the main need quite reasonably appears to be sheltered residential and/or working conditions with compassionate care. This group has bedevilled statistics on mental handicap for years. It contains a considerable minority of so-called simple schizophrenics, often severely under-func-

tioning as a result of past illness, for whom the acute stage was long ago. For some mental handicap hospitals it constitutes a large proportion of admissions, and of course, it is a group for whom care needs to be provided somewhere.

2. *Those in the general community scoring less than IQ 70.* They constitute 3 per cent of the general population. The mentally ill among this group are the stock-in-trade of the community psychiatrist's out-patient clinic, but recent statistics for this group are few.

3. *In-patient populations of hospitalized mentally handicapped.* Two analyses of mental illness among defectives admitted under the 1913 Act reported in the literature are detailed (Table 9.1). The figures are similar and reflect the selective admission to psychiatric hospitals of the community mentally ill. As Heaton Ward (1977) notes the proportion of mentally ill among mentally handicapped admitted to hospital varies markedly depending on the hospital and the consultant. Quoting statistics by Primrose (1971), Craft (1971) and Reid (1972), he suggests that up to 60 per cent

TABLE 9.1

Mental illness in the institutionalized

| Type of mental illness | 1280 patients (Penrose 1938)* | | | | 314 patients (Craft 1958)† |
|---|---|---|---|---|---|
| | IQ 76–95 (dull) | IQ 50–75 (feeble-minded) | IQ 21–49 (imbecile) | IQ 20 (idiot) | IQ 38–93 (imbecile and feeble-minded) |
| Idiopathic epilepsy | 30 | 57 | 81 | 42 | — |
| Psychoneurosis and perversion | 56 | 53 | 20 | 3 | 91 |
| Affective psychosis | 4 | 17 | 3 | — | — |
| Schizophrenia | 8 | 11 | 16 | 13 | 13 |
| Subtotals | 98 | 138 | 120 | 58 | |
| Totals | 414 (32%) | | | | 104 (33%) |

\* Royal Eastern Counties Institution.
† Royal Western Counties Institution.

of admissions suffered from 'all forms of psychiatric disorder' including personality disorder, neuroses and psychoses. However, as anyone admitting patients to a psychiatric hospital will know, the label 'personality disorder' often tells one as much about the labeller, as the labelled.

4. *Mentally handicapped children*. Descriptions of mental illness among retarded children are rare, except for autism (see Chapter 24).

A rather fuller account of psychiatric causes of retardation is given here than in former editions, partly because useful practical accounts elsewhere in the literature are lacking, partly because the recent extension of psychiatric community practice has opened up new areas of activity, and partly due to the recent arrival of powerful new treatment agents. Much of what follows is based on personal community practice.

## SCHIZOPHRENIA

*History*. The term was first used by Bleuler (1911) to delimit the mass of asylum psychoses described as dementia praecox by Kraepelin (1896). The old German term *pfropf-schizophrenie* was used to describe the illness in the mentally handicapped.

*Incidence*. The schizophrenias are widespread round the world. Expectation during a person's life to age 65 has been given as 0.9 (Shields 1978) and 1.1 per cent (Slater & Cowie 1971). On average a person unrelated to a schizophrenic has a 1.0 per cent possibility of developing the illness during his life. Elsewhere in the world the incidence is said to be low among the Hutterite sect of North America and in Iceland, high in Northern Sweden, Norway and Geneva. Among hospitalized mentally handicapped in-patients Penrose (1938) found 3 per cent, Craft (1958) 4 per cent and Heaton Ward (1977) 3.4 per cent.

*Genetics*. Twin studies provide the best data, and are well reviewed by Slater and Roth (1974) who provide the following data:

*Expectation of schizophrenia*

| | |
|---|---|
| In general population | 1.0% |
| Among the family of a schizophrenic | |
| In non-blood relatives: | |
| Adopted siblings | 1.8% |
| Spouses | 2.1% |
| In blood relatives: | |
| First cousins | 2.6% |
| Nephews and nieces | 3.9% |
| Grandchildren | 4.3% |
| Half siblings | 7.1% |
| Parents | 9.2% |
| Full siblings | 14.2% |
| Dizygotic co-twins | 14.5% |
| Dizygotic twins (same sex) | 17.6% |
| Children | 16.4% |
| Children of two schizophrenics | 39.2% |
| Monozygotic twins (living apart) | 77.6% |
| Monozygotic twins (living together) | 91.5% |

They also review family studies showing schizophrenia, manic depressive psychosis and atypical psychoses to 'breed true'. Children born to a parent with one type of psychosis thus do not develop the other. They say there is no reported instance of a monozygotic twin pair in which one is schizophrenic and one manic depressive. Slater and Roth (1974) calculate a gene frequency of 0.015 for schizophrenia, for an incidence of 0.9 per cent lifetime expected illness in the general population, 97 per cent of schizophrenics being heterozygous and 3 per cent being homozygous. They suggest that only 26 per cent of heterozygotes develop schizophrenia, which is in line with arguments earlier in this book of variation in target organ specificity, and environmental precipitation in the development of frank illness (see for instance inborn errors of metabolism and phenylketonuria, p. 66). Identification of any inborn errors of metabolism underlying schizophrenia continue to elude investigators. *Pfropf-schizophrenie*, that is schizophrenia associated with mental defect, has been repeatedly investigated. Most workers (for instance, Sjogren and Larsson 1959) find a higher proportion of schizophrenia among the severely mentally handicapped than among the general population (see later).

*Clinical features.* The schizophrenic illnesses are primarily associated with disturbance of affect, feeling and communication. The primary signs, described by Bleuler (1911) of (1) thought disorder, (2) disturbance of volition, (3) primary delusions, (4) emotional disturbance, are found with the mentally handicapped, together with secondary disturbances of (5) catatonia and (6) hallucinations. However their elucidation is considerably impaired firstly by the defect in communication between the mentally handicapped person and his peers, and even more so between him and a highly qualified professional from a cultural background which often gives little discussion in common.

In the general population half the schizophrenic psychoses occur among people already abnormal in behaviour or physique, the so-called schizoid personality. Such people are cold in feeling to others, they may be shy, sensitive and retiring or even aggressive, demanding and brusque, but above all unfeeling. As shown by photographic, X-ray and morphological studies their bodily type is statistically more commonly thin and etiolated. Such people tend to be cyanosed, have poor peripheral circulation and cold skins and palms. Both with these, and with the half who develop a psychosis 'out of the blue', the affection may develop, over a period of days or weeks, any or all of the following conditions in the mentally handicapped:

1.  Thought disorder, mainly confusion, in the absence of fever, inability to explain what is being felt, puzzlement, occasional attacks on fellow workers due to unexplainable suspicions.

2.  Disturbance of volition, or loss of drive as a cardinal feature of the illness in the mentally handicapped, and compared with the general population this may be the most important feature. Less common is hyperexcitability with furious activity in all directions.

3.  Primary delusions are rarely found with the strength of those with average intelligence. The mentally handicapped usually feel themselves overshadowed by brighter people of ordinary ability and accept disapproval of their primary and strongly felt delusions, although continuing to be deluded.

4.  Disturbance of feeling sense is com-

mon; in the ordinary person with schizophrenia this is exemplified by apathy and listlessness towards his loved ones. So many people with mild mental handicap have been brought up under deprivative circumstances and have not learnt to love and 'feel' for others, that this sign is difficult to elucidate, and is better checked out with relatives and friends.

5.  Catatonia seems to be more common with the mentally handicapped. The following case history describes such a case.

6.  Hallucinations, like delusions above, seem rarely to be held with strength by the retarded. They are most commonly seen among the group who refuse medication.

Using the classic categories, case histories may best describe the forms.

## SIMPLE SCHIZOPHRENIA

Gwyneth, a 25-year-old retarded girl of mental age 7, was referred to out-patients by her retired parents, who loved her well. There was a three month history of apathy, listlessness, disinterest at the adult training centre, where she had formerly excelled. She spurned her handicapped boy friend, rose at night to make tea and use the record player, and slept by day. On examination there were no abnormal physical signs, she was not feverish, hypothyroid or hyperglycaemic. She thought her food tasted queer, needed the record player on at night to 'drown her thoughts', had lost all interest. She had a chest X-ray and multiphase investigation at out-patients, was placed on phenothiazines and deteriorated. She was admitted to hospital, had depot flupenthixol, explained she had spat out the previous tablets, and improved steadily during her three months stay. One year later, now off tranquilizers, she was 'back to her old self'.

Clearly, there are a number of physical conditions which needed to be excluded, but the cardinal features of the diagnosis were her loving parents' report of lost 'feeling' sense, her thought confusion on examination and the training centre's report of loss in drive. She has not relapsed four years later.

## HEBEPHRENIC SCHIZOPHRENIA

Geraint aged 22 was a known ESN(M) schoolboy who was sacked as a labourer for increasing slowness and presented with a one year history of shyness and retardation. Within a month he had become wild, confused, cold, threw bricks at cars, drove one car into the mountains, burnt another. On examination he had a residual cerebellar syndrome from birth anoxia, but was afebrile and otherwise well, had incongruous affect, was noisy, muttered to himself, laughing uproariously as he denied hearing voices, and explained hitting his mother as 'she provoked me'. All investigations were negative. He needed compulsory admission thereafter, had heavy oral phenothiazine medication and recovered rapidly. Discharged home after five months, he attends the hospital as a day patient, and two years later has remained fit.

## CATATONIC SCHIZOPHRENIA

Alec was a quiet, shy youth of 19 when brought to clinic by his divorced mother with a six month history of behaviour disorder. She said he had over-reacted to the recent loss of his father, taking to his room to play records, going to bed in boots and clothes, laughing insanely and 'freezing' when reprimanded. On out-patient examination he was in good physical health, had a mental age of 9, read comics and the TV Times, was thin, peripherally cyanosed, hypotensive, and had a slow pulse. He was afebrile. He was diagnosed as reacting to the loss of a father who had taken him everywhere with him. Alec had a remittant course over the next two years, each time responding to hospital admission and relapsing at home. He entered a beautiful new hostel, but reacted to a continuing destructive staff row by going to bed and staying there. He fed, but became partly incontinent. When next seen in hospital he had large bed sores in both heels, gangrene of the skin and side of one foot, was mute, manneristic and catatonically stuperose with a history of severe recent febrile illness. The diagnosis was now uncertain, and he had no drugs whilst being investigated in hospital over the next fortnight. He made a dramatic recovery, the result of much staff cosseting, and minimal drugs were needed. Thereafter investigations were all negative and he was not diabetic.

This case history shows a schizophrenic reaction both to negative and positive environmental handling. It was the first catatonic 'second degree' bed sore with gangrene the writer had seen since 1957. Three years later Alec remains well, on drugs.

## PARANOID SCHIZOPHRENIA

Leonard was a rigid, meticulous man of 40 when first brought to clinic by his mother. There was a ten-year history of increasing suspicion, with recent violence. On examination he was a neat man of mental age 12 in excellent physical health. He was cold, unfeeling, suspicious and believed his mother had systematically poisoned him. He spat out oral out-patient phenothiazines, and after throwing his mother downstairs twice, breaking limbs, he was hospitalized and proved extremely violent, needing depot neuroleptics and sedatives to quieten him. Although 10 years later he is still in hospital only slightly improved, he works well, and visits shops unaccompanied.

As with many of average intelligence, the prognosis was always poor.

## PFROPF-SCHIZOPHRENIE

As Sjogren and Larsson (1959) showed, schizophrenia is statistically more common in the severely handicapped. More recently Hoffer and Osmond (1962) lent substantiation to the association by finding an unidentified substance they called 'malvaria' causing a mauve spot on paper chromatography, present in the urine of both schizophrenics and mental retardates.

Clinically schizophrenia in the adult mentally handicapped is common (between 3 and 4 per cent of in-patients) and is notable by the lack of communication, resistance to change, 'unpredictable' bouts of aggression, but amenability to staff handling between episodic outbursts.

There are probably several reasons why schizophrenia appears to be common among mentally handicapped in hospital and community:

1. Apart from the 'expected' incidence of 1 per cent among the population under IQ 70, others initially 'dull normal' (that is, originally scoring IQ 71–85) are partly alleviated from schizophrenia, but are still substantially retarded on IQ testing, functioning and scoring under IQ 70.

2. A group of socially incompetent people of higher ability, never IQ tested, whose residual schizophrenic deficit suggests to social workers and adult training centre staff that their needs are best served in a centre for the handicapped.

3. The group of partly recovered childhood autistics are included (Chapter 24). Once of near-normal ability, they may function at a mentally handicapped level in adolescence and beyond.

4. Those with organic brain syndromes may be counted, including metabolic errors such as phenylketonuria, who show schizophreniform signs, and in whom treatment of the original syndrome is only partially successful.

*Further tests for schizophrenia.* Biochemical tests are usually negative in schizophrenia although various esoteric, and variably replicated, tests are positive, such as that by Hoffer and Osmond (1962).

*Treatment and outcome.* As to outcome Slater and Roth (1974) give the data in Table 9.2 for those of average ability. With improved care and drugs, the rates appear to advance. However, there are so many variables involved that it is difficult to compare one group with another, for instance, the selection of initial cases, the definition of remission, usage of drugs et cetera. In the UK only 10 per cent of first admissions remain in hospital continuously for two years or more and the social recovery rate for first attacks is 80 per cent according to a recent *British Medical Journal* editorial (1977). Thus there are grounds for believing that most uncomplicated first attacks of schizophrenia in the handicapped end in social recovery, but there are no such results reported. Elegantly illustrating the effect of environmental variables Leff (1976) described the London follow-up shown in Figure 9.1. The co-variance of drugs

TABLE 9.2

Outcome in schizophrenia

|  | No. of patients | % total remissions | Length of follow-up (years) |
|---|---|---|---|
| Chenley and Drew (1938) | 500 | 12 | 2–12 |
| Kant (1941) | 308 | 6.6 | 7.5–10 |
| Rennie (1939) | 500 | 24.5 | 9–20 |
| Kelly and Sargent (1965) | 84 | 31 | 2 |
| Voliant (1964) | 103 | 40 | 1.5 |

and environmental factors is clear. Many books have been written on treatment of schizophrenia (for a detailed discussion, see Leff (1976) and Slater & Roth (1974)). Among important variables for the mentally handicapped, as for those of average ability with schizophrenia, the following are all important:

1. Drugs. Phenothiazines are symptomatically most effective in acute schizophrenia by injection or as a syrup for more rapid

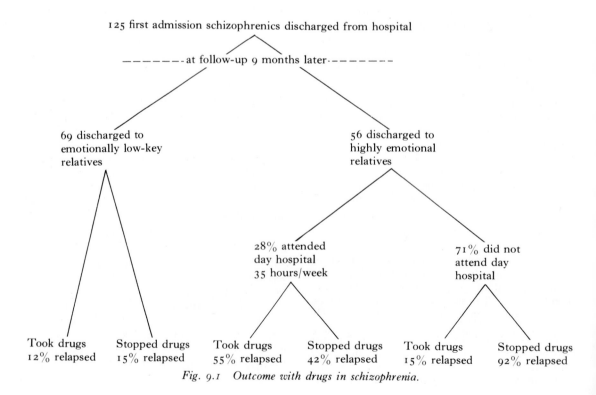

Fig. 9.1   *Outcome with drugs in schizophrenia.*

effect; chlorpromazine 100–1000 mg/day is the best known and still useful; haloperidol 6–30 mg/day is extremely effective for short-term control; flupenthixol decanoate 25–50 mg/day i.m. is useful for maintenance therapy.

2. Psychotherapy. A compassionate and understanding care approach is essential, and communication by facial expression, hand and touch is more effective with the handicapped than tone of voice.

3. Work therapy. The stimulation of daily work is as effective in preventing deterioration as with normal people.

4. Physical treatment such as ECT may be needed on occasion.

5. Surgery by way of stereotactic section is rarely necessary. The writer has felt the need to refer only one such in 20 years of practice.

## DEPRESSION AND MANIA: UNIPOLAR AND BIPOLAR AFFECTIVE ILLNESS IN THE RETARDATE

*History, numbers, incidence.* The numbers of retardates diagnosed as having affective illness has always been low compared with the general population. Among in-patient populations Penrose (1938) found 6 per cent, Reid (1972) 1.2 per cent and Heaton-Ward (1977) 1.2 per cent. Among retarded out-patients Neustadt (1928) found 8 per cent, and Craft (1958) 6 per cent among retardates seen as out-patients at the Maudsley Hospital, London.

*Genetics.* Slater and Roth (1974) quote Stenstedd's (1959) work with approval that 12 per cent of first degree relatives of those affected by manic depression are also affected, the result of a dominant gene of partial effect. The results of most recent researchers agree with this model for bipolar (manic and depressive swings) but for the three times more common unipolar (depression only swing) a different genotype of partial dominance is postulated. The issue is important, for there is some evidence that the first responds better than the second to monoamine oxidase inhibitor drugs. Also, if genetic

endowment is important, and retardates react to their endowment as others do, it seems probable that many depressive reactions in the retardate are misdiagnosed or under-diagnosed.

*Clinical features.* Retardates can in fact show instances of frank depression just like those of the general population, with sorrow, apathy, loss of interest in food and in sleep, loss of weight, even suicidal threats. Reid and Naylor (1976) have been the most recent to emphasize such illnesses. Such extreme illnesses are indeed less common than in the general population, for by and large the retardate is a happy person who seems to be protected by his retardation from severe depression. Indeed there is evidence that suicide is more common as intelligence advances, particularly among psychiatrists and psychologists! Much more common among retardates is a moderate depressive reaction in which apathy and listlessness are the main features with over-emphasis on somatic complaints. Other signs of true depression are lack of appetite, loss of weight, light sleep, little work interest, no contact or communication, retardation of activity worse in afternoons, self-pity and hypochondriasis.

In clinical practice among adult retardates, psychiatric retardation from depression is most common following bereavement or institutionalization. Unfortunately the lack in communications skills, the lack of verbal complaint by the retardate or his dead next of kin, and the inability of staff to compare present unit inactivity with past home activity leads to infrequent remedial action. The elucidation of delusion or guilt are difficult in the retarded and are usually expressed as puzzlement or doubt. Parents do notice change and the nurse or care staff may gain data about change in behaviour during the course of quiet, unstressed conversation with them.

## MASKED, OR SOMATIC, DEPRESSION IN THE DULL

In his book on masked depression Kielholz and his associates (1973) make it quite clear that the more dull the person the more likely is his depressive illness to be 'masked', or

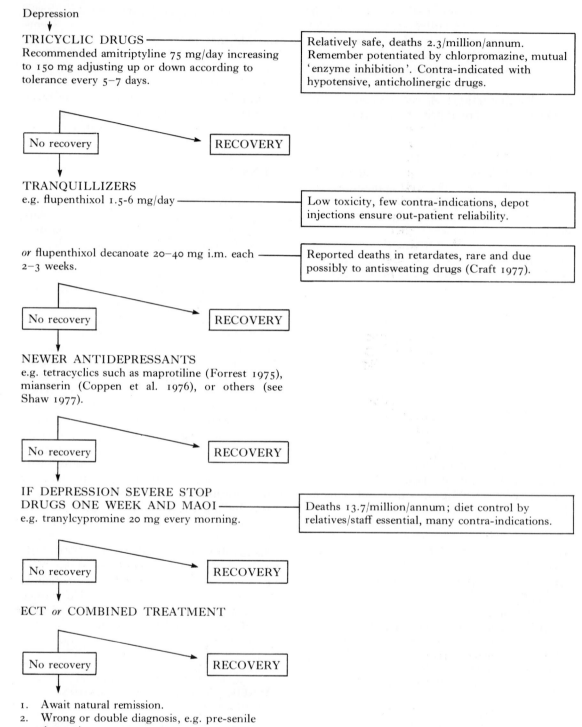

Depression

TRICYCLIC DRUGS
Recommended amitriptyline 75 mg/day increasing to 150 mg adjusting up or down according to tolerance every 5–7 days.

Relatively safe, deaths 2.3/million/annum. Remember potentiated by chlorpromazine, mutual 'enzyme inhibition'. Contra-indicated with hypotensive, anticholinergic drugs.

No recovery          RECOVERY

TRANQUILLIZERS
e.g. flupenthixol 1.5-6 mg/day

Low toxicity, few contra-indications, depot injections ensure out-patient reliability.

or flupenthixol decanoate 20–40 mg i.m. each 2–3 weeks.

Reported deaths in retardates, rare and due possibly to antisweating drugs (Craft 1977).

No recovery          RECOVERY

NEWER ANTIDEPRESSANTS
e.g. tetracyclics such as maprotiline (Forrest 1975), mianserin (Coppen et al. 1976), or others (see Shaw 1977).

No recovery          RECOVERY

IF DEPRESSION SEVERE STOP
DRUGS ONE WEEK AND MAOI
e.g. tranylcypromine 20 mg every morning.

Deaths 13.7/million/annum; diet control by relatives/staff essential, many contra-indications.

No recovery          RECOVERY

ECT or COMBINED TREATMENT

No recovery          RECOVERY

1.  Await natural remission.
2.  Wrong or double diagnosis, e.g. pre-senile dementia.
3.  Possibility of stereotactic surgery.

*Fig. 9.2    Treatment of depression in the retardate (after Shaw 1977).*

'somatized'. It is said that 20 per cent of the depressions appearing in a general psychiatric out-patient department are likely to be 'masked' through overemphasis on somatic complaints, and among those who are illiterate (usually below IQ 75 in the UK) three-quarters will not complain either of depression or of change in sleep rhythms. Among such subjects in the general out-patient department the prime complaints were headaches (40 per cent), abdominal symptoms (36 per cent) and cardiac symptoms (32 per cent), particularly pain or distress on activity. The illiterate members of a general psychiatric out-patient department are coextensive with the members of the general population who could appear at a mental handicap clinic, and could well be the same members brought by their social worker or mother complaining of behaviour disorder centred on bowel or bladder preoccupation. In an important paper on the subject Kreitman et al. (1965) showed the chronicity of marked depression. Fifty per cent of their patients had been ill for more than 10 years and one for 30 years. Yet during this time there had been partial remissions so that the history within a hospital or without of considerable variation in functional level in a person who continuously complains of head or bowel preoccupation without identifiable cause, should raise the suspicion of chronic masked or somatic depression. Supporting factors for the latter would be the gloomy outlook, lack of enjoyment or happiness usual for the mentally handicapped, and apathy, listlessness and disinterestedness compared with behaviour in former years as described by relatives. In cases of doubt, a trial of treatment would seem to be indicated providing one can help any improvement with day work or stimulus to guard against coexistent institutional neurosis or apathy which may be a parallel diagnosis. Some writers have suggested that institutional neurosis and somatic depression lie behind the substantial differences in functioning level of institutionalized retardates found in hospitals which serve similar populations but have different proportions of mentally ill, severely subnormal, moderately subnormal and mildly subnormal.

*Treatment and outcome.* Prevention is clearly better than cure and where depressive illness from bereavement is predictable, careful introduction of change is best. The mentally handicapped, like other people, need work, need to be loved and to have environmental stimulus.

Where drug treatment is indicated the flow chart (Fig. 9.2) may help.

*Differential diagnosis.* This is from other psychogenic causes of secondary retardation in those with primary intellectual deficit; from schizophrenia (see previous section) and other causes of retardation due to 'dementia' (see Table 9.3), particularly hypothyroidism and anaemia, both common in Down's syndrome. In the latter there is a slow pulse, low blood pressure and metabolic rate, and for anaemia paleness and a diagnostic blood film.

MANIA

*History and incidence.* Mania and hypomania are rare in the retarded but dramatic when they occur.

*Genetics.* See discussion of bipolar affective illness (p. 151).

*Clinical features.* There is episodic excitement and overactivity without precipitating cause and in the absence of provocation such as in the furores of epileptics the excitement continues at night. There may be much overeating without weight gain, or indeed weight loss. In extreme cases overactivity, lack of sleep and food lead to intercurrent illnesses, even death.

*Further tests.* The excitement of schizophrenic catatonia has a cold affective quality, that in epilepsy will have marked spike and wave complexes in the EEG. In 'myxoedema madness' there will be a low metabolic rate and protein-bound iodine.

*Treatment and outcome. Acute phase*: true mania is highly episodic, and in acute illnesses drug dosage will have to be similarly variable. Thus sedatives such as barbiturates, or intramuscular valium have been used in the past, for example sodium amytal up to 180 mg orally, two or three times daily, valium 10 mg i.m. as required. Most workers now believe paraldehyde 10 cc i.m. as required

TABLE 9.3

Differential diagnosis of progressive retardation in the adult mentally handicapped (for children, see Table 4.3)

1. *Environmental*
   Lack of stimulation
   Extreme malnutrition
     especially protein
   Anaemia
   Avitaminosis eg thiamine
     B6, B12, niacin, folate
   Drugs and poisons
   Barbiturates
   Alcohol
   Bromides
   Tranquillizers
   Organic phosphates

2. *Metabolic*
   Hypothyroidism
   Hypoglycaemia
   Porphyria
   Uraemia
   Hepatic narcosis
   Hepatolenticular degeneration

3. *Infections*
   Chronic meningitis
   Syphilis
   Cerebral abscess
   Sub-acute sclerosing
     panencephalitis*

4. *Tumours*
   Gliomas
   Meningiomas
   Secondary carcinomata

5. *Mechanical*
   Subdural haematomata
   Occult hydrocephalus
   Continuing epilepsy
   Brain trauma
   Fractured femur
   in elderly

6. *Degenerative*
   Alzheimer's/Pick's disease*
   Huntington's chorea*
   Arteriosclerosis*
   Collagen disease (eg giant
     cell arteritis)
   Senility*

7. *Psychiatric*
   Depression, masked,
     unipolar or bipolar
   Schizophrenia

* denotes those conditions of progressive retardation that are not treatable.

has been superseded by more efficient drugs such as haloperidol.

Haloperidol 10–30 mg i.m. is the initial drug of choice in acute excitement, followed after 1–2 hours by a second dose, size dependent on reaction. Extrapyramidal side effects are uncommon, and it is safe to watch for early finger tremor before giving antiparkinson drugs. The main side effect and risk is fall in blood pressure below systolic 100 mm. Total haloperidol in a physically fit man may reach 40–80 mg per day in the first few days. Once mania subsides oral dosage should be started, this route warranting twice the dosage as given by injection and continued over the next week or two. In the brain-damaged, one must remember the occasional hypersensitive reaction, and use a lower test-dose first.

*Longer term treatment.* There are three considerations here. Firstly those with rare episodes responding to highly provocative situations, or under close residential control, may be judged to need no further long-term treatment. Haloperidol can be slowly reduced over a month or so.

Secondly the depot injection flupenthixol decanoate 20–40 mg every 2 to 3 weeks can be used as maintenance, and aids fearful relatives or lonely care staff. The two drugs are compatible, and the changeover from haloperidol can be effected quickly and safely during the fortnight following the first test-dose of sensitivity of 12.5 mg flupenthixol. This has the advantage of needing review every 2 to 4 weeks or so with the opportunity to check progress and counsel care agents.

Thirdly, in true mania or bipolar affective illness maintenance lithium must be considered. There are few reports to guide one in its successful or effective use with other causes of excitement, but many reports of success in mania and depression. A daily divided dose of 1000–1200 mg lithium salt a day for a fit person should produce the optimal therapeutic level of 0.6–1 mmol/l. The dose must be varied according to need, and the side effects of tremor or other adverse result. Serum levels must be checked, twelve hours after the last dose, after the first five days and weekly thereafter. Since degrees of brain damage may increase sensitivity to lithium as with other neuroleptic drugs this is clearly a taxing regime for relatives and doctors, needing time and careful monitoring.

In the absence of controlled trials to the contrary, most clinicians will opt for a care regime which will take from the above what they need, and transfer on to safe neuroleptics such as haloperidol up to 40 mg/day when crises are long past. Habituation to all these drugs occurs and there is much to be said for discontinuance of neuroleptic medication after a year to assess need, avoid progressive hepatic intoxication in the susceptible, allow re-use of a re-efficacious drug on relapse, and also because environmental care may have improved as a direct result of people reconsidering their attitudes following illness.

## PROGRESSIVE RETARDATION

Progressive retardation in an adult mentally handicapped person is here meant to describe a deterioration in mental and physical performance which is not accounted for by reference to the original cause of mental handicap. For instance, if the original cause for mental handicap is Huntington's chorea, muscular dystrophy, or one of the lipidoses, it is to be expected that the original genetic misendowment will lead to progressive deterioration throughout life. This is not so for chromosomal anomalies such as Down's or Klinefelter's syndromes, where the affected person might be expected to gradually improve his abilities in early adult life even reaching some levels of output which may be close to the 'normal'.

Some mentally handicapped, particularly Down's syndrome subjects, develop an unexplained and unexpected downturn in early or middle life which cannot be ascribed to their chromosomal anomaly. In order to make a complete second-stage diagnosis it is necessary to proceed along normal medical channels by way of a good history, intellectual and neurological examination, with further investigations.

A *good history* is important in establishing the previous functioning level of the person concerned. Intelligence tests may or may not have been done in the past; a better guide is often the social level at which the person concerned is functioning, the tasks he is able to do at the training centre, and his hobbies at home.

*Physical examination* allows the causes of progressive retardation to be divided into three categories:

1. Those associated with medical and laboratory signs of disease, for example, hypothyroidism, avitaminoses, meningitis, fractured femoral lead.
2. Those associated with other neurological signs but no general medical disease, for example, Huntington's chorea, the ataxias, subdural haematoma, low pressure hydrocephalus.
3. No neurological or medical features, for example Alzheimer's and Pick's diseases, senile dementia.

*Further investigations* will naturally follow upon findings as above, and it should be remembered that hypothyroidism has been reported to affect between 5 and 10 per cent of Down's syndrome subjects, and that avitaminoses though rare, have consistently been reported among those taking aberrant diets.

True pre-senile dementia has been described by a number of writers to occur in Down's syndrome subjects, but others dispute this. Crome and Stern (1967) and others describe pre-senile plaques as occurring in the brains of Down's syndrome subjects in the early thirties, ten years earlier than expected for subjects in the general population. The true significance of this is not clear as the appearance of senile plaques varies greatly in ageing brains, and like 'normal' people some Down's syndrome subjects die relatively early, from what clinically appears to be senile dementia; whilst other subjects now live on to their seventies, their faculties unimpaired. It seems wise to conclude at this juncture, that the genetic programming for Down's syndrome subjects includes a higher propensity to lethal developments such as leukaemia and lack of immune defence, but for pre-senile dementia is unproven.

*Treatment* must follow diagnosis. As with those apparently 'dementing' in the general population, one should not now be content with this simplistic label for deterioration in an adult retardate. Table 9.3 is provided to remind the practitioner of likely causes and their investigations. It remains to emphasize the recent research showing that hypothyroidism can affect over 10 per cent of ageing

Down's syndrome subjects and other retardates; that frequent epileptic fits cause cell fall-out; and that anti-epileptic drugs can themselves cause mental intoxication. All these are common causes of progressive retardation in the adult retardate.

## BIBLIOGRAPHY

Bleuler, E. (1911) *Dementia Praecox, or The Group of Schizophrenics*. New York: Int. Univ. Press.
*British Medical Journal* (1977) Editorial. *1*, 733.
Coppen, A., Gupta, R., Montgomery, S., Ghose, K., Bailey, J., Burns, B. & De Ridder, J. J. (1976) Mianserin hydrochloride; a novel antidepressant. *Br. J. Psychiat.*, *129*, 342–5.
Craft, M. J. (1958) *Mental Disorders in the Defective*. Royal Institution, Starcross, Devon.
Craft, M. J. (1960) Mental disorder in a series of English out-patient defectives. *Am. J. Ment. Defic.*, *64*, 718–24.
Craft, M. J. (1967) *Psychopathic Disorders*. Oxford: Pergamon.
Craft, M. J. (1971) A North Wales experiment in subnormality care. *Br. J. Psychiat.*, *118*, 199–206.
Craft, M. J. (1977) Letter re toxic effects of depot tranquillizers in mental handicap. *Br. med. J.*, *1*, 835.
Crome, L. C. & Stern, J. (1967) *Pathology of Mental Retardation*. Edinburgh: Churchill Livingstone.
Forrest, A. (1975) Maprotiline. In: Murphy, J. E. (ed.), *Research and Clinical Investigation in Depression*. Northampton: Cambridge Medical Publications.
Heaton-Ward, A. (1977) Psychosis in mental handicap (the Blake Marsh Lecture 1976). *Br. J. Psychiat.* *130*, 525–33.
Hoffer, A. & Osmond, A. (1962) The association between schizophrenia and two objective tests. *Can. med. Ass. J.*, *87*, 641–6.
Kielholz, P. (ed.) (1973) *Masked Depression*. Bern: Hans Huber.
Kraepelin, E. (1896) *Psychiatrie*. Leipzig: Thieme.
Kreitman, N., Sainsbury, P., Pearce, K., & Costain, W. R. (1965) Hypochondriasis and depression in out-patients at a general hospital. *Br. J. Psychiat.*, *III*, 607–15.
Leff, J. (1976) Assessment of psychiatric and social state. *Br. J. Clin. Pharmacol.*, *3* (3/Suppl. 2).
Neustadt, R. (1928) *Psychoses of Defectives*. Berlin: Karger.
Norris, V. (1959) *Mental Illness in London*. Maudsley Monographs. London: Institute of Psychiatry and Chapman Hall.
Penrose, L. S. (1938) A clinical and genetic study of 1280 cases of mental defect (Colchester Survey). *Spec. Rep. Ser. med. Res. Coun.*, No. 229. London: HMSO.
Primrose, D. A. (1971) A survey of 500 consecutive admissions to a subnormality hospital from 1 January 1968 to 31 December 1970. *Br. J. ment. Subnorm.*, *27*, 25–8.
Reid, A. H. (1972) Psychoses in adult mental defectives. *Br. J. Psychiat.*, *120*, 205–18.
Reid, A. H. & Naylor, G. J. (1976) Short cycle manic depressive psychosis in mental defectives, a clinical and physiological study. *J. ment. Defic. Res.*, *20*, 67–76.
Shaw, D. (1977) The practical management of affective disorders. *Br. J. Psychiat.*, *130*, 432–51.
Shields, J. (1978) Genetics. In: Wing, J. K. (ed.), *Schizophrenia: Towards a New Synthesis*. London: Academic Press.
Sjogren, T. & Larsson, T. (1959) Changing age structure in Sweden and its impact on mental illness especially senile psychosis. *Bull. Wld Hlth Org.*, *21*, 560.
Slater, E. & Cowie, V. (1971) *The Genetics of Mental Disorders*. Oxford: Oxford University Press.
Slater, E. & Roth, M. (1974) *Clinical Psychiatry*, 4th ed. Baltimore: Williams & Wilkins.
Stenstedt, A. (1959) Involutional melancholia. *Acta psychiat. neurol. scand.*, *34*, Suppl. 127.

# CHAPTER 10

# MEDICATION

## MICHAEL CRAFT

It is sad to have to record in 1979 that the mode of action of many psychiatrically active drugs is not fully known. It is probable that this is because the role of neurotransmitter agents themselves in mental disorder is poorly understood, and the respective roles of dopaminergic, cholinergic and other systems are still being unravelled. Psychiatrically active drugs can be divided into:

1. Major tranquillizers, such as the chlorpromazine group.
2. Minor tranquillizers, such as sedatives and anti-anxiety drugs.
3. Antidepressants.
4. A more general group, which includes the anticonvulsants described in detail in Chapter 25 (see p. 337).

The following list provides a convenient analysis of psychotropic drugs which can be used with the retardate; the first three groups are discussed in this chapter. Drugs for the epileptic are described in Chapter 25, and for the violent in Chapter 26.

1. *Major tranquillizers.*
   Antipsychotic and antischizophrenic being non-hypnotic sedatives:
   a. Phenothiazine group, e.g. chlorpromazine best known, 75–500 mg/day; thioridazine (Melleril) 75–500 mg/day latest derivative; or fluphenazine decanoate 10–15 mg depot i.m.
   b. Thioxanthines, e.g. flupenthixol 10–40 mg depot i.m.
   c. Butyrophenones, e.g. haloperidol 3–5 mg/day up to 40 mg or more.

2. *Minor tranquillizers.*
   Lacking antipsychotic effect and with a calming, hypnotic action:
   a. Diazepam (Valium) 6–60 mg/day.
   b. Nitrazepam (Mogadon) 5–10 mg each night.
   c. Barbiturates e.g. phenobarbitone.
3. *Antidepressants.*
   a. Primarily mood elevating: tricyclics, e.g. imipramine 30–300 mg/day.
   b. Disinhibiting: monoamineoxidases, e.g. tranylcypromine 10–30 mg/day (Parnate).
   c. Stabilizing: lithium 250–1500 mg/day.
4. *Older drugs.*
   a. Frank sedatives: alcohol, paraldehyde, phenobarbitone.
   b. Frank stimulants: amphetamine, marijuana.
   c. Anti-epileptic: phenobarbitone, etc.

A golden rule for those concerned with drug administration is that they should use those drugs with which they are most familiar, but a second rule is that although one might not be the first to use a powerful and potentially dangerous new drug, one should not be the last either. Since research continues apace throwing more light on the usage of old drugs and fresh light on the specificity of new, the scene is always changing, and it behoves one to keep up to date.

In general, old drugs have wide actions and many side effects, some good, some bad. For example phenobarbitone appears three times in the list above, respectively as a minor tranquillizer, sedative and anti-epileptic agent. It has many other effects, two of them causing addiction and anaesthesia, tending to diminish its usage in contemporary medicine. In fact successful drug treatment depends largely on improving the specificity of drugs one uses, apart from accurate diagnosis of need. To understand specificity it is essential to understand the mode of action of drugs and thus appreciate the significance of their use, or abuse.

## MAJOR TRANQUILLIZERS

The most commonly used tranquillizer until quite recently was chlorpromazine. Discovered by accident in the early 1950s and co-inciding with social changes that allowed the discharge of over half the population of many mental hospitals it has a variety of side effects. Like all other major tranquillizers it blocks dopamine-mediated synapses in the brain. As a result the presynaptic neurone increases its production of dopamine to overcome the block at the postsynaptic receptor and initially there is an increase in the CSF concentration of homovanillic acid, the principal metabolite of dopamine. Originally noted in rats, this has recently been verified in humans and seems to be a type of neuronal feedback system.

In support of the blockade theory, the phenothiazines with the most antipsychotic activity have parts of their molecular structure very similar to dopamine, and those without this similarity are less active.

The side effect of extrapyramidal signs in man (and catalepsy which is the equivalent in animals) is due to this blockade. True Parkinsonism results from structural deterioration of dopaminergic neurones in the nigrostrictal projection in the human brain and this is aided by levodopa, a replacement synthetic dopamine. One can understand why levodopa is ineffective in drug-induced Parkinsonism where there is already an over-production of natural dopamine unable to be effective because of the drug-induced blockade. It seems that another type of neuronal feedback is responsible for tardive dyskinesia, a potentially permanent twitching of face, shoulders and head. This is probably due to overcompensatory induced oversensitivity to dopamine by the neurones, which often

becomes more obvious when the drug–dopamine blockade is removed.

A further side effect of chlorpromazine, as of other major tranquillizers, is its anti-emetic effect due to the chemoreceptors for chlorpromazine also being receptive to the dopamine-agonist amorphine. As stated before, chlorpromazine is one of the least specific early tranquillizers and others of its side effects concern skin–light sensitivity, corneal clouding and liver dyscrasias. These have led to its diminished use in recent years.

There are relatively few dopamine-sensitive pathways in the human brain, but in the rat part of the limbic system concerned with emotion is so mediated. This links the olfactory tubercles, amygdaloid nucleus, frontal cortex and other areas. It is not yet clear how extensively the limbic system is dopamine-mediated in man but there is evidence that the more dopamine-like the major tranquillizer is, the more effective and more anti-schizophrenic is the drug. This poses problems in drug usage, since it is also unclear whether this system is more highly developed in some humans than in others, or more used, or genetically more sensitive. It is also known that there are different rates of drug breakdown in gut and liver, presumably genetic in origin, from human to human.

Another important side effect of major tranquillizers is their degree of anticholinergic activity. This neurotransmitter system is far more widespread in man and overdosage results in anticholinergic blockade with dry mouth, blurring of vision, constipation, vasodilation, tachycardia and hypotension, often highly unpleasant.

There are other widespread effects, and since humans vary in their sensitivity due to variations in receptor sensitivity, drug breakdown and competition with other enzyme systems (even drugs), some patients become much more loath to continue treatment than others. It is estimated that over two-thirds of patients do not take medication as ordered and nearly half do so in ineffective or erratic dosage. In addition the sedative side effects of some tranquillizers like chlorpromazine potentiate other sedatives, including alcohol, whereas newer tranquillizers, for example flupenthixol, can be a cortical neuro-stimulant whilst exerting limbic taming.

The metabolism of chlorpromazine is exceedingly complex, over 150 different metabolites having been identified. Some of these breakdown products are much more active than others. Most of the enzyme systems involved will be genetically endowed. Thus great variations between human response occur. For instance, in some patients the gut-wall metabolizes most orally ingested drugs and the rest may be broken down in the liver with a low plasma level reaching the brain. This is the reason why some patients need enormous doses, and others are sensitive to small doses. Since different drugs compete, and smoking interferes with metabolism, the range of variables is great. In general, fast metabolizers respond poorly and slow metabolizers well to this and other such drugs. Injection is one answer, but is painful with chlorpromazine. Intramuscular fluphenazine or flupenthixol in oily bases are effective. This also avoids erratic or absent self-medication. The two new families, the thioxanthines and the butyrophenones, are both more specific and easier to give by injection as a depot preparation.

In summary: chlorpromazine has been the most extensively investigated of the major tranquillizers and is metabolized along a variety of pathways, and has many side effects. Thioridazine (Melleril) 75–500 mg per day is more specific, with less side effects, as also are the butyrophenones such as haloperidol 3–5 mg per day. For certainty of administration the depot injections fluphenazine decanoate 10–15 mg i.m. and thioxanthines (flupenthixol 10–40 mg i.m.) have been developed.

MINOR TRANQUILLIZERS

Minor tranquillizers are numerous and vary from drugs inducing anaesthesia and death such as alcohol and barbiturates, through hypnotics such as nitrazepam, muscle relaxants (diazepam) and anxiolytics of minor effect (benactyzine). In general barbiturates are widespread cell depressants which reduce oxidative metabolism throughout the body. By depression of neuronal membrane transmission and inhibition of oxidation in liver and brain all activity is reduced, particularly nerve cells involved in involuntary and repetitive action such as the reticular-activating system. Hence the association with addiction, anaesthesia, death.

Recently the benzodiazepines have been introduced. Because of their specificity of action upon the limbic system rather than the cortex, a high dose correlation with tranquillization can be achieved causing taming rather than general sedation. Some members are metabolized very slowly, one, desmethyldiazepam, taking 48 hours. This leads to more reliability in action with fewer of the troughs and peaks of four times daily medication with such as chlorpromazine. Another result of specificity is safety, overdosage producing oblivion without coma, in contrast with barbiturates where oblivion often equates with coma. In fact addiction is rare with diazepams, and withdrawal effects slow, steady and slight. Biochemically there is little neuronal loopback either, a side effect of barbiturates resulting from their widespread inhibition. Barbiturates also cause a loopback stimulation to liver microsomal enzyme systems, resulting in a paradoxical increase in metabolism of other drugs ingested, which thereby become less effective.

The specificity of action of benzodiazepines for the limbic system has led to their being called a 'chemical amygdaloidectomy'. This is a reference to the extreme taming effect of surgical removal of both such lobes in animals. The benzodiazepines appear to act on a further neurotransmitter system. This is the gamma amino butyric acid (GABA) inhibitory neurotransmitter system which inhibits parts of the reticular-activating system. Barbiturates also have this action because of their general cell and membrane inhibition throughout the brain and body, but their action on the reticular system is particularly important. The benzodiazepines appear to be more specific in the inhibition of the limbic system.

Whilst there is little genetic variation in innovation of systems between man and man, there is far greater variation between man and animal. For instance, when severe electroshock stimulation is given to rats, there is an increase in noradrenaline secretion from the cerebral cortex, which can be blocked in rats by benzodiazepines. It is by no means certain that the same action occurs in man.

The metabolism of benzodiazepines is quite different to chlorpromazine. They are broken down in a regular way with slight variation between man and man, suggesting there is little genetically endowed difference between the pathways open to different humans. In addition most early metabolites are active which means there is a long half-life, and only slight difference between different drug members so far as their action is concerned.

In contrast, propranolol (500–1000 mg per day) is a beta adrenoceptor blockader acting mainly on peripheral neuroreceptors with little central action. Here the sympathomimetic response reduces peripheral somatic sensation. Thus hand trembling, palpitations and gastrointestinal overactivity are reduced, with little action in the brain. When the anxious patient is blockaded by the drug and thus protected from palpitation, he may feel relieved from his main somatic symptoms previously reinforcing his mental feelings of illness.

## ANTIDEPRESSANT DRUGS

Antidepressant drugs are the third group of drugs to be much used and sometimes abused. Recent mental health surveys have shown that some 67 per cent of older women in the general population in Australia had taken drugs during the year prior to review. Up to 15 per cent had been on tranquillizers and 5 per cent on antidepressants (Schacht et al. 1976). There are similar figures from Britain and the United States. These figures make drug interaction possibilities ·quite alarming, and for a new client there is much to be said for filling up a standardized information sheet before first interview.

### The tricyclics

The tricyclics, for example imipramine 75–300 mg, share with many other drugs the oxidative enzyme systems in the liver as the main metabolic disposal method. Thus chlorpromazine and others will share or compete for this enzyme system and the more the drugs, the slower their total elimination. Once again increased competition may also increase production of the enzymes, with later increase in metabolism. The genetic endowment for this varies. Thus depending on high or low enzyme concentrations an ordinary dose of tricyclics prescribed with other sedatives and

tranquillizers may cause an unexpectedly rapid rise in plasma level and marked side effects inducing the patient to stop usage. For example plasma levels ranging from 48 to 238 ng/ml have resulted from test doses of 150 mg nortriptyline (Kragh-Sorensen et al. 1973). Unfortunately the same authors show that there is no direct relationship between plasma level and response with this drug, both high and low levels being less effective than the medium. In contrast, using imipramine the response tended to improve as dose increased until side effects became apparent (Gram et al. 1976).

Other side effects of tricyclics are well known such as their tendency to exacerbate coronary artery disease when physically stressed, with a frightening number of deaths among middle-aged men when snow first falls in Chicago. Also important are atropine-like actions synergistic with anticholinergic compounds to produce glaucoma, with blindness, paralytic lens, and retention of urine.

### Monoamine oxidase inhibitors (MAOI)

The monoamine oxidase inhibitors, for example tranylcypromine 30 mg per day inhibit enzymes metabolizing amines including noradrenaline, adrenaline, histamine and dopamine. These enzymes protect the body internally by degrading the transmitter amines between synapse and neurone, whilst externally they destroy the amines which might flood in from the gut, after cheese or excess beer. It is well known that on MAOI medication the ingestion of tyramine, the most active amine to stimulate catecholamine release, may provoke a hypertensive crisis. Such a crisis can be caused by 25 mg tyramine, contained in 2.5 litres of beer, 300 grams of mature cheese, or 4 pickled herrings. In addition MAOI react with a variety of drugs containing tyramine-like agents; with tricyclics; between different MAOI members, and some sedatives.

Finally one MAOI, phenelzine, is believed to be metabolized by acetylation. The gene for fast acetylation is dominant to slow, and possessed by only 46 per cent of the UK population. Thus there is a major genetic difference between the way one half of the population will react to this drug compared with the other.

MORTALITY AMONG USERS OF
PSYCHOTROPIC DRUGS

As daily papers make clear, many new drugs are powerful, lethal, and their use needs a careful balance between use and abuse. Leff's (1976) research on maintenance dose in schizophrenia has shown that the emotional pattern of a home and adequacy of day work are often more important factors than drugs in preventing relapse; drugs can better be discontinued among well-supported patients.

In depression, Guze and Robins (1970) estimated that 15 per cent of affected individuals died by suicide, and assumed the rather high estimate of six illnesses a lifetime. Shaw (1977) quotes Girdwood's (1974) figures of the following deaths/million prescriptions:

| | |
|---|---|
| Imipramine | 3.6 |
| Chlorpromazine | 8.6 |
| Tranylcypromine | 13.7 |
| Phenelzine | 17.2 |

However, deaths per million prescriptions is not the same as deaths per illness. Many patients remain on comparatively low doses and many prescriptions for a sizeable portion of their lives. Nevertheless the inference is clear, the risks from suicide in depressive illness are likely to be far greater than the risks from any of the drugs used in treatment.

The older psychotropic drugs (group 4 in the list on p. 157) have been used for a very long time. The risks for alcohol are well known, whilst for others such as barbiturates, amphetamines, marijuana, the generality of their actions and likelihood of addiction has caused many to be superseded by drugs more accurate in action.

In the review article on treatment of depression Shaw (1977) eschews the various divisions into unipolar, bipolar, involutional, endogenous and reactive depressions current in the field. He concentrates on effective use of the antidepressants under review. In view of the various metabolic pathways available to individuals of differing genetic endowment to degrade drugs presented to them, it is not surprising that there is considerable variation in effectiveness of these drugs. The review infers that diagnostic differentiations between for instance endogenous and reactive depressions may be less important than the individual's genetic endowment in metabolic efficiency. In consideration of an antidepressant for example, there are at least five variables, respectively:

1. Degree of gut ingestion and breakdown.
2. Degree of metabolism by the liver.
3. Effectiveness of blood–brain barrier.
4. Degree of antagonism or potentiation by other drugs.
5. Genetically-endowed variation in susceptible neuroreactors among parts of the nervous system.

The last is most important for the doctor. Whilst it is difficult to estimate drug levels in the cerebrospinal fluid, it is possible to estimate drug levels in the blood.

These variables have been teased out in the case of chlorpromazine, a classic variable action psychotropic drug. We do not know how many other psychotropic drugs have variable actions with different people due to different endowments, but we have now reached the stage of either monitoring blood drug levels to gauge effective medication level, or using drugs with a more reliable (specific) action. There is now little excuse for using drugs up to the level of toxicity.

To summarize: the use of psychotropic drugs is intimately concerned with how they are deployed. If to specificity of diagnosis is added specificity of drug action, more effective treatment will result. There are no 'safe' drugs which are therapeutically active, but there can be safe doctors.

BIBLIOGRAPHY

Girdwood, R. H. (1974) Death after taking medicaments. *Br. med. J.*, *1*, 501–4.
Gram, L. F., Reisby, N., Ibsen, I., Nagy, A., Dencker, S. J., Beck, P., Petersen, G. O. & Christiansen, J. (1976) Plasma levels and antidepressant effect of imipramine. *Clin. Pharmac. Ther.*, *19*, 318–24.
Guze, S. B. & Robins, E. (1970) Suicide and primary affective disorders. *Br. J. Psychiat.*, *117*, 437–8.

Kragh-Sorensen, P., Asberg, M. & Eggert-Hansen, C. (1973) Plasma-nortriptyline levels in endogenous depression. *Lancet*, *1*, 113–15.

Leff, J. (1976) Assessment of psychiatric and social state. *Br. J. clin. Pharmacol.*, *3* (3/Suppl. 2).

Schacht, P., Brown, J., Brown, R. & Schonfield, C. (1976) *The Redcliffe Health Survey*. Brisbane: Queensland Department of Health.

Shaw, D. M. (1977) The practical management of affective disorders. *Br. J. Psychiat.*, *130*, 432–51.

# THE USE AND ABUSE
# OF THE LABORATORY

## ALAN RUNDLE

In the United Kingdom, laboratory services are based on a three tier system. The lowest tier is based on a hospital or district serving a community of 100 000 to 300 000, and is responsible for providing the full range of the simpler routine investigations and acting as the intermediate between the clinician and the two higher tiers. The second tier is a specialized regional laboratory whose main function is to provide new, technically complex or infrequently requested analyses more quickly or economically than is possible on a local basis; it usually serves several districts within one administrative region. The third tier, similar in function to the regional service but serving a number of regions, is the supra-regional assay service. In most countries where socialized medicine has not been introduced, the two latter tiers are often replaced by commercial laboratories. At hospital or district level, the laboratory service is usually composed of four or more single-discipline departments, although in some hospitals the existence of separate departments is inappropriate and related disciplines are associated in a combined department, with each department being managed by a head who carries responsibility for the organization of the department.

Although there are a few notable examples in which the pathology of mental handicap represents a specific entity, the investigations requested are those common to both the acute services and the general practitioner. With mental handicap there is the additional problem that the laboratory is usually sited near the general hospital, often some distance from the location of the mentally handicapped

patients. Whereas it is customary in the acute field for the clinicians to be in daily contact with laboratory personnel, in mental handicap this is very rarely the case. The very isolation of the specialty means that close discussions should be carried out with the local laboratory on any non-routine problems with which assistance is required. The pathologist is particularly concerned with complicating features arising from the causative nature of the handicap which either preclude some investigations (for example those requiring a subjective evaluation by the patient) or suggest investigations not normally encountered in the acute field. An example is abnormal metabolites arising from inborn errors of metabolism. The laboratory staff will suggest what help may be the most effective, which investigations are advised and what specimens are required. The pathologist can, if necessary, assist in the interpretation of results.

## COLLECTION OF SPECIMENS

Increasing workloads and automation have resulted in many investigations being carried out at specified times daily, and it is important that the specimen should be taken as early as possible and delivered in time for the investigation to be carried out and reported on the same day. More complex investigations, such as serum vitamin assays and plasma lipo-proteins, are only carried out weekly, whereas the rarer investigations, such as serum testosterone and prolactin, may be batched for financial reasons and only carried out on specified days of the month. If an analysis is regarded as urgent it is essential to make contact with the laboratory staff personally so that the appropriate degree of priority can be given to the tests. The collection of certain specimens, particularly those involving serial blood examinations, for example cortisol stimulation tests, prolactin response to bromocryptine, et cetera, or timed urine collections may be better performed in the laboratory, and arrangements for such tests should be made with the laboratory. Only dry-sterilized glass or disposable syringes should be used for the collection of blood or cerebrospinal fluid. Blood should be taken by venepuncture with a minimum of venous stasis, and after the needle has been removed from the syringe, the blood should be gently expelled into the container. If the container contains anticoagulant, this should be dissolved in the blood by inverting the stoppered tube slowly several times.

## Containers

There are no general rules on which container to use for which specimen, individual laboratories will advise on local requirements. A large American commercial laboratory lists no fewer than 40 containers (Bio-science Laboratories 1975). Universal containers (20 ml), 4, 50, 100 and 200 ml glass containers, sputum containers and plastic 24-hour urine containers should be obtained from the local hospital laboratory services.

## Transmission and storage of specimens

*Bacteriological specimens.* Specimens should be handed into the laboratory as soon as possible after collection. If for any reason a specimen cannot reach the laboratory on the day it is taken, it can often be kept overnight in a refrigerator at 4°C or, if the specimen is a swab, it can be put in a transport medium (obtainable from the laboratory) and kept at room temperature. If bacteriological examination is to be made, the specimen should be taken before antibiotic or chemotherapy has been started. If this is not possible a note of the treatment and its duration should be stated on the request form. Absorbent wrapping should be used for postal packages to absorb contents in case of breakage, and such packages should be marked 'Fragile with care (pathological specimen)'.

*Biochemical and haematological specimens.* Most of the assays in these two disciplines are relatively stable in plasma, serum or urine at ambient temperatures. A few, particularly small peptides such as ACTH, AVP and calcitonin are unstable in biological fluids due to the action of proteolytic enzymes, and specific protocols will be available. Additionally some hormones and drugs may absorb onto the surface of glass tubes, and the laboratory will advise on the special precautions required.

## Clinical information and patient identification

Probably the greatest single abuse of the laboratory services arises from the failure to complete the request form adequately. In cases presenting new problems of diagnosis or management, it is essential that request forms should be completed with every relevant detail, because without full information it is impossible to examine a specimen adequately, or to report on it constructively. For example, date of onset of illness, its nature, date and time when the specimen was taken and details of any treatment can be relevant to the selection and interpretation of the investigations carried out. Full details of treatment, if any, should always be given as the use of anticonvulsant drugs is widespread in mental retardation. The most common of these, phenobarbitone, phenytoin and primidone, are known to cause secondary changes in a number of systems including decalcification of bones, with fracture, caused by a disturbance of the hepatic hydroxylation of vitamin $D_3$ to 25-hydroxycholecalciferol, stimulating microsomes resulting in the elevation (that is 'induction') of serum enzymes of microsomal origin (for example, gamma glutamyl transpeptidase, alkaline phosphatase), reduction in serum bilirubin, increased urinary excretion of 6β-hydroxycortisol, reduced serum calcium, elevated excretion of D-glucaric acid, folate deficiency, megaloblastic changes (occasionally macrocytic anaemia). An up-to-date account of these and other changes resulting from anticonvulsant therapy is given in Richens and Woodford (1976).

*Degree of urgency.* Although most pathology laboratories provide a round-the-clock service, only the most urgent specimens should be sent outside normal working hours as usually only a skeleton staff is on duty. Any urgent specimens should be clearly marked together with instructions for contacting the requesting physician, for example phone Dr X on Ward Y. Generally speaking, laboratories are reluctant to report results verbally as this is a ready source of errors, and such requests should be kept to the minimum.

## NORMAL VALUES

Within the laboratory services there are various opinions on what constitutes a normal value. Generally speaking, the normal range is that within which 95 per cent of healthy adults' figures should fall, although in some specific incidences the 97th percentile may be used, or even $2.5 \times$ the normal median is quoted. Normal ranges may vary with the technique used by the laboratory (Holtzman et al. 1974). Additional errors can occur between samples, several radioassays are known to be affected by the protein concentration in the serum (digoxin, vitamin B assays, renin activity measurements, and some steroid assays) (Leyendecker et al. 1972). Appropriate tables of normal values are issued by local laboratories with the data based on local variations in technique.

## SPECIAL PRECAUTIONS WITH HIGH-RISK PATIENTS

The increased frequency of the presence of the antigen for hepatitis B in the serum of institutionalized mentally retarded subjects in general, and subjects with Down's syndrome in particular, poses a problem in sample-collecting peculiar to the mentally handicapped. Simple precautions, for example the use of gloves, during venepuncture should eliminate the risk to the phlebotomist, and it is the procedure adopted in the author's hospital, St Lawrence's, Caterham, to assume all subjects are high-risk unless the contrary has been established. Screw-capped specimen containers should be used for dispatch of the specimen to the local laboratory; these containers should be placed in individual plastic bags separate from the request form and both the specimen and the request form should be clearly labelled high-risk. Any spillage should be swabbed with strong hypochlorite,

and in the case of accidental inoculation the advice of the local bacteriologist on the use of specific immunoglobulin in the prevention of hepatitis B should be obtained. Additional care should be taken in the disposal of syringes, needles and swabs used on high-risk subjects.

## PATHOLOGY OF THE MENTALLY RETARDED

In the second section of this chapter a brief outline of the investigations found to have general application to the mentally retarded will be given. This should not be considered in any way to be exhaustive and is confined to the routine tests of most general application together with those screening tests which, if available, have been found to be of special interest to the clinician in mental handicap.

### ROUTINE BIOCHEMISTRY

The common biochemical investigations are those found in acute medicine and general practice, that is, blood sugar, blood urea, electrolytes, serum enzymes, proteins, thymol turbidity and bilirubin for liver function, total lipids and lipid typing, cholesterol and thyroid function. Most of these are self-explanatory. Liver function assessment will depend on the tests carried out at the local laboratory but experience in mental retardation at St. Lawrence's suggests that routine estimation of gamma-glutamyl transpeptidase should be carried out. As previously explained (see p. 164), a large percentage of the mentally handicapped are under treatment with anticonvulsant agents which induce liver enzymes to cause a 'pathological' rise in alkaline phosphatase. An elevation in serum levels of alkaline phosphatase may also be due to osteomalacia. The estimation of gamma-glutamyl transpeptidase will differentiate between the two side effects as this enzyme is of liver origin only. Since an effect on the liver is a common feature of anticonvulsants, we try to monitor liver function in treated patients while well, to allow a more accurate interpretation of liver function when hepatitis is suspected. Thyroid function has been added to the list of 'routine' estimations since experience has shown that abnormal thyroid function is more common among the mentally retarded than in a normal population. In one survey on thyroxine alone no fewer than 18 cases classified as hypothyroid were found in 224 non-Down's subjects, and 12 cases in 109 Down's subjects. There is strong evidence that Down's subjects over 45 years of age show a much higher frequency of thyroid defects (for review see Rundle & Sylvester 1978). Although there is still some controversy on what constitutes a toxic serum lead level in the mentally retarded, and even if treatment with chelating agents is clinically justified, at St Lawrence's it is routine to estimate the serum lead levels of all new patients, and to estimate the lead levels annually in children below 14 years and all pica subjects, as lead paint has not been eliminated entirely from the hospital environment.

## SPECIFIC BIOCHEMISTRY

Any clinician interested in the pathology of mental handicap should first become acquainted with the standard work by Crome and Stern (1972). It is most unlikely that any one laboratory will be able, on request, to carry out the wide range of specialized investigations which may arise in mental handicap. Discussion with the local chemical pathologist or biochemist on specific case histories is essential before requesting serum or urine chromatography, urinary sediment analysis, serum organic acid screening or any of the other non-routine tests for neurometabolic disorders.

Some clinicians advocate the preliminary screening of all patients with a series of simple routine urine spot tests such as ferric chloride for phenylketonuria, histidinaemia, tyrosinosis, maple-syrup urine disease and alcaptonuria, the 2.4-dinitrophenylhydrazine test for ketones for phenylketonuria, maple-syrup disease, tyrosinosis and children with hyperglycinaemia, and the nitroprusside test for cystinuria and homocystinuria. Such spot tests in experienced hands can often yield useful information, but there is a tendency to overestimate the sensitivity of the test, and to neglect the need to regulate the pH of the urine before tests are carried out.

The routine screening of anticonvulsant drug levels in serum is now well established, and is a facility being offered by more pathology departments each year. The most common estimations are carbamazepine, sodium valproate, ethosuxamide, primidone, phenytoin and phenobarbitone. The methodology will differ between laboratories, with colorimetry, radio-immune assay, enzyme-multiplication techniques, gas-liquid chromatography and high-pressure liquid chromatography all being in common use, and the 'normal therapeutic serum level' will depend on the method adopted. The value of such a screening programme may be indicated by the increase in work-load since the facility was first initiated at St Lawrence's:

| Year | Number of requests |
|---|---|
| 1974–75 | 269 |
| 1975–76 | 306 |
| 1976–77 | 583 |
| 1977–78 | 637 |
| 1978–79 (estimated) | 850 |

The provision of this screening programme has not only contributed by reducing both the number of drugs given and the dosage, but has indicated those subjects where malabsorption could be seen to occur and has served as a test of compliance with dosage instructions. However, one word of warning, the most reliable methods (and the most sensitive) are the radio-immune assay, gas-liquid and high-pressure chromatography and the enzyme-multiplications techniques, all of which require not only expensive equipment but also considerable expertise and are thus very expensive investigations, at least initially; before embarking on a large-scale screening programme the clinician should consult the local laboratory.

## CYTOGENETIC INVESTIGATIONS (KARYOTYPING)

Chapter 5 on chromosomal anomalies indicates the paramount importance of chromosomal investigations to anyone involved in mental handicap, and it has become incumbent on any clinician in this specialty to be able at least to read the cytogeneticist's report. The introduction of banding techniques and specific staining methods in the last few years has enabled the cytogeneticist to explore the micro-architecture of the chromosome in some detail as well as the grosser chromosomal errors such as trisomy, translocation and deletions. To oversimplify the value of cytogenetic investigations, the results can be subdivided into three main categories: those abnormalities which allow a diagnosis and in which the relationship between the chromosomal defect and the mental handicap is established, for example, the trisomies; chromosomal abnormalities such as re-arrangements, deletions et cetera, which are relatively rare and may or may not contribute to the mental retardation; and the third type, usually minor changes in chromosomal architecture which although probably not conferring a serious handicap may be of academic interest in the establishment of gene maps.

The extent to which genetic screening is available varies. Whereas some cytogenetic laboratories may restrict requests to those cases which have genetic counselling implications, others may welcome all specimens of clinical interest. Close cooperation between the specialist in mental handicap and the cytogeneticist is essential both at individual case and screening levels. At all times the clinician must take into consideration that chromosome investigations are highly labour-intensive and are among the most costly investigations offered by the laboratory.

## BACTERIOLOGY AND VIROLOGY

With the exception of the hepatitis B antigen, there is little specific to be said of bacteriology and virology in mental handicap. The identification of organisms and sensitivity tests are those routinely carried out in general medicine and should pose no problems. Serum hepatitis (long-incubation hepatitis) is associated with the presence of a serological entity, Australia antigen ($HB_s$ Ag), and whereas the short-period incubation form hepatitis A is predominantly an illness seen outside the hospital environment, hepatitis B is seen classically (though not exclusively) within hospitals or in subjects who have acquired it within hospitals or institutions. A comparison of the two types of hepatitis shows considerable differences (Table 11.1).

$HB_s$ Ag is found at some stage of the hepatitis

TABLE 11.1

Comparison between hepatitis A and B

| | Hepatitis A | Hepatitis B |
|---|---|---|
| Incubation (days) | 15–50 | 50–60 |
| Willowbrook Hospital, New York State | MS1 | MS2 |
| Australia antigen | Absent | Present |
| Method of infection | | |
| Parenteral | + | + |
| Oral | + + | + |
| Faecal | + + | + |
| Urinary | + | + |
| Seasonal incidence | Autumn & winter | All year |
| Age preference | Children & young adults | All ages |
| Severity | Usually mild | Severe |

B illness in most patients and the detection of this antigen is essential for the detection of the healthy carriers of the disease and the affected but symptomless carriers (for example, subjects with Down's syndrome) or other persons with immunological deficiencies. The oral/faecal route of spread of hepatitis B, in addition to the more common parenteral route, is probably the cause for the high frequency of the disease among institutionalized mentally retarded subjects.

The approach of the clinician to the increased frequency of hepatitis B antigen in populations of the mentally retarded is often either to ignore it as being overestimated or to take the view that the necessary prophylactic precautions would cause unnecessary fears among the staff; occasionally such precautions are established leading to a severe curtailing of the activities of the mentally retarded and a diminution of the quality of life. The screening of the $HB_s$ Ag was established some years ago at St. Lawrence's, and this is limited to all cases of Down's syndrome annually, any case of suspected jaundice and all new admissions. Any positive cases are then considered as high-risk, the ward and any training department concerned with that patient are notified and the case notes and ward lists are amended to show high-risk. Initially this process caused some fears among the staff, but these were allayed when it was explained that 'high-risk' really meant risk to the laboratory staff, and that other members of staff would not be at risk if they exercised elementary precautions such as the use of rubber gloves whenever there was any possibility of their coming into contact with the blood of a high-risk subject. This close monitoring of the high-risk patients has led to a dramatic decrease in the frequency of the number of carriers:

| Year | % of Down's subjects $HB_s$ $Ag +$ |
|------|------|
| 1974 | 32 |
| 1975 | 29 |
| 1976 | 16 |
| 1977 | 7 |
| 1978 | 5 |

In the last three years there have been no new cases of Down's subjects being detected as positive when previously shown to be negative. A recent report (Kingham et al. 1978) from a mental handicap hospital in southern England found 22 per cent of Down's syndrome and 6 per cent of other handicapped in-patients to be positive for $HB_s$ Ag. Among these there was a high prevalence of a new marker antigen which was thought to indicate chronic active liver disease, without symptoms.

In the detection of the $HB_s$ antigen, three methods are in general use, electrophoresis which is less sensitive than passive haemagglutination tests which in turn are less sensitive than radio-immune assay. For screening purposes as outlined above, the haemagglutination tests which are available commercially have been found to be ideal. The radio-immune assay methods pick up more positive carriers but are too sensitive for practical purposes. The haemagglutination tests require little expertise and no specialized equipment and can, in the hands of any clinician, provide the necessary information to bring about a reduction in the number of high-risk patients that have been noted.

## RESEARCH

An important and legitimate function of the laboratory service is to collaborate in clinical research and to be prepared to undertake or supervise other research in pathology. It must be emphasized that such research demands development of new ideas that are based on concepts of medicine and pathology and not solely on technical methods and advances. Before requesting help from the laboratory in a research project the clinician must be aware of the following factors:

1. Most research is expensive.
2. Badly designed research is even more expensive.
3. Repeating other people's work (with modifications) is not research.
4. Research is often boring and even laboratory staff rebel sometimes.
5. Unfinished research reduces cooperation next time.

Before involving the laboratory, the clinician must first have an idea (rarer than one may think), have a working knowledge of the literature on the subject, and be ready to limit the project to a programme which can be achieved. All too often the clinician will approach the laboratory with a project which will involve the estimation of a large number of parameters on the grounds that the number of subjects will be limited to a mere handful, without realizing that even if the sample is large enough to employ the statistical treatment of the resulting data, the multivariate nature of the data can be time consuming in its analysis. The correct design of any research project must start, not finish, with the knowledge of how the data will be analysed statistically. Although, and perhaps because, computers are now becoming readily available, the evaluation of the data is becoming more sophisticated with both parametric and non-parametric techniques, sequential analysis, cohort analysis and discriminant function analysis becoming commonplace. Each of these statistical techniques will dictate the size of the sample, the size and nature of the control group, the information gathered on the test groups and the validity of the final conclusions. When the project has been designed, the laboratory will suggest methodology based partially on cost, partially on time and equipment available and partially on the degree of sensitivity the project requires. Once these preliminaries have been agreed the clinician should be willing to contribute his time and effort in the sample and/or data collecting.

## FUTURE TRENDS

The advent of new techniques, particularly radio-immune assay methods, in the last few years is allowing the clinician access to more sophisticated data at a local laboratory level. This is particularly true of all the hormone investigations—thyroid, adrenal, gonadal, pituitary and particularly the hypothalamus–pituitary axis. At no time has the clinician been able to study the physiological changes concomitant to mental handicap as he can now, and it behoves everyone in this field to persuade the pathologists that the mentally handicapped have the right to such investigations, although the results may only have a marginal effect on the subsequent treatment of the patient. Increasing use of the newer investigations will lead to increased knowledge of the underlying abnormal mechanisms and inevitably the chance to correct some of these. To quote an example, the availability of a relatively simple assay method for prolactin has led to a clearer understanding of its central role at peripheral tissue level, and additionally its involvement not only with post-partum galactorrhoea but with reduced fertility in general. The subsequent availability of dopamine-agonists acting on the release of the prolactin-inhibiting factor and possibly correcting the reduced fertility is seen as having obvious advantage in the normal, but will create social and ethical problems if advocated for the mentally retarded. If we advocate a normalization of the mentally retarded in the community, with an expectation of as normal a life as is possible, will we be able ethically to refuse the investigations and possibly the corrective treatment leading to that most basic of human activities, the right to reproduce?

## BIBLIOGRAPHY

Bio-Science Laboratories (1975) *The Bio-Science Handbook. Specialized Diagnostic Laboratory Tests*, 11th ed. 7600 Tyrone Avenue, Van Nuys, California 91405.

Crome, L. & Stern, J. (1972) *Pathology of Mental Retardation*, 2nd ed. Edinburgh: Churchill Livingstone.

Holtzman, J. L., Shafer, R. B. & Erickson, R. R. (1974) Methodological causes for discrepancies in radio-immune assays for digoxin in human serum. *Clin. Chem.*, *20*, 1194–8.

Kingham, J. G., Macguire, M., Paine, D. H. D. & Wright, R. (1978) Hepatitis B in a hospital for the mentally subnormal in southern England. *Br. med. J.*, *2*, 594–5.

Leyendecker, G., Wardlaw, S. & Nocke, W. (1972) Gamma globulin protection for radio-immune assay and competitive binding saturation analysis of steroids. *J. clin. Endocr. Metab.*, *34*, 430–3.

Richens, A. & Woodford, F. P. (1976) *Anticonvulsant Drugs and Enzyme Induction*. Amsterdam: Elsevier.

Rundle, A. T. & Sylvester, P. E. (1978) Growth and maturation. In: Wortis, J. (ed.), *Mental Retardation and Development Disabilities*, vol. X. New York: Bruner Mazel Inc.

# III

# PSYCHOLOGY AND EDUCATION

# CHAPTER 12

# TRAINING, EDUCATION AND REHABILITATION: AN OVERVIEW

## PETER MITTLER

The last 20 years have seen a renewed interest in the possibilities of active and systematic teaching methods. These methods have not only been applied to children of school age but also to very young children and to adults. The emphasis now is on ways of helping mentally handicapped people to learn new skills and to 'unlearn' behaviours which restrict their opportunities for development. These methods have achieved a good deal but have not yet been used to the best advantage. In fact, we have only just begun to develop effective teaching methods; much of the knowledge already available has still not been communicated to professional staff or to parents.

There are of course limitations to what can be achieved, but we can no longer be confident that we know what those limits are. Current emphasis is more on the problems we have in teaching than on the inability of mentally handicapped people to learn. The evidence now available from both research and practice strongly suggests that mentally handicapped people are capable of learning to a far greater extent than was previously thought possible. Given systematic teaching and time to learn, even profoundly handicapped people can learn new skills. However, we cannot simply expose people to the conditions of learning and hope that they will benefit. Learning cannot be left to chance; it has to be actively fostered.

## THE PSYCHOLOGIST'S CONTRIBUTION

Psychologists have made an important contribution, as members of multidisciplinary teams, to the development of training and rehabilitation programmes for mentally handicapped people. Although few in number, they have worked increasingly through nursing and teaching staff in hospitals and schools and also through parents, helping to design and evaluate training programmes for the training unit, as well as for individual clients. Their contribution rests largely on a knowledge of normal and abnormal human development, the nature of learning processes, and delays and disorders of learning; above all, they have developed particular skills in the last ten years or so in using systematic principles of teaching based on operant psychology.

The distinctive nature of the psychologist's role has undergone major changes in the last ten years or so. He is no longer as preoccupied with individual assessment for assessment's sake, or with the administration of standardized tests of intelligence or attainment; instead, he is concerned with the planning of learning and developmental objectives both for individuals and for groups. He uses assessment only as a starting point for designing programmes of intervention. Furthermore, his concern is not only with the individual but with ways in which both the human and the physical environment can be used to reinforce learning. Above all, he is interested in helping people to use what they have learned in real life and not just in training situations.

In order to do this, psychologists must work through other people by helping them to acquire some of the skills and techniques of systematic assessment and teaching. In particular, they have been active in helping both parents and professional staff to carry out basic assessments, to make decisions on short-term teaching objectives based on the needs of the individual and to use systematic principles of training based on behavioural principles, such as shaping, prompting, fading, modelling and, above all, reinforcing appropriately and consistently. These methods have been taught to parents, nurses, teachers, social workers and others in direct practical teaching situations with opportunities to try them out under the supervision of experienced people. The psychologist's contribution therefore lies increasingly in his work with other practitioners; he acts as a consultant and as a resource to help them to adapt and apply psychological methods of teaching and training.

Psychologists should therefore be available as members of multidisciplinary treatment teams; their particular contribution lies in defining individual teaching objectives, in designing systematic methods by which these objectives may be attained, and in methods of recording and evaluating the individual's response to teaching.

## SYSTEMATIC TEACHING

The essence of systematic teaching lies in the identification of an appropriate short-term teaching objective; this takes the form of a statement of precisely what it is that the person will be able to do after teaching, that he was unable to do before. This contrasts with the rather general statements of global aims which are frequently made but which do not lend themselves to objective evaluation. For example, it is difficult to define the point at which a person can be said to be 'independent', to have 'adjusted to the demands of the community', or even to have learned to dress, feed or toilet himself. These general aims have to be broken down into small steps which can be easily defined and therefore measured. We should always be able to evaluate whether or not objectives have been reached. If we have succeeded, we move on to the next objective; if not, we carry out a more detailed analysis to try to make the task simpler, and begin to teach again.

In other words, if the child fails to learn, we re-examine our own teaching methods; we do not blame the child for being too handicapped to learn.

What, then, are these methods? Baldly summarized, such a systematic approach contains a number of essential components:

## ASSESSMENT

Assessment is essentially a task for those who are going to teach the child, whether they are teachers or parents. Assessment is not only a matter of administering specialized intelligence tests, but involves an attempt to establish what the child can and cannot do, so that a teaching target can be related to his immediate needs. *Assessment therefore defines the entry point to the curriculum.*

Assessment has been traditionally seen in terms of formal, standardized normative tests which have been used largely as instruments of classification and for placement purposes. Such tests compare the performance of any given individual with the performance of representative samples of non-handicapped people on whom the test had been standardized. Intelligence tests such as the Binet or the Wechsler scales have been used to exclude children from the educational system—thus, children with IQs below 55 or 50 were formerly declared unsuitable for education in school.

Although the use of tests to determine the placement of children in one type of school rather than another has now fallen out of favour, intelligence tests still have some value in individual cases. They may reveal hidden strengths or provide evidence of under-estimation of abilities in one or more areas of functioning; they may also be used to prevent misclassification, for example in cases where an adult has been treated as mentally handicapped even though his level of intellectual ability is outside the ability range specified by classification systems such as that of the World Health Organization or the American Association on Mental Deficiency. In practice, no-one should now be regarded as mentally handicapped unless his tested abilities fall below a level of two standard deviations from the mean, that is an IQ of under 70 on a test where the mean is 100 and the standard deviation is 15 points (Mittler 1973, 1978).

One criticism of the administrative use of tests merely as a means of classification is that they provided little or no information to the teacher which could be used as the basis for a programme of teaching. The test items themselves are, of course, deliberately chosen to exclude the possibility of special training, and are thus largely devoid of suggestions for curriculum content. By their very search for items measuring 'pure intelligence', the tests have largely lost their educational validity.

These criticisms apply more strongly to the traditional intelligence tests than to some of the more recently developed measures. For example, there are now an increasing number of developmental checklists containing more or less detailed step-by-step items covering the various aspects of development. The best known of these is the series of charts developed by Gunzburg (1976) known as the *Progress Assessment Charts*, covering various aspects of development from the preschool to the adult stage; the strength of these charts is that they were specifically designed with the needs of the mentally handicapped in mind, and were also designed to lead to a programme of teaching. Other developmental checklists are now being developed for use by parents, and can also be used by care staff. The essence of such charts is that they not only specify a target behaviour but also the whole range of steps needed to reach that target (for example, Jeffree & McConkey 1976).

The question of educational validity is less relevant for developmental checklists concerned with earlier stages of development because many of the items do at least have a certain 'face of validity'. Items concerned with self-care skills, such as self-feeding, dressing, toileting, are obviously highly relevant to the design of teaching programmes. However, this is not necessarily the case with some of the items dealing with fine and gross motor skills. For example, many of the scales include items concerned with block building; children are credited with points for building towers of blocks of a certain size or configuration. Yet teaching a child to build with blocks is not necessarily a high priority for

a teacher. There may be skills which the child will need before he can begin to build with blocks.

Kiernan and Jones (1978) in arguing this position have developed a detailed assessment battery, known as the Behaviour Assessment Battery (BAB), based on interview schedules as well as on various types of structured and unstructured observations and test settings. The scales are designed for profoundly handicapped children, and include specific behavioural items concerned with visual inspection and search strategies, tracking, exploratory and constructive play, grasping and reaching skills, response to sounds, perceptual problem-solving and social skills.

Such checklists should wherever possible be completed with the help of parents. Not only are parents likely to have more detailed knowledge of what a child can and cannot do, but their knowledge is based on experience in a much wider variety of natural settings. It is well known that handicapped children may show a certain behaviour in one setting but not in another—for example a child may speak in longer sentences, or use certain toys and play materials quite differently, depending on whether he is at home or school. These differences can form a useful foundation for collaboration between home and school; effective teaching begins when parents and teachers sit down together to share their knowledge of the child.

Charts and assessment scales are obviously not enough, however. They should be supplemented by detailed observations of behaviour in a variety of structured and unstructured situations. This calls for a simple system of recording which can be used to plan teaching and as a means of evaluating progress.

SELECTION AND ANALYSIS OF THE TASK

The assessment process should always lead to the formulation of a plan of development which is related to the needs of the individual child. On the basis of their detailed knowledge of the invidual, teachers will need to make certain decisions and to choose between different priorities. It is not always a matter of teaching a person to take the next step in his development in, say, self-care or language or motor skills. It is often necessary to try to isolate and identify the nature of the difficulties that he may be experiencing in reaching the next stage; there may be a problem in acquiring an essential component or sub-skill. For example, in teaching a child to learn to use a spoon, it may be necessary to teach him to look at the spoon or, if he is physically handicapped, to retain his grip on the handle. An analysis of the task to be taught does not always result in the identification of all the steps required to learn; it is sometimes necessary to move sideways and to teach a skill that is not directly related to the main task.

It may also be necessary on occasion to try to deal with a severe behaviour problem before teaching new skills; for example head banging or a marked mannerism such as rocking may need to be brought under control before developmental teaching can begin.

Mentally handicapped adults are now taught a wide range of skills which are not normally taught at all and for which we largely lack any systematic teaching methods. Within the framework of social education programmes, adults are taught to use public facilities, such as buses and post offices, how to plan a weekly budget and spend money wisely, how to deal with door-to-door salesmen and about the problems of hire purchase agreements; how to make choices, how to deal with over-protective or over-anxious adults who want to do everything for them, but also how to ask for help when it really is needed. They are prepared for interviews by using simulation or rehearsal procedures, sometimes with videotape, and taught how to deal with difficult questions and with stressful situations (Gunzburg 1973; National Development Group 1977).

### PRESENTATION OF THE TASK

Having analysed the task and identified the steps needed to teach it, the task can then be taught one step at a time. Various methods have been developed to help the child to learn. For example, the systematic use of shaping may involve the teacher doing the whole task for the child at first, and then gradually fading the prompt in very small stages over a number of trials, the speed of fading depending on the child's response. In teaching a child to use a spoon without spilling, the child may be physically guided through all but the last of the sequence of actions, and then taught to complete more and more of the actions for himself, with as much help as is necessary. Various forms of 'chaining' methods are also used.

The use of systematic reward has been found to be highly effective in teaching mentally handicapped people, and the principles of reward training are now better understood. However, reward training is only a means to an end; before we begin to use rewards, we need to have selected a teaching objective that is relevant to the needs of the person we are teaching. Reward training can easily be misused to teach people to do the things that we want, and that are convenient to us, rather than meeting the needs of the individual. The very effectiveness of reward training makes it necessary to be cautious about the uses to which it is put. It is not merely a matter of providing sweets or praise when people learn something that we want them to learn; a good deal is now known about the wide range of training techniques that can be used, and how they can be varied—for example, in changing from food rewards to secondary rewards, from continuous reinforcement to more irregular schedules, the use of tokens and so on. These methods have to be learned and practised. They are not necessarily always obvious or 'common sense'. (Perkins et al. (1976) give a useful summary of behavioural methods.)

### EVALUATION AND MONITORING

If the teacher has set a specific and definable objective, it should be possible to evaluate whether or not it has been achieved. This can be done by means of a simple record system or by special short test sessions in the form of 'probes'. These enable changes to be made in the course of the teaching; for example, if teaching is not successful, then the task to be taught may need to be broken down into even smaller steps, or the method of reinforcement may need to be modified.

*The most important test is whether the person uses what he has learned.* This is perhaps the most difficult challenge of all. It is one thing to teach a child to acquire a skill in the classroom; quite another for him to use it outside the teaching situation. Teachers are therefore very concerned at the present time with methods of teaching the child to generalize his learning from one setting to another (see Baer and Stokes (1977) for a useful summary of the main methods).

Evaluation need not be confined to an examination of the progress made by individuals but can usefully be applied to the training unit. Hospitals, residential facilities, day centres and schools are increasingly feeling the need to define both their general aims as well as specific objectives and then to devise procedures by which they can monitor the extent to which the objectives are being achieved. This has led to the development of various guidelines itemizing specific elements of good practice not only in respect of training but also for other aspects of the work of the unit. These will obviously vary depending on the nature of the unit, the needs of its clients and the resources available to its staff. Berry and Andrews (see Chapter 19) describe Australian experience in the use of the Program Analysis of Service Systems (PASS) devised by Wolfensberger and Glenn (1975); similarly, the Accreditation Council for the Mentally Retarded (1975) in the USA has published detailed standards for both community and residential agencies. In England, the National Development Group for the Mentally Handicapped is also developing specific service guidelines for the use of staff; interim suggestions have been made for the work of day centres for adults (NDG 1977) and for hospitals (NDG 1978).

## TRAINING IN RESIDENTIAL UNITS

Although there is a great deal of discussion about the long-term future of residential institutions, one of the most pressing needs is to provide training and rehabilitation facilities for the many thousands of people who are living in hospitals and other residential establishments. The purpose of such training is to help as many people as possible to leave hospital in order to live and work in the community; those who for any reason cannot do so should be given opportunities to achieve maximum independence by learning new skills and extending their abilities to the full.

Principles and practices of training with special reference to residential units have been most recently set out in the National Development Group's hospital report referred to above (NDG 1978); suggestions for the reorganization of staff training have been made by the Committee of Enquiry into Nursing Care (the Jay Committee) (DHSS 1979).

Although many striking changes have been made in hospitals for the mentally handicapped, many of the improvements have been concerned with the creation of a more homely, domestic environment. Hospitals have been improved out of all recognition; large barrack-like wards have been divided into smaller units; curtains, carpets, lockers, divans, personal clothing and many other improvements have contributed greatly to creating living conditions which are both more dignified and more individual than the classic conditions described by Goffman (1961) as characteristics of the 'total institution'—block treatment, depersonalization, social distance and rigidity. If mentally handicapped people are ever going to leave hospital and live in the community, it is obviously essential to do everything possible to simulate community conditions within the hospital and to allow residents to experience the realities of community life before they are discharged. Furthermore, principles of normalization demand that even those who are unlikely to be discharged should be helped to live as normally as possible and 'in the least restrictive setting'.

Although a reasonably homely and domestic environment is the essential basis for a training programme, it is no substitute for direct teaching. Merely creating the conditions for learning is not enough. For example, the easy chairs in a ward might be moved from their institutional position around the walls of the 'day room' into groups of three or four around a low coffee table on the expectation that this would encourage residents to interact with one another. Unfortunately, it cannot be assumed that this will happen; levels of interaction between residents are often very low and it may take much more than a rearrangement of chairs for people to begin to talk to one another. Similarly, we cannot assume that increasing the number of staff on a living unit will necessarily lead to better standards of care, to higher levels of staff interaction with residents or to the development of additional skills in residents. Indeed, there is evidence from research that this does not happen unless specific steps are taken to ensure that it does (King et al. 1971; Pratt et al. 1977).

We now realize that staff attitudes and practices are fundamentally important in determining outcomes. Surveys of different types of day and residential units have provided evidence of enormous variations in what staff actually do, even when they are working with identical staff ratios and with people with very similar levels of need and dependency. Two adjacent wards containing very similar residents may be years apart in provision of domestic amenities and training opportunities and in the way they treat residents. Even though both may provide a warm caring environment, residents in one ward may be encouraged to learn to do things for themselves, such as make their own beds, prepare simple snacks, clean and dust their own living areas and develop self-care skills in dressing and eating independently. Their neighbours may have all these things done for them on the grounds that it is quicker and more convenient for staff to do these jobs themselves.

The absence of clear policies for training is perhaps most clearly seen in community hostels for mentally handicapped people. There are hostels where residents are actively discouraged from making their own beds or preparing simple snacks on the grounds that domestic staff are employed for this purpose; similarly, staff are reluctant to introduce training programmes to help residents to develop their self-care skills or to learn to live more independently on the grounds that the hostel is their home and that it is not normal for non-handicapped people to come home in the evening to a training programme.

## BASIC TRAINING PRINCIPLES

It would be quite wrong to apportion praise or blame to staff adopting one or other of the practices outlined above. If blame lies anywhere, it is to be sought in failure to define staff roles, and in the absence of clearly stated aims and policies for the unit as a whole.

We therefore conclude this chapter with a summary of basic principles of training adapted from the National Development Group's report on hospitals (NDG 1978). More detailed statements and examples can be found in Gardner (1971) and in Perkins et al. (1976).

1. A training programme will not be fully effective unless all staff who work with a resident are informed about his training. This means that all staff should be aware of the training objectives set for a particular resident with whom they work, the details of his progress so far and the way he or she has reacted to other parts of the training programme.

2. Never accept present level of functioning or even the first response to training as an indication of the person's potential ability. There is often little or no relationship between the individual's initial performance and the level that he can achieve after training.

3. Never underestimate what can be achieved. There is now ample evidence that the abilities of mentally handicapped people have been greatly underestimated, often by those who know them best and have worked with them for many years. Mentally handicapped people respond well to the challenge of demand, but the demand must be clear and unambiguous, and the teaching must be properly planned and organized.

4. Never rely on general stimulation and exposure to a rich and stimulating environment alone. This is useful as a general background for the structured teaching which is essential to success.

5. Set a precise, measurable objective. This means deciding exactly what it is you wish the resident to do that he could not do before. An objective must be distinguished from a general aim. Examples of aims include 'helping children to achieve their potential' ... 'adjust to the demands of society' ... 'lead a satisfying life', et cetera. All these are admirable aims, but they cannot be measured. An objective should be measurable in such a way that there can be no doubt about whether or not it has been achieved. Examples of objectives might be: wets the bed less than once a week; points to nose on request; gets in and out of bath without help.

6. The selection of a teaching objective should arise from the process of ongoing

assessment which results in a statement of needs. Assessment can be carried out both by the use of developmental or behavioural checklists and by systematic observation and recording of the resident's behaviour in ordinary living and learning situations. The teaching objective is not necessarily developmental, that is, it does not have to be the behaviour which would be likely to be reached next; it may be a behaviour problem which needs to be tackled first. Assessment should therefore lead to a consideration of priorities.

7. All staff should agree upon a common form of behaviour rating so that the progress made by a resident can be evaluated by the staff of various disciplines who work with him.

8. The training objective may need to be broken down into a series of sub-goals, representing steps in the teaching programme. For example, if the objective is that the trainee should learn to clean his teeth, a task analysis may result in the specification of a series of steps that will need to be taught before a specified training criterion is reached, for example pick up . . . hold . . . wet toothbrush; remove toothpaste cap; apply toothpaste; replace cap; brush outside . . . biting . . . inside surfaces; fill cup with water; rinse . . . wipe mouth; rinse brush . . . sink: put brush and cup away.

9. More detailed task analysis may be necessary if the trainee is failing to move from one sub-goal to another.

10. Reinforce immediately, consistently, appropriately. A reinforcement is an event that can be shown to change behaviour and which increases the probability of a given behaviour occurring; it cannot be arbitrarily determined by the trainer. Therefore it is necessary to find a reward that the trainee really wants. Sometimes this is obvious, for example, a sweet or particular food, but the trainer should never assume that what he thinks is a reinforcer will actually work as one. Sometimes it is possible to determine which reinforcer will work by giving the person several choices between two or more objects and seeing whether he expresses any consistent preferences.

Having found a reinforcer, it is imperative that there should be no delay between the desired behaviour occurring and the delivery of the reinforcement, as it is essential that the reinforcement is connected only with the desired behaviour. This requires practice; nothing is easier than accidentally reinforcing something inappropriate.

Consistency is essential, at least at the beginning of a training programme. Every single occurrence of the behaviour should be reinforced. Later it may be possible to experiment with different 'schedules', for example, rewarding every other instance of the behaviour, but this has to be done very gradually.

Although every single correct response or approximation to a correct response may need to be reinforced in the early stages of training, it is worth trying to work by very small degrees to reinforcing more intermittently. There are many techniques for moving from continuous reinforcement to less regular reinforcements; for example, if a light pat on the head and praise are paired with a food reinforcement, it may be possible to 'fade' the food out very slowly, leaving just the physical contact or even verbal praise alone.

Once the trainee is working for a reward, it is possible to withhold it for a very short period if he is not attending or cooperating. The trainer can turn his head away or even his back for a few seconds, and resume training when there is some evidence of a resumption of the desired behaviour.

11. Accept any approximation to the 'correct' behaviour at first, and reward it immediately; then increase the difficulty of the task by very small steps. If there is failure, decrease the size of the learning steps even further.

12. Give maximum help at first, almost doing the whole task for the trainee, and then gradually decrease the help by very small steps.

This help may take a variety of forms. It may involve physically guiding the trainee through a whole sequence of movements, and then reducing the amount of guidance by small steps; demonstrating the whole procedure for him (modelling) and then training him to carry out one component after another; it may be necessary to train general imitation behaviour, for example, by rewarding the trainee for exact imitation of the trainer's behaviour on the instruction 'Do this'.

13. Ensure that the trainee has the oppor-

tunity to use what he has learned in real situations. No training programme can hope to succeed if the trainee can only show evidence of learning with one person or in one setting. If he has learned to use a washing machine in the hospital, he will need to learn to use a launderette in the nearest town. This requires time and organization, but the principle of training for generalization applies at every level. For example, it is important that all staff working on a ward should not only know the training objectives for each resident, but also the training methods being used. If a particular sound made by the trainee has been linked with the arrival of a drink, the same result should follow if the sound is made in the presence of another member of staff.

## SUMMARY

This chapter presents a brief overview of some of the main principles of training, education and rehabilitation. It is based on the premise that the abilities of mentally handicapped people have been greatly underestimated and that even the most profoundly handicapped person is capable of learning, provided he is taught by systematic methods and given time to learn.

Systematic teaching is based on careful assessment of what the individual can do, using observational methods and behavioural and developmental checklists; decisions on what is to be taught should be based on the assessment process and should result in a precise statement of a behavioural objective which will identify exactly what the individual will be able to achieve after teaching that he could not achieve before. The application of these principles in the work of residential facilities is briefly examined.

Chapter 13 considers ways in which a developmental approach can be applied to handicapped infants from the first weeks of life and how their families can be helped to create situations that will actively assist their development.

## BIBLIOGRAPHY

Accreditation Council for the Mentally Retarded (1975) *Standards for Residential Facilities for the Mentally Retarded.* Chicago: Joint Commission on Accreditation of Hospitals.

Baer, D. M. & Stokes, T. F. (1977) Discriminating a generalisation technology. In: Mittler, P. (ed), *Research to Practice in Mental Retardation,* vol. 2. Baltimore: University Park Press.

Department of Health and Social Security (1979) *Report of the Committee of Enquiry into Mental Handicap, Nursing and Care* (Jay Committee). London: HMSO.

Gardner, W. I. (1971) *Behaviour Modification in Mental Retardation.* Chicago: Aldine.

Goffman, E. (1961) *Asylums: Essays on the Social Situation of Mental Patients and Other Inmates.* New York: Doubleday.

Gunzburg, H. C. (1973) *Social Competence and Mental Handicap,* 2nd ed. London: Baillière Tindall.

Gunzburg, H. C. (1976) *Progress Assessment Charts.* Stratford: Social Education Publications.

Jeffree, D. M. & McConkey, R. (1976) *P.I.P. Developmental Charts.* Sevenoaks: Hodder and Stoughton Educational.

Kiernan, C. C. & Jones, M. C. (1978) *Behaviour Assessment Battery.* Windsor: NFER Publishing Co. Ltd.

King, R., Raynes, N. & Tizard, J. (1971) *Patterns of Residential Care.* London: Routledge & Kegan Paul.

Mittler, P. (1973) Purposes and principles of assessment. In: Mittler, P. (ed.), *Assessment for Learning in the Mentally Handicapped.* Edinburgh: Churchill Livingstone.

Mittler, P. (1979) *Problems and Policies in Mental Handicap.* London: Methuen.

National Development Group for the Mentally Handicapped (1977) *Day Services for Mentally Handicapped Adults.* NDG Pamphlet 5. London: DHSS.

National Development Group for the Mentally Handicapped (1978) *Helping Mentally Handicapped People in Hospital.* London: HMSO.

Perkins, E. A., Taylor, P. D. & Capie, A. (1976) *Helping the Retarded: A Systematic Behavioural Approach.* Kidderminster: Institute of Mental Subnormality.

Pratt, M. W., Raynes, N. V. & Roses, S. (1977) Organisational characteristics and their relationship to the quality of care. In: Mittler, P. (ed.), *Research to Practice in Mental Retardation*, vol. 1. Baltimore: University Park Press.

Wolfensberger, W. & Glenn, S. (1975) *Program Analysis of Service Systems.* Toronto: National Institute of Mental Retardation.

# EARLY STIMULATION OF THE SEVERELY HANDICAPPED CHILD

## CLIFF CUNNINGHAM

They (the mongol) are usually able to speak; the speech is thick and indistinct, but may be improved very greatly by a well-directed scheme of tongue gymnastics. The coordinating faculty is abnormal, but not so defective that it cannot be greatly strengthened. By systematic training, considerable manipulative power may be obtained.

J. Langdon Down, 1866

In his classic paper identifying the mongol (Down's syndrome) Down set forth three directions for study. The first concerned the isolation of physical and organic characteristics upon which to base a classification; the second concerned descriptions of behavioural characteristics; and the third, suggestions for improving attainments and skills through systematic instruction. Like much of the early history of mental handicap, it was the first two themes which dominated the study of Down's syndrome. By comparison the third theme was sadly neglected until recently. This is somewhat ironic as it would appear that the prime motivation for Down's interest was to improve the care and development of the mentally handicapped.

Developments in the last 30 years have certainly begun to redress this neglect. The cumulative results of many enlightened research and educational studies have clearly demonstrated that the potential of mentally handicapped children and adults has been seriously underestimated. The use of systematic training and educational procedures has shown that they are capable of achieving much higher levels of performance and learning than previously supposed and further that the level of performance is relatively independent of IQ or initial performance (Clarke & Clarke 1974).

Unfortunately, until this decade, these developments have not generally included the very young child. In 1973 Dybwad, who had just completed an extensive tour of the major countries of the world, could state:

> The scarcity of any kind of interest in early intervention for the severely handicapped, particularly by the medical profession, is really nothing short of phenomenal.

This chapter is primarily concerned with intervention procedures for the mentally handicapped infant in the first two years of life. It takes a pragmatic approach in considering the recent developments in this field and the extent to which present optimism is justified.

The following general points will help to familiarize the reader with the ensuing discussion.

1. The infants considered here are those who have a recognized primary syndrome or condition such as Down's syndrome*, associated with delayed development or future intellectual retardation, or whose development in the first months of life is so impaired that future severe retardation is highly probable. However, the presence of such a condition or syndrome does not necessarily predict the extent of future handicap. A number of infants with such conditions will not eventually fall into the handicap range, that is, less than two standard deviations below the

* For description of the four possible genotypes in Down's syndrome, see pp. 49–50. *Ed.*)

norm on IQ scales. Indeed an early pessimistic prognosis can lead to such low expectations on the part of those persons providing for the care of the infant that a degree of *secondary* handicap ensues—an example of a self-fulfilling prophecy.

2. Most of the information available in this field has arisen from work with Down's syndrome infants, this being the commonest single condition in mental handicap and easily recognizable at birth. The prognosis for this condition is probably one of the most favourable of the recognized conditions associated with mental handicap, thus whilst the findings from Down's syndrome infants can provide useful models, generalizations to other conditions must be made with caution.

3. Whilst there has been a decreased *incidence* in mental handicap at birth, particularly of Down's syndrome, there has also been a decreased rate of mortality. This has resulted in an increase in *prevalence* in the population. No longer can the birth of such children be considered as a short-term problem for parents or society; instead it demands the provision of an education for a normal lifespan.

4. Increasing emphasis is being given to family care for such children. This calls for services which will help the family care for the handicapped child in the home and for changes in attitudes and support from the community.

5. In the case of some conditions which result in mental handicap such as phenylketonuria, medical treatments have been noticeably successful. However, in the majority of conditions results have been less successful. Medical treatments of Down's syndrome, for example, using thyroid or pituitary extracts, vitamins, siccacell, 5-hydroxytryptophan and serotonin therapy have not produced sustained beneficial effects (Share 1976) and do not appear to be any more successful than providing increased support for parents and stimulation for the infant. However, such infants are now generally more healthy, as suggested by the reduced mortality.

6. The increased knowledge of early child development and the evidence from research of the importance of stimulation during infancy, have considerably altered the conception of the infant from that of being a mere passive recipient of information to that of an organism actively participating in interactions and being responsive to early stimulation. If this is important for the normal infant, it is all the more so for the handicapped infant who is less well equipped to profit from his experiences.

7. Studies with animals have suggested that early experiences significantly affect future development and result in successful adaptation to the environment. These studies frequently show accelerated maturation of the nervous system and body chemistry. In a review of this field Callaway (1970) concluded that enriched experience can be shown to modify almost every structure and physiological function that can be measured and it may obviously be expected to modify the behaviours based on these structures and functions. Whilst caution must be maintained in applying the results of animal studies to humans, it would appear reasonable to assume that early experience can affect the development of basic structures and behaviour.*

## EARLY INTERVENTION

### THE DISADVANTAGED CHILD

A number of positive guidelines can be inferred from early intervention with disadvantaged (as distinct from mentally handicapped) pre-school children. Relatively large and permanent gains can be achieved if:

1. The child is enrolled in the programme from an early age.
2. The parent is closely associated with the programme and used as a co-therapist, and if 'home-rearing' is considered as a major variable in the intervention.
3. The programme has specific and developmentally appropriate objectives and is based on relatively systematic teaching approaches rather than general enrichment.
4. The programme is maintained over long enough periods of time.

* For a discussion of the recent research linking brain stimulation with increased brain blood supply and nutrition, see p. 138. *Ed.*

5. Steps are taken to provide for generalizations of the learning to new situations (Stedman 1977).

Thus any early intervention programme must consider both the child and the most appropriate stimulation for him, also the parent, the home and the most appropriate support and training.

The importance of the home is supported by studies comparing home-reared and institution-reared handicapped children. The findings also contradict the suggestion that such infants are better placed in residential provisions at birth—a proposition still advised by some physicians. (See p. 368.)

HOME VERSUS INSTITUTION

A number of studies have consistently reported that infants and young children raised in the relatively restricted and unstimulating environments found in many institutions perform at lower developmental levels than those raised under favourable home conditions. These findings include both 'normal' infants and mentally handicapped infants. In the case of Down's syndrome infants, it was found that the effects of institutionalization were relatively immediate and possibly permanent. Children reared at home for the first years of life before entering an institution were in advance of those placed in the institution from birth. This benefit was maintained even after several subsequent years of institutional care. Significant differences in developmental attainment were also found between home-reared and institution-reared infants by the second year of life (Carr 1975; Francis 1971). These findings are supported by studies which have changed the nature of stimulation provided in institutions. Improved functioning has been reported for mentally handicapped children (Lyle 1959), premature infants (Solkhoff et al. 1969) and 'normal' infants (White 1971).

Thus it can be concluded with some confidence that young mentally handicapped children are responsive to environmental conditions from infancy and that favourable home rearing is of great importance to their development. It is also important to note that it is not only the development assessed by standardized tests that is improved, but the whole 'style' that the child develops in interacting with his environment. Francis (1971) reports that the home-reared Down's syndrome infants showed more initiative and exploration in play than those raised in the institution.

However, these comparative studies do not indicate that home rearing per se produces optimal development, merely that institutional rearing can further the handicapped effect. Again this needs qualification. Institutions do not necessarily increase the handicap. It is the lack of stimulation, such as is provided by the one-to-one care-taking situation usually found in the home, that appears to be critical and not all institutions necessarily depress performance (Tizard & Tizard 1974).

INTERVENTION IN THE HOME

Given the implication that the infant will develop best if raised in his own home, it is essential to consider the nature and effect of the stimulation provided in the home. There is evidence to support the following contentions:

1. Home rearing alone may not provide this structured development of the infant.
2. Parents can be trained to provide this structured stimulation.
3. Intervention, via the parent, facilitates the development of the mentally handicapped infant.

*Home rearing*

There is some evidence that suggests the possibility of a 'hidden deprivation' effect even in 'good quality' homes. Both Francis (1971) and Jeffree and Cashdan (1971) reported observable differences in the type of interactions which took place between the parent and normal sibling and the parent and the handicapped child. Jones (1976) found that the phasing of mother and infant behaviour differed significantly between the interactions with Down's syndrome infants and normal infants in the first year of life. Typically the mothers of the Down's syndrome infants were more directive and there were more instances of vocal 'clashes' rather than phased turn-taking.

## Parent training

Much evidence exists indicating that many parents of mentally handicapped children are eager to help their child and are willing to spend much time and effort to this end. Indeed a major cause of anguish for many parents is the feeling of hopelessness and helplessness, and wanting to do something for their child. Consequently, many state that they gain considerable satisfaction from being shown what they can do to help their child, regardless of the eventual level of achievements.

It is reasonable to assume that a necessary prerequisite for parents who are going to help their infant, is a positive feeling toward the child and a belief that they can provide such help. The importance of parent counselling beginning prior to the disclosure of the diagnosis is discussed in Chapter 23.

With respect to parent training a number of generalizations can be made. Firstly, the socio-economic and educational level of the parents is not generally correlated with their ability to learn and apply techniques for training and stimulating their child. However, parents experienced in obtaining information from lectures and written material obviously find this more helpful than those without such experience. The latter need far more individual assistance. Recent studies indicate that demonstrating the techniques with the child is probably the most effective approach for all parents (Nay 1975) and that validated instructional manuals are particularly useful (Heifetz 1977).

Secondly, parents gain much from small discussion groups with other parents whose children have similar difficulties. Such groups should not exceed ten to twelve parents, should be planned and organized with clearly stated objectives in agreement with the parents, and if possible, be led by an experienced person. This person can be another parent who has had previous experience with small groups, a knowledge of the content for discussions and sufficient personal skills to lead the group, refraining from a too authoritative or a too relaxed style.

Thirdly, whilst parents can learn and apply these techniques they need continual support and advice. Mental handicap is a permanent condition lasting the individual's lifespan.

Particular note should be given to the changing nature of the handicapped child—the problems of infancy are obviously different from those of toddlers, adolescence and adulthood.

Fourthly, having convinced parents that their efforts can help the child, and conversely therefore, that lack of effort or misappropriate management can hinder the child, parents can become increasingly anxious that they are not doing enough.

## Parent intervention

Various attempts have been made to train the parent to work with the very young handicapped child (Cunningham 1976). Some involved regular visits to the home, devising structured play and training, showing the parent how to use these and how to evaluate the results. Others brought parents and children into special classes where trained personnel taught the child whilst the parents were given advice and instruction on how to help. A third approach trained the parents in the content and techniques of early stimulation with limited professional access to the children. Each of these approaches has its advantages and disadvantages and, as yet, no evidence exists to support any one in particular. Suffice it to say that domiciliary visits provide much necessary information on home circumstances, extend the possibility of including other members of the family and provide concentrated effort on parent and child whilst clinic, school or workshops provide the opportunity to meet with other parents. A comprehensive approach providing for both these aspects would seem most advisable, particularly in the early years.

With few exceptions, such approaches report a high level of parent satisfaction and changes in the child's performance. However, they generally lack control groups, frequently report gains and seldom isolate crucial variables.

## Intervention studies

There are studies of intervention with Down's syndrome infants from the early months of life comparing the treated group with non-treated groups (de Coriat et al. 1968; Ludlow 1979). The studies typically provide the parents with advice on early child development and methods of stimulation. They have assessed the results using standardized infant tests and shown significant difference between the treated and non-treated groups. One of the earliest of these (de Coriat et al. 1968) provided 'psycho-motor' stimulation from birth and assessed the subjects on the Gesell Scales of Infant Development at six monthly intervals until five years of age. The difference between the two groups was significant throughout; at five the median IQ score was 61 for the treated group and 42 for the non-treated group.

Of noticeable interest is the study of Dr Ludlow (Ludlow 1979), working in a situation closely comparable to the community health physician and child health clinic. She compared three groups of Down's syndrome children from the first years of life. One group was reared in institutions, and the other two were home reared; the parents and children of one of the home-reared groups regularly attended a developmental clinic and were given advice and support, in the other group the parents had no access to such facilities and received no regular counselling. She found consistent significant differences between the three groups from the first year of life, as assessed on the Griffiths Scale of Child Development and later on the Stanford-Binet Intelligence Scales. The differences were of a similar magnitude to the de Coriat study (de Coriat et al. 1968) and had persisted up to nine and ten years of age.

Studies reporting more advanced development of Down's syndrome infants compared with previous expectations and control groups regularly appear in the literature (Hayden & Dmitriev 1975; Rynders & Horrobin 1975). Hayden and Haring (1977) have also reported increased development for 94 Down's syndrome children enrolled in a structured preschool programme from 6 months to 6 years and particularly emphasize that the longer the child has been in the study the greater his gains. One of the few controlled studies aimed at cerebral palsied infants including a large proportion who were also mentally handicapped is that of Scherzer, Mike and Ilson (1976). Twenty-four children under the age of 18 months were observed for a minimum period of six months in either experi-

mental or control physical therapy programmes. The study used a double-blind design and found definite positive changes in motor, social and management areas in favour of the experimental group. However, the authors noted that the younger the infant and the greater his global deficit the less evidence there was for change. They suggest that for the very young CP infants stimulation in modalities other than motor should be given greater emphasis at this early developmental period. This observation is most significant. It indicates the present lack of information on the interrelationships between content, techniques, etiology and the developmental process in intervention studies.

Thus, taken together, the results of early intervention studies with mentally handicapped infants clearly suggest that it is possible to facilitate both developmental rate and management. Parents gain considerable support from such activities and generally are capable of learning the necessary techniques and content.

The remainder of this chapter will consider some of the major aspects of early intervention, beginning with a discussion of the 'nature' of mental handicap.

## PRIMARY AND SECONDARY HANDICAP

There are two kinds of restriction impinging on the development of handicapped children; those resulting from primary conditions such as chromosomal anomaly, deafness, blindness or severe brain damage, and those resulting from secondary conditions such as parental handling, environmental deprivation or inadequate treatment of the primary condition. Figure 13.1 gives an example of interrelationship between primary and secondary handicap. It presents the cumulative percentages for the attainment of sitting without support, compares the results of a number of studies of Down's syndrome infants with one study of normal infants. The data from the Carr (1975) and Cunningham (1976) studies are for the item 'sits alone steadily' from the Bayley Scales of Infant Development which quote a range of 5 to 9 months, mean of 6.6 months for this item. The remaining stud-

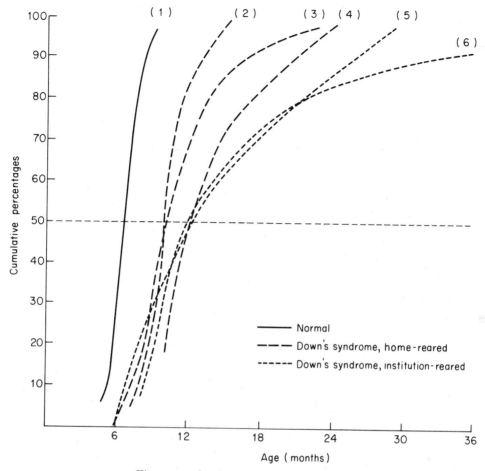

*Fig. 13.1   Age for sitting without support.*

(1) NELIGAN & PRUDHAM (1969). Normal infants n = 3831. Born 1960–62 City of Newcastle. Data collected by health visitors from parent reports and direct observation.

(2) CUNNINGHAM (1976). Down's syndrome infants n = 67 home-reared. Born 1973–77 Manchester area. Data collected by researchers at six-weekly assessments in home.

(3) SHARE & VEALE (1974). Down's syndrome infants n = 123 home-reared. Born 1960–65 New Zealand. Data obtained from parent recollections.

(4) CARR (1975). Down's syndrome infants n = 47 (40 home-reared, 7 institution-reared). Born 1963–64 London area. Data obtained by researchers at six-monthly assessments in home.

(5) Taken from several studies noted in PENROSE & SMITH (1966), indicating range and means and including both institution-reared and home-reared infants.

(6) SHARE & VEALE (1974). Down's syndrome infants n = 26 institution-reared.

ies use the Gesell definition, 'sits unsupported and erect for one minute' (which includes no support by the arms). The range quoted from the Bayley standardization and that of the Neligan and Prudham (1969) survey are very similar. The Neligan and Prudham and the Share and Veale (1974) surveys are both based upon parent recollections of the age when the behaviour was attained, whilst the Cunningham and Carr studies are based upon assessments by qualified personnel. Thus the former studies may have some error, erring toward a slightly earlier age than the latter. Given the discrepancies the studies are still quite consistent.

If we assume that the curve for the normal

infants (curve 1, Fig. 13.1) reflects the 'matur-ational' development of sitting without sup-port—that is, whilst it may be possible to shift the curve more to the left using training procedures it will maintain the same shape—curve 2, which closely approximates this shape, may reflect the 'maturational' curve for Down's syndrome infants. Thus the dis-tance between curves 1 and 2 might represent the delay in development directly resulting from the inherent handicapping condition. This is called the primary handicapping con-dition. The distances between curves 2, 3, 4, 5 and 6 might reflect the effect of varying experiences which appear necessary to facili-tate the development of sitting in such infants. This is called the secondary handicapping condition. Curves 5 and 6 which are for pre-dominantly institutionalized Down's syn-drome infants indicate far more delay in attaining the behaviour than curves 2, 3 and 4 for home-reared infants. Curve 2 consisted of infants whose parents were visited in the home every six weeks and given a high level of support and specific advice on stimulation.

These secondary conditions are complex and as yet not fully determined, however a number of points can be isolated.

*Level of stimulation*

The parents may or may not provide the same level of stimulation given to the normal child. They may believe that such stimulation is of little use, that the child is unable to gain from it. They may be fearful of doing 'something wrong' and as a result not even try to do things which intuitively they feel are necessary. They may prevent the child from mastering skills such as feeding, dress-ing, walking and so on, because it is more convenient to do such things for the child, or because they have such low expectations of the child's potential that they feel he will never attain such skills. Their work or family commitments, lack of family or service sup-port and organizational ability may not allow them to find the time to provide the oppor-tunities for the child to learn and develop.

Through embarrassment or inconvenience they may not take the child out, particularly if he looks different or is difficult to manage. Exclusion from such everyday experiences

as shopping, meeting a variety of people, see-ing different places is particularly damaging to the handicapped child.

*Environmental feedback*

The child may also be deprived of many experiences as a result of the primary condi-tion. Extremely slow development on the part of the infant together with the parents' inabil-ity to note small changes or understand the significances of small responses may lead the parents to give up their efforts to stimulate the child, to settle for less than is possible. In this case a detailed knowledge of child development and training in observation can be most useful.

The infant may not have the same range of social interactive skills such as smiling, facial expressions or eye gaze as the normal infant. This in turn may affect the very heart of the mother–infant interaction and, as was noted on p. 184, unwittingly lead the mother to abnormal stimulation and interaction, so further depriving the infant of opportunities to respond and to learn.

The mentally handicapped person also has an inability to utilize everyday experiences due to specific deficits in his learning pro-cesses. Considerable evidence exists to sup-port the presence of learning deficits in men-tally handicapped children and adults, par-ticularly in attentional mechanisms and in their ability to learn spontaneously from their experiences, for example, the ability to direct their attention to relevant stimuli; to analyse and synthesize incoming information; to abstract and generalize and to do this without the aid of an adult (Clarke & Clarke 1974). Unless the parent is aware of these learning deficits and is trained in methods to compen-sate for them, the infant will receive less than appropriate stimulation. This is reflected in the sitting-without-support example dis-cussed above and shown in Figure 13.1. The differences between the curves increase rela-tive to the delay in achieving the behaviour. Thus the slower the infants the more suscep-tible they appear to environmental factors. If we assume that the slower infant has a greater degree of deficiency, then these data would support the notion of specific learning deficits. Further, the primary handicap is not just made up of inherently determined slow growth but also of specific learning difficulties. It is the effect of these that can be compensated for by structured stimulation.

## The child's rate of development

There is considerable variability within the mentally handicapped population. If one compares the range of sitting without support in the quoted example between the normal infants and the Down's syndrome infants, it is immediately apparent that the latter has a wider distribution. Thus even with an early behaviour like sitting and an apparently discrete condition like Down's syndrome, the variability is immense. Consider how much greater this will become as the individual gets older.

This concept of variability within the mentally handicapped population has many implications for practice. Firstly, it strongly supports the need for early intervention. Secondly, and perhaps of importance to the physician faced with the parents of a recently diagnosed infant, it cautions against too simplistic predictions of future attainments on the following grounds:

1. The greater variability found in the population reduces the possibility of predicting future individual progress.

2. It is particularly noticeable in the quoted example that the delay in development due to the secondary handicaps appears to be even greater for the slower infants than that due to the primary handicap for this sitting behaviour. If one accepts that development is hierarchical and that later abilities are built upon early ones, then developmental delay will be cumulative. Thus the cumulative effects of the secondary handicap may be considerable. When we examine older handicapped children and adults, it is possible that a relatively large proportion of the handicap is secondary and could have been prevented. Evidence quoted earlier for the long-term effects of early stimulation on Down's syndrome infants would support this. Thus it is unwise to base future prognosis of the degree of handicap on observations of older individuals who have not received optimal stimulation from the early years.

## The additive effect of multiple handicaps

All too often the primary condition and the degree of resulting handicap are confused as being the same. The loss of sight in one eye represents a 50 per cent loss of the visual receptive mechanism, yet the resulting handicap is very small and is determined by the individual's lifestyle. The level of handicap will also be determined by the overall ability of the individual. A partial loss of hearing in a child of normal intelligence may have minor handicapping results as he can compensate for the loss. However, the same level of impairment in a mentally retarded child who cannot compensate for the loss may be far more handicapping, Indeed, the interaction between the two impairments may produce a greater handicap than the sum of the separate disabilities.

To summarize, in assessing any child one has to consider his primary handicap, the specific nature of the environmental experiences available to him and the extent to which these are conducive to cognitive, emotional and physical growth. From what has been said above it is obvious that the all too common assumption that middle-class articulate parents will provide a good environment is unwarranted and dangerous. Similarly, the converse assumption of impoverished, less educated parents providing poor environments is unacceptable. Each case must be examined in detail in relation to the infant's abilities and handicaps, and parental attitudes, resources, motivations, knowledge of child development and treatment taken into account.

Diagnosis, assessment and treatment planning will now be considered in more detail.

## DIAGNOSIS, ASSESSMENT AND TREATMENT PLANNING

Diagnosis and assessment are the necessary first steps to treatment. They have two functions: (1) to predict future problems and hence preventive treatment, and (2) to analyse existing problems and prescribe treatment. For the parent of the mentally handicapped infant both functions are crucial. They are desperately in need of information which will tell them what the future may hold, what the child may or may not achieve. They also need to know what they can do now to help their infant.

If we accept the evidence that treatment can prevent the occurrence of a secondary handicap and that it should commence as soon as possible, early diagnosis is essential.

Mental handicap is diagnosed in infants when:

1. A condition is recognized which is consistently associated with delayed development and future intellectual impairment.
2. Assessments of the infant's rate of development indicate abnormally slow progress.

Diagnosis of mental handicap in the infant should always lead to assessments of actual and potential development. This is achieved by examining the infant on standardized scales of child development. These scales are made up of descriptions of typical infant behaviours arranged in hierarchical order. A number are closed tests only available to 'qualified' personnel (Bayley 1969; Griffiths 1960); others have been developed by paediatricians for the purpose of developmental screening (Illingworth 1963; Sheridan 1968). These scales indicate both the rate and the level of development. The level is expressed by the mental age (MA) and the rate by the developmental quotient (DQ). The mental age represents the mean score for the population at a given chronological age.* Generally the DQ is calculated by dividing the MA by the chronological age and multiplying by 100.† This same method is used in intelli-

gence tests to arrive at the IQ and in both cases the mean quotient for the population is 100. Thus the infant or child is considered to be mentally handicapped when his DQ or MA is significantly below average. By correlating the DQ with the later IQ, it is possible to ask how much these early assessments foretell later ones. In the case of mentally handicapped populations, the correlations are higher than with normal children and infant tests are considered to be more efficient predictors of later ability for such infants. Even so they are not high enough to allow useful predictions of individual scores (Carr 1975). However, as Carr noted, if a Down's syndrome infant scored at a high level between 10 and 36 months he is unlikely to score at the lowest level at four years or later and vice versa. After the age of two years the correlations become increasingly higher and more predictive and 'offer a valuable source of intellectual estimate by the time the child is four years of age' (Fishler et al. 1969).

Thus where infants are found to be functioning at a significantly lower than average level (that is, more than two standard deviations below the norm) on developmental tests, there is a high probability that they will show some level of retardation in later years. Certainly, such findings suggest the need for treatment. However, neither the recognition of the condition nor developmental assessments before the age of two can be used with confidence to predict individual progress.

Predictions do improve when a clinical appraisal includes such factors as the quality of response, the child's general alertness, responsiveness, concentration and attention. For instance, Illingworth's success in predicting mental handicap in the first year of life is not just as a result of using standardized tests of infant development, but also because he used these instruments in conjunction with a very full consideration of the child's previous history, rate of development, and relevant physical and neurological findings. For a full discussion of these issues the reader is referred to Illingworth (1963, 1971). In a sense, by taking into account clinical impressions, medical history and environmental factors in making an appraisal of the developmental abilities one is more

---

* If the mean score at 8 months of age is 21, then any infant gaining a score of 21 can be designated as having an MA of 8 months regardless of his chronological age.

† There is some dissatisfaction with this method of deriving a quotient as it fails to take into account the variance of the population. The Bayley Scales of Infant Development, for example, use this variance and produce a Developmental-Index (DI), not a DQ. This has implications for practice. For example, an infant aged 18 months may obtain a raw score of 103 on the mental scale. This would produce an MA of 12 months and a DI of 50. However, if the DQ is computed it would be $\frac{12}{18} \times 100 = 66$.

closely approximating the 'spirit' in which developmental testing was pioneered by Gesell (1940).

Another problem in assessment of mental handicap is the presence of plateaux. A plateau is best described as a period when little or no measurable change can be ascertained using standard developmental tests. Most children, normal and retarded, develop in a step-by-step fashion—the spurt at puberty, for example, is well documented. However, it is very common for the young child with Down's syndrome to obtain the same score or fail the same items for several months, whatever scale is used.

An obvious problem is that if the child is assessed at the beginning of a plateau the DQ will be higher than if he is assessed at the end of the period. Similarly, whilst the child's mental age will remain the same, the assessor may draw different inferences as to his potential from these assessments. Thus regular and frequent assessment is essential if a more reliable statement of potential is to be obtained. Assessments based on a single examination can be very misleading and may seriously affect decisions concerned with placement of the child for educational treatment.

These plateaux should not be considered as times of no development. Whilst they are often apparently related to specific difficulties, they frequently correspond to periods when the quality of response is being improved, and much consolidation of the behaviours is taking place. This is apparently a slower process in mentally handicapped children. Plateaux also reflect the difficulty children have between steps in developmental advance. The step-size (that is, the level of difficulty and the time it will take to develop the next behaviour) between increments is apparently neither too large nor too small for normally developing infants; however, less is known about how mentally handicapped infants develop between increments. This is particularly important when one begins to use developmental scales to direct treatment.

Before discussing treatment, let us summarize the use of developmental tests so far:

1. For normal infants developmental tests have little predictive value for future assessment of intelligence.

2. By two to three years the correlation between the developmental and intelligence scales is more useful and increases with age.

3. Developmental scales have a higher predictive value for children scoring abnormally low in the first two years but this does not allow for accurate individual prediction.

4. Improved predictive value is achieved if clinical impressions of alertness and responsiveness, medical history—particularly evidence of neurological or sensory impairment—and environmental factors are taken into account.

5. Assessment should be continuous and not based on a single examination.

TREATMENT: THE USE OF
DEVELOPMENTAL SCALES

Developmental scales are important tools in the treatment of severely handicapped infants. They provide:

1. A description of the hierarchical order of development of behaviours, the one leading to the next.

2. An indication, taken from the age norms, of when behaviours can be expected.

3. Measures of present performance, rather than future potential, and hence some indication of particular strengths and weaknesses.

4. A profile of the range of behaviours which make up normal child development, and which by implication are necessary for the normal development of the whole child.

The first stage in planning treatment is to decide what it is we want the child to acquire. This is something which is relevant to the needs of the child and which he is ready to learn, that is, which we can expect him to acquire in the immediate, not the distant, future. Developmental scales provide, at least partially, the initial outline of necessary present levels of ability and forecast the next logical step for the child. By noting specific areas of strength and weakness a profile of the child is attained which further suggests key areas for detailed observation and intervention. Developmental scales can also

TABLE 13.1

Mean ages and range for achieving early developmental behaviours in infants with Down's syndrome

| Behavioural item | Mean age in months | Range in months | No. of babies |
|---|---|---|---|
| *Gross motor* | | | |
| Holds head up for 15 seconds | 3 | $1\frac{1}{2}$–$5\frac{1}{2}$ | 24 |
| Balances head and holds it steady when swayed | 5 | 3–$8\frac{1}{2}$ | 31 |
| Rolls from back to front and front to back | 8 | 4–11 | 37 |
| Sits without support for one minute or more | 10 | 7–$15\frac{1}{2}$ | 37 |
| Sits steadily for 10 minutes or more and is well balanced | 11 | $8\frac{1}{2}$–$15\frac{1}{2}$ | 35 |
| When lying down pulls himself up to sit | $14\frac{1}{2}$ | $8\frac{1}{2}$–24 | 35 |
| Pulls to standing position on furniture | $16\frac{1}{2}$ | 10–24 | 33 |
| Walks with hands held | $17\frac{1}{2}$ | 10–30 | 30 |
| Stands alone | $21\frac{1}{2}$ | $15\frac{1}{2}$–36 | 29 |
| Walks 3 or more steps without support | 24 | $15\frac{1}{2}$–42 | 27 |
| *Fine motor* | | | |
| Holds cube using fingers against palm | $4\frac{1}{2}$ | $1\frac{1}{2}$–7 | 30 |
| Grasps cube, using thumb and fingers to hold it | $6\frac{1}{2}$ | 4–10 | 34 |
| Can pick up object size of currant | 12 | $8\frac{1}{2}$–$15\frac{1}{2}$ | 35 |
| Picks up object size of currant using thumb and forefinger only | 20 | 12–36 | 31 |
| *Adaptive* | | | |
| Visually follows dangling ring in circular movement | 3 | $1\frac{1}{2}$–$5\frac{1}{2}$ | 18 |
| Grasps dangling ring | 7 | 4–11 | 36 |
| Picks up cube | 8 | $5\frac{1}{2}$–10 | 36 |
| Holds 2 cubes | 8 | 4–11 | 35 |
| Picks up neatly and directly | 10 | 7–14 | 37 |
| Pulls ring by string deliberately | $11\frac{1}{2}$ | 7–17 | 36 |
| Removes cloth to find hidden toy | $13\frac{1}{2}$ | 10–21 | 35 |
| Puts cube in cup | $16\frac{1}{2}$ | 10–24 | 34 |
| Attempts to imitate scribble | $15\frac{1}{2}$ | 10–21 | 35 |
| Puts 3 cubes in cup | 19 | 14–30 | 29 |
| Puts a peg in pegboard two or more times | 23 | 17–36 | 24 |
| Builds a tower of 2 cubes | 22 | $15\frac{1}{2}$–30 | 26 |
| *Social* | | | |
| Smiles when touched and talked to | 3 | $1\frac{1}{2}$–$5\frac{1}{2}$ | 18 |
| Approaches image in mirror | $6\frac{1}{2}$ | 4–10 | 37 |
| *Communication* | | | |
| Vocalises to smile and talk | 4 | $1\frac{1}{2}$–$8\frac{1}{2}$ | 28 |
| Turns to sound | 7 | 4–11 | 36 |
| Says da-da, ba-ba etc. | 11 | 7–18 | 37 |
| Reacts to 'no' | 14 | 11–24 | 35 |
| Responds to familiar words by gestures etc. | $13\frac{1}{2}$ | 10–18 | 35 |
| Jabbers expressively | 18 | $12\frac{1}{2}$–30 | 35 |
| Says 2 words | 22 | $15\frac{1}{2}$–30 | 25 |

The data presented is the result of a study of early development in Down's syndrome. The infants were visited every six weeks and assessed on the Bayley Scales of Infant Development, for the first 2 years of life. (Reproduced from Cunningham and Sloper (1978) by courtesy of the publishers.)

provide a means of recording progress—an essential encouragement to the intervener, be he parent or professional. Many intervention programmes have successfully used developmental scales as a basis for their curricula. At present these emphasize gross motor and sensorimotor development and are less informed on socio-emotional behaviours and such areas as alertness, responsiveness and attentional skills. It is to be hoped that increasing knowledge of these areas will be used to enlarge these curricula and so maintain as complete a development of the whole child as possible.

Generally, the hierarchical order of the behaviours is well established, but there are particular exceptions. In the area of gross motor development normal children frequently do not crawl but bottom-hitch and some apparently walk before they crawl. Such discrepancies are even more noticeable with mentally handicapped infants. Down's syndrome infants, for example, frequently clap hands and throw balls before they crawl or walk even though such items appear later on developmental scales. Similarly, some behaviours seem more sensitive to treatment, for example, scribbling with a pencil or looking at picture books, and so appear earlier in the repertoire of 'trained' infants than would be suggested by their order in the scales. Such observations reinforce the contention that it is necessary to look at the particular behaviours in terms of the skills needed to attain them rather than normative placement on a scale.

Thus whilst assessment on a developmental scale provides an initial statement of the child's strengths and weaknesses, it is necessary to follow this by more detailed observation and analysis of the skills that might develop next. This is important for mentally handicapped infants, as the step-size between behavioural items noted in the scales may be too large or too complex for them. The more severe the mental handicap, the more likely this will be, and the more essential will be a detailed analysis of the required skill. Thus one moves from the normative basis of child development to an approach which emphasizes specification of the present level of skill or behaviour and the next smallest step required to achieve a new behaviour. In other

words, asking what the child can do and will do next, rather than what he should or might do. Looking at development in this manner makes chronological age redundant. The recently published Behaviour Assessment Battery (Kiernan & Jones 1977) is an example of this type of criterion-reference assessment. It attempts to define operationally crucial early behaviours, arrive at performance levels and sequence them in a series of small steps. The Battery has been devised specifically for profoundly handicapped individuals and can be used by psychologists, doctors, nurses and teachers.

Parents, however, do feel the need for some idea of what their child may achieve and when this can be reasonably expected. In the case of Down's syndrome several studies have collected data which can provide some information (Carr 1975; Share & Veale 1974) and our own 'norms' are given in Table 13.1. However, it is crucial to understand that these conclusions are based on current research studies whose subjects may not have been provided with optimal stimulation, and thus may not indicate optimal progress.

The model is then as follows:

1. Assess the child to determine strengths and weaknesses.
2. From this assessment, outline a provisional plan of available behaviours, and select the behaviours which are considered necessary for treatment.
3. Analyse these behaviours and produce a series of logically ordered steps. Each step should be as small as possible. Further detailed observation of the child is also frequently necessary, for example, to determine hand preference, posture problems, interests et cetera.

As an example, let us consider the behaviour of finding a hidden object under a cloth. This is part of object permanence. It appears at about 8–9 months in normal development. In most standard infant tests the previous item related to this, at about 6–7 months, is looking for a fallen object, that is, one dropped off the edge of the table. Thus according to development scales, there are approximately two months between these items. If the handicapped infant is progressing at a slower rate then this difference could be much longer. Thus having established that he is beginning object permanence in looking for the dropped object we must ask what are the next steps leading to finding an object hidden under a cloth and later a cup.

One sequence of behaviours could be the following:

1. When the infant is holding a noisy rattle and looking at it, cover it with a light cloth.

   The criterial behaviour or objective is that the child will remove the cloth and look at or manipulate the rattle on say four or five successive attempts.

   In practice, behaviours occur which themselves can be seen as sub-criterial behaviours or smaller steps. Typically, the infant reacts in one of the following ways:
   a. He drops the rattle and plays with the cloth, showing no further interest in the rattle.
   b. He drops the rattle so as to play with the cloth, but then attends to the rattle when he realizes it has dropped or when he hears it land.
   c. He shakes the rattle and cloth, often displacing the cloth.
   d. He pulls the cloth off with the other hand and attends to it but still holds on to the rattle, sometimes 'banging' the two together.
   e. He removes the cloth, and attends to the rattle.

These sub-behaviours vary greatly according to the child and his ability level. Thus observation of what the child does during his attempts to attain the behaviour are crucial. Frequently, difficulties are observed and new objectives must be worked out. Hence, the teaching is also part of the testing and *vice versa*. If one has a sufficiently detailed curriculum the need for testing is redundant and one just teaches.

The next steps, all of which could be further broken down depending upon the individual child's interaction with the teaching situation, are as follows:

2. Removes cloth from silent object held in hand.

3. Attains an object from the table, when the hand and object are covered by the cloth at the moment of grasping.
4. Removes cloth from large noisy object which is placed on the table and gently moved, for example, a squeezy doll or ball.
5. Removes cloth from half-hidden smaller object.
6. Removes cloth from large silent object which is gently moved.
7. Removes cloth from still, silent objects of any size.

In all cases the infant would be expected to attend to the hidden object either with sustained visual inspection or reach and manipulation.

*Useful techniques for teaching behaviours*

In teaching the behaviours a number of basic techniques are useful.

Firstly, the attention of the child is essential. Thus in placing the object on the table one would make sure the infant was looking at it before hiding it. Indeed one can frequently make the task easier by waiting until the infant starts to reach for the desired object before covering it.

Secondly, *prompts* are used. These may be physical prompts, such as guiding the child's hand to the cloth, forming a grip, and removing the cloth. These are particularly useful with mentally handicapped infants. There are visual prompts, such as shaking the object or pointing to it to attract attention. There are auditory prompts, such as tapping the object, or using a noise-making object, to attract attention; also verbal prompts, such as 'look', 'find', 'give' and so on which instruct the child to perform a particular behaviour. Prompts are useful to make the step-size smaller and to shape the new behaviour by a series of small steps which gradually become more and more like the final criterial behaviour. Most people intuitively use prompts but seldom plan how to reduce them. The art of teaching the child is knowing when to use the prompts and how to fade them out.

Each completion of a successful behaviour

or sub-behaviour should be reinforced by *rewarding* the child immediately after the behaviour has been demonstrated. A reward is anything which increases the likelihood of the behaviour being repeated. Simply, it is something which gives the child pleasure. Obviously, an interest in the task is the best means of rewarding the child and in the above example one would choose objects which the child appears to want and will try to attain. However, telling the child he is 'good', smiling, tickling, hugging, kissing can all be used to reinforce and are used naturally by most parents. With very impaired children it is sometimes necessary to resort to more tangible rewards such as food or drink, but this is something of a special case. The important principle in using rewards is to be consistent and immediate.

It is obvious that the method of assessing the child's progress in achieving these critical behaviours will be different from the initial assessment using standard scales. The standardized scale assessment, for example, cannot really indicate if the treatment techniques are actually working. Similarly, by the time they indicate that little progress is being made, much effort and opportunity have been wasted. Thus data is needed which is more specific, more immediate and directly related to the task under treatment. The main approach is to record continuously during the teaching. Such recording methods use frequency, duration or time taken to respond. In the example of finding the hidden object one can record the number of times the child

successfully uncovered and obtained the object. This would be the frequency.

In special cases of poor responsiveness or alertness, one might also note the time taken to respond and complete the behaviour. If one were training grasping of an object, sitting or standing, one might measure duration, that is, how long an object was held, how long the child sat or stood. Similarly, for transferring objects from hand to hand one would use frequency, and possible latency of response, and for walking, the number of steps taken. One would also need to record whether a prompt was used to achieve the behaviour or not. Figure 13.2 represents a possible chart for finding an object hidden under a cloth. Each day five trials were recorded at the end of the training sessions. As can be seen, the first day required constant prompting, but by the fourth day the infant had succeeded in five successful performances and thus it was decided to move on to the next step in the programme. This was achieved quite quickly and the child was ready for the third step. If no change had been recorded over several days one would have to assume a deficiency in the training, and the task, the infant's abilities and the teaching techniques would have to be re-analysed.

The detailed breakdown and recording techniques noted here are time consuming and one must ask to what extent they are necessary and practical, particularly for the parent. Parents can certainly understand and use these techniques but do not really have the time to develop them. Thus professional

| DATE | 1.2.78 | | | | | 2.2.78 | | | | | 4.2.78 | | | | | 5.2.78 | | | | |
|---|---|---|---|---|---|---|---|---|---|---|---|---|---|---|---|---|---|---|---|---|
| TRIAL | 1 | 2 | 3 | 4 | 5 | 1 | 2 | 3 | 4 | 5 | 1 | 2 | 3 | 4 | 5 | 1 | 2 | 3 | 4 | 5 |
| 1. Uncovers noisy rattle held in hand — with prompts | √ | √ | √ | √ | √ | √ | √ | √ | | | √ | | | | | | | | | |
| 1. Uncovers noisy rattle held in hand — without prompts | | | | | | | | | √ | √ | | √ | √ | √ | √ | √ | √ | √ | √ | √ |

| DATE | 6.2.78 | | | | | 7.2.78 | | | | | | | | | | | | | | |
|---|---|---|---|---|---|---|---|---|---|---|---|---|---|---|---|---|---|---|---|---|
| 2. Uncovers silent object held in hand — with prompts | √ | √ | | | | | | | | | | | | | | | | | | |
| 2. Uncovers silent object held in hand — without prompts | | | √ | √ | √ | √ | √ | √ | √ | √ | | | | | | | | | | |

Fig. 13.2   *Recording chart: finding the object hidden under a cloth.*

support is important, not only to provide objectives, task analysis and recording methods but also to analyse difficulties. However, the use of such techniques is relatively new and the extent to which they are necessary in relation to the individual child under treatment is unclear. The general answer is that the more handicapped the child, the greater his difficulties and the slower his progress, the more need there is for very detailed analysis, teaching and recording. Certainly, more investigation is needed to indicate the level of effort needed to obtain 'optimal', or acceptable, rate of development. However, the intending intervener who has limited resources should not be put off by the apparent effort needed. Much improvement has been demonstrated with Down's syndrome infants by merely providing parents with checklists of normal development derived from standardized scales, some insights into the use of observation, analysis, and shaping and prompting techniques, and much optimistic support and encouragement. It is very possible that future studies may find that in many cases this is sufficient.

The above discussion of treatment and assessment is necessarily brief and the reader is referred to such texts as Haring and Brown (1976) for details of analysis and teaching techniques in pre-school handicapped children. Also available are packages and outline programmes for professionals to work with parents, for example, the Portage Project (Shearer et al. 1972), or practical books directed to parents (Cunningham & Sloper 1978).

## CONCLUSIONS AND FUTURE NEEDS

There is sufficient evidence to demonstrate that the provision of early stimulation has a positive effect on the development of many young handicapped children, particularly those with Down's syndrome. Further, the provision of support and training for the parents is an essential part of this and also provides a necessary therapy for the parents.

There is sufficient information concerning early child development, techniques of stimulation, techniques and approaches to parent training and a knowledge of parental needs from which to build early services.

The climate is favourable. Both the Court Committee (DHSS 1976) and the Warnock Committee (DES 1978) have outlined in some detail a framework for the development of such services.

This is not to argue that more research and investigation are unnecessary. There is insufficient information on the interrelationships between programme content, techniques, etiologies and the stages of development of the infant. How intensive does early stimulation need to be? Does it vary with developmental level or with areas of development or both? How much, and how little, effort do parents have to make to expect optimal development? Does this vary with age or etiology? There is some evidence to suggest that home visiting on a fortnightly basis is no more effective than on a six-weekly or two-monthly basis in the first two years of life (Cunningham & Sloper 1977) and may be less effective (Sandow & Clarke 1978). There is little information regarding individual differences of infants, parents and families and their interaction with various intervention approaches.

However, many of these questions will only be answered as more and more services are set up and evaluated. Thus we have the opportunity to turn the present isolated pockets of provision and investigation into a nationwide service such that all parents of young severely handicapped children should feel that they have had the best available help from the moment the infant's condition was diagnosed.

## BIBLIOGRAPHY

Bayley, N. (1969) *Bayley Scales of Infant Development*. New York: The Psychological Corporation.
Callaway, W. R. (1970) *Percept. Cogn. Def.* Monograph no. 1, 1–34.
Carr, J. (1975) *Young Children with Down's Syndrome*. IRMMH Monograph no. 4. Sevenoaks: Butterworth.

Clark, A. D. B. & Clarke, A. M. (1974) Mental retardation and behavioural change. *Br. med. Bull.*, *30*, 179–85.

Cunningham, C. C. (1976) Parents as therapists and educators. In: Kiernan, C. C. & Woodford, P. (eds.), *Behaviour Modification with the Severely Retarded*. IRMMH Study Group 8. Amsterdam: Elsevier.

Cunningham, C. C. & Sloper, P. (1977) Down's syndrome infants: a positive approach to parents and professional collaboration. *Health Visitor*, *50*, 32.

Cunningham, C. C. & Sloper, P. (1978) *Helping your Handicapped Baby*. London: Souvenir Press.

de Coriat, L. F., Theslenco, L. & Waksman, J. (1968) The effects of psychomotor stimulation on the I.Q. of young children with Trisomy-21. In: Richards, B. W. (ed.), *Proceedings of the 1st Congress of the International Association for Scientific Study of Mental Deficiency* (Montpellier, Sept. 1967). Reigate: Michael Jackson Pub. Co. Ltd.

Department of Education and Science (1978) *Special Educational Needs*. Report of the Committee of Enquiry into the Education of Handicapped Children and Young People (Warnock Committee). Cmnd. 7212. London: HMSO.

Department of Health and Social Security (1976) *Fit for the Future*. Report of the Committee on Child Health Services (Court Committee). Cmnd. 6684. London: HMSO.

Down, J. L. H. (1866) Observations on an ethnic classification of idiots: clinical lectures and reports, London Hospital. Reprinted in: Jordan, J. E. (ed.), *Perspectives in Mental Retardation*. Carbondale, S. Illinois: University Press, 1966.

Dybwad, G. (1973) See discussion in: Clarke, A. D. B. & Clarke, A. M. (eds.), *Mental Retardation and Behavioural Research*, p. 226. IRMR Study Group 4. Edinburgh: Churchill Livingstone.

Fishler, K., Graliker, B. V. & Koch, R. (1969) The predictability of intelligence with Gesell Developmental Scales in mentally retarded infants and young children. *Am. J. ment. Defic.*, *69*, 515–25.

Francis, S. H. (1971) The effects of own home and institutional rearing on the behavioural development of normal and mongol children. *J. Child Psychol. Psychiat.*, *12*, 173–90.

Gesell, A. (1940) *The First Five Years of Life: A Guide to the Study of the Pre-school Child*. New York: Harper & Row.

Griffiths, R. (1960) *The Abilities of Babies*. London: University of London Press.

Haring, N. G. & Brown, L. J. (eds.) (1976) *Teaching the Severely Handicapped*, vol. 1. New York: Grune and Stratton.

Hayden, A. H. & Dmitriev, V. (1975) Early developmental and educational problems for the child with Down's syndrome. In: Friedlander, B., Kirk, G. & Sternitt, G. (eds.), *The Exceptional Infant*, vol. III. New York: Brunner/Mazel.

Hayden, A. H. & Haring, N. G. (1977) The acceleration and maintenance of development gains in Down's syndrome school-age children. In: Mittler, P. (ed.), *Research to Practice in Mental Retardation*, vol. 1. Baltimore: University Park Press.

Heifetz, L. J. (1977) Behavioural training for parents of retarded children: alternative formats based on instructional manuals. *Am. J. ment. Defic.*, *82*, 194–203.

Illingworth, R. S. (1963) *The Development of the Infant and Young Child*, 2nd ed. Edinburgh: Churchill Livingstone.

Illingworth, R. S. (1971) The predictive value of developmental assessment in infancy. *Devl. Med. Child Neurol.*, *13*, 721–5.

Jeffree, D. M. & Cashdan, A. (1971) The home background of the severely subnormal child: a second study. *Br. J. med. Psychol.*, *44*, 27–33.

Jones, O. (1976) Mother-child communication with pre-linguistic Down's syndrome and normal infants. In: Schaffer, H. R. (ed.), *Studies in Mother–Infant Interaction*. London: Academic Press.

Kiernan, C. & Jones, M. (1977) *Behaviour Assessment Battery*. Windsor: NFER Publishing Co. Ltd.

Ludlow, J. R. (1979) Study of a group of children in Kent, suffering from Down's syndrome. *J. ment. Defic. Res.*, *23*, 29–44.

Lyle, J. G. (1959) The effect of an institution environment upon the verbal development of imbecile children. 1. Verbal Intelligence. *J. ment. Defic. Res.*, *3*, 122–8.

Nay, R. W. (1975) A systematic comparison of instructional techniques for parents. *Behav. Therapy*, *6*, 14–21.

Neligan, G. & Prudham, D. (1969) Norms for four standard developmental milestones by sex, social class and place in family. *Devl. Med. Child Neurol.*, *11*, 413–22.

Penrose, L. S. & Smith, G. F. (1966) *Down's Anomaly*. Edinburgh: Churchill Livingstone.

Rynders, J. E. & Horrobin, J. M. (1975) Project EDGE: The University of Minnesota's Communication

Stimulation Program for Down's Syndrome Infants. In: Friedlander, B., Kirk, G. & Sternitt, G. (eds.), *The Exceptional Infant*, vol. III. New York: Brunner/Mazel.

Sandow, S. & Clarke, A. D. B. (1978) Home intervention with parents of severely subnormal, pre-school children: an interim report. *Child: care, health and development*, 4, 29–39.

Scherzer, A. L., Mike, V. & Ilson, J. (1976) Physical therapy as a determinant of change in the cerebral palsied infant. *Paediatrics*, 58, 47–52.

Share, J. B. (1976) Review of drug treatment for Down's syndrome persons. *Am. J. ment. Defic.*, 80, 388–93.

Share, J. B. & Veale, A. M. O. (1974) *Developmental Landmarks for Children with Down's Syndrome (Mongolism)*. Dunedin, New Zealand: University of Otago Press.

Shearer, P., Billingsley, J., Froham, A., Hilliar, J., Johnson, F. & Shearer, M. (1972) *The Portage Guide to Early Education*. Portage, Wisconsin: Co-operative Educational Service Agency.

Sheridan, M. (1968) *The Developmental Profiles of Infants and Young Children*. London: HMSO.

Solkhoff, N., Yaffe, S., Weintraub, D. & Blase, B. (1969) Effects of handling on the subsequent development of premature infants. *Develop. Psychol.*, 1, 765–8.

Stedman, D. J. (1977) Important Considerations in the Review and Evaluation of Educational Intervention Programmes. In: Mittler, P. (ed.), *Research to Practice in Mental Retardation*, vol. 1. Baltimore: University Park Press.

Tizard, J. & Tizard, B. (1974) The institution as an environment for development. In: Richards, M. P. (ed.), *The Integration of a Child into a Social World*. Cambridge: Cambridge University Press.

White, B. L. (1971) *Human Infants Experience and Psychological Development*. New Jersey: Prentice-Hall.

# CHAPTER 14

# EDUCATING MENTALLY HANDICAPPED CHILDREN

## PETER MITTLER

In Britain at the present time, well over 80 per cent of mentally handicapped children live at home with their families; even the most severely handicapped go to special schools every day. Fewer than 5000 children are resident in hospitals for the mentally handicapped, and the government is trying to reduce the numbers in hospital even further. This is being done by a policy of providing residential facilities near the children's own homes rather than in large hospitals and by ensuring that those facilities are run along homely and domestic lines. However, the children who are still resident in hospital also attend school in the hospital; these hospital schools are run by the education authorities and are staffed by qualified teachers.

England and Wales now have over 400 special schools for some 33 000 mentally handicapped (ESNS) children. Hardly any children are in special classes attached to ordinary schools. Most of the classes in the special schools cater for between eight and ten children, and the majority are staffed by two people—one teacher and a care assistant or nursery nurse. The staffing ratios may be as high as one adult for three children, particularly for those children with profound multiple handicaps, perhaps a quarter of the total in day special schools, but as high as a half in hospital schools.

Government calculations suggest that each total population unit of 100 000 people will need to provide special school places for at least 75 ESN(S) children; but this number does not allow for the need for school places to be retained for those young people who might benefit from remaining at school after the age of 16. In theory, children can remain at special schools up to the age of 19, if it is in their interests to do so, but there are very few children over the age of 16 at special schools at the present time, mainly because there is no space for them. This may change for the better, partly as a result of better provision, partly because the sharply falling birth rate is beginning to result in fewer children entering special schools.

Although the current outlook in Britain is certainly one of optimism and enthusiasm, we are faced with many serious and intractable problems which cannot be solved by enthusiasm or extra finance alone. We shall need to consider some basic issues: What should be the aims of education for these children? How early should education begin? How relevant are existing educational methods to this population? What kind of curriculum and what kind of teaching methods are suitable? What kind of teachers do we need, and how should they be trained? What kind of educational provision should be made for further education after school?

### What do we mean by education?

Underlying all these questions is the need to attempt some definition of what we mean by education for this group of children.

*Education is concerned with everything which actively helps an individual to learn new skills and abilities.*

Seen in this light, education is much broader than schooling; it is a process which begins at birth, which involves the parents in depth and detail, but which should also extend throughout adulthood. The school is only an interlude in the process of education, and the school-leaving age, whether it is 16, 19 or any other age, merely marks the end of one of several stages in the education of the individual. After he leaves full-time schooling, society must find other means of continuing to provide opportunities for him to develop his skills and abilities. Eleven years of compulsory education is certainly not enough for a mentally handicapped person.

If we accept such a broad view of education, we shall have to learn to take special education out of the school and into the community. Teachers will not only work with pupils in special schools, but will also be concerned with helping those who are not teachers to develop skills as special educators. This includes parents of the mentally handicapped, as well as nurses and residential care staff.

The general aims of education are the same for the mentally handicapped as for anyone else. General aims are necessarily expressed in global terms. For example, the goals of education are often expressed in terms of personal autonomy and independence; specialists in the education of handicapped children are fond of saying that children should be able to 'achieve the maximum of their potential', be helped to 'adjust to the demands of the community and to take their place in society'.

Terms like autonomy and independence can be useful and need not be vague; a child increases his independence by learning to walk, and by learning to speak just as much as by learning to read. The fact that some skills are at a more advanced level than others does not make the teaching of basic skills any less educationally important. However, we are confronted by a very special challenge

—that of teaching children to acquire skills which do not normally have to be taught at all. How often in our experience as parents or as teachers of ordinary children do we have to plan consciously and systematically to teach a child to look, to listen, to reach out for objects, to play with toys or dolls, to explore his environment, to enjoy the company of human beings? Perhaps the most exciting challenge of all is that of teaching a child to understand and speak his own language.

## NORMAL DEVELOPMENT AS A CURRICULUM FRAMEWORK

Given the vagueness of the general aims of education for the mentally handicapped, what should be the source of the curriculum, and how shall we decide what we are going to teach?

This is a difficult and controversial question at the present time, and one which seems to be subject to substantial changes from time to time. Although many workers in this field are content to base their work on the framework provided by our knowledge of normal child development, this may not provide all the signposts we need. For example, teachers working with mentally handicapped children in the 1960s were strongly influenced by the movements in British infant and nursery education; these placed a strong emphasis on providing a rich and stimulating environment, and on encouraging the child to take advantage of a wide range of materials and learning opportunities. The choice of materials was influenced by the overall developmental level of the child; there was therefore an emphasis on nursery school toys and methods, since the developmental level of many of the children corresponded to the levels of 'mental age' encountered in nursery schools, that is, between $2\frac{1}{2}$ and 5 years.

However, it could not be assumed that toys and play materials for young normal children were necessarily suitable for much older mentally handicapped children, even though their levels of mental development might be comparable to those of younger children. The fact that a fifteen-year-old young person has a mental age of three years does not mean that he should be educated only according to the methods and principles suitable for normal three-year-olds.

These methods were themselves a reaction against the rather formal 'sense training' methods which had been used in many schools, based loosely on influences deriving from the work of Seguin, Itard and others. However, the methods were applied to groups of children and were not sufficiently related to the needs of the individual. Thus it was not uncommon to see rows of children sitting in desks, each child engaged in the same task of threading beads or completing identical form boards.

Psychological research began to raise questions about the validity of approaches based on free activity and on 'learning by doing' and suggested that mentally handicapped children had specific difficulties in spontaneous and incidental learning; it could not therefore be assumed that the child would learn merely by being exposed to the conditions for learning which were suitable for other children (Clarke & Clarke 1974).

Here again, our knowledge of normal development is useful as a general framework because it provides signposts for the teacher in search of a curriculum. But the signposts are sometimes few and far between and do not provide enough detailed or specific guidance to help the teacher to travel from one landmark to another.

The emphasis has now shifted towards a systematic teaching strategy. An attempt is being made in many schools to achieve a balance between stimulation and structure by retaining a lively child-centred, stimulating environment as a background, while at the same time using structured methods as a foreground.

The need for more structural methods has undoubtedly been more widely recognized in the past five years or so, not only because of the findings of research but because teachers themselves felt dissatisfied with the results of existing methods and seemed to be actively seeking for a more systematic approach without at the same time abandoning what they regarded as the most valuable elements of the infant and nursery school approach.

*One expression of this more rigorous approach to education is the principle that everything a mentally handicapped child is to learn will have to be taught.*

## EDUCATION FROM BIRTH

If education is concerned with everything that actively helps an individual to learn and to develop, then means must be found of providing educational experiences to handicapped children from the first weeks of life. This can be done by helping the family to adopt an educational approach and to be active in fostering the development of the child.

This does not mean that highly specialized treatment procedures must necessarily be brought into the home. Some children may well benefit from certain exercises and activities, but many others will need little more than the ordinary games, activities and experiences which help normal infants to learn and to develop. Mothers often assume that handicapped babies are 'different' and that expert advice is necessary before anything new can be attempted; for example, they may fear that a brain-damaged child will be subject to fits if too much stimulation is provided or if demands are made for a child to do something new.

Problems involved in fostering the development of handicapped infants are discussed in Chapter 13, and in a handbook for parents of children of this age by Cunningham and Sloper (1978). Although very little is known about the needs of handicapped infants and their families, particularly about the long-term benefits of very early intervention, it is becoming clearer that some form of intervention and early help is at least called for by the parents who often feel isolated and uninformed at this early stage and who may not in the normal course of events gain access to help and services for some years. Systematic early help is likely to give parents confidence that they can achieve results with their child and dispel the feeling that they are coping entirely without support and understanding from professionals. One of the most impressive developments of the 1970s has been the demonstration of the contribution that parents can make to the development of their handicapped child. Parents have been helped to observe, assess and record the skills and behaviours of their child, to set realistic goals that he can achieve in a short time and to develop methods that they can use in their own home to help him to reach those targets.

A variety of approaches has been developed to help parents to work in depth and detail with their own child (see O'Dell 1974 and Cunningham 1976 for reviews). Some involve highly prescriptive programmes of behaviour modification, while others merely help parents to set objectives but leave it to them to decide the means by which these objectives will be attained. Some projects involve groups of parents meeting in regular workshop sessions, others involve direct work with home visitors. It is clear that we have only just begun to harness the considerable resources which families can provide once they are fully involved in partnership with professional staff.

The Court Committee on Child Health Services (DHSS 1976) has recently suggested the establishment of District Handicap Teams covering population units of about 240 000 people, including some 60 000 children (the size of the average health district since the 1974 reorganization of the National Health Service); these teams are intended to provide a focus of help and services for handicapped children and for parents who are in any way concerned about the development of their child. The multidisciplinary teams will consist of paediatricians, nurses, psychologists, teachers and social workers, and are intended to provide not merely skilled assessment but a programme of treatment and intervention suited to the needs of the child and the family. The teams might be based on a Child Development Centre attached to the local district general hospital or might for certain purposes be sited in a school or other community setting. However services are organized to suit local needs and conditions, it is essential that skilled help is available to families from the very beginning, so that they can work in partnership with professional staff in fostering the development of their child (see Spain & Wigley 1975, and National Development Group 1977 for discussions on the organization of services).

Children who are under school age are increasingly being helped to use the ordinary resources available to non-handicapped children of the same age, for example, pre-school playgroups, nursery classes and schools, day nurseries; many also go to special schools for mentally handicapped children from the age of two onwards, and seem to derive great benefit from doing so. If they go to schools and centres designed primarily for ordinary children, it is essential that staff should be able to gain access to people with special experience in working with mentally handicapped children. The Child Development Centres and District Handicap Teams proposed by the Court Committee may carry out detailed assessments and begin to work out programmes of teaching based on the needs of the individual, but they will need to work closely with people who are involved with the child on a day-to-day basis, that is, the family and the staff of the school or unit attended by the child. It is not enough simply to place a handicapped child in a 'normal' environment in the hope that he will benefit simply by being exposed to conditions that help other children; more active and systematic methods may be needed to help him to learn.

## SPECIAL SCHOOLS

Special schools are currently being criticized not so much for what they do or fail to do but because they run counter to the principle that handicapped children should wherever possible be educated with ordinary children. Merely placing a handicapped child in an ordinary school does not guarantee integration, any more than placing him in a special school necessarily involves segregation. It is basically a question of planning and organization.

Special schools of the future are likely to function increasingly as resource centres for teachers and children in ordinary schools. Staff of special schools will work not only with their own children but with children and staff in other schools and in the homes of families. They will work with children who are not yet at school, and perhaps also with those who have already left. The schools themselves can provide not only skilled advice on methods of teaching handicapped children but can also provide resource materials such as teaching machines, specialist materials for teaching language, reading or numbers, and advice on the advantages and disadvantages of these methods. Schools can also house toy libraries for handicapped children and provide a local forum for advice on practical problems of teaching. They can also develop film and videotape libraries, so that staff and families can readily observe a demonstration of a particular teaching programme in action. Advice on aids and appliances and means of helping children to use or adapt to them can also be provided.

### Planning for the individual child

The truism that no two children are alike applies nowhere more forcefully than in schools for the mentally handicapped. The range of individual differences even within a single classroom is likely to be considerable. The children will vary in chronological age and level of development, they are likely to have additional physical, sensory or motor handicaps and the task of teaching them may be further complicated by emotional disturbance or behaviour disorder.

The teacher's first task, therefore, is to carry out a thorough assessment of the child in order to design a programme of remediation and learning that is geared to his specific needs and difficulties. It is now recognized that this cannot be done by a conventional intelligence test, but requires a prolonged period of systematic observation and experimental teaching in which different educational methods and approaches are applied and evaluated.

The needs of the individual mentally handicapped child can rarely be met by traditional educational methods. For one thing, the developmental level of many of the children will correspond in some respects to those of the pre-school child. The teacher will therefore be concerned with many aspects of development and behaviour that are usually undertaken by the mother of a normal child before he reaches school. Teaching a child to feed, dress and toilet himself requires the same level of professional skill and application as teaching him to speak or even to read, and no simple distinction can be made between the teaching of self-care skills and the teaching of cognitive skills. The teacher will need to devise means of helping the child to pay attention, and to discriminate between relevant and irrelevant materials; he may have to be taught to look at objects, to learn about the physical properties of his environment and to be carefully and systematically exposed to different shapes, sizes, sounds and materials. Many children have to be taught to play, or helped to understand other people's facial expressions.

The normal child rarely has to be taught to do any of these things, but nothing can be taken for granted in the case of a mentally handicapped child, and it can never be confidently assumed that a child will acquire these skills without special help. Not only do these skills rarely feature in the usual curriculum even for normal three-year-olds, but little attention has so far been given to the methods and techniques by which they may be taught. The teacher's task is therefore a highly demanding and difficult one, for which conventional teacher training does not usually provide an adequate introduction.

The foundation of a systematic and individualised approach to teaching is provided by the assessment process, which should result in the specification of precise teaching objectives. These objectives may need to be very carefully defined, so that each learning task is broken down into small and finely graded steps. Teaching has to begin at a point where the child is likely to be successful; the demands on the child can then be gradually increased until it is clear that he has temporarily reached a limit, at which point suitable remedial procedures might be introduced. The important principle here is that the task to be taught should be precisely defined by the teacher and attainable by the child.

## THE TEACHING OF LANGUAGE AND COMMUNICATION SKILLS

It may be useful at this point to illustrate these general principles in one curriculum area. Language and communication teaching can be considered as an example, because it is an area of common concern to parents as well as teachers and to the community as a whole.

A recent survey of the language abilities of some 1400 children in 19 special schools in the north west of England (Swann & Mittler 1976) showed that, of those children aged 16 years who were about to leave school, about one-fifth had not reached the stage of speaking single words; nearly a quarter were not yet able to combine two words and about 43 per cent were not yet speaking in grammatical sentences.

The survey also showed a rather depressing picture of little or no growth in language abilities between the ages of about six and fourteen. The youngest children—those between three and six—showed an encouraging rate of growth, but the rate of growth of the older children in language skills was disappointingly slow. The survey results bear out other evidence which suggests that mentally handicapped children tend to show particularly marked delays in language development. Recent work clearly shows that mentally handicapped children can be taught to develop language and communication skills, but that systematic and structured methods are necessary if they are to learn, and above all if they are to learn to use language in ordinary life. During the 1960s and until very recently research workers reported a number of studies in which language was largely taught in rather artificial one-to-one 'clinical' sessions. It is only very recently that more emphasis has been placed on the teaching of language in ordinary, natural settings, such as the home, in shops, on public transport and in the playground. In order to learn to speak, children need to have something to say, and someone to talk to. This is why it is both more natural and more effective to involve families from the outset in systematic attempts to teach language skills.

It is now accepted that language can be taught long before the child begins to speak. The roots of language lie in the child's first attempt to communicate; we have to build on these foundations in the case of mentally handicapped children, and try to help them to learn that any form of communication is rewarding. Communication may begin with no more than a look or a smile, and then gradually develop towards gesture.

One of the most dramatic educational developments in the past few years has been the gradually increasing use of systematic sign languages with mentally handicapped people (Kiernan 1977). Some of these are modifications of sign languages used by deaf people; others are no more than a few basic signs, such as signs for me, you, give, yes, no, eat, drink, toilet, signs for certain objects or activities. These signs build bridges between the silent child and those around him, and it is on such foundations that communication can be built.

We also find increasing interest in teaching children to learn to listen, to learn that certain sounds are associated with certain activities, and to learn that listening can be enjoyable. A number of studies have shown that even profoundly handicapped children are able to express choice for one type of sound rather than another, for example, by moving a large switch they can choose to listen to one type of music rather than another.

Learning to play is also recognized as one of the essential foundations of language development; children are therefore being taught to play symbolically and representationally, for example, pretend games, games with dolls—indeed, any game in which one thing is made to stand for or symbolize another (Jeffree et al. 1977).

The goal of language is, of course, to teach a child to speak in words, phrases and sentences and finally to use words to communicate meaning and intention. Here again, techniques are being developed to do this, using principles of assessment and task analysis. The teacher may begin with a programme of imitation training, in which the child is trained to imitate large movements of the body; these are then localized to the head, mouth or tongue; finally the child is taught to imitate sounds and words.

There is some ground for optimism about recent developments in language teaching. Considerable progress has been made, and a number of publications are becoming available which provide detailed guidance on the range of methods that can be used (Schiefelbusch & Lloyd 1974; Berry 1976). Some language-teaching programmes have also become available on the commercial market, for example, the Peabody Language Development Kit, Goal, Distar and Jim's People (Leeming et al. 1979).

## CREATIVE ACTIVITIES

Although the approach to education outlined here is broadly behavioural, and relies to a large extent on assessment, developmental planning, task analysis and prescription, there is no reason why educational experiences for these children should be sterile or lacking in enjoyment. Of course, success in learning and in the attainment of goals is a reward in itself, but it is important to allow plenty of time for creative activities, for enjoyment and for free activity, since these bring their own reward and are as important to the total development of the child as the attainment of formal learning goals (Stevens 1976).

It is therefore important to provide opportunities for children to benefit from creative activities, such as drama, music, physical education, swimming, games, sports and a wide range of recreational activities. These are an essential part of their education and of their personal development, since such activities can often provide the means of self-expression and a source of satisfaction.

## TEACHER TRAINING

Teacher education is the central question of special education for the mentally handicapped. The preparation of teachers has been badly neglected in many countries, with the result that modern well-equipped schools are often staffed by teachers who are inadequately trained for this demanding work, and who are left without a proper network of professional support and advice. The training of teachers to work with the mentally handicapped deserves as much priority as the erection of buildings and schools. Even in countries where much of the responsibility is delegated to colleges and other teacher-training institutions, some central guidance and initiative is required in this area. This could take a number of forms:

1. A national plan to ensure a minimum number of qualified teachers in special schools by a specified date, to be reached by annual targets.

2. A series of local teacher-training pro-

grammes, to ensure that every teacher working with handicapped children has the opportunity to take a basic course in special education, followed by more advanced refresher courses, workshops and short courses of in-service training. Financial incentives should be available.

3. Encouragement needs also to be given to the creation of a network of local support systems for teachers, so that each teacher and each school can call on the advice and support of specialists. For example, there should be a 'special education resource centre' within reach of every school. This might be a 'Teachers Centre' with an extensive supply of curriculum materials, including films, cassette tapes, videotapes and other material illustrating a variety of methods and techniques used in special education. Ideally, this should be centrally organized on a national basis, and supported by government departments.

4. Advanced programmes of teacher education and research are also essential to a healthy system of special education. Certain universities and colleges should be regarded as 'centres of excellence', and provide a range of advanced courses, including Master's and Doctoral programmes.

5. Some central guidance and initiative is also required to ensure that research and development are properly disseminated and critically evaluated by teachers. This can be done through teacher workshops and discussion groups, as well as by more conventional means, such as publication.

## CONCLUSIONS

Education for the mentally handicapped is a lifelong process. Because it neither begins nor ends in school, one of our most urgent tasks is to extend its best concepts and practices outside the school and into the community.

Educators should be involved in the development of a handicapped child from the first weeks and months of life. Their task is to assess the needs of the child and to plan actively to assist his development.

Teachers should learn to work in the closest possible partnership with the child's family, and to involve them in depth and detail in furthering the child's development. Experience in many countries has not only shown that this is possible, but that handicapped children learn better and more lastingly when their families are actively involved than when teaching is carried out by teachers alone.

A special school for mentally handicapped children need not therefore work only with those children who attend every day; it can also act as a resource centre for all mentally handicapped children in a given area, whether they attend the school or not. This means in practice that some members of the school staff may be employed to work as 'home teachers', working largely or wholly with families, while using the resources of the school as a base for their operation. They would then be able to call on the advice and help of their colleagues, and use the material resources of the school, such as learning materials, special toys and educational apparatus.

Recent developments have opened up a wide range of opportunities for teaching. The application of systematic methods of developmental planning, based on a thorough assessment of the needs of each child as an individual, has shown that the development of even the most profoundly handicapped can be actively furthered. It is equally clear that it is not enough merely to expose children to the conditions of learning; they have to be actively taught.

Finally, one of the main tasks for special education for the future lies in its extension to adults. This has hardly begun.

It now seems obvious to us that education of the mentally handicapped is not only worthwhile on humanitarian grounds but is technically and humanly possible to a greater extent than we previously thought. We need to convey this to the general public, to teachers in the normal sector, and to educational administrators who determine the resources that are to be given to special education.

## BIBLIOGRAPHY

Berry, P. (ed.) (1976) *Language and Communication in the Mentally Handicapped.* London: Edward Arnold.

Clarke, A. M. & Clarke, A. D. B. (1974) Experimental studies: an overview. In: Clarke, A. M. & Clarke, A. D. B. (eds.), *Mental Deficiency: The Changing Outlook*, 3rd ed. London: Methuen.

Cunningham, C. C. (1976) Parents as educators and therapists. In: Kiernan, C. C. & Woodford, P. (eds.), *Behaviour Modification with the Severely Retarded.* Amsterdam: Elsevier.

Cunningham, C. C. & Sloper, P. (1978) *Teaching Your Handicapped Baby.* London: Souvenir Press.

Department of Health and Social Security (1976) *Fit for the Future.* Report of the Committee on Child Health Services (Court Committee). Cmnd. 6684. London: HMSO.

Jeffree, D., McConkey, R. & Hewson, S. (1977) *Let Me Play.* London: Souvenir Press.

Kiernan, C. C. (1977) Alternatives to speech: a review of research on manual and other forms of communication with the mentally handicapped and other non-communicating populations. *Br. J. ment. Sub., 23,* 6–28.

Leeming, K., Coupe, J., Swann, W. & Mittler, P. (1979) *Teaching Language and Communication to the Mentally Handicapped.* London: Schools Council Curriculum Bulletin No. 8. London: Evans Methuen Educational.

National Development Group for the Mentally Handicapped (1977) *Mentally Handicapped Children: A Plan for Action* (pamphlet 2). London: DHSS.

O'Dell, S. (1974) Training parents in behaviour modification: a review. *Psychol. Bull., 81,* 418–33.

Schiefelbusch, R. L. & Lloyd, L. (eds.) (1974) *Language Perspectives—Acquisition, Retardation and Intervention.* Baltimore: University Park Press.

Spain, B. & Wigley, G. (eds.) (1975) *Right from the Start: A Service for Families with a Young Handicapped Child.* London: National Society for Mentally Handicapped Children.

Stevens, M. (1976) *The Educational and Social Needs of Children with Severe Handicap.* London: Edward Arnold.

Swann, W. & Mittler, P. (1976) A survey of language abilities in ESNS children. *Special Education: Forward Trends, 3,* 24–7.

# CHAPTER 15

# HOSPITAL SCHOOLS FOR THE MENTALLY HANDICAPPED

## GORDON BLAND

There are in England and Wales approximately 65 hospital schools for the mentally handicapped.* In an area of education which is essentially dynamic it is impossible to be more accurate. Since the publication of the last official figures new schools have increasingly been built outside the confines of the hospital; other schools have been united to form more efficient units, and some schools have ceased to exist with the drop in hospitalized children. The 65 schools are administered by the Department of Education and Science whilst operating in a health service setting.

The task of defining a hospital school is difficult. In some cases the hospital itself is identified with a residential school in its grounds, although both are autonomous; in other cases the school is an organization within a hospital but without identifiable headquarters, whilst, in the majority of cases, there is a school building within a hospital complex in which the child population of the hospital is educated. Though there is some debate about the effectiveness of the latter pattern of educational provision there is evidence to show that within this type of structure it is possible to create an educational system which permeates all areas of hospital life and extends beyond the confines of the hospital itself. It is this pattern of provision which will be considered, and in this connotation that hospital schools will be discussed.

The number of children and young persons being educated in such schools is approximately 4420 of whom some 1150 are over the age of 16 years (all figures from Bland 1978).

* For Scottish figures, see DES (1978).

Some 420 children and young persons are resident in the community and attend hospital schools daily. Though there are variations in the age-range of students the age of admission tends to be from two to five years and the leaving age from 16 to 19 years.

It is estimated that 2.7 per cent of the students function at an intellectual level less than two standard deviations below the norm; 2.7 per cent function at a level between the second and third standard deviation below the norm; 12.3 per cent lie between the third and fourth standard deviation below the norm; 37.7 per cent are placed between the fourth and fifth standard deviation below the norm; and 44.6 per cent are beyond the fifth standard deviation below the norm. Though these estimated levels of intellectual ability are not in themselves reliable predicators of performance they do indicate the wide range of ability for which educators must cater in hospital schools as compared with schools in the community, and when considered in combination with additional handicaps these intellectual handicaps serve to stress the enormity of the teaching task.

Bland (1978) estimates that approximately 30 per cent of pupils suffer from severe physical handicaps, including a high incidence of non-ambulant cases. Twenty-six schools sampled recorded over 5.5 per cent suffering from hemiplegia; 6.6 per cent suffering from paraplegia; and 13 per cent suffering from tetraplegia. Though the categories are not mutually exclusive, a sample of 48 schools showed 8.5 per cent of pupils suffering from serious defects of vision excluding total blindness and 3.5 per cent with total loss of vision.

Almost 7.5 per cent of the 3554 children surveyed were reported as having serious loss of hearing, and 79 per cent of these were reported as having serious speech defects or total lack of speech.

Since incorrigible behaviour has frequently been the deciding factor between retention in the community and hospital placement it is not unusual to find aggressive and destructive behaviour in approximately a quarter of the hospital school population. In addition to the profoundly handicapped pupils who are behaviourally disturbed there is in many schools a small but declining proportion of mildly handicapped young persons referred to hospital by the courts for treatment. These are usually more accurately described as sociopaths, coming from unstimulating and undesirable home environments with a history of petty crime, truancy from school, and/or sexual promiscuity. There may be, also, a very small percentage of young persons with psychopathic tendencies.

### THE TEACHING PROGRAMME

It has been noted that the range of provision in the hospital school must be wider than that in the community school. Though differences of approach and emphasis exist and must be examined there are certain basic principles which are common to both types of school. These have been described in Chapter 14, and may be summarized briefly as follows. The needs of each individual pupil must be assessed carefully and continuously in a functional manner and must be related to his physical, social, intellectual and moral development. At any moment in time priorities will need to be ascertained; clear and precise teaching goals will need to be set, and the resultant teaching task will need to be analysed into realistic sub-goals or stages. The attainment of these goals must be approached through skilled application of stimuli found to be effective in the individual case, appropriate reinforcement of positive responses, and continuous monitoring of the teaching programme and of both sides of the teacher/pupil relationship. There must at the same time be constant recording of this data feedback.

Teaching the mentally handicapped is still in its infancy and still tends to be empirical and eclectic. It is essential to know which approaches are likely to be the most effective with a particular pupil; what interests can be exploited; what form of motivation can be employed; and what is the most effective reinforcer. Recording of such observations leads inevitably to the other aspect of data feedback, the longitudinal study. It is an acknowledged essential of the teaching programme that individual records be kept over a period of years, showing the goals achieved, that is, the skills mastered at particular times in particular areas of development. Especially valuable are those developmental scales which give a guide to programming and provide at any one time a holistic assessment of the pupil as a social being (see Chapter 12 for a description of developmental scales). Many schools both in the community and in hospitals have used over a long period the Gunzburg Progress Assessment Charts and, though other developmental scales are often used in conjunction with these, the former tend to be repositories of long experience and to be particularly valuable for both diagnosis and prognosis. Whatever the teacher's preference, monitoring of individual programmes and recording of observations is vital to effective teaching.

In the decade ending in 1977 the mean ratio of teachers to children in hospital schools for the mentally handicapped in England and Wales has been reduced from one to twelve to a ratio of one to six. At the same time there has been a considerable increase in the amount of ancillary help for the teacher by way of classroom aides, usually with nursery nurse training. With the inclusion of these additional members of the teaching team the mean ratio of adults to children in the schools is now one to three. Consideration of the teaching approaches appropriate to these pupils will confirm the view that this apparently generous ratio is not ideal. It does allow, however, in many hospital schools, a measure of specialization and an opportunity to implement individual programming.

It will be apparent that in almost all hospital schools there still exists a need to group students for teaching purposes and to use group methods to some extent alongside individual teaching. It may be that the teaching assistant can work with a group whilst the teacher attends to individual programmes or the converse might be appropriate. The use of specialist teachers or peripatetic teachers might supplement further the time which can be devoted to individuals who can be withdrawn for remedial teaching on a one-to-one basis or can receive more attention from an enhanced teaching team. It would seem that classroom availability rather than numbers of teachers determines the size of class groups but, in general, six to ten children comprise a class in a hospital school.

Criteria for placement in a particular group include physical, social and intellectual development, behavioural pattern, particular interests, reaction to other students, reaction to particular members of the teaching team and, to some extent, the pupil's preference. It must be emphasized that groupings, like programmes, must be under constant review and that whilst there must be a high degree of stability in both staffing and teaching approach a degree of flexibility must be retained in respect of class groupings. Differing rates of progress and changing interests and abilities soon destroy the homogeneity of a group; transfers of pupils, if considered likely to prove beneficial, must be implemented without impediment.

In school or on the ward the teaching programme ranges from the application of physical stimuli to multiply handicapped students on the one hand to the teaching of civics with a high content of reading, writing and arithmetic on the other. It seems hardly likely, therefore, that there can be a common approach to the wide range of educational needs. At the one end of the spectrum the student's experience has been limited and may well have been arrested because of restricted movement due to physical defect. At the other end there has been, in the vast majority of cases, social and intellectual deprivation because of unstimulating home environments. In both cases, for very different reasons, the student has had neither the motivation nor the opportunity to explore a rich and wide environment but has lived in a confined world, the boundaries of which have been fixed by accident of birth.

Paradoxical though it may appear to those who see hospitals in the context of total institutions, unstimulating and dehumanising,

the theme common to all teaching programmes in the hospital school is the experiential approach. Basic to every individual programme is the provision of an environment in which the student can extend his experiences by his own efforts or, where necessary, with the close involvement of the teacher. Three approaches of particular value and relevance can be described.

## THE ENACTIVE STAGE

The first of these approaches is based on an adaptation to teaching technique of Bruner's enactive stage of representation (Stones 1966). This is applicable to the profoundly multiply handicapped student who is unable to communicate his experiences in language or to respond to language stimuli and who, because of his physical handicap, is unable to extend his experience by motoric means. At this stage the approach must be largely physical, though language must accompany all activity, and the teacher is required to become an extension of the student. The student may explore his own body only because his teacher moves the student's hands to clasp each other; to stroke his hair; to examine his facial features, and so on. In an adaptation of the 'baby bouncer' of appropriate size he can feel his feet but, of even greater importance, he can escape from a perceptive world of ceilings and unflattering views of people who tower over him to a world of normal angles and perceptions. Change of position and of activity at regular intervals is essential but change of environment from classroom to gymnasium, hydrotherapy pool or open grassland is equally essential. This physical approach leads naturally to patterning which in turn requires a generous provision of teaching staff, but at all times there is a need, however limited the response might appear, for a wide variety of environmental provision for motoric and sensory experience. There is a close correlation between enhanced physical health and strength and intellectual response.

As a guide to the types of experience which might be provided one might follow the recommendation of Cunningham (1974), and concentrate on the experiences normally encountered at mother's knee. The teaching area must provide for personal comfort; for feeding;

for physical manipulation by the parent figure; for bathing, and dabbling in the kitchen sink; for a roll on the hearthrug; for a bounce on the bed; for a rummage through the pan cupboard, and for involvement with the activities of baking day, the teacher being more or less involved according to the student's physical and intellectual ability.

The teaching environment must be organized to cater for the needs enumerated. Ideally the floor area should be large and should give ample space for a shallow pool, a sandpit, mini-trampolines, walking aids and suspended harnesses, large multicoloured foam shapes and mattresses, and various types of wheeled chairs and platforms for self-propulsion. Toilet accommodation should be conveniently sited. Toys, too often adult projections of childhood needs, are not as necessary as a variety of everyday objects of varying shape, texture, colour and sound.

Though much of the stimulation and motivation tends to emanate from the members of the teaching team, at this stage of development a degree of operant conditioning is possible. In particular, social reinforcement of responses frequently and obviously creates a desire to repeat the action which has been rewarded. This applies particularly to triplegic cerebral palsied students whose low level of social and intellectual functioning is attributable in a large measure to their physical disability. However, it is significant that amongst these profoundly mentally and multiply handicapped students intrinsic reinforcement is often evident. The sheer joy of a particular activity provides strong motivation for its repetition.

Increasingly hospital schools for the mentally handicapped are being regarded by teaching staff as bases for the exploration of a wider environment. Almost all schools have one minibus at least; many have camping equipment; several have mobile caravans, and one or two have canal barges. It is not unusual for a teacher to specialize in environmental studies and to work full time assisting individual teachers to organize educational visits to the nearby towns, swimming pools, ice-rinks, zoological gardens, railway stations, farms, places of natural interest, and adventure training camps. With facilities such as those described, students at the enactive stage can be taken out of the hospital environment and

teaching involvement can be both intensive and extensive.

The work of the teacher at this stage, then, requires both versatility and adaptability. In many areas of teaching, however, there will be an obvious need for the guidance and assistance of other professionals. Of at least equal importance is the need for continuity of the teaching programme and consistency of approach to the student's needs. These matters will be discussed in a later section.

## THE ICONIC OR 'CONCRETE' STAGE

Bruner's thesis, that it is essential for an amount of motor activity or practice to take place before a mental picture of a sequence of acts can be formed, seems an appropriate basis for a teaching approach. In considering the iconic stage as applicable to one section of the school's student population the difficulty exposed by Bruner must be taken into account. Briefly this is that iconic representation tends to shade into symbolic representation and that it cannot therefore be assumed that group or individual learning is at one level only at all times. From a teaching point of view the emphasis is still on an experiential approach with a high degree of physical involvement. The main distinguishing feature is that the children learn more easily from the example of the teacher and by imitation generally. There is less need for members of the teaching team to identify physically with the student but there is a greater need to communicate enthusiasm and to stimulate curiosity by creating a challenging and stimulating environment within the school and by exploiting a wide variety of situations in the community at large.

Though there will still be some emphasis on the skills learned incidentally by the non-handicapped child—the mother's knee approach—the pattern will tend to be analogous to the infant and lower primary school stage where a child is extending his experiences beyond the home circle and developing both social skills and social attitudes.

At this stage the accompaniment of activities with language becomes increasingly important, as does the stimulation of efforts to communicate. Within a variety of situations and with a wide range of possible activities it should be possible to discover some focus of interest for each student and to encourage his motivation to pursue that interest by supplementing his intrinsic reinforcement with the highly valued social reinforcement of approving adult contact.

Though the teaching groups may be a little larger than those at the enactive stage a generous provision of teaching team members is necessary so that there may be daily opportunity for individual teaching alongside the group approach. The use of a measure of group teaching must not be taken to imply a formal teaching approach. The classroom is better regarded as a base from which the student may explore the environment of the school, the hospital and the community at large.

There should be generous play areas in which the student may develop concepts with or without the intervention of language. He should learn, for example, the relationship between himself and familiar everyday objects. He may climb the 'mountain' in the playground by the gentle spiral route, by steep steps or by a more adventurous direction. He may choose to descend rapidly by the slide or to return by one of the other routes. In other words this one provision presents a variety of physical experience and the opportunity for choice. He may cross the playground pond by means of the stable but irregularly spaced stepping-stones, by a very unstable plank of wood or by a highly stable stone bridge. He may be provided with an opportunity to discover that the cubic block is relatively stable, the cylindrical block is less stable and the sphere most unstable if he wishes to balance on these. He needs the opportunity to relate colour and texture to his own experiences. The asphalt surface is unkind to his knees when he falls; the grass is green and soft; the sand will run through his fingers but can be moulded to shape. It would be wrong to anticipate the reaction of the student to the mud patch. One can but say that it should not be a reaction conditioned by fear of disapproval after a period of experimentation with it!

Many of the experiences can be reproduced to some extent in the gymnasium where apparatus can provide a variety of learning activities and the opportunity to experience changes of shape, texture, mobility, speed and height. In the wider sphere the children at this stage of development can benefit greatly from regular trips into the community as described earlier and can participate in camping holidays, holidays afloat and simple programmes of adventure training.

It will be obvious that in such an active approach to education there must be regular opportunities for the development of self-help skills. There should be well-planned toilet blocks with generous provision for washing and bathing activities so that although toilet training is incidental it is a regular feature of the teaching programme. Communication skills must be given high precedence but these again will range from activities to develop the throat muscles, for example, blowing exercises, the chewing of solid foods prepared in the Domestic Science Room to the use of microphones and amplifying equipment or interclass telephones. With the help of specialists children with sensory defects may be withdrawn for regular periods of instruction and all children may be screened by specialists in, for example, audiology.

To summarize, at this stage the teaching approaches already discussed will be applied. Children will be assessed both by their teachers and by specialists and provision will be made for specific defects. The approach to learning will be an experiential one in which the student through his own activities will learn to relate himself to an ever-widening environment and though his base may be a school within a hospital there need be no limits to the learning environment.

THE SYMBOLIC OR 'ABSTRACT' STAGE

As applied to the teaching of mentally handicapped students this stage may be taken to refer to increased facility in the use of language which removes to some extent the dependence of the student on the immediate environment. Verbal instructions can be understood and their implications appreciated; the written word can be interpreted and applied, and transfer of learning from one situation to another is facilitated.

The students often placed in this category are the mildly handicapped and the educationally retarded young persons who might be described as sociopathic and/or psychopathic. The approach to teaching is still largely experiential but both method and matter tend to be conditioned by problems peculiar to this group.

The majority of students not only have a history of failure and disapproving adult reactions but they are fully conscious of these and tend to adopt strategic approaches towards their teachers varying from defensive to offensive attitudes. They need desperately to achieve success so that adult approval may not only be forthcoming but may be obviously merited. Programmes must therefore be planned after careful assessment of the individual's aptitudes and abilities to provide the opportunity for early and recurring successes and for the simplification of tasks should these prove to be too difficult.

In general the students are highly motivated to gain approval, and reinforcement by social means is usually most effective. The teaching approach needs to be mildly permissive if sound assessment of needs is to be made. Young persons of this kind when admitted to hospital frequently adapt their strategies to maximize their own comfort and avoid confrontation with authority. They pay lip service to the mores of the institutions and appear to undergo a change of attitude. On return to the community at large they adapt just as readily to the mores of a familiar peer group and to their former deviant behaviour. Whilst the groups discussed earlier require the teacher to be involved physically in the training programme this particular group of students requires the teacher to be involved in a sense with their emotional needs. Without real empathy between teacher and student attitude change is extremely difficult. With real empathy dramatic changes can often occur. An apparently tough and hardened young rebel can be transformed by a word of praise or a mild display of affection and subsequently make efforts to please 'his friend'. Regrettably this kind of reaction is an implied criticism of the student's former family, associates and teachers. There is a heavy responsibility placed on the teacher to monitor his own approaches and reactions and to ensure that the pattern of behaviour he sets is worthy of imitation.

The curriculum, briefly, for this group consists of a concrete approach to numeracy, a graded approach to reading supplemented by as much creative writing as possible, a variety of approaches to creative activities in art and craft, a vocational approach to certain crafts and domestic skills, and a wider and more sophisticated approach to environmental activities. At this stage swimming and life-saving certificates may be obtained, and awards under national schemes may be secured; sporting activities may take place with schools from the community; camps may be set up further afield and in cooperation with other schools and youth organizations. There are increasing opportunities to accept responsibility for less competent students in camp or in barge crews. There is increasing participation in adventure training and in community projects. In general there is no clear dividing line between school and environmental activities, the latter arising naturally out of the former. Though the need for social reinforcement has been stressed it is often possible at an early stage to note the intervention of intrinsic reinforcement.

## BEHAVIOURAL PATTERNS

It will be obvious that the approach to education in hospital schools has been simplified and abbreviated in the preceding descriptions chiefly because it has much in common with the approach in any school for the mentally handicapped. However certain areas of difference have been revealed which would bear closer examination.

Reference has been made to the fact that in very many cases the decision to admit to hospital has been made on the basis of the pupil's incorrigible behaviour, with an estimated one-quarter of the hospital school population suffering from some form of disturbed behaviour. It should be noted that this proportion includes the 5 per cent of young persons whose behaviour has been adjudged antisocial and requiring treatment. It is difficult to generalize across such a wide range of handicap, from the brain-damaged profoundly handicapped child to the mildly handicapped delinquent, yet they have in common their exclusion from the community at large, from home and school and contemporaries. In the former group both home and school may have found their behaviour intolerable and unmanageable; in the latter case the delinquent may have rejected or been rejected by the school or by the home or by both. The first and immediate requirement of the hospital school is that it must accept. There is no educational alternative; no lower rung on the ladder of rejection. The only path open is that which leads to a return to the community, a community which will demand standards of behaviour good enough to cross a very demanding threshold of tolerance.

In the school situation acceptance of the individual and of the challenge he presents needs a measure of tolerance and understanding. Assisted by the comparatively stable ward environment and possibly by drug therapy, the teacher is able to observe behavioural patterns; to ascertain in some cases cause and effect; to provide in all cases outlets for physical activity; to discover interests and stimulate these and to reinforce positively desirable patterns of behaviour. In short, the basic approach is one of behaviour modification. Results may be achieved dramatically or over an extremely long period according to the causative factors.

Robert, a profoundly mentally handicapped boy, was admitted to hospital at the age of ten with a history of uncontrollable behaviour. He had been excluded from residential and community schools for the mentally handicapped because of his destructive and violent behaviour. The suspected cause was encephalitis at the age of nine months. His mental age could not be ascertained and he was said to have no educational attainments. After a short time in hospital he was admitted to school and placed in a class of hyperkinetic children where the emphasis was on gross motor activities including music and movement. In a very short time he became amenable and responsive to his teachers and made significant progress in social skills.

At the age of 15, however, he began to smother his head and body with his own faeces. Careful observation showed that this occurred on a particular weekday before close of morning school. After two weeks of placing Robert in a playroom with a wide variety of equipment, and after several false starts or clues, he began to show great interest in the piano. Realizing that his faecal activities regularly followed a music lesson the teacher who was observing opened the piano for him. Astonishingly he began to play chords and to reproduce hymns and traditional songs which were regularly played by his teachers. He was allowed to play daily for as long as he wished and there was no further undesirable behaviour. The root of his regressive behaviour was obviously the frustration he felt on the termination of the music lesson and the removal of the record player.

Paul was a similarly hyperactive boy with a long history of violent behaviour which had seriously affected his family and had led to his rejection from schools in the community. He was obviously bright by comparison with the other pupils but had no speech. He was quick to anger and usually broke the nearest window when enraged. It was noted quite soon that he had a passionate interest in water and loved to turn the hosepipes on the walls of the school if unobserved. He was given long periods of water play during which times his behaviour was logical and intelligent but, more significantly, he now revealed real talent as an artist. He illustrated not only places and buildings from his own town but began to illustrate in unmistakeable detail his experiences in school and on his ward. Often these were humorous in a sophisticated way. By combining words with his pictorial communication his teachers were able to help him to build up a reasonable working vocabulary. His behaviour was intelligent, cooperative and wholly reasonable, and belatedly it was found that he was profoundly deaf. He had reacted aggressibely but with displacement of affect to the frustration he suffered at being unable to communicate his wishes to those around him. Once he was able to communicate his frustration, his maladaptive behaviour ceased.

## LABELLING OR STEREOTYPING

It is to be hoped that careful screening at an early age may in future reduce the chances of sensory defects leading to maladaptive behaviour as described in the case histories above. However, it is still a common experience, especially in hospital schools, to find that a gross physical defect, or a deviant behavioural pattern, or a recognizable handicapping syndrome has monopolised the perceptions of teachers and care staff alike and blinded them to underlying sensory defects which are the fundamental obstacle to learning. In some cases, indeed, the greatest obstacle to learning is a secondary handicap arising out of the failure to diagnose this sensory deprivation. Stereotyping is implicit in this problem.

In one school teachers were well aware that many Down's syndrome children had little or no speech and were late in beginning to speak. It had been noted, also, that these children often whispered when commencing to speak. Malformation of throat muscles and limited intellectual capacity were to be expected along with other stigmata common to Down's syndrome children, but the clues could have pointed just as easily to hearing impairment. In fact, when the audiologist tested all the Down's syndrome children, every one of them was found to have a hearing loss and the educational approach was adjusted to allow for this defect.

Another aspect of stereotyping experienced by one headmaster was that of a girl whose inability to read had throughout a great part of her school career been attributed to limited intellectual capacity following brain damage as a result of phenylketonuria. Several years after her return home she was tested by an optician and spectacles were prescribed. She now reads simple texts and writes fluently though phonetically, whilst attending evening classes for retarded readers.

The hospital school may be a school of last resort but it is just as often a school which provides an opportunity within a stable environment for a reappraisal of the student's problems and potential comparatively unbiased by previous history and experience. But are the schools equipped to re-assess, re-programme and reform?

### THE TEACHERS

Although the degree of severity of handicap in these schools is increasing it is significant that the quality and training of teaching staff is improving more rapidly than in any other field of education. Only ten years ago it could be said that in hospital schools for the mentally handicapped in England and Wales some 23.5 per cent of head teachers had no teaching qualification, whilst 82 per cent of assistant teachers were similarly unqualified. At the present time (Bland 1978) less than 6 per cent of head teachers are qualified by a Declaration of Recognition of Experience and all others are trained teachers. Of these over 43 per cent have additional university certificates or diplomas in education, nearly 12 per cent have degrees and 4 per cent have higher degrees. Of the assistant teachers 19 per cent are unqualified but many have specific skills as, for example, in music, crafts and physical education. Of the 81 per cent who are qualified, 6 per cent have additional certificates or diplo-

mas and over 11 per cent have degrees including a minority with Master's degrees and Doctorates. This reflects not only a highly desirable form of positive discrimination but a response to the challenge which is posed by the educational needs of the profoundly and severely mentally and multiply handicapped pupil. The approach to education which has been described, demands highly skilled and versatile teachers. It cannot be questioned that the response to this need has been very largely met in the hospitals for the mentally handicapped, and though these hospital schools may have been regarded by some as the lowest rung of a ladder of rejection they are being used increasingly as areas of excellence in education to which children can be sent from the community for short-term treatment.

It would seem, therefore, that in the area of education the hospital school cannot be associated justifiably with any disadvantages, real or supposed, which are attributed to hospitals for the mentally handicapped. However, there are even stronger grounds for the refutation of these unfavourable stereotypes.

### SPECIALIST SERVICES

In spite of the high and improving qualifications of teachers in hospital schools there are areas of diagnosis and treatment which are beyond the skills of even the most versatile teacher, and the guidance of specialists is essential. This is as true in the community school as in the hospital school, and in both areas there is a dearth of certain specialists. It is not possible to estimate the amount of help available in community schools but the statistics for hospital schools are available and it is the writer's contention that in spite of very obvious shortages in the latter service the position in respect of specialist services is probably superior to that in the community. It is certain that in the hospital schools which have developed interdisciplinary approaches as a matter of policy there exist models of good practice unsurpassed and, possibly, unmatched by any community school.

For pupils with serious defects of hearing in hospital schools, some 360 in total, slightly more than 37 per cent have help or advice from teachers of the deaf, and nearly 30 per cent have the help of an audiologist. Of the 580 pupils suffering from blindness or serious defects of vision some 25 per cent have specialist help. Slightly more than 30 per cent of pupils suffer from serious physical defects and although only 12 per cent have the help of remedial gymnasts some 80 per cent have help from physiotherapists, nearly 10 per cent having full-time help. Nearly 80 per cent of pupils have serious speech defects or are speechless, but in spite of a general shortage of speech therapists 67 per cent have some help from such specialists. Finally, 67 per cent of all children benefit from the services of clinical psychologists and nearly 50 per cent have access to educational psychologists.

It would be easy to take the converse of these figures and show the deficiencies in specialist help but, as stated earlier, the true picture is one of areas of low interdisciplinary cooperation contrasted with a growing number of areas of excellence. The significant aspect is that a number of the specialists mentioned are employed by the health service and not by the local education authorities responsible for hospital schools. Quite frequently the speech therapist is a health service employee whilst psychiatric consultants, physiotherapists and clinical psychologists are essentially employees of the hospital service. It is to their credit and to the credit of the health service that help is given to the pupils and their teachers; that whether in school or on the ward the residents are still the responsibility of all professionals involved in the total therapeutic programme. The teachers for their part are grateful for the specialist help and advice provided from within the hospital. When this is allied with the help of education advisers, Her Majesty's Inspectors, local authority-based specialists and resource centres, the hospital school teacher is conscious not only of strong supportive help but of being integrated in a multidisciplinary and wholly appropriate approach to the education of the handicapped.

## THE HOSPITAL ENVIRONMENT

It may well be that the pupil in a hospital school is deprived of a normal home environment and of contact with the community at large. The dictum that a bad home is better than a good institution receives far more support than it merits in the light of many research programmes following the findings of Speer (1964) and Stippich (1964), and environmental deprivation is an oft-quoted culpable factor. Is this stereotype justified and to what extent?

In the description of the educational programme (see pp. 208–9), the hospital school was referred to frequently as a base for wider exploration rather than the sole location of educational activities. One of the schools examined in depth with respect to educational programmes places so much emphasis on contact with the community at large and expansion of the child's educational environment that a teacher is employed full time, arranging journeys and camping holidays covering an area from the Scottish Lowlands to the south coast of England. Every teacher over the age of 25 years with a current driving licence is allowed to drive the two minibuses; camping equipment includes a camping trailer tent, continental frame tents and a mini-marquee; there is a six-berth trailer caravan for use with delicate children or as a sick-bay; there is a twelve-foot sailing dinghy, and a fifty-foot barge is at present being fitted out as a floating classroom. The local swimming pool is used regularly. Pupils go ice-skating and horse-riding. Nursing staff of the hospital as well as schoolchildren from local secondary schools join in all or most of the activities. But is this a representative picture?

Nearly 80 per cent of the hospital schools in England and Wales have the use of a minibus, and 93 per cent arrange trips outside the hospital as part of the educational programme. At least 56 per cent of schools organize camps for their pupils; whilst another 4 per cent arrange holidays afloat on the canal system. Some 6 per cent arrange adventure training holidays and at least 16 per cent arrange horse-riding lessons. The picture is again one of areas of excellence but with these highly desirable practices spreading rapidly. It is pertinent to ask how many pupils in the community at large travel to school in a private vehicle and return home by the same means without venturing in the meantime beyond the perimeters of the school grounds. However, the question of home accommodation and its superiority to hospital accommodation remains.

It must be acknowledged that although the trend is towards a reduction in size of ward populations there are still many children housed on large and comparatively over-populated wards. It must be noted, however, that less than 0.5 per cent are now on wards housing more than 40 residents whilst over 27 per cent are on wards housing less than 20 residents. This bears favourable comparison with many of our noted public school dormitories.

More significant is the fact that nearly two-thirds of the children are on wards with residents of both sexes, and three-quarters are on wards with staff of both sexes. The trend is towards small wards or villas with groups of six to eight residents with nursing staff assuming the roles of house mother and house father. The villa, like the school, is becoming a base for exploration and play activities with liaison between the two professions, teacher and nurse, becoming closer. The nurses spend a period in the children's school as an integral part of their training, and contact, with a reciprocal flow of information between ward and school, is maintained. In very many hospitals there is clear evidence that the teaching function is being supported by the nursing staff with a decline in the obsession for clinically clean wards. Sand and water, paint and paste and even mud, all are condoned and encouraged so that the child may enjoy as normal a home environment as possible. In these activities young people from local schools make regular contributions after school hours, fulfilling the roles of elder brothers and sisters. In this way the most desirable of all educational approaches is achieved, the tripartite involvement of teacher–family–child, with the needs of the child paramount.

## PARENTAL CONTACT

It would be an overstatement to say that the nursing staff can wholly fill the role of parent. Shortages of staff or illness of the 'professional parent' may imperil the parent–child relationship, but where a comparatively stable staffing arrangement is possible it may be said justifi-ably that a rich home environment with a continuing educational component can be created. In many ways this is a more profitable arrangement from a child's developmental aspect than an unstimulating and/or uncaring home, and is an arrangement which may well compare with that of a good home in the community in its degree of parent–teacher cooperation in the interests of the child.

Yet is there a degree of deprivation in the sense that a child is out of contact with his natural parents? Any opinions on the emotional aspects of this question would be fraught with value judgements of doubtful validity. The facts of the matter from an educational point of view can be examined briefly.

Too often in the past admission to a hospital has been the result of a crisis situation traumatic to the pupil and, to some extent, to the staff receiving him: 'We just have a brand new face in and we have to fit him in.', 'You strip him off and examine him and try to find what he is in for' (Bland 1970). And from some mildly handicapped pupils: 'My mother brought me here to see if she could get me any better. I kept being a nuisance.', 'I came here for the spoons I knocked off.', 'It was the court—for a holiday while my mother was having a baby.' (Bland 1970). In the case of mildly handicapped pupils such situations tended to lead to increasing resentment of parents as time passed and the true situation became apparent whilst, at the same time, parental guilt feelings tended to grow. The teacher in school was all too often aware of the emotional pressures but had little or no contact with parents. What, if any, improvement has been made since the above quotations were recorded?

With the introduction of sectorisation the tendency towards crisis admissions has declined significantly. The consultant psychiatrist is no longer confined largely to hospital duties but is responsible for, and to, a particular community. During his frequent clinics in his particular community he is accompanied usually by a senior nursing officer and by any other professional whose help in counselling and decision-making might, in his opinion, be needed. In this way probable admission and placement can be discussed with parents, social workers in the community or in the hospital, and with those who might be concerned with the care of the potential resident in the future. With increasing frequency a further step is now taken. The parent or guardian is given a brochure on the hospital and its amenities. This is followed by a visit when all relevant aspects of hospital life can be shown to the parents and, if it is felt desirable, to the child. This will involve a visit to the school if the proposed resident is of school age. If it is felt that sufficient evidence is still not available for a placement the child may stay for a time on an assessment unit before being allocated to a ward and to an educational programme.

In these ways contact with natural parents is now being made, before admission takes place, by a variety of professionals likely to be involved in the remedial programme. From the point of view of the school this contact is maintained as often as possible through the parent member of the school governors, by frequent school open days and by invitations to sports days and concert performances. The hospital for its part organizes one-to-one days, open days, sports days et cetera. The withdrawal of children to meet parents in a formal visiting-room is a thing of the past and parents are welcomed into school when it is in session to see their children in a 'working situation'.

When the isolation of hospital sites is taken into account, together with the number of children rejected in some measure by parents, it is encouraging to note that 94 per cent of schools in England and Wales claim some face-to-face contact with parents whilst nearly 35 per cent have from 25 to more than one hundred such contacts annually. When the contact with natural parents is considered alongside the continuous cooperation in an educationally orientated programme with nurses acting *in loco parentis*, the hospital school may claim to have attained more nearly than the community school the ideal of the tripartite approach to education.

Implicit in this cooperation, close monitoring of progress by all disciplines involved, and interchange of information and expertise, is the desire to return the pupil to the community at large as soon as possible. To this end the degree of involvement of the social services which appertained before admission must be maintained so that the child or young person may be returned home under the same thorough assessment or re-assessment procedures as those giving rise to admission to hospital. All head teachers in England and Wales now attend case conferences, over 93 per cent of these attending regularly. Although contact with officers of the social services in schools is less frequent than contact in case conferences there is evidence of growing liaison and nearly 60 per cent of head teachers are regularly consulted by, or send reports to, community-based officers of the social services. Children in hospital schools for the mentally handicapped need not be forgotten nor isolated. Strong links with the community can be maintained; parental care can be continuous and rich both in fact and by proxy; the hospital environment can be made stimulating with an interdisciplinary approach to education, whilst at the same time acting as a base for wider environmental experience of a rich and varied nature. The very valid charges made by Goffman (1961) against total institutions are invalid when applied to a therapeutic community: the stereotyped criticisms of hospital schools are equally invalid when applied to educationally orientated communities. The hospital school, indeed, may enjoy a net advantage over the community school, though it is sufficient to prove only less disadvantage than is often postulated. In one respect, however, the hospital school may in many cases enjoy a considerable advantage. This is in the area of continuing or further education.

## FURTHER EDUCATION

In many community schools for the mentally handicapped there is a comparatively rigid leaving age of 16 years. At the same time there is a dearth of adult training centre places and little or no opportunity of placement in open industry. It is not unusual for the ex-pupil to remain at home, almost inevitably regressing educationally and placing a heavy responsibility on parents. Though some hospitals provide further education at the age of 16 the usual practice is for the pupil to remain in school until the age of 19 and for that leaving age to be applied somewhat loosely so that he or she might remain in school until an alternative training programme is available. In this way continuity of education can be assured.

In most hospitals there are industrial training units with an educational component but many have availed themselves additionally of the facilities provided by the further education service under the Department of Education and Science. The 1959 Mental Health Act amended that part of the 1944 Education Act which excluded the vast majority of mentally handicapped adults from educational provision. As a result the handicapped person may now enrol for classes at any further education establishment. A comparatively small number of hospital residents do enrol for tuition in colleges of further education but many hospitals have found it more convenient to have classes and courses arranged on their own premises. A number have extensive daytime educational programmes and/or evening classes. These are organized by the local education authority. Teachers are appointed and paid by the local authority whilst the hospital authority, acting in *loco parentis*, provides its residents with materials for their particular classes. Students pay no fees although the education authority may recover the costs from the 'no area' pool.

An example of the typical evening centre is one which was formed as a social club for Brockhall Hospital residents in 1959 and which proved so popular that in 1961 it was adopted as an evening centre by the local education authority. Attendance is strictly voluntary as is choice of class or activity. Out of a population of nearly 1400 adult residents 450 attend the 70 classes provided on two evenings each week. These classes include civics, woodwork, pottery, art, crafts, music, ballroom dancing, music and movement, beauty culture with hairdressing, flower arrangement, photography, catering, home economics, physical education including swimming and games, horticulture, tailoring and dressmaking. Emphasis is upon social relationships rather than excellence of products and to that end there is a refreshment period during each session, whilst each evening concludes with all students meeting for an informal dancing session in the main hall of the hospital. During this the Students' Council meets and

makes recommendations. Teachers are recruited from within the hospital as well as from the community. Sporting fixtures are arranged with community organizations and young persons from the community regularly join in activities.

The voluntary nature of attendance and choice of class is in a sense a weakness, although it is too highly valued by students for anyone to change it. It may be of great advantage for a particular student to concentrate on, for example, reading skills. If he can be persuaded to join a civics group all is well, but if he prefers swimming his wishes must be respected. The answer to this problem is to organize day-release classes to which he can be directed, as an apprentice in the community would be directed by his employer. Approximately 75 per cent of hospitals in England and Wales now have further education classes provided by the education authority. Of these 44 per cent have day classes and 56 per cent have evening classes. The percentage of residents involved in further education in these hospitals ranges from a little over 3 per cent to 53 per cent, the mean being slightly more than 16 per cent. This is a valuable and growing educational area which, together with the training provisions of the hospital service, gives not only continuity of education but an approach to the problem of leisure pursuits, the latter being in many ways more important than work skills in promoting successful reintegration.

Continuity of education in the sense of provision for all ages is, therefore, well and widely established. As regards the provision of the local education authority, however, there are breaks in day-to-day continuity because of the traditional lengths of terms or semesters interspersed with staff holidays of varying lengths. Continuity is essential for the carefully planned programmes. Both with children in school and adults in further education attendance at classes is considered a privilege and a pleasure. At Brockhall the evening centre is still referred to as 'The Club' after 17 years as an official evening centre. There is a need to break away from the established paradigm and to restructure the teaching approach according to the needs of the handicapped residents. Teaching hours must be flexible to allow meal-times to become a cooperative teaching activity between nurses and teachers; the holidays of teachers need to be so arranged that the service may be continuous or with a minimum of short breaks. The long summer closure of some hospital schools coincides usually with an increased child population in the hospital as a result of short-term admissions designed to give parents a rest or a holiday. When the burden is thrown entirely on other disciplines there is not only interruption of the teaching programme but interruption or disruption of interdisciplinary relationships.

At the present time one school practises a four-term year and slightly more than 40 per cent of hospital schools practise a system of staggered holidays for teaching staff. In a number of schools which close for normal holidays teachers attend their hospital voluntarily to assist in play activities. The will is there and the practice of reducing school closures will spread. The hospital school can become an educational system which permeates all aspects of hospital life, involves all disciplines and caters for all residents. In such a case the hospital may well be deemed a school. It is important that it should function as such and that its gates should be open to the community at large.

## FUTURE DEVELOPMENTS

The trend is towards the admission to hospital of the profoundly mentally and physically handicapped child and to a reduction in population of the mildly and moderately handicapped. The former are the children who will find the greatest difficulty in being integrated in community schools and who will present difficulties in transport and interdisciplinary cooperation if the hospital school is removed to a campus in the community. They may well suffer additionally from loss of continuity of programme if separated from further educational provision and hospital provision for training and sheltered employment. In the long term the community may meet all needs and be able to duplicate all services now provided in hospital. In the short term, however, the move to an integrated and interdisciplinary approach to education should be encouraged. To this end both teachers and nurses should be prepared to examine present practices and to reform them wherever the interests of the residents can be better served. The practice of flexible teaching times and staggered holidays should become general.

The increasing expertise of teachers in hospital schools should be exploited by primary care teams in the community with a view to reducing the incidence of secondary handicaps. The same expertise might justify increasing use of the hospital school for relatively short-term care, for diagnosis, for programming and for the resolution within a stable environment of behavioural disorders. In brief, the hospital school of the future should conform to the model of comprehensive and continuous educational provision described in this text and should merit recognition as an area of educational excellence rather than as a school of last resort.

## BIBLIOGRAPHY

Bland, G. A. (1970) *The effects of an educational programme in the area of communication on the social and intellectual functioning of mentally handicapped adults in hospital.* Unpublished thesis, University of Bath.
Bland, G. A. (1973) Some architectural requirements for a scientific approach to teaching the mentally handicapped in hospital schools. In: Gunzberg, H. C. (ed.), *Advances in the Care of the Mentally Handicapped.* London: Baillière Tindall.
Bland, G. A. (1978) *Ten Years On: A Follow-up Study of Education in Hospitals for the Mentally Handicapped.* National Council for Special Education, 1 Wood Street, Stratford-upon-Avon, Warwickshire.
Cunningham, C. (1974) The relevance of 'normal' educational theory and practice for the mentally retarded. In: Tizard, J. (ed.), *Mental Retardation.* Sevenoaks: Butterworth.
Department of Education and Science (1978) *The Education of Children in Hospitals for the Mentally Handicapped.* HMI Series No. 7. London: HMSO.

Goffman, E. (1961) *Asylums: Essays on the Social Situation of Mental Patients and Other Inmates*. New York: Doubleday.

Gunzberg, H. C. (1976) *Progress Assessment Charts*. Stratford: Social Education Publications.

Speer, G. S. (1964) Mental development of children of feeble-minded and normal mothers. In: Stevens, H. A. & Heber, R. (eds.) *Mental Retardation: A Review of Research*. Chicago: University of Chicago Press.

Stippich, M. E. (1964) The mental development of children of feeble-minded mothers. In: Stevens, H. A. & Heber, R. (eds.) *Mental Retardation: A Review of Research*. Chicago: University of Chicago Press.

Stones, E. (1966) *An Introduction to Educational Psychology*, pp. 177–8. London: Methuen.

# CHAPTER 16

# ADULT EDUCATION AND TRAINING

## PETER MITTLER AND EDWARD WHELAN

Although there has been a statutory obligation to provide education facilities for all children including the mentally handicapped in Great Britain since 1971, there is no corresponding statutory obligation on local authorities to provide day services for all mentally handicapped adults who are much more numerous and who often have urgent need of such facilities. The main form of community provision for mentally handicapped adults in Great Britain is the Adult Training Centre (ATC).

It is only recently that ATCs have come to be regarded as the potential focal point of expertise in mental handicap for adults living in the community. New thinking about the future role of the ATC presents challenges concerning the provision of places, the training and deployment of staff and the best use of professional and financial resources. The overall target is to offer education in its widest sense to the adult mentally handicapped citizen.

## GOVERNMENT POLICY

The current statistics are shown in Table 16.1, with approximately 37 000 adults attending daily in England. The Government's White Paper, *Better Services for the Mentally Handicapped* (DHSS 1971) set a target of 150 ATC places per 100 000 population by 1991 (a total of 70 000 places). This goal has been confirmed (DHSS 1976, 1977b), but the task is a large one for it requires the provision of about 2400 new places each year, together with a corresponding increase in staff. This postulates an

average annual revenue increase of 6.5 per cent over five years and a capital outlay of about £6 million a year over the same period (based on 1975 prices). While the severe restrictions on public expenditure are bound to have an adverse effect on progress towards the 1991 target, there are signs that local authorities are putting more emphasis on their

TABLE 16.1

Adult Training Centres

| | |
|---|---:|
| Total number of ATCs (England only) (March 1976) | 385 |
| Total number of students (England only) | 36 638 |
| Number of places for severely mentally handicapped with gross physical difficulties | 1099 |
| Number of managers and instructors | 3100 |
| Other staff | 2018 |

From DHSS (1977a).

day services for the mentally handicapped (for example, more severely handicapped people are beginning to be offered places in the special care units). Joint Funding is one way in which financial restrictions can be overcome, and it represents a particularly good use of NHS money, since it should ultimately prevent unnecessary hospital admission for long-term care (see p. 228).

The authors gratefully acknowledge the contribution of their colleague Dr Barbara Speake to the work reported in this chapter and the editorial help received from Michael and Ann Craft.

## ADULT TRAINING CENTRES

The first national survey of ATCs in England and Wales was carried out in 1974 by Whelan and Speake, with the support of the DHSS; it was based on the responses of 305 centres (78 per cent) catering for nearly 25 000 trainees (Whelan & Speake 1977; see also Jackson & Strutters 1975; Schlesinger et al. 1979). The survey provides a substantial amount of information about the work of ATCs, the people who attend and the staff who run them.*

### THE TRAINEES/STUDENTS

#### How are people referred to ATCs?

It might be thought that most trainees come straight from ESN(S) schools but, as will be seen from Table 16.2, only 40 per cent come from this source. ESN(M) schools also feed in some school-leavers and as many as 15 per cent are referred by community agencies, suggesting that they did not come straight from school.

TABLE 16.2

Source of trainees

|  | No. | % |
|---|---|---|
| ESN(S) school or Junior Training Centre | 9469 | 40.5 |
| ESN(M) school | 2651 | 11.3 |
| Community or social agency | 3586 | 15.3 |
| Other ATC | 3238 | 13.9 |
| Subnormality hospital | 1784 | 7.6 |
| Mental illness hospital | 735 | 3.1 |
| Sheltered workshop | 222 | 0.9 |
| Other source | 1693 | 7.2 |
| Total | 23 378 | 100.0 |

From Whelan and Speake (1977).

The economic situation of particular areas is bound to have an effect on the pressure for places in ATCs.

It may well be that the rising unemployment figures for school leavers will increase the number of admissions of young people straight from ESN(M) and other special schools. This

* Copies of the survey can be obtained from Dr Whelan at the Hester Adrian Research Centre, University of Manchester.

is another argument for emphasizing a positive rehabilitation approach, for many of these youngsters should be able eventually to take their place in sheltered or open work situations.

#### Age of trainees

The National Survey found that the population of trainees was predominantly a young one, 44 per cent being under the age of 25 and 63 per cent under the age of 30 (Table 16.3). In addition, some 80 per cent live at home with at least one member of their family.

TABLE 16.3

Age of trainees

| Age | No. | % |
|---|---|---|
| 16–19 | 4361 | 18.2 |
| 20–24 | 6167 | 25.8 |
| 25–29 | 4623 | 19.4 |
| 30–39 | 4555 | 19.1 |
| 40–49 | 2235 | 9.4 |
| 50–59 | 1490 | 6.2 |
| 60+ | 457 | 1.9 |
| Total | 23 888 | 100.0 |

The value of continuing education, together with the feasibility of establishing closer working links between the centre and the trainee's family cannot be questioned. If the average age of the trainee population is to be prevented from increasing annually, ATCs will need to achieve a steady throughput of trainees into employment, other forms of training and further education.

#### Types of handicap

It will be seen from Table 16.4 that nearly four out of five trainees are rated by staff as having 'mental handicap only' and that the number with additional handicaps is still fairly small, although there are signs that this proportion may be increasing. In fact, over 92.7 per cent of trainees have mental handicap, whether alone or in combination with some other condition. The service may therefore be described as a fairly specialized one, although some local authorities are now experimenting with more generic centres catering for a wider range of disabilities.

TABLE 16.4

Types of handicap

|  | No. | % |
|---|---|---|
| Mental handicap only | 19 037 | 79.7 |
| Mental and physical handicap | 2615 | 11.0 |
| Physical handicap only | 253 | 1.1 |
| Mental handicap and mental illness | 812 | 3.4 |
| Mental illness only | 911 | 3.8 |
| Unknown or other | 260 | 1.1 |
| Total | 23 888 | 100.0 |

## Educational, social and work abilities

The National Survey provides data about the abilities of some 24 000 trainees in 1974, summarized in Tables 16.5 and 16.6. These tables are of interest for what they tell us about the

TABLE 16.5

Summary of educational and social attainments

|  | Able | Not able | Not known |
|---|---|---|---|
|  | (percentages rounded) (No. = 24 251) | | |
| Talks in sentences | 69 | 14 | 17 |
| Counting and measuring | 38 | 41 | 22 |
| Reading | 26 | 53 | 21 |
| Recognition of colours | 59 | 20 | 21 |
| Telling time | 34 | 43 | 23 |
| Use of money, including budgeting | 28 | 54 | 18 |
| Use of telephone | 23 | 55 | 23 |
| Writing | 29 | 48 | 23 |
| Signature | 41 | 37 | 22 |
| Public transport | 28 | 50 | 22 |
| Post Office procedures | 21 | 53 | 26 |
| Prepares basic meal including shopping | 24 | 51 | 26 |
| Personal hygiene | 52 | 23 | 26 |
| Health hazards | 28 | 38 | 34 |
| Honesty | 53 | 11 | 37 |
| Normal courtesies | 62 | 12 | 26 |
| Use of medical, dental, social services | 17 | 49 | 34 |
| Sexual responsibility | 19 | 28 | 54 |
| Could live on own | 6 | 63 | 31 |
| Can take own medicine | 18 | 46 | 36 |

TABLE 16.6

Summary of work attainments

|  | Able | Not able | Not known |
|---|---|---|---|
|  | (percentages rounded) | | |
| Has appropriate work attitude | 50 | 32 | 19 |
| Works without close supervision | 40 | 44 | 15 |
| Recognizes tools | 48 | 30 | 22 |
| Uses hand tools only | 50 | 29 | 21 |
| Uses powered machinery | 20 | 54 | 26 |
| Can show sustained effort | 38 | 40 | 22 |
| Can adapt readily to a different task | 41 | 38 | 21 |
| Able to work accurately with few mistakes | 35 | 46 | 19 |
| Works at acceptable speed | 38 | 39 | 23 |
| Checks own work | 20 | 56 | 24 |
| Works cooperatively with others | 61 | 17 | 22 |
| Expresses work preferences | 34 | 40 | 27 |
| Contributes to own product design | 4 | 44 | 52 |

Tables 16.5 and 16.6 adapted from Whelan and Speake (1977).

trainees and about the activities of the training centres themselves. The percentages in the 'Not known' column are surprisingly high.

Tables 16.5 and 16.6 serve as reminders that no generalities can be made about what is an 'average' centre. Indeed it may even be said that no two centres are alike, either in respect of the trainees as a whole or in new admissions. Some centres cater for a large number of severely mentally handicapped people, others contain a majority of trainees who seem to have considerable educational, social and work attainments.

### THE ACTIVITIES OF ADULT TRAINING CENTRES

It is virtually impossible to give a comprehensive report of the activities of the centres. They have changed rapidly in recent years, due partly to changing attitudes—particularly to changes in the availability of suitable sub-contract work—and partly because of the fluctuating economic and employment situation. Another factor is that many managers have considerable autonomy and can stamp their individual mark upon the direction the centre takes. While some centres remain very work-orientated, devoting much time to the manufacture of their own products or sub-contract work, others are concentrating more and more on social and further education, using work as only one means to that end. The majority of centres, however, seem to be trying to arrive at a curriculum providing both social education and work training, and to arrive at a balanced programme of activities. This positive attempt to achieve a balance has sometimes led to criticisms that the centres try to be 'all things to all men', and to the view that some differentiation of functions is needed (see pp. 227-8).

## Work activities

The National Survey provides a picture of work activities carried out by trainees.

> Over 63 per cent of trainees were said to be engaged in work which did not require tools, for example, packing, sorting or labelling, or work which required only non-powered hand tools. We might conclude from this that most trainees were engaged in basic and general pre-vocational training. However, there are also indications ... that more specialized training is available in some ATCs in such areas as laundry work, horticulture and industrial sewing.

There is evidence too that centres are rejecting sub-contract work which involves inflexible timetables and deprives trainees of broader-based activities. Many centres make their own products; the list is long and varied, including concrete block making, ornamental concrete work, toy manufacture, boat building, industrial ceramics, jewellery and pottery, garden furniture, wrought iron work, candle making, paint spraying, car washing.

Some centres are also finding paid work for groups of trainees outside the centre; for example, local authorities employ mentally handicapped people to work on public amenities such as parks and gardens. Some are currently using the Job Creation Scheme for

this purpose, demonstrating the ability of mentally handicapped people to do a useful job for the community. Some trainees enter open employment: one of the best-known examples is that reported by Lowman (1975). In his capacity as manager of a food preparation factory in Great Yarmouth, and working closely with the local ATC, he successfully employed a large number of mentally handicapped workers in food preparation. He reported that, with careful preparation in both the job requirements and the accompanying social demands, his own workers were able to accept the mentally handicapped as workmates. He suggested that a member of the ATC staff should work as a peripatetic instructor in the factory, providing a bridge between the mentally handicapped workers and the rest of the factory. This staff member may only be needed at the early stages, but his help should be freely available at other times as well. Lowman also recommended that a member of the factory's personnel section should be responsible for the handicapped workers on a day-to-day basis to ensure their familiarity with the layout and routine of the factory.

## Social education

However well trained a mentally handicapped person is in work skills, his level of social competence will be an important factor in determining whether he remains in open employment. For this reason centres have always tried to ensure that the trainees received social education and training. The major influence has been the work of Gunzburg who developed the *Progress Assessment Charts* which provide a checklist of basic social skills and can be used as a foundation for a training programme (Gunzburg 1973, 1976). Social education must cover both self-help skills—how to make a telephone call, how to go to town on public transport, how to handle money—and appropriate interpersonal behaviour—waiting in queues, not interrupting other people's conversations, and so on. It is these kinds of social skills which may make all the difference between the success or breakdown of a placement in open or sheltered employment. There are a number of specific techniques which can be used to help trainees acquire and practise the necessary social skills.

These include 'modelling' of behaviour appropriate to a particular situation, and role-play activities. In this way trainees can benefit from concentrated experiences, and appropriate behaviour and overlearning can take place. Mock interviews, group situations and simulated work experiences can help the trainees rehearse how they would cope with the kind of difficulties likely to be encountered. Video-recording equipment is likely to be an increasingly important resource for this type of training.

Many mentally retarded adults are seriously handicapped by their lack of competence in language and communication skills. Some have problems with articulation, making it difficult for them to be understood; others have only very limited language skills; some under-function by limiting themselves to one or two words for example, when in fact they may be capable of more complex sentence constructions. It has become increasingly clear that little reliance can be placed upon simply 'encouraging conversation' or upon general language stimulation. As in other priority areas, centre staff must make use of systematic, structured approaches in teaching communication skills. Not all centres are in a position to call on outside specialist help, but simple assessment of language ability can be carried out by staff in association with parents (see Kellett 1976 for an example of teachers developing a survey of language abilities in a number of ESN(S) schools). There is also a growing interest, particularly in special care units, in the use of basic sign and gesture 'language' for those who have not yet developed speech (Kiernan 1977).

Social education must include the teaching and practice of basic number skills—counting, measuring, weighing, use of money, budgeting, telling the time and so on. Those who cannot read need practice in recognition of signs, for example, Entry, Exit, Men, Ladies. Many centres are now teaching literacy skills, a welcome trend as a number of trainees are leaving special schools just at the point where they are beginning to respond to reading teaching. The Adult Literacy Programme can be of help, as also the BBC programmes specially designed for the purpose of developing literacy skills. In addition, the BBC has prepared a series of 24 television programmes specifically aimed at mentally handicapped young people and adults ('Let's Go').

Although many of the skills we have mentioned can be taught by a systematic structured approach, it is just as important to create and take advantage of opportunities to allow trainees to put into practice what they have learnt. The mentally handicapped often experience difficulties in transferring skills acquired in one setting into another, where people and place are unfamiliar. Accompanied and unaccompanied visits to the local town to carry out specified shopping, or simply buying a cup of tea in a cafe, can be important learning experiences. The centre staff have to achieve a balance between structured teaching and the need to practise what has been learnt in everyday situations both at the centre and outside.

### Further education

There is currently a great deal of interest in the education of mentally handicapped adults. Colleges of further education and adult education are beginning to open their doors to disabled people generally, including the mentally handicapped. They are learning that it is not just a matter of providing ramps for wheelchairs and special toilets for disabled people, but of trying to make provision for their learning needs and allowances for their learning difficulties. Just as a severely handicapped person may be able to sit in his wheelchair in a lecture room, but be unable to write quickly enough to take notes, to see the blackboard or to hear the teacher's voice, so a mentally handicapped person may need some courses specially adapted for his needs and may need to be taught skills which would never be taught to non-handicapped students.

More needs to be learned about the work of further education (FE) teachers and the ways in which it might best complement the work of ATC staff. Some real difficulties must be recognized. Although the FE college may offer valuable facilities and experiences not easily obtained elsewhere, FE teachers are not formally qualified at the present time to work with mentally handicapped students, and a high proportion have no qualifications for FE teaching in general. There is also a great deal of insecurity among ATC staff due to the proposed phasing out of the Diploma in the Teaching of Mentally Handicapped Adults, and its replacement by the Certificate in Social Service. ATC staff have strongly expressed their wish for extended and more appropriate training; in the light of their concern for professional recognition, some ATC staff fear that their work will be 'taken over' by FE teachers. Indeed, these fears may be confirmed by the recommendations of the Warnock Committee (DES 1978) that the 'educational component' of the work of ATCs should be provided by the education service.

The Warnock report also recommends, however, that the basic training of all FE teachers should in future contain a substantial component dealing with students with special needs, including the mentally handicapped, that each FE college should designate one member of staff with specific responsibilities for meeting the needs of disabled students, and that at least one college in each region should specialize in the provision of courses for such students. There will clearly have to be a substantial expansion of training facilities for staff of FE and adult education colleges, and it is to be hoped that ATC staff will be able to take full advantage of such facilities to work in closer partnership with staff working in colleges.

In the meantime, two points might be emphasized here. In the first place, it is the expressed wish of members of the National Association of Teachers of the Mentally Handicapped (NATMH) that ATCs as a whole should become the responsibility of education departments rather than social service departments. Whether or not the Department of Education and Science will agree to this—and it is not among the recommendations made by the Warnock Committee—there is no reason why fruitful working links should not be established between ATCs and FE colleges at local level. This is in the interests of the trainees and of inter-professional respect and collaboration. NDG Pamphlet 5 (1977) suggests a number of ways in which such links can be developed. Secondly, it must be clearly understood that any FE teacher who works part or full time in an ATC is responsible to the manager of the ATC, in the same way that anyone working in a special school is responsible to the head teacher.

## PROSPECTS FOR ATC TRAINEES

We end this section on the work of the ATCs with a comment on the prospects of habilitation for trainees. The National Survey looked at the numbers of trainees leaving ATCs during the previous years for either open or sheltered employment. Out of a total of 24 252 students only 934 (less than 4 per cent) entered open employment; and only 97 (0.4 per cent) entered sheltered employment; some 18 per cent returned to the centres within one year. It is perhaps relevant that only a third of those entering open employment had had any experience of similar work while attending the centres. At first glance it is curious that it seems ten times harder for a mentally handicapped person to enter sheltered rather than open employment. The main reason for this appears to lie in the shortage of sheltered workshop places (for example, Remploy) for mentally handicapped people. However, current trends, encouraged by government backing, seem to be towards more sheltered workshops and sheltered work placements for people with handicaps of all kinds, including a contingent of mentally handicapped adults. In addition, more employers are now being encouraged to discover the real potential of handicapped people as employees.

Furthermore, habilitation should not only be measured in terms of the achievement of employment. A major contribution has been made by training if it results in a mentally handicapped adult acquiring the social skills which will enable him to maintain himself in hostel, sheltered housing, foster home or lodgings when his parents can no longer care for him. To enable this to happen, ATC staff need to keep careful records of trainees' progress and difficulties, backed up by effective programmes of training and a periodic review system. Gaps in work or social skills which are highlighted can then be tackled systematically. Tables 16.5 and 16.6 have shown that staff have not yet assessed the capabilities of many trainees. Without knowledge, prospects cannot be realistically assessed.

## PROPOSALS FOR CHANGE

Proposals for the development and future direction of the centres have come from a variety of sources (for example, NSMHC 1977) and there is a good measure of agreement in the field as a whole about the direction in which progress is possible. Many of these proposals were incorporated in the National Development Group's recommendations and hinge on a number of principles:

1. Development of community links using the centre as a key resource for mental handicap in the community, with both staff and trainees ('students') making fullest possible use of the whole range of local agencies and resources.

2. Differentiation of functions and management structure within the centre which involves the establishment of four functional sections: admission and assessment; special care; development and activity; and advanced work.

3. Methods of training: the adoption of a broadly educational programme which involves a full assessment of the needs of each individual, leading to the design of a programme of activities which is closely related to those needs, making it possible for students to develop their skills, abilities and interests with the aid of systematic and structured teaching.

## Development of community links

The extent to which the centres are able to develop links with community resources such as further education colleges, leisure centres and clubs, depends on the availability of staff to promote and foster these links. Many people, professionals and general public alike, are unfamiliar with mentally handicapped people and have quite erroneous ideas about their behaviour and potentialities. We have discussed the contribution of an ATC staff member as the initial 'bridge builder' for mentally handicapped workers in a factory (see p. 224); this bridge-building role is equally relevant as mentally handicapped people are encouraged to make use of community facilities. The NDG pamphlet makes many other detailed suggestions for ways in which better working relationships can be established and developed between the centres and other agencies.

Just as the function of a centre is diminished by isolation from the community at large,

so valuable training opportunities are lost if there is not good liaison with the parents/carers of its clientele. However, in saying this, it must be remembered that the trainees are adults, not children, and have rights and responsibilities of their own. It is a waste of time for staff and parents to agree on a certain objective if the trainee has not been consulted and is either totally ignorant of, or opposed to, that particular goal. It is precisely because there are legitimate doubts about what constitute appropriate goals that a working relationship with parents/carers is essential. There will then be opportunity to discuss both specific and general aims.

## Differentiation of functions within the centres

Because needs and abilities of trainees in most centres are so variable, it is virtually impossible to devise a programme to cater for all of them satisfactorily. Recent reports have recommended that there should be much greater differentiation of functions within ATCs. The National Development Group suggests four functions which need not necessarily take place in different buildings, although some social services departments prefer different centres to have different emphases. The four functions are: admission and assessment; special care; development and activities; and advanced work.

*Admission and assessment.* The National Survey indicated that the needs of many trainees are inadequately assessed. It is therefore suggested that each new entrant should spend a period in an assessment section, during which his basic skills and abilities will be tested and observed in a wide range of carefully designed situations, for example, use of tools; social independence; relationships with other people; educational attainments, leisure interests. Naturally the family or hostel/hospital care staff have an important part to play at this point as they have a unique knowledge of the trainee. As admission to the centre will represent a new stage in the life of the entrant, the family may find it profitable to discuss the more adult needs of their son or daughter. It is important that staff should be provided with reliable and relevant information by those who refer the individual to the centre and that this should form the basis of the centre's own initial assessment.

*Special care.* Although ESN(S) schools cater for almost every child, no matter how severely or profoundly handicapped, ATCs do not have a corresponding legal obligation. In fact, the *Model of Good Practice for ATCs* issued in 1968 by the (then) Ministry of Health specifically discouraged ATCs from taking 'special care cases'; in 1974 only 13 per cent of ATCs had identifiable special care units, although 60 per cent of ATCs had trainees whom they regarded as special care cases. Thus a serious deficiency in the current system lies in the paucity of provisions for the most handicapped school leaver. It is naturally a cause for great concern to many parents, faced with the task of full-time care of their severely handicapped son or daughter when they can no longer go daily to school. It is not surprising that hospital placement is often sought but could be avoided.

The NDG pamphlet recommends strongly that the centre of the future should have provisions for the whole range of handicapped people living in the community and makes suggestions for ways in which the most severely handicapped can be fully integrated into the centres and catered for appropriately. Special care units are an obvious example of how to put joint funding money to good use. By this method money can be transferred from the National Health Service to social services departments for schemes that are in the interests of both services. Special care units ease the pressure on parents and help to prevent unnecessary and costly permanent admission to mental handicap hospitals. Joint funding has already been used in many areas to build/adapt, equip and staff special care units.

*Development and activities section.* This will constitute the core of the new social education centre, encompassing social and further education as well as work training. The balance between these component parts will be based upon the needs and abilities of each trainee/student as ascertained by the assessment section. The overall aim is to help each mentally handicapped person to learn and/or practise the social and work skills which will help him to progress to as independent a life

style as possible. Once again, partnership with parents/carers is of the utmost importance if these skills are to be utilized.

*Advanced work.* As we have seen from the National Survey, the number of trainees moving on to open employment in 1974 was under 4 per cent. There are many reasons for this, including the national economic climate, the general high level of unemployment, and the drop in the number of unskilled jobs. But we have also seen that only a third of those moving into open employment had had any experience of similar work while in the centre. As yet there is no systematic policy of training for work and much more collaboration is necessary with the whole range of statutory and voluntary organizations dealing with unemployment or training for work. Thus the most able group of trainees have not had suitable provision made for their abilities. The NDG pamphlet therefore recommends the setting up of an advanced work section in each centre.

These sections would aim at providing realistic pre-work training, with emphasis on both the work aspect—time keeping, understanding pay slips and deductions, job hunting, being interviewed—and the social demands of the job—how to address the foreman, how to react to teasing and so on. Many of the routines, for example eating in the works canteen, can be seen as important and often neglected aspects of pre-work training.

*Methods of training*

How can all these improvements be implemented? The main burden falls on the staff of the centres who are being asked to take on more responsibility for active programmes of training and rehabilitation, linking this with the resources available in the local community.

The new emphasis of the centres is based on an educational approach, requiring detailed assessment of each entrant's needs and capabilities. This assessment, although utilizing the expert skills of outside specialists (for example, psychologists) and the unique knowledge of parents/carers, is seen as the responsibility of the staff themselves, that is, of those who will be doing the necessary teaching. A number of assessment methods have been developed; the National Development Group's pamphlet contains a list; see also Clarke and Clarke (1974).

Systematic teaching must rely on the setting of precisely defined teaching goals. This is the basis of related systems such as goal planning and behaviour modification. Whatever approach is adopted, a knowledge of behavioural methods is essential to a systematic training programme; such techniques and procedures are well described (Perkins et al. 1976). At present most staff have not been trained in these teaching methods, and one of the most important needs is not only to provide opportunities for learning about such methods, but also opportunities to try them out in their own work setting. Indeed, much more is now known about the needs of mentally handicapped people and of the most effective ways of teaching them. Consequently staff need a longer and more specialized course of training than the current one-year Diploma course if they are to acquire the knowledge, skills and appropriate professional attitude necessary for their work.

## CONCLUSIONS

Mentally handicapped adults can continue to learn and develop new skills and abilities, if they are given time and are taught by structured teaching methods. The number of people in ATCs is due to double by 1991; this chapter has pointed to some of the new directions these centres might take and has discussed the findings of the first National Survey together with the main recommendations made by staff associations, by parents and by the National Development Group for the Mentally Handicapped.

Adult training and education are important areas for the future. Like non-handicapped citizens, most mentally handicapped people have potentialities which may be developed to allow them and their relatives a more enriched and rewarding life. It is essential to develop staff enthusiasm and to provide staff with the necessary knowledge and skills to enable them to develop the abilities and personalities of the mentally handicapped to the full.

## BIBLIOGRAPHY

Clarke, A. M. & Clarke, A. D. B. (eds.) (1974) *Mental Deficiency: The Changing Outlook*, 3rd ed. London: Methuen.

Department of Education and Science (1978) *Special Educational Needs*. Report of the Committee of Enquiry into the Education of Handicapped Children and Young People (Chairman Mrs H. N. Warnock) Cmnd. 7212. London: HMSO.

Department of Health and Social Security (1971) *Better Services for the Mentally Handicapped*. Cmnd. 4683. London: HMSO.

Department of Health and Social Security (1976) *Priorities for Health and Social Services in England*. London: HMSO.

Department of Health and Social Security (1977a) *Adult Training Centres for the Mentally Handicapped and Day Centres for the Mentally Ill at 31st March 1976*. A/F76/8. London: DHSS.

Department of Health and Social Security (1977b) *The Way Forward*. London: HMSO.

Gunzburg, H. C. (1973) *Social Competence and Mental Handicap*, 2nd ed. London: Baillière Tindall.

Gunzburg, H. C. (1976) *Progress Assessment Charts*. Stratford: Social Education Publications.

Jackson, S. & Strutters, M. (1975) *A survey of Scottish Adult Training Centres*. Glasgow: Scottish Society for the Mentally Handicapped.

Kellett, B. (1976) An initial survey of the language of ESNS children in Manchester: the results of a teachers' workshop. In: Berry, P. (ed.), *Language and Communication in the Mentally Handicapped*. London: Edward Arnold.

Kiernan, C. (1977) Alternatives to speech: a review of research on manual and other forms of communication with the mentally handicapped and other non-communicating populations. *Br. J. ment. Subnorm.*, *23*, 6–28.

Lowman, P. (1975) Permanent employment in industry for the mentally handicapped person. In: Elliott, J. & Whelan, E. (eds.), *Employment of Mentally Handicapped People*. King's Fund Paper 8. London: King's Fund Centre.

Ministry of Health (1968) *Model of Good Practice for ATCs*. London: HMSO.

National Development Group for the Mentally Handicapped (1977) *Day Services for Mentally Handi-capped Adults*. NDG Pamphlet 5. London: DHSS.

National Society for Mentally Handicapped Children (1977) *Minimum Standards for ATCs*. London: NSMHC.

Perkins, E. A., Taylor, P. D. & Capie, A. C. M. (1976) *Helping the Retarded: A Systematic Behavioural Approach*. Kidderminster: Institute of Mental Subnormality.

Schlesinger, H., Whelan, E., Ronan, M. & Davies, S. (1979) *Industry and Effort: A Survey of Day Work Centres*. London: Spastics Society.

Whelan, E. & Speake, B. R. (1977) *Adult Training Centres in England and Wales*. Manchester: National Association of Teachers for the Mentally Handicapped, Hester Adrian Research Centre, University of Manchester.

# IV

# SOCIAL WORK AND RESIDENTIAL CARE

# CHAPTER 17

# SOCIAL WORK AND MENTAL RETARDATION

## MORA SKELTON AND CYRIL GREENLAND

'The mentally retarded person has, to the maximum degree of feasibility, the same rights as other human beings.'
Declaration on the Rights of Retarded Persons, United Nations General Assembly, December 1971

Written in 1971, these remain challenging words. The implications for the social planning needed to bring them to life for retarded people, and for people with other handicaps, are tremendous. All professional people dealing with retarded individuals and their families must react to this challenge, but social workers most of all, since the challenge is in the field of social action.

This chapter deals with the role of the social worker on the therapeutic team, and with his role in the community in relation to retarded people and their families. Chapter 18 discusses the social worker's role in residential services.

## THE SOCIAL WORKER ON THE MULTIDISCIPLINARY TEAM

The composition and function of the multi-disciplinary team was described in Chapter 2. The multidisciplinary team draws together appropriate specialists on behalf of a particular client; it is a familiar approach in Britain, the United States and Canada. In Britain teams consulting on cases of mental retardation are usually located in the institutions for the mentally retarded, but teams are also assembled to discuss particular cases in paediatric hospital clinics, with regard to school entry and leaving, and at other times as indicated.

The thrust toward provision of specialized services for retarded or otherwise handicapped people, long urged by parent associations because of the lack of suitable services for the handicapped, is currently being replaced by a movement on the part of these same parent groups to make generic services available to all, even those with special needs. Specialized services for particular groups would continue to be available only where necessary.

The widespread acceptance of the Seebohm Committee recommendations (HMSO 1968) in July 1968 led to the rapid development of an integrated social service system in England and Wales, and in Scotland. The Social Services Acts which followed enabled local authorities to provide social services to special groups such as the mentally retarded on a generic basis.

Following the adoption of the government White Paper *Better Services for the Mentally Handicapped* (DHSS 1971), social workers in England and Wales have become employees of the municipalities, working from area social work offices, and carrying an undifferentiated caseload of persons in need, rather than specializing in a particular problem, such as mental retardation. Exceptions occur when social workers are seconded to an institution for retarded people. In Canada and the United States the team approach to the problem of mental retardation is more common, on both an in-patient and an out-patient basis; it is also more common for social workers who deal with the mentally retarded to have specialized in this aspect of social work. It would seem that the function of the social worker on such a team is similar on both sides of the Atlantic, with the exceptions to be noted below.

In the team approach to handling the problem of mental retardation, the social worker undertakes to identify the social factors operating in the background and in the current functioning of the mentally retarded person which might have contributed to the development of his condition, or to the problem of his adjustment. Sometimes the family strategy which was developed to deal with the situation breaks down at a critical point, for instance when the retarded person reaches adolescence with its new problems and challenges.

If this is indicated, the social worker undertakes counselling with the retarded person and his family with a view to amelioration of the problem and achievement of maximum functioning. He identifies those community supports which might enable the retarded person to carry on productively in the community if possible and, where appropriate, supports for the family. His should be the listening ear through a follow-up period after contact with the team, and in fact at any time when changing circumstances, or the passage of time, bring new problems.

Generally, in working with a diagnostic and treatment team, the social worker carries responsibility for intake (the selection of cases for the team); social diagnostic evaluation of the individual or family situation; individual and group counselling when required; participation in interdisciplinary case planning; training and research in the area of social work; referral to the appropriate community resources; and follow-up.

This is the model of task assignment within the team which was originally developed and which is still very widely followed, but other models are utilized as well. One variation is to handle the case in this way until a diagnostic formulation has been made and a management plan developed, then to assign all aspects of follow-through to one team member whose area of expertise seems particularly important for the case. A speech therapist might at this point perform many of the functions usually assigned to other team members, for instance, often in consultation with another team member having particular expertise in the area of communication skills. It should be noted that in addition to the usual medical model of the multidisciplinary team, in which the physician was usually the team leader, other models are making their appearance in the field of mental retardation. A member of any of the team disciplines may be the team leader.

The ensuing discussion is based on the traditional model of social work responsibility within the team, described above and still by far the most widely utilized model. The discussion commences with reference to a landmark piece of advice to the treatment team from a consumer of the service, Mrs Letha L. Patterson. In June 1956 Mrs Patterson, herself the mother of a severely retarded son, recorded 'Some Pointers for Professionals' which still have meaning for the whole assessment and treatment process, especially for the social work member of the team (Patterson 1956):

1. Tell us the nature of our problem as soon as possible.
2. Always see both parents (if the case involves a child).
3. Watch your language (use readily understandable terms).
4. Help us to see that this is our problem and don't impose solutions).
5. Help us to understand our problem.
6. Know your resources.
7. Never put us on the defensive.
8. Remember that parents of retarded children are just people (with a mixture of strength and weakness).
9. Remember that we are parents and that you are professionals.
10. Remember the importance of your attitude towards us.

## INTAKE

Intake is a vital period in the client's contact with the team, often colouring his whole perception of the service offered and his ability to use it. Even if there is a waiting list for a full assessment a preliminary discussion with the intake social worker at home or in the office should be speedily available upon request or on referral. It may be that the case is not a suitable one for the team, and in that event alternative services should be described and, if desired, a careful referral made. The intake worker should be prepared to follow through with the referral to make sure that the client actually receives service.

Admission criteria or waiting lists at other agencies may in effect deny service at a time when it is urgently needed. The intake worker may need to deal with community agencies on behalf of his client. If the case is a suitable one for the team, the intake worker is in a position to set priorities for service and, if necessary, to react immediately to an emergency situation.

For most cases the intake period is concerned with assembling relevant facts and developing a careful social diagnosis of the situation as it presents itself, and the factors which have brought it about. With the client's consent or, in the case of a child, that of his family, relevant information from all sources is collected, so that the team need not duplicate work done elsewhere. The retarded person's own perception of his situation, and the nature of the help he is seeking from the team, is ascertained. If the retarded person is a child, the parents' assessment of the situation is sought and the nature of their expectations of service, so that the response of the team can relate to parental expectations. The retarded adult's perception of his situation may differ from that of his family. For instance, a family might overprotect its retarded member and refuse to let him emancipate himself from their care when he becomes able to function on his own. This is a dilemma which the staff must deal with when making a management plan with the client and his family.

Most people turn to a mental retardation service with reluctance—new parents may approach it with dread. The intake worker should inquire why the clients chose to approach the service at the time they did and what other advice they had received, in order that the team should respond to the clients' concerns and to their degree of understanding.

The intake worker must be prepared to receive inquiries and conduct initial interviews with sensitivity to the anxiety and distress and—sometimes—anger which retarded clients and their families may be feeling. In a second great landmark statement D. Boyd describes *The Three Stages in the Growth of a Parent of a Mentally Retarded Child* (1950):

1. *Why did this happen to us?* At this stage the parent feels cheated, and his thoughts for the moment are on himself. The child is not yet seen as a real person. In most cases the parent moves on to stage 2.

2. *What can we do for our child?* This is the frame of mind of most, but not all, parents who come to an assessment centre. They are reaching out for help.

3. *What can be done for these people?* Not all parents are able to reach this stage of interest in retarded persons as a group.

Parents who come to the assessment centre may be in any one of these stages, and in time of stress they may regress from a later to an earlier stage. It is apparent that parents in stage 1 may appear to be rejecting and cold to the child. At one time such parents were viewed by a clinic team accustomed to a psychoanalytic approach as psychiatric patients, and suitable subjects for treatment. It is now suggested that symptoms of stress can be essentially normal in some circumstances, and that the family's reactions should not be handled too directly until the initial shock is over, and until practical management suggestions and community supports have been offered and utilized. At every stage stress should be on family competence and problem-solving potential. Most families can then move from stage 1 into partnership with the team in helping their retarded member.

This is not to say that there are no seriously troubled families or seriously disturbed retarded people, but they are the exception rather than the rule (see also Chapter 9.)

The intake worker maintains a contact during the waiting period—which hopefully will not be long—until the case is seen by the treatment team, and is available if service is required in the meantime. If possible the intake worker carries the case to its conclusion.

THE CASE IN PROGRESS

*Preliminary team discussion*

Usually the assessment or treatment team is made up of persons whose area of expertise seems to be needed in the particular case, as indicated by the intake summary, and by hospital or other reports assembled by the intake worker.

The social worker presents to the team the social dynamics of the case as they appear to be indicated by the intake interviews, so that team members can visualise the situation and have some indices of social strengths as well as weaknesses in the picture.

## Assessment procedure

The social worker often functions as the facilitator in this process, introducing the client and family, interpreting the function of the various team members to them, answering the client's questions. On occasion the worker functions as advocate for the client and family, phrasing for the client questions he has voiced earlier but is hesitant to voice now. The worker tries to minimize the problem of service delivery, concerning himself with the timing of interviews if the clients come from a distance, problems connected with transportation, care of other children in the home, and the client's understanding of what is going on. The goal is to develop a sense of partnership between the team and the client and his family.

## Assessment reporting

Assessment teams and clinics differ in their way of imparting assessment findings to families or to the retarded person himself. In some cases the entire team sits down with the family in order that each member can comment on his findings and be available for questioning. This can be a rather frightening procedure for unsophisticated clients. If it is utilized, the team members should endeavour to behave in an informal manner, which invites questions and discussion.

In other settings the team leader states the combined findings of all team members. In any case the social worker, in his role as client advocate, should try to ensure that the family or the retarded person has understood the information given him. This reporting session should be frank, within the limits of the information available. 'Just be honest with us', said one parent.

Whenever possible visits to the centre should be seen as the establishment of a partnership between a family who have a handicapped member and a professional team who have some of the expertise required to help them.

It is not easy to give the information that a child is retarded, and it is not easy for parents to take the information in, especially for parents to whom the idea is new. Many parents recall that on the occasion when the diagnosis was first given them, the physician may have continued to elaborate but that they (the parents) were too upset to be able to grasp what he was saying. Wolfensberger and Meno-lascino (1970), in an article on discussions with parents, called this condition 'novelty shock', and recommended that every interpretation interview to new parents, hearing the diagnosis for the first time, be followed up by a second of a very similar nature to make sure that the information is understood, and to reply to questions which may have occurred to the parents in the meantime.

In their effort to understand, most people move from what they know in trying to grasp something new. The professional staff should ascertain from family members what their understanding of the problem is, and move from there in adding the clinic findings. The parents' own perceptions of a child's problems are important, but some parents have seen their questions go unanswered. One family reported that they have five children, two of whom are retarded. The parents say that they asked for genetic counselling, but came away without knowing whether or not the retardation was of a type which might re-appear in their normal children's offspring. It is apparent that the parents should have persisted in their questioning, but this can be difficult for parents who are in a strange place, speaking to people who seem busy, important or in a hurry. One parent complained:

A parent must cajole, promise, con or threaten several people to make it known that he or she is serious about knowing the condition of the child; what it is called in layman's terms; what are the possible short- and long-term complications. As a parent you are entitled to this information.

Another parent wrote, with regard to a large government facility:

My personal feeling is that the parent feels that he puts his child into a government bureaucracy mill and has no say in the decisions concerning his offspring. The parents have no identity.

All parents make mistakes. Parents of a retarded child have sometimes pressed their child too hard, or have overprotected him. Such mistakes need to be corrected, but parents should never be made to feel guilty about them. People on the defensive find it hard to ask for help, or to use it constructively.

It would appear that there is always the danger of development of negative feelings on the part of parents towards clinic personnel who are giving them bad news, without being able to offer them a cure for the situation. Parents are quick to sense if they are being patronised, put off, or—as one parent put it—pacified.

A diagnostic assessment is not enough. To be of use to parents or to the retarded person himself, the diagnosis must be understood, and should lead to some form of management plan.

Parents have complained that their children were admitted to a mental retardation facility for investigation, sometimes for months, with very meagre reporting back of findings. Probably the investigation produced many negative as well as positive findings. These too should be shared with the family. Lack of information can produce unhelpful results, with parents feeling that staff do not expect them to understand, or that the information was not considered suitable for them to hear.

When the retarded person is a child the team should always try to see both parents. An upset mother should not have to try to interpret the clinic findings to her husband, whose perception of the problem may be different from hers, and whose questions may be different from those she has asked. The present trend is to include brothers and sisters in the clinic interpretation and, wherever appropriate, the retarded person himself. Team members should rely on plain speaking. Unfamiliar language—such as use of medical, social work or psychological jargon—contributes to the parents' sense that they have not been 'told anything'. One couple emerged from such an interview under the impression that their severely retarded child would become normal in seven years' time. Parents cannot be expected to relate to or retain material which they have not really understood. As has been noted earlier, it is one of the particular tasks of the social worker to be sensitive to the degree of satisfaction or dissatisfaction the client or his family are feeling with regard to the relaying of information, and to function as their advocate to try to maximise the usefulness of this part of the service.

If it is not appropriate for the entire team to see the retarded person and his family a second time for discussion of their findings, the social worker should certainly do so, in order to deal with questions which may still linger in the clients' minds.

CASE PLANNING

Immediately related to information given is the development of a management plan for the retarded person and his family. In parts of Canada and the United States this is called the Individual Program Plan (IPP) and a team member, often the social worker, has the responsibility of seeing that the treatment steps, or referrals, recommended in the plan are carried out.

Whenever possible the family and the retarded person should take part in this planning session, as should the extended family or other interested persons, if appropriate. Where no family exists, or is not interested, a client surrogate might take part, an individual who is alive to the client's best interest. The Eleanor Roosevelt Developmental Services in Albany, New York State, is an excellent example of this practice. A parent volunteer, paid by the state, is in attendance at all case conferences and case planning sessions, both of individuals who are in an institution and those who are living in the community, if no parent is available or if the parent needs help in understanding the information.

Sometimes physicians or maternity ward staff, out of concern for the parents' mental health, will advise hospitalization for a newborn child with Down's syndrome or otherwise handicapped infant, without sufficient thought as to what is best, or even possible, for the baby himself—or for the parents in the long term. One parent said: 'We may never be at peace with a solution which was reached for us.' In fact the solutions may change as time goes by, and families make successive adaptations to the changing requirements of their situation. The retarded young person or adult should be consulted and have a choice of living and work plans.

At this juncture the social workers' knowledge of the community resources and supports available is all-important. A programme plan calling for non-existent remedies is of no use.

Wolfensberger and Menolascino (1970) talk of the reality stress of raising an atypical child, and suggest that it is not possible to accurately assess the degree of upset in a family until after the 'novelty shock' has worn off and reality stress factors have been met as far as possible.

For the retarded young person and adult the support of an appropriate referral can be crucial.

The social worker must be aware of the availability of both generic services and specialized resources in the area—nursery schools, community accommodation plans, parent associations, government facilities, protective service workers (see p. 245), and in Britain, the social security benefits available. As we have noted earlier, referrals to other agencies should be followed up by the team social worker to make sure that they are appropriate, and that the service is, in fact, being given.

## FAMILY COUNSELLING

At the conclusion of the assessment period the team may recommend a further social work contact to the family, in order to consolidate the service and extend it through further help in problem solving and planning for the future. The assistance offered might be a series of individual and family interviews, or a supervised group experience with other parents, discussing similar difficulties, or other types of support which might be needed. Referral might be to the social worker on the team or in another specialized setting, or to a generic family service agency in the community.

Because the team often functions in a diagnostic and assessment setting, clients are frequently families with young retarded children, and the parents may be learning for the first time about the nature of the child's problem. Older children may be brought to the team at a time of crisis, such as starting or leaving school, or with regard to a particular management problem, such as poor social behaviour—biting, hitting, swearing, over-eating. Young adults and adults may present themselves or come with their families for advice about planning for work, a place to live, sexual counselling, or some specific problem in adjustment to living in the community. Requests for placement away from home may be made with regard to a person of any age, when problems arise in home management, for instance, or when the maturing retarded individual seeks to emancipate himself.

The normal life cycle of any individual begins with complete helplessness and dependence on his family, and gradually progresses through various stages of maturation to independence at which time the individual usually leaves home and starts up a social unit of his own. The stages of this transition prior to independence usually take place within a family and are highly dependent upon the family's physical and emotional support, teaching and example. The retarded person progresses through his developmental stages slowly and with greater difficulty, depending on the degree of his handicap, the climate of his family, and the quality of support and stimulation given him. The retarded child needs the nurture and support of his own home as much as, or more than, a normal child, in order to achieve his potential. The substantially handicapped person may not be able to become independent of his family without specialized community support.

The presence of a retarded child in a family of otherwise intellectually normal people is in almost all instances a stressful experience. Margaret Adams (1971) sees three important components in the chronic state of stress: stress related to the disability itself, which will vary in degree and kind with the severity of the handicap; stress related to the continuing dependency of the retarded individual, which may reach a crisis point at any of the major milestones, birth, starting or leaving school, adolescence, or leaving home; and stress related to the degree of vulnerability of the family. A well-functioning family unit will be more able to cope with the added stress of having a retarded child. A troubled family, or one which has made a poor adjustment to the problem, may find it overwhelming without help.

Olshansky (1970) still speaks for many parents when he writes:

Almost all families with mentally defective children experience what I call 'chronic sorrow' which I feel is an understandable, non-neurotic response to a tragic fact. The sorrow is chronic and lasts as long as the child lives.

Schreiber and Feeley (1970) described the anxieties and concerns of groups of siblings of retarded children, and the value to them of a series of 'sibling seminars' in which they could talk their problems out as a group.

To the task of helping these families the social worker should bring the same skills and techniques which serve his colleagues in other settings; plus an understanding of the nature of developmental disorders and their influence on individuals and family function; plus a thorough knowledge of appropriate community resources and of effective referral procedures.

Three aspects of social work service to the family seem to stand out: crisis intervention, support and availability. Focus of the contact can vary from help in solving a particular problem to the development of insight into difficulties which have become complicated by emotional overtones. The short-term task-oriented contact, lasting 4 to 6 weeks with the possibility of follow-up contact as needed is usually preferred by both client and worker to more prolonged discussions with a diffuse focus.

The strength of families (and of retarded people) has perhaps been underestimated in the past. As community supports increase in number and quality, and as the problem of mental retardation is increasingly seen as only one of a spectrum of difficulties a family might be called upon to face, and is freed from the added stress of secrecy and shame, the family response to having a retarded child may become less catastrophic than was formerly the case. The parent of a retarded adult commented recently that, while the problem of chronic sorrow still remains, 'the new generation of parents seem more hopeful and carefree than we were. They seem more able to take things in their stride.' The time when team members viewed parents of retarded children as potential psychiatric patients is long since past. Long-term counselling for the multi-problem family belongs with the generic community agency.

Mention has already been made of the importance of the team social worker's basic knowledge of all aspects of developmental handicap, so that he can recapitulate and interpret the team's findings as often as necessary, and intervene effectively in his counselling of the client. The community social worker in a generic agency will need to inform himself about mental retardation and, with the client's consent, obtain a report on the team findings in a particular case. Sometimes community agencies report difficulty in obtaining adequate reports from medical, psychiatric and mental retardation specialists. It is important that the best interest of the client is served, and that the treatment team does not withhold information which is needed by a community agency.

Mention has also been made of the importance of the social worker's knowledge and use of appropriate community resources—infant stimulation programmes, specialized or integrated nursery schools, developmental day care programmes, schools, baby-sitting and other parental relief programmes, financial support in the home (such as the attendance allowance in Britain for families with a retarded member at home). The older child or adult may need sheltered or training workshops and work placements, a range of community living options when the time comes to leave home, information about pensions and allowances and leisure-time activities which may be available to him. The social worker should be aware of community supports for the individual such as We are People First (1975), a handicapped people's group in Oregon, USA, and individual helping agents such as protective service workers and citizen advocates (see p. 245).

Parents offer support to one another through the large voluntary organizations active in most parts of the western world, and through a wide variety of mutual support programmes, such as Pilot Parents in the USA, in which new parents who wish this service can be matched with an experienced couple who have come to terms with the challenge of bringing up a retarded child, or Extend-a-Family (USA) in which an interested family extends hospitality to a retarded child from time to time to give the child's own family respite when needed.

Sometimes the family of a retarded client is made up of individuals who are themselves of limited intelligence. Counselling would then focus on tasks to be performed to solve or ameliorate problems experienced by the family in relation to the retarded client. In a minority of cases, if the problem is a severe one, it may become necessary to intervene on behalf of a child born to seriously handicapped parents. The Milwaukee experiment (Heber et al. 1972) undertook to greatly enrich the stimulation available to children of a group of retarded mothers included in the experiment and seemed to improve the functioning level of the children involved above that of any of their siblings. Similar projects are reported elsewhere. In Montreal, Canada, a vigorous approach to the nutrition of expectant mothers with a history of premature or distressed infants, assisted these mothers to carry the child involved to term, and produced healthier, full-weight babies. Community social workers and public health nurses (health visitors in the UK) are in an advantageous position to spot at-risk pregnancies and infants in marginal social settings, whether the parents are retarded or not, and to cooperate to arrange a better start in life for the infant or young child.

## COUNSELLING RETARDED PEOPLE

The trend today is to enable retarded people to remain in the community, and to return to the community those retarded people who have been living in institutions but who are able to make this change. Many retarded people now living into their middle years would formerly have died relatively young (sufferers from Down's syndrome, for example). The increasing numbers of adult handicapped people are now adapting to social living in the community; emancipating themselves from home; interacting with people of all ages, with their employer, with people of the opposite sex.

Inadequate social skills can prevent a retarded person from enjoying life in the community, or obtaining otherwise suitable training and employment. Training to improve social skills can be obtained in a variety of ways on a personal counselling basis, as part of the experience offered in a community residence or sheltered workshop or school, or through a supervised group experience.

The task of training retarded people who lack communication skills by use of behaviour modification techniques, particularly using positive reinforcement, is an important one. Some social workers have become proficient in these training methods, and are able to help families to carry out programmes at home, but the majority of social workers refer cases in need of this kind of help to their colleagues in psychology.

### Sexual problems

Because many retarded people are leading more normal lives in the community, problems related to sex present themselves to both the family and to retarded people themselves. Families worry about possible pregnancy and about protecting the person who is an adult physically, but perhaps not mentally. Often parents who have been realistic in permitting their retarded family members to grow in other areas are frightened about this one and find it hard to instruct and prepare their retarded son or daughter to function in a socially acceptable yet satisfying manner. They worry about the daughter returning late from the workshop, or the son who wants to leave home, uneasily aware that they as parents may not have prepared their retarded adult children adequately to cope with possible sexual exploitation or abuse.

The staff of an urban counselling service for young adults whose average age was 18–30 years and who were potentially employable found that sexuality was a prime source of concern for this group of retarded people as well. Group discussions revealed the existence of a wide range of bits of sophisticated knowledge, plus gaps in basic understanding, plus much misinformation on the topic. The majority of the members of the group felt uncertain in their relationships with the opposite sex, very 'normal' at 14 years, but causing much anxiety to a person in his late twenties.

The staff of the agency found it was relatively easy to give information and counselling to this group. The retarded clients, when encouraged to do so, would speak frankly of their concerns, expected an equally frank response from staff, and were able to act upon the suggestions made to them.

Pre-marital counselling, instruction in the use of contraceptives, and abortion counselling are other areas where help should be given.

Much of the counselling needed would fall within the area of service offered by a generic service. (See also Chapter 27.)

*Feelings about being retarded*

Not too long ago literature on counselling retarded people dealt almost exclusively with the task-oriented interview as though retarded people could not be expected to think about, let alone speak about, their disability and their feelings. Counselling agencies have found that on the contrary many retarded people in the community were very aware that they were different from those about them, and could articulate their concerns about it. Counselling should then be concerned with developing a healthy self-concept and self-acceptance. A group setting is helpful, so that individuals can feel less alone with their problems.

The task of living with a handicap is not an easy one. People with mild or borderline degrees of retardation suffer because they are able to perceive a difference between their own level of competence and that of those about them. They need counselling so that their hopes and aspirations are geared to the level of their abilities.

*Independence*

When the retarded person leaves home or moves into a community setting from an institution, it is to be expected that lack of judgement, based on inexperience, may present problems. Assistance with budgeting, finding accommodation, obtaining medical and dental care, using public transport, shopping, eating in restaurants, and many other social skills needs to be given. Experience seems to show that the majority of difficulties retarded adults meet in the community can be solved with help from social services. Very few problems seem to need legal action, though this may be required in some cases. For this reason many authorities hesitate to use legislation providing legal guardianship for retarded adults, fearing to withdraw rights which the retarded person could, with help, learn to exercise.

Some adult retarded people and their families may need help in developing a healthy relationship after separation. Often ambivalent feelings remain, related to past problems. Emotional support from the family continues to be important to retarded people living on their own.

In the past the abilities of retarded people have been underestimated. Just as retarded people can perform a job well if it has been broken down into component parts, so most retarded people can cope with the difficulties of everyday living if taught the necessary skills in manageable segments. However, the difficulties they face in trying to manage in a complex society should not be underestimated. People who have been institutionalized and are now living in the community face particular difficulty, because so many aspects of community life are new to them, and because they are not accustomed to making decisions for themselves. Many retarded people do not wish to reveal the extent of their handicap and pretend to understand what is said to them when in fact they do not, thus provoking anger and rejection from employers and others. Another problem expresses itself in poor judgement, often the result of a lesser capacity for learning by experience and for transferring learning from one situation to another. Thus crises repeat themselves, especially when the problem occurs in slightly different guise.

An array of supports is needed, but none more than the sympathetic counsellor—whether friend, family, citizen advocate or social worker—some-one to whom the retarded person may turn when in doubt. It is important that this person be available when needed. Counselling at these times should usually be task-oriented, often training-oriented, with concrete solutions worked out for concrete problems. Goals should be modest, and both client and worker should feel genuine pleasure when these goals are achieved.

Edgerton's book *The Cloak of Competence* (1967) and the follow-up report (Edgerton & Bercovici 1976) describe the adjustment of a large group of retarded persons discharged from an institution into the community. The book and follow-up report illustrate the struggle of the group to assume the 'cloak' and no longer appear as handicapped persons. They also reveal the importance for most of the retarded people who survived in the community, of finding a friend, landlady, employer, family member, spouse, who could give sympathetic counsel. This was the lifeline in most cases. Since the time of Edgerton's first study professional helpers for handicapped persons have multiplied, but they need not, and cannot, take the place of such friends. Speaking of the experience in Britain, Bayley (1973) says: 'Care given by official services of the welfare state can only hope to be effective when they live with, support, and are supported by the informal caring that goes on throughout society.'

Leisure time poses a problem for many retarded people living in the community. Almost invariably they are in poor financial circumstances and cannot afford to go to the cinema or to pay for other forms of entertainment. Drop-in centres (day centres in the UK) which offer fellowship and teaching in appropriate social behaviour as well as suggestions for inexpensive leisure pursuits are helpful. The retarded person who is socially isolated also dreads holidays and weekends.

In spite of all these difficulties, when retarded people have been allowed to express themselves freely, as in the series of weekend conferences sponsored by the Campaign for the Mentally Handicapped (1972–1975) in Britain or the We are People First Conferences in Oregon, USA, they have opted for independent living. One young lady featured in a film of the We are People First Conference of 1976 said: 'I want to be my own person. I don't want someone looking over my shoulder.'

Mental retardation service agencies must involve retarded clients in the planning of services for their welfare. They know their own needs.

## USING GENERIC SOCIAL SERVICES

> The main stream of social work in America has not demonstrated a concern for retardation and its social implications commensurate with that given to other problem areas, or with the needs of this client group. (Adams 1971)

Current thinking is that this alienation of retarded people from the rest of society should be brought to an end. One expression of this belief is that retarded and otherwise handicapped people and their families should use generic agencies wherever possible and seek specialized services only where necessary. Relegation of retarded clients and their families to a specialized corner for services has tended to contribute to the social isolation of this group, supports the stereotype that retarded people are fundamentally different from other people, and limits the range of services available to them, leaving gaps in the provision.

Every family who approaches a counselling agency has a problem, concerning which the agency worker must inform himself, in order to be of help. Families of retarded people, and the bulk of mildly retarded persons themselves, are not much different from other clients. For the agency worker it is a matter of assisting the client to use his own strengths and the supports available in the community to reach an accommodation with his problem.

Care must be taken not to refer a vulnerable retarded person or his family to a generic agency which is not yet ready to accept the responsibility of serving them.

Some aspects of service still seem to call for a specialized approach, such as the counselling on sexuality described above, or finding the strengths in relatively severely handicapped people. Diagnosis and treatment of the mentally ill retarded person is perhaps another area of specialization. Integration of service to retarded people is sometimes accomplished by placing a social worker experienced in this field in the agency to function as a consultant to staff at least for a time; or the therapeutic team might function as consultant to the community agency.

## THE COMMUNITY SOCIAL WORKER AND MENTAL RETARDATION

The first part of this chapter outlined the role of the social worker as a member of the therapeutic team. This is the traditional role in relation to retarded people. Over the years, in response to pressure from parents' groups, specialized services for retarded children and adults were developed. In some areas social workers have specialized in working with retarded people and their families in institutions, and in community agencies, day nurseries, community residences or sheltered workshops.

We live, however, in changing times. New philosophies have emerged in the past 10–15 years which seek recognition of retarded or otherwise handicapped people as legitimate members of the community with the right to live in the community; they also seek to encourage more accepting attitudes in the community toward people who differ from the norm in any way. Again, it is the parent-centred voluntary groups who have pioneered and pressed for these changes. The social work role has been vitally affected by the move back to community living. New specialized jobs have been created on the one hand, for instance the hiring of protective service workers in some parts of the United States and Canada (see p. 245). On the other hand, social workers in the whole spectrum of generic agencies are being challenged to adapt their method of serving their clients to suit the needs of handicapped people now living in the community.

We will now discuss some of the recent changes in the philosophy and practice of working with retarded and otherwise handicapped people, in the light of their influence on the social worker's role.

*Phasing down of large institutions*

Until 10–15 years ago, it was generally thought in many parts of Canada and the United States (somewhat less so in Britain) that a wise and appropriate disposal of retarded people who could no longer be cared for at home was admission to an institution, which tended to be large and isolated from community living. There seemed to be no other alternative. Social work literature of the 1950s and early 60s shows that considerably more attention was given to the social work skills necessary to relieve parental guilt about institutionalizing a retarded family member than to the need for provision of suitable options and opportunities for the retarded person and his family in the community, or to the retarded person's rights as an individual and as a citizen.

In the 1960s there were several widely publicized exposés of neglect and malpractice in large institutions for the mentally retarded in the United States, exemplified by Blatt (1966) in his report of conditions in the Willowbrook and Belchertown State Hospitals. These reports stimulated a re-appraisal of the use of large institutions for retarded people, summed up in the report of the President's

Committee on Mental Retardation (1976), *Changing Patterns in Residential Services for the Mentally Retarded.* In Canada the major recommendation of the Williston Report (1971) was that large institutions in Ontario should be phased down in favour of community supports and services which would enable most retarded people to remain in the community, and enable many of the residents of large institutions to return to the community. This trend will be dealt with in more detail in Chapter 18.

It is now becoming generally recognized that the great majority of retarded persons do not need to be in an institution and, indeed, may be harmed by it. Retarded and otherwise handicapped people should remain in the community. Most can function in the community, utilizing the community supports and services available to all citizens to help them deal with community pressures. Others will need specialized services.

Planning for discharge into the community of residents of institutions who are ready for this change is a team undertaking within the institution, often in cooperation with a community-based discharge committee representing the community into which the individual will be discharged. Successful discharge depends upon the availability of a suitable array of community living and work plans.

Difficulties in adaptation can be expected when long-term institutionalized residents undertake to live in the community, simply in terms of culture shock. In spite of this there are many success stories, exemplified by the following letter written by a former resident who had spent many years in an institution for retarded people. After leaving the institution for a community group home she wrote:

[The group home] is different then any plase I have ever been. None of the staff has ever acted as if there better then us. They joine right in & help us. Like shopping for the right kind of clothes. They take us to Shopping Plassas & we look at all the different stores before we buy anything. We pick out what we like. They sugest if the couler or Price is what we want or is there anything eles we need morre. But it is up to us to say, buy ... I go to Bingos by my self. They do not stop me frome doing.

"I went out & got my own job which is just a crose the road ... I like it very much. I am no longer afraid to meet Pepole as I have been showen that I am just as good as the next persoin...

"I only wish that there was some how I could tell every one how I feel, as I was in (an institution) for over 24 years. I know how it use to be & how it is now.

"I have never felt so good & happy as I do now. I will close for now as I am going to the Store By My Slefe.

Yours truly,
Dora

Perhaps in the long run the most fruitful efforts will be those directed towards maintaining retarded people who are already in the community, through the development of community supports, thus avoiding the use of institutions wherever possible.

### Normalization and integration

During the past few years workers in the field of mental retardation have been using a recently manufactured word which has become increasingly important in discussion of planning for any type of handicap. The word is 'normalization'.

The normalization principle was developed in Denmark in 1959 by Bank-Mikkleson, and enlarged upon by Bengt Nirje of Sweden in 1969. The theory developed out of concern for institutionalized retarded people, living in an atmosphere of unvarying stereotyped routines. It is concerned with their need for growth-producing change, however handicapped they might be. The theory has been further elaborated by Nirje (1976). Wolfensberger (1972) carried this thinking several steps further. Retarded people, wherever they live, should indeed learn the normal rhythms of living, but he was also concerned about the *way* they were taught. He sees the normalization process as: 'The use of means which are as culturally normative as possible in order to establish, maintain, and support patterns of behaviour which are as culturally normative as possible.' Normalization does not mean ignoring the presence of mental retardation in an individual, and forcing 'normal' expectations upon him.

In lay terms normalization means, first, that retarded people should be brought up, trained and sustained in the community by the same means as are employed for the rest of the population. Living, school and working conditions should not separate retarded people from others in the community. Secondly, the behaviour patterns taught to, or acquired by, retarded people should be those which one would normally find among persons of the same age in the community—with regard to appearance, behaviour in public, earning one's living, self-care, leisure-time activities and so on.

Practical implications of the principle of normalization include the utilization of generic educational, employment, housing, recreational and other opportunities by retarded people in ways that will enhance their development and growth; the provision of a normal range of choices to retarded people; opportunities for physical and social integration into the life of the community; recognition of the dignity of risk; and interpretation of the human and legal rights and positive potentialities of retarded citizens to the general public and to specific groups in society.

A companion word for normalization is integration, which means, in this context, the integration of retarded and otherwise handicapped persons into the mainstream of community living, wherever possible.

It is necessary to temper enthusiasm with good sense. Rhoades and Browning (1977) observe that, improperly understood, pressure for 'normalized' behaviour can harass a retarded person. Thompson (1976) points out that some retarded persons will need a great deal of help and that institutions should not be abandoned until adequate community supports become available to take their place

Mentally retarded people display a wide range of degree of handicap, and cannot be planned for as a homogeneous group. However, there is a great deal of evidence that retarded people have been undervalued and their abilities have been underestimated. The great majority can, and do, manage in the community with support.

More study is needed to determine the most useful kinds of support needed by severely handicapped people, especially those who are without families. Individuals displaying severe behaviour problems, including trouble with the law, also need special consideration. What degree of support and protection should be extended to a retarded individual who engages in behaviour which is destructive to him, such as excessive drinking or promiscuity, when he sees others about him indulging in the same behaviour? Experience has shown that a relatively small proportion of retarded people will experience major problems in community living on their own, while others will be more successful than was anticipated.

It is important to remember that the potential for adjustment to community living is an individual matter, and that the majority of retarded people are only mildly handicapped.

## Generic services

One logical outcome of this kind of reasoning is that wherever possible, retarded people should be served by generic agencies, as members of the general public. Many of these agencies, including psychiatric services, have a history of 'screening out' retarded applicants for their services on the grounds that they cannot benefit from insight therapy. It is now suggested that such services work towards adjusting their methods and their expectations in order to successfully serve mildly retarded people, who make up the great majority of the retarded population.

## Specialized community supports

As has been noted above, the term 'mental retardation' is applied to a wide range of degree of handicap, from those few at one end of the spectrum who need every sort of care, to the mildly affected individual who carries an almost invisible handicap at the other. At the risk of contradiction, we make a plea for a place in society for the majority of retarded people and also for specialized training and supports to assist the more handicapped to live comfortably in the community.

A recent study by Lambert and Bowman (1977) demonstrated that there are major lacks of continuity in services for retarded adults in Ontario, Canada—an area which might seem relatively well served. Many graduates from special schools and classes for retarded people dropped out of sight upon graduation, not into sheltered workshops, not to jobs, but simply to sit at home or live in isolated and impoverished circumstances. Less than one in five received help from any professional

person. Those who are concerned for the right of retarded people to live in the community need to be concerned about the quality of life there. Surely the 'rightful place' of a retarded or otherwise handicapped citizen is not at the bottom of the social scale, in poverty!

Specialized community supports in the UK and North America for retarded people in the community include the following:

*Community accommodation options.* These range from group homes to a variety of individual living plans in apartments and boarding homes, with varying degrees of supervision. Some accommodation plans are temporary, for training in social skills. Others are long-term. Adoption and foster homes may be considered as appropriate options for children and adolescents.

*Vocational placements.* These include sheltered or training workshops, supervised work stations in industry, on-the-job training, and subsidized or specialized businesses.

*Help from individuals in the community.* Protective service workers or family support workers: In some areas of Canada and the United States, young people are hired by government to offer community-based support to adult retarded citizens in need of help, or to families with young retarded members.

Citizen advocacy programmes in Canada and the United States: In these programmes an interested volunteer is matched with a retarded adult seeking this service. The 'advocate' takes an intense and friendly interest in his 'protégé', and when necessary, seeks to represent the retarded person's interests as though they were his own. Social workers frequently undertake the matching of advocate and protégé, and offer back-up support. (See Wolfensberger & Zauha 1973.)

In the United Kingdom individualized help may be provided by local authority social services.

*A centralized planning and referral service.* This is desirable within a manageable area, to plan for the specific needs of that area and prevent gaps and overlaps in services, and to try to prevent retarded individuals from becoming lost among available services. Social work agencies and other appropriate services are usually involved.

*Financial support.* This enables a family with a severely retarded child in the home to pay for domestic help and special aids or equipment. A means test is usually involved.

## Public education and public awareness

Community living for significantly handicapped people cannot succeed without public acceptance and support. A great number of mildly handicapped people have always lived in the community, but people who display noticeable differences from the norm may meet rejection.

Elkin (1976) in a study carried out in Saskatchewan, Canada, discovered severe problems in the attitude of the general public towards retarded people, which would militate against successful integration. Answers to questions designed to elicit attitudes made it clear that public expectation of the capabilities of retarded persons was very low. When respondents were invited to consider a retarded person being placed near or close to them, they became less enthusiastic. They did not want a retarded person living next to them or working beside them. All the changing and adapting seemed to be required of the retarded person, and little of the rest of the population.

## CHALLENGES AHEAD

Traditionally, social workers have been interested in supporting the rights of disadvantaged people, including retarded and otherwise handicapped persons. Many are convinced that the majority of handicapped people belong in the community as part of the citizen body, with community supports and services appropriate to their needs. A sizeable group of citizens including some social workers and other professionals do not see this step as a natural consequence of a belief in the handicapped person's rights as a citizen. Some of the areas for further work to bring about a better understanding would seem to include the following:

1. Promotion of the idea of community living for retarded people. Their problems do not require that they be shut away. Their rights as citizens demand the provision of alternatives.

2. Generic services should equip themselves to serve handicapped people. Specialized services should be used only where necessary. Care must be taken not to withdraw a specialized service before the generic service is ready.

3. A comprehensive service and support system should be developed in the community to assure continuity of service, and to assist handicapped people to obtain needed services.

4. Retarded persons and their families must be included in the planning and execution of services for them. Social workers are well placed as advocates for retarded people to bring this about.

5. Innovative programmes should be developed for severely handicapped persons in the community.

6. Experimentation in industry and commerce should be encouraged, to pinpoint jobs which could be performed by retarded or otherwise handicapped people.

7. Prevention of preventable mental retardation and other handicaps should be a priority in public health systems. Social workers should be interested in identifying at-risk pregnancies and young children in their work load, and obtaining help for them.

This list of challenges is not exhaustive. Planning for retarded people was simpler in the safe and silent days of the relatively indiscriminate use of large institutions. Once the retarded person was seen as a fellow citizen with all the rights of citizenship, it became necessary to work towards securing a place in the community for him.

Involved as the profession is with pressing problems, social workers can be in danger of failing to take advantage of opportunities to bring about social change. Social workers, together with members of other professions, parent associations and the retarded people themselves, should become involved in political action to return these citizens to their rightful place in society. These changes will not be easily achieved, and continued vigilance is necessary.

BIBLIOGRAPHY

Adams, M. (1971) *Mental Retardation and Its Social Dimensions*. New York: Columbia University Press.

Bayley, M. (1973) *Mental Handicap and Community Care: A Study of Mentally Handicapped People in Sheffield*. London: Routledge & Kegan Paul.

Blatt, B. (1966) *Christmas in Purgatory*. Boston: Allyn & Bacon.

Boyd, D. (1950) *The Three Stages in the Growth of a Parent of a Mentally Retarded Child*. New York: National Association for Retarded Citizens, Inc.

Campaign for the Mentally Handicapped, Conference Reports: *Our Life* (1972), *Listen* (1973), *Participation* (1974), *Working Out* (1975). 96 Portland Place, London W1.

Department of Health and Social Security and Welsh Office (1971) *Better Services for the Mentally Handicapped*. Cmnd. 4683. London: HMSO.

Edgerton, R. B. (1967) *The Cloak of Competence*. Berkeley: University of California Press.

Edgerton, R. B. & Bercovici, S. M. (1976) The cloak of competence: years later. *Am. J. ment. Defic.*, *80*, 5, 485–97.

Elkin, L. (1976) *A Question of Rights*. 229 Lansing Street, Moose Jaw, Saskatchewan, Canada.

Heber, R., Garber, H., Harrington, S., Hoffman, C. & Falender, C. (1972) *Rehabilitation of Families at Risk for Mental Retardation*. Madison: University of Wisconsin.

HMSO (1968) *Report of The Committee on Local Authority and Allied Personal Social Services*. Cmnd. 3703. London.

Lambert, C. & Bowman, K. (1977) *Program Planning for Retarded Adults*. Ontario Association for the Mentally Retarded, 1373 Bayview Avenue, Toronto, Ontario, Canada.

*Letter from Dora*—available with Dora's permission from the Ontario Association for the Mentally Retarded (see above).

Nirje, B. (1976) The normalization principle. In: The President's Committee on Mental Retardation, *Changing Patterns in Residential Services for the Mentally Retarded*, revised ed., Washington D.C.

Olshansky, S. (1970) Chronic sorrow: a response to having a mentally retarded child. In: Schreiber, M. (ed.), *Social Work and Mental Retardation*. New York: The John Day Company.

Patterson, L. L. (1956) Some Pointers for Professionals. *Children 1*, 3, 13–17. US Dept. of Health, Education and Welfare, US Government Printing Office, Div. of Public Documents, Washington D.C.

President's Committee on Mental Retardation (1976) *Changing Patterns in Residential Services for the Mentally Retarded*, revised ed. Washington D.C.

Rhoades, C. & Browning, P. (1977) Normalization at what price? *Mental Retardation*, *15*, 2, 24.

Schreiber, M. & Feeley, M. (1970) Siblings of the retarded: a guided group experience. In: Schreiber, M. (ed.), *Social Work and Mental Retardation*. New York: The John Day Company.

Thompson, C. R. (1976) Social work and interdisciplinary case discussions. In: Johnston, R. B. & Magrab, P. R. (eds.), *Developmental Disorders: Assessment, Treatment, Education*. Baltimore: University Park Press.

*We are People First of Oregon* (1975) (brochure). PO Box 5208, Salem, Oregon, USA.

Williston, W. B. (1971) *Present Arrangements for the Care and Supervision of Mentally Retarded Persons in Ontario*. Ontario Division of Health.

Wolfensberger, W. (1972) *Normalization—The Principle of Normalization in Human Services*. Toronto: National Institute on Mental Retardation.

Wolfensberger, W. & Menolascino, F. J. (1970) A theoretical framework for the management of parents of the mentally retarded. In: Menolascino, F. J. (ed.), *Psychiatric Approaches to Mental Retardation*. New York: Basic Books.

Wolfensberger, W. & Zauha, H. (1973) *Citizen Advocacy and Protective Services for the Impaired and Handicapped*. Toronto: National Institute on Mental Retardation.

[*also recommended*] Begab, M. J. & Richardson, S. A. (eds.) (1975) *The Mentally Retarded and Society: A Social Science Perspective*. Baltimore: University Park Press.

# CHAPTER 18

# RESIDENTIAL CARE

## MALCOLM SAVAGE

The roots of present residential services in western society rest in the developments that have occurred in the past 150 years. In the first decades of the nineteenth century, mental retardation began to be recognized as a specific state of man, and for the first time, specialized services began to develop. Early programmes represented an attempt to cure the condition, and concentrated on offering education and training. Since their aim was high, these early developments were thought to have failed, and the era of large institutions began. These were a particular feature of Victorian society, and were developed for many other deviant groups as well as for the mentally retarded. The particular feature of these institutions was that the residents carried out all their day-to-day activities within the walls of the institution and were not expected to return to community living, as had the individuals involved in the earlier training centres. Such institutions have continued to be a part of services up until the present day and their development in North America has tended to follow that of Western Europe with a distinct time lag of about twenty-five years. Wolfensberger (1976) has traced the dynamic developments in institutional care over the past century and has related these to the many changes that have occurred in attitudes towards the mentally retarded.

After the Second World War, a new wave of activity began throughout the western world and led to the development of community-based services for the mentally retarded and other handicapped persons.

Within these new service networks, residential care was offered as a specific programme entity, thus distinguishing this system from the previous institutional programmes where residential care was a necessary prerequisite for a person to qualify for the other institutional education and training activities.

Most western countries now have a range of residential facilities, some small, some large. The quality of care varies greatly, but there has fortunately been an increasing awareness of the relationships between institutional structure, size, method of caring and the resultant quality of life. Goffman (1961) revealed the general nature of large institutions which he defined as 'total institutions' that, to varying degrees, tended to be dehumanizing and resistant to involvement and change. King et al. (1971) and Tizard et al. (1975) have examined the patterns of child care and administrative organization involved in a number of children's residential services in the United Kingdom whilst Vail (1966) described the dehumanizing effect which he found in many institutions in North America. Klaber (1966) examined a number of institutions in the United States and attempted to evaluate their care, often with confusing results. For example, in his sample, the oldest most inefficient institution was found to have the most self-sufficient and happiest residents!

Whilst the present pattern of residential provisions in many countries demonstrates a patchwork of various poorly related services, there are changes occurring within larger institutions. Braddock (1977) gives statistics indicating that in many parts of the United States, institutional size is decreasing, and the number of community group homes is increasing. Despite this trend, he indicates that the total number of persons in institutions is still increasing, and Scheerenberger (1976a and b) indicates that of 167 institutions surveyed in the United States, 20 per cent were still increasing in size.

## TYPES OF RESIDENTIAL FACILITIES

Existing residential facilities demonstrate a number of different organizational structures, with considerable variation in size and form. The large institutions continue to survive in most countries except in those where service development is recent and where there was no inheritance of old structures and systems from the nineteenth century.

The particular features of such institutions are their size, which may vary from 500 to 5000 residents, and the fact that all offer a multiplicity of care and training programmes. Such programmes are residentially based, and will frequently be designed to cover the whole range of needs of the retarded. Thus they will have educational and rehabilitation programmes as well as medical and nursing services for the more severely handicapped. These large institutions are most frequently divided into smaller administrative units or sub-hospitals in order to obtain greater efficiency and more effective personalized programming. Despite the many efforts to reorganize such structures, the large institutions continue to have great difficulty in offering effective services, because of their size, isolation and the complexity of their administrative structure.

A second type of institution can also be found in some countries. These are smaller in size, often with between 200 and 500 residents. Their development results from recent attempts to find a more efficient form of service, although still based on the old concept of multiple programmes within the same structure. This type of institution will usually have a unified administration, a smaller range of professional services, and a far less complex bureaucratic structure. However, it is doubtful if such institutions offer much of an improvement over the older structure, and they in fact represent an adaptation of an outdated system, rather than a new development.

A third form of institutional care is also found in many countries. These are the nursing homes and special care units that have been developed for specific groups of the mentally retarded, usually for severely handicapped children and adults. They vary in size from 25 to 100 residents, and were developed to offer specialized services. Normally they lack professional staff and have simplified organizational structures. Facilities of this type can be effective, but often insufficient emphasis has been given to the quality of care, and to the importance of integrating such facilities into the complete service network. Too easily, they can exist in isolation from the mainstream of other community services, and if this happens, the quality of care offered may deteriorate.

A fourth form of residential service includes group homes, residences, hostels and half-way houses which have developed in recent years. Their main feature is their small size and they offer residential care as part of a network of services so that the residents will go out to school or work, and for recreation. With this basic form, many of the drawbacks found in the large institutions are avoided, and a more normal life style is possible for the residents. It must not be thought, however, that these small units are the complete answer to the problem of the provision of residential care. There has to be a great deal of emphasis on staff training and education, and provision of a range of consultant and supervisory services from outside has to be well organized. A small group home can also become isolated and is particularly vulnerable to becoming ingrown and over-protective of its residents.

The last form of residential care is what has become known in the United States as 'alternatives to residential care'. With the development of more comprehensive community support programmes for handicapped adults, and for families with handicapped children, it is now possible to develop foster homes, boarding homes and supervised apartment living as viable alternatives to other more complex structures. These developments are exciting because they offer a style of life within the normal structure of society and avoid grouping large numbers of the handicapped together. In such a system of care, quality of staff, supervision and coordination of services become very important, as well as a need for flexibility so that the needs of individuals can be met without having to battle with an entrenched bureaucracy.

## THE SOCIAL WORKER AND RESIDENTIAL CARE

Within the large variety of residential services, the role of the social worker will vary considerably. The large institution has a very complex administrative structure, composed of sub-hospital units and also of professional departments. Unfortunately the situation becomes more complex with the modern emphasis on individual programme planning, and with the introduction of greater numbers of professional staff. With this increased complexity, more and more energy goes into maintaining the bureaucratic structure which inevitably leaves fewer resources for programme development. The social worker in such a setting will frequently be much concerned with encouraging staff cooperation and coordination to assist in effective programme planning for individual residents and their families, particularly at times of admission and discharge. Considerable effort also has to be expended on achieving coordination with community-based programmes. Relationships with residential care staff are most important, but can be difficult to achieve beacuse of the complex administration, departmental rivalries and physical remoteness.

In the small single unit institutions, the less complex structure usually allows for more time to be spent on programme planning and for direct work with clients. The social worker is more likely to achieve a satisfactory working relationship with a small functioning team of professional and non-professional staff without the divided loyalties of the larger institutions. A major difficulty remains the remoteness of the organization from the community which it serves.

Smaller community institutions and group living facilities are unlikely to have social workers on their staff, and most commonly the social worker is employed in a consultant or supervisory capacity or as part of the community-based services. A network of community-based social workers can provide support to retarded persons who live in the mainstream of society, and can assist individual clients to use appropriate programmes and services, whilst at the same time assisting services to understand clients' needs, and to design programmes to meet them.

The whole question of the relationship of social work staff to direct care staff is most important, particularly if one is concerned with the quality of services to the resident and his family. In large centres, direct care staff have often been seen more as nursing staff, and they appear to have little in common with social workers in their training and priorities for care. Thus in some large institutions one can still find the direct care staff more concerned about cleanliness and clothing, than about whether the resident is happy and well adjusted. As one parent recently complained, 'I just don't know how the staff could be so busy in the ward with my daughter, and not realize that she can communicate well, and can say when she needs the toilet. They were treating her like a little child who was incapable.' This kind of criticism is often expressed to social workers by parents and only the cooperation between care staff, parent and social worker can achieve the understanding necessary to avoid such unfortunate occurrences, and to establish common goals for staff, families and residents.

Within smaller community facilities, the

direct care staff do not regard themselves as nursing staff. Their experience, and sometimes training, usually gives them much in common with social work staff. They are likely to have a more personal involvement with the residents, and also to have a more intimate relationship with families and with the staff of social resources and training programmes. The outside social worker will often be more of a consultant, assisting in care planning, and in direct counselling in situations where more intensive involvement is necessary. The social worker will also have skills to offer in helping the staff achieve harmonious relationships with the neighbours and their communities. Specialized training programmes for the staff of group homes for the mentally retarded have been slow to arise, but hopefully, in time, will be developed along the lines of the training programmes for child care workers and staff of other children's group homes. Such programmes usually include courses in understanding individual needs, family dynamics and the organization of community services. Their development would undoubtedly assist in achieving a better level of programming and greater appreciation of realistic goals for residential care.

## THE ROLE OF THE SOCIAL WORKER

The social worker will usually work in association with other professional staff; sometimes when the relationship is close, the term *team work* is used. In other circumstances *collaboration* is the more appropriate term used to describe a less structured working relationship. In any service system a number of tasks must be carried out in order to give an effective service. Attempts are usually made to assign tasks to specific members of staff, on the basis of their training, experience and effectiveness. The difficulties occur in the areas of service where different staff share common expertise. Solutions to this kind of team organizational problem range from prescription to mutual consensus. When describing the typical roles of social workers it has to be recognized that rigid boundaries do not exist, and that in some settings tasks may be carried by other staff. In these circumstances the social worker may not carry out the tasks, but should see that they are completed by an appropriate member of the collaborating group.

A further complication of any discussion of the social worker's role in relation to residential units is the nature of the organizational structure. If social work services are organized in the community on a generic basis, this can lead to organizational distance between the residential units and the workers involved in the generic services. Problems of inaccessibility and communication will often result, and considerable attention has to be given to coordination of the two areas of service. In some North American districts there are specialist community-based social workers who visit residential units from an area-based service. In others, the social workers are institutionally based, and will often have considerable difficulties coordinating with community services which may serve overlapping geographical areas and use different criteria for admission to their facilities.

It is to be hoped that in the future there will be better planning of comprehensive community-based services, so that residential services are clearly related to all other services for the mentally retarded. If this is achieved, coordination becomes a necessary concern of the whole system and would not then be assigned to any particular social worker.

The tasks carried out by social workers fall into a number of broad areas. Firstly those of a *concrete* nature will involve arranging pre-admission visits, assisting families to relate to services and forming the supportive relationships involved in finding accommodation or work. Secondly there are tasks related to particular individuals and families with demonstrated needs, which may take the form of advocacy, or casework using skills in social diagnosis, case planning and various methods of counselling. Thirdly there are tasks related to *communication* and effective collaboration with colleagues and agencies. Finally there are tasks related to *administration* such as the development of policies,

programmes and services, staff development, education, community awareness,
consultations, supervision and research.
Obviously the functions of social workers
will, to a large extent, depend upon the
nature of the setting in which they work.
In large institutions there will be a greater
emphasis on roles related to administration,
communication, internal coordination and
community liaison. In small community
units the emphasis is more likely to be on
programme supervision and counselling.

## PLANNING FOR RESIDENTIAL CARE

At one time, admission to a residential service for the mentally retarded was the only
means of obtaining service for the individual. That necessitated a child or adult
leaving the protection of his family, which
clearly represented a dilemma for many
parents. This is still largely true for a few
North American areas, but is probably not
so in Scandinavia and other Western European countries. Now that there are, in
most communities, some services which
relate to the needs of individuals who
reside within those communities, residential
services have become more specialized.
Kugel (1976) discusses the current needs
for residential care in the United States,
and considers four main groups of retarded
persons who require care:

> Those with difficult or objectional
> behaviour.
> Those with severe physical impair-
> ment.
> Those who have committed major
> crimes.
> Those from a background of poverty.

He appears, however, to have overlooked
the fact that there are now a large group
of mentally retarded adults who have been
the recipients of community services, and
who have developed the capacity to live in
some degree of independence from their
family of origin. Many may be able to
reside in apartments or boarding homes,

others may need hostels or community
group homes. It is clear that they represent a large number of our retarded
citizens, and that services must continue to
develop a variety of living options to meet
their needs. At last there is now a possibility that parents do not have to fear the
unknown future expressed by them as
'what will happen when I die?' In many
countries we are facing a major change in
philosophy involving a recognition of the
rights and needs of our mentally retarded
adult citizens, particularly the right to live
in their own communities with comfort
and decency.

Given the variety of training, educational
and vocational programmes now operating
in many Western countries, a variety of
residential services will be necessary to
meet the needs of children and adults.
Firstly, there should be counselling and
advocacy staff who can offer continued
support to those who either continue to
live with their families, or who are able to
live independently in their own communities. Secondly, there should be group living facilities which can offer a secure home
for those who can stay in their own communities, but who are unable to continue
to live with their families or to live on
their own.

Those for whom there are no suitable
training, educational or vocational programmes within their own communities,
will need residential provisions which are
available in conjunction with such specially
organized programmes. For example, a
child may require a specialized educational
programme and may need to move to
another city where there is a suitable class.
Provision has to be made for him to live
in that city, hopefully with the opportunity
of returning to his family at weekends.
This form of service is particularly applicable to countries with sparse rural populations, such as Western Canada. It is probably not necessary for the residential and
training programmes to be offered under
the same roof.

Another distinct type of residential programme is that which offers training in independent or community living. Some
adults who have been sheltered in their

own families or in institutions will need special residential programmes which can offer them training and experience, and assist them to achieve their maximum potential for independence.

There may also be a need for a small number of specialized residential programmes which give training as well as offering residential care. Such a facility will offer highly specialized programming which cannot be obtained in a community setting because of the particular client's needs, or because of the scarcity of highly trained staff. Examples may be programmes for some multiply handicapped children and adults, programmes for the retarded who are in conflict with the law, programmes for those who have severe behavioural problems, and programmes for those who have special vocational training needs, most particularly when these are associated with behavioural difficulties.

When a family has difficulty in providing care for a mentally retarded member, the prospect of seeking care outside the family group may provoke anxiety, often accompanied by feelings of guilt and failure. It is necessary, therefore, that the professional staff discuss the question of residential care with an understanding of the parents' feelings. It is all too easy for the outside observer to see the difficulties that may exist within a family and in his anxiety to help resolve the problems, the principles of good counselling can be easily forgotten.

Frequently it is the task of the social worker to assist the family to resolve their dilemma. This requires that a residential care facility has contacts with families long before any decision about admission is made. Admission to a residential unit should only be planned after a comprehensive assessment of the retarded person's needs, and a thorough exploration of other helping services within the community. If such an assessment reveals that residential care should be made available, the family and the retarded person must be immediately involved in a process enabling them to make a decision which they can live with, and not have to regret.

Parents do not want others to take over their problems, rather they require adequate and honest information which can help them reach a decision. It is necessary that they have an opportunity to visit residential facilities, meet the staff who provide care and find out enough about the facility to give them a clear picture of its functioning, particularly as to whether it will meet the needs of their family member. The social worker should be available to the parents so that they can express and discuss their impressions and their concerns. If it is possible, they should be helped to meet other parents who are either struggling with similar decisions or who have come through the same agonizing process.

Probably all parents fear 'giving up' their children, because they too easily see it as a result of their own failure as parents. Their decision to request admission for a family member can be made immeasurably easier if they can see the future care of their child as a shared responsibility where parents and residential staff have complementary roles, and can feel they are not abandoning the responsibilities of parenthood.

When adults are the persons for whom admission is considered, then they too must be involved in the admission process, so that they can participate in the decision and not feel abandoned or rejected by their families.

THE PROCESS OF ADMISSION

Families should be given time to come to terms with their feelings about the admission of a family member. Crisis action should be kept to a minimum and used only when the immediate family circumstances indicate it is necessary. How difficult it must be for parents to have to wait for months or years for a suitable vacancy and then be given only a few days notice that the vacancy is there. Undoubtedly, sensitive pre-admission planning can make it much easier for a family, and for the individual who is having to enter the new world of a residential facility.

Unfortunately, the problems of family and institutional relationships do not end here. Skarnulis (1977) has pointed out clearly how the institution's and the families' needs are often polarized, leading to feelings of alienation and abandonment which he calls a 'cycle of conflict'. How often are parents still told that they should not visit their child in the first weeks 'so that he can settle down'? As one parent stated; 'When my son was admitted, I felt that I should visit often and I was really angry when I was told not to visit for the first month. I felt that I was not needed anymore.' Many paediatric hospitals and units encourage mothers to stay with younger children. Why do so many institutions still practise the opposite policy?

Social workers and other members of staff should ensure that they use the parental contacts at the time of admission as an opportunity for parents and children to deal with their feelings. Long history-taking should be avoided, and in any case there is no reason why such data could not be obtained at an earlier time.

Parents need to see where their family member is going to live and sleep, and will feel far more satisfied if they can have personal contact with the care and programme staff. How helpful it can be when staff are concerned enough to telephone parents at home to tell them how their child is progressing. The social worker should ensure that parents do have such personal contacts and they should be careful never to stand between parents and staff.

Unfortunately many hospitals and residential centres do not take such care, and subsequently another polarization can occur. Just at the point when parents have adjusted to life without the family member in their home, the institution will begin to demand contacts and visiting in a manner which fits their perception of the needs. A father put his reaction to this very concisely; 'When my son was admitted they did not want me around and tried to get rid of me as quickly as possible. Now they want me to go at their convenience in the middle of the day and I am in a trap because if I don't turn up they will say that I am not interested.'

The importance of the relationship between the staff of residential facilities and the families of the residents cannot be over-emphasized. Policies should be clearly worked out, and staff should always be on the alert to the difficulties that continually occur. Residential centres should see their role as one of assisting families to care for their family members, and must beware of the paternalism of the Victorian institution. It is less than ten years since the brass plate was removed from the door of one Ontario institution. It said 'Visiting Day, the First Sunday of the Month'.

## THE PERIOD OF ADMISSION

The early weeks are difficult for the residential staff. They receive strangers into their unit, must get to know them and then work out a programme to meet their needs. A large number of people are often involved in this process. Social workers will usually participate by contributing the information gained by their contacts with the other family members and with community programmes. All too often assessment teams are proficient at completing this task, whilst the programmes developed are not as well worked out. Even more frequently, the results are not shared with either the resident or his family. Too often one still hears that old institutional cry, 'nobody tells me anything!'

Individuals and families must be involved in programme planning, and in some centres are actively involved as participants in the case-planning process. Community programme personnel should also be involved in the same manner since they may have intimate knowledge of individual needs, and may also be involved in later community placement plans.

There should be a clear understanding by all parties as to the needs of the resident, the roles of staff, families and community services. Parents and residents alike must also be aware of their rights, and should feel comfortable in their personal relationships with staff and with the patterns of communication that are set up. Difficulties in this area are not unique to large institutions. One parent of a resident of an Australian group home writes 'The communication problem is not solved by the independent living situation.' Parents need to be able to communicate with staff, and to have opportunities to discuss values implicit in the operation of the residence (van Pelt 1977).

In residential facilities which undertake long-term care, there is the additional difficulty for residents caused by the illness and death of their parents. Such persons can feel abandoned and neglected without the stimulation which they used to receive from their parents' visits, and from holidays with their families. Attention has to be given to such situations, so that the interest of other family members, relatives or volunteers is maintained. A healthy residential centre is one that has a continual interaction with its community, with personal visitors for all its residents. Some large institutions have schemes for 'foster grandparents' in order to combat the lack of personal human contact. Such schemes encourage senior citizens who have love to spare, to visit severely handicapped residents who are often so much in need of personal contact and interest.

## PLANNING FOR DISCHARGE

The manner of discharge planning is set by the whole tone of the residential centre, particularly by the way that it deals with admissions. This is summed up by that common phrase 'discharge begins at admission'. Discharge planning presents few problems for a centre which has a clear purpose, well thought-out programme planning, clear residents' rights and continuous relationships with both the families of its residents and its community agencies. The problems of discharge planning arise mainly from unilateral action. When an administration sets forth on a programme to reduce the size of an institution, it will eventually meet with resistance in those other parts of the system that have no investment in the plan. Staff, parents and community will almost inevitably take a stance of opposition. If a family unilaterally decide to take their child home,

then resistance will often come from administration and programme personnel. If a resident takes the action into his own hands it is often labelled 'absconding' or 'discharge against medical or professional advice'. Likewise if the social worker is seen to be the initiator of discharges, the resistance will occur in many other parts of the system, and in fact, social workers are often regarded as scapegoats because of the failure of the system to work smoothly.

It should go without saying that discharge should be the ultimate step for as many residents as possible, who have been participants in the programmes set up to meet their needs and to foster their independence. The success of such plans will always depend upon the participation of the resident, his family, the care and programme staff, the professional staff, community agencies and the administration. The social worker may have many roles to play throughout the process, but most frequently works in the area of cooperation with the resident's family, and in finding and liaising with appropriate community resources.

## AFTER DISCHARGE

When an individual resident returns to live in the community, special services are necessary in the period of transition. This responsibility most commonly falls on social work staff, who should have been participants in previous planning processes. In many large institutions the social worker will go out from the institution to give support and counselling, although in other centres it may be the responsibility of community-based workers who liaise with the institution. Community-based support and counselling services should always be available, as it is clearly preferable that they be situated within the community provided there is a close liaison with the residential facilities.

The existence of such services makes good discharge planning much more effective, but does not decrease the responsibility of residential centres to make good programmes and planning available to its residents.

## DILEMMAS OF THE RESIDENTIAL
## SOCIAL WORKER

There are many difficulties inherent in the roles that are frequently assumed by social workers in residential settings. It is necessary that these difficulties be understood by all staff if there is to be harmony and good working relationships. In order to know families, communities and community services, it is necessary for the worker to be physically present in the community, away from the residential centre. Frequently other staff will say that 'you should be out there and not sitting behind a desk'. Unfortunately, it is often the same staff who also say 'but you are never here when we want you'. The majority of the other staff at a residential centre are engaged in tasks that require them to be in the centre, and are often unaware of the dilemmas that the social worker faces.

Another dilemma is of a similar, but more serious nature. The social worker is frequently in contact with parents, social agencies, parents' associations and other groups involved in community-based services. Not only will such workers be involved in discussing other people's viewpoints of the residential centre, but they will also be the recipients of adverse criticisms and comments. Since they are bound to perceive the institution as being one of a number of community services, it is almost inevitable that they will come into conflict with the residential staff who rarely leave the centre, who never meet parents and other agencies, and who, as a result, often develop an increasing myopia seeing the residential facility as the central and most important component of services to the mentally retarded.

The problems are compounded with the complexity of communication networks in large institutions, where staff work rotating shifts. It is no wonder that social workers are often caught between institutional staff who see them as traitors, and community agencies or families who take out their wrath on them, because of service inefficiencies. It is also common in these times when many institutions are decreas-

ing in size, for the residential staff to feel that their careers are threatened. It is not surprising that social workers are seen as the cause of the difficulty since they are frequently involved in planning the discharges which lead to the reduction in size.

These difficulties are inherent in the social worker's role in large institutions. The impact can be lessened if there is an understanding administration, which encourages a community awareness within the organization. It would be ideal if all administrative, professional and programme staff could be involved in community programmes, which would assist in keeping a balanced perspective. Social workers themselves can help if they encourage two-way communication between communities and residential centres. They should also ensure that community and parental contacts are available to as many staff as possible at all levels in the organization structure.

## DILEMMAS OF RESIDENTIAL
## SERVICES

Present residential services have their origins in two very different philosophies. On the one hand, large institutions still survive with their developing programmes and various attempts to reduce size and reach out into their communities. On the other hand, there are an increasing number of small residential services, often developed out of community needs by community groups.

These two aspects of residential care present a dilemma to government, to staff, to parents and to communities. Attempts at integration into one service network have met with varying degrees of success. Governments continue to fund both, without always thinking through the effects of developing services from this polarized situation.

Parent groups are often themselves divided. Whilst some parents call vociferously for the abolition of large institutions, others remain suspicious of the new developments and prefer to call for the modernization of old institutions and the building of smaller new institutions. These parents appear to prefer the security offered by the larger structures which they see as more likely to survive the vicissitudes of government funding and policy changes.

The older institutions inherited many features from previous generations which make it difficult for them to adapt to modern service patterns. Many still occupy old outdated buildings. In recent years there have been many efforts to increase the efficiency of their organization, but the results have been disappointing. The larger institutions have a very complex pattern of department and unit organization with consequent bureaucratic and communication complexities. Their size alone makes it impossible to produce the individualized humanitarian services which the community has come to expect. They are often in relatively isolated rural communities, which means that they can never be well integrated with the services of the metropolitan areas that they were designed to serve. In recent years most have greatly improved their staff complements, and have also employed greater numbers of qualified professionals. Unfortunately, they remain largely cut off from the mainstream of services, which encourages a form of institutional paranoia. Institutional staff frequently feel isolated from their colleagues in other services, and feel that their views are ignored, and that they, themselves, are treated as second-class citizens in the professional community. Their knowledge of programming, developed particularly in the services of the severely handicapped, is often ignored and they are rarely consulted by those designing and setting up new programmes.

Staff in community facilities have tended to regard all institutions as bad, ignoring the writing of the Clarkes (1976) and others revealing that even large institutions can be better than 'bad' homes. When developing new provisions, planning groups ignore the roles that the large institutions have continued to perform. Community residential facilities have been developed most frequently for the mildly and moderately retarded, and very few have been designed for the more severely handicapped with physical and emotional prob-

lems. In addition, the overall development of alternative community living facilities has been painfully slow. Braddock (1977) reveals that in 1973 there were still only 374 Community Residences in the United States. More hopeful is his finding that an increasing number are being opened each year. These residences are small group living facilities, situated in the community and operated either by community groups, or by governments that are committed to community-based services. However, facilities now in existence would only service the population of one moderate sized institution. Isolation, poor programming and inadequate staff training are not the prerogative of the large institution. Some of the newer units have failed to learn the lessons of their predecessors. This is clearly illustrated by such authors as Murphy (1972) who points out there are 'Back Wards' in small group living facilities as much as in big institutions.

In the meantime, institutions continue to survive. In the United Kingdom and Canada, they have been subject to frequent public enquiries and scandals lowering their public image and their often already low staff morale. In the United States there have been an increasing number of court actions which have established the rights of the residents to receive treatment according to their needs. This has brought great pressure to bear on governments and administrations. Yet the institutions continue to care for large numbers of severely and profoundly retarded children and adults, whose needs others have largely ignored. Much remains to be done, and ways have to be found to develop an effective framework for a network of residential services that can serve community needs and make optimum use of available resources of money and staff.

Community alternatives to institutional care have developed only very slowly, and if governments await the initiative of the community groups, a patchwork of provisions which do not offer service equally to all populations will tend to develop. There is continuing questioning as to standards and staffing. Tinsley et al. (1973) discuss many of the unanswered questions concerning the development of community residences. In most countries the answers have been slow to emerge.

Skarnulis (1977) and others involved in the Eastern Nebraska Office of Retardation (ENCOR) describe the development of Alternative Living Units relating to a 'core' unit together making a residential programme. By this means care has been provided for very small groups of severely and profoundly retarded children and adults without the need for larger residential units. In refusing to accept the 'residential assumption' they have developed hand in hand with other educational and training programmes. Unfortunately few areas have had the courage to initiate such schemes because of the difficulties in changing existing inefficient and often ineffective provisions.

## THE FUTURE OF RESIDENTIAL CARE

We now know so much more than those early pioneers of the nineteenth century, and yet many of the principles that they expressed are valid today. We know that the vast majority of mentally retarded persons do progress and can develop skills which enable them to participate in community life, even though many may never develop complete independence. We know that training and educational programmes must be based on the needs of each individual and since the vast majority have always remained in the community, these programmes must be closely related to family life and other community services.

There is evidence from provisions such as those in Nebraska that even the most severely disturbed and handicapped can be served in small groups in a community setting. The problem is how to progress to this from the current position. Obviously large institutions will not disappear overnight, and reduction in size does not alone resolve the problem. Governments must face the serious political consequences of progress and initiate a planned process of change. Most institutions can reduce considerably in size, with their existing staff and facilities serving the resulting smaller

populations more effectively. However, this only defers the issue of what will happen when problems of over-staffing occur and staff redundancies must be faced.

Some way has to be found to utilize the budgets and staff of such institutions in a more dynamic way to enable a gradual changeover to alternative styles of living for the mentally retarded. The first necessity is for larger institutions to involve themselves in their communities, and reorganize their structures so that sub-units can offer services to specific small geographic communities. All levels of staff must be encouraged to relate to their colleagues who are already engaged in community settings, so that there develops a mutual respect and a shared responsibility for programme development. Out-patient, home management and day programmes should develop which use the expertise of staff, and which can draw on the resources of the institution. Particular emphasis must be given to the development of specialized technology for low-incidence categories of the severely handicapped. At initial stages such training programmes may take place in the institution, but the aim should always be that the participants move to community residential units so that true integration of service is achieved. Residential care staff must be utilized in such training programmes and must also be encouraged to participate in day care if the past polarization of service is to be destroyed.

Staff of existing community units must also seriously examine their own beliefs and systems. Small size is not of itself a golden answer to service effectiveness. More recognition has to be given to family support programmes which provide the direct help that a family requires and not just what rigid services dictate it should need. Day programmes must develop in such a way that their existence is known in the community where they can be seen as being effective, and where the clients have an opportunity to be recognized as fellow citizens who should have equal rights and opportunities. Residential services must be closely related to all other community services; living units should be small scale so that they can be accepted by their neighbours in the community, and should be involved closely with the families of their residents. They should be less obvious than schools, vocational centres and other such training facilities, but all need to be closely linked so that supplementary resources are available to the living units and also to families who are supporting mentally retarded members within the family unit.

Service networks must be planned to meet the needs of limited-size populations, preferably of between 50 000 and 100 000 persons. Liaison and communication become very complex if the scale is larger. Planning must clearly be the responsibility of community groups with considerable assistance from government in the form of expertise, finance and other material resources. This is most likely to entail the establishment of regional and district budgets, backed up by legislation which would allow the flexible use of all resources.

Given such developments, the role of social work staff would undergo considerable change. Small specialized residential units for those with severe emotional and physical handicaps would still require social work staff whose major roles would be in case management and counselling services to families. Most social workers would be involved in direct counselling and support services to families and individuals, as well as case-planning activities to ensure that accessible services are available in an effective personal manner to all mentally retarded persons. The emphasis has to be on the rights of handicapped persons to receive service according to their needs within their own communities, so that they may live with respect and dignity.

## BIBLIOGRAPHY

Braddock, D. (1977) *Opening Closed Doors: The Deinstitutionalization of Disabled Individuals.* New York: The Council for Exceptional Children.

Clarke, A. M. & Clarke, A. D. B. (1976) *Early Experience, Myth and Evidence.* London: Open Books.

Goffman, E. (1961) *Asylums: Essays on the Social Situation of Mental Patients and Other Inmates.* New York: Doubleday.

King, R. D., Raynes, H. V. & Tizard, J. (1971) *Patterns of Residential Care.* London: Routledge & Kegan Paul.

Klaber, M. M. (1966) *Retardates in Residence: A Study of Institutions.* University of Connecticut, U.S.A.

Kugel, R. B. (ed.) (1976) *Changing Patterns in Residential Services for the Mentally Retarded.* President's Committee on Mental Retardation, Washington, DC 20201.

Murphy, H. P. M. (1972) *Foster Homes: The New Back Wards.* Dept. of National Health and Welfare, Health Program Board, Ottawa, Canada.

Scheerenberger, R. C. (1976a) *Deinstitutionalization and Institutional Reforms.* Springfield, Illinois: Charles C. Thomas.

Scheerenberger, R. C. (1976b) *Public Residential Services for the Mentally Retarded.* National Association of Superintendents of Residential Facilities for the Mentally Retarded, U.S.A.

Skarnulis, E. (1977) *The Residential Assumption,* Presentation for the National Association of Social Workers, U.S.A.

Tinsley, D. J., O'Connor, G. & Halpern, A. S. (1973) *The Identification of Problem Areas in the Establishment and Maintenance of Community Residential Facilities for the Developmentally Disabled.* Working Paper 64. Eugene, Oregon: University of Oregon.

Tizard, J., Sinclair, I. & Clarke, R. V. G. (eds.) (1975) *Varieties of Residential Experiences.* London: Routledge & Kegan Paul.

Vail, D. R. (1966) *Dehumanization and the Institutional Career.* Springfield, Illinois: Charles C. Thomas.

van Pelt, J. D. (1977) A parent looks at independent living. *Aust. J. ment. Retard.,* 4, 5, 1–3.

Wolfensberger, W. (1976) The origin and nature of our institutional models. In: Kugel, R. B. (ed.), *Changing Patterns in Residential Services for the Mentally Retarded.* President's Committee on Mental Retardation, Washington, DC 20201.

# CHAPTER 19

# EVALUATION OF RESIDENTIAL PROVISION

## PAUL BERRY AND ROBERT ANDREWS

Contemporary patterns of residential provision vary considerably between countries, and within countries a wide range of facilities may be observed. Based on this 'variety' of residential provision the following types of facilities can be described, at least in terms of their physical characteristics.

1. Hospital provision has for many decades been the traditional and most common form of residential care for mentally handicapped people. Although there is a strong international trend away from such provision there will always be a need for hospital-based services for a small proportion of the mentally handicapped.

2. Home-based residential provision is now afforded to a large and growing number of mentally handicapped people, particularly children of school age. Such provision follows the basic principles of normalization (Wolfensberger & Glenn 1975), and an internationally accepted philosophy of family-based provision. In Britain this type of support is provided for about 80 per cent of families with a mentally handicapped child, but this percentage varies from country to country.

3. Fostering and adoption are further alternatives to natural family-based domiciliary provision. Although the identification and training of suitable foster parents is often difficult, this kind of provision is essentially a viable community-based alternative.

4. Family-group homes within the community are rapidly becoming the major alternative to larger institutional settings whenever a mentally handicapped person cannot live with his own family. Such provision attempts to give a home-like setting for handicapped people within the community and therefore should be situated within reach of appropriate educational and vocational establishments.

5. Larger homes in the community are also provided in some countries including Australia and the Netherlands. These purpose-built facilities provide accommodation for some 20 residents or more.

6. Short-term residential care has an increasingly important role to play in the overall provision of residential services for the mentally handicapped. This type of provision enables families to be involved in activities (such as holidays) which otherwise might be impossible, and provides relief from family pressures. Parents frequently advocate this type of provision as one of their most important needs.

The residential provisions afforded to the mentally handicapped range, then, from the normal family home (the most natural and *micro* level of such provision), through to the larger hospital type of provision (the *macro* level), which is the least normalizing.

The over-riding and essential element in any residential service is the way in which it meets the developmental needs of its clients. It is clearly important, therefore, that the efficiency of all these systems be evaluated, and the relative deficiencies in *client* terms be documented. There is little doubt that smaller establishments resembling home-like provision can improve the learning and social development of the clients, as Tizard in his classic Brooklands experiment has shown

(Tizard 1964). It was also shown in the early 1960s that learning improvements can take place in hospital settings if appropriate changes are made. Essentially the 'rule of thumb' for residential facilities for the mentally handicapped should be 'home if possible; if not, as home-like as possible; when such provision is inappropriate then care in hospital should be geared to a stimulating and learning atmosphere.'

## THE EVALUATION OF SERVICES

### DEFINITION AND LEVELS OF ASSESSMENT

Evaluation may be described as the systematic process of measuring the relative efficiency of a service in attaining its defined objectives. An appropriate evaluation will be able to answer a number of questions concerned with how well a service system, or programme, is achieving its aims. Continuing evaluation is essential for successful monitoring of service provision and for developing better services which are more informed, streamlined and suited to the particular needs of the clients in the programme. In many respects,

as will be seen, evaluation has its roots in individual assessment.

Assessment is seen to be the foundation stone of intervention; without appropriate assessment, intervention programmes and hence the facilities in which they are implemented have no systematic basis and their effectiveness will be undermined.

As with residential provision, evaluation has a number of levels, and these are also presented as ranging in their characteristics from the micro to macro levels. Figure 19.1 gives a diagrammatic analysis of these levels. It will be noted that four specific levels of evaluation are suggested, together with the components of service delivery appropriate to each level. The interaction between each level is emphasized and it may be useful to consider the points at which communication and information dissemination are more (or less) adequate. The four levels of the model are briefly discussed below.

The first level, the level of individuals within the system, is the ultimate micro level of analysis. Unless it can be demonstrated that a programme within a facility actually produces systematic and effective change and development in the psycho-social characteristics of the mentally handicapped (and those

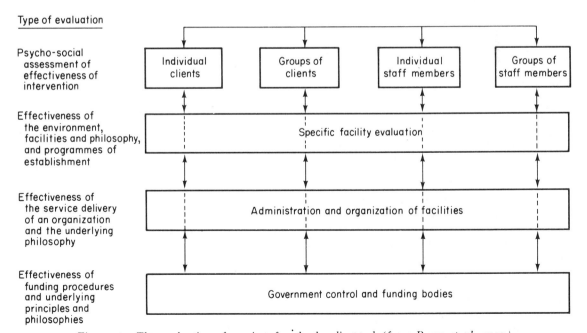

Fig. 19.1   *The evaluation of services for the handicapped (from Berry et al. 1977).*

whose job it is to actualize the programmes) then the whole *raison d'être* of the programme requires scrutiny of staff practice and training.

At the second level the specific role of the establishment is investigated. Basically this evaluation considers the facility as a whole, as an appropriate facilitator of the aims and objectives of the organization under which it is administered. It includes such factors as appropriate buildings and fitments, the construction of curricula, the ways in which staff are recruited and trained and provision of a comprehensive service for the clients.

Evaluation of the organization, the third level, relates the philosophies and procedures of an agency's administration to the actualization of the programme. It also investigates the degree to which the administrators, at this level, are effective as change-agents in the system of service delivery.

Finally, at the fourth level, the funding bodies, for instance government departments of social security, and voluntary charitable organizations, are evaluated. Such issues as the extent to which they are able to control and direct the philosophies of the organization towards a comprehensive set of services for the handicapped are explored. The issues of adequate funding and the appropriate use of resources, top level political decisions, are considered here.

Clearly it is important to establish a comprehensive and coherent policy from government or agency to client level, all this within the context of a specific social system. Of course, a four-tiered basis of evaluation such as this is ideal but extremely difficult to establish; it is nevertheless possible given appropriate resources and cooperation from all levels as indicated.

For a comprehensive evaluation of services each aspect of the service offered needs to be developed. Although a wide variety and number of psychological assessment techniques are openly available for the evaluation of learning in the mentally handicapped, there is little evidence that they are employed in the development of the majority of programmes. Hence, even where methods of evaluation do exist they are infrequently used. Of course in some areas of evaluation (especially system-centred evaluation) there are a very limited number of methods actually available. In addition, residential programmes are not often seen as developmental and therefore it may not be generally appreciated that they should be evaluated at the first level.

## EVALUATION TECHNIQUES

At the individual or first level (client or staff) a number of assessment techniques are readily available for immediate use by residential staff. For example, a residence may wish to evaluate the effectiveness of a programme to develop communication skills. Before-and-after measures can be effected in a number of ways. A checklist approach could be undertaken, such as that devised by Kellett (1976). This technique requires minimal training, and measures four different aspects of language: comprehension, production, articulation and gesture. The development of personal social skills can be measured by devices such as the Progress Assessment Chart (Gunzberg 1963), or by simpler devices such as that devised by the Wessex Health Care Evaluation Research Team (National Development Group for the Mentally Handicapped 1977). This technique covers aspects of development important for performance in residential settings, such as toiletting and walking skills, through to language, defects in vision, hearing and speech, as well as basic reading, writing and number abilities. Also included in this questionnaire is a brief analysis of behaviour problems. The form can be completed very quickly by residential workers and can be most useful in the evaluation of clients.

At the level of specific facility evaluation, two particular methods, currently available and comparatively well documented, will be discussed below. These are the Program Analysis of Service Systems (Wolfensberger & Glenn 1975), and the programme entitled *Standards for Community Agencies* (Joint Commission in Accreditation of Hospitals 1973). In addition, the use of the 'delphi' technique in evaluation will be discussed.

### Program Analysis of Service Systems (PASS)

PASS is a procedure for the objective measurement of the quality of a wide range of human management service projects, systems and agencies. It is based on a number of ideological or value systems; the most important of these is the principle of normalization, which is broken down into practical implications for service delivery.

The procedure is equally applicable to small and large institutions and facilities whether they are based on education, medical, welfare or other practices. It is also applicable to the evaluation of community services and attitudes, in fact to virtually all we think and do in relation to the handicapped.

Wolfensberger (1972) has discussed in depth the principle of normalization as a rationale for human management. Briefly, this principle calls for the use of 'means which are as culturally normative as possible, in order to establish and/or maintain personal behaviours and characteristics (in a potentially deviant person) which are as culturally normative as possible.'

The PASS system evolved from the identification of certain needs in evaluating services, and as an evaluation procedure is claimed to meet all of these needs. These are presented below as a statement of the purposes PASS is designed to fulfil.

1. To provide a quantitative analysis of the quality and adequacy of human services.
2. To identify how programmes are related to the principle of normalization.
3. To enable continuous or repeated assessment of services.
4. To enable comparative studies in evaluation of services.
5. To provide a system of accreditation of services with the objective of providing appropriate funds for continuation and/or development of programmes.
6. To provide a teaching tool for service personnel related to the normalization principle to the extent that services could be continuously evaluated by staff in respect of these defined criteria.
7. In evaluation, to provide a specification of whether 'the right to treatment' is being met.

Wolfensberger and Glenn (1975) have described the mechanics of administering PASS and analysing the results obtained. With respect to the content, a diagrammatic analysis of the areas and structure of PASS is given

in Figure 19.2. An example of the item of 'normalization' may also serve to clarify the system. This is outlined briefly in Table 19.1 and illustrates the nature and scope of the programme ratings in that area.

TABLE 19.1

An example of the structure of the PASS system

---

*Item area*
normalization

*Items*
A. physical integration
B. social integration

*Sub-items and ratings*
A. physical integration
  1. proximity (i)
  2. access (ii)
  3. physical context (iii)
  4. size or dispersal (iv)

B. social integration
  1. socially integrative interpretations
    *a.* programme and facility labels (v)
    *b.* building perception (vi)
  2. socially integrative programme structures
    *a.* deviant staff contact (vii)
    *b.* other deviant contact (viii)
    *c.* socially integrative social opportunities (ix)

---

The broad bases of the ratings (i)–(ix) in Table 19.1 are as follows:

  i. *Proximity.* The physical distance of the facility from population centres, with reference to social integration.
  ii. *Access.* The lack of physical barriers to access to the facility, with transportation a key factor.
  iii. *Physical context.* The proximity of the facility to socially integrative physical resources, for example community facilities in an integrative location.
  iv. *Size or dispersal.* The size of the facility and of the community, with reference to the number of 'deviant' persons in the location of the facility and the ability of the location to assimilate them.
  v. *Programme and facility labels.* Are they appropriate and not detrimental? Do they give a perception of non-deviant?

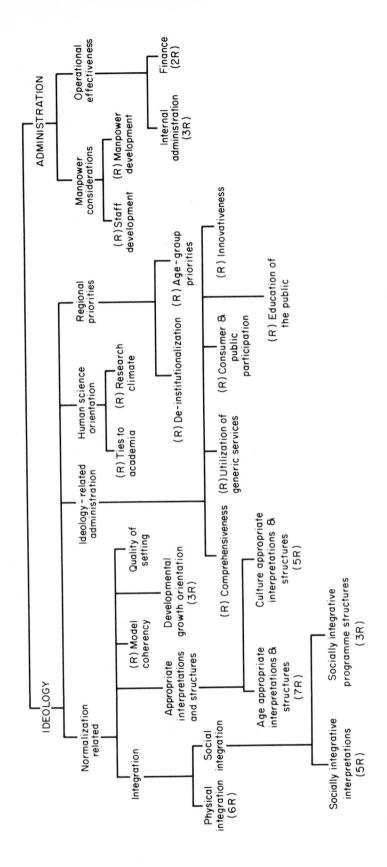

Note: some areas have been reduced to actual rating headings (R). The number of ratings in each area is indicated in other cases.

Fig. 19.2    A diagrammatic analysis of the areas and structure of the Program Analysis of Service Systems (from Berry et al. 1977).

vi. *Building perception.* The past and present use of the buildings; general appearance, non-prominence.

vii. *Deviant staff contact.* The percentage of habilitated staff employed.

viii. *Other deviant contact.* The amount of contact by 'clients' with other deviants.

ix. *Socially integrative social opportunities.* The opportunity for the clients to interact or engage in 'normative' activities, such as in residence, recreation, social interactions and developmental activities (including education).

Full descriptions of each of the 50 items of PASS are given in the PASS manual.

It should be noted that the expression of the normalization principle in PASS is based on rating areas which were judged by the authors to be important reflections of normalization in service delivery. Likewise, the weighting given to each rating is also a judgement of the authors.

*Administration of PASS.* Evaluations using PASS are carried out by a team of assessors independently evaluating the agency or facility. Data is gathered from ratings based on familiarization through written descriptions, interviews and site visits. A total score for each facility, which can range from −947 to +1000, using the Wolfensberger and Glenn procedure, is based on the averaged ratings of the four raters over the 50 items in the analysis, but comparison between programmes on all 50 areas of the evaluation is possible. This has the advantage of identifying the extent to which programmes vary as well as highlighting strengths and weaknesses.

*Standards for Community Agencies (serving persons with mental retardation and other developmental disabilities)*

The Joint Commission in Accreditation of Hospitals (1973) has developed a very detailed survey questionnaire for evaluating standards for residential facilities for the handicapped. This procedure also invokes the principle of normalization, as indicated by the following statement:

The essential requirements for a normalized environment include a physical environment that is as home-like as possible, and in which residents can be divided into small groups, for which specific direct-care staff are responsible, so that there can be individualized attention to the developmental needs of residents, rather than merely large-group or mass care routines.

This process of accreditation has five main aspects which are given in Table 19.2.

The process of accreditation is two-fold. First the facility is sent copies of the questionnaire which are completed by the appropriate officer(s) of the establishment. These are then returned to the Council with any other documentation which may be required. The Council then conducts a site survey and its surveyors observe very closely whether the programme actually pertains to the needs of the clients. The programme is then either formally granted accreditation or the facility is provided with a report which indicates how it can improve its programme to the level of the standards laid down by the Council.

Although the Council's approach to accreditation and evaluation is both time consuming as well as very intricate, it aims to provide consumers of the services offered with a precise statement of the adequacy of the services, and in addition the facility itself is given evidence of its accountability to the people it aims to service.

*The delphi technique*

In many ways evaluation is directed to future practices and policies, and involves judgements about these. In recent years research directed towards the development of judgements about future policies and events has made considerable use of the delphi technique. A very comprehensive review of the development and potential use of this procedure was recently published by McGaw et al. (1976). McGaw and his associates had been involved in a study which looked at the future of teacher education in Australia, when they compiled the material reported. Another useful review is available in Schipper and Kenowitz (1976).

The delphi technique was originally used for forecasting in such areas as industry and defence. As such it had been employed to forecast technological change. Recently, however, its use has been extended to educational

TABLE 19.2

Process of accreditation: requirements and number
of standards

| Requirements | Number of standards |
|---|---|
| I. Provision of active habilitation programming to each resident | |
| A. General requirements | 20 |
| B. Interdisciplinary process | 17 |
| C. Evaluation and programme planning | 48 |
| D. Management of programme delivery | 8 |
| E. Resident training | 23 |
| F. Behaviour management | 27 |
| G. Attention to resident health needs | 64 |
| H. Habilitation services | 42 |
| I. Staff training and consultation | 14 |
| J. Staffing | 24 |
| K. Documentation | 21 |
| L. Facilities and equipment | 12 |
| | |
| II. Provision of services within a normalized and normalizing environment | |
| A. General normalization | 20 |
| B. Community integration | 11 |
| C. Integration of multihandicapped | 7 |
| D. Rhythm of life | 10 |
| E. Physical environment | 24 |
| | |
| III. Assurance of the rights of residents and their families | |
| A. General rights-assurance | 13 |
| B. Rights of residents | 43 |
| C. Rights of families | 18 |
| | |
| IV. Effective administrative practices | |
| A. General administration | 39 |
| B. Communication | 5 |
| C. Records | 19 |
| D. Research | 8 |
| | |
| V. Maintenance of a safe and sanitary environment | 70 |
| Total | 607 |

and social areas and evidence suggests that it is a promising procedure in these areas. There seems to be little doubt as to its potential value in looking ahead in the areas of rehabilitation and services for the handicapped.

The technique systematically processes individual judgements about problems and issues to give a useful consensus concerning desired ends. This consensus can be reached without bias if the procedure is conducted without the formation of groups, and with anonymity of the participants. In this way the technique, generally employing a number of rounds (usually three) in which the judgements of the participants are sought, can be used to predict future patterns of services, based on the expectations and knowledge of individuals associated with the field under study.

In the area of future special education, for example, a pioneering piece of research employing this technique was carried out by the National Association of State Directors of Special Education (Schipper & Kenowitz 1976) to forecast future events in the United States affecting the education of exceptional children in the year 2000. For the study, 121 special education administrators representing all regions in the United States initially generated 800 future event statements, which, through a process of screening and elimination, were reduced to 60 event items. The participants then predicted when each would occur and, in a later round, were asked to check their own predictions against the median predictions of the total group of respondents. They were also requested to justify their views. In this way 60 hypothetical future events with a median year of expected realization were achieved to a 65–70 per cent consensus level. The results were expressed both in expected years of achievement and in terms of the level of value placed on the events by the participants. Highly valued events predicted by 1980 indicated that due process procedures would be guaranteed for all exceptional children in all public schools, and that two states in the United States of America would have standardized guidelines and regulations for non-public schools serving handicapped children.

The delphi technique is seen to be a useful

tool in future developments in the evaluation sphere. To date a number of evaluation procedures available at the facility level have been based on author judgements about desirable standards and future characteristics of services. A more adequate way of deriving these would be to sample the opinions and judgements of a wide range of users, administrators and professional workers, and use the results of such a study as the basis for evaluation instruments.*

*An example of facility evaluation*

As an example of the conclusions which can be drawn from evaluation of services for the mentally handicapped the results of a recent study by Berry et al. (1977) can be noted. This study evaluated 36 programmes for the moderately to severely mentally handicapped in three States in Australia. The sample included nine of each of the following: schools, residential units, sheltered workshops and activity therapy centres. The methods of evaluation used were the PASS system (see pp. 262–5 for details), and questionnaires which sought a wide variety of information about equipment, facilities, staffing and other aspects of facility operation, to enable detailed descriptions of facilities to be undertaken

Each establishment was visited by four experienced raters for one half-day. During these visits the raters assessed the facilities and held extensive discussions with both administrators and staff. All other available information on the facilities was also used in the evaluation.

The findings in respect to residential services for this Australian study included the following:

* Such a study is currently being undertaken by the authors.

1. There was a wide range of quality in the services evaluated, and some failed to meet adequate levels of performance.
2. There was an urgent need to train basic programme staff for work in residential services.
3. Wide differences existed between the voluntary organizations which administered the facilities, in both philosophy and service delivery.
4. There was a need for increased numbers of small community-based living units for the mentally handicapped in Australia.
5. There was a need to train staff and administrators in the use of appropriate evaluation techniques.
6. Organization and programmes needed to specify their goals more clearly, and the means to be adopted to achieve them.
7. There was a need for self-evaluation by facility staff.

CONCLUSIONS

Evaluation of services for the mentally handicapped, including residential services, will be an important part of service provision in the years ahead. A number of levels of evaluation have been identified, and evaluation techniques are emerging to help meet the requirements of evaluation at each level. These techniques will doubtless continue to be developed, and new procedures will also emerge. If they are conscientiously and appropriately employed by service providers, future provision for the mentally handicapped will better meet the developmental and other needs of clients, and the accountability expectations of the societies which support them.

BIBLIOGRAPHY

Berry, P., Andrews, R. J. & Elkins, J. (1977) *An evaluative study of educational, vocational and residential programmes for the moderately to severely mentally handicapped in three States.* Research report to the Department of Social Security, Canberra, Australia.
Gunzberg, H. (1963) *Progress Assessment Chart (P.A.C.)* (Form 1, Form 11). London: National Association for Mental Health.
Joint Commission in Accreditation of Hospitals (1973) *Standards for Community Agencies serving persons with mental retardation and other developmental disabilities.* Chicago, USA.

Kellett, B. (1976) An initial survey of the language of ESN(S) children in Manchester: the results of a teachers' workshop. In: Berry, P. (ed.), *Language and Communication in the Mentally Handicapped*. London: Edward Arnold.

McGaw, B., Browne, R. K. & Rees, P. (1976) Delphi in education: review and assessment. *Aust. J. Educ.*, *20*, 1, 59–76.

National Development Group for the Mentally Handicapped (1977) *Mentally Handicapped Children: A Plan for Action*. Pamphlet 2. London: DHSS.

Schipper, W. V. & Kenowitz, L. A. (1976) Special education futures: forecast of events affecting the education of exceptional children, 1976–2000. *J. special Educ.*, *10*, 4, 401–13.

Tizard, J. (1964) *Community Services for the Mentally Handicapped*. Oxford: Oxford University Press.

Wolfensberger, W. (1972) *The Principle of Normalization in Human Services*. Toronto: NIMR.

Wolfensberger, W. & Glenn, L. (1975) *Program Analysis of Service Systems: a system for the quantitative evaluation of human services*, 3rd ed. Toronto: NIMR.

# V
# THE LAW

# CHAPTER 20

# THE LAW RELATING TO MENTAL HANDICAP IN ENGLAND AND WALES

## LARRY O. GOSTIN

There are approximately 110 000 severely mentally handicapped people in England and more than 350 000 with mild mental handicap. In 1975 nearly 60 000 were in residential care, 50 000 in hospitals (78 per cent of these patients had been resident for five years or more) and over 10 000 in lodgings, foster homes and similar accommodation (DHSS 1976b).

These mentally handicapped people have been designated a priority group for expenditure in the health and social services sector. The intended aims are to ensure that they have a satisfying environment (which should, as far as possible, be within the general community) and to provide education, social stimulation and purposeful occupation and employment so as to develop and exercise skills to their full potential (DHSS 1976b).

Despite the broad aims of government there are thousands of mentally handicapped individuals who are arbitrarily excluded from essential services and financial assistance (MIND 1977). Others are deprived of liberty and rights of citizenship solely on the basis of their handicaps (Gostin 1975).

Increasingly, mentally handicapped people and their families are turning to the law for redress (*In re D*). This chapter examines the impact of law on issues which have previously been considered as within the exclusive domain of the medical profession.

## THE LEGISLATIVE FRAMEWORK FOR MENTALLY HANDICAPPED PEOPLE IN HOSPITAL

### INFORMAL ADMISSION: MENTAL HANDICAP HOSPITALS AND ALTERNATIVES

The Royal Commission on the Law Relating to Mental Illness and Mental Deficiency (1957) considered that whenever possible a mentally handicapped person should be admitted to hospital without formality of any kind. Section 5 of the Mental Health Act 1959 implements this recommendation and authorizes admission to a mental handicap hospital on the same basis as admission to a general hospital. The patient need not sign an application form or obtain a medical recommendation, and there is no statutory requirement of a fixed notice of intention to leave.

The mentally handicapped person is often incapable of understanding the implications of hospital admission and of giving consent. Section 5 of the Act does not require his consent, but only that he should not positively object. Accordingly, admission is not on a 'voluntary' basis but on a 'non-volitional' or 'informal' basis.

For a proposed patient below the age of 16, a request for informal admission must be made by the parent or guardian. If a parent wants a child to be informally admitted, and a hospital will take him, no legal authority will accept the child's inability or refusal to consent as sufficient to bar admission.

In 1975, 96 per cent of the 12 939 admissions to mental handicap hospitals and units in England were arranged informally (see Table 20.1). Children under the age of 15 comprised 42 per cent of all admissions in that year, of whom 2863 were under the age of 10 (DHSS 1978).*

International disquiet has been occasioned by the extensive use of informal admission into hospital without appropriate safeguards. A mentally handicapped person is normally unable to give a meaningful consent to admission or to subsequent decisions taken on his behalf. Further, the parent or guardian may not always take decisions which are fully in the best interests of the child. Various efforts have been made to resolve this problem. For example, the Swedish Mental Retardation Service has advised county directors that infants and pre-school children should not be cared for in institutional settings, except for some specific physical condition. Where such a mentally handicapped child's own family proves unable to manage, care is provided in some 'other family home'. This position has now been buttressed by the recent Swedish law which provides a publicly paid spokesman for every vulnerable mentally handicapped person. This measure allows these spokesmen to question closed care provisions where normal settings would suffice (Herr & Gostin 1975).

In the United States a constitutional position is emerging which would require notice and a hearing prior to the admission of non-consenting minors to mental handicap institutions (see Chapter 22).

The British Government does not recognize a legal component in the resolution of this problem and has thus dissociated itself from the American position. There is apprehension that the use of procedural safeguards in the absence of a coherent national policy on the provision of community accommo-

dation and care will result in hardship for mentally handicapped people. Care in a hospital ward is sometimes considered more humane than homelessness or neglect in the community.

The approach of the British Government is to revise substantially the role of the hospital services within a projected period of 15 to 20 years. Currently, a considerable part of the functions of mental handicap hospitals is to provide long-term residential accommodation. The Government estimates that between one-half and one-third of the residents of these hospitals could be relocated in the community if appropriate housing were available (Hansard, 15 January 1976). The Government response is to reduce the number of in-patient beds by one-half over the projected period. The only patients to be eligible for long-term placements will be those who require constant nursing care under specialist supervision—for example, patients with severe physical disability or serious behaviour disorder (DHSS 1971, 1976b). There is also to be a corresponding increase in community housing and fostering arrangements; augmented education, occupation and training services are to be available in the community or in existing hospitals on an out-patient or day-patient basis (see Table 2.1, p. 24).

## COMPULSORY ADMISSION TO HOSPITAL

Mental disorder is broadly defined in Section 4 of the 1959 Act as mental illness, severe mental handicap, mental handicap, psychopathic disorder and 'any other disorder or disability of mind'.* Two of these—mental illness and severe mental handicap—might be regarded as major disorders; mental handicap and psychopathic disorder being minor disorders. Significant legal consequences flow from this distinction.

Mental handicap is defined in Section 4 as a state of arrested or incomplete development of mind which is susceptible to medical treatment or other special care or training. A severely mentally handicapped person is

---

* Statistics for hospital admission are now computed separately for England and Wales. See Welsh Office (1978).

* Section 4 of the 1959 Act uses the term *subnormality*. The Department of Health and Social Security (1976a) has indicated that this term will be replaced in amended legislation by *mental handicap*, and this latter term has been used throughout.

one who is incapable of living an independent life or of guarding himself against serious exploitation.

Table 20.1 provides a breakdown of the use of compulsory admissions to mental handicap hospitals and units for 1975. Two overviews emerge from the figures: first, the majority of admissions to hospital were for social rather than medical reasons; second, only 4 per cent of the total admissions were on a compulsory basis.

*Admission for observation in case of emergency (Section 29)*

In any case of urgent necessity, a mentally handicapped person may be admitted for emergency observation under Section 29 of the Mental Health Act, on the basis of one medical recommendation, preferably by a medical practitioner who has some previous acquaintance with the patient, normally his general practitioner. In addition, an application must be made by a mental welfare officer, who is an approved social worker, or by any relative as defined in Section 49 of the Act. The authority to detain expires after 72 hours from the time of admission unless a second medical recommendation is obtained within that period to satisfy Section 25 (see below).

TABLE 20.1

Mental handicap hospitals and units: admissions by legal status and source of referral

| Legal status | Source of referral | | | | | | | |
| | All admissions | Family doctor | Courts and police | Social services departments | Other persons and authorities | Psychiatrist Out-patients | Domiciliary visits | Other |
| --- | --- | --- | --- | --- | --- | --- | --- | --- |
| Informal: | | | | | | | | |
| Admissions for social reasons | 7476 | 1012 | 13 | 2393 | 2576 | 938 | 74 | 470 |
| Admissions for other than social reasons | 4933 | 808 | 48 | 697 | 1331 | 426 | 75 | 1548 |
| Detained under Section* | | | | | | | | |
| 25 | 71 | 8 | 2 | 22 | 22 | 2 | 7 | 8 |
| 26 | 110 | 7 | — | 10 | 47 | 3 | 5 | 38 |
| 29 | 59 | 12 | 2 | 16 | 23 | 3 | 2 | 1 |
| 30(2) | 2 | — | 1 | — | — | — | 1 | — |
| 60 (without S. 65 restriction) | 135 | 3 | 81 | 1 | 25 | 2 | 2 | 21 |
| 60 (with S. 65 restriction) | 63 | 11 | 13 | 4 | 26 | — | — | 9 |
| 135 | 1 | — | — | 1 | — | — | — | — |
| 136 | 1 | — | — | — | 1 | — | — | — |
| Other | 88 | 3 | 54 | — | 23 | 1 | 3 | 4 |
| Totals | 12939 | 1864 | 214 | 3144 | 4074 | 1375 | 169 | 2099 |

From DHSS (1978) Table D4: Legal Status.

* Only those sections of the Act which have broad significance for mentally handicapped people are discussed in the text. Sections 30 and 136 are, therefore, not included. Briefly, Section 30 authorizes the medical practitioner in charge of the treatment of an informal patient to detain him for three days. Section 136 gives a police officer power in defined circumstances to take a person who appears to be mentally disordered to a place of safety (a hospital or police station) for 72 hours. Sections 60 and 65 relate to mentally abnormal offenders; these sections are briefly discussed later in this chapter. All of the foregoing provisions are fully explained and analysed in Gostin (1975, 1977).

The figures given in Table 20.1 indicate that nearly one-quarter of all applications for civil (as opposed to criminal) admissions to mental handicap hospitals purport to be of 'urgent necessity'. Conceptually, one would not expect that intellectual retardation itself would require emergency intervention in quite so high a proportion of cases. There is also substantial empirical evidence which suggests that the procedures under Section 29 are misused (Barton & Haider 1966).

The ease of application under Section 29, along with its extensive and improper use, has resulted in disquiet expressed by government agencies throughout the years (Ministry of Health 1967; Hospital Advisory Service 1975; DHSS 1976a). Recently, the Department of Health and Social Security reported that it intends to introduce a procedure for close monitoring of the reasons given for admissions under Section 29, to ensure they are made only in cases of genuine emergency, and not for administrative convenience. The Department is also considering the adoption of proposals by the National Association for Mental Health (MIND) and the British Association of Social Workers for crisis intervention units in the community, intended to reduce substantially the need for emergency admissions into hospital (DHSS 1976a).

*Admission for observation (Section 25)*

A person may be compulsorily admitted to hospital for observation for 28 days under Section 25 of the Act on the grounds that he is suffering from a mental disorder which warrants his detention in hospital under observation, with or without medical treatment, and that he *ought* to be so detained in the interests of his own health or safety or for the protection of others.

An application under Section 25 must be made by the nearest relative or by a mental welfare officer. The application must be founded upon the recommendations of two medical practitioners, one of whom must be approved by the Secretary of State as having special experience in the diagnosis or treatment of mental disorder. The recommendations must be signed on or before the date of the application, and must be given by prac-titioners who have personally examined the patient either together or at an interval of not more than seven days (Mental Health Act 1959, Section 28).

The purpose behind an admission for observation is that the patient can be taken to hospital for assessment for a limited period. Because the admission is for observation, there is no safeguard provided, such as a tribunal which is available to a patient admitted for treatment (see Section 26 below).

Now, 20 years later, the greater availability of community-based assessment services should obviate the need for compulsory observational admissions to hospital. Further, there are comparatively few countries in the western world which now operate procedures for observation. The only other European country is Denmark, where the Law of 1938 provides for observation on a *voluntary* basis for six months. The United States and Canada have no jurisdictions which provide for observational detention (WHO 1978).

*Admission for treatment (Section 26)*

A person may be compulsorily admitted to hospital under Section 26 for treatment for a period not exceeding one year, on the grounds that he is suffering from a mental disorder which warrants his detention for medical treatment, and that it is necessary for his health or safety, or for the protection of others, that he should be detained. The application for admission has to be made by the nearest relative or by a mental welfare officer, and must be supported by two medical recommendations in the same way as an application for observation under Section 25.

Section 26 requires a specific diagnosis to be made. If a person is classified as suffering from one of the minor disorders (for example, mental handicap) and is over the age of 21, he may not be admitted under Section 26. However, if such a person was admitted before the age of 21, the hospital could continue to detain him up to the age of 25. If a person is classified as suffering from a major disorder (for example, severe mental handicap) he may be admitted and detained at any age. The authority to detain, under Section 26, may be renewed for one further year, and for subsequent periods of two years. The renewal is effected by the responsible medical officer, who must furnish a report to the hospital managers in accordance with Section 43 of the Act.

A patient may apply for a Mental Health Review Tribunal within six months, following his admission under Section 26. He may also apply at any time during each period of renewal. The nearest relative may apply on behalf of the patient up to twelve months after admission, and in any subsequent period of twelve months. The nearest relative may also exercise a 'discharge order'. However, the Act gives the responsible medical officer the right to override this if, in his opinion, the patient poses a danger to himself or others. This in turn gives the relative an augmented right to apply for a tribunal within 28 days following the doctor's decision to override the discharge order (see Mental Health Act 1959, Sections 31, 43, 47, 48 and 49).

Mental Health Review Tribunals are independent bodies with the power to discharge patients. They consist of a lawyer (the chairman), a medical member (a consultant psychiatrist) and a lay member.

The primary criticism of the tribunal is that the patient must take the initiative to apply before its jurisdiction can be invoked. Empirical research has shown that only about 12 per cent of those eligible to apply for tribunals actually exercise their right (Gostin 1975).

Regrettably, the kind of patient who is likely to spend much of his hospital time making detailed arrangements for his tribunal is not necessarily the kind of patient who most needs to be heard. It may well be, for example, that a mentally handicapped person who has been in hospital for five years and whose case has been overlooked should have his case reviewed. He may not be aware that he has a right to a tribunal, or he may be too submissive and unassertive to interrupt his daily routine in order to apply. Such a person neither takes the initiative to apply for a tribunal, nor has the capacity to question the judgement of professionals and family members who may take decisions which affect his life. Yet he may be precisely the kind of patient whom the tribunal may want to hear from. To overcome this it has been sug-

gested that automatic periodic references to tribunals should be introduced for patients who lack the initiative to apply. The Government appears to have accepted the proposal in principle, and may introduce it as part of its general review of the Mental Health Act (see below).

## Guardianship (Section 33)

The procedure and criteria for reception into guardianship under Section 33 of the Act is in most respects the same as an admission to hospital for treatment under Section 26. The duration of the guardianship order and the right to apply to a Mental Health Review Tribunal is also the same as for an admission for treatment.

The person named as guardian may be either a local social services department or any person accepted by the department. The guardian has all such power as would be exercisable by the father of a person under the age of 14.

The number of mentally handicapped people under statutory guardianship in England and Wales has dropped from 1132 in 1960 to 134 in 1974 (DHSS 1976a). Apparently, it is no longer regarded as appropriate to the needs of the people involved. One reason for this may be the emphasis of this form of guardianship on supervision and control. A feasible alternative could be provided by a facilitative guardianship, emphasizing the positive aspects of guidance, help and advice. The facilitator guardian already operates in Sweden. He has responsibility for supporting the person in taking major decisions, in obtaining a fair share of resources, and in obtaining the most appropriate (for example, the least restrictive) service.

## Powers of courts to order hospital admission or guardianship (Section 60)

In pursuance of Section 60 of the Act, a court may authorize a person's admission to a specified mental handicap hospital or place him under guardianship of the local authority social services department. The effect of a Section 60 order is virtually equivalent to an admission for treatment under Section 26 or a civil guardianship order under Section 33 of the Act. The essential difference is that the nearest relative cannot exercise a discharge order in respect of a Section 60 patient. In addition, the age limits laid down in Sections 26 and 44 for the admission and detention of mildly mentally handicapped people do not apply to Section 60 patients.

The following conditions must be fulfilled if a hospital or guardianship order is to be made. First, the person must have been convicted of an imprisonable offence. A magistrate's court may make a hospital or guardianship order in respect of a severely mentally handicapped person without recording a conviction if satisfied that he committed the act or made the omission charged. Secondly, the court must be satisfied, on the written or oral evidence of two medical practitioners, that the offender is suffering from a mental disorder of a nature or degree which warrants his detention in hospital or admission into guardianship. Thirdly, the court must be of the opinion, considering all the circumstances, including the nature of the offence and character and antecedents of the offender, and the other methods of dealing with him, that the most suitable method of disposing of the case is a Section 60 order. Finally, a hospital order cannot be made unless the admission of the offender to the hospital specified in the order has been arranged; he must be admitted to that hospital within 28 days from the date on which the order is made. In practice, this means that the court must be satisfied that the hospital specified in the order is willing to accept the offender. It may specify a special (maximum security) hospital such as Broadmoor, Rampton, Moss Side or Park Lane, if the offender is thought to be dangerous; otherwise he will normally be admitted to an ordinary National Health Service hospital in his home area.

In making a hospital order, the court is placing the patient in the hands of doctors, and is nominally foregoing the imposition of punishment. Therefore, unless the order is coupled with a restriction order under Section 65, the court and Home Office relinquish control over the patient; either the responsible medical officer (RMO) or Mental Health Review Tribunal (MHRT) can discharge the patient at any time.

## Hospital orders with restrictions (Section 65)

A Crown (superior) Court may consider, having regard to the nature of the offence, the antecedents of the offender and the risk of his committing further offences if set at large, that it is necessary for the protection of the public, to also make an order under Section 65 of the Act. This restricts the offender's discharge from hospital. The restriction order may be either without limit of time or for a specified period. In 1975 the proportion of restriction orders made for fixed periods was only 3 per cent (Home Office 1976).

A person admitted to hospital with special restrictions under Section 65 is not subject to the civil provisions of the Act (Part IV), relating to the duration, renewal and expiration of the authority for the compulsory detention of patients. This means that neither the RMO nor the MHRT has the power to grant a leave of absence, a transfer to another hospital or a discharge without the consent of the Secretary of State for Home Affairs.

No restricted patient may apply to a MHRT, nor may his nearest relative. The Home Secretary, however, may at any time refer his case to a tribunal for its advice. The patient can make a written request that his case be referred to a tribunal not sooner than one year after the relevant order is made and once in any subsequent two-year period. The Home Secretary must refer the case to the tribunal within two months of receiving a properly made request.

The tribunal has no power over a restricted patient and no authority to discharge him. It may only *advise* the Home Secretary in the exercise of his discretionary powers. The patient or his representative are not informed of the tribunal's recommendation. Further, the Home Secretary does not give reasons and there is no appeal against his decision. In the years 1970 to 1975 the Home Secretary rejected the tribunals' recommendations for discharge in 40 per cent of all cases (Gostin 1977).

*International remedies.* The European Commission of Human Rights is currently reviewing the lawfulness of Section 65 under Article

5 of the European Convention (*X, Y and Z v. United Kingdom*).

> Everyone who is deprived of his liberty by arrest or detention shall be entitled to take proceedings whereby the lawfulness of his detention shall be decided speedily by a court and his release ordered if the detention is not lawful.

The issue before the Commission is whether the patients (detained for periods disproportional to the gravity of their offences) were provided with a periodic judicial review of the lawfulness of their detention.

### THE PATIENT'S RIGHT TO REFUSE TREATMENT

Informal patients in mental handicap hospitals (or their guardians) can legally refuse to consent to treatment. They have the same remedy against receiving treatment to which they do not consent as do patients in any other kind of hospital: they have a common law right to sue for assault.

Generally, an action for assault will be successful if the patient has been treated without his (or his guardian's) informed legal consent. However, treatment can be given without consent in the case of urgent necessity, for example when the patient has become unconscious. The professional carrying out the treatment would then defend himself on the grounds that he acted in good faith and in the best interests of the patient, and that urgent necessity made it impracticable to seek consent. Indeed, if the professional had not treated the patient in such circumstances, he might have been liable in an action for negligence.

The general right of the informal patient to refuse treatment may be infringed through the threat of a compulsory order, loss of privileges or other sanctions. It may also be infringed if the patient or his guardian is inadequately informed of the purpose or side effects of the treatment, or of his legal right to withhold consent.

The state of law as regards the compulsory patient is not so clear, despite representations by the Department of Health and Social Security that detained patients cannot legally refuse treatment. The issue can be reduced to this: does the Mental Health Act 1959 alter the ordinary right of the person to use the common law remedies of court against an unauthorized touching? Section 26 of the Act allows compulsory 'admission for treatment' if two medical practitioners are satisfied that the patient is suffering from a mental disorder which warrants his detention for medical treatment. To some, the word 'warrants' carries with it the necessary implication that treatment which is warranted may be imposed. According to this view, compulsory detention is itself a plenary deprivation of rights which necessarily includes the imposition of lesser infringements such as compulsory treatment.

To others, the word 'warrants' does not also authorize professionals to give treatment without consent. The 1959 Act authorizes compulsory admission but says nothing of the powers over treatment.

Sections 25 and 29 authorize 'admission for observation' in express contradistinction to an 'admission for treatment'. These sections state that the person must be suffering from a mental disorder which warrants detention in hospital under observation and adds the proviso, 'with or without other medical treatment'. (Does it imply that observation itself is a form of treatment?)

The legality of the imposition of treatment has not been tested in court, but the Secretary of State for Social Services has announced that the Government will clarify the position in its forthcoming amendment of the 1959 Act. Preliminary indications are that the responsible medical officer will be given the express right to impose treatment on detained patients, subject to certain safeguards for procedures of a hazardous or irreversible character (DHSS 1976a).

### MENTAL HANDICAP: IN OR OUT OF THE MENTAL HEALTH ACT?

The Department of Health and Social Security is currently reviewing the Mental Health Act and has published a Consultative Document setting out its preliminary analysis of the issues. Although compulsory admission affects comparatively few mentally handicapped people, the Department saw this as the sole issue deserving review. The question was put: should the mentally handicapped be removed from the jurisdiction of the Mental Health Act? (DHSS 1976a).

The inclusion of mental handicap in the Act is primarily criticized for implicitly equating it with forms of psychiatric incapacity such as mental illness and psychopathic disorder. The premise of the Act is that psychiatric illness may cause antisocial behaviour. The 'illness' can be cured and the behaviour corrected through compulsory hospitalization.

Whatever the merits of this model in relation to the psychiatrically ill, it appears inapplicable to the handicapped. Mental handicap does not of itself result in disruptive or antisocial behaviour. The factors which may warrant the detention of a mentally handicapped person are more usually attributable to a concomitant psychiatric disorder than to intellectual retardation and diminished social competence. Moreover, uncomplicated intellectual deficit by the time of adulthood is not usually susceptible to medical treatment. Simple deficit is likely to result from genetic prenatal or postnatal damage influencing the ability to learn and reason. By adulthood it is less likely to be 'curable' in a health context in the same sense as an illness, as open to improvement by education training and social care. This hardly warrants compulsory hospital admission.

The language of the Mental Health Act, an advance in 1959, indicates that mental handicap was forced into a legislative straight-jacket which really applied to the psychiatrically ill. The Act presupposes that the handicap, having initially manifested itself, will cease to exist after a period in hospital. Thus, an important criterion for the discharge of a Section 26 patient is that he no longer suffers from mental handicap (Mental Health Act 1959, Section 123). Similarly, a person can be admitted to hospital under Sections 25 or 29 purely on the basis of a developmental disability. The question should be asked: what needs of a mentally handicapped person are met by detaining him for 72 hours or 28 days? Medical intervention as a measure of crisis intervention, or for a short period of observation, is based less on intellectual handicap, but more upon a supervening disability, that is, behaviour or personality disorder. Admission could therefore be accom-

plished without including mental handicap within the jurisdiction of the Act.

The opposing view is that the need for compulsory admission arises because of an impairment in an individual's reason and judgement or his appreciation of the effect of his behaviour on himself or others. The impairment of judgement may render the person unable to care for himself in the community or may lead to behaviour which is offensive to other people. It would be difficult to deny that mental handicap could not, in any circumstances, have such an effect.

The resolution of these issues is in the hands of the Department of Health and Social Security, which must decide upon the criteria necessary for compulsory hospitalization. The question to be asked is whether it would be appropriate to authorize the detention of an individual solely because of his inability to lead an independent life in the community. If this were the legislative standard, it might unfairly include the severely physically handicapped, the aged, the chronically infirm, and so forth. So too, the question should be asked whether the intolerance of the community toward non-conforming or irresponsible behaviour, not amounting to dangerous behaviour, would be an over-broad criterion for compulsory admission to hospital. (For a comparison with the law of the United States, see the case of *Donaldson* v. *O'Connor* in Chapter 22, p. 296.)

### THE LEGISLATIVE FRAMEWORK FOR MEETING THE NEEDS OF THE MENTALLY HANDICAPPED IN THE COMMUNITY

Legislation in England and Wales places great emphasis on the deficits in a person's intellectual capacity and the need for custodial care. In this way, the law may neglect the everyday needs of mentally handicapped people. What are the needs of these people? What is the legal framework available to ensure these needs are met? Are there any procedures available to the handicapped person when government arbitrarily fails to meet a basic human requirement?

The basic needs of any human being, particularly the handicapped, are for a home, food, medical care, education and training, marital and sexual expression and, if necessary, protection from harm.

Great Britain does not have a written constitution, as does the United States, on which these rights can be based. Rather, each element of a handicapped person's life-needs is dealt with through a number of fragmented statutory and administrative provisions. There follows an exposition of the rights of a mentally handicapped person to the fulfilment of some of his basic life-needs. Other less fundamental rights are described elsewhere by the author and include the right of access to the courts, to correspond by post, to drive a motor vehicle and to vote (Gostin 1975, 1977).

## THE NEED FOR A HOME

DHSS figures on reasons for admission show that substantial numbers of people enter mental handicap hospitals and other specialist facilities primarily for domiciliary and social reasons. The institution, therefore, has a distinct 'hotel' or 'asylum' function, providing lodgings for vulnerable people with no home. Existing legislation has the effect of encouraging local government to adopt such an approach, in which fundamental 'housing' needs are obscured by a need for 'care'. In the following section the relevant provisions under health and social service legislation are explained; most mentally handicapped people who have no-one to care for them either find their way into hospital or into medium-sized establishments built in accordance with these provisions. Thereafter, ordinary housing legislation is explained; a case is made for more general use of these provisions for the benefit of handicapped people (see Tyne 1976, 1977).

### Residential provision under health and social service legislation

Most of the special residential care legislation in England and Wales is derived from the National Assistance Act 1948. Section 21(1) of that Act places a *duty* on local social services departments to provide 'residential accommodation for persons who by reason of age, infirmity or any other circumstances are in need of care and attention which is not otherwise available to them.' Subsection (2) specifies that in the exercise of this duty departments should provide accommodation of various descriptions suited to the needs of the individual. (For more recent manifestations of this statutory principle, see Local Authority Circular 13/74 (DHSS 1974b).)

A further but relatively less used provision is contained in Section 29 of the 1948 Act which *empowers* local social services authorities to 'make arrangements for the welfare of persons who are blind, deaf or dumb, and other persons who are substantially and permanently handicapped by illness, injury or congenital deformity'.

National Assistance Act accommodation is not directly referrable to the ordinary housing needs of mentally handicapped people, although some clearly will benefit (for example, the aged or those with accompanying physical disabilities). Domiciliary provision arranged in pursuance of Section 21 is principally used for old people or the temporarily homeless, while provision under Section 29 is associated with workshop places for disabled people of various descriptions.

The Health Services and Public Health Act 1968 is more directly applicable to mentally handicapped people, although the point should be reiterated that it, like other health service legislation, is principally designed for the physically or psychiatrically ill. Section 12 of that Act lays down that 'a local authority shall, with the approval of the Minister, and to such extent as he may direct, make arrangements for . . . the prevention of illness and for the after care of persons suffering from illness and for the care of persons who have been so suffering.' 'Illness' is defined in the National Health Service Act, as amended by the Mental Health Act, to include 'mental disorder'. This provision has been implemented by Local Authority Circular 19/74 (DHSS 1974c) which *directs* social services departments to provide residential accommodation for mentally disordered persons ordinarily resident in their areas. This would include residential homes, hostels, group homes, minimum support facilities or other appropriate accommodation. An important domiciliary arrangement made under this provision is the standard mental handicap hostel with 24 beds.

The foregoing is concerned with special residential provision for mentally handicapped people. This is directly related to a person's need for care, which is provided in moderately-sized segregated accommodation. This may not accord with the needs of mentally handicapped people for their own homes—ensuring a sense of identification, privacy and freedom from the stigma and regimentation associated with specialist facilities.

General housing legislation does offer mentally handicapped people some opportunity for ordinary housing, but they have been regarded in the past as 'in need of care and attention', even if their handicaps have been relatively mild.* This operates to exclude them from housing legislation and make them eligible for special residential care legislation.

*General housing legislation*

The Housing Act 1957 requires local housing departments to consider the needs of their area and to prepare schemes for providing housing to meet these needs. They are empowered under this Act, and under the Housing Act 1974, to provide a range of accommodation which would be suitable for many mentally handicapped people, including single dwellings, bed-sitters and hostels.

The Housing (Homeless Persons) Act, which came into force on 1 December 1977, is a potentially important development for mentally handicapped people. The Act imposes a duty on housing departments to provide accommodation for homeless people with a priority need. Section 2 of the Act specifically states that a mentally handicapped person and his family are in such need.

The joint circular on Homelessness (DOE 1974; DHSS 1974a) suggests that what may be described as the 'Hidden Homeless' is

not a recognized category. People who remain in institutional care only because there is no alternative provision in the community do not meet the standard of being 'literally without shelter or likely to lose in the immediate future what shelter they have'.

Thus, if mental handicap hospitals sought to discharge the 'Hidden Homeless' would they be entitled to assistance under the 1977 Act?

*Cost effectiveness*

MIND, in its evidence to the currently sitting Royal Commission on the National Health Service, produced a cost-benefit analysis of the various forms of accommodation for mentally handicapped people: hospitals, medium-sized hostels, small housing units designed to cope with highly dependent children ('Wessex Units') and ordinary lodgings, foster homes and unsupervised group homes (MIND 1977).

The 'hotel' function of mental handicap hospitals costs in the region of (1977) £90 per in-patient per week, exclusive of interest charges on capital loans. This was considerably higher than the average cost of maintaining a mentally handicapped person in a local authority staffed hostel which stood at £33 per week. Other less restrictive domiciliary arrangements were still less expensive. The single exception was the Wessex Units, where the revenue costs were comparable with those of conventional hospitals. However, it was concluded that these units were more cost-effective as they took a higher proportion of severely handicapped children. It was also shown that the capital costs of these units were less than mental handicap hospitals.

THE NEED FOR EDUCATION

*Legal provisions*

The Education Act 1944 (Section 8) requires every local education authority in England and Wales to ensure that there are sufficient schools in their areas to provide full-time primary and secondary education to all children between the ages of five and sixteen. The schools are not deemed to be sufficient for the purposes of the Act 'unless they are sufficient in number, character and equipment

* MIND is to institute a court action to compel a local authority to accept financial responsibility for housing mentally handicapped twins (aged 18) in the community; the action is intended to prevent an unnecessary 'social' admission to a mental handicap hospital.

The particular local authority is refusing to pay the cost of maintaining the twins in the community because it is alleged that they are not 'ordinarily resident' in its area. Every other authority which has been approached has similarly denied responsibility.

to afford for all pupils opportunities for education offering such variety of instruction and training as may be desirable in view of their different ages, abilities and aptitudes . . . including practical instruction and training appropriate to their respective needs'.

In addition to the statutory duties placed on the local education authority, there is a duty imposed on the parents of every child of compulsory school age to ensure that their child receives education, 'either by regular attendance at school or otherwise' (Section 36).

The standard of education which the local authority and the parent must arrange for each child is 'full-time education suitable to [his or her] requirements' (Sections 8 and 36).

These general legal provisions apply to all children, whether or not they suffer from a mental or physical handicap. However, special considerations apply to the education of handicapped children.

Local education authorities, in carrying out their duties to provide primary and secondary schools, are required to have regard 'to the need for securing that provision is made for pupils who suffer from any disability of mind or body by providing, either in special schools or otherwise, special educational treatment, that is to say, education by special methods appropriate for persons suffering from that disability' (Section 8). A general principle has been laid down in Section 10 of the Education Act 1976 that such special educational treatment should be provided in ordinary schools, subject to practical or financial difficulties. Section 10, however, will not come into force until the Secretary of State for Education and Science so orders.

Until 1 April 1971, when the Education (Handicapped Children) Act 1970 came into operation, a local education authority could avoid its responsibilities for the education of a handicapped child by classifying him under Section 57 of the 1944 Act as 'incapable' of receiving education at school. However, the 1970 Act provides that no further use should be made of the powers contained in Section 57; the section is, therefore, repealed. Now, the duty imposed on every local education authority is to ascertain what children in its area require special educational treat-

ment. This extends to all mentally handicapped children. The 1970 Act also states that local health authorities under Section 12 of the Health Services and Public Health Act 1968 shall no longer have the power or duty to provide training for children who suffer from a disability of mind.

The Department of Education and Science issued a circular on 22 September 1970 in which it explained the effect of the 1970 Act (DES 1970). The key sentence is: 'No child within the age limits for education . . . will be outside the scope of the educational system.'

The statutory duty now imposed on local education authorities (LEAs) to provide 'special educational treatment' for every mentally handicapped child does not necessarily mean that the child must receive education at school. Section 56 of the 1944 Act allows LEAs to provide education elsewhere, although only in 'extraordinary circumstances' and with the consent of the Secretary of State in each particular case. Despite these limitations, the then Ministry of *Education* gave LEAs blanket approval under Section 56 for their general arrangements in respect of mentally handicapped children (Min. Ed. 1950). This general approval means that the LEAs very rarely seek the permission of the Secretary of State in an individual case. It is difficult to see what statutory authority there is for this informal practice that has developed between the Department and local authorities.

The Department, however, has made one point clear. If the child is excluded from school under Section 56, it is the duty of the authority to ensure that the child receives other appropriate education, such as home tuition. Despite the strict statutory requirements to educate children at school—except in extraordinary circumstances—19 per cent of the 6860 children aged under 19 in mental handicap hospitals in England in 1975 were not participating in educational activities. These children were excluded from education ostensibly for the following reasons: severity of their mental and physical disabilities, behaviour problems, and lack of educational facilities (DHSS 1977). Of those receiving some education, many were in makeshift programmes falling below the statutory standard of 'full-time education suitable to [the child's] requirements'. Moreover, as the case study below illustrates there are children who, after exclusion from school, remain in the parental home without any kind of education, training or support. In 1975, 2377 educationally handicapped children, and 472 severely mentally handicapped children had been awaiting admission to a special school for more than one year (DES 1975).

### Enforcement machinery

The statutory duties placed upon local education authorities by the Education Act 1944 may be enforced by the Secretary of State in accordance with Section 99 of that Act.

Under Section 99, any interested person may make a complaint to the Secretary of State that a particular local authority has failed to discharge its duties to provide education to a mentally handicapped child. However, as has already been pointed out, the Secretary of State has given indiscriminate approval to local authorities under Section 56 to educate children 'otherwise than at school'. In these circumstances, it is perhaps unrealistic to expect him to hold a particular authority in default under Section 99. The more important legal question is whether a court of law will be prepared to review the discretion of the Secretary of State in holding under Section 99 that the local authority was not in default of its duties.

The issue was first presented to the courts in *Watt* v. *Kesteven County Council* where a parent applied for an order of *mandamus* to compel a local education authority to carry out its duties to educate his mentally handicapped child. The application was rejected by the Court of Appeal. Lord Denning said:

> I would not like to say that there can be no cases under the Act, in which an action would lie, but I do not think an action lies in this case. It is plain to me that the duty under Section 8 (to make schools available) can only be enforced by the Minister under Section 99 of the Act and not by action at law.

This dictum was quoted with approval in *Wood* v. *Ealing Borough Council*. The earlier case of *Passmore* v. *Oswaldtwistle U.D.C.* laid down the general rule that where an Act provides its own administrative machinery for enforcement of any duties in the Act (as does Section 99), that constitutes grounds for refusing *mandamus*. However, it is of significance that, in the above cases, the administrative machinery had not been tried; if an applicant first used the administrative procedures available, and failing that, applied for *mandamus*, the court might be more amenable.

### An illustrative case study

Dwight Francis was born in 1962. In 1968 he was classified as educationally subnormal and sent to Northgate ESN school. In September 1971 he was suspended from school because the headmaster found him a disturbing influence and difficult to control. Since then he has been living at home with his parents, and has received no proper education. The Northamptonshire Education Authority (NEA) has approached 27 schools, but none has accepted Dwight. The NEA also discussed the possibilities of home tuition but, according to the Francis family, no tutors have ever come to the house to teach Dwight. Thus, in the past five years, Dwight has not received the education to which he is entitled by law.

In response to a Section 99 complaint filed by MIND, the Secretary of State held that the NEA was not in default of its duties because blanket approval under Section 56 had been given by the Department, and because the NEA made reasonable attempts to find a place for Dwight during the last five years.

In early 1978 Dwight became 16 years of age and the NEA maintained that it no longer had a statutory responsibility to provide education, as Dwight was beyond school age. A request was made on behalf of the parents in pursuance of Sections 18 and 114 of the Education Act 1944 to provide education until the age of 19. This request had the effect of extending the legal obligation of the NEA to provide appropriate education.

MIND's Legal Department has been granted legal aid on behalf of Dwight, in order to bring an action to compel the Secretary of State to direct the NEA to carry out its duties under the 1944 Act.

If the court does decide to examine the substantive issues in Dwight's case, there are many questions which will be explored. For example:

> What is the standard of education which a local authority must provide in order to fulfil its statutory duties?
> Is it sufficient to provide a mentally

handicapped child with an unfulfilled promise of home tuition and short-term residential assessments?

If a child attends a day centre, training school or mental handicap hospital, can the Secretary of State or the court examine the curriculum in order to assess whether 'full-time' and 'suitable' education is provided?

Can the local education authority discharge its duties by making reasonable attempts to arrange for education? Or must it ensure that there is a sufficient range of alternatives to meet the needs of all kinds of children, regardless of the severity of the handicap?

Can the Secretary of State legally give blanket approval under Section 56 for the general arrangements made for special education in a particular area? Or must it give approval in each individual case after reviewing the particular needs of the child?

In sum, the mentally handicapped child's basic need for education is adequately provided for under the law. The pitfalls, however, are deep and occur largely as a result of improper government implementation of the legislation. The immediate future of handicapped children under the education system is, in the final analysis, dependent on the will and power of the judiciary to intervene.

## THE NEED FOR MARITAL, SEXUAL AND OTHER SOCIAL EXPRESSION

The right to marry, to bear children, to sexuality, sociability and privacy, are central to the life of a physically and mentally able person. It is otherwise for the mentally handicapped. The law lays down certain boundaries which cannot be transgressed. The circumstances in which the mentally handicapped are cared for in practice frequently impose further restrictions on the exercise of such rights.

### Marriage and divorce

There is nothing in English law to prevent a mentally handicapped person from going through the ceremony of marriage, provided none of the usual impediments apply (for example, consanguinity or age) nor any objection is raised, as below. The granting of a marriage licence is discretionary, and an intended marriage may be prevented by voicing dissent to the publication of banns or entering a caveat against the issue of a common or special licence. If a caveat is entered, the licence cannot be issued until the caveat is withdrawn or alternatively until a judge certifies that it ought not to obstruct the granting of the licence. Thus, it is possible for a third party, if he feels the marriage to be misguided, to prevent or substantially impede the ceremony.

In the case of people detained under a section of the Mental Health Act, they will require leave from their responsible medical officer to attend the ceremony. (A person detained with restrictions under Sections 60/65 of the Mental Health Act will require the consent of the Home Secretary.)

The fact that one or both of the partners to the marriage is severely mentally handicapped may give grounds for obtaining a decree of nullity or divorce. Under Section 12 of the Matrimonial Causes Act 1973 a marriage is voidable where either party did not validly consent to it in consequence of unsoundness of mind. The court is not concerned with any general definition of unsoundness. It will ask whether at the date of the marriage the person was capable of understanding the nature of the marriage and the obligations and responsibilities which it involved (*Estate of Park*). The contract of marriage is a simple one which does not require a high degree of intelligence to comprehend and, therefore, there is a strong presumption, *prima facie*, that the consent is valid. Mere backwardness or impaired intelligence is not enough to void an otherwise legal marriage.

A marriage is also voidable under Section 12 if at the time of the marriage either party, though capable of giving a valid consent, was suffering (whether continuously or intermittently) from a mental disorder within the meaning of the Mental Health Act 1959 of such a kind or to such an extent as to be unfitted for marriage. Here, the court will ask whether the person is capable of living in a married state and of carrying out the ordinary duties of marriage (*Bennett* v. *Bennett*). A voidable marriage is one which the parties may choose to continue or to have dissolved within the first three years. It is not a nullity from the beginning as is a void marriage.

The sole ground for divorce is the irretrievable breakdown of the marriage. However, it must be established that the reason for the breakdown comes within one of five categories, which can be loosely summarized as: adultery, unreasonable behaviour, desertion, two years separation with consent of the Respondent, and five years separation without the Respondent's consent. (Matrimonial Causes Act 1973, Sections 1 and 2.)

In practice, there may be important obstacles to the marriage of mentally handicapped people. There are, for example, financial and social problems in finding a home and paid employment, both essential for building a family unit. Objections may also be raised by parents and staff who, having devoted kindness and care to the individual since infancy, may consider him unsuitable for an adult institution like marriage. Yet marriages come in many forms and mentally handicapped people are no less capable of expressing love and commitment than 'normal' members of the community. (See also Chapter 27.)

*Freedom of sexual expression*

Mentally handicapped people are seen by the law as being particularly vulnerable to exploitation in the area of their sexuality. It is an offence for a man to have unlawful (extra-marital) intercourse with a severely mentally handicapped woman. It is also an offence for a man on the staff or employed by a hospital or mental nursing home to have unlawful sexual intercourse with a woman receiving treatment for other forms of mental disorder (including mild mental handicap) in that hospital or home (Mental Health Act 1959, Sections 127 and 128; see also Sexual Offences Act 1967, Section 1). In both of these offences it is a defence for a man charged to prove he did not know and had no reason to suspect that the person was mentally handicapped.

It is interesting to note that these offences can only be committed by a man and that the law does not consider it possible that patients require protection from the sexual advances of a woman, whether or not in a position of responsibility over them.

Clearly, to the extent that mentally handicapped people may be more suggestible and less able to protect themselves from the advances of those who are ill-intentioned or may seriously harm them, the law needs to provide safeguards.

However, in so doing, there is a danger that mentally handicapped people may be deprived of the pleasure and affection that sexual expression brings. The question to be asked is whether the proper balance has been struck between protection against exploitation and ordinary enjoyment of sexual expression.

LEADS FOR THE FUTURE

Legislative reform must begin with recognition that the needs of mentally handicapped people are the same as those of all citizens, together with some special needs associated with their handicaps. The 'general need' services are those which are legally mandated for all members of the community: housing, education, medical care and social services. Each service is provided by the appropriate department of local government. Under current law, mentally handicapped people are sometimes denied equal access to these statutory services, simply on the basis of their disabilities. Instead, a comprehensive, if sometimes sub-standard (MIND 1977), service is provided in a segregated facility— either a hospital or medium sized hostel. A more humane and normal alternative is to provide a complete community-support system based on ordinary residential housing; legal authorization for the support services already exists in large measure. Delivery of primary medical care is available through a general practitioner under ordinary National Health Service legislation. Under these provisions, medical requirements may be clearly identified and dealt with by appropriate specialist referrals or by admission to a general hospital, when the need arises. There is also a statutory right to home nursing services for those with chronic physical, developmental or behavioural disabilities. So too, education can normally be provided in ordinary schools, and social support and training in day-care facilities.

Mentally handicapped people also require special services, not readily available under ordinary welfare legislation. The first objective should be to strengthen the families of mentally handicapped people by providing practical, material and advisory assistance (Bayley 1973). Families may need a good laundry service, respite from total care, meals-on-wheels, advice on welfare benefits and professional assistance in ensuring that their full and fair entitlement is received, aids to daily living and, in the case of multiply handicapped children, adaptations to premises or re-housing. Social services departments are authorized to provide these special services, but accord them a low priority because there are no mandatory duties within existing law. Legislative changes giving mentally handicapped people and their families an enforceable right to these services would provide a foundation for building a viable community alternative to institutional care. In addition, a 'mentorship', or citizen's advocate, programme, similar to the Swedish model described earlier, would enable mentally handicapped people to take full advantage of existing and proposed services.

There are also medical (prevention and early detection), para-medical (speech therapy, physiotherapy and chiropody) and psychological services which are particularly referrable to the needs of mentally handicapped people (DHSS 1971). These should be more readily available in the community according to individual needs, and may also require special legislative and financial arrangements for proper implementation.

### The needs of a child

The analysis suggested above can be simply illustrated by examining a fairly standard response by local authority social services departments to mentally handicapped children in the community. The professional gives primary attention to the child's disability, not to his normal emotional needs. He is referred to as 'mentally handicapped', and a social response is formed on that basis. In some ways, parents seem to manage better than professionals because they see the person as a child, not solely as a disabled individual.

What would a social worker do if a 'normal' child and his or her family were unable to cope? The answer is that the social worker would provide support to ensure that the child had, as far as possible, a natural healthy development. All children have material needs for a home, education and medical care; they also have emotional needs for love, warmth, attention and friendship. These are accomplished by professional, practical and financial support and assistance for the family. If the family situation is irretrievable, other alternatives are examined, such as fostering. This is the preferred caring response to a child in need. However, the response may be wholly different in the case of a developmentally disabled child who requires special attention. This child, although not medically ill, may be channelled into a health care system, where he may spend his childhood days within the confines of a hospital ward, in an isolated institution, attended, *inter alia*, by doctors and nurses; his friends may be limited to those with physical and mental handicaps equivalent to, or more severe than, his own.

Admission to a hospital setting, which may heighten a child's disabilities, is virtually always on an informal basis. Accordingly, there is no statutory review of the propriety of admission, nor of the consequences of long-term residence; the legal and social fiction being that the placement is made with the meaningful consent and in the best interests of the child. The proposals made in this chapter (see also Gostin 1975) reflect the belief that the State cannot weigh the interests of mentally handicapped children and adults by a standard lower than that which it applies to other people who are dependent or in need of care.

## BIBLIOGRAPHY

CASES

*Bennett* v. *Bennett* (1969) 1 All E.R. 539.
*Estate of Park* (1953) 2 All E.R. 1411.
*In re D* (a minor), Times Law Report, Sept. 18, 1975.
*X, Y and Z* v. *United Kingdom*, European Commission of Human Rights; application nos. 6998/75,
    6870/75 and 7099/75.
*Passmore* v. *Oswaldtwistle U.D.C.* (1898) A.C. 387.
*Watt* v. *Kesteven County Council* (1955) 1 Q.B. 408.
*Wood* v. *Ealing Borough Council* (1967) ch. 354.


STATUTES AND ADMINISTRATIVE REGULATIONS

Department of Education and Science (1970) Circular 15/70. London: HMSO.
Department of Environment (1974) Circular 18/74. London: HMSO.
Department of Health and Social Security (1974a) Circular 4/74. London: HMSO.
Department of Health and Social Security (1974b) Circular 13/74. London: HMSO.
Department of Health and Social Security (1974c) Circular 19/74. London: HMSO.
Education Act 1944. London: HMSO.
Education Act 1976. London: HMSO.
Education (Handicapped Children) Act 1970. London: HMSO.
Health Services and Public Health Act 1968. London: HMSO.
Housing Act 1957. London: HMSO.
Housing Act 1974. London: HMSO.
Housing (Homeless Persons) Act 1977. London: HMSO.
Matrimonial Causes Act 1973. London: HMSO.
Mental Health Act 1959. London: HMSO.
Ministry of Education (1950) *Manual of Guidance–Special Services*. London: HMSO.
National Assistance Act 1948. London: HMSO.
Sexual Offences Act 1967. London: HMSO.


BOOKS AND ARTICLES

Barton, R. & Haider, I. (1966) Unnecessary compulsory admission to a psychiatric hospital. *Med. Sci.*
    *& Law*, 6, 3, 147.
Bayley, M. (1973) *Mental Handicap and Community Care: A Study of Mentally Handicapped People*
    *in Sheffield*. London: Routledge & Kegan Paul.
Department of Education and Science (1975) *Statistics of Education*, vol. 1, p. 54. London: HMSO.
Department of Health and Social Security (1976a) *A Review of the Mental Health Act 1959*. London:
    HMSO.
Department of Health and Social Security (1976b) *Priorities for Health and Personal Social Services*
    *in England: A Consultative Document*. London: HMSO.
Department of Health and Social Security (1978) *In-patient statistics from the mental health enquiry*
    *for England, 1975*. Statistical and Research Report Series No. 17. London: HMSO.
Department of Health and Social Security and Welsh Office (1971) *Better Services for the Mentally*
    *Handicapped*. Cmnd. 4683. London: HMSO.
Department of Health and Social Security and Welsh Office (1977) *The facilities and services of mental*
    *illness and mental handicap hospitals in England and Wales (1975)*, Table 18. Statistical and Research
    Report Series No. 19. London: HMSO.
Gostin, L. (1975) *A Human Condition: The Mental Health Act from 1959 to 1975. Observations, Analysis*
    *and Proposals for Reform*, vol. 1. London: MIND.
Gostin, L. (1977) *A Human Condition: The Law Relating to Mentally Abnormal Offenders*, vol. 2. London:
    MIND.
Hansard written parliamentary answer by Dr David Owen, then Minister of State for Health (15 January
    1976).

Herr, S. & Gostin, L. (1975) Volunteering handicapped children for institutions. *Oxford Medical School Gazette*, xxvii, 2, Michaelmas term, p. 86.

Home Office (1976) *Criminal statistics, England and Wales 1975*, Table XIX (a). London: HMSO.

Hospital Advisory Service (1975) *Annual Report for 1974*. London: HMSO.

MIND (The National Association for Mental Health) (1977) *Evidence to the Royal Commission on the National Health Service with regard to Services for Mentally Handicapped People*. London: MIND.

Ministry of Health (1967) *Annual Report for 1966*. London: HMSO.

Royal Commission on the Law Relating to Mental Illness and Mental Deficiency (1957). London: HMSO.

Tyne, A. (1976) Residential provision for mentally handicapped adults. *Social Work Today*, 7, 163–4.

Tyne, A. (1977) Mental handicap, housing need and the law. *Housing Monthly* (June), 7–11.

Welsh Office (1978) *Statistics of psychiatric hospitals and units in Wales 1975 and 1976*. London: HMSO.

World Health Organization (1978) *The Law and Mental Health : Harmonizing Objectives. Guiding principles based on an international survey*, Curran, W. J. & Harding, T. W. (eds.). Geneva: WHO.

# CHAPTER 21

# THE LAW RELATING TO MENTAL HANDICAP IN SCOTLAND

## LARRY O. GOSTIN

The Mental Health (Scotland) Act 1960 broadly defines mental disorder as 'mental illness or mental deficiency however caused or manifested'; in this chapter, the term *mental handicap* will be used instead of the term *mental deficiency*. The 1960 Act (which is currently under review) does not define mental deficiency and does not differentiate, for the purposes of hospital admission, between mental illness and mental deficiency. The recently published White Paper on the Mental Health Act 1959 of England and Wales did not remove mental handicap from the jurisdiction of Part IV of the Act (DHSS 1978); the Scottish Home and Health Department, for pragmatic reasons, is expected to adopt the same approach.

This chapter contains a legislative review and analysis of admission to hospital in Scotland. Special emphasis is placed on drawing distinctions between provisions in England and Wales and those in Scotland.

### INFORMAL ADMISSION TO HOSPITAL

The law relating to non-compulsory admission to hospital in Scotland is virtually identical to that in England and Wales. (Compare S. 5(1) of the 1959 Act with S. 23(3) of the 1960 Act.) Thus, admission of an adult is based, not upon an informed legal consent, but upon the absence of any positive objection to hospital care. Admission, therefore, is termed 'informal' (not 'voluntary') and is effected as in a hospital for physical treatment, that is, without substantive or procedural for-

mality. The admission of a mentally handicapped child is founded upon the substituted consent of the parent or guardian; the law would not ordinarily recognize any objection of the child to admission.

As in England and Wales, the Mental Health (Scotland) Act 1960 does not provide any statutory review of the need for informal admission. It maintains a legal position that mentally handicapped people are capable of understanding the implications of informal admission and of objecting where appropriate. However, informal patients in Scotland are within the protective jurisdiction of the Mental Welfare Commission. The Commission has already drawn attention to the inappropriate use of hospitals for residential purposes (Mental Welfare Commission 1975).

### INVOLUNTARY CIVIL ADMISSION TO HOSPITAL

In Scotland there are two principal procedures for compulsory civil admission: an *emergency recommendation* and an *application for admission*. There are also powers comparable to Sections 22, 135 and 136 of the Mental Health Act 1959. The Mental Health (Scotland) Act 1960, Section 103, empowers a Mental Health Officer or a Medical Commissioner from the Mental Welfare Commission, upon obtaining a warrant, to enter a private premises of a mentally handicapped person in need of protection or care, and to remove that person to a place of safety for 72 hours. Section 104 of the 1960 Act authorizes a police officer to remove to a place of safety for 72 hours a person whom he finds in a public place and who appears to be mentally handicapped and in need of care or control. 'Place of safety' in both contexts means a hospital or residential home for people suffering from mental disorder or any other suitable place, whose occupier is willing temporarily to receive the patient; unlike England, it does not include a police station unless, because of urgent necessity, there is no alternative.

## EMERGENCY RECOMMENDATION

Emergency admission under Section 31 of the Mental Health (Scotland) Act 1960 is founded upon the recommendation of one medical practitioner who need not have formal qualifications or experience in the field of mental handicap. There is no requirement for an application as in Section 29 of the 1959 Act, but if practicable the practitioner must obtain the consent of a relative or a Mental Health Officer. (The MHO is an approved social worker; this is equivalent to the Mental Welfare Officer in England and Wales.) The requirement of obtaining consent is waived in cases where the patient is already in hospital. The 1960 Act provides that, although the patient is already in a health care setting, the use of emergency powers under Section 31 is valid. Thus, Section 31 fulfills the role of Section 30 of the 1959 Act in respect of patients already in hospital on an informal basis.

In making a recommendation under Section 31, the practitioner must state that it is urgently necessary for the patient to be admitted to hospital but that compliance with the usual formalities of an application for admission would occasion undesirable delay. The recommendation authorizes the patient's involuntary admission to hospital for a period not to exceed seven days. The order cannot be renewed as it is conceived as a preliminary to an application for admission.

Since there are no procedural safeguards for this seven-day period, this order is in stark contrast to other compulsory provisions of the 1960 Act. The Sheriff (who is comparable to an English circuit court judge) has no jurisdiction in respect of a Section 31 admission and there is no other formal procedure to ensure that recommendations comply with legal criteria and current professional concepts relating to the needs of mentally handicapped people. The vulnerable position of Section 31 patients is exemplified by the fact that there is no statutory duty to notify the Mental Welfare Commission of their admission.

## APPLICATION FOR ADMISSION

An application for admission under Section 24 of the 1960 Act authorizes the detention of the patient in hospital for a period not to exceed one year. The period may be renewed for a further year and thereafter for periods of two years at a time. The grounds and procedures for admission are set out below. A renewal is effected by a report from the Responsible Medical Officer to the management, a copy of which must also be sent to the Mental Welfare Commission. This is virtually identical to Section 43 of the 1959 Act but, instead of the RMO examining the patient, he must obtain a medical report from another doctor before deciding upon renewal. On renewing the order the management must inform the patient (if over the age of 16) of his right to appeal to the Sheriff for discharge. The role of the Sheriff in this context is similar to that of the Mental Health Review Tribunal in England and Wales.

### Grounds

The patient must be suffering from a mental disorder which requires or is susceptible to medical treatment* and is of a nature or degree which warrants the patient's detention in hospital for such treatment. A further ground is that 'the interests of the health or safety of the patient or the protection of other persons cannot be secured otherwise than by such a detention'.

The Scottish Act does not expressly divide mental disorder into major (severe mental handicap and mental illness) and minor (simple mental handicap and psychopathic disorder) disorders as in Section 26 of the 1959 Act. However, in Scotland a patient cannot

* The term *medical treatment* as used in the grounds for admission includes nursing, and also includes care and training under medical supervision.

be made the subject of an application for admission (or be received into guardianship) over the age of 21 if his mental deficiency is such that he is capable of living an independent life and guarding himself against serious exploitation. If a mentally handicapped patient is admitted before attaining the age of 21 he or she may continue to be liable to detention until the age of 25. When the patient reaches the age of 25 the Responsible Medical Officer must obtain a report from another doctor. Detention may be continued either if the patient is suffering from a lower grade deficiency (that is, such that he cannot live independently or guard against serious exploitation) or if he would be likely to act dangerously to himself or others (S.23). In such cases, the patient and his nearest relative must be informed, and either of them may appeal to the Sheriff within 28 days from the patient's twenty-fifth birthday (S.40).

*Procedures*

Admission under Section 24 of the 1960 Act must be founded upon an application made either by a Mental Health Officer or by the nearest relative and the recommendation of two medical practitioners, one of whom must have been approved by a Health Board as having special experience in the diagnosis and treatment of mental disorder. If an MHO makes an application he must take such steps as are reasonably practicable to inform the nearest relative. Unlike Section 27(2) of the 1959 Act, the nearest relative cannot prevent the application being made, but has the right to object to its approval by the Sheriff.

In Scotland, every application for admission must be submitted for approval to the Sheriff within seven days of the last medical examination. He can make such inquiries and hear such people as he thinks necessary. The Sheriff must hear any objections from the nearest relative, but he need not hear the patient unless he wishes. He cannot refuse an application without offering to hear the applicant. The Sheriff's hearing must be in private if the patient or applicant wishes or if the Sheriff sees fit.

There is a substantial difference between Scotland and England in the way an order is reviewed. In Scotland this is done by a Sheriff, who because he is acting in a legal capacity can take evidence on oath. He is thus in a position to check the legality and the points of law on both admission and continued detention. In England the Mental Health Tribunal is a tribunal sitting informally. Although it is not in a position to take evidence on oath, it does have a medical member, usually of the status of consultant psychiatrist. It is therefore able to discuss the medical aspects of both admission and continued care, and if necessary is able to discuss the need for continued treatment with the Responsible Medical Officer. In Scotland the Sheriff would normally only question the medical appropriateness of admission when the patient or nearest relative provided actual evidence on the issue. There is no statistical data on the number of applications which fail to receive the Sheriff's approval, but they are rarely actively contested and the number of refusals is therefore probably quite small.

The RMO and the Mental Welfare Commission provide additional safeguards for the liberty of the subject. Both are under a mandatory duty to discharge patients who are not mentally disordered or where detention is not necessary in the interests of the patient's health or safety. The nearest relative also has a qualified power to discharge which is similar to that in England and Wales.

CRIMINAL ADMISSION TO HOSPITAL

Traditionally, mentally abnormal offenders have been exempt from ordinary penal measures on the grounds that they are not legally responsible for their behaviour. It is maintained in law that a person who does not have full comprehension when committing a criminal act cannot be held legally responsible for it. In Scotland, a finding of not guilty by reason of insanity will be made (Criminal Procedure (Scotland) Act 1975, S.174(2)) if, at the time of the offence, the defendant was suffering from 'some mental defect . . . by which his reason was overpowered, and he was thereby rendered incapable of exerting his reason to control his conduct and reactions' (*H.M. Advocate* v. *Kidd* 1960). The court then has no choice but to order the person's detention in the state hospital, or, if there are special reasons, in some other specified hospital. (The state hospital, Carstairs, is maintained for patients requiring special security. 1960 Act, Ss. 89 and 90.) The order has the same effect as a hospital order with restrictions without limit of time (see below).

Another traditional justification for exempting the abnormal offender from ordinary penal measures is that he is too mentally disordered to stand trial for the offence charged. In Scotland, if the defendant is unable to understand the course of proceedings at the trial, he may be found insane in bar of trial. The result of such a finding is that the defendant will not stand trial; instead he will be detained in the state hospital, or, if there are special reasons, another specified hospital under a hospital order with restrictions of unlimited duration (1975 Act, S. 174). (A Sheriff court dealing with a person charged under summary procedure may make a hospital order with or without restrictions. 1975 Act, Ss. 375 and 376.) A fundamental criticism of a finding of insanity in bar of trial is that a person may be detained in a maximum security institution under special restrictions on discharge without any finding in respect of the offence with which he was charged (Gostin 1977). The Thompson Committee on Criminal Procedure in Scotland (Scottish Home and Health Department 1975) has recommended amendments to this plea which are intended to ensure that there is always a finding of fact in relation to the criminal charge.

Persons found not guilty by reason of insanity and insane in bar of trial account for only a small proportion of the total number of people admitted to hospital under a court order in Scotland. These traditional legal procedures have largely been supplanted by a 'utilitarian' approach. A High Court or a Sheriff Court may make a hospital order if it finds (on the basis of two medical opinions) that the offender is suffering from a mental disorder of a nature or degree which would warrant his admission under Section 24 (1960 Act, Ss. 55–59; 1975 Act, Ss. 175–176 and 376–378). The court must not specify a state hospital unless satisfied on the medical evidence that special security is needed and there

is no other alternative. A hospital order has a similar effect to that of Section 24. The only provisions which do not apply are those relating to approval by the Sheriff, the qualified discharge order by the nearest relative, and the age limits for detention of patients with higher grade mental handicap.

The court can make a hospital order subject to special restrictions on discharge (1960 Act, Ss. 60 and 61; 1975 Act, Ss. 178 and 379). As in England and Wales, this means that the patient can receive a discharge, transfer or leave of absence only by, or with the consent of, the Secretary of State. The conceptual difficulty of delegating to a member of the executive unfettered authority over the discharge of psychiatric patients is that political factors may be taken into account and an over-cautious approach assumed (Gostin 1977). The case of X v. United Kingdom, pending against England at the European Commission of Human Rights, has clear significance in the Scottish context because of the similarity of provision. Indeed, the Scottish provisions may be regarded as less satisfactory in respect of the standards set by the European Convention. This is because the Secretary of State does not act on the basis of advice given by a Mental Health Review Tribunal; the discharge decision in Scotland rests solely with the executive who is not advised by a quasi-judicial authority.

## THE MENTAL WELFARE COMMISSION

The Mental Welfare Commission for Scotland was established under Section 2 of the Mental Health (Scotland) Act 1960. The Commission is a body corporate which must consist of no fewer than seven and not more than nine commissioners, appointed by the Queen on the recommendation of the Secretary of State as amended by the National Health Service (Scotland) Act 1972. Among the commissioners appointed, there must be a minimum of one woman, one lawyer and three medical practitioners. At present, the policy of the Commission is not to have a majority of medical members.

The Mental Welfare Commission is charged with the duty 'generally to exercise protective functions in respect of persons who may, by reason of mental disorder, be incapable of adequately protecting their persons or interests'. The Commission's jurisdiction, therefore, includes all mentally handicapped people who are incapable of protecting themselves, whether they are situated in a hospital, in residential accommodation, or in the community.

In addition to this broad responsibility to protect mentally disordered persons, the Commission has specific powers and duties. First, the Commission is authorized to discharge any patient (save those subject to special restrictions on discharge) detained under compulsory powers. The very fact that the Commission possesses the statutory power of discharge may influence the exercise of professional discretion in respect of the use of compulsion. However, the Commission rarely exercises this power (Hoggett 1977; Greenland 1969).

The second specific duty of the Commission is to 'make enquiry into any case where ... there may be ill treatment, deficiency in care or treatment, or improper detention [or where property may be exposed to loss or damage]'. The Commission must bring such instances to the attention of the hospital management or local authority, and must bring other matters important to the welfare of mentally disordered people to the attention of the Secretary of State.

Finally, the Commission has the duty to visit regularly all patients who are compulsorily detained in hospital or subject to guardianship, and to allow an opportunity, on request, for a private interview to any such patient. The Commission's policy is that each hospital, and each patient in the care of an unrelated guardian, should be visited at least twice a year. The fact that there are currently a greater proportion of informal patients does not, in the Commission's view, detract from the need for regular visitation.

The Commission's work is widely regarded in international circles as one of the most interesting organizational structures for the protection of mentally disordered people. The Commission's most distinctive features are as follows:

1. Its unfettered jurisdiction over subject matter. Notably, it is not expressly excluded from dealing with issues of clinical judgement as in the case of the Health Service Commissioner in England and Wales.

2. It is not restricted in its jurisdiction over mentally disordered people who may require protection and assistance. Its powers in respect of informal patients and persons under guardianship and in the community are particularly important.

3. Its comprehensive powers of enquiry and visitation need not be triggered by specific complaints.

On a practical level, the Commission is criticized for its reluctance to exercise its powers to discharge patients and to examine matters of clinical judgement. A structural deficiency is that the Commission has no positive power (apart from discharge) to enforce its findings; it may only advise the appropriate government authority.

## DISCUSSION AND LEADS FOR THE FUTURE

The clear impression gained by an examination of the Mental Health (Scotland) Act 1960 is that mental deficiency is inappropriately regarded as fully equivalent to psychiatric illness. The Act is designed to encourage informal admission to hospital. However, there is no recognition of the fact that mentally handicapped people, unlike some people suffering from mental illness, can seldom give informed consent to admission. In its current review of the 1960 Act, the Scottish Home and Health Department should consider the possibility of enacting separate procedures for the informal admission of mentally handicapped people. Positive guardianship designed to inform the handicapped person of statutory benefits and community alternatives, and to aid him in making decisions, may prove beneficial in the Scottish context. The Department may also consider whether a need exists for a multidisciplinary or judicial (for example, the Sheriff) review as a condition precedent, or subsequent, to informal admission.

The compulsory powers in the 1960 Act also lack clear relevance to mentally handicapped people. The express duty placed on the Mental Welfare Commission and on the RMO to discharge involuntary patients if they are no longer suffering from mental deficiency, and the requirement that the mental deficiency must be susceptible to medical treatment, are not compatible with current concepts of mental handicap. Uncomplicated intellectual deficit is not regarded as solely a medical problem; retardation will not go into remission or respond completely to medical treatment as do some forms of psychiatric illness.

The same observations can be made, perhaps with greater force, in respect of emergency recommendations for admission under Section 31. Simple intellectual deficit would not require compulsory admission to hospital as a matter of urgent necessity. Even where such urgency did exist as in the case of a mentally handicapped person with a supervening behavioural disorder, the crisis would not normally extend for a period of seven days. Section 31 attempts to achieve several purposes within a single provision: in addition to its use as a measure of crisis intervention, it purports to be a holding order for patients already in hospital (analogous to Section 30 of the 1959 Act) and a preliminary to full admission (analogous to Section 25 of the 1959 Act). In attempting to accomplish highly divergent functions, Section 31 does not accomplish any one of these satisfactorily. The Home and Health Department should consider reducing the seven-day period and enacting reasonable monitoring provisions and safeguards in respect of Section 31. If the Department considers that there is a need for a short-term order as a preliminary to full admission, or a holding order, these should be dealt with separately and on their own merits.

Like its counterpart south of the border, the Scottish Mental Health Act is under review. It is to be hoped that the resulting new legislation will reflect the changes which have occurred in the professional approach to mentally handicapped people and their needs.

## BIBLIOGRAPHY

CASES

H.M. Advocate v. Kidd, 1960 J.C. 61.
X v. United Kingdom, European Commission of Human Rights: application no. 6998/75.

STATUTES

Criminal Procedure (Scotland) Act 1975. Edinburgh: HMSO.
Mental Health Act 1959. London: HMSO.
Mental Health (Scotland) Act 1960. London: HMSO.
National Health Service (Scotland) Act 1972. London: HMSO.

BOOKS AND ARTICLES

DHSS (1978) A Review of the Mental Health Act 1959. London: HMSO.
Gostin, L. (1977) A Human Condition: The Law Relating to Mentally Abnormal Offenders. London: MIND.
Greenland, C. (1969) Appealing against commitment to mental hospitals in the United Kingdom, Canada and the United States: an international review. Am. J. Psychiat., 126, 538–42.
Hoggett, B. (1977) Mental Health and the Law. Sevenoaks, Kent: Butterworth.
Mental Welfare Commission of Scotland (1975) No Place To Go. Edinburgh: HMSO.
Scottish Home and Health Department (1975) Criminal Procedure in Scotland (Second Report). Cmnd. 6218. Edinburgh: HMSO.

# CHAPTER 22

# CURRENT LEGAL CONCEPTS IN MENTAL RETARDATION IN THE UNITED STATES: EMERGING CONSTITUTIONAL ISSUES

## LARRY O. GOSTIN

A written constitution and judicial review of legislative and executive action sets the United States apart from Great Britain and other western countries in respect of the rights and services provided to mentally retarded people. This chapter sets out the constitutional doctrines developed in the last decade which have had a profound effect upon the status of mentally retarded people. The chapter further proposes a framework for distinct and separate roles for the legislature and judiciary. The former should provide appropriate resources and an integrated long-term programme for the development of community alternatives to hospital care, while the latter should conduct its civil commitment or other compulsory hearings with formality of procedure and informality of atmosphere.

## INVOLUNTARY COMMITMENT STANDARDS: A SUBSTANTIVE DUE PROCESS ANALYSIS

In pursuance of the substantive due process clause of the fourteenth amendment of the United States Constitution, all actions taken by the State which affect an individual's person or property must be reasonably related to a valid government interest. Moreover, State actions which deprive an individual of a fundamental (constitutionally protected) interest—such as the restriction of liberty, travel and association produced by compulsory civil commitment—must be justified by a substan-

tial or compelling government interest. The traditional State interests in the civil commitment of the mentally retarded are the police and *parens patriae* powers.

### POLICE POWER

Police power enables the State, as the sovereign, to make laws and regulations for the protection of public health, safety, welfare and morals. Involuntary civil commitment for society's protection, rather than in the exclusive interests of the mentally retarded citizen, constitutes an established exercise of police power. The statutory commitment standard, which is almost universally applied to the mentally retarded person under the State's police power, is 'dangerousness to others'. In order to determine whether this government purpose is 'compelling' there must be an examination of the gravity, nature and probability of the potential harm to the public. Such an examination has led to a judicial and legislative rejection of this criterion in several jurisdictions; it has been supplanted by a standard of 'imminent dangerousness' based on 'recent overt behaviour'.

### Recent overt act

As was indicated in Chapter 20, there is no established causal relationship between mental retardation *per se* and dangerous behaviour. This suggests that the Government could not show a reasonable relationship between preventive confinement of the mentally retarded and a substantial State interest.

While there is evidence that in extremely limited circumstances, psychiatric illness may be positively correlated with dangerous behaviour, there is inevitably significant scope for false positive predictions (see Gostin 1975). Research indicates that accurate psychiatric prediction of dangerous behaviour requires, at a minimum, evidence that the individual was previously engaged in the conduct which is being predicted (Kozol et al. 1972). The 'overt behaviour' standard is based on the constitutional requirement that only grave and genuinely probable future harm to others should form the basis for civil commitment and loss of liberty. Overt dangerous behaviour is subject to empirical verification, which allows the decision-maker to evaluate independently the observations and recommendations of the clinician (see *procedural due process*, p. 298). Further, it subjects the clinician to a readily identifiable standard of self-evaluation, by requiring documentation of the specific behaviour upon which the recommendation is based.

The opposing view is that it is improper to wait until a person commits a violent act before confinement is lawfully permitted. However, society does not authorize the preventive detention of other groups (for example, ex-offenders or socio-economically deprived people in inner cities) on the basis of sociological and psychological predictions of predilection for violence.

## PARENS PATRIAE

The *parens patriae* power of the State has its origins in the English common law where the king had the authority to act as 'the general guardian of all infants, idiots and lunatics' (*Hawaii* v. *Standard Oil Co.*) The sovereign, as father of the country, was responsible for the care and custody of 'all persons who had lost their intellects and become incompetent to care for themselves.' In the United States the *parens patriae* power is vested in the legislatures and is used to protect the mentally retarded citizen from harm. The threshold constitutional requirement under this power is the incapacity of the individual to care for himself and to evaluate his need for hospital admission. In such a case, the State must act in the best interests of the individual; it may not involuntarily detain a prospective patient without a full determination that he will benefit from hospital care. Further, there is a dicta in the case of *In re Ballay* that 'without some form of treatment the state justification for acting as *parens patriae* becomes a nullity'.

### Grave disablement

The statutory commitment standards which have been applied to the mentally retarded under the State's *parens patriae* power are 'dangerousness to self' or 'in need of care and treatment'. This latter standard is particularly imprecise; it is not strictly related to the State's *parens patriae* power to protect the well-being of citizens who cannot care for themselves.

If a mentally retarded person is capable of caring for himself in the community there is no apparent constitutional authority for confinement under the *parens patriae* power. In pursuance of this constitutional principle, certain State legislatures have enacted a standard of 'grave disablement' for involuntary admission. Compulsion under the *parens patriae* power is only permitted where a person, because of mental retardation, is not able to provide for basic personal needs for food, clothing or shelter in order to sustain life.

This criterion has been criticized by those who feel it unnecessarily circumscribes the class of people who may be admitted to hospitals for the mentally retarded. A retarded person may not be gravely disabled, but may nonetheless benefit from hospital care and treatment. The criticism, however, devalues the individual's interest in a free and normal community life. If a person is able to live alone or with support in the community, care in a restricted setting is unjustified. One could go further and cogently argue that it is improper to confine a person even if he is incapable of independent life in the community. In such cases, the State has a humanitarian responsibility to provide the support necessary for community existence. If a person's incapacity to live independently were the universal criterion for compulsory detention, it could have equally unjust consequences for the elderly, the physically handicapped and the chronically infirm.

## O'CONNOR V. DONALDSON: CONSTITUTIONALLY PERMISSIBLE STANDARDS FOR INVOLUNTARY CIVIL CONFINEMENT

Mr Kenneth Donaldson had been confined for nearly fifteen years in a Florida State Mental Hospital. He had made frequent requests for his release which were rejected by the medical superintendent, notwithstanding undertakings given by responsible persons to care for him if necessary. Mr Donaldson had never engaged in behaviour which posed a danger to himself or others. Further, his confinement was of a custodial nature, as he had not participated in any therapeutic programme designed to alleviate his disability.

The United States Supreme Court held that the medical superintendent of the hospital, as an agent of the State, violated Mr Donaldson's right to liberty. The State may not confine a person solely because of mental disorder without demonstrating a constitutionally adequate purpose under its police or *parens patriae* power: 'In short, a state cannot constitutionally confine without more* a non-dangerous individual who is capable of surviving safely in freedom by himself or with the help of willing and responsible family members or friends.'

The necessary implication of the *Donaldson* case is that the 'in need of care and treatment' standard commonly found in state statutes for the involuntary commitment of the retarded is not constitutionally adequate without a showing that the individual is incapable of living in the community, either independently or with voluntary support. This suggests that the 'grave disablement' standard may be constitutionally mandated in the exercise of the State's *parens patriae* power.

A number of questions arise, for instance:

1. If a person were capable of being in the community with support, would the State be required to provide residential and social assistance in the absence of willing family or friend?

2. Does the Supreme Court's statement, 'confinement without more' mean that con-

---

* The term *without more* is legal parlance and means that something more than confinement must be made available to the individual.

---

finement would indeed be constitutionally adequate if treatment was provided?

3. Would the Supreme Court accept the State interest in protecting the public under the police power without any evidence of recent overt behaviour?

These interesting issues still await definitive constitutional construction by the court.*

## THE LEAST RESTRICTIVE ALTERNATIVE DOCTRINE: DE-INSTITUTIONALIZATION AND NORMALIZATION

There is a well-established principle in the United States that the means used to give effect to a government interest, even if the interest is valid, indeed compelling, cannot infringe upon a constitutionally protected freedom to an extent greater than is necessary to promote that interest (*Shelton* v. *Tucker*). This principle, termed the 'least restrictive alternative', may be applied to compulsory civil commitment standards. In committing a mentally retarded person to hospital, the State purports to serve its traditional functions of safeguarding the public (police power) and providing protection, care and treatment for the individual (*parens patriae* power). However compelling these concerns may be, commitment also intrudes on the constitutionally protected freedoms of liberty and association. Accordingly, in constitutional theory the State cannot confine a mentally retarded person in hospital on an involuntary

---

* An interesting subsidiary issue in the *Donaldson* case is the personal financial liability of the medical superintendent for the violation of the patient's constitutional right to liberty. The jury returned a verdict at the Federal District Court against Dr O'Connor and a co-defendant, with awarded damages of $38 500, including $10 000 in punitive damages. The Court of Appeal affirmed the judgement and award despite Dr O'Connor's defence that he had acted in good faith.

The Supreme Court vacated the judgement and award of the Court of Appeal and remanded the case to the court to consider whether Dr O'Connor should be liable for monetary damages. The criteria for this decision, as set down in *Wood* v. *Strickland*, is whether Dr O'Connor 'knew or reasonably should have known that the action he took within his sphere of official responsibility would violate the constitutional rights of [*Donaldson*], or if he took the action with malicious intention to cause a deprivation of constitutional rights or other injury to [*Donaldson*].' The matter has still to be resolved.

basis if its interests could be as effectively served in a less restrictive community setting, for example, a hostel, group home or, in the case of children, fostering (Chambers 1972). This principle has been affirmed in several lower courts by construction of relevant commitment statutes (for example, *Covington v. Harris*) and by constitutional due process analysis (for example, *Lessard v. Schmidt*; *Welsch v. Likins*; *Stamus and US v. Leonhardt*). The least restrictive alternative doctrine, however, has not been definitively determined by the United States Supreme Court in relation to civil commitment. Indeed, the court has refused to hear an appeal on this very issue for 'want of a substantial federal question' (*State v. Sanchez*).

The doctrine may be applied in two ways. The first application requires an exploration of community alternatives prior to involuntary admission to hospital. Here, the judicial authority responsible for determining the propriety of involuntary admission is charged with the duty to search for effective community care settings which are less restrictive than hospital confinement. The standard has been expressed as follows:

> No person shall be admitted to the institution unless a prior determination shall have been made that residence in the institution is the least restrictive habilitation† setting feasible for that person. (*Wyatt v. Stickney*)

The second application of the doctrine relates to the restrictions placed upon an individual while in confinement. Here, the State cannot confine a person in conditions which are more secure than necessary to meet its goals. Thus, the State would be compelled to transfer patients who can function in relative autonomy from highly controlled hospitals and wards to more normal environments, for example, away from segregated institutions to smaller, perhaps individual, residences located in the community. This approach has had a significant effect on institutions for the mentally retarded in states where legal actions have been filed. For instance, in the Willowbrook State School in New York, mental retardation experts testified that only 250 residents within a popu-

lation of 5700 required confinement in an institutional setting and the court's order required a corresponding reduction of the school population within six years (*New York State Association for Retarded Children v. Carey*). At Beatrice State School in Nebraska a similar planned reduction in the resident population was ordered (*Horacek v. Exon*).

## De-institutionalization

The de-institutionalization of mentally handicapped people can result in tragedy if humane community settings do not exist. Dependent mentally retarded people have found themselves 'dumped' on the streets without support, put into private nursing homes with inadequate staff and facilities, and sent back to family homes where they are unwanted. Vulnerable mentally retarded people find themselves being re-admitted to institutions (termed the 'revolving door syndrome') or suffering hardship or death in an uncaring community (Barnett 1978). The sterile choice for too many mentally retarded citizens is between inhuman and degrading conditions in large institutions (for example, the Willowbrook case cited above) and neglect, isolation and rejection in the community.

### Implementation of community alternatives

The following is a suggested strategy for the implementation of community alternatives.

*1. Helping judges to find alternatives.* The task of assessing alternatives to hospital care bristles with difficulties. It demands continuing familiarity with the range and capacity of habilitation approaches and facilities which exist in the community. Judges or committing agencies, if unaided by professional staff, are unlikely to make sensible decisions about community alternatives. Thus, to give the principle teeth, courts need continuing professional advice in respect of available alternatives (see Chambers 1972).

*2. Can community provision be constitutionally mandated by the courts?* The extent to which the courts can compel State legislature to provide new alternatives depends largely on whether the doctrine itself can be invoked for this purpose. The basic constitutional principle is expressed in *Wyatt v.*

† For definition of term *habilitation*, see p. 303.

*Stickney*: 'inadequate resources can never be an adequate justification for depriving any person of his constitutional rights'. The concept of affirmative action found its most complete expression in the case of *Morales* v. *Turman*:

> This procedure (enquiry into least restrictive alternative) is hollow if there are in fact no alternatives to institutionalisation. The State may not circumvent the Constitution by simply refusing to create any alternatives to incarceration; it must act affirmatively to foster such alternatives as now exist only in rudimentary form, and to build new programs suited to the needs of hundreds of children that do not need institutional care.

In the Willowbrook case, the court construed the term 'possible alternatives' to mean those which meet the needs of the individual, irrespective of the financial and administrative considerations of the State.

The judicial principle of affirmative action is still in its infancy; it requires development and monitoring in order to achieve a more humane and appropriate community service for the developmentally disabled.

### Normalization

The principle of the least restrictive alternative can be recast within a normalization framework. The Swedish principle of normalization (subsequently adopted in several American jurisdictions) is defined as 'making available to the mentally retarded patterns and conditions which are as close as possible to the norms and patterns of mainstream society'. The consequent goal of normalization is to provide mentally retarded people with the opportunity to live, wherever possible, in the community, and to provide the support and education necessary to enable them to achieve their maximum potential.

## INVOLUNTARY COMMITMENT PROCEDURE: A PROCEDURAL DUE PROCESS ANALYSIS

The Fourteenth Amendment of the United States Constitution has a procedural, as well as a substantive, component, which states that no person may be deprived of his life, liberty or property without procedural due process of the law (termed 'natural justice' in European courts). The procedural protections afforded by the Fourteenth Amendment are not absolute; each procedural element is only required to the extent that it is necessary for accurate decision-making and does not frustrate substantial State objectives. Thus, the precise procedural guarantees vary according to the circumstances of the case; a balancing test is employed which measures the magnitude of the individual interests and the importance of the particular procedure in protecting them against the counterveiling State objectives.

The United States Supreme Court is yet to consider whether the procedural due process clause applies to involuntary civil commitment. Its recent jurisprudence in respect of juveniles strongly indicates that it would require similar safeguards in the civil confinement of the developmentally disabled. The Federal Court of Appeal in *Heryford* v. *Parker* expressed the established legal principle:

> Where, as in both proceedings for juveniles and mentally deficient persons, the state undertakes to act in *parens patriae*, it has the inescapable duty to vouchsafe due process.

The particular procedural elements required by lower federal courts in respect of civil commitment are briefly outlined below.

### Notice

In *Lessard* v. *Schmidt* the Federal District Court held that the prospective patient must be given notice designed both to inform him of his rights under the commitment statute and to facilitate the preparation of his defence.

### Full and fair hearing

*Emergency detention prior to hearing.* States have a compelling interest in hospitalization as a measure of crisis intervention; in such cases the State need not provide a hearing during the duration of the emergency.

*Preliminary hearing.* A preliminary hearing on the limited issue of whether there is 'probable cause' for continued detention under the commitment statute must be provided within a reasonable period of time following emergency admission. Courts have been divided on the period required prior to a preliminary hearing. In *Fhagen* v. *Miller* and *Logan* v. *Arafeh* courts upheld emergency statutes which authorized confinement for 15 and 45 days respectively without a hearing. Other courts (*Lessard* v. *Schmidt*; *In re Barnard*) have held that the State must provide a preliminary hearing within 48 hours. The latter view appears to be constitutionally preferred (Developments 1974).

*Full hearing.* There is no definite judicial ruling on when a full hearing by an independent authority must take place. The court in *Lessard* determined that this must occur within 14 days of the preliminary hearing.

### Right to appointed counsel

Adversarial legal counsel appointed by the State is a well-established element of procedural due process (*Heryford* v. *Parker*).

### Trial by jury

The preferred constitutional view is that the right to a jury trial is not required in civil commitment (cf. *McKeiver* v. *Pennsylvania*).

### Standard of proof

Inferior courts in *Lessard* v. *Schmidt*, *In re Ballay* and *Proctor* v. *Butler* have determined that 'beyond a reasonable doubt' is the standard constitutionally applicable to civil commitment. Other courts have considered 'clear, cogent and convincing' a more acceptable civil standard (*In re Levias*; *In re Stephenson*).

### Privilege against self-incrimination

The Federal District Court in *Lessard* v. *Schmidt* held that the right to remain silent was an element of due process in civil commitment. However, the exercise of this right could prevent the State from conducting psychiatric, psychological and educational testing. This would substantially impair the State's ability to exercise its valid objectives through commitment. *Lessard* would thus appear to be incorrect in this respect.

### Examination by an independent mental retardation professional appointed by the court

The Federal District Court in *Dixon* v. *Attorney General* held that an examination by an independent professional appointed by the court was a procedural due process guarantee in relation to civil appointment.

### OBSERVATIONS AND LEADS FOR THE FUTURE

Mental retardation professionals often attribute high social costs to the provision of criminal due process standards in the civil commitment of the developmentally disabled. The allocation of scarce financial and human resources in order to erect a cumbersome legal edifice appears unjustified, particularly in the light of the economic starvation within the health and social services. There is also professional concern for the prospective patient who will experience putative trial procedures. The procedures are markedly similar to those devised in the social ostracism of the Victorian era. In particular, the process of certification through a magistrate was interpreted as both implicitly attaching moral blame to the individual and explicitly punishing him with judicially sanctioned loss of liberty. The repeal of these legal procedures in 1959 by the British Parliament was welcomed in North America and the Commonwealth as an important development in legislative and public attitudes toward mentally retarded people.

The social cost attributed to formal judicial procedures by professionals and historians (Jones 1972) warrants consideration. Procedural safeguards are only justified to the extent that they improve the accuracy of the decision-making process or achieve some other benefit for the prospective patient. There is no empirical evidence that decisions made by courts or administrative bodies are more accurate than those made by professionals. In fact, judges, magistrates and tribunals have sometimes shown themselves to be reluctant guardians of the liberty of mentally retarded citizens; they sometimes conduct superficial factual enquiries and act as 'rubber stamps' for medical authorities.

There is, however, an inherent value in

impartial decision-making to which the retarded, as citizens, should be entitled. The judicial process, despite its undoubted financial cost, is regarded as a fundamental prerequisite to the deprivation of liberty or property in the United States. It would be invidious to exclude arbitrarily the developmentally disabled from the same procedural protections which are afforded to other citizens. A society devalues itself when it judges the freedom of its vulnerable members by standards lower than those ascribed to others.

Can the prospective patient receive a full and fair hearing without incurring all of the attendant social and financial costs? The hallmarks of the administration of justice are openness, fairness and impartiality. The decision-maker requires full information regarding the prospective patient's behaviour, the proposed habilitation programme and the reason why it must be implemented in an institutional setting, and a complete assessment of community alternatives (termed a 'social enquiry' report). The following is a suggested modification of the American system which could provide a fair measure of protection for the patient.

### The decision-maker

The decision-maker need not be a 'court', with its inevitable formality and association with the criminal process. A multidisciplinary tribunal which is independent of the executive and the parties to the case, guarantees impartiality and fairness. The English Mental Health Review Tribunal, comprised of a legal chairman, a psychiatrist and a lay member, is one possible model (Gostin 1975).

### Formality of procedure and informality of atmosphere

Formality of procedure is required to ensure an ordered determination of the facts. The atmosphere need not be formal, so long as the tribunal respects the dignity of the parties.

### Unnecessary criminal procedures

There are certain procedures associated with a criminal court which inject an element of rigidity and formality of atmosphere, without necessarily providing assistance in the fact-finding process. Such procedures include a jury trial, a 'probable cause' hearing, proof 'beyond a reasonable doubt', strict rules of evidence, the right against self-incrimination, a full written transcript, oaths and subpoena powers. These can be required at the discretion of the tribunal if they are held to be important in determining the facts.

The above proposals are made in order to reconcile the interests of the individual and the State: the patient must not be excluded from accepted standards of procedural justice, while the government must provide an economical and factual determination without the accompanying stigma and trauma of a criminal due process hearing.

## THE DISTINCTIONS BETWEEN VOLUNTARY AND INVOLUNTARY ADMISSION

### VOLUNTARY ADMISSION OF ADULTS

There is a lack of clarity concerning voluntary and involuntary admissions to hospitals for the mentally retarded. Although termed 'voluntary', most statutes do not require a formal determination concerning the capacity of the prospective patient to give an informed consent. It has been observed that the passivity commonly found in prospective patients cannot be taken as a meaningful acceptance of institutional care (Cohen 1966); the classification 'non-protesting patient' is a more accurate description.

The very concept of 'voluntariness' may be regarded as a legal and social fiction. Institutional care is normally justified by the severity of the mental and developmental disability which renders a person incapable of life in the community. Given the extent of the intellectual handicap necessary to justify total care, it is paradoxical that a mentally retarded person should be thought capable of understanding and choosing hospitalization. Even if the capacity of the prospective patient to consent to admission were accepted, it would not be regarded as a truly voluntary decision if there were no meaningful choice among alternatives. In many States there is inadequate residential and social support in the community.

The retarded person with nowhere to go and no-one to care for him has only one realistic option, that is, to remain in hospital.

The opportunity for community life is further limited by the demonstrated deficiencies in education and habilitation within State institutions; the individual often is not assisted in attaining greater autonomy and in adapting to non-regimented community norms. By failing to introduce the patient to the world outside institutional walls and locked wards, the State does not offer a meaningful opportunity for a more normal life in open society (see Herr 1974).

## VOLUNTARY ADMISSION OF CHILDREN BY PARENTS

In most states parents or guardians can admit their children to institutions for the mentally retarded without independent reviews of the propriety of hospital care. In such cases even protesting children are designated as 'voluntary' patients. The child's dilemma is that he cannot leave the hospital without the approval of the parent or guardian who sought the initial admission and, as a voluntary patient, he has no legal grounds upon which to challenge his confinement. The child who seeks discharge, therefore, has no recourse except to those who agreed to the original admission, that is, his parents and the hospital authorities (see Ellis 1974).

The legal assumption that the interests of the parents necessarily coincide with those of the child is not supported by the facts. For the parents, long-term management of a child considered to be mentally retarded may be expensive, time consuming and emotionally draining. Any choice of treatment or habilitation alternatives which would reduce the expense or supervision required for the care of such a person might be attractive, whether or not there is correlative benefit to the child. The parent, therefore, may not be sufficiently objective to make judgements which are fully in the best interests of the child. Moreover, parents are often provided with a false choice: either to maintain the handicapped child at home without material support and respite from care, or to assent to his admission to hospital. The concerned parent, without assistance and without a sufficient understanding of the detrimental effect on the child's development, may provide the necessary substituted consent for voluntary admission.

## A CHILD'S RIGHT TO DUE PROCESS OF LAW

The fact that the individuals to be admitted are children does not make constitutional protections any less applicable. Children do possess a recognized interest under the due process clause. The child's constitutional interests have traditionally been allied to those of his parents. The US Supreme Court has protected the integrity of the family unit against unreasonable government interference and has established a presumption in favour of parental control:

> The child is not the mere creature of the State; those who nurture him and direct his destiny have the right, coupled with the high duty, to recognize and prepare him for additional obligations. (*Pierce* v. *Society of Sisters*)

The Supreme Court, however, has upheld the authority of the parent only where the interests of the parent and the child coincide. The parent does not have a constitutional licence to take a decision which brings significant harm to the child (*Prince* v. *Massachusetts*; *Jehovah's Witnesses* v. *King County Hospital*). The federal district courts in Pennsylvania (*Bartley* v. *Kremens*), in Tennessee (*Saville* v. *Treadway*) and Georgia (*J. L. and J. R.* v. *Parham*) have recognized the potential conflict of interest between the parent and the child in the commitment process. These courts have decided that the child is entitled to a due process hearing prior to a final determination regarding commitment. The Supreme Court has noted probable jurisdiction in the *Parham* case; it was argued in September 1978.

## THE CONFLICTING INTERESTS OF THE STATE, THE PARENT AND THE CHILD

### Parham v. J. R.

*Parham* v. *J.R.* is a class action filed by two children who allege that they and other similarly situated children in Georgia State Mental Hospitals were deprived of liberty without due process of law. Under the Georgia Code, minors under the age of eighteen may be 'voluntarily' committed to a state hospital following an application made by the minor's parent or guardian, and a determination made by a state-employed physician that the child is in need of treatment. At no time prior to commitment is the decision of the state physician subject to review by an independent authority. Release of the child following habilitation or treatment depends upon the willingness of the parent or guardian to re-accept the child. In the case of a child who is already in State custody, release depends upon the State's ability to secure a foster home. If no foster care is located, the child remains indefinitely hospitalized.

In the Parham case, independent experts, and employees at the state hospital, testified that long-term hospitalization is likely to have a detrimental effect on the development of the child. The child may modify his behaviour to succeed in an institutional setting, making him less capable of independent existence in a more normal environment.

### The conflicting interests

In the conflict-evoking situation of the 'voluntary' admission of a protesting child by his parent, the Supreme Court must reconcile the competing interests of the parent, the State and the child. The parental interest is in directing the child's growth and development without interference. The decision to temporarily admit a child to an institution for needed habilitation may not be materially different from other decisions within the traditional scope of parental authority, for example, admission to a general hospital for medical treatment, attendance at a boarding-school, confining the child to his room or isolating him from peer relationships. It is significant that the parental decision to admit a mentally retarded child to an institution is often the end product of a disturbed parent–child relationship. An adversarial hearing, with separate legal counsel for the parent and the child, may cause further deterioration of this important relationship. The procedure itself may impede any future bond between parent and child; this could permanently deny the child the opportunity for the love and intimacy of a normal family.

The legitimate objectives of the State are to uphold the family unit and to provide appropriate care for troubled and disabled children. A procedure which enables an impartial decision-maker to receive reliable and complete information would not, by itself, curtail the State's objectives. However, a formal judicial atmosphere which frightens, confuses or stigmatises the child might cause psychological damage, without any accompanying benefit to the fact-finding process. The provision of legal counsel and a formal procedural hearing also may not constitute the most productive way of allocating scarce resources to a damaged family.

In *Planned Parenthood of Missouri* v. *Danforth* the Supreme Court recently decided that the child may have constitutional interests separate from those of his parents. The distinct interest affected by voluntary commitment procedures is the liberty of the child. An orderly and independent process, however informal, would give recognition to this interest. But liberty, without more, may be meaningless to a disabled child. Parents and children together require supportive services in the home and in the community; without such assistance, the child's interest in freedom will remain hollow.

Assuming the Supreme Court reaches the question of which process is due, it may focus on the apparent capacity of the respective parties to take responsible decisions concerning admission. For example, the court may differentiate between a parental decision to temporarily place a child in hospital for habilitation or respite from care as against long-term hospitalization with the intention of abandoning the child. If parents permanently relinquish their duty of care, they should also forego the right to decide what is best for the child. An intention to abandon demonstrates an effective parental incapacity or unwillingness to act on behalf of the child.

The court may also examine the competency of the child to make his own decisions. In this regard the court could differentiate between a mature minor and a young child or infant. The court has already recognized the legal autonomy in certain circumstances of children over the age of fourteen (*Planned Parenthood of Missouri* v. *Danforth*; *Bellotti* v. *Baird*). If the court does recognize a special status for mature minors it would also have to address the issue of whether this referred to chronological or developmental age; if it chose the latter, there would be inevitable difficulty in determining whether a particular mentally disordered child had the developmental and emotional maturity to make a decision concerning the propriety of his own hospital care.

The court is expected to decide that children do have a constitutional interest in procedural safeguards prior to a final determination regarding commitment. However, the court may find that a full criminal due process hearing is harmful to the child, particularly where the admission is for a limited period of time or where the child is chronologically or developmentally immature. Accordingly, the process required by the court may involve flexible procedures and an informal atmosphere. Such a decision would adequately reconcile the competing tensions of the child's right to liberty and his right to healthy development.

## THE RIGHT TO HABILITATION: EMERGING CONSTITUTIONAL THEORIES

The concept of a constitutional right to treatment was originally established for the mentally ill. Then in the case of *Wyatt* v. *Stickney* the federal district court found that where the right to appropriate care was concerned, no distinction could be made between the mentally ill and the mentally retarded. Furthermore, 'because the only constitutional justification for civilly committing a mental retardate is habilitation, it follows that once committed, such a person is possessed of an inviolable constitutional right to habilitation.'

The term *habilitation* is defined in *Wyatt* as the acquisition and maintenance of those life skills which enable a mentally retarded person to cope more effectively with the demands of his own person and of his environment and to raise the level of his physical, mental and social efficiency. (See Appendix, pp. 372–5. for the minimum constitutional standards for habilitation established in *Wyatt*. See also *Declaration of General and Special Rights of the Mentally Handicapped* (United Nations 1971)). More specifically, habilitation is a constellation of legal rights for mentally retarded people facilitating the remediation of their delayed learning process in order that they might develop their maximum growth potential by the acquisition of self-help, language, personal, social, educational, vocational and recreational skills (Mason & Menolascino 1976). (As some institutionalized residents have never had an opportunity to acquire these skills, the term *habilitation* rather than *rehabilitation* is used.)

The United States Supreme Court has never affirmed the right to treatment or habilitation. Nevertheless, there is strong support for this right emanating from State statutes and from the United States Constitution (see *Halderman* v. *Pennhurst*).

The doctrinal bases for the constitutional right to treatment or habilitation are set out below. These are important because, depending upon the constitutional theory, certain residents (for example, the dangerous mentally retarded or those under a 'voluntary' status) may be excluded from the benefits which accrue.

### DUE PROCESS OF LAW

It will be recalled that, under the substantive due process clause of the Fourteenth Amendment, any significant deprivation of liberty or property must be justified by a permissible governmental goal. Where the State's interest in commitment is the *parens patriae* rationale that the individual is incompetent and in need of treatment, the basis for the detention is considered void if a minimally adequate standard of treatment is not forthcoming. As expressed by the court in *Wyatt*:

> To deprive any citizen of his or her liberty upon the altruistic theory that the confinement is for humane therapeutic reasons, and then fail to provide adequate treatment, violates the very fundamentals of due process.

This basic due process theory applies to non-dangerous patients compulsorily detained in pursuance of the State's *parens patriae* power. However, there are judicial indications that this reasoning might be extended to include dangerous patients detained under the State's police power. In so doing, courts have employed a *quid pro quo* rationale. Long-term detention, as a matter of due process, is generally permitted only when an individual is proved, in a hearing with substantial procedural guarantees, to have committed a specific act defined as an offence against the State. In addition, this detention is generally for a period of time proportional to the gravity of the offence. Thus, when these central limitations on the State's power to detain are missing, there must be a *quid pro quo* extended by the State to justify confinement. The most generally recognized *quid pro quo* is treatment or habilitation.

The *quid pro quo* theory is sensible in that it implicitly recognizes the general legal prohibition against preventive confinement, that is, confinement *in case* a dangerous act will occur in the future. If a mentally retarded patient, detained solely because of his dangerousness, is not provided with treatment designed to ameliorate this dangerous propensity, the propensity will persist, as will the basis for the confinement; the patient will be subject to potential life-long detention without committing any criminal offence.

This concept has two inherent difficulties. Firstly, it assumes that future dangerousness in a mentally retarded person can be reliably and validly predicted. Secondly, it assumes that a causal relationship generally exists between the condition for which treatment is provided (mental retardation) and the future dangerous behaviour. The law presumes that the provision of minimally adequate treatment will reduce the dangerous propensity. As indicated previously, there is a good deal of evidence that both of these assumptions are incorrect. If this is so, it may therefore be argued that detention on the basis of mental retardation and dangerousness —whether or not treatment is provided— is improper. Put in constitutional terms, the only legitimate State purpose for civilly confining the dangerous retarded person is to ameliorate his dangerous propensity through habilitation and to return him to society. This purpose is not reasonably related to either confinement (detention without reasonable prospect of amelioration of the dangerous condition) *or* the duration of the confinement (which could be unlimited or until the dangerous propensity desists).

## CRUEL AND UNUSUAL PUNISHMENT

In *Robinson* v. *California*, the United States Supreme Court held that incarceration for the crime of being a narcotics addict violated the Eighth Amendment's prohibition against cruel and unusual punishment, since the sanction was imposed not for specific behaviour but for a mere status. Relying on *Robinson*, several lower courts have held that confinement for mental retardation without the provision of an adequate habilitation programme is also unconstitutional (*Halderman* v. *Pennhurst*; *Welsch* v. *Likens*; *Martarella* v. *Kelley*). Unless a mentally retarded person is provided with habilitation, the detention is because of the mere status of being intellectually disabled, a condition over which he has no control. Other courts have indicated that poor institutional conditions (for example, physical deprivation, lack of basic sanitation, overcrowding, inadequate diet, unchecked violence, inadequate medical care) might violate the Eighth Amendment (cf. *Rozecki* v. *Gaughan*; *Horacek* v. *Exon*; see also *Haines* v. *Kerner*).

The right to habilitation based on the Eighth Amendment has been called into question by recent cases which suggest that the sanctions in a statute are punishment only when the intent of the legislature is punative. (*Ingraham* v. *Wright*; *Johnson* v. *Glick*). Where the 'intent' concept is adopted, the Eighth Amendment may only be applicable in criminal cases. The counter to this argument is that the 'impact' of detention is more important than the expressed intent of the legislature. Confinement without habilitation and in conditions which are degrading to human dignity is indistinguishable from penal confinement and should be deemed to constitute punishment.

## PROBLEMS WITH EXISTING HABILITATION THEORIES

### Voluntariness

The 'due process' and 'cruel and unusual punishment' theories of a right to habilitation do not strictly apply to voluntary patients. This makes a mockery of the right for it

# THE LAW IN THE UNITED STATES 305

would be both unfair and impractical to provide a different standard of care depending upon the legal status of the institutionalized resident. Courts have thus far circumvented this doctrinal difficulty by presuming that all residents—regardless of their label—are detained against their will because mentally retarded people designated as 'voluntary' may not understand their alternatives or are physically and mentally unable to indicate their desire to leave the institution. However, it has not received recognition by any of the higher federal courts, so the application of the right to habilitation to the voluntary patient therefore remains a vexing problem to the American constitutional lawyer.

## Legitimating institutions

The question should be asked regarding the right to habilitation for the institutionalized resident: how can the rights of persons inside institutions be protected without legitimating the institutions themselves? The existing constitutional theories on the right to habilitation only apply to patients in institutions; conspicuously omitted from the benefits of this right are mentally retarded people in hostels, group homes and those living with their families. In implementing the right to habilitation the courts have required the expenditure of large sums of money to improve services, staffing and conditions in American institutions. This may cause the legislatures to fund newer, bigger and ostensibly better institutions. However, it will also necessarily divert scarce resources from the development of needed community alternatives.

A habilitation theory based on an equality norm for all mentally retarded people in institutions and in the community has been developed, but the theory is still in its nascency and has received the complete support of only one lower court (*Halderman* v. *Pennhurst*).

## EQUAL ACCESS TO HABILITATION AND EDUCATION

The Fourteenth Amendment to the United States Constitution provides that no person shall be denied equal protection of the laws. The Supreme Court has held that 'equal protection does not require that all persons be dealt with identically, but it does require that

a distinction made have some relevance to the purpose for which the classification is made' (*Baxstrom* v. *Herold*). In judging the relationship between the classification and State purpose the court has developed a two-tiered analysis. Under the standard equal protection analysis, the court will accept any reasonable relation between the classification and State goals (the 'rational basis' test). However, where the classification affects a fundamental (constitutionally protected) interest or where the classification itself is suspect, the court will require a 'substantial or compelling' reason for the classification (*Dunn* v. *Blumstein*; see also Developments in the Law 1969). Where the court decides that a classification must be measured by a strict equal protection test, it is normally signalling the outcome of the case; the court has very rarely found a State interest to be sufficiently compelling to uphold the classification (Gunther 1972).

## Equal protection theories

There are two equal protection theories. The first is that a classification for the purpose of involuntary civil commitment infringes upon the residents' fundamental interests in liberty, association and travel; it must therefore be measured by a strict scrutiny equal protection analysis. It is suggested that the only compelling justification for commitment is habilitation, and failure to provide habilitation vitiates the classification (Halpern 1976).

The second equal protection theory is not based upon institutional residence, but upon the delivery of minimally adequate services to a class of citizens identified as 'mentally retarded'. This theory is not restricted to habilitation but applies to a conglomeration of community rights and needs, for example, education, training and non-restrictive zoning (Kindred et al. 1976). Equal protection under the law does not require a State to provide equal services to every citizen; it does require that if specified services are offered, some minimal opportunity be made available to similarly situated individuals. For example, there is nothing in American constitutional law which requires a State to provide habilitation, education and care for children in general. However, if a State chooses to provide any of these services for its 'normal' children, it must provide some such services for all children.

Neither of these two equal protection theories have received affirmance by a superior Federal Court.

*'New equal protection'*. The most promising development in forging a fresh constitutional theory to benefit the mentally retarded is the 'new equal protection' (Gunther 1972; Burt 1976). The doctrinal basis for this equal protection analysis is not the rigid two-tiered structure, but a means-related analysis. There are indications from recent Supreme Court cases that the court would critically review legislation which had a broad detrimental impact on a disadvantaged class. Here, the court would carefully balance the particular harm occasioned by a classification against the legislative purpose. The judicial requirement in relation to any 'semi-suspect' classification would be that it must have a substantial relationship to legislative purposes.

The new equal protection doctrine mandates that a classification based upon a disadvantaged minority such as the mentally retarded, which has an enormous effect on their well-being, should be held to violate the Fourteenth Amendment. Moreover, under the doctrine of *Brown* v. *Board of Education*, habilitation and education for mentally retarded people in segregated institutions may be considered inherently unequal, particularly in light of the evidence concerning the physical and psychological damage engendered by institutional residence. By this test, isolation of mentally retarded people in remote large-scale institutions would be presumptively unconstitutional; it would augur the end of such institutions, except perhaps for individuals with chronic multiple disabilities, and affirmatively require the State to provide equal and, whenever possible, integrated habilitation and education for mentally retarded people in the community.

## RIGHT TO PROTECTION FROM HARM

The catalogue of abuse towards institutionalized mentally retarded citizens documented by American courts has been sobering. Insti-

tutional environments have been shown to be physically harmful to residents. Living conditions have been unsanitary and without adequate human amenities. Naked mentally retarded people have been found huddled in the corners of institutional wards or isolated for years in small rooms. There has also been excrement and urine on ward floors and walls; many toilet facilities did not have towels, soap or toilet paper, and some were in a state of disrepair. Impoverished institutional conditions and inadequate resources have also resulted in the intellectual and developmental deterioration of residents. Mentally retarded people have lost social skills, including the ability to communicate, and have learned maladaptive or aggressive behaviour. On a more disturbing level, residents have been subject to physical harm and abuse. Scaldings, loss of the function of eyes, ears or limbs, bruises, scalp wounds, medical neglect, and even death were typical elements of the testimony to the courts.

In *New York State Association for Retarded Children* v. *Rockefeller* a federal district court in New York found that residents of Willowbrook State School for the Mentally Retarded did not have a constitutional right to habilitation because many were not subject to formal legal compulsion. The court, however, did accept that these residents had a constitutional right—whether founded upon due process or cruel and unusual punishment—to protection from harms such as those documented above. Based upon a number of cases dealing with minimal conditions in prisons, the court held that the right to protection from harm included protection from assaults, correction of conditions which violate basic standards of human decency, provision of adequate medical care, opportunity for exercise and outdoor recreation, normal temperature conditions, and basic sanitation and hygiene. The court noted in a subsequent judgement that, in respect of the relief provided to plaintiffs, the right to protection from harm was not significantly different from the right to habilitation. The court explained that 'harm can result not only from neglect, but from conditions which cause regression or which prevent development of an individual's capability' (*New York State Association for Retarded Children* v. *Carey*).

## IMPLEMENTING CONSTITUTIONAL STANDARDS

Courts which have enunciated a right to habilitation or right to protection from harm* have established three baᶜ'c standards for implementation of the constitutional guarantees:

1. *Humane physical and psychological environment*, consisting, *inter alia*, of the right to dignity, privacy and humane care.

2. *Qualified staff in numbers sufficient to provide adequate habilitation*, specifying minimum staffing ratios.

3. *Individualized habilitation plans*, requiring a comprehensive assessment of the resident's medical, social, educational and psychological needs; an individual programme and time-table for meeting those needs and returning the person to the community; and a post-institutionalization plan for the support and care of the resident following discharge from hospital.

A more complete description of the foregoing standards are contained in the Appendix (see pp. 372–5). The financial cost of implementing these precise requirements on a national basis would be significant. Respondent State governments have maintained that the allocation of resources is a traditional legislative function which should not be usurped by the judiciary. Notwithstanding this argument, courts have required States to provide adequate funds to bring institutional conditions up to these minimum standards: 'inadequate resources can never be an adequate justification for the State's depriving any person of his constitutional rights' (see cases cited in *Welsch* v. *Likins*, p. 499).

Professionals have similarly maintained that it is inappropriate and impractical for the judiciary to regulate clinical matters; they

have suggested that the adequacy of habilitation and treatment is essentially a 'non-justicable' question that must be left to the discretion of relevant professionals. The US Supreme Court expressly discounted this argument in *O'Connor* v. *Donaldson* (n. 10): 'where "treatment" is the sole asserted ground for depriving a person of liberty, it is plainly unacceptable to suggest that the courts are powerless to determine whether the asserted ground is present.'

The courts could monitor the constitutional right to habilitation without restricting legitimate professional discretion, that is, they would not pick and choose among various forms of habilitation and thereby overturn the decision of competent professionals. The courts would not proscribe specific forms of habilitation for particular patients, but would determine whether some form of habilitation recognized by responsible professionals was being provided. In conducting that review, courts would ordinarily look to efforts made in good faith by professionals to provide habilitation within a broad range of accepted practice. The 'right to habilitation' would, at least, condemn the warehousing of non-dangerous persons in institutions so substandard that there was virtual unanimity among responsible mental retardation professionals that a reasonable level of habilitation was not being provided (see Gostin 1975).

## SUMMARY AND CONCLUSION: A ROLE FOR THE LEGISLATURE

A notable characteristic of American federalism is that domestic policy is now substantially determined by the courts; the judiciary has introduced its own social morality to ensure reasonable access to services for minority groups. The concept of 'judicial moralism' has found no greater expression than in the interface of medicine and law. This chapter has described a mental retardation service which has, in part, been devised and implemented by judges. It would be improper to be over-critical of judicial intervention, particularly as it has come in the wake of chronic legislative and executive neglect of the needs

---

* There is still need for clarification concerning the extent to which the right to protection from harm requires positive programmes of habilitation. *New York State Association for Retarded Children* v. *Carey* does suggest that, without individual habilitation programmes, residents suffer from intellectual and developmental deterioration. Positive habilitation may therefore be regarded as a requisite component of the right to protection from harm.

of mentally retarded people\*. Nonetheless, it is regrettable that important policy decisions in respect of the mentally retarded have had to be taken within the narrow context of litigation. The courts are limited by the particular facts and issues raised in the immediate case; they are only able to set *minimal* standards based upon non-specific constitutional principles; and they are ill-equipped to assure long-term compliance with, and implementation of, their judgements. Indeed, the elements which go to make up the development of effective services—planning, budgeting, building and operating—are traditionally legislative functions, and comprehensive interference by the judiciary may prove ineffective. It may also strain the relationship between the three branches of government.

Conspicuously absent from American policy is a comprehensive legislative assessment of the needs of mentally retarded people and a long-term programme designed to meet those needs. (Compare the fragmented approach of the United States illustrated by judicial intervention on a case-by-case basis with the integrated approach in the British White Paper *Better Services for the Mentally Handicapped*, described in Chapter 20.) If the United States is to achieve effective and humane integration of mentally retarded people into ordinary homes, schools and industries, it will have to build and adapt community resources in sufficient numbers; it will have to educate the wider community to be more tolerant of disabled people; and it will have to reduce society's false reliance on total institutional care for its handicapped members. The proper role of the judiciary is not to devise and implement this policy, but to construe it and to provide sensitive arbitration in cases where individuals have been subject to discrimination solely by reason of their handicaps.

* Although the US Congress has essentially neglected the needs of mentally retarded people by failing to allocate sufficient resources for community development, it has passed legislation to promote their status and civil rights. For instance, the Developmentally Disabled Assistance and Bill of Rights Act 1975 (implemented 1977) provides a non-inclusive bill of rights for the developmentally disabled, for example, rights to appropriate medical services, a nourishing diet, and the right to an individualized habilitation programme. The most significant aspect of this Act is its requirement that states, as a condition of receipt of federal funding, set up an agency to provide protection and advocacy for the developmentally disabled. Such agencies must be independent of state facilities serving developmentally disabled people; must advise, protect and intercede on behalf of the developmentally disabled; and must pursue 'legal, administrative and other appropriate remedies'.

# BIBLIOGRAPHY

## CASES

*Bartley* v. *Kremens*, 402 F. Supp. 1039 (E.D.Pa. 1975), *dismissed as moot, Kremens* v. *Bartley* 52 L. Ed. 2d 184 (1977).
*Baxstrom* v. *Herold*, 383 U.S. 107, 111 (1966).
*Bellotti* v. *Baird*, 96 S.Ct. 2857 (1976).
*Brown* v. *Board of Education*, 347 U.S. at 493 (1954).
*Covington* v. *Harris*, 419 F. 2d 617 (D.C. Cir. 1966).
*Dixon* v. *Attorney General*, 325 F. Supp. 966 (M.D. Pa. 1971).
*Dixon* v. *Weinberger*, 405 F. Supp. 974 (D.D.C. 1975).
*Donaldson* v. *O'Connor*, 493 F. 2d 507 (5th Cir. 1974), *vacated*, 422 U.S. 563 (1975).
*Dunn* v. *Blumstein*, 405 U.S. 330 (1972).
*Fhagen* v. *Miller*, 29 N.Y. 2d 348, 278, N.E. 2d 615, 328, N.Y.S. 2d 393, *cert. denied*, 409 U.S. 845 (1972).
*Haines* v. *Kerner*, 404 U.S. 519 (1972), *aff'd*, 456 F. 2d 854 (1972).
*Halderman et al.* v. *Pennhurst State School and Hospital*, C.A. No. 74–1345 (E.D.Pa. Dec. 23, 1977. Order made March 17, 1978. Reported in *Mental Disability Law Reporter*, Sept.–Dec. 1977, p. 201.)
*Hawaii* v. *Standard Oil Co.*, 405 U.S. 251, 257 (1972), *quoting* 3 W. Blackstone, *Commentaries*, p. 47.

*Heryford* v. *Parker*, 396 F. 2d 393 (10th Cir. 1968).

*Horacek* v. *Exon*, 357 F. Supp. 71 (D. Neb. 1973), consent decree entered in August 1975.

*Ingraham* v. *Wright*, _____ U.S. _____ , 97 S.Ct. 1401 (1977).

*In re Ballay*, 482 F. 2d 648 (D.C. Cir. 1973).

*In re Barnard*, 2 Johns. Ch. 232, 236 (N.Y. 1816).

*In re Levias*, 517 P. 2d 588, 590 (Wash. 1973).

*In re Stephenson*, Docket No. 48390 (Ill. Sept. 20, 1977), reported in *Mental Disability Law Reporter*, vol. 2 (1977), pp. 169–72.

*Jehovah's Witnesses* v. *King County Hospital*, 278 F. Supp. 488 (Q.D. Wash. 1967), aff'd *per curium*, 390 U.S. 598 (1968).

*J.L. and J.R.* v. *Parham*, 412 F. Supp. 112 (M.D. Georgia 1976), *probable jurisdiction noted by U.S. S.Ct.* May 31, 1977.

*Johnson* v. *Glick*, 481 F. 2d 1028 (2d Cir. 1973).

*Lessard* v. *Schmidt*, 349 F. Supp. 1078 (E.D. Wisc. 1972), *vacated and remanded on other grounds*, 414 U.S. 473 (1974).

*Logan* v. *Arafeh*, 346 F. Supp. 1265 (D.Conn. 1972).

*Martarella* v. *Kelley*, 349 F. Supp. 575 (S. D. N. Y. 1972).

*McKeiver* v. *Pennsylvania*, 403 U.S. 528 (1971).

*Morales* v. *Turman*, 383 F. Supp. 53, 125 (E.D. Tex. 1974), *rev'd* 535 F. 2d 864 (5th Cir. 1976), *reinstated*, 430 U.S. 322 (1977).

*New York State Association for Retarded Children* v. *Carey*, 393 F. Supp. 715 (E. D. N. Y. 1975).

*New York State Association for Retarded Children* v. *Rockefeller*, 357, F. Supp. 752 (E. D. N. Y. 1973).

*O'Connor* v. *Donaldson*, 422 U.S. 563 (1975).

*Parham* v. *J.R.*, _____ U.S. _____ (1978).

*Pierce* v. *Society of Sisters*, 268 U.S. 510 (1910).

*Planned Parenthood of Missouri* v. *Danforth*, 428 U.S. 52 (1976).

*Prince* v. *Massachusetts*, 321 U.S. 158 (1944).

*Proctor* v. *Butler*, Nos. 7737 and 7738 (N.H. Nov. 16, 1977), reported in *Mental Disability Law Reporter*, vol. 2. (1977), pp. 169–72.

*Robinson* v. *California*, 370 U.S. 660 (1962).

*Rozecki* v. *Gaughan*, 459 F. 2d 6 (1st Cir. 1972).

*Saville* v. *Treadway*, 404 F. Supp. 430 (M.D. Tenn. 1974).

*Shelton* v. *Tucker*, 364 U.S. 479 (1960).

*Stamus and U.S.* v. *Leonhardt*, 414 F. Supp. 439 (S.D. La. 1976).

*State* v. *Sanchez*, 80 N.M. 438, 457 P. 2d 370 (1968), *appeal dismissed*, 396 U.S. 276 (1969).

*Welsch* v. *Likins*, 373 F. Supp. 487 (D. Minn. 1974), *aff'd in part and remanded in part*, 550 F. 2d 1122 (8th Cir. 1977).

*Wood* v. *Strickland*, 420 U.S. 308 (1975).

*Wyatt* v. *Stickney*, 325 F. Supp. 781 (M.D. Ala. 1971); 344 F. Supp. 373, 344 F. Supp. 387 (M.D. Ala. 1972) *aff'd in part, remanded in part, decision reserved in part sub nom*, Wyatt v. Aderholt, 503 F. 2d 1305 (5th Cir. 1974).

## STATUTES AND ADMINISTRATIVE REGULATIONS

Developmentally Disabled Assistance and Bill of Rights Act 1975, sections 111 *et seq.*, PL94–103, 42 U.S.C. sections 6000 *et seq.*, *amending* PL88–164. Relevant provisions at 42 U.S.C. sections 6010, 6011, 6012.

Developmentally Disabled Assistance and Bill of Rights Regulations, 42 *Federal Register* 5273 *et seq.* (January 27, 1977).

## BOOKS AND ARTICLES

Barnett, C. (1978) Treatment rights of the mentally ill nursing home residents. *U.Pa.L. Rev.*, *126*, 578.

Burt, R. (1976) Beyond the right to habilitation. In: Kindred, M. et al., *see below*.

Chambers, D. L. (1972) Alternatives to civil commitment of the mentally ill; practical guides and constitutional imperatives. *Mich. L. Rev.*, *70*, 1107.

Cohen, F. (1966) The function of the attorney and the commitment of the mentally ill. *Tex. L. Rev.*, *44*, 424–47.

Developments (1974) Civil commitment. *Harv. L. Rev.*, *87*, 1190.

Developments in the Law (1969) Equal protection. *Harv. L. Rev.*, *82*, 1065.

Ellis, J. (1974) Volunteering children: parental commitment of minors to mental institutions. *Calif. L. Rev.*, *62*, 840.

Gostin, L. (1975) *A Human Condition: The Mental Health Act from 1959 to 1975. Observations, Analysis and Proposals for Reform*, vol. 1. London: MIND.

Gunther, G. (1972) The Supreme Court 1971 Term—in search of evolving doctrine on a changing court: a model for a newer equal protection. *Harv. L. Rev.*, *86*, 1.

Halpern, C. (1976) The Right to Habilitation. In: Kindred, M. et al. *see below*.

Herr, S. (1974) Civil rights, uncivil asylums and the retarded. *U. Cinn. L. Rev.*, *43*, 679.

Jones, K. (1972) *A History of the Mental Health Services*. London: Routledge & Kegan Paul.

Kindred, M., Cohen, J., Penrod, D. & Schaffer, T. (eds.) (1976) *The Mentally Retarded Citizen and the Law*. New York: The Free Press.

Kozol, H. L., Boucher, R. J. & Garofalo, R. F. (1972) The diagnosis and treatment of dangerousness. *Crime and Delinquency*, *18*, 371.

Mason, B. G. & Menolascino, F. J. (1976) The right to treatment for mentally retarded citizens: an evolving legal and scientific interface. *Creighton L. Rev.*, *10*, 124.

United Nations (1971) *Declaration of General and Special Rights of the Mentally Handicapped*. New York: U.N. Department of Social Affairs.

# VI
# SPECIALIZED AREAS

# CHAPTER 23

# PARENT COUNSELLING

## CLIFF CUNNINGHAM

There can be few, if any, professionals associated with handicapped children who have not experienced the frustrated and aggressive outpourings of parents. The criticisms of these parents usually concern either a lack of practical support and advice or difficulties encountered in getting information and assistance from the service agencies, or a lack of sympathy, sensitivity or genuine feelings of concern on the part of the professional person. It is not uncommon for the professional to assume that this aggression is inevitable; that it is the irrational and misdirected release of emotions of anxiety and guilt at having given birth to a handicapped child. As one physician put it, 'there is no way of breaking bad news without the parent hating you for it', and similarly a social worker, 'some parents are never satisfied because what they really want is for us to cure the handicap.'

Whilst there is some truth in this, the assumption that such aggression is inevitable is unwarranted. Parents who feel they were told 'badly' will frequently relate the experience many times, even years later, as though trying to reduce their original feelings of shock and aggression. Yet parents who state that they were told 'well' seldom refer to this time except in terms of their feelings of shock and sadness, and appear more ready to seek support from the service agencies. Similarly, Cunningham and Sloper (1977a) report that all the parents of Down's syndrome children in their study who felt they were told of the diagnosis 'well', wished to speak to the 'teller' again soon after the disclosure whilst all those who felt they were told bluntly and unsympathetically wanted

to speak to someone soon after the disclosure, but not to the 'teller'.

It is not only the way the professional talks to the parent that can cause conflict. Several studies on the problem of telling parents the diagnosis of Down's syndrome have reported complaints by parents that they were not told together, that they were not told soon enough, that they were told in front of a large number of people and no privacy was available, that the baby was not present and that they were not given any or enough information (Gayton & Walker 1974; Pueschel & Murphy 1976; Cunningham & Sloper 1977a).

Two points can be made to illustrate the range of problems. If one assumes that the person who does the initial telling must do it well and sympathetically and even then is likely to incur the parents' 'irrational' aggression, then why do so many physicians tell only one spouse who is then left to inform the other? The above surveys found that only 20 to 30 per cent of parents were told together, that 60 to 80 per cent would have liked to be told together, and that in 50 to 60 per cent of the cases one spouse was left to inform the other.

The second point concerns the issue of when to tell the parent of the diagnosis or suspicion of some handicap being present. Surveys with Down's syndrome infants report that about 90 per cent of parents want to be informed of the diagnosis in the first week after birth and many as soon as possible. The sooner parents were told the greater was their satisfaction with the timing. Many parents told later than they would have liked felt that they had been 'cheated', 'that there was something to hide'. This suggests to them that there is a stigma in having such an infant and is hardly conducive to developing a positive approach to the child. An anomaly arises when one finds that surveys repeatedly report that 50 to 60 per cent of the parents of Down's syndrome infants suspect something is wrong in the first 48 hours after the birth. The problem is even more confounded by many parents reporting that it was the changes in the hospital routine or reactions of the staff that made them suspicious, as in the two instances following:

> I knew something was wrong as soon as he was ... born. They all looked at each other and went very quiet. Some other people then came in ... but when I asked was he all right, they said he was fine and not to worry ... but I knew they knew all the time, so why didn't they say something instead of keeping me wondering and worrying all that time.

> [Similarly] I guessed she wasn't all right. She was always the last baby brought up from the nursery after feeding and people—doctors, students and nurses and that—kept popping in to see us but never seemed to want anything.

Thus parent counselling involves not only the way we talk to parents but the whole way we organize the treatment of the parents and the baby. If an improvement is to be made with respect to the parents' expressed dissatisfaction, it is necessary to understand that the counselling begins prior to the diagnosis being given, and continues for many months afterwards. Thus it must include all agencies who will come into contact with the family.

Counselling is necessary and worthwhile for two reasons. Firstly, it can prevent the development of aggression towards the very services on which the parents rely. In many cases such agression can prevent the parents from seeking advice. If parents find out about the condition themselves, the trust relationship between the parents and the physician can be undermined. All too frequently this will affect the parents' relationships with other associated agencies and can lead to their failing to cope, or to their developing maladaptive practices in trying to cope with their child's handicap. Secondly, parents can help the development of the handicapped infant or child through intervention procedures (see Chapter 13). In turn, helping the infant can act as a powerful therapy for the parent. However, such intervention cannot begin until the parent is willing and ready to seek advice.

In the remainder of this brief chapter, guidelines for this early counselling will be given. (The reader is also directed to the publication of Spain and Wigley (1975) for a more detailed discussion.)

## THE INITIAL PROBLEM

Table 23.1 is a schematic overview of a model of the reactions and possible treatment following the disclosure of the diagnosis. It is adapted from the work of Hall and Grunewald (1977) and the available literature.

Progress through the various phases depends upon several variables:

1. Parents' past experience of mental handicap or any severe childhood disorders, previous difficulties with childbirth and other offspring, whether they have other children, have waited for many years to have a child and so on.

2. Philosophy, covering parents' hopes, strivings and the values they place on various abilities. Often parents who particularly value intellectual skill have greater difficulty in accepting mental handicap than a physical handicap and *vice versa*. Fathers often find it more difficult to accept the child through irrational association with their 'manhood' or fear for the family as a whole. Some parents fear a child who will be disfigured or look peculiar.

3. Life-style, covering the difficulties that the child may cause in the present life-style of the family.

4. Relationship between partners. A knowledge of the parents, their relative strengths and weaknesses, support for each other and so on can be most useful.

5. Personality. This is particularly complex, but any instability or personality disorder can become disproportionately crucial at this time. Information from the family doctor can be most important.

6. How the parents and the infant are treated.

TABLE 23.1

Model of psychic crisis at disclosure of handicap

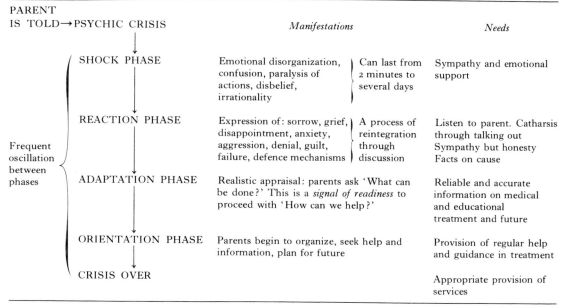

| PARENT IS TOLD → PSYCHIC CRISIS | Manifestations | | Needs |
|---|---|---|---|
| SHOCK PHASE | Emotional disorganization, confusion, paralysis of actions, disbelief, irrationality | Can last from 2 minutes to several days | Sympathy and emotional support |
| REACTION PHASE | Expression of: sorrow, grief, disappointment, anxiety, aggression, denial, guilt, failure, defence mechanisms | A process of reintegration through discussion | Listen to parent. Catharsis through talking out Sympathy but honesty Facts on cause |
| ADAPTATION PHASE | Realistic appraisal: parents ask 'What can be done?' This is a *signal of readiness* to proceed with 'How can we help?' | | Reliable and accurate information on medical and educational treatment and future |
| ORIENTATION PHASE | Parents begin to organize, seek help and information, plan for future | | Provision of regular help and guidance in treatment |
| CRISIS OVER | | | Appropriate provision of services |

Frequent oscillation between phases

Adapted from Hall and Grunewald (1977).

The first four variables are somewhat intangible and there is relatively little information to guide the person responsible for the parent at this time. Clearly, someone who knows the parents is important. The family doctor, obstetrician or health visitor may have essential information which would suggest how best to treat the parents. However, the following guidelines may be given:

1. The majority of parents wish to be informed of the diagnosis as soon as possible. They are retrospectively extremely sensitive to any attempts to hide the information from them or to reassure them falsely. If disclosure is particularly delayed and the parents are aware of the infant's need for special treatment, they can feel that their child may have been 'held back' because of the delay.

2. Most parents feel that the child should be present at the time of the telling. If this is not possible then they should have access to him immediately afterwards.

3. The majority of parents wish to be told together. In the case of a single-parent family, the presence of a close relative or friend is useful, particularly if the diagnosis is given when the parent is attending out-patient services.

4. The diagnosis should be given in a private place where there is not likely to be any disturbance. Similarly, parents often resent the presence of other professionals at this time.

5. There should be adequate time for the information to be given, questions asked, emotions expressed. The parents should not feel that the professional is anxious to get away. This is often interpreted as being a lack of sympathy or disinterest in the child.

Parents are extremely sensitive to people's reaction to the new baby at this stage. Particularly, they note any suggestion that the baby is 'not worth bothering about', has 'little value'. It is essential that those professionals responsible for the infant and parents at this time show the parents that they do value the infant whilst still honestly and realistically appraising the handicapping condition. If the professional cannot feel any value in the infant, then it would be far better to delegate the disclosure and earlier interviews to someone who does.

Several guidelines can also be given regarding the way one talks to the parent:

Avoid all unnecessary jargon.

Do not give a lecture but let the parents ask questions; let them talk and be prepared to listen.

Allow pauses in the conversation. Give the parents time to think, and remember that silence often precedes embarrassment or difficult statements.

Try to get the parents to make statements, to talk about and discover their own feelings, values, hopes, disappointments and so on.

Choose words carefully. An odd expression such as 'had you not noticed something peculiar or strange about the baby' can be misinterpreted out of all proportion.

Be as objective as possible in giving information about the baby, neither over-positive nor particularly negative.

Do not avoid honest responses, for example, saying that a particular question cannot be answered.

Try to give an accepting attitude to parents and child. Avoid any indications that the parents may be inadequate, for example, by talking in so complicated a manner that they do not understand, or by suggesting that the child needs extra expertise which they do not have.

*Organization of services*

Organization of services at this time is also crucial. Parents should have the opportunity for a further appointment with the professional or another informed person as soon as possible after the initial disclosure. At the first meeting the trauma is so great that little information is taken in. However, once this shock phase is over parents will need frequent opportunities to meet with professionals for support and information. If the person who did the initial telling cannot be available to maintain this contact, it is best if he introduces a new agent who can be available. It is best if as few people as possible are concerned with providing the support and advice. Once the initial diagnosis and interviews are over, the paediatrician may play a less active

role, with health visitor or community mental handicap nurse as the major resource. The family may need casework help from a social worker, as well as information about benefits available and local branches of parental organizations.

Some parents find great comfort from meeting with another parent who has a similarly handicapped child. However, not all parents are ready to do this and so one must ask first if they would like such a meeting and not arrange it automatically. It is also worthwhile carefully considering who the other parent should be. Merely having a handicapped child is not a sufficient criterion for being able to help a fellow parent at this time.

As far as possible the 'normality' of how parents and infants are treated in the hospital or baby clinic should be maintained. Particular emphasis on special treatment appears to upset a number of parents. It is also necessary to ensure that everyone dealing with the parents takes a similar approach and is aware of the treatment being given. Team meetings to review the position are essential.

The provision of early treatment shows the parents that they are not alone, and helps to prevent feelings of guilt, loss of esteem and undue anxiety. Care must be taken that the parents' own responsibility for their child is not implicitly denied by an over-emphasis on professional expertise. After all, parents are in the best position to help the baby develop.

*Parents' need for information*

The imparting of accurate information is essential. Parents often complain that they meet with conflicting information or advice from professionals. They also seek out books and again find conflict, usually because of out-dated information such as poor prognosis for mortality or achievement, or such stereotyped banalities as 'they are all very humorous, 'they all love music and are good mimics'!

If parents are going to develop a positive relationship to the infant they must feel they know him and understand him. It is a common psychological phenomenon to feel apprehensive or alienated from things we do not understand. How much more this must happen if it is your own child. Similarly, feelings of guilt over producing such a child can best be reduced if accurate statements of causality are given and understood. The parents of the brain-damaged child for which no causal explanation can be given, often suffer a great deal and need much support and guidance over a long period. In all cases, however, one must help the parent to realize that knowing the cause does not necessarily help the child; that even where a cause is known the variability and individual differences found are so great that it is of minor value. What is important is for parents to realize that they can help the child by giving him love and care and special stimulation to achieve his potential, to do as well as he can.

Thus, regardless of the handicapping condition, all parents ask the same questions:

*What is the handicap? How was it caused?* Though many professionals assume that parents do not want too much detail or cannot understand the technicalities associated with such a question, our experience is that the majority of parents do want as much information as is available. What upsets them is being given the information in so complex a way that they do not understand and consequently feel even more useless and frustrated. Having understood the information, however, they can gain much satisfaction and feel less alienated from the infant.

*What is the future? What will he do and not do?*
To answer this question the professional must be honest and realistic. So often we can only say we are not sure of the future. If we use examples of adults with a similar handicapping condition we cannot tell to what extent the eventual achievement was due to primary or secondary factors (see Chapter 13). Variability again is so great that precise predictions are impossible. Frequently, professionals present a very negative picture emphasizing what the infant may not do. It is essential to provide a balanced overview, emphasizing generalizations but noting both positive and negative aspects. Above all parents appreciate an honest attempt to answer their queries.

*What can we do to help?*
It is essential that parents are not given some weak platitude such as 'treat them as normal' but are given detailed explanations of practical help which they can give. Obviously this must be continuous and aimed at small achievable stages of development.

It is unfortunate that the majority of parents of handicapped infants currently feel that they do not receive sufficient accurate information. Many would like access to well-explained written information (for example Smith and Wilson (1973)) as well as discussion. However, the professional must check that such information is up to date. In such a varied situation as mental handicap, impinging as it does on so many disciplines, this is exceedingly difficult for one individual. The well-organized multidisciplinary team has a major part to play in this provision (see Chapter 2) and needs to supply itself with booklets for further reading by parents.

NEED FOR CONTINUING SUPPORT

However, it is not just the first period which is crucial. Mental handicap is a permanent condition lasting throughout life. Parents need a constant service providing information, support and physical or financial assistance which reflects the development and changing needs of the child. For example, the majority of infants with Down's syndrome are not significantly delayed in their development until late into the first year of life. Thus the parents begin with a state of shock and anxiety, then within weeks adapt to the knowledge of the condition. They start to look for signs of handicap, of delay, but seldom see any. This can lead to a 'euphoric period': 'He is not really that handicapped, he will be high grade.' It is only when the major milestones, such as sitting unaided, do not appear towards the end of the first year that the parents first appreciate the reality of the handicap. This can produce a different trauma for the parents and again counselling is important. Yet by this time many of the services which were constantly available in the first weeks have ceased (Cunningham & Sloper 1977b).

Similarly, in conditions such as severe microcephaly and spina bifida, once the parents have accepted the diagnosis they settle down and care for the baby. However, as the child grows and ceases to be a baby in terms of physical size, many crises appear. The fact that the parents are coping with the handicapped baby does not mean that they will be able to cope when he is older.

This pattern of change repeats itself throughout the life of the child: 'What shall I do about school', 'Should I let him play out in the street', 'What should I do about sex education, 'Will I know when he has reached puberty', 'What sort of work placement would be best', 'Should I think of some part-time residential placement' and so on.

Changes in the parents will also affect planning and provision. Some parents are unwilling or unable to visit clinics or parent groups, especially on a regular basis. Thus at first a domiciliary service is needed. Even when they are willing to visit outside agencies they may still prefer and require individual treatment and meetings on their own ground where they feel less threatened.

One point which cannot be overstated is the tremendous strength and support parents gain from knowing there is someone whom they can trust and who is always available. A telephone number and the knowledge that someone will contact them periodically, even just to see if everything is all right and to inquire how the child is getting on, is always appreciated.

## SUMMARY

Well-organized parent counselling is essential. It must take account of the parents' changing pattern of needs, must be regular and continuous, and must meet these needs. If these criteria are fulfilled, it will be possible to predict and prevent problems arising rather than hastily meeting them when crises occur. Above all, counselling must never be withdrawn in the face of frustration and aggression, nor must hostility be met with hostility, no matter how disguised.

## BIBLIOGRAPHY

Cunningham, C. C. & Sloper, P. (1977a) Parents of Down's syndrome babies: their early needs. *Child Care, Health and Development, 3,* 325.

Cunningham, C. C. & Sloper, P. (1977b) Down's syndrome infants: a positive approach to parent and professional collaboration. *Health Visitor, 50,* 32.

Gayton, W. F. & Walker, L. (1974) Down's syndrome: informing the parents. *Am. J. Dis. Child., 127,* 510–12.

Hall, E. C. & Grunewald, K. (1977) Unpublished report. The National Board of Health and Welfare, S-10630, Stockholm, Sweden.

Pueschel, S. M. & Murphy, A. (1976) Assessment of counselling practices at the birth of a child with Down's syndrome. *Am. J. ment. Defic., 81,* 325–30.

Smith, D. W. & Wilson, A. A. (1973) *The Child with Down's Syndrome (Mongolism).* Eastbourne: W. B. Saunders.

Spain, B. & Wigley, J. (eds) (1975) *Right from the Start: A service for families with a young handicapped child.* London: National Society for Mentally Handicapped Children.

# CHAPTER 24

# AUTISM AND ITS RELATION TO MENTAL RETARDATION

## ROBYN BENCE AND JOHN RENDLE-SHORT

In a paper entitled 'Autistic Disturbance of Affective Contact', Kanner (1943) described a syndrome of behaviour not previously considered as a unique entity. The eleven children whose behaviour he studied were unable to relate to other people; Kanner called this condition 'extreme autistic aloneness'. The children also exhibited delay in speech acquisition together with abnormalities of language, an obsessive desire to maintain sameness but an excellent rote memory. Kanner stressed that the condition was found from early infancy and considered that it could represent an inborn disturbance of affective contact.

Although the term *autism* had originally been coined by Bleuler in 1911, it was not used by him for the type of disorder to which Kanner referred. Bleuler used the term to describe an atypical thought process in schizophrenics.

It is of interest that descriptions of 'autistic-like' behaviour have been found dating prior to the present use of the term *autism*. Humphries and Humphries translated *The Wild Boy of Averyron* by Jean-Marc-Gaspard Itard (1799). Itard was a physician into whose care a boy named Victor was given. Itard described the boy's conduct which was characteristic of infantile autism. He showed no affection, was absolutely inattentive, did not focus on objects or people and was selectively deaf. He resisted changes in his environment.

Witmer (1922) described the behaviour of Don and attempts that were made to educate him. Don's behaviour, like Victor's, was typically autistic. Don had an unusual attachment to a particular object, a card. He also showed a lack of attention to other objects and people. Neither Don nor Victor ever became normal but functioned as mentally retarded.

After Kanner's article was published, there was a dormant period and then a spate of articles appeared, mostly concerned with etiology and management.

Since 1943, there has been a difference of opinion by authorities concerning the causation of infantile autism. This diversity may be broadly categorized into two main streams:

1. Views based on organic theories.
2. Views based on non-organic theories which are either psychodynamically or behaviourally oriented.

The purely organic theories postulate different types of neurological impairments. Diffuse brain impairment was suggested by Rimland (1964) while Hutt et al. (1965) considered a more specific disability such as a disturbance of the reticular system.

Ruttenberg (1971) differentiated between what he called primary and secondary autism. He considered that primary autism was caused by some form of neurological disorder while secondary autism was a response to an inadequate environment. Ruttenberg therefore suggested two conditions, one organically based, and one related to environmental factors.

Authorities who follow a psychodynamic approach include Edelson (1966) and Bettelheim (1967). Edelson regarded all schizophrenic behaviour (in which he included infantile autism) as a mourning reaction caused by a perceived loss of maternal love, whereas Bettelheim interpreted autistic behaviour as a denial of self as a defence against threats from a world perceived as hostile and rejecting. O'Gorman (1967) followed Kanner and related infantile autism to a lack of the normal relationships with parents, particularly the mother. He considered that the cause of the condition could be an excessively stressful environment or some organic predisposition.

More recently Rutter (1972) has suggested that infantile autism develops as a central disorder of cognition which involves impairment of both comprehension of language and defects in the utilization of language or conceptual skills in thinking.

## CAUSATION

It has been a fairly common finding in the history of medicine that the evolution of knowledge of a new disease follows a set pattern. Initially there is a description of the symptom complex, then it is realized that harboured under this umbrella title are a number of conditions of varying etiology. Lastly the stage is reached when it is appreciated that though the cause and mode of presentation may be different, the practical management and end result have much in common, and so it is with autism.

Looking at the original infantile autism complex, what can we tease out from it, to refine the concept? We will first consider the age of presentation. Some people have considered infantile autism under the general heading of 'Juvenile Schizophrenia'. However, it is now appreciated that this condition, which merges into ordinary adult schizophrenia, rarely commences below the age of 8 years, whereas there is almost universal agreement that the initial symptoms of infantile autism always commence under the age of 30 months. Sometimes the two conditions are brought together under the heading of 'Juvenile Psychosis' but this merely clouds the issue. Thus there is a period of approximately six years during which psychotic symptoms do not commence. Children with infantile autism (commencing before 30 months) can continue to manifest their autistic symptoms throughout childhood.

The fact that the onset of infantile autism is confined to the first three years of life is important diagnostically; it also has etiological implications, for this is the time, of all times, when a child should be developing his powers of communication.

We must now consider the genetic implications. Several pairs of identical twins with autism have been described and we have had one such pair under our care. Other instances of two cases of autism in a family have been reported but so far no convincing genetic inheritance has been established. The importance of establishing a possible genetic causation is twofold.

Firstly, it would mean that the parents (and especially the mother) were only secondarily causative. This is important because following Kanner's original description of autism there has been a school of thought that considered the disorder to lie in the mother rather than the child. Hence the term 'the refrigerator mum'.

Secondly, it is probable but not certain that the condition would have commenced from birth. This is important because a difficulty we encounter when we try to elucidate the causation of infantile autism in a particular case is that it is very rare and therefore always unexpected. It is never diagnosed at birth. Thus the history the doctor obtains is always retrospective by at least 10 months, and indeed the diagnosis is rarely made under a year. Moreover the symptoms almost always have to be viewed through the eyes of the mother. 'Was the child ever normal?' 'Did something happen or was the child always strange?' Many mothers state that the child was normal until an 'event' or 'events' occurred. Examples of such 'events' can be cited. A child was reported as being quite normal till he witnessed his mother giving birth to a new baby in the back of a taxi-cab. Another child was normal until, when running along the beach, he fell with his face into the sand and was only resuscitated with difficulty. A further child was normal until he went into hospital, where his leg was placed in plaster. The plaster was too tight and the child yelled with pain and was thought to be autistic from that time onwards. Three possibilities obviously arise:

1. The 'event' really was the cause of the subsequent autism.

2. The child was abnormal but the mother had not noticed this fact previously. Retrospectively she picked on the 'event' to account for his progressive deterioration.

3. The child was normal but vulnerable, and the 'event' precipitated and hastened the inevitable onset of autism.

The male/female ratio in infantile autism is often given as 3 to 1. The more rigidly the criteria for making the diagnosis are applied the more does this ratio hold. If, however, the term *autistic* is applied to children who manifest only a few of the normal symptoms of infantile autism and particularly if in addition, they have features of other disorders such as cerebral palsy or rubella embryopathy, the sex ratio drifts away from the marked male predominance. This would probably be even more striking if it were not for the fact that males tend to predominate in some of these handicaps.

Sometimes autism is found in children in whom we have reason to expect mental retardation. A notable example of this is untreated phenylketonuria. A child of 6 years was admitted to hospital with all the usual symptomatology of infantile autism and the diagnosis was in no doubt. In particular her eating habits were bizarre and extremely restricted so that she had quite severe infantile scurvy. The purpose of hospitalization was to correct her feeding problems and to treat the scurvy. The ward sister testing the urine routinely for phenylketonuria, found it positive. It then became apparent that the child had phenylketonuria which had been unrecognized up to that time and had never been treated. On other occasions, autism may be found in children with cerebral palsy of a type in which we might expect there to be concomitant mental retardation.

In yet other instances, the primary pathology does seem to lie with the parent. As might be anticipated this is usually the mother, since ordinarily she has most contact with the child. Thus a psychotic mother under our care induced autistic-like symptoms in her child which rapidly remitted when the mother was admitted to hospital for therapy.

## CLASSIFICATION

We can now suggest a tentative classification of autism (Rendle-Short 1969).

*Group 1 (a).* In accordance with the classic Kanner disorder, children in this group present with a clear history of symptoms originating during the first year of life.

*Group 1 (b).* These children develop symptoms during the first 30 months of life, after an acute 'event'. This may be physical, for instance after an illness which is often only mild or moderately severe; or psychological, such as a severe shock. However, careful inquiry sometimes establishes that a mild degree of abnormal behaviour existed before the 'event'. Whether this is really so, or whether the parents are now viewing the child's early behaviour with hypercritical and enlightened hindsight, it is not possible to say.

*Group 2.* This group covers children whose autistic signs and symptoms are secondary to gross mental retardation or in association with handicaps arising from an organic brain lesion, for example, rubella deaf/blind.

*Group 3.* These children present as clinically autistic, but their behaviour is related to some specific psychological trauma without preceding abnormal behaviour. The autistic symptoms disappear when the specific trauma is alleviated, or the environment is manipulated.

From the above it will be obvious that a crucial question is arising. Is the relationship between autism and mental retardation that of cause and effect? If so, which is the cart and which the horse? Does mental retardation lead to autism; does autism lead to mental retardation or is there an equation autism $\rightleftarrows$ mental retardation? Unfortunately, ordinary psychological testing rarely helps to distinguish between the two. Autistic children are notoriously difficult to test because of lack of cooperation and attentiveness. The so-called 'islets of normality', which often consist of a bizarre memory for facts (for example, a page of a telephone directory), help to differentiate between the two but, on the whole, formal testing has grave limitations.

One way of looking at autism is as a disruption of bonding. In recent years increasing attention has been paid to the fact that a mutual, two-way bond should develop between the normal, loving mother and her child. It is somewhat similar to the imprinting whereby a newborn animal relates to the first large, moving object it sees and follows it at all times. The classical example of this is of Konrad Lorenz swimming in the Danube followed by a brood of goslings. However bonding differs from imprinting in that the relationship in bonding is primarily from the maternal side. It can easily be disrupted by early separation of mother and child. Failure of bonding seems to be an important factor in the statistically increased incidence of child abuse of babies who were separated from their mothers at birth to be cared for in premature nurseries. Many factors can destroy the reciprocal bond between mother and child. Geographic separation is one. Lack of response on the part of the child is another important factor. The child may fail to respond to the mother's blandishments because of mental retardation, illness, blindness or some organic disorder. If the child will not smile at the mother, the mother gives up smiling at the child. Just as the child can be deprived of the mother's love and stimulation, so the mother can feel deprived, and think that the child does not need her. Many mothers of autistic children will say that the young baby seems to be comforted most by being left alone, not, as they had hoped and expected, by being picked up and cuddled.

Bond disruption can be due to many factors. It can be primarily at the maternal or at the child end. It can be passive or active. Classically the autistic child 'cuts off', that is, he separates himself from adults by ignoring them or by engaging in some cut-off behaviour which occupies his attention exclusively, for example, spinning objects is a favourite one.

Not only does mental retardation disrupt the bond between mother and child but, as a corollary, cut-off behaviour by a potentially normal child results in diminished love and stimulation by the mother, lowered opportunity for child/mother interaction and therefore decreased opportunity for learning. The child therefore becomes 'mentally retarded',

even if he was not previously. One of the most important aspects of this is in language and communication. Characteristically children who are autistic do not speak or, if they do, they develop speech late. In those older children who do speak, there is often a failure to use language to convey meaning to others. Thus there is a tendency to repeat familiar phrases rather than to construct original remarks. Immediate or delayed echolalia may also be present. Sentences or phrases heard previously may be stored and uttered later without appropriate alterations. As a result an autistic child may refer to himself as 'you'.

Hermelin (1971) presented results of experiments to provide the beginnings of an analysis and explanation for the various aspects of linguistic functioning of the autistic child. The findings include the following:

1. Both autistic and normal children recalled stressed words better than unstressed words.

2. Whereas mentally handicapped children tend to differentiate between words and sounds, autistic children do so to a far lesser degree. They tended to respond to intensity or to some other stimulus.

3. In an experiment designed to determine the ability to pattern incoming verbal stimuli, normal and retarded children recalled items in related groups significantly more frequently than autistic children.

4. While normal and mentally handicapped children had no difficulty constructing a non-verbal series with elements analogous to language operation, autistic children had great difficulty conceiving items in an orderly sequence.

5. Although mentally handicapped children were able to recall sentences far more easily than unconnected words, there was no significant difference between the recall of sentences and unconnected words for autistic children.

In brief, Hermelin's findings demonstrated that autistic children have an intact immediate auditory memory span. Their recall strategies are of an 'echo-box' type memory store. They are unable to distinguish between meaningful and meaningless, structure and randomness.

To the autistic child the world would

appear chaotic and unpredictable. Their obsession with repetitive, ritualistic behaviour and their desire to maintain sameness may well be an attempt to put order into the disorder in which they live.

## DIAGNOSIS

As an aid to diagnosis, Creak (1961) described and classified the behavioural characteristics of autistic children into a nine point scale. O'Gorman (1967) modified the nine points and later, Clancy et al., (1969) presented the results of a study to extend the nine point scale. Their aim was to determine: whether the syndrome could be distinguished as a separate entity; which symptoms, as interpreted by the parents, were characteristic of the syndrome; more diagnostic criteria.

The results of their study indicated that 14 behavioural symptoms were the major manifestations of autism:

1. Stand-offish manner: communicates very little with other people; treats them as objects rather than people.
2. Great difficulty in mixing and playing with other children.
3. Strong resistance to any learning of new behaviour or skills.
4. Resists change in routine.
5. Acts as if deaf.
6. No eye contact.
7. Repetitive and sustained odd play.
8. Not cuddly as a baby.
9. Unusual attachment to particular objects.
10. Marked physical overactivity.
11. Spins objects, especially round ones.
12. Prefers to indicate needs by gesture.
13. Lack of fear about realistic dangers.
14. Laughs and giggles for no apparent reason.

Clancy et al. (1969) recommended that if 7 or more of the 14 manifestations were present then a diagnosis of autism should be considered. However, the 14 manifestations do not distinguish a child with true autism from one with primary mental retardation and autistic symptoms.

Rutter (1971) considered that autism was

a disorder beginning before the child reaches 30 months of age, in which three major abnormalities are all present:

1. An autistic-type failure to develop interpersonal relationships.
2. A delay in speech and language development.
3. Ritualistic or compulsive phenomena.

Rendle-Short and Clancy (1969) suggest the following definition: 'Autism is a clinical state, transient or persistent, characterized by a failure to develop or sustain normal relationships with human beings, and associated with an exceptional degree of self-involvement.'

### PROFILE OF AN AUTISTIC CHILD

How does a doctor recognize an autistic child when he is first brought to see him, unlabelled? This will depend to a considerable extent on the causation of the autism, which will in turn determine the age at which the child first gave rise to anxiety. Children in Group 1 will present early, 1(a) under a year and 1(b) some time later. For convenience we will consider these together. As in all difficult diagnostic problems, the keys to success are awareness and alertness. The doctor must know that autism exists and something of its usual manifestations, and then he must be alert to apply his knowledge to the particular child in front of him. In the United Kingdom an infant will probably be first seen by a health visitor, a general practitioner or in hospital casualty. Only later will he go to a paediatrician and much later still to a psychiatrist. The story will be that the child is 'different'. He is obviously not normal but yet he does not conform to the expected pattern of behaviour of a child who is physically sick, deaf, neurologically impaired or mentally retarded. Each diagnosis is considered in turn but has to be rejected, for example, deafness: the infant takes no notice of his mother's voice, and certainly does not speak, yet is obviously delighted at the sound of an aeroplane overhead. Or again, the child, though physically able to walk, can only be induced to do so under certain well-defined circumstances such as when pushing a chair down a certain corridor. The commonest misdiagnosis is probably mental retardation. As previously explained, this is natural because the child may indeed be mentally retarded (Group 2), and even if not, he acts as such because of his cut-off behaviour and later he will become functionally mentally retarded for the same reason. However, at this early age the secondary retardation is not so apparent. If the child is primarily mentally retarded, or has some severe neurological handicap, this is usually obvious. Later the child develops autistic cut-off features in addition. He ignores people, refuses to make eye contact, collects objects, adheres to a strict regime, which may result in serious feeding problems, and so on. As will be discussed later, from the point of view of practical management, these autistic features often assume great importance as they can be so disrupting to the family. Irrespective of etiology and mode of presentation, we feel that therapy needs to follow the same general lines, although with varying expectations of success depending on the degree of primary mental retardation and the severity and duration of the cut-off behaviour.

We have attempted above to present a word picture of a young child with autism but it must of course be realized that no two cases are the same.

## ASSESSMENT

All therapy properly begins with assessment. This should include a full physical and neurological examination by a paediatrician, audiometric assessment, psychological assessment, reports from other agencies which have previously dealt with the child and assessment by staff specially trained in working with autistic children. These would ideally include a speech therapist, an occupational therapist, a physical educationalist and a teacher.

In the classical Kanner disorder, the paediatric examination usually reveals little that is abnormal but, if the child is suffering from the autistic syndrome, there may be evidence of the primary disorder, for example cerebral palsy, mental retardation or deafness.

Formal evaluation should be carried out by a psychologist, although it must be admitted that, because of lack of cooperation, this may be of limited value.

*Suggested formal assessment scales*

> Merrill Palmer (IQ)
> Denver Developmental Screen Test (development relative to age)
> Vineland Scale of Social Maturity (social development)
> 14 Point Scale ⎫
> 19 Point Scale ⎬ autistic characteristics
> Rimland Scale of Autism
> Peabody Picture Vocabulary Test ⎫
> ⎬ speech and language development
> Illinois Test of Psycholinguistic Abilities ⎭

It is because formal assessment is so frequently limited that informal assessment by therapists and teachers becomes an important tool. Table 24.1 lists the items which could be considered in this informal assessment, and includes queries relating to each item that any examiner should consider when observing a child who is at risk of being autistic.

It is most important that the child is not assessed in an environment such as the doctor's surgery or the therapist's room which is out of context with his normal daily routine and behaviour patterns. Flexibility is vital if significant signs and symptoms are not to be missed.

## TREATMENT AND MANAGEMENT

The history of the treatment of autistic children, both in its theory and practice, has been beset by widely differing viewpoints. This may be observed both from the literature and also by discussion with practitioners involved in therapy.

The most prominent methods advocated have been psychotherapy, behaviour modification and educational programmes. Theories of etiology influence techniques of treatment. Not unnaturally, therapists and educationalists who hold to a particular theory of causation develop methods consistent with that theory.

Therapists who hold to non-organic

TABLE 24.1

Informal observations

1. *Social factors*
1.1 *Avoidance of eye contact*
   Does he seek eye contact?
   Does he give eye contact when it is requested by the examiner?
   Does he give eye contact to himself or examiner in a mirror? (Often autistic children will more readily give eye contact in a mirror than in a face-to-face situation.)
1.2 *Awareness of others*
   Does he show interest in people around him?
   Is he aware of his peers? (Some autistic children show some interest in adults but ignore the existence of peers.)
   Does he differentiate between his parents and others? (Some young autistic children give a false impression of being well behaved as they do not react to separation from parents. This is often significant.)

2. *The child's play*
   Does the child play appropriately? (Does he push a toy car along the ground rather than spin its wheels?)
   Does the child have any imaginative play?
   Does the child play without direction?

3. *Extremes of activity*
   Is the child hyperactive or hypoactive? (An autistic child may display both extremes of activity during the same day.)
   Is he excessively passive, rigid or tense? (Often his physical state is inappropriate to the environment.)

4. *Inappropriate emotional reactions*
   Does the child have tantrums which are not appropriate to the situation? (The autistic child who obsessively lines up objects may become inconsolable if an object is bumped out of line.)
   Does the child have abnormal detachment? Is he non-reactive? (A vivacious therapist or teacher can be completely demoralized by the lack of response from autistic children who stare

through what should be a most entertaining experience.)

5. *Repetitive and bizarre mannerisms*
   Does the child flick or spin objects, walk on his toes, repeatedly carry out rhythmic behaviour, for example, rocking or slapping himself or an object, laugh inappropriately? (The autistic child can have hysterical or inappropriate laughter.)

6. *Verbal language*
   Does the child have a language disorder?
   Does he have the ability to communicate through verbal language? (Autistic children either lack speech or have severely limited speech. Many writers consider that a severe language problem is the most common characteristic of autism.)
   Is the child echolalic?
   Does he comprehend his own speech?
   Does he use abnormal patterns of speech? (Frequently an autistic child will refer to himself as 'you' and use a set repertoire of phrases or sentences which may not be appropriate. One little boy who cannot cope with pressure always says he wants to go to the toilet when asked to participate. No matter how many times he goes to the toilet he still parrots the same response to a demand.)

7. *Uneven ability*
   Does the child have a well-developed splinter skill? (Many autistic children show particular skill in one area, for example, building a complicated tower or tracing the drainage system of a building. These skills are usually repetitive, obsessional and relatively useless. One boy had the clever obsessional mathematical skill of working out mentally how old, to the day, any person would be. This interest included both dead and alive people and he requested dates of birth incessantly.)

theories of causation tend to use psychotherapy techniques. For example Bettelheim (1967) put forward one approach involving psychotherapy. He advocated residential treatment for autistic children in order to uncover the underlying psychodynamic mechanism which he postulated as the cause of autism.

Behaviour modification provides a different approach. An early study of behaviour modification with psychotic children was undertaken and reported by Ferster and De Myer (1961). This study was carried out in strict laboratory conditions with purely mechanical responses from the children being reinforced. Subsequent research in behaviour therapy has been broadened to include non-laboratory conditions and behaviour modification has been applied to a wide range of behaviour. Behaviour modification generally involves modifying specific behaviours such as attending responses, speech, social skills, imitative responses and the elimination of inappropriate behaviours. Both positive and aversive conditioning has been used by researchers such as Lovaas et al. (1965, 1966).

Whereas pure behaviour therapy techniques are often restricted by the number of children who are able to receive treatment at any one time, educational programmes are able to provide training and education for groups of autistic children. Wing (1966), Weston (1965) and Lotter (1966) all advocated an educational approach. Such an approach is generally based on remedial teaching methods, the aims of which are to develop basic skills, particularly in communication. Nevertheless, psychotherapy and/or behaviour modification can also be incorporated into an educational approach.

Training centres throughout the world cater for different age ranges. Facilities should of course be provided for autistic people of all ages from pre-school to adults. However we believe that the greatest emphasis should be placed on assessment and treatment of very young children. Unfortunately it is rarely that children younger than 2 years are diagnosed as autistic and appropriately treated.

## FACTORS INFLUENCING THERAPY AND OUTCOME

A child's prognosis is dependent on a number of factors, including:

1. Factors inherent in the child.
   a. Severity of autism.
   b. Level of intelligence.
   c. Other complications, for example, deafness, epilepsy and primary mental retardation
2. Treatment.
   a. Length of treatment.
   b. Intensity of treatment.
   c. The age of the child when treatment was commenced.
3. Environment.
   a. Institutionalization or family care.

b. Access to treatment facilities: many children have difficulty in obtaining treatment because of geographic isolation.
c. Ability of parents to carry out home programmes.

Children with low intelligence and severe autistic behaviour have the poorest prognosis. However a child's prognosis and the success of treatment should not be considered as synonymous. It is axiomatic that retarded children cannot be given normal intelligence. However, successful treatment should ensure that a retarded child functions at his optimal level of ability in all areas. With the majority of autistic children it is unrealistic at this stage of our knowledge to anticipate complete normalization of function. The prognosis for severely autistic children must be considered poor if development of normal function is the goal. However, treatment can achieve significant improvement in behaviour. Some areas of particular difficulty for autistic children are spontaneity and flexibility. Even if an autistic child is able to talk and communicate, language problems persist in the majority of cases.

Practitioners with substantial experience in the therapy of autistic children often find it difficult to give correct prognosis. The following case history illustrates this. Allan at 3 years of age appeared to the diagnostic team to be mildly autistic. Within the first 6 months of treatment his response was promising. However, his development then levelled out and after 8 years of treatment and education, it is now obvious both to his parents and the therapists that his initial response and presentation belied the severity of his condition.

Allan's case history cannot be adequately explained. Many other children who were in similar programmes to him and whose early prognosis appeared less promising have been successfully integrated into the community.

### THE THERAPY PROGRAMME

Strategies are more important than detailed programme content and although content should in no way be ignored or disregarded, the emphasis in this chapter will be on strategies and techniques.

In evaluating a therapy programme the following points need to be taken into consideration.

*The child.* The response of the child to treatment and education and his progress in social and emotional development, perceptual, motor, living and academic skills.

*The programme.* How the content, treatment, structure and techniques meet the needs of the child individually and in groups, and how that programme aids and trains the parents and provides services in the home.

*The staff.* The mix of professional staff so as to provide a broad and thorough service. The quality of in-service training of professional staff and the role of auxiliary staff.

*The environment.* The adequacy of the buildings, individual rooms and equipment and community facilities.

*Programme review.* This must be undertaken at all levels.

*Programme content.* This can be considered within the following areas, which are broken down into sub-groups:

1. *Social and emotional development*
   Eye contact
   Taking turns
   Awareness of others
   Concern for others
   Self-control
2. *Activities of daily living*
   Toilet training
   Eating and drinking skills
   Self-care: dressing, washing
3. *Motor skills*
   Fine motor: manipulations, perceptual motor skills
   Gross motor: balance, coordination, specific skills, e.g. swimming, skating
4. *Perceptual skills*
   Visual, auditory and tactile: discrimination, matching, sorting, identifying

Further information will be found in the numerous textbooks dealing with the treatment and education of handicapped children.

PRACTICAL STRATEGIES
AND TECHNIQUES

One of the most important facets in treating an autistic child is the establishment of eye contact. This is a realistic place to start treatment. The procedure followed is given here in detail, both because of its intrinsic importance but also as an illustration of the kind of techniques which can be employed. A one-to-one situation is established with the child and the therapist in a room with minimal or no distraction. The only equipment required is a bubble pipe and bubble-making liquid. The therapist blows bubbles into the air so that the child becomes interested in them. The child's attention is drawn to the bubbles and he is shown how to chase and break them. When this is achieved he is rewarded. The pipe is then moved to the front of the therapist's face and the child told to look at the therapist with the pipe near her face. The pipe is then gradually removed but eye contact is still demanded.

If difficulty is experienced in obtaining the child's attention it may be helped by placing the pipe near the child, lifting it to his face level and drawing it back towards the therapist's face which should be on the same level as the child.*

In general it is preferable to avoid food rewards for autistic children. However these may be needed with very difficult children. It is more advantageous to use social or praise rewards associated with warm physical contact such as a rub on the cheek. It is better to teach the child to enjoy and expect this type of reward rather than instituting food rewards which have later to be eliminated.

Limit-setting is very important with autistic children. The teacher or therapist must be in charge at all times. Demands should not be made that the therapist cannot enforce. It is better that the therapist ignores a situation if she cannot actively change or avoid it.

A child is asked to undertake some activity. If he does not respond he is asked again and at the same time taken physically through the activity; for example, if the child fails to come when he is called, the therapist must be prepared to go to the child and take him to the point where she was, at the same time repeating the request to come. He is then rewarded as if he had come by himself. The

---

* This activity of bubble blowing was originally outlined by Clancy and Rendle-Short (1968) as a technique for communication therapy in autistic children.

rationale is that it is important to create situations in which the child can be rewarded.

Autistic children have no innate desire for reward. They have to be taught the value of a reward by constant repetition. It is therefore important that confrontations caused by continuing unfulfilled demands are avoided by the therapist actively assisting the child to obtain his reward.

If the therapist makes a demand which the child cannot fulfil (a situation which a competent therapist should avoid), she should assist the child to complete the task without making it apparent to the child that she had lowered her expectations. The child should then be rewarded as if he had completed the task unassisted. The therapist should at all times be *firm, confident, kind, consistent* and in full control of any situation.

## PARENT INVOLVEMENT

Parent training and the use of parents as co-therapists are concepts which have, with good cause, become fashionable in recent times. A social worker is an essential member of the staff if parent involvement is to be taken seriously, as she acts as a liaison between staff and parents and aids parents in reaching an understanding and acceptance of the handicap of their child. It is, however, important that families are not overtaxed by unreasonable demands and that the rights of all family members are taken into account in family programmes.

Members of the family should visit the centre regularly. Mothers are normally the most frequent visitors as other family members have commitments during working hours. Home programmes should be undertaken with a teacher or therapist and a social worker. Parents must be shown and taught how to keep simple records and the information given to the parents by the therapist should be detailed and explicit. Daily monitoring by telephone is often necessary.

The following case history illustrates the value of a home programme.

Johnny's mother had reported that difficulties occurred from the time that her son arrived home from school. He threw his bag on the footpath and refused to pick it up and bring it inside.

At dinner he would eat meat and potatoes only and then only out of his blue 'bunny plate'. He also demanded that his sister eat from her pink 'bunny plate' but that she should be served after him. After his bath he insisted that his sister put on her pyjamas piece by piece but only after he did and in the express order that he did. The mother's difficulty in this situation was to know where to begin. The most promising area was some modification of the child's eating pattern. Therefore, it was resolved that Johnny was to commence eating green vegetables; no other problem was to be tackled at this stage.

It is important to note the following rules for both physical and parent programmes:

Do not try to change too much at once. Take one step at a time; each step must be very small.

On the first day of his programme, Johnny was presented with his normal main course for dinner, that is, meat and mashed potato but one pea was added. The family's record shows he objected to this change (one pea!). Nevertheless, the rest of the family, as instructed, proceeded with the meal and for the first time ever they ate dessert without him as he did not eat his pea. His dessert was in fact put before him to show him that he was entitled to eat it but only after he was prepared to eat the single pea. After a terrible scene he finally ate the pea and was allowed to eat his dessert.

The number of peas on his plate was steadily increased; two peas on the second night, then three and four, adding one more on each subsequent night until finally he was introduced to a variety of vegetables and was prepared to eat the same food as the rest of the family. The other problems were dealt with step by step in the same fashion.

It should be said that not every programme brings radical changes. However, all programmes can be successful if carefully designed and monitored. Johnny's parents contacted the centre daily during the programme and the various problems that arose were resolved. A diary was also kept by them.

The success of this programme was not only that Johnny's behaviour was modified, but more significantly that the parents undertook the therapy themselves and they learned to control the situation rather than being controlled by Johnny.

## THE STAFF

Professional, ancillary and voluntary staff who have contact with the children should have the following qualities: tolerance, warmth, empathy, sense of humour, initiative, imagination, ability to be confident, firm, consistent but kind, ability to work as a member of a team, ability to cope with noise.

They must also be satisfied by small returns for all the effort invested. All teachers and therapists should have appropriate professional qualifications, a knowledge of child development and an ability to design a programme for the children. In addition, it is useful for some members of the team to have experience of education for handicapped children, remedial education, physical education and infant or kindergarten level training. Therapy should be given both in groups and individually, and the children discussed by the staff, both formally and informally.

## ENVIRONMENT

The education of autistic children should take place not only in the centre but also within the community: in shops, parks, swimming pools, skating rinks, horse-riding facilities, private homes and many other places. The ultimate aim is that the child eventually leaves the shelter of the centre to re-enter the community for the final stages of training in social behaviour, learning physical skills and use of language.

## THE FUTURE

The short-term aim of all autistic training centres is to rehabilitate the children to such a degree that they can enter the community at a level appropriate to their intelligence and social and physical ability. Therapy at present therefore is largely educational.

In the long-term, perhaps drugs will be developed which will influence the physiological abnormality from which these children may suffer but this day is a long way off yet.

## BIBLIOGRAPHY

Bettelheim, B. (1967) *The Empty Fortress: Infantile Autism and the Birth of the Self*. New York: The Free Press.

Bleuler, E. (1911) *Dementia Praecox, or The Group of Schizophrenics*. New York: International University Press.

Clancy, H. & Rendle-Short, J. (1968) Infantile autism: a problem of communication. *Aust. J. Occupational Therapy*, *15*, 3, 7–29.

Clancy, H., Dugdale, A. & Rendle-Short, J. (1969) The diagnosis of infantile autism. *Devl. Med. Child Neurol.*, *11*, 432–42.

Creak, M. (1961) Schizophrenia syndrome in childhood. *Br. med. J.* 2, 889–90.

Edelson, S. R. (1966) A dynamic formulation of childhood schizophrenia. *Dis. nerv. Syst.*, 2, 610–15.

Ferster, C. B. & De Myer, M. K. (1961) The development of performance in autistic children in an automatically controlled environment. *J. chron. Dis.*, *13*, 312–45.

Hermelin, B. (1971) Rules and language. In: Rutter, M. (ed.), *Infantile Autism: Concepts, Characteristics and Treatment*. Edinburgh: Churchill Livingstone.

Hutt, S. J., Hutt, C., Lee, D. & Ounsted, C. (1965) A behavioural and electroencephalographic study of autistic children. *J. psychiat. Res.*, *3*, 181–97.

Itard, J. M. G. (1799) *The Wild Boy of Averyron, trans*. Humphries and Humphries (1932). New York: Appleton Century Crofts.

Kanner, L. (1943) Autistic disturbance of affective contact. *Nerv. Child.*, 2, 217.

Lotter, V. (1966) Epidemiology of autistic conditions in young children: prevalence. *Social Psychiat.*, *1*, 3, 124–37.

Lovaas, O. I., Freitag, G., Gold, V. J. & Kassorla, I. C. (1965) Experimental studies in childhood schizophrenia. 1. Analysis of self-destructive behaviour. *J. exp. Child Psychol.*, 2, 67–84.

Lovaas, O. I., Schaeffer, B. & Simmons, J. B. (1965) Building social behaviour in autistic children by use of electric shock. *J. exp. Personality Res.*, *1*, 99–109.

Lovaas, O. I., Freitag, G., Kinder, M. I., Rubenstein, B. D., Schaeffer, B. & Simmons, J. H. (1966) Establishment of social reinforcers in schizophrenic children on the basis of food. *J. exp. Child Psychol.*, *4*, 109–25.

O'Gorman, G. (1967) *The Nature of Childhood Autism*. Sevenoaks, Kent: Butterworth.

Rendle-Short, J. (1969) Infantile autism in Australia. *Med. J. Aust.*, *2*, 245–9.

Rendle-Short, J. & Clancy, H. (1969) *Autism: A seminar*. Brisbane: University of Queensland.

Rimland, B. (1964) *Infantile Autism*. London: Methuen.

Ruttenberg, B. A. (1971) A psychoanalytic understanding of infantile autism and its treatment. In: Churchill, D. W., Alpern, G. D. & De Myer, M. (eds.), *Infantile Autism: Proceedings of the Indiana University Colloquium, 1968*. Springfield, Ill.: Charles C. Thomas.

Rutter, M. (ed.) (1971) *Infantile Autism: Concepts, Characteristics and Treatment*. Edinburgh: Churchill Livingstone.

Rutter, M. (1972) Childhood schizophrenia reconsidered. *J. Autism Child Schizo.*, *2*, 315–37.

Weston, P. T. B. (1965) *Some Approaches to Teaching Autistic Children: A collection of papers*. Oxford: Pergamon Press.

Wing, J. K. (ed.) (1966) *Early Childhood Autism*. Oxford: Pergamon Press.

Witmer, L. (1922) Don: A curable case of arrested development due to a fear psychosis in a 3-year-old infant. *Psychol. Clin*, 1919–22, *13*, 97.

# CHAPTER 25

# EPILEPSY AND MENTAL RETARDATION

## DESMOND POND

It is now well accepted that mental retardation is a symptom and not a disease, and the same should apply to epilepsy, but in many places there is still a suspicion that epilepsy is a disease, especially when the word is preceded by the adjective 'idiopathic'. However, epilepsy should always be regarded as a symptom of some underlying brain damage and/or disorder, though in practice it may not be possible to establish the exact nature of the disorder in spite of exhaustive investigations. Therefore in discussing the association of the two symptoms—epilepsy and mental retardation—it is axiomatic that their occurrence together is usually not coincidental, but that both result from some underlying brain disorder.

In the past thirty years a great deal has been learnt about the physiological disturbances occurring in epileptic discharges, for details of which various standard works may be consulted (Corbett et al. 1975; Meldrum 1976; Laidlaw & Richens 1976). All these studies confirm and amplify Hughlings Jackson's definition of epilepsy as a sudden excessive discharge of the grey matter of the brain. The massive neuronal discharge tends to be hypersynchronous and self-sustaining. The various forms of attack seen depend on where in the brain the discharge begins, its pathways of spread over the cortex, and the effects of the temporary post-ictal paralysis that the discharge leaves behind. The classical grand mal, or major, seizure represents a generalized maximal discharge of the whole intact brain. Its most typical form is seen in the convulsion of electric-shock treatment unmodified by relaxant and anaesthetic drugs. Clinically it

is the commonest form of seizure, since epileptogenic lesions in almost any area of the brain appear sometimes to be able to cause generalized seizures, though they may at other times produce other forms of attack. If the brain is grossly damaged the fit pattern may be atypical; for example, a seizure may begin in a hemiplegic limb (often making it move more than it can ever be moved voluntarily); then, if and when the discharge becomes generalized, the character of the movements on the hemiplegic side is distinctively different from movements on the unparalysed side.

### CLASSIFICATION

A simple clinical classification of epileptic attacks is shown in Table 25.1. The essential division is between partial seizures involving only a part of the brain (at any rate in the earlier stages of the attack) and generalized attacks involving more or less all parts of the cerebral cortex. The latter are then divided into convulsive (grand mal) and non-convulsive (various kinds of absence or petit mal) attacks. A classification of epilepsy involves more than just the fit pattern, but also the etiology and pathogenesis, the latter being mainly understood in terms of the distribution of the abnormal excessive hypersynchronous neuronal discharges that are the *sine qua non* of epilepsy and best seen in

Special thanks are due to Dr J. A. Corbett, Hilda Lewis Unit, Bethlem Hospital, for his help in the preparation of this chapter.

TABLE 25.1

Classification of epilepsy

I. *Generalized fits*
　　A. Grand mal
　　B. Petit mal
　　　1. Absence attack
　　　2. Myoclonic seizures

II. *Focal fits*
　　A. With simple symptoms
　　　1. Motor seizures
　　　2. Sensory seizures
　　　　*a.* Somatosensory
　　　　*b.* Visual
　　　　*c.* Auditory
　　　　*d.* Olfactory and gustatory
　　　　*e.* Visceral and autonomic
　　B. With complex symptoms
　　　*a.* Automatisms
　　　*b.* Psychic experiences
　　　*c.* Emotional and mood changes
　　C. Absence attacks
　　D. No aura but focal origin

III. *Focal fits secondarily generalized*
　　Indicated by:
　　A. Aura preceding grand mal
　　B. Focal EEG discharge preceding genera-
　　　lized discharge
　　C. Focal events during or prefacing a grand
　　　mal fit
　　D. Focal aftermath to grand mal fit

From Marsden (1976).

the electroencephalogram (EEG). It is important to determine as far as possible the nature
of the patient's epileptic attacks as the probable site of the causal epileptogenic lesion
may be deduced from the onset of the seizure.
Also, the choice of appropriate medication
may depend on the type of seizure (see p.
339).

## EPILEPTIC SYNDROMES ASSOCIATED WITH RETARDATION

Several particular syndromes of epilepsy are
associated with mental retardation. One of
the best known is the *syndrome of infantile
spasms* that goes by various other names; for
example, Blitz-Nick und Salaam Krämpfe

attacks in Germany, and 'hypsarrhythmia', a
popular name coined by Gibbs in the United
States, to describe the characteristic EEG
picture (Gibbs & Gibbs 1965). Jeavons and
Bower's (1964) monograph is still the best
account of this serious syndrome. It begins
usually in the early months of life with sudden
brief spasms of trunk and limbs that may
be very varied in appearance and often associated with generalized seizures. The condition
runs a stormy course and, even with intensive
treatment and cessation of attacks, most
children become severely retarded. It is also
of interest that several workers have noticed
that, as the attacks die out, the residual clinical
picture resembles that of early infantile autism
in many cases (Kolvin et al. 1971; Taft &
Cohen 1971). The cause has been ascribed
to different cerebral conditions, such as malformations, lipidoses and brain damage, but
the etiology is unknown in about half of the
cases. These latter children seem to develop
normally up to the time of the onset of the
spasms, whereas those with known or presumed causes are often abnormal from birth.

The *Lennox syndrome*, or petit mal variant,
is similar to infantile spasm and may, in fact,
simply be a version of that disorder that
begins somewhat later in life but still in the
pre-school period. As suggested by its name,
there is a typical EEG picture of slow spike
and wave, which is more regular than the
hypsarrhythmia of infantile spasms. The
minor seizures may be so continuous that
they merit the description of minor status
epilepticus, and the condition tends to run
a fluctuating but downhill course (Gastaut
et al. 1966; Chevrie & Aicardi 1972).

A rare syndrome within this general group
has recently been described by Bower and
Jeavons (1967). The condition has been chris-
tened the '*Happy Puppet Syndrome*' from the
bizarre physical appearance and jerky movements of the infants. The baby suffers from
numerous minor seizures that bring it into
the general category of infantile spasms but
the EEG never shows the typical hypsar-
rhythmic pattern of general disintegration of
the record with irregular high voltage, spikes
and other complexes. Instead, the EEG shows
more regular and symmetrical slow spike and
wave. The etiology of this syndrome is unknown.

## 'EPILEPTIC DETERIORATION'

Apart from the cases just described in which the epileptic attacks appear merely to complicate a clinical picture that has other distinguishing features, for example, neurological signs or a metabolic disorder, there are some cases in which the epileptic attacks appear the chief, if not the only, clinical symptom. In fact, there is reason to believe from observations at neurosurgery and post-mortem, that all these patients do have acquired brain damage, but not in areas that produce clinical signs elicitable by routine methods. Although the terms *epileptic dementia* and *epileptic amentia* are sometimes used, these terms are not appropriate even when applied to these groups of patients. The terms suggest firstly, that all persons with epilepsy may deteriorate, which is manifestly untrue; and secondly, that the deterioration is directly due to the fits, which is arguable, since some patients will have as many fits as the most deteriorated cases, and yet will not deteriorate. If the attacks and the mental state of retarded patients grow steadily worse in spite of anticonvulsant treatment, one can be sure that the underlying brain disorder is progressive.

## RELATIONSHIP OF FITS TO AGE AND OTHER FACTORS

Other factors besides the site of origin of the attacks affect their form and frequency. The age of the subject is very important for, as is well known, epileptic attacks are much more common in children than in adults. Although the total incidence of epilepsy in the retarded is so much higher than in people of normal intelligence, the relationship to age is similar in both groups. For instance, in the Camberwell Survey (Corbett et al. 1975) of all severely retarded children known in a population of 175 000, a quarter of these under the age of 5 had had a fit in the past year compared with only 5 per cent between the ages of 10 and 15.

However, the reasons why epilepsy is much commoner at the younger ages may not be the same in the mentally retarded as in normal people. In the former, for example, at the younger ages there may be a number of children with severe brain damage who subsequently die. Nevertheless, follow-up studies of static neurological disorders, such as cerebral palsy, show less epilepsy in older than in younger children, so it appears as if the liability to epilepsy depends on a factor related to maturation that may be operative whether or not the brain is damaged.

Exceptions to the general rule that seizures tend to become infrequent, or even die out, with ageing, are autism and Down's syndrome. Rutter et al. (1967) report that in a proportion of those with autism, the epilepsy may not appear until adolescence, some years after the establishment of the psychosis. Recently, Veall (1974) has shown that patients with Down's syndrome also have an increasing tendency to epilepsy as they get older. Seizures, of course, do become more frequent if there is an underlying progressive neurological disorder, such as lipidosis, and one cannot rule out the possibility that the underlying cerebral disorder in Down's syndrome, and possibly some cases of autism, is also progressive.

The age factor is also operative in the so-called febrile convulsions, which are short major seizures occurring with sudden rises of temperature mostly between the ages of $1\frac{1}{2}$ and 3 years. There is a strong family history in these cases and, in contrast to most other forms of epilepsy, little evidence of any acquired brain damage. Such simple seizures do not create any special problems in young mentally retarded children, but for the reasons already mentioned any epileptic attack in these children should be taken seriously and regarded as part of an underlying brain disorder until as far as possible proved otherwise and shown to be benign.

Attacks, especially in children, are often precipitated by physiological stresses such as metabolic disturbances, for example, hypoglycaemia. Convulsions are sometimes seen associated with the tetany of rickets, so-called spasmophilia, but it is unclear why the neuronal irritability of hypocalcaemia manifests itself sometimes with the peripheral disturbance of tetanus and sometimes with the central disturbance of the convulsion.

The generally increased biological vulnerability of boys rather than girls, noted by Rutter (1970) and others, is shown by the increased frequency of both severe mental retardation and seizures in boys compared with girls.

The published figures vary according to the nature of the samples surveyed. According to Kirman (1965) about one quarter of the patients had epilepsy in the Fountain Hospital, London, a 600-bed hospital, which at that time took many of the in-patient children with mental handicap from South London. A similar figure was obtained both at the Maudsley Hospital (Pond, unpublished) and in the mental handicap consultation service at University College Hospital (Tredgold & Soddy 1963). Margerison (1962) reported from another hospital that nearly 20 per cent of the mildly and 42 per cent of the severely mentally handicapped were epileptic. Primrose (1966) in his survey of a Scottish hospital for defectives found that (to use the old terminology) 11 per cent of the feeble-minded, 20 per cent of the imbeciles and 33 per cent of the idiots were epileptic. According to A. F. Tredgold in early editions of this book, the proportion of epilepsy rose to over 50 per cent in the lowest grade, the idiots. The differences between the figures at any one level of intelligence are most likely to result from admission policies and other social factors rather than any real differences between the hospitals and the areas surveyed. All authors, though, agree that the more severely retarded the patients, the more likely are they also to have epilepsy. Tizard and Grad (1961) carried out a survey of ascertained mentally handicapped in the London area, that is, those known to the statutory authorities whether or not they were in hospital. They found that about 18 per cent of the children had epilepsy, whether they were at home or institutionalized; whereas in the case of the adults, there were significantly more cases of epilepsy in the institutionalized, 25 per cent, than in those at home, 13 per cent. Similar figures were found by Corbett et al. in their Camberwell survey (1975). They found that of children with severe retardation, that is, with an IQ under 50, one-third had a history of seizures at some time during their life, and 19 per cent had had at least one fit during the previous year. At the higher level of the educationally subnormal, that is, with IQs roughly between 50 and 70, both the Isle of Wight survey (Rutter et al. 1970) and the National Child Development Study (Peckham 1974) suggest that about 3 to 6 per cent of these children had epilepsy. To show how high these figures are, it should be mentioned that the prevalence of any form of epilepsy at any time of life in the normal population is between 0.5 per cent and 1 per cent.

Conversely, studies of the prevalence of mental retardation in people with epilepsy have usually suggested that the average intelligence of non-institutionalized epileptics is near normal. However, according to Pond and Bidwell (1960) about 10 per cent of their general practitioner series who were of school age had educational problems due to low intelligence and a rather higher proportion of adults reported such difficulties in their childhood. Gudmunsson's (1966) survey of epileptics in Iceland showed that about 7 per cent of them had IQs below 75, which is several times the expected rate.

## PREVALENCE BY TYPE OF MENTAL RETARDATION

The sporadic occurrence of epilepsy in almost all the different disorders associated with mental handicap has been described in isolated case reports too numerous to specify here. Those disorders in which the fits are the sole, or at least predominant, symptom, have already been described (p. 332). Epilepsy occurs in about one-third of patients with phenylketonuria and similar metabolic disorders. In these disorders affecting all cerebral neurones, major and minor seizures of generalized type occur, for example, myoclonic jerks, focal or generalized absences of up to 30 seconds with or without irregular movements. Typical Jacksonian focal cortical seizures of adult type are comparatively rare. On the other hand, focal cortical seizures, with or without grand mal, occur in patients with anatomical damage, whether acquired by trauma, infections or vascular lesions, as opposed to those with biochemical disorders.

Among children with cerebral palsy, the various series reported by Illingworth (1958) suggest that epilepsy occurs in about 50 per cent of spastics (especially hemiplegics) and in the lower proportion of 25 per cent of athetoids. The reason for the differences between the two groups is possibly related to the fact that the predominant damage is in the basal ganglia and subcortical areas in athetoid subjects, and in cortical areas in the spastic. The percentage with epilepsy is less at the higher than at the lower levels of intelligence as shown particularly in Hansen's (1960) large series from Denmark that covered all cerebral palsies, including those of normal intelligence. Epilepsy is rare in kernicterus and cretinism.

## STATUS EPILEPTICUS

Status epilepticus is defined as serial seizures which occur without recovery of consciousness between attacks. A series of grand mal convulsions in this way is a medical emergency and requires urgent treatment (see p. 377). The condition was fairly common in retarded epileptics, and an important cause of death, but modern anticonvulsant régimes have made it a rarity. For no obvious reason, some epileptics appear to be more liable to have status than others.

Occasionally, status epilepticus is the first attack from which young children suffer, usually with a fever and neurological signs, such as hemiplegia. Attacks of status may alternate between one side and the other. Gastaut et al. (1960) have described it as H.H.E. (hemi-convulsions, hemi-plégie, épilepsie). Other forms of epilepsy (most commonly temporal lobe attacks) may then start months or years later. As Ounsted et al. (1966) showed, a proportion of these cases may be moderately retarded as is also the case with temporal lobe epilepsy following a known insult such as head injury or meningitis.

Permanent neuropathological changes as a result of epileptic attacks have been energetically discussed for many years. In particular, the characteristic lesions of Ammon's horn in the deep temporal areas have been regarded as cause and/or effect of epileptic attacks. It now appears certain that only severe grand mal attacks or status epilepticus with anoxia can, in fact, cause such lesions, though the pathogenic mechanism is still poorly understood. It is discussed by Norman in Ounsted et al. (1966), and by Margerison and Corsellis (1966). Ounsted et al. are concerned particularly with the role of status epilepticus in young children in subsequently producing epileptogenic lesions in the temporal areas, and the typical picture of temporal lobe epilepsy. A similar sequence of events can result from birth injury which increases the chances that anoxic mechanisms are important. It is, however, difficult to understand the exact distribution of lesions purely as a result of an anoxic episode, particularly when the effects may be predominantly unilateral. Margerison and Corsellis (1966) report the neuropathological and clinical findings in a number of epileptic patients who had clinical temporal lobe epilepsy. In those from a hospital for the mentally handicapped, these lesions were widespread in many areas of the deep and superficial structures of the brain besides the temporal area.

## RELATIONSHIPS BETWEEN EPILEPSY AND BEHAVIOUR DISORDER

The general principles underlying the relationships between epilepsy and behaviour disorders in people with mental retardation are similar to those in children of normal intelligence. Five factors need to be taken into account, although their relative importance will vary from case to case:

1. The general genetic or constitutional endowment of the child.
2. The brain damage or disorder which is causing the symptom of the epileptic attacks.
3. The effects of the epileptic attacks themselves.
4. The psychological environment of the child.
5. The anticonvulsants and other drugs used in therapy.

In subjects with severe mental retardation the underlying brain lesion tends to be much more extensive than in epileptic persons of normal intelligence and thus tends to exert a more important influence on psychological function, affecting intelligence more than

TABLE 25.2

Classification of psychiatric symptoms in epileptic (ictal) patients

*Pre-ictal Phase*
1. As cause of psychological symptoms, ? 'Working up to a fit'.
2. As effect of psychological conditions:
   *a.* Specific triggers, e.g. musicogenic epilepsy; self-induced photic stimulation.
   *b.* Non-specific, e.g. tension, excitement.

*Ictal*
Loss of consciousness, total or partial.
Elementary (and ? complex) sensory experiences (auras).
? Epileptic equivalent.

*Post-ictal*
Confusional states
'Furors', fugues.

*Inter-ictal*
Non-episodic behaviour disorders, neurotic symptoms.
Effects of underlying brain-damage.
Effects of medication.

personality. Apart from brain damage due to status epilepticus, the effects of the epileptic attacks themselves are transitory.

The behavioural associations of epilepsy may be divided into pre-ictal, ictal, post-ictal and inter-ictal, and these will be discussed briefly in that order (see Table 25.2). Little is known physiologically about the pre-ictal condition that could throw light on the behaviour disorders sometimes seen before major attacks. (The aura is, of course, not strictly speaking pre-ictal as it is a manifestation of a local epileptic discharge and therefore ictal.) On the other hand, psychological and physiological stresses may precipitate attacks in a number of patients. One such condition is the so-called startle seizure, which is not uncommon in hemiplegic cerebral palsy with retardation. A sudden loud noise or other shock can cause the hemiplegic limb to go into tonic spasm, pushing the patient over, and sometimes followed by a brief generalized seizure.

Ictal disorders, with rare exceptions, such as focal myoclonic jerks, are accompanied by disturbances of consciousness. They are usually easily recognized, except in some in-stances of continuous minor seizures sometimes known as petit mal status or absence status, which present as a confusional state that is often difficult to diagnose in the patient with severe mental retardation.

Particular caution is required in the use of the term *epileptic equivalent*, which suggests that children may suffer from paroxysmal disturbances of behaviour which have an epileptic basis, although they are not accompanied by any of the typical signs of an attack. Sudden outbursts of temper and violence were particularly liable to be regarded as having such an epileptic basis, especially in the older literature. The idea of an epileptic equivalent is sometimes mixed up with the concept of the epileptic personality or constitution for which there is also really no evidence at all.

Post-ictal behaviour disorders usually take the form of short-lived confusional states which may be maintained by brief minor epileptic attacks passing almost unnoticed, but serving to continue the general disruption of cerebral activity. Episodic behaviour disorders that are related to ictal or post-ictal states are likely to respond to treatment with anticonvulsants, and this may be an important diagnostic point as non-ictal disorders do not usually respond this way. The inter-ictal group contains most of the important chronic psychological disturbances which have no direct relationship to the seizures nor are they the result of 'subclinical' neurophysiological disturbances.

Even without accepting the idea of there being a specific epileptic personality, many authors have considered that mentally retarded people with epilepsy, like epileptic people of normal intelligence, are particularly liable to certain symptoms such as aggressive behaviour and either hyperactivity or hypoactivity. The latter refers to the slowness or 'stickiness' of response seen in some chronic adult epileptic patients. Eyman et al. (1969) in a study of three large hospitals found that hyperactivity was more common in mentally retarded patients with seizures than in those without. Aggressive behaviour, speech problems and difficulties in eating and dressing were also more common, but this may well have been a reflection of the more severe degree of retardation of the patients with epilepsy who are likely to be selectively admitted for these reasons. In this study, however, all the patients were institutionalized, and drugs were thought to play an important part in causing behaviour disturbance.

In the Camberwell study (Corbett et al. 1975) there was no significant difference between the frequency of behaviour disturbance in epileptic and non-epileptic retarded children. This interesting finding may be due to the fact that most of the seizures occurred in early infancy, that only a quarter of the children were institutionalized, and that fits were particularly frequent in children with severe cerebral palsy who, in many instances, would be physically incapable of demonstrating severe behaviour disturbance. It does, however, hold even when the children with cerebral palsy are excluded. It must be remembered that mentally retarded children usually live in a protected environment and may not be subject to the same psychosocial stresses, for example, peer group rejection, which interact to cause emotional disturbance in children of normal intelligence with epilepsy. Another important factor may be that other important handicaps, for example, specific language and perceptual disorders, which are particularly associated with behaviour disturbance in retarded children, are less commonly associated with seizures.

In the Camberwell study seizures were more often found in retarded children with hyperkinetic behaviour disorders than in those without, confirming the results of other studies with children in the normal range of intelligence (Ounsted et al. 1966). They were less frequent in those with childhood psychosis apart from those instances where symptoms of this condition followed infantile spasms. As mentioned previously, children with the autistic syndrome seem particularly likely to develop seizures in later adolescence and this has been reported in up to 36 per cent of cases (Rutter et al. 1967).

## THE TREATMENT OF EPILEPSY

### OUT-PATIENT SERVICES

The additional handicap of epilepsy places particular problems on families and others caring for the mentally retarded. Anxiety and fear for the life of the child engendered by the seizures themselves frequently compound the sense of partial bereavement caused by the presence of the handicapped child in the family. There are particular difficulties in providing substitute care for the mentally retarded in the community who have severe and frequent seizures; this may be a key factor leading to long-term hospital care (Tizard 1963), although with the advent of modern powerful drugs almost all cases can now be controlled (Shorvon et al. 1978). It follows that there is a particular need for people with epilepsy and mental retardation to have ease of access to out-patient services for epilepsy. Special investigations, such as EEGs and neuroradiology, will need to be carried out in hospital. As routine hospital visits are often difficult for the severely mentally retarded, and as there is a special need for staff counselling, continuing supervision and monitoring of blood anticonvulsant levels may be best carried out by the same team of specialists visiting special schools, adult training centres or residential units in which the handicapped person works or lives.

### USE OF DRUGS

Little is known about the effects of anticonvulsant drugs on the behaviour or intellectual performance of people with mental retardation. Patients are often maintained on multiple drugs over periods of many years; only over the past few years, following the introduction of methods of monitoring blood levels of these drugs, has it been possible to get a clearer picture of the situation in the retarded where clinical signs of intoxication may be difficult to elicit.

The management of status epilepticus of both major and minor types has been facilitated by the introduction of intravenous benzodiazepines, though Tassinari et al. (1972) have reported that paradoxically these drugs may precipitate what they call tonic status in children with the Lennox syndrome. Diazepam 10 mg in 2 ml may be given intravenously in about two minutes, and is usually immediately effective. The intramuscular route is of no value as it is absorbed slowly.

This drug must be followed by a longer-acting anticonvulsant, such as phenobarbitone or phenytoin, given at first parenterally, if necessary, and then orally as soon as the patient can swallow. A second intravenous dose of diazepam can be given in one or two hours, or even earlier, if status recurs in spite of further anticonvulsant medication. Sodium valproate (Epilim), 600 mg for an adult in single dose, is also very effective. The maintenance dose is 20–40 mg per kilogram body weight in enteric-coated tablets.

Status in small children is often precipitated by a rapidly rising high fever, and this should be treated with tepid sponging et cetera. The cause of sudden status in an otherwise well-controlled epileptic should always be carefully sought as it may be precipitated by some new event (for example, cerebral haemorrhage). Continuing status epilepticus is, of course, a medical emergency that may need the full service of an intensive care unit used to dealing with deeply unconscious patients who may need intubation et cetera, while under the anaesthesia and muscle relaxants needed to control the attacks.

Intoxication and treatment effectiveness are better indicated by monitoring blood levels than by giving increasing amounts of drugs until toxic signs (for example, nystagmus) are produced, then reducing the dose below this level. Recent evidence suggests that neurological side effects, albeit in a subtle form, may be seen with serum anticonvulsant levels lower than those conventionally accepted as the upper limit of normal. Reynolds and Travers (1974) also found that psychomotor slowing and intellectual deterioration were more frequent in mentally retarded than in normal patients. This may be due to the difficulty in eliciting neurological signs of intoxication in people who are already likely to show clinical evidence of neurological disorders.

Among the other chronic disturbances in metabolism which are likely to go undiscovered in people with mental retardation are those which involve folic acid and calcium. Both these require regular monitoring, although the clinical effects of folate depletion in children receiving long-term anticonvulsants is still a matter of debate (Bowe et al. 1971). However, it is now well established that in both children and adults there is a higher prevalence of folate deficiency in demented epileptic patients (Reynolds 1973). There have been a number of reports of calcium deficiency in patients receiving long-term anticonvulsants and this has been confirmed recently in mentally retarded patients with epilepsy (Viukara et al. 1972).

The indications for the use of different anticonvulsants are similar in retarded patients to those in people of normal intelligence (see Richens (1976) for the best recent account, and Table 25.3.) There is much to be said for a determined attempt, where possible, to use the minimum number of drugs chosen from those with proven low toxicity, bearing in mind the additional burdens placed on those caring for the retarded. Particular attention needs to be given to the practical aspects of any administration. For example, anticonvulsants often have to be given to the retarded child in elixir form; it is important to bear in mind that some anticonvulsants, such as phenytoin, do not stay in suspension easily, and unless the bottle is shaken vigorously, considerable variation in drug dose is likely to occur. Similarly, many retarded patients have difficulties over chewing food and teeth-brushing, and so are likely to develop gingivitis consequent upon anticonvulsant-induced gum hypertrophy. The correct combination of drugs may take some months to establish, but once established the dosage should not be varied too frequently. The usual rule is that anticonvulsants are not reduced until the patient has been fit-free for about two years. Drug reduction should then be carried out slowly over some months to avoid precipitating further attacks by sudden withdrawal.

The drug control of abnormal behaviour is unsatisfactory as anticonvulsants often have no effect on such disturbances. The exception is sulthiame (Ospolot) which has been reported as useful in retarded patients with aggression and hyperactivity (Al-Kaisi & McGuire 1974). However, sulthiame is a powerful inhibitor of the metabolism of phenytoin and phenobarbitone, whose sedative effect is thereby prolonged (Green et al. 1974). Although controversial, amphetamine is still sometimes of value, especially in hyperkinetic disorders, but large doses (up

TABLE 25.3

Drugs of choice in the various types of epilepsy

| Type of epilepsy | EEG | Drugs of 1st choice | Therapeutic blood level (μ/ml) | Range of maintenance dose (mg/day) |
|---|---|---|---|---|
| Grand mal | Spike & wave | phenytoin | 10–25 | 150–600 |
| Focal motor & sensory | Focal spikes or sharp waves | carbamazepine | 4–10 | 600–1600 |
| | | phenobarbitone | 14–38 | 60–240 |
| | | primidone | 14–38 (as phenobarb.) | 500–1500 |
| | | sodium valproate | — | 1000–2400 |
| Psychomotor | Temporal spikes & sharp waves | As for Grand mal but phenobarbitone ineffective | | |
| Minor myoclonic & akinetic | Polyspike & wave 2 per second spike & wave | ethosuximide | 38–100 | 750–1500 |
| | | sodium valproate | — | 1000–2400 |
| Petit mal absences | 3 per second spike & wave | ethosuximide | 38–100 | 750–1500 |
| | | sodium valproate | — | 1000–2400 |
| | | troxidone | <700 | 900–2100 |

From Richens (1976).

to 30 mg a day) may be required. Tranquillizers, such as chlorpromazine and haloperidol, are also sometimes of value, but should always be given together with anticonvulsants owing to their slight tendency to increase the number of fits in some patients. The dosage varies widely between patients so it is advisable (especially in children) to start with small doses, and work up until an effect is obtained. Among anticonvulsants, sodium valproate is said to have the extra advantage of being a minor stimulant rather than sedative.

Although anticonvulsants are the mainstay of treatment, other methods should be mentioned that are of value in special situations. Steroids are of value in the early treatment of infantile spasms which are usually quickly brought under control thereby. Unfortunately, they have less influence on mental development, as is shown by the fact that so many former sufferers finally come into the care of the services for the mentally handicapped. Once the attacks have died down, steroids are of no value, although small doses of anticonvulsants will probably still be needed. The benzodiazepines and sodium valproate are

likely to be particularly useful. In spite of the drugs, some children may continue to have sudden disabling myoclonic jerks of the trunk which, when involving the trunk flexor muscles, may 'jack-knife' the patient to the floor with enough violence to hurt the head. For such persons some form of helmet may be needed to protect the brain against possible further traumatic damage.

SURGERY AND TEMPORAL LOBECTOMY

Surgery has a very limited place in the treatment of epilepsy, although when properly used it can produce dramatic improvement, even cure. One specific operation is hemispherectomy which is indicated in patients with uncontrolled seizures and signs of extensive permanent damage to one hemisphere, such as hemiplegia and hemianopia. Sturge–Weber's disease, vascular lesions affecting the whole territory of the middle cerebral artery and birth injuries are the commonest known causes. These children often show severe behaviour disorders as well as epilepsy, and this is also usually improved. The operation has been regarded as a great success, although unfortunately an occasional, usually fatal, complication is now recognized in which years later the cavity fills up with a massive haemorrhage, often unavailingly treated by a further craniotomy.

A less radical procedure, designed only to prevent the spread of the abnormal discharges to the opposite hemisphere, is section of the corpus callosum. There are other even more experimental procedures, such as lobotomy, the making of focal lesions (in the amygdaloid, for example) and the implantation of stimulating electrodes in the cerebellum.

A well-established operation is, of course, temporal lobectomy, but it is very rarely indicated in mentally handicapped persons. This is because it is likely that the deep temporal lesion (such as mesial sclerosis) whose excision is the *sine qua non* of the operation, is, in fact, much more extensive and accompanied by other cerebral lesions that together are responsible for the retardation.

In view of the many possible procedures involving a surgical approach to the brain, consultations with a neurosurgeon would seem indicated whenever a retarded person has an intractable epilepsy not due to a progressive neurological disorder, especially if it is accompanied by a behaviour disorder and/or there is clear evidence of a focal origin to the attacks. The whole subject of surgery in epilepsy is authoritatively reviewed by Richardson (1976).

### THE ELECTROENCEPHALOGRAM

The electroencephalogram (EEG) is a record of such electrical activity of the brain as can be obtained through the intact skull. Only gross changes in electrical activity can be recorded in this way because of the attenuation of the potential differences caused by the distance between the brain and the electrodes, and the physical properties of the skull and overlying tissues. EEG, as a routine clinical laboratory investigation, is mainly concerned with epilepsy in all its aspects, largely because the potential changes produced during epileptic attacks (and often between overt seizures) have characteristic, easily recognizable forms, usually of a much higher ampli-

tude than normal. The current clinical practice of EEG is best described by Driver and MacGillivray (1976), and Harris (1972) has most recently reviewed the EEG in severely retarded patients.

### RECORDING METHODS AND TECHNIQUES

For most routine recordings the subject lies quietly on the couch or in a chair, opening and closing his eyes on command. In addition to the basic resting record, certain simple stimuli are usually applied, of which the commonest is overbreathing. This produces a slight alkalosis that often increases the instability of the EEG, especially in children, and may produce epileptic disturbances in records that up to then did not show any such change. Another common provocative technique is intermittent photic stimulation using a very short high intensity flash at varying frequencies, between about 1 and 30 flashes per second.

The routine methods of recording require the subject to be cooperative and to be able to lie still for minutes. This is not always easy to obtain in young children, especially in restless mentally handicapped ones. Sedative drugs are often administered in order to quieten the patient, but these may greatly alter the basic EEG tracing, since the most obvious of all EEG changes are closely related to the level of consciousness or awareness. However EEG abnormalities are more often seen in the sleeping than the waking records of the retarded.

In recent years several new techniques have moved from the experimental stage to routine clinical use in the larger centres. There are, for example, various mainly computerized techniques which enable responses to regular stimuli too small to be seen in a routine trace, to be 'averaged' so that the random variations to cancel out and the specific cerebral responses can be identified. Transistorized components also enable EEG signals to be transmitted from electrodes fixed on the head of a freely moving subject to the main amplifiers and write-out, so that cerebral activity can be recorded in a wider and more natural range of situations. Electro-corticography and chronic implanted electrodes, of course, require neurosurgical cooperation.

A standard tracing of any one adult varies little from time to time, but children's records are more variable. In addition, the processes of maturation produce marked changes in the record up to the teens. The rate of these changes varies very much from child to child so that at any one age group a wide variety of EEG tracings can be obtained. The commonest EEG abnormalities are those associated with epilepsy in all its forms and reference should be made to various standard texts for details of the EEG changes such as spikes and spikes and waves, both focal and diffuse, in the different forms of epilepsy. Destructive or invasive lesions of the brain also produce EEG changes, particularly if they are large and rapidly growing; that is to say, lesions which cause oedema in the surrounding brain substance which is still in physiological contact with the rest of the brain, thereby producing abnormal, usually slow, activity. The lesion itself, whether tumour, abscess or porencephalic cyst is, of course, electrically silent, and if large enough may produce an area of flatness in the tracing. This silence can sometimes be more easily seen if the subject is given a barbiturate drug to produce sleep, as the normal barbiturate-fast activity is sometimes more obviously asymmetrical than are the asymmetries of normal rhythms.

## EEG: APPLICATION AND INTERPRETATION

Something may now be said about the particular application of these general principles to the EEGs of retarded patients. Since severely mentally handicapped subjects have some sort of acquired brain damage, the EEG reflects the effects of such destruction, with no characteristic picture for retardation as such, and there are no clear correlations between any EEG phenomena and the level of mental handicap. That there are relationships between EEG data and intelligence has been affirmed, and denied, so the problem clearly awaits further study, preferably with more subtle analyses of the EEG data.

It is convenient to discuss changes seen in retarded subjects with and without epilepsy since the epileptic discharges frequently overshadow all other abnormalities. Useful reviews are by Clevenger (1968) and Harris

(1972). Abnormalities of all kinds are more common in older than younger children, probably mainly because good records are difficult to obtain in young children and standards of normality are very wide. Records of severely retarded subjects more often show abnormalities than the mildly handicapped, as would be expected from the much greater incidence of gross brain damage in the severely retarded. The average alpha frequency in adult retardates without brain damage does not differ from normal though the scatter may be wider, and maturation with age seems to occur as usual.

Focal spikes or spikes and waves are often seen over an epileptogenic lesion; for example, a nodule of tuberous sclerosis, or an old abscess or head injury scar. This epileptic activity is produced by the brain around the dead tissue which remains in functional contact with the rest of the brain. The focus can appear at quite a distance from the responsible lesion. This is particularly true with discharges that may originate from lesions in the uncus and amygdaloid areas. These appear to project onto any area of the cerebral cortex from the posterior temporal to the inferior frontal regions. The discharges may also fire across to the other hemisphere; for example, in Sturge–Weber disease the affected hemisphere may appear almost electrically silent, and spikes and waves of all forms appear on the apparently normal hemisphere. These latter discharges will often disappear after a hemispherectomy, proving their projected origin.

During actual epileptic attacks the EEG picture becomes very complicated, and generalized abnormalities are usually seen. The generalized myoclonic activity which is so often found in mentally handicapped subjects is usually accompanied by massive, generalized irregular high-voltage multiple spike complexes.

EEG abnormalities are commonly found in other infantile illnesses associated with seizures, with possible sequelae of retardation and continuing epilepsy, such as cerebral trauma, infections and the various encephalopathies associated with epilepsy. While there are few clear correlations between underlying pathology and EEG abnormalities, EEG studies during the acute stages of these illnesses are important as they may indicate the possible extent of brain damage in relation to later defects. Other than incidental fluctuations in the EEG pattern related to change in seizure frequency and intercurrent illnesses, the EEG in retarded epileptic children with static brain lesions tends to show rather little change or improvement over time (Harris 1972) and the EEG may therefore be of great value in distinguishing those causes of retardation which are due to progressive disease. The EEG is of particular value in the diagnosis of minor status epilepticus and temporal lobe epilepsy in the retarded child. In the latter condition recordings made during sleep are often especially useful.

Epileptic activity in the form of spikes or spikes and waves (both generalized and focal) is sometimes seen in retarded subjects even when they do not have clinical attacks of any sort. The possible clinical significance of this specifically abnormal activity is unknown as it does not necessarily presage the later onset of epilepsy. The use of anticonvulsants in such cases does not usually cause any improvement in intelligence level or behaviour, nor, as far as we know, does it prevent later epilepsy.

The EEG in Down's syndrome is reviewed by Ellingson et al. (1970) and the sleep patterns by Clausen et al. (1977). There appears to be general disorganization of the waking record with excess of slow activity for the age (that is, a general 'immaturity'), but the responses to eye opening and closure, overbreathing et cetera, are not abnormal. Sleep lasts longer than normal (? an institutional effect) but is more broken. On the other hand, the records of those with hypothyroidism do frequently appear to be abnormal by reason of the low voltage of all activity (especially in babies) and the presence of more slow activity than is usual at later ages (Harris et al. 1965). These changes are reversed by the administration of thyroid in those cases that do respond intellectually to the hormone, but not in the unresponsive cases. The metabolic disorders such as phenylketonuria usually produce generalized irregular spike and wave activity that may from time to time appear asymmetrical, but usually, with repeated or long tracings, the activity shows no constant focus or lateralization. In the lipidoses, Cobb et al. (1952) thought there was a fairly typical picture of irregular spike and wave activity occurring on a background of generalized abnormalities.

Patients with large destructive lesions, for example, porencephalic cysts, may show asymmetries with flatness of normal rhythms, particularly of the barbiturate-induced fast activity as has already been mentioned. Patients with predominantly sub-cortical or basal ganglia damage, for example, kernicterus, usually have normal or doubtfully normal records with a moderate amount of symmetrical slow activity. Foley (1968) found that in the general group of cerebral palsies the athetoids had the most normal records with less chance of deterioration in the EEG over the years, in contrast to spastic, hemiplegic children. Although the EEGs of a considerable number of palsied children deteriorate, the worsening, surprisingly, is not closely correlated with clinical deterioration or the late development of epilepsy.

Following an acute head injury, the EEG is often grossly abnormal for a few days corresponding to the period of concussion and confusion. EEG and clinical improvement are usually parallel, but sometimes the EEG may remain normal even when there is an obvious residual neurological deficit, for example, hemiplegia. The reason for this is probably that a small lesion of the motor cortex may produce irreversible disturbance of motor ability, but the normal cortex around the lesion produces normal rhythms and there is no area of silence. On the other hand, sometimes months after the injury, the EEG begins to become abnormal again with the presence of epileptic activity that is usually the prelude to post-traumatic epilepsy. It is important to stress that the EEG may remain quite normal even when there is other unequivocal evidence of brain damage.

EEGs are also of value in sorting out the possible causes of dullness or slowness in retarded epileptics, especially when it is episodic. If such episodes are due to drug overdosage, the EEG will usually show a symmetrical 'ironed-out' appearance with rhythmic fast and slow activity. If they are due to frequent minor or 'subclinical' attacks, then the record will show very frequent or even continuous generalized irregular epileptic discharges, such as spikes and spikes and waves. On the other hand, if the frequent attacks are focal (especially temporal lobe) in origin, then unless an actual seizure is recorded, the record may show generalized irregular, perhaps asymmetrical, very slow activity, and little or no evidence of the focus of origin. Finally, if the dullness is psychogenic, in the nature of emotional withdrawal, then the EEGs will resemble the tracings obtained when the patient is in his normal livelier state, whether they be then normal or abnormal.

## SUMMARY

A correct diagnosis of the type of 'fit' and of the nature of the underlying cause, are essential for correct treatment. Epileptic attacks are now classified into:

1. Generalized seizures, divided into convulsive (grand mal) and non-convulsive (petit mal).
2. Focal seizures, including those with motor, sensory or complex auras.
3. Focal seizures leading on to generalized fits.

Almost all causes of retardation may be associated with epilepsy, but it is particularly common in metabolic disorders and lesions affecting the cerebral cortex. Types of epileptic attacks, such as infantile spasms ('salaam' attacks or hypsarrhythmia), Lennox attacks and Happy Puppet type, are especially associated with mental retardation. However, epilepsy is not always associated with retardation or deterioration. As in normal subjects attacks tend to become less frequent as the child ages. Rare exceptions are autism and Down's syndrome. If deterioration occurs in spite of correct treatment, it is probable that both fits and retardation are due to a progressive underlying cause. Epilepsy is more common the more retarded (and the more brain-damaged) the retardate; thus between 0.5 and 1 per cent of the general population have

a history of an epileptic fit, among those with IQ 50–70 it is 3 to 6 per cent, and among those with less than IQ 50, 33 per cent have a history of one or more fits.

Episodic behaviour disorders may be related to actual epileptic attacks if there is a disturbance of consciousness. Terms like epileptic equivalent can be misleading. Continuing behaviour disorders and other psychological disturbances are the result of the combined effects of two or more of the following factors: underlying brain damage, anticonvulsants, nature and frequency of attacks, psychosocial factors and (possibly) genetic predisposition.

The use of drugs in epilepsy has been revolutionized over the last ten years by the new techniques of measuring blood levels of drugs. Blood levels may differ substantially between two people of the same weight on the same dose of the same drug, owing, in part, to their different genetic endowment for absorption and metabolism of the drug. Monitoring blood levels is better than increasing dosage until toxic effects appear because people differ markedly in level of toxic response, and some may be put off taking the drug altogether. In addition, poor speech makes toxicity more difficult to identify in the retarded. Over the last ten years the indications for new drugs have been clarified, and the use of barbiturates has decreased (see Table 25.3). The drug treatment of status epilepticus is now much facilitated by the technique of intravenous benzodiazepines (see page 337). New techniques of intubation and intensive care are not reviewed here. Surgical treatment of epilepsy in the retarded is seldom possible, although experimental procedures, such as electrode implants, are being developed.

The electroencephalogram (EEG) is of great importance in initial diagnosis of the type of epileptic attacks, and recent research is reviewed. It is also useful in continuing care; for example, it can help distinguish between the dulling effect produced by overdosage (a flat EEG), numerous minor attacks (generalized irregular discharges in the EEG), or psychogenic causes (no change from patient's previous EEG).

BIBLIOGRAPHY

Al-Kaisi, A. H. & McGuire, R. J. (1974) The effect of sulthiame on disturbed behaviour in mentally subnormal patients. *Br. J. Psychiat.*, *124*, 45–9.

Bowe, J. C., Cornish, E. J. & Dawson, M. (1971) Evaluation of folic acid supplements in children taking phenytoin. *Devl Med. Child Neurol.*, *13*, 343–54.

Bower, B. & Jeavons, P. M. (1967) The 'Happy Puppet' syndrome. *Archs Dis. Childh.*, *42*, 298–302.

Chevrie, J. J. & Aicardi, J. (1972) Childhood epileptic encephalopathy with slow spike and wave: a statistical study of 80 cases. *Epilepsia*, *13*, 259–71.

Clausen, J., Sersen, E. A. & Lidsky, A. (1977) Sleep patterns in mental retardation: Down's syndrome. *Electro-encephalography & clin. Neurophysiol.*, *43*, 183–91.

Clevenger, L. J. (1966) EEG studies relating to mental retardation. *Ment. Retard. Abstr.*, *3*, 170–8.

Cobb, W. A., Martin, F. & Pampiglione, G. (1952) Cerebral lipidosis: an EEG study. *Brain*, *75*, 343–57.

Corbett, J. A., Harris, R. & Robinson, R. G. (1975) Epilepsy. In: Wortis, J. (ed.), *Mental Retardation and Developmental Disabilities*, vol. VII. New York: Brunner/Mazel.

Driver, M. V. & MacGillivray, B. B. (1976) Electro-encephalography. In: Laidlaw, J. & Richens, A. (eds.), *A Textbook of Epilepsy*. Edinburgh: Churchill Livingstone.

Ellingson, R. J., Menolascino, F. J. & Eisen, J. D. (1970) Clinical EEG relationships in mongoloids confirmed by karyotype. *Am. J. ment. Defic.*, *74*, 645–50.

Eyman, R. K., Caples, L., Moore, B. C. & Zachofsky, T. (1969) Retardates with seizures. *Am. J. ment. Defic.*, *74*, 651–9.

Foley, J. (1968) Deterioration in the EEG in children with cerebral palsy. *Devl Med. Child Neurol.*, *10*, 287–301.

Gastaut, H., Poirier, F., Payan, M., Salamon, G., Toga, M. & Vigouroux, M. (1960) H.H.E. Syndrome: Hemiconvulsions, hemiplegia, epilepsy. *Epilepsia*, *1*, 418–47.

Gastaut, H., Roger, J., Soulayrol, R., Tassinari, C. A., Regis, H. & Dravet, C. (1966) Childhood epileptic encephalopathy with diffuse slow spike and waves (otherwise known as petit mal variant) or Lennox syndrome. *Ann. paediat. (Paris)*, *13*, 489–99.

Gibbs, F. A. & Gibbs, E. L. (1965) The electroencephalogram in mental retardation. In: Carter, C. H. (ed.), *Medical Aspects of Mental Retardation*, pp. 112–35. Springfield, Ill.: Charles C. Thomas.

Green, J. R., Troupian, A. S., Halpern, L. M., Friel, P. & Kanarek, P. (1974) Sulthiame: evaluation as an anticonvulsant. *Epilepsia (Amst.)*, *15*, 329–50.

Gudmunsson, G. (1966) Epilepsy in Iceland. *Acta neurol. Scand.* Suppl. *25*, 43.

Hansen, E. (1960) Cerebral palsy in Denmark. *Acta psychiat. Scand.* Suppl. *146*.

Harris, R. (1972) EEG aspects of unclassified mental retardation. In: Cavanagh, J. B. (ed.), *The Brain in Unclassified Mental Retardation*, pp. 225–42. Edinburgh: Churchill Livingstone.

Harris, R., Della Rovere, M. & Prior, P. C. (1965) Electroencephalographic studies in infants and children with hypothyroidism. *Archs Dis. Childh.*, *40*, 612–17.

Illingworth, R. S. (1958) *Recent Advances in Cerebral Palsy*. Edinburgh: Churchill Livingstone.

Jeavons, P. M. & Bower, B. D. (1964) Infantile spasms. *Clinics in Developmental Medicine*, *15*. London: Heinemann.

Kirman, B. H. (1965) The pathology of certain syndromes. In: Hilliard, L. T. & Kirman, B. H. (eds.), *Mental Deficiency*, 2nd ed. Edinburgh: Churchill Livingstone.

Kolvin, I., Ounsted, C. & Roth, M. (1971) Cerebral dysfunction and childhood psychosis. *Br. J. Psychiat.*, *118*, 407–14.

Laidlaw, J. & Richens, A. (eds.) (1976) *A Textbook of Epilepsy*. Edinburgh: Churchill Livingstone.

Margerison, J. H. (1962) The incidence of temporal lobe epilepsy in a hospital population of mental defectives. In: *Proceedings of the London Conference of the Scientific Study of Mental Deficiency*, pp. 210–16. Dagenham: May and Baker.

Margerison, J. H. & Corsellis, J. A. N. (1966) Epilepsy and the temporal lobes. *Brain*, *89*, 499–530.

Marsden, C. D. (1976) Classification in epilepsy. In: Laidlaw, J. & Richens, A. (eds.), *A Textbook of Epilepsy*. Edinburgh: Churchill Livingstone.

Meldrum, B. S. (1976) Neuropathology and pathophysiology. In: Laidlaw, J. & Richens, A. (eds.), *A Textbook of Epilepsy*. Edinburgh: Churchill Livingstone.

Ounsted, C., Lindsay, J. & Norman, R. (1966) Biological factors in temporal lobe epilepsy. *Clinics in Developmental Medicine*, *22*, 1. London: Heinemann.

Peckham, C. (1974) National Child Development Study (1958 Cohort). Personal communication.

Pond, D. A. & Bidwell, B. H. (1960) A survey of epilepsy in fourteen general practices. II. Social and psychological aspects. *Epilepsia*, *1*, 283–99.

Primrose, D. A. A. (1966) Natural history of mental deficiency in a hospital group and in the population it serves. *J. ment. Defic. Res.*, *10*, 159–89.

Reynolds, E. H. (1973) Anticonvulsants, folic acid epilepsy. *Lancet*, *1*, 1376–8.

Reynolds, E. H. & Travers, R. D. (1974) Serum anticonvulsant concentrations in epileptic patients with mental symptoms. *Br. J. Psychiat.*, *124*, 440–5.

Richardson, A. E. (1976) Neurosurgery. In: Laidlaw, J. & Richens, A. (eds.), *A Textbook of Epilepsy*. Edinburgh: Churchill Livingstone.

Richens, A. (1976) Clinical pharmacology and medical treatment. In: Laidlaw, J. & Richens, A. (eds.), *A Textbook of Epilepsy*. Edinburgh: Churchill Livingstone.

Rutter, M. (1970) Sex differences in children's responses to family stress. In: Anthony, E. J. & Koupernik, C. (eds.), *International Year Book of Child Psychiatry, vol. 1: The Child and His Family*. New York: Wiley.

Rutter, M., Graham, P. & Yule, W. (1970) *A Neuropsychiatric Study in Childhood*. London: Spastics Int. Med. Pub.

Rutter, M., Greenfield, D. & Lockyer, L. (1967) A five to fifteen-year follow-up study of infantile psychosis. II. Social and behavioural outcome. *Br. J. Psychiat.*, *113*, 1183–99.

Shorvon, S. D., Chadwick, D., Galbraith, A. W. & Reynolds, E. H. (1978) One drug for epilepsy. *Br. med. J.*, *1*, 474–6.

Taft, L. T. & Cohen, M. J. (1971) Hypsarrhythmia and infantile autism: a clinical report. *J. Autism Childh. Schizo.*, *1*, 27–36.

Tassinari, C. A., Davet, C., Roger, J., Cano, J. P. & Gastaut, H. (1972) Tonic status epilepticus precipitated by intravenous benzodiazepine in 5 patients with Lennox-Gastaut syndrome. *Epilepsia*, *13*, 421–35.

Tizard, J. (1963) *Community Services for the Mentally Handicapped*. Oxford: Oxford University Press.

Tizard, J. & Grad, J. C. (1961) *The Mentally Handicapped and their Families*. Maudsley Monograph No. 7. Oxford: Oxford University Press.

Tredgold, R. F. & Soddy, K. (1963) *Tredgold's Textbook of Mental Deficiency*, 10th ed. London: Baillière Tindall and Cox.

Veall, R. M. (1974) Survey of epilepsy among mongols in subnormality hospitals. *J. ment. Defic. Res.*, *18*, 99–106.

Viukara, N. M. A., Tannisto, P. & Kauho, K. (1972) Low calcium levels in forty mentally subnormal epileptics. *J. ment. Defic. Res.*, *16*, 192–5.

# CHAPTER 26

# THE VIOLENT AND DANGEROUS PATIENT: ASSESSMENT AND TREATMENT

## MICHAEL CRAFT

Incidents of violence are common enough in the general population, all too common in fact. Wife- and husband-beating, violence on the football terraces, vandalism in public buildings, all feature in our daily newspapers. Crimes involving violence to person or property are increasing.

Violence can be defined as the actual delivery of aggressive feelings to other humans or material things. Many people would differentiate between verbal violence, and actual bodily harm.

Naturally the public has a right to be protected against those who have proved themselves capable of violence. Prison sentences deal with many, and for those whose mental disorder leads them to aggressive behaviour, the psychiatric hospital is the proper setting. Here we hit upon a paradox, for violence is frightening, disruptive and destructive and all too often a psychiatric hospital will refuse to admit someone on the grounds that it does not have the necessary treatment facilities available. Thus the very people who need time away from the community (asylum) are excluded from such a setting. The illogical end point is that hospitals only accept those unlikely to cause any upsets at all.

What follows here is a discussion on the assessment and treatment of the violent and dangerous patient, outlining both theory and practice.

### THEORIES OF AGGRESSION

There are four major explanatory theories of aggression.

*Psychoanalytical theory* explains aggression as one of the instinctual forces driving people towards the twin poles of love and destruction. Freud outlined what he called 'the death wish'. According to this theory, the release of aggressive energy in actual violence allows the individual to reduce aggressive feelings for a while. It has a 'cathartic effect', allowing the internal reservoir of aggressive feelings to spill over from time to time, in aggression towards people or property. Thus agricultural workers who have a physically more violent occupation than office workers are felt to be less subject to frustration, which can be one result of pent-up aggressive feelings. The damming-up of aggression can cause other deleterious results by working through the subconscious of the individual. The outcome can be destructive, with reactions such as guilt, over-strict morality, over-eating, excessive smoking, alcoholism, anxiety and tension states; or constructive, when aggression is diverted to physical outlets such as gardening, sawing wood, mountain climbing and walking. The theory suggests that treatment might be needed for both too much and too little deployment of actual aggression if the norm of society does not allow adequate expression.

*Learning theory* does not accept the above view, but sees aggression as one type of learned behaviour. According to this theory childhood temper tantrums and frustration develop before aggression by adolescents or adults; if young children with frequent temper tantrums are rewarded for their aggressive behaviour by extra attention, if not downright rewards or bribes from parents, such as sweets or pocket money 'to keep them quiet', they learn that aggression pays dividends.

It is very difficult to test theories of aggression in the laboratory because aggression is so disruptive to humans, and few experiments would stand up to ethical approval. Such experiments as have been reported are more war-game types than the study of emotional fury.

It is easier to carry out experiments with animals. With rats, for example, experiments have shown that overcrowding stimulates aggression, and that increased aggressive behaviour can be developed by rewarding those who win fights. In this way mice have been trained to be highly aggressive through repeated successes with submissive adversaries, and these highly aggressive mice have also been trained to become markedly non-aggressive following punishment by better-trained mice warriors. However the former were not sexually inactivated, which rebuts the psychoanalytic theory that inhibition would result from submission.

*Group dynamics theory* explains aggression as a development of interpersonal relationships. One human is less likely to be aggressive to himself when alone, than if he is in a crowd in a confined space. Most people are susceptible to group emotion such as in a 'rock' concert or football match, especially if there has been a physical deprivation for some hours before, such as queuing in the rain and lacking food.

The fourth explanation of aggression is the *neurophysiological theory*. Certain types of brain damage are known, from both animal experiments and accidental damage in man, to cause the recipient to be more aggressive. This is probably by interference with centres of inhibition. Such results have been interpreted as supporting both psychoanalytic and learning theories, and are well observed in people with extensive brain damage from birth, who have frequent epilepsy thereafter. The term *epileptic personality* is here a misnomer for although there are some hundreds who are indeed selectively admitted to hospital on account of their aggressive behaviour disorder, they are likely to be just the most severely affected of the half-million epileptics in the United Kingdom. (See also pp. 335–7.)

In animal experiments damage to parts of a cat's thalamus causes it to show 'thalamic rage' when the unfortunate animal, apparently contentedly purring and drinking milk, responds to a pin-prick with a three-second burst of extreme, spitting rage before resuming its purring and drinking. Twenty years ago tracts leading to the thalamus from the frontal lobe used to be severed in humans, in the operation known as prefrontal leucotomy. These earlier operations gained a bad reputation because they often left an apathetic, listless individual without reactions. Now, as a result of the advance of knowledge in recent years, smaller tractotomies are effected, using stereotactic surgical techniques, often in the temporal lobe. In drug-resistant temporal lobe epilepsy with psychotic episodes, or violent aggressive outbursts, it may be possible to excise the discharging focus. Sometimes the focus is in the amygdaloid nucleus, a large collection of brain nuclei on the antero-medial wall of the temporal lobe. By means of high frequency electrical stimulation, the suspect nucleus or focus can be located and stereotactic division of small tracts between the medial and lateral nuclei bodies is possible. In successful cases the result is decreased emotional hyperactivity, fewer fits, less EEG activity from the discharging focus, and fewer anti-epileptic drugs required thereafter. There should be no deadening of personality as a result.

## THE ASSESSMENT AND AVOIDANCE OF DANGER

Clearly, identification of the circumstances which can lead to a violent incident is the most effective avoidance, but once such a situation has developed, methods of treatment and of handling are crucial to limit the amount of damage done.

Violent situations can be unpredictable, but most do develop out of a situation that builds up over time. Anyone who has visited a number of public bars can identify the atmosphere that develops before a violent outburst occurs. Exactly the same is true of situations that develop in a residential or other community, and once assessed may be avoided. One can divide the factors behind a potentially dangerous situation into the historical situation, the susceptible group, the potential protagonist, and the provocative incident.

### The historical situation

The background is often the same in these situations. A group of people with violent records are shut in together on a ward or in a unit, not necessarily with keys, but by physical environment. There may well be lack of work opportunities and/or limited leisure activities, leading to boredom and a build-up of energy and tense atmosphere. This is the general background against which violent incidents occur and are remembered. Each watches to ensure no-one is more favoured than he, each may come to feel he has a legitimate grievance and that he is not able to secure redress within the limitations that obtain. He feels the people who are with him are either cold or unfeeling, or antagonistic. In a residential home or psychiatric hospital it is usually possible to identify the potentially violent situation.

### The susceptible group

Property can be damaged by one violent person on his own, but much more damage is done by a group in violent action. In a residential situation such action takes time to build up, and needs a susceptible group. By this is meant a group of people, some of whom may have a history of violence; who may be placed together against their own wishes, and dislike each other in consequence; who may have a hatred of authority figures resulting from their own parental handling or teachers or police later on. The nurse or care assistant faced with the responsibility of managing this group may not be in a position to separate or scatter such an ill-matched assembly, but it may be worth-while trying. The allocation of different jobs in different areas may be possible. The attempt to get people to talk, even to laugh together, may help. Stories from the day's newspaper, the radio, or even gossip—preferably constructive—about people known to the group may gain their attention.

### The potential protagonist

The potential protagonist is the one likely to break into violence given the right historical situation, the presence of a susceptible group, and appropriate provocation. Indeed, there may be several such persons in the group and the flashpoint of one may be triggered by a different stimulus to another. It is rare for the potential protagonist not to show signs of the coming explosion. There *are* those trained to violence and skilled at concealing their feelings, such as soldiers, *mafiosa*, or professional criminals, who may give no sign of the violence to come. Experience of Glaswegian soldiers in an English bar or the film *The Godfather* reminds one that with such people there may be no facial or bodily sign that one is about to be beaten up, stabbed or mugged. It is debatable whether these people should be called more 'normal' than those about to be described, but it is true that by training—the result of learning theory—the more 'normal' the average soldier, the better can he school himself to swift and efficient violence.

This is not so for psychiatric patients or those in a residential situation. Because of their historical background and upbringing, usually full of conflict between felt feelings and taught good behaviour, the clash between emotions is almost always expressed in facial and bodily signs. Such signs have to be looked for, and weighed against knowledge of that person's past behaviour. For instance, the quiet reserved introvert may need much greater provocation to reach his flashpoint of violence than the habitually noisy extrovert. Each human is genetically differently endowed in the way he may respond to stimulus so that there is considerable variety in the signs different humans can present in the face of stress or provocation.

*Negative signs* foretelling the protagonist's outburst may be his sudden silence, his retirement to a corner, or the absence of facial colour in one who reacts to stress by an overactive sympathetic nervous system.

*Positive signs* foretelling an outburst are a flushed face, for one with an overactive parasympathetic system, or the result of high blood pressure; tense, twitching face; eyes that fail to look at one directly; jerking hands, a body that is agitated and hops from one foot to another; fists that clasp and unclasp.

Psychiatry is full of signs to see if one knows what to look for and has been taught to understand what one sees. It is very rare for a person under psychiatric care to cause violence that is completely unsignalled.

## The provocative situation

It is an old saying that what stimulates one person may sedate another, or in modern idiom, 'turns on' or 'turns off' the adolescent, the commonest group at issue. It is also true that a group of persons who know one another well will know each one's tender spots.

In a potentially explosive situation the provocation leading to violence needs to be only very slight. A look, a gesture, a bodily touch or a word may be enough for those who wish to think ill of it. If the situation is as explosive as this it may be too late for prevention; but prevention is certainly best.

### PREVENTATIVE MEANS

The brooding group, or the irritable man or woman may have been thus all morning. Before they find an outlet for their feelings, it should be possible to scatter or divert them. The potential protagonist may be in a complaining mood, objecting to his chair, his clothing, his food or the weather. It may be that he dislikes the look on a person's face. By himself without too many other people around, it is usually possible to avoid the chance provocative gesture which may trigger him off. If those surrounding him are cheery his attention may be diverted. If his interest is gained so that he can be helped to laugh with somebody about something emotionally neutral it may be possible to lower the rising head of steam within him. Obviously, one should never laugh *at* such a person, one has to work hard at trying carefully to laugh *with* him. Since a great deal of time may need to be spent with such a person, the organizer of the group in which the situation is building up may need to detail one or two people to take this as their task for a while.

Lack of communication between resident and resident, or resident and care staff, is a common background to a rise in tension. The brooding person may be unable to communicate his resentment, it may be that others are unwilling to hear him. The care staff member who recognizes this problem has gone half-way to solving it because he is clearly using his powers of perception to receive non-verbal signals from his residents.

Non-verbal communication is more important than verbal; it has been called the primary signalling system among animals, including humans. Humans hardly have the raised fur of the dog, or tense tail of the rabbit to signify fight or fright, but the same hormone, adrenaline, circulates in their system to cause eye change, 'goose pimples' on the skin, blanching of the face and tension in the muscles of the body, all signs which can be identified by perceptive staff. Non-verbal replies could be to sit with the resident, smile with him, hold his/her hand, place a hand on the shoulder or walk with him. There may be limits to non-verbal communication, set by the resident's background. Readers will have experienced the repudiation of their proffered touch or handshake by someone perhaps in unrequited sexual tension who 'cannot bear to be touched' by male or female, as the case may be.

Sexual tension is in fact a prime cause of violence at any age after puberty. Many people become resentful at their own tension, unrequited need for love, company or sex-release, and furious if others indulge in front of them. Non-verbal displays of fury result, because at any ability level these needs are difficult to describe in words. Preventive methods depend on forecasting need, providing mixed wards, socials, dances, outings, fostering companionship. In some cases, partnership results, and since the need for love is as important for the retardate as the normal, Chapter 27 is devoted to this need.

Confinement even in an unlocked room or ward is a further cause of tension building up. This can be avoided by timely outings, walks, the release of energy in outdoor pursuits or in winter by day-room activities. The purpose is not only to provide constructive activities but also to provide the opportunity to meet other companions.

Verbal communication, also called man's second signalling system, is the route which comes easiest to staff. Yet there are six ways of saying the same thing, even a simple word like 'yes', and the perceptive staff member will use the sensitive instrument of voice, like music, to soothe if not the savage beast, the brooding human.

The domineering or provocative staff member is another part of the equation which may build up to violence. There are some staff with a loud voice, a hectoring manner, an abusive style and a flow of expletive more appropriate on a parade ground. Such staff may be well meaning but if they cannot adjust their manner it is better for senior staff to intervene rather than to allow matters to proceed to the point of an enquiry where all the unit's dirty linen will be washed.

Yet despite difficulties, there must be places in the community for those who are formed in a violent or dangerous mould, and psychiatric hospitals are one place for those particularly liable to violence. In such places it is usually possible to organize an activity schedule, or work task which allows for the deployment of surplus energy otherwise liable to be used in an explosive outburst. Digging, breaking up stone, even a long walk are effective ways to dispel energy, but obviously the task should be chosen with the potentially violent person very much in mind. For instance, a fork or spade could easily become an offensive weapon! In such situations it may also be possible to use a sedative agent, or tranquillizing agent, to soothe the irritable. It must be remembered, however, that like the use of alcohol which is a potentially provocative agent, sedation may well remove a degree of the person's self-control or restraint.

## THE TREATMENT OF THE VIOLENT

### PERSONAL RESOURCES

Drugs and quiet side-rooms are very much secondary resources in the treatment of the violent. They are undeniably important as back-ups, but the primary resource is the staff member whose work gives him responsibility for the care of the susceptible groups discussed above. The ward sister portrayed in the film *One Flew over the Cuckoo's Nest* is a prime example of the destructive use of a human resource. Not too far outside the field of psychiatry, Makarenko, the Russian educationalist, used his own personality to inspire thieving and murderous juveniles

orphaned by the Soviet civil war to build an enthusiastic farm commune. In the United Kingdom, the first governor of Lowdham Grange Borstal selected some of the most violent and aggressive delinquents in the English borstal system to march north to Lowdham and camp with him while they built a new Borstal on the ruins of a derelict farm. He so inspired them that there were few runaways and many asked to stay informally after their sentence ended. These are extreme examples of the force of personality, but they serve as reminders that it is possible to inspire, exhort and cajole the most unlikely people and constructively channel their energies.

In the treatment setting the person caring for an unruly group must appreciate that the best tools he has for handling them are his own will and body. Both verbal and non-verbal signals are sent and received. Both must match up.

*Negative signals* should not be given by the staff member. If by one's face and with one's body one shows fury, tension or annoyance, it is quite possible that these signals will be interpreted by the violent person as provocation to fresh mischief. Equally if by one's face and with one's body, one shows fear, anxiety or tremulousness then the violent person may feel it safe to proceed to an exhibition of greater fury.

*Positive signals* have to be taught to, and displayed by, care staff. The naturally self-confident caring person may feel that he yet has sufficient control over the situation to reason with, turn aside, or play down the violence exhibited so far. He marches in firmly, with cheerful smile, firm voice and experience gained from years of successful evaluation of such emergencies and takes the violent person away from the provoking situation, to lead him to a quieter or more constructive place to chat to him. At this stage a cup of tea is often regarded as a panacea, a quiet side-room away from noise and distractions of other people may be useful in which to talk calmly, steadily and stolidly to show that all may be accepted if not forgiven. Such evaluation and experience in the caring person is not an inborn flair, it is a learning experience for the staff member. The most effective exponent of this I ever met was a small Cornish casualty sister serving the Plymouth dockyards. We young doctors were scared stiff of her, but so were the dockyard navvies, I was pleased to note.

It is crucial for the caring person to decide correctly if he still has control of a changing situation. It is possible that the violent person has sufficient remaining control, so that after breaking, smashing or hitting, he will have 'blown his top', and be ready to accept direction, even reproof. If so, then the sooner his interest is diverted to a fresh area of activity, the better. If violence is escalating it is important to know at what level one should call for help. It is an old adage, that it takes one to start a fight but three to impose peace. Better that these three men are called early, rather than so late in the day that much destruction is caused, or many join in.

Discipline and love are both needed to raise children to successful adulthood; both are needed with violent humans for long-term success. A firm face and clear eye looking straight at the protagonist aid with one; a friendly smile and a gentle hand may help with the other. One cannot be certain which recipe of firmness or love is best for a particular broth which is boiling, this is the art of diagnosis and treatment of a particular human situation. In any case each recipe can be argued at length by staff at the interminable conferences so much a feature of residential units, but when all is said and done at such meetings, most who talk will not have been present to assess the non-verbal signals which passed at the time between group members, potential protagonists and staff.

Reference has been made to violence and alcoholism before, for the use of alcohol by people with a grudge is well known. Unfortunately alcohol is a slowly absorbed drug and first removes the self-restraint people commonly feel and may even give false courage before stupor occurs. Thus in a psychiatric hospital or residential home, where the potentially violent customer arrives after visiting the bar it may be necessary to identify the situation, and make a discrete retreat to summon help, rather than attempting to deal unaided with the situation once violence escalates. Alcohol is not the only agent which may release violent behaviour and it is as well to remember that one cannot always go by the smell of a person's breath in identifying how drugged he might be.

Drug-addiction units illustrate how much experience helps in containing the violent. These units treat aggressive and immature personalities who use alcohol, as well as other drugs. Staff learn and depend upon special techniques and experience in dealing with such people. Much rests on knowing the individuals well enough to refer in companionable terms to their family, and items of shared background experience. Staff get to know the people who matter to a resident, those who have an influence, so as to build up a special relationship which at times of stress can be used constructively.

## Patient and staff signals

One must remember that the person who has initially damaged property, and may have progressed to arson or assault on other humans may become very guilty about the severity of his feelings. He may go from anger to weeping, from elation to depression. The calm interval here may be a sign of danger. He is best presented with a pair of staff eyes that reflect calmness and understanding, which are unwavering and never leave his face. If these eyes show that their owner is understanding and compassionate, is a good listener to tales of woe, as well as tales of hostility, all may be well. It is best not to leave the violent person alone in a situation where he can cause harm to himself as well as material damage, for self-destruction is always a possible end-point to the extremely violent. Equally, when those in a violent state have recovered to some extent, it is even less wise to leave them then, in case the swings of mood lead to another outburst of destruction.

## PHYSICAL MANAGEMENT OF THE VIOLENT

### Action

If two patients are fighting, the nurse must first estimate his chances of success in stopping them, and then plan his intervention, including the way his face, his body and his arrival are seen by the participants.

Surprise and noise level are useful. A sudden arrival may daunt fighters, a quiet voice or sudden shout 'What's this?' may surprise them. With children, or underdeveloped handicapped, two forceful hands may part fighters easily; whilst women fighters may respond with shame to a male nurse and *vice versa*. It is said that Newcastle pub landlords always call their wives to part drunken males!

One axiom for care staff is to use only that little bit more force adequate to subdue violence in progress; this might be termed 'approved escalation'. Thus two staff separating two patients fighting with teeth and nails are justified in dragging each back by their coat arms. A charge nurse who first knocked to the ground a severely physically handicapped male who threatened to bite him, and then kicked in his face and ribs, in temper at the end of a long day, was asked by the subsequent enquiry to resign, being judged guilty of 'gross escalation'.

A second staff axiom is to avoid damage to the patient. One should part fighters from behind, holding the clothes of the upper arm or upper leg to avoid fractures. A sitting patient can be similarly pinioned in his chair.

In the past physical methods of restraint such as strong garments or the use of chains or ropes were used, but these are now outmoded. Sometimes a side-room, or quiet room is necessary for peace, quiet and segregation and discussion with a staff member. If there are very few staff, or many helpless persons about, it is on rare occasions necessary to seclude or isolate the violent person in a locked room. Most residential units require this event to be recorded and reported to avoid later charges of improper incarceration.

## The law

*Common law* recognizes a duty on the *ordinary citizen* to prevent someone else wilfully damaging himself or a weaker citizen, but prosecutions are rare. The duty on a paid care staff, parent or teacher to prevent damage to their charge is higher; for example, some are convicted each year in the United Kingdom for being drunk in charge of a child.

The law lays a duty on police, staff and parents to use only that force just necessary to subdue continuing violence, 'approved escalation'. A person is also entitled to defend himself and his charges, so for example *in extremis* it is a valid defence to manslaughter if a citizen kills believing himself to be about to be murdered.

*Pountney* v. *Griffiths* (1975) has clarified the position on 'control' of potentially violent patients. This case stemmed from a Broadmoor patient, detained during Her Majesty's pleasure, alleging that at the end of visiting time a nurse had punched him on the shoulder, which was denied. The magistrates convicted the nurse. The nurse appealed and the conviction was quashed on a technicality, as the patient had failed to obtain the permission of the High Court to proceed as required by Section 141 of the 1959 Mental Health Act. More importantly the House of Lords dismissed the patient's counter appeal, Lord Edmund Davies laying down case law; 'The conception of detention and treatment *necessarily implies* that the staff of the hospital, including the male nurses, can and on occasion must, use reasonable force in order to ensure that control is exercised over the patient'.

Whilst this appears to apply to those detained under the Mental Health Act, and common law would include restraining patients from harming others, it is wise for staff needing to restrain the habitually violent informal patient, to ask their Responsible Medical Officer to use compulsory powers (Sections 26, 29, 30) to cover those in need.

## Drugs

Drugs are commonly used to impose quiet, and most require medical prescription.

*Alcohol* is the oldest sedative, and the most common drug to be self-prescribed by those who feel violent. It is noted here, because like other sedatives, in the early stages of sedation it causes loss of self-control and possible escalation of violence. Due to variable and erratic uptake from the stomach there follows a lengthy period of failing coordination during which injury to the head may compound the sedation. It is not recommended.

*Diazepam* (Valium) 10 mg by intramuscular or slow intravenous injection is most effective for the violent. Orally 10–20 mg by tablet or syrup is effective. It needs a medical prescription and is recommended.

*Chlorpromazine* (Largactil) 50 mg by intramuscular injection, 100–300 mg by tablet or syrup is hallowed by long usage in patients who are violent. It is safe, can be repeated two or three times in the day for the extremely violent and has been standard medication in casualty departments for drunkards for many years. It has to be given as a result of medical prescription and is recommended.

*Haloperidol* (Serenace) 3 mg orally is now often used. It probably has fewer side effects than chlorpromazine and is more slowly absorbed and metabolized. Side effects are rare. A medical prescription is necessary. It is recommended.

*Paraldehyde* 5 cc by intramuscular injection, up to 15 cc in divided injections, has been used for many years. Whilst sterile, these injections are painful and have to be given by an experienced person; since the violent person may dislike injections, this presupposes there are plenty of staff to aid the therapist. It is therefore of limited use.

## AFTER-CARE

Following a violent incident, it is essential that the person concerned should be advised how he might better handle himself in future. Strong emotional feelings are not forgotten, indeed they provide some of the longest lasting memory traces of all. It is never wise to ignore studiously an aggressive incident afterwards. Once it has died down the person in charge can often suggest better ways of displaying feeling than the way the aggressor chose. After the incident is over, it is a good time to try to redress any grievances possible, to offer work or activity which better deploys energy felt, to re-arrange sitting, sleeping or living arrangements between people who cannot understand each other, even to allow restitution of damage done by willing work offered.

We live in a litigious age. It is therefore essential to have a proper record noted of the circumstances of the incident, the people concerned and what actually happened written down as soon as possible after the event has closed. Because strong memories may remain of emotion felt, those involved may well describe the incident in more lurid terms elsewhere. It therefore behoves one to show the record to those in authority who are therefore better prepared to avoid a recurrence. More staff may be needed, a re-deployment of personnel, more opportunities for work, and informed discussion of what was done and what could better be done may all be indicated.

## CONCLUSION

The assessment of danger and the treatment of violence are highly important in the psychiatric hospital. Few are born to success with either, success comes with experience and the careful recognition and evaluation of signals or signs shown by clients. The art of constructing an effective nurse or care assistant team is that they do build up this expertise, this confidence, and when a crisis occurs do not flee behind the counter as does the stereotype barman in the late-night Western film but assess danger, prevent upset and treat violence itself as constructively as possible.

## BIBLIOGRAPHY

Department of Health and Social Security (1976) *The Management of Violent, or Potentially Violent, Hospital Patients.* London: HMSO.
Home Office and Department of Health and Social Security (1975) *Report of the Committee on Mentally Abnormal Offenders* (Butler Committee). Cmnd. 6244. London: HMSO.
*Pountney* v. *Griffiths* (1975) 2 All E.R. 881 H.L.
Royal College of Nursing (1972) *Care of the Violent Patient.* London: RCN.
Smith, A. C. (1979) Violence. *Br. J. Psychiat., 134,* 528–9.
South East Thames Regional Health Authority (1977) *Guidelines to the Nursing Management of Violence.* [20-minute film, may be hired]

# CHAPTER 27

# PERSONAL RELATIONSHIPS AND PARTNERSHIPS FOR THE MENTALLY HANDICAPPED

## ANN AND MICHAEL CRAFT

Social and personal relationships are essential to the human condition. The bonds of friendship and love we form with other people enrich the quality of life we enjoy, and this is as true for the graduate of the Special School as of the University. Mentally handicapped people may be disadvantaged in many respects, but with education and counselling they can be aided to both give and receive personal satisfaction and pleasure in their relationships with others.

### SEX EDUCATION

The basic philosophy behind all education is that the individual who is taught learns and, in learning, internalizes what is taught, with the result that his behaviour is directed in socially acceptable ways and his life is enriched. Sex education, if it is to be judged by the same criteria as other areas of education, has to aim at the maximum possible degree of knowledge and understanding concerning sexual behaviour (for a discussion of this point, see Harris 1974). This is the object whether those being taught are mentally handicapped or normal.

What should sex education cover? Obviously it has to impart physical and biological facts, for ignorance can only mean vulnerability. A girl, mentally handicapped or otherwise, cannot choose to avoid having a baby if she knows nothing of contraception, and a mentally handicapped girl may not even know that intercourse is connected in any way with pregnancy. Sex education must also look at relationships and their implications. If people can be helped to understand themselves and their own needs better, they gain insight into the feelings and needs of others. Lastly, sexual relationships, partnership and marriage have to be put in social and ethical context, for all societies develop rules which govern such behaviour.

Is there any evidence showing the advantages or disadvantages of sex education? It is only comparatively recently that such programmes have had a place in the curricula of many of our schools. At this stage not enough research has been done to determine long-term effects. The few studies to date relied on the subjects' ability to recall having had sex education. It is extremely difficult to tease out at a later stage the amount, the quality or the manner in which instruction was given. Schofield (1968) found that among his sample of teenagers sex education seemed to have had remarkably little effect on their subsequent behaviour. However there was evidence to show that what the schools term 'sex education' may not be recognized as such by the students, for there is often a lack of frankness in the approach. There was evidence also that formal teaching in this area came too late, many youngsters did not pay attention to the teacher because they felt (albeit erroneously) that they knew it all already.

Scandinavian countries are often held up as models of sexually liberal or overly permissive societies (depending on one's viewpoint). In Sweden sex education in schools has been compulsory since 1956 and a recent report showed that 90 per cent of the population are in favour of such teaching, including information about contraceptive use (Proposed Guidelines for Sex Education in the Swedish School System 1974). Although premarital sexual intercourse was felt to be acceptable if the partners were in love, marital faithfulness was advocated by 90 per cent of the married people interviewed, young and old alike. It is interesting to note that, as in Schofield's survey, what the education authorities call a comprehensive sex education programme falls short of pupil expectations; 80 per cent of the students would like more information than is currently given. Only 20 per cent of teachers showed any interest in that area of the curricula, the rest felt they had not received sufficient professional training for the task. This reminds us that sex education is a sensitive and sometimes personally disquieting subject, and one where it is most important that the teacher feels at ease with his presentation and his students. While no statistics are quoted in the Swedish report for illegitimate births or legal abortions, the strong confirmation of the idea of marital fidelity is an indication that sex education has not led to the lowering of moral standards that some people feared. In England and Wales we know that since 1972 the total of extramarital pregnancies has been falling. It is likely that not only an increased awareness of contraceptive methods among the at-risk population but also improved contraceptive practice (Edmunds & Yarrow 1977) are contributory factors. The handicapped proportion of the population could equally well benefit from increased knowledge and the greater availability of contraceptive advice and methods.

We know that sex education—that is, learning about sexuality—does not take place only in a planned, formal setting. Indeed the attitudes which determine our approach are mostly acquired without conscious effort or thought by a learning process which begins from the time a human baby is born and which continues throughout life. This learning is by no means straightforward for humans often do not acquire the information

and responses which will aid them to form and maintain mutually satisfactory adult relationships. Literature abounds with examples of the haphazard and sometimes traumatic way many normal people have learned 'the facts of life'.

The mentally handicapped are doubly disadvantaged in this area as those who care for them frequently try to suppress their expressions of sexuality, and unlike their normal counterparts they cannot usually obtain information from their peers. Many parents and care staff believe that the less a mentally handicapped child knows about sex the better it will be for all concerned. Implicit here is the assumption that the mentally handicapped will remain asexual beings until awakened by the magic wand of knowledge. This simply is not so, the mentally handicapped, even if profoundly retarded, have sexual feelings and drives like everyone else, and most develop normal secondary sexual characteristics.

For a number of reasons sex education is of *special* importance with this intellectually handicapped group as they need more help, not less, towards understanding their bodies and their emotions. As Kempton (1972) points out, the mentally handicapped frequently over-respond to attention and give affection indiscriminately in return, commonly because of poor social teaching. It is socially acceptable in our society for a child to show affection by touching and kissing adults, some of whom are strangers to him though they are friends or relations of his parents. In normal children this behaviour is expected less and less as the child grows up, but mentally handicapped children are often encouraged to continue long after their normal brothers and sisters. Anyone who has visited a mental handicap hospital will have experienced demonstrations of inappropriate affection from residents. What is cute and touching in a five-year-old mongol girl is inappropriate in a fifteen-year-old. Indiscriminate affectionate behaviour can so easily be exploited.

Another reason why the mentally handicapped need sex education is that by definition their judgement and reasoning ability are limited. They do not by themselves think through the consequences of their actions.

Frequently, and often with the best will in the world, those who care for the mentally handicapped foster dependence and obedience. This creates another danger, for the mentally handicapped youngster may do what is asked of him without question and therefore stands in danger of being used and exploited sexually. Their peer group is usually just as ignorant and they lack the reading techniques to use books to fill gaps in knowledge. They may know isolated facts, but do not link them together or do so in a way which defies human physiology. To summarize, they lack the skills which would give them some defence against exploitation, and enable them to satisfy their social and sexual needs without bringing them into conflict with the law.

There are some who feel that the giving of sex education stimulates students to experiment, but it is the common experience of teachers that this is not the case, rather, anxiety is relieved and the student is helped to understand his own confusing emotions. Conversely lack of formal instruction does not seem to deter people from sexual performance, whether they are mentally handicapped or normal.

Do the mentally handicapped require different curricula for sex education? Basically the same ground needs to be covered as with normal children, although more repetition and revision will be necessary. One of the foremost Americans involved in sex education for the mentally handicapped, Dr Sol Gordon (1972), suggests that the following points need to be put across to care staff, administrators, teachers and the mentally handicapped in any teaching programme:

1. Masturbation is a normal expression of sex more common in young than old.
2. All sexual behaviour involving the genitals should be done in private. Institutions and hostels not built for privacy should clearly define what is a 'private' area, for example, one's own bed or the bathroom, as opposed to the 'public' day-room.
3. Any time a physically mature boy and girl have sexual intercourse they risk pregnancy.
4. Both partners should use birth control methods unless they are both clear about

wanting to have a baby and the responsibilities that go with child-rearing.
5. It is unlawful to have sexual intercourse with a girl under 16. In general, society prefers people to be adults (over 18) before they have intercourse.
6. Adults are not permitted to use children sexually.
7. The most effective way to avoid development of homosexual activity involves risking heterosexual activity.
8. In the final analysis sexual behaviour between consenting adults (whatever their mental age), whether it is homo- or hetero-sexual, should be no-one else's business, providing there is little risk of unwanted pregnancy, and neither participant is harmed.

Such programmes are always best placed in the context of social living, that is, personal relationships and responsibilities (Craft & Craft 1978). Each biological 'fact' has social aspects. For instance, the onset of puberty causes physical and emotional changes in the adolescent. The social aspects are many, for example: preparing for adulthood; understanding oneself and others; menstrual hygiene; accepting that masturbation is normal, but should be done in private; girl friends/boy friends; different kinds of love; behaviour on a date, et cetera. The only limiting factor is the ability level of the individual or group. For instance, some girls will be able to grasp only very simple elements of menstrual hygiene, others can be trained and encouraged to cope with their 'periods' by themselves, yet others will be able to understand what happens when they menstruate and the biological implications.

It is self evident that in teaching it is necessary to communicate, so the language and presentation must suit the individual or group. The sexual parts of the body and the act of sexual intercourse have many colloquial names and the teacher must be prepared to use the terms most familiar, while introducing correct terminology. Most mentally handicapped youngsters have difficulty in dealing with abstract concepts, so slides, illustrations, pictures, films, models, will all help to clarify the subject on hand. Role-playing games can widen repertoires of behaviour (Craft & Craft 1978).

Ignorance is hardly ever bliss, and as far as the mentally handicapped are concerned it will never 'solve the problem' of sexuality. It may well compound any difficulties. Like all human beings the mentally handicapped have a right to sexual fulfilment, and it follows that they also have a right to education which will help them achieve that fulfilment without offending, exploiting or hurting others, or being exploited or hurt themselves.

## COUNSELLING

Counselling involves both a response to specific situations which have arisen, and preparation for future events and behaviour. It is a process which is an integral part of helping the handicapped to help themselves. Anyone can find himself cast in the role of counsellor, whether parent, teacher, care staff or trainer. Not everyone is at ease with the task. Adults in close contact with mentally handicapped people should either be prepared to answer questions themselves about personal and sexual matters, or to refer the questioner immediately to another adult who can handle the subject. Fobbing off only raises anxiety levels. If the actual moment is inconvenient, set aside a time in the near future there and then, and make sure the date is kept. Counselling should never be merely the giving of advice or directions, for it needs to be an exploration of the situation as the mentally handicapped person sees it, and a working-through of the alternatives available.

### PERSONAL RELATIONSHIPS

Care staff find themselves in the same position as parents when it comes to counselling in the area of friendships and personal relationships. In adolescence there is usually an upsurge of interest in the opposite sex and friendships become more intense. At best, friendships stimulate, aiding mental development and promoting an enthusiastic response to life and its rich possibilities. Some relationships, however, can hurt rather than help, and just as normal parents promote friendships with some of their children's circle and not others, so care staff would be expected

to give frank encouragement or discouragement to those in their charge.

The mentally handicapped may need extra help in maintaining relationships because they are likely to lack the social skills which minimize frictions. They may not be good at recognizing mood signals, or at considering another's feelings. At a more practical level they may find it difficult to make telephone calls, write letters or keep dates. It is well known that having a girl friend or boy friend can produce great improvements in social abilities! (Edgerton & Dingman 1964.)

Particularly at the adolescent stage (which may well stretch into the twenties) friendships may be intense but short-lived, making the erstwhile friends miserable for a time. Normal adolescents learn by these experiences and mentally handicapped youngsters should be allowed this same opportunity. It is all part of growing up. Professionals may be called upon to advise parents with children at this stage; those with an only child are especially vulnerable and are likely to feel it is the handicap, not adolescence, that is causing difficulties. It can be very comforting for parents to discover through informal discussions with other parents that their child is not the only one presenting 'problems', and that others have found ways of coping. Social workers and voluntary organizations can arrange these informal meetings.

### PRE-MARITAL COUNSELLING

There will be couples who become serious about each other, remain together for months rather than weeks, and begin to talk of marriage. Usually one or both will have a place in a system of care and the possibility exists of providing a more structured counselling service.

For example, at one mental handicap hospital an Operational Policy on interpersonal relationships sets out guidelines for residents and staff. A couple talking of marriage are expected to 'go steady' for three months, and the implications of this are explained to them, that is, each should look after the other, not make dates with anyone else, and demonstrate by their mutual concern that their partnership is a constructive one. If all goes well during the three months and the pair wish to become engaged, a meeting is held with the couple, their next of kin and care staff. An arbitrary engagement period of six months is set, although it may be longer before the marriage takes place. The giving of a ring and a party announce the couple's formal intentions to everyone.

During the *engagement* period staff will take the initiative in counselling the pair, both separately and together on what sex means in and out of marriage, the birth control methods usually needed, meeting each other's emotional needs, and the art of living together. Domestic training, cooking, budgetting and saving should also be covered, and the couple aided to think realistically of future plans. Obviously no two couples are exactly alike and counselling must be individually tailored. Are both mentally handicapped? If so, how competent are they expected, or proving, to be in looking after themselves? Were one or both brought up at home or in an institution? No studies have yet compared the marriages or child-rearing of those originally raised in institutions with those living all of their lives in the community, and it may well be that the former lack the models on which to base their own marital behaviour.

Counselling sessions should also explore the question of children. The couple will doubtless have views on the subject. Do they want children? How old is the wife? Do they understand that any woman over 35 runs a higher risk of having a handicapped child? Is the cause of their retardation known? If so, is there a genetic component? Are the couple likely to be mature enough to cope with the complete dependence of a child over many years? What do they feel are the advantages and disadvantages of parenthood? How financially independent are they likely to be? What sort of accommodation do they have? Many normal couples wait until they have settled down in marriage together before starting their family, and this has much to commend it. A mentally handicapped couple who wish for children can be advised to do the same. Others will not want the additional responsibility of children and will need counselling on appropriate methods of birth control. Here sterilization is probably the simplest and most effective method, for after comple-

tion no more attention is needed. It does raise the vexed question of informed consent, as mentally handicapped people are often easily influenced by authority figures. There is a risk of regret, but of course that is so for everyone undergoing the operation regardless of handicap.

## POST-MARITAL COUNSELLING

We know that marital maladjustments, especially in the early stages of the partnership, are extremely common among normal partners. It might thus be expected that this would also be so where the couple are mentally handicapped, and here post-marital counselling can be of great benefit. It may only be a small problem, but it may be magnified because the couple do not have the interpersonal skill to handle it. For example one mentally handicapped wife in our Welsh survey (Craft & Craft 1976) had been orphaned at an early age and had lived in well-ordered homes and institutions nearly all her life until marriage. Always a neat and tidy woman, she complained in tears to the social worker that however much she appealed to her husband, Paul, he refused to hang up his clothes and they lay as they fell around the bedroom. A woman-to-woman chat about the shortcomings of husbands in general, introducing the idea that other wives also get upset sometimes by their partner's habits, reduced the mountain to molehill size, and a talk to Paul prompted him to be more thoughtful.

The maladjustment may be a sexual one and then detailed and experience-linked counselling will be needed. Another couple in the same survey illustrate this point. During their engagement Gareth and Helen explored with a counsellor the subject of marriage, and the responsibilities it would entail, in depth and detail. Once they were married staff assumed all was well until in fact the partnership reached crisis point. The *words*, even the *pictures* used beforehand, did not match with their *experience*. Gareth was sexually unskilled and his first attempts at intercourse were clumsy. Not surprisingly Helen 'froze', making penetration impossible. This situation continued for almost a year until they were counselled about their specific difficulties. It was found that Helen was rather small and a minor operation made intercourse physically more comfortable for her. Gareth was prompted to be more gentle, Helen relaxed more and both gained enormously in satisfaction.

Counselling is a vital part of the support service professionals can offer the mentally retarded. The cardinal points to remember are that the counsellor must spend time listening, and that he must talk *with* the persons concerned, not *at* them.

## THE SEVERELY MENTALLY HANDICAPPED

We have concentrated on counselling the moderately and mildly mentally handicapped in this section because both in practice and statistically they contribute the vast majority of those who need such services. In every 1000 general population, there are 31 who are mildly handicapped (above IQ 50) and 4 who are severely mentally handicapped. Few of the latter will be able to establish or sustain meaningful sexual partnerships, although there are some who do (Craft & Craft 1978). In the literature, reviewed elsewhere, there are no detailed references to this particular area of concern (Craft & Craft 1978).

Most of the severely mentally handicapped need instruction at a very basic level. Behaviour reinforcement underlies the teaching of modest behaviour, that is, disapproval for a girl lifting up her dress in company, repeated praise for her pulling up her pants properly or for a boy fastening his flies after toiletting. Modest behaviour may also be encouraged by the parental teaching of masturbation, instilling the principle that masturbation, like going to the toilet, is a private activity. Thus the severely handicapped person has to learn that pleasurable personal reward may follow private masturbation; parental or care staff disapproval will follow a public exhibition. Parents who have taught their severely handicapped son or daughter to masturbate, report much reduction in tension and subsequent improvement in public behaviour.

Commonly, a psychiatrist or another professional is called upon to give practical advice and counsel where a sexual offence has been committed by a severely mentally handicapped person. The reactions of parents, public and court can be explosive. Comparatively few 'offenders' are taken to court, but when they are, the psychiatrist has to be aware of the fate which may overtake subjects who are unable to speak for themselves. They may be adjudicated 'unfit to plead' and ordered to be detained indefinitely during Her Majesty's Pleasure in a special hospital, by judges who insist on the letter of the law. Most magistrates will accept a solicitor's plea of 'guilty' for someone who cannot speak, and will then discuss constructive measures which may include probation with a condition of psychiatric treatment.

The majority of 'offenders' do not reach this stage; nonetheless, the recriminations, upset and parental anxiety following an incident can be traumatic for all involved. The professional must be as clear as possible as to the exact nature of the offending action and the circumstances surrounding it. It is salutory to remember that one human's hand on the knee of another human can constitute an indecent assault, given an adverse set of circumstances. The severely mentally handicapped male offender is usually indicted for sexually playing with younger boys who are his mental peer group. It is also common enough in new housing estates for such males to be used as a sexual butt by local adolescents, and then blamed for whatever has occurred. They may enthusiastically handle training-centre staff or other trainees, or delight in the sensation caused by open and flamboyant masturbation, perhaps standing at a window. Severely mentally handicapped females are less likely to find themselves before the courts, but it does happen. In general they run a greater risk of being sexually exploited.

The professional investigating the circumstances of the offence and background of the offender must proceed carefully, for a destructive over-reaction is all too common. If a court case is involved, a remand, giving time for a written report, allows emotions to settle down. A social history may show a disrupted family life, lack of affection at home, or warring parents, all factors which commonly produce personality disorder in the juvenile delinquent of average intelligence. They are just as capable of producing aggressive or attention-seeking personalities in the severely handicapped. Such parents may have given little or no character training, they may be erratic, or actively encourage delinquent behaviour by the pleased expressions on their faces, even while expostulating to the professional.

While the severely mentally handicapped person may not be able to describe why he is upset, it is commonly found that a recent incident in public, or perhaps a new arrival at the training centre, has provoked the trainee or taught him or her the wrong behaviour. For example, a girl may have been approached sexually, or a boy upset by an aggressive newcomer. If future provocation can be avoided by a simple move from one work-room to another, so much the better.

The most common 'offence' is inappropriate masturbation. Although a physical examination rarely yields positive results, it should be carried out. The girl may have been venereally infected by a chance meeting in a park, she might perhaps have tight fitting clothes which irritate. Infected urine and diabetes have also been indicted. Likewise, the boy may have a tight prepuce with balanitis. It is more likely, however, that the professional's role will be one of counselling parents and training-centre staff, and generally 'letting the steam' out of the situation. Emotions may be so high that one or two sessions need to be devoted to mere listening to complaints before people are ready to move towards a constructive treatment programme. For the severely handicapped boy, fatherly instruction on masturbation in bed or in the toilet gradually teaches the appropriate time and place. Training centre cooperation by the prompt removal of the boy to the toilet area at the first sign of masturbatory activity makes it clear to the trainee what behaviour is expected where.

Sterilization and castration are sometimes requested, often on the erroneous assumption that sexual interest and behaviour will then cease. A contraceptive pill or an intrauterine device can effectively protect the girl for the risk years of puberty, whilst Kinsey reminds us that peak sexual activity for boys is during the years 15–18, so that time is in favour as the years progress. The sexual activity of trainees, as of ordinary adults, wanes with age. Continuous administration of contraceptive medication may also avoid menstruation for some trainees when necessary. Medication to decrease male sexual drive is now available in the shape of cyproterone acetate 100 mg b.d., an anti-androgen preparation marketed as Androcur. This has replaced the use of oestrogens for males, now known to cause breast hypertrophy and testicular atrophy. Cyproterone is associated with neither of these, and the effects wear off within a few days of the drug being stopped. It is thus particularly useful during the hypersexual phase of adolescence.

Given time the prognosis is remarkably favourable. For a minority, where a deviant personality exists, residential admission and perhaps even long-term hospitalization is occasionally necessary. For most of the remainder, careful and concerted behaviour reinforcement by training-centre staff and parents is almost always effective over a two-year period, perhaps with the administration of cyproterone for particularly active males. Minor tranquillizers and sedatives may also help over an active period, but as usual oversight is required, for such medication can cause a decrease in ability levels which are already low.

In general then, it is the task of the professional to ventilate the feelings and tensions usually engendered by the overt sexual behaviour of severely mentally handicapped people. Courts, while protecting the public, need professional advice in opting for the most constructive way of dealing with an offender. Parents, often having denied the sexuality of their handicapped offspring, need skilled counselling to allow them to accept sexual expression as a normal development, but one which needs to be directed in socially acceptable ways.

## MARRIAGE

In recent years there has been much talk about the right of the mentally handicapped to as normal a life as possible. It is normal in nearly every society for the majority of adult males and females to be married at least once in the course of their lives. In

Western societies this is not true for those citizens labelled 'mentally handicapped'. Their legal and social status has been such that relatively few have ever married. Normally it is the married couple which forms the stable unit to produce and raise the next generation. It is this association of marriage with parenthood which led the guardians of society to make sure that as few mentally handicapped people as possible married or produced children. Indeed, in many parts of the United States sterilization was the condition of discharge to the community. The fear that the mentally handicapped will produce retarded children in great numbers is still with us. However, nowadays methods of birth control are available to all and no-one need produce children they do not want or more children than they can cope with. Marriage does not necessarily involve parenthood, and parenthood does not necessarily involve an unlimited number of children.

## THE LITERATURE

### A caveat

Reviews of the literature concerning marriages where one or both partners are mentally retarded have appeared elsewhere (Hall 1974; Craft & Craft 1976). We would like to add a caveat. In our opinion there has been a tendency to confuse two separate populations; (1) those in the community and institutions below IQ 70 who have reached or are near their potential; and (2) those admitted to mental handicap hospitals (often through the courts) after deprivative upbringing and personality disorder, originally scoring IQ 70–95+ who can still legally be labelled 'mentally retarded'. Obviously the life chances for these two populations are rather different. Those in group (2) may offend again, but it is highly likely that their IQs and abilities will rise over a period of time, so that eventually they will need little or no official care and guidance, and will merge with the general population (Clarke & Clarke 1953; Craft 1959). This has implications for the studies following up marriages among those labelled mentally retarded. In Britain we know that the interpretation of the 1913 Mental Deficiency Act encompassed many people of dull normal intelligence who pre-

sented social problems, as well as those with intellectual deficit, and thus included, for example, unmarried pregnant young women of average intelligence in receipt of 'poor relief'. The 1959 Mental Health Act facilitated the discharge of such people and on follow-up (Shaw & Wright 1960; Mattinson 1975) many were found to have married and settled down. The situation in the United States was not dissimilar. Floor et al. (1975) surveyed 214 discharges from a residential institution, 80 of whom had married. The mean IQ on discharge from the total sample was 76 (male 78.1, female 71.3). Among the reported characteristics of the subjects, mention is made that 'All are orphans, or have families who are inadequate, disinterested or unwilling to accept the individual after discharge. The majority were institutionalized as adolescents, were referred from public agencies, and received State support.'

Personality disorders and insufficient social skills to get along amicably with family and the world at large are characteristics by no means limited to one section of the intelligence distribution curve; many extremely intelligent people are socially handicapped. Such deficits are measured against family or community tolerance, and in general they are perhaps more *noticeable* and *less tolerated* among the dull normal, who for various reasons come into conflict with family or outside authority. Dull normal adolescents in social classes IV and V seem to be particularly vulnerable. Just as they are more likely to acquire the labels of 'delinquent' and 'psychopath', so they run a higher risk of being termed 'mentally retarded'.

This risk does exist for others too, especially when there is family tension. For instance, at an outpatient clinic for the mentally handicapped a psychiatrist colleague was asked to see a university professor's son, thought by his parents to be 'behaviourally disordered' and 'retarded' They wanted their diagnosis made official both to excuse James' 'failure' and to give them the authority to control his adult activities. James was a very ordinary young man of 19 with an IQ in the 90s, who had not been able to live up to the high academic standards expected. The fact that the only thing he seemed to be happy doing was stripping and reassembling oily car engines was a further cause of household dissension. Not surprisingly the frustrations of never, ever being able to satisfy his parents led to a rebellion which included a poor work record, drinking bouts and brushes with the law.

James was 'socially and mentally handicapped' only to the extent that he did not fit the parental image. He soon solved his own 'problem' by leaving home and the district, getting a car mechanic's job and marrying a girl of similar intellectual level. The professor and his wife solved their 'problem' by speaking of James as being 'in engineering'.

We need to remind ourselves that mental handicap is a dynamic, not a static, concept. It should be used to reflect *current* functioning, not past disabilities, especially among those once underfunctioning in intelligence because of personality disorders.

The subjects of the marital studies present further difficulties. Some studies look at couples where both partners have been labelled 'mentally retarded', others where there are partners of normal intelligence, still others are made up of subjects from both groups. Some studies look only at those discharged from mental handicap hospitals, often after long periods in an institution; others include retardates who have always lived in the community.

A number of studies are biased because of the method of selecting subjects. Unless there is a register of all mentally handicapped people in a particular area, or one is doing a follow-up of a cohort discharged from an institution, difficulties arise in locating subjects. The obvious and frequently used procedure is to contact social agencies, but if a couple is known to welfare departments it is probably because they have needed help of some kind. There must be other couples who manage without official assistance, but who are virtually untraceable. Results of such studies have to be viewed against this background.

### The marital studies

The marital studies have to be approached with caution. Besides the difficulties relating to the two populations and the subjects discussed above, each has to be viewed against its own social background, both in time and space. For example Shaw and Wright (1960) give a divorce or permanent separation rate of 20 per cent. From the standpoint of 1978 this does not sound excessive, but in terms of a follow-up done in the 1950s it compares unfavourably with statistics for the general population.

Support services vary enormously from area to area, and can be vital in keeping problems to a minimum. In Britain the disappearance of the Mental Welfare Officer with the reorganization of Social Service Departments meant that in many areas mentally handicapped people were no longer visited regularly, and thus the chance to prevent or deal with problems before they escalated was missed.

None of the studies we have looked at have a control group. Admittedly this would be hard to do, but the danger of the inappropriate use of middle-class standards is well known. It would be interesting also to compare the quality of life experienced by mentally handicapped married couples in the community as opposed to single retardates. Floor et al. (1975) did so briefly and found that handicapped married couples saved significantly less and owed significantly more than the single retardates. However, 'single persons tend to show a greater frequency and variety of social and personal problems than do married persons'.

Is it possible using pointers from the literature to predict whether a marriage will be of benefit to a particular couple? Edgerton (1967) concluded '. . . it would seem that the sexual and marital lives of these retarded persons are more "normal" and better regulated than we could possibly have predicted from a knowledge of their pre-hospital experiences and their manifest intellectual deficits.' Mattinson (1975) looked at four obvious factors which might be of predictive value: recorded IQ score, length of time spent in hospital, behaviour in hospital and early history and background of deprivation. None of these factors on her sample of 32 couples correlated significantly with the achievement scores attained. Hall (1974) lists 18 factors appearing in the literature, which if present in significant number and/or degree, can affect the 'success' of a marriage involving a retarded individual, for example, emotional disturbance of one or both partners; faulty childhood background; both partners being retarded; poor socio-economic background; length of institutionalization; absence of sex education. As might be expected many of these 18 factors have a bearing on the stability of any marriage. Yet the reactions of human beings to each other and to circumstances are often *not* predictable. For example, with one couple in our own survey where the wife is classified as mentally handicapped, and the husband has episodes of schizophrenia (Craft & Craft 1976), nine of these factors might be said to be present. True, their day is not complete without a row and both acknowledge the partnership to be unsatisfactory, but for the 28 years the marriage has lasted they have been apart only when one or other has needed to be hospitalized. Even then, full use is always made of opportunities to visit the sick or disturbed partner. As Hall (1974) says, '... certain needs may be met in a marital partnership that cannot be met elsewhere'. We will return to this point in the section on subjective assessment.

## Social functioning

Bearing in mind the difficulties in the literature, what do the studies tell us about the daily functioning of couples where one or both partners are retarded?

Several studies stress the importance of the support the couple receive in day-to-day living. This may be support from an official agency, or a private individual, someone Edgerton (1967) terms a 'befriender'. This is often a relative, but may be a neighbour, landlord or employer, someone who in many ways mediates between the couple and the world, particularly officialdom. All but one of the 12 couples on Andron and Sturm's (1973) survey depended on others in varying degrees for everything from advice to money.

In our survey of 45 Welsh couples (41 intact marriages), where one or both partners were mentally handicapped, 13 received no support from social agencies (Craft & Craft 1979). Two couples lived in hospital married quarters with all the support that such entails,

a further 4 were in lodgings under a hospital guardianship scheme; the remaining 20 lived in the community and received help from social agencies/relatives/friends. This varied from intensive (at least weekly visits) to very infrequent help. Support may also be generated by the partnership itself. Mattinson (1975) reported a high number of couples (19 out of 32) who organized marital activities on a complementary basis, that is, the activities of husband and wife are different and separate but fitted together form a whole, with the skill of one partner supplementing the inability of the other. She writes: 'In many instances the active fit or complement made the whole greater than the sum of the two parts. This is true of many marriages, but with this group of subnormal people it seemed to be a particularly striking characteristic.'

As might be expected the problems the couples encountered were many and various, but not substantially different from those met within the general population.

Those who are handicapped are particularly vulnerable to the fluctuations of the economic climate. At the time of Shaw and Wright's (1960) survey 29 per cent of the mentally handicapped husbands were not in employment. In Mattinson's (1975) study 14 husbands were employed irregularly and 6 were unemployed regularly; 12 were in regular employment. In our Welsh survey just over half of the husbands and one-third of the wives were in regular employment, either in an ordinary job or in sheltered workshops. One mentally handicapped wife had lost her schizophrenic husband his job by insisting on accompanying him into the ditches he was supposed to be digging to ensure 'the bugger got up to no mischief'!

Some spouses run foul of the law. In Shaw and Wright's (1960) study 42 of the 197 husbands and 11 of the wives had come before the courts for a variety of offences. Of the 64 spouses in Mattinson's (1975) survey, 14 had been charged with offences since marriage, mostly for larceny. Andron and Sturm (1973) report 9 of the 24 retarded people being surveyed were known to have had some police involvement, but comment: 'Most of the offences described seemed to be the result of suggestibility and vulnerability of many of the members of this group and their ignorance of the complexities of the law.'

Parenthood can present problems to some families. Shaw and Wright (1960) report that almost a third of families with one or more children were known to the National Society for the Prevention of Cruelty to Children or the Children's Department because of neglect or cruelty. There was evidence that families with three or more children were less successful from the point of view of social adaptation than small families. Of the 40 children born to the couples on Mattinson's (1975) survey, 6 (from 3 families) had been committed to the care of the local authority and 34 were being looked after by their parents. Of the 13 families with children under school age, 10 needed regular or intensive support or advice from health visitors or social workers, but none of the children appeared to be in dire need.

Other studies mention that previous sterilization is seen by many spouses as an inerradicable stigma and wives may use their childlessness as an excuse for all the difficulties present in the marriage (Edgerton 1967). Andron and Sturm (1973) and Craft and Craft (1976) mention the disappointments some couples feel at not being able to have a family.

As for many normal couples, housing can be an area of major difficulty. Those in council and public housing are reasonably secure, but many are not so fortunate and find themselves in rented accommodation of the worst sort. Living on top of one another in a small, dank and dismal room can exacerbate marital difficulties. At present available placements in hostels and sheltered housing complexes are the exception rather than the rule for retarded married couples. In the future there may be changes. In a care system it seems just as sensible to cater for those who need support in units of two as it does for individuals who require substitute homes and help in daily living.

The spouses who have had little or no experience of family life and therefore few models on which to base adult behaviour, may have interpersonal difficulties because of this. Care staff in institutions are usually neutral in affection for each other, or else do not openly display loving behaviour. Staff may be careful to avoid becoming overfond

of those in their charge because it is likely they and/or their patients will move on. The mentally handicapped raised in such care systems do not see the give-and-take of married life and may find it hard at first to adjust both sexually and emotionally to the needs of their partner.

Our own initial survey indicated that although the nature of the problems experienced may alter with marriage, they do not significantly increase. Of course marriage is not a cure-all, either for the general or the retarded population, but neither is it a relationship beyond the capacity of those below a certain level of intelligence. True, some mentally handicapped spouses may need more help than others to keep the partnership viable, but these are usually people who would require support whether married or single. None of the studies revealed an excessively high divorce or separation rate for their subjects. The next section may help us understand why this is so.

### Subjective satisfaction

In the last resort marriage is a contract between just two people and so it is the partners themselves who must be the final judges. What does the partnership mean to them? Do they feel themselves worse or better off? Is there a discrepancy between their expectations of the relationship and perceived reality (an important potential source of discontent in marriages)?

Edgerton (1967) reports that marriage for the discharged retardate is a highly meaningful status to achieve, it emphasizes a newly won position as a free and full member of the outside world. It is seen as a proof of normality. Marriage can also give a sense of relief because the couple are past the danger of being arbitrarily parted by a care system which all too often ignored friendships and personal preferences. As one Welsh couple expressed it, 'We're completely together, no one can separate us. It's just great, you know.'

Do the couples feel themselves better or worse off in the married state? Most seem to prefer being married, and given their often appalling past histories, it is hardly surprising that they draw much satisfaction from having a home of their own, a place in the community and a sense of family, one special person who cares very much about them. Of the 32 intact marriages surveyed by Mattinson (1975) 25 were considered by the spouses to be preferable to being single. Andron and Sturm (1973) report: 'All but one man said that married life was better than single life. The overwhelming reason given was the companionship marriage provided in contrast to their previous social isolation.' Floor et al. (1975) looked at 54 couples and rated the marital relationships: eight had divorced, 15 were untraceable; of the remaining 31, 18 partnerships were considered to be being maintained satisfactorily, even though there were symptoms of stress in some.

In our Welsh survey of 45 marriages (1 divorced, 1 broken by death, 2 broken by involuntary separation, 41 intact) 18 partnerships were judged to be mutually supportive; in 3 marriages one partner was heavily dependent on the other, but this was in no way resented, rather it was an integral part of the satisfaction; 14 partnerships were judged to be affectionate, although there were some symptoms of stress; in 4 marriages one partner resented the dependency of the other; two couples said they regretted their marriages, but had made no attempt (for 28 and 19 years respectively) to actually part. One husband sums it up: 'Marriage? It do beat being single!' (Craft & Craft 1979).

A number of studies, both British and American, say that many of these partnerships are characterized by a certain social isolation; they are what Mattinson (1975) calls 'cocooned', that is, with few relationships outside the marriage. Andron and Sturm (1973) report: 'For most of the couples each spouse seemed to be the other's best friend and companion.' Twenty-two of our Welsh couples either kept very much to themselves or had contact mainly with family.

We know from studies of marriages and marital breakdown that shared expectations tend to cement the partnership, while divergent views of the relationship impose an often fatal strain upon it. Commonly, the experiences of the mentally handicapped lead them to expect very little. They are often unidealistic about the marital state, and take things very much as they come. This may serve to increase their chance of happiness. As Mattinson (1975) comments, '(The) reality was usually so much better than anything they had known before; and an awareness of their limitations and often considerable ignorance of what went on in other people's homes enabled them not to overreach themselves and search for the finer subtleties of living.'

CONCLUSION

We have seen that in personal terms many marriages between mentally handicapped people are 'successful', even when they present problems to others. Improving the quality of life experienced by the retarded is the ultimate aim of our services. Bearing in mind that more mentally handicapped people are likely to marry in the future, how can we better prepare them for marriage and aid them after marriage?

The conclusions from our own study of 45 handicapped married couples (Craft & Craft 1979) which was the first following the recent extended allowance system in the UK, was that most could be successful. Four areas are important:

1. Sex education and counselling programmes in special schools, institutions and hostels, designed to help the retarded understand their own needs and those of others.
2. Family planning advice and genetic counselling services staffed by professionals skilled in working with mentally handicapped people.
3. Support services, readily available. The flexibility of systems of care needs to be greater so that hostels and small group homes can offer places as readily to married couples as to single people.
4. Sheltered housing now needs to be developed. Whilst hostels and staffed small group homes have been an advance on big institutions, the main drive for the future will need to be provision of council houses and flatlets. Here there can be much service input to help a couple settle in which can be withdrawn as need diminishes. Thus both capital cost and service cost can be optimized.

## PARENTHOOD

In nearly all societies the normative pressure on married couples to become parents is very strong. The advent of safe and effective contraception has made it theoretically possible for ordinary couples to choose not to have children and there are discernible trends in this direction. Yet, according to one study only one per cent of the population of the United States considers marital union without a child to be a desirable state (Silka & Kiesler 1977). What relevance does this have for mentally handicapped people in the community, who do their utmost to assume 'the cloak of competence' (Edgerton 1967) and pass as ordinary citizens? On the one hand they are subject to normative pressures; on the other, they are likely to encounter serious opposition if they attempt to fulfil their reproductive potential. The disapproval voiced by parents and professionals is remarkably strong given that the term *mentally handicapped* covers a very heterogeneous group of people and that properly controlled studies of parental competence are extremely scanty.

Any consideration of parenthood in this context of mental handicap has to explore a number of different areas: potential and actual fertility; the possibility that the offspring of mentally handicapped parents will themselves be handicapped; the competency of mentally handicapped parents both to care for their children and to create family environments which stimulate, not dampen, development.

### FERTILITY

Fertility has two aspects: the biological capacity to reproduce, and effective reproduction, that is, the numbers of children actually produced. With regard to the first aspect, most of the mentally handicapped are fertile at a biological level although there are obvious exceptions such as Klinefelter's and Turner's syndromes. However, it is the social position of the mentally handicapped, particularly the severely retarded, which militates against the actual reproduction of children. Kirman (1975) states '... in the main the effective reproductive capacity of the feeble-minded

below IQ 70 is very limited and below IQ 50 it is statistically negligible.' This of course may change in the future as more of the mentally handicapped remain in the community, or marry while in care.

To compare effective reproduction we need to look at longitudinal studies. In analysing some of the data collected by the Minnesota Institute of Human Genetics, Higgins et al. (1962) show clearly that there is no correlation between measured intelligence and family size. The lowest IQ group, because of the small numbers who reproduce, have no more children per person than do the higher IQ groups. Although most professionals know of couples they judge to be mentally retarded who have large numbers of offspring, this may well result from ignorance of birth control methods; and as we have seen in the literature concerning married couples, 'problem families' who are dull and have members with unstable or inadequate personalities may be labelled 'mentally retarded' even when their measured intelligence is above 70.

### USE OF CONTRACEPTIVE TECHNIQUES

In the past, it was assumed that mentally retarded persons did not have the judgement, foresight or control required to use contraception. Although this assumption has been repeatedly questioned, there have been very few attempts to discover which method might be most appropriate. Oral contraceptives are now thought suitable for mildly retarded women who are supervised and have high motivation, and intrauterine devices (IUD) for those who lack supervision (LaVeck & de la Cruz 1973). Sterilization was first used on an involuntary basis as a condition of discharge from hospital. Voluntary sterilization is now a well-known method of contraception in the general population, and with sensitive counselling it is frequently the choice of mentally handicapped couples.

While family planning services for normal clients have greatly expanded in the past decade, there have been few systematic attempts to provide retarded individuals or couples with family planning training. An American research team looked at the possibility of providing a service for the mentally handicapped and made several recommendations (David et al. 1976). They suggested that use should be made of the normal family planning provisions, but that selected staff should receive training in working with retarded clients. Hospital staff and parent groups should be made more aware of the existence of services to facilitate their effectiveness. The pilot survey showed how difficult it was to reach the target group (only 47 mentally handicapped clients came forward in a seven-month period, 41 of them coming from one large institution), so it would be advantageous to make others in the community (citizens and professionals) aware of the needs of the mentally handicapped, the availability of local services, and the benefits which would be obtained from responsible sexuality and prevention of unwanted pregnancies. Maclean (1979) gives an interesting account of five years' experience of a family planning clinic held in a mental handicap hospital in Britain.

It is of relevance to note that among the 45 couples we surveyed (Craft & Craft 1979) relatively few children had been produced (30 in 14 families). Six wives were past child-bearing age at marriage, nine spouses had been sterilized prior to marriage. The rest appear to have coped with their marital fertility in a responsible manner. Six wives were pregnant at the time of their marriage. After the birth of these first children, one wife started taking oral contraception, one husband had a vasectomy. Two more had another child each, then the wives started to take the contraceptive pill. The remaining two had three children each before starting contraception. The situation at the time of the survey was as follows:

11 wives relied on oral contraception.
3 wives were fitted with IUDs.
13 spouses had been sterilized.
10 wives were post-menopausal.
2 couples were not using any method (one had two children, the other rarely had intercourse).
2 not known (both married 3 years and no pregnancies).
4 marriages not intact.

No accidental pregnancies have occurred so far, and although this is a small-scale survey,

it does perhaps indicate that with help and advice, mentally handicapped people are more capable of limiting their fertility than was previously thought.

THE INHERITANCE OF
HANDICAP

In the not-so-distant past when the laws of genetic inheritance were less well understood it was thought that parents who were handicapped (mentally or physically) were highly likely to pass on their disability to any offspring they produced. Eugenicists vociferously deplored what they saw as the disproportionate 'reproduction of the unfit' which could have only disastrous effects on the national 'gene pool' (see p. 5). While the laws of genetics are still not perfectly understood, we know enough to realize that 'handicapped parent' does not necessarily mean 'handicapped offspring.' As was pointed out in Chapter 1, the vast majority of the mentally handicapped have IQs above 50, with no detectable genetic causation for their retardation. Most of the remaining small proportion of severely and moderately handicapped adults are genetically impaired, and risks to any children can be estimated by genetic experts. In this latter group are chromosome 21 trisomies (Down's syndrome), and while there is no known case of a fertile male, the few females who have conceived run a one in two risk of passing on their extra chromosome to their children.

In the literature, studies of mentally handicapped parents estimating the percentage of retarded children vary enormously in their results. Hall (1974) reviewed 31 such studies dating from 1913 to 1965. The percentage of retarded children produced ranged from 2.5 to 93.2. As Hall points out, these estimations vary so much because of differences in the studies themselves. Some of the obvious variables are: retardation in one as opposed to both parents; psychometric assessment of IQs; type of retardation of parents (for example, genetic or social); IQ level of parents; percentage of death rate in children; prenatal factors relating to socio-economic level (malnutrition of fetus, prematurity et cetera).

One of the most comprehensive of the studies is an American one reported by Reed and Reed (1965). The Minnesota Institute of Human Genetics selected 289 in-patient retardates with IQs below 70 who had been institutionalized between 1911 and 1918 and traced first the patients' grandparents and then the latter's descendants forward to 1961. They could thus compare a group of in-patient retardates with a group of 'normal' people in the community with similar genetic (and environmental) background. The sample eventually covered up to seven generations and included more than 80 000 people. The records available for 7778 of the children descended from the grandparents of the hospital retardates show that in the 89 instances where both parents had IQs under 70 nearly 40 per cent of the children were also retarded (although it is worthy of mention that the *average* IQ of these children was 74). Where only one parent had an IQ below 70, 15 per cent of the children were retarded (54 per cent had IQs above 90); and of the 7035 children with neither parent retarded, 1 per cent were retarded. It is generally accepted that children's measured intelligence tends to show a reversion towards the norm compared with their parents; this is as true for the children of the very bright as for those of the very dull.

Reed and Anderson (1973) constructed a model of 100 000 persons to describe the general population, and suggested that 17 per cent of the retarded children in the model population would have at least one retarded parent. The model thus predicts that the remaining 83 per cent of retarded children in any generation have both parents in the normal range of intelligence, retardation occurring as a result of abnormal mutations, recessive genes and other chance pre- and post-natal factors.

## ASSESSMENT OF PARENTAL COMPETENCE

Trying to assess the adequacy of mentally handicapped parents is by no means a simple matter. By what criteria do we judge the adequacy of any parent? Individuals in different stratas of society would give different answers. We know from the British National Child Development Study (Davie et al. 1972) that by the age of 7 there are major differences between the children of various social classes in health, skills and scholastic attainment.

The literature is very scanty on this point of parental competence, and there is a notable absence of controls matched for such vital factors as social class and family income. What does seem certain is that the intelligence of the parents is only one of the many factors which have a bearing on child care. Other factors to take into consideration are the degree of marital harmony and stability, the psychiatric health of the parents, financial income, the number of pregnancies and the number of live children, use of support services, use of family planning, and whether or not the parents have histories of being institutionalized.

## ENVIRONMENTAL FACTORS

We do know that environment can play an important part in the development or retardation of intelligence. A study by Barbara Tizard and colleagues (Tizard & Rees 1976; Tizard & Hodges 1978) showed that their 2-year-old institutionalized subjects with a mean IQ of around 94 (slightly backward) developed in markedly different ways as they underwent different fates, and a statistically significant difference in their IQs arose between the groups when retested. Amongst their findings, those adopted before the age of 4, when tested at 8, had a mean IQ of 115. Those adopted after $4\frac{1}{2}$ had a mean IQ of 101 aged 8. Those who remained in institutions had a mean IQ of 99. Those restored to their parents after the age of $4\frac{1}{2}$ had a mean IQ of 93 when tested at 8. The study of environmental variables is, however, complex, and the original papers should be studied for the many related variables involved, including the vexed question of how far bonding between child and parent affected the degree of communication, and thus of language, established.

In the United States it is estimated that 75 per cent of the identified population of mentally retarded persons come from the 'cultural–familial' group, that is, where no plausible organic explanation is applicable. Usually, of course, because there is little or no overt pathological expression of the retardation early in life, it is not until school age is reached that detection is possible.

Garber (1975) reported a project carried out by the University of Wisconsin Research and Training Center where a technique for the early detection of cultural–familial retardation was devised and tested. The research centred on a 'slum' district of Milwaukee which had an extremely high prevalence ot retardation together with the lowest median educational level, the lowest median family income, the greatest population density per living unit and the highest rate of delapidated housing in the city. Maternal intelligence proved to be the best single predictor of intellectual development in the offspring. Interestingly, on infant intelligence tests, two-year-old children of mothers above *and* below IQ 80 did almost equally well, but after the infancy period the first group (mothers' IQ >80) appeared to maintain a fairly steady intellectual level, while the second group of children (mothers' IQ <80) exhibited a marked progressive decline in their intellect. A survey of fathers showed that of the mothers below IQ 70, 62 per cent had husbands who also scored below 70, and only 14 per cent had husbands who scored over 100; by contrast, not one of the mothers scoring above IQ 100 had a husband below IQ 80.

While at first sight the survey data seem to point to hereditary determinants of cultural–familial mental retardation, the researchers' casual observations suggested that the mentally retarded mother living in the 'slum' area creates a social environment for her offspring which is distinctly different from that created by the 'slum dwelling' mother of normal intelligence.

The researchers began to test what in fact was a social deprivation hypothesis by selecting a sample of children and intervening in their lives at a time prior to the decline in intellectual level to try and prevent that decline and hopefully permit normal intellectual growth. They screened all mothers of babies born in the survey area over a year, identifying mothers with IQs less than 70. Forty mothers were drawn from the subject pool and assigned randomly to the experimental or the control group. The researchers posited that if the children in the experimental half reach the age of 7 or 8 and show normal intelligence then it will have been shown to be possible to prevent mental retardation occurring at the present high frequency in this group. If the children function at a retarded level then it will be shown that intensive exposure to learning experiences is not sufficient to displace their genetic predispositions for intellectual functioning.

Intervention with the experimental group began in the home soon after the mother returned from hospital. The mothers and children then attended an Infant Education Center, the mothers for a rehabilitation programme to help them with skills and to modify the environment they create or control for their children; the infants for an intensive programme of sensory and language stimulation thought to be relevant for the development of intellectual abilities.

Testing was carried out at regular intervals. At the ages of 48 and 57 months the Wechsler Preschool and Primary Scale Index (WPPSI) test was administered. The experimental group scored 114 (SD 8.6) and 113 (SD 4.7) (but none below 100), while the controls scored 84 (SD 10.1) and 81 (SD 10.1). At 66 months the experimental group had a mean score of 123 (SD 7.6), while the controls had a mean of 92 (SD 9.4). At the latest reported testing point of 96 months there is a differential of 20 or more points between the two groups (Garber & Heber 1977). One-third of the control group children have IQs below 75 on the Wechsler Intelligence Scale for Children (WISC); by contrast the lowest scorers among the experimental group children are two with IQs of 88. Thus all the children in the experimental group are functioning within the normal range of ability. It remains to be seen whether this will be maintained in the adverse social conditions these children are still encountering.

While there must be caution in the interpretation of such data because of the hazards of infant and child measurement and the training received by the experimental group which sometimes overlapped with items sampled in the tests, the implications of this research are wide ranging. Obviously, it is not practical to intervene in the lives of all children at risk, but it does point out an important area where it may be possible to prevent (rather than cure or ameliorate) the development of a very common form of retardation.

CONCLUSION

Although we know that the mentally retarded do not produce a disproportionately large number of children, we also know that their risk of having a handicapped child is greater, mainly for environmental reasons, than the risk facing a normal couple. However, that risk is statistical, and as we have discussed in the section on counselling, each couple is unique and ideally should have individual advice. There are couples who know they could not cope with the burden of parenthood, and nowadays no-one need have unwanted children. There are others who long for a family of their own, often this is an idealized dream as they have little or no practical experience of real babies who scream, need nappies changed, have teething troubles. A number of studies looking at handicapped couples have reported the use of child substitutes, usually a pet who has affection lavished upon it. Other authors suggest that mentally handicapped people help in play groups and nursery schools and act as 'godparents' for children in hospital who do not receive many visitors.

While there is no real agreement on the skills necessary for good parenting, we know from the various studies on marriages between mentally handicapped people that many such couples do give what is judged to be at least adequate care to their offspring. It may be that these children would fare even better away from their natural parents, but that leads into the problematical realms of social engineering. In such a world it would not only be those of below average intelligence who would be in danger of losing their children.

EPILOGUE

The principle of normalization has far-reaching consequences, covering as it does all aspects of life. Modern research has shown that many of society's fears concerning the sexuality of retarded people were ill-founded. With education, counselling and support in the area of relationships, mentally handicapped citizens can be aided towards a better understanding of themselves and others, towards personally satisfying and socially satisfactory partnerships, and an overall enrichment of life. In order to do this they need areas of privacy when single, and protection from unwanted risks. Handicapped married couples may well support each other better than care staff supported them as single people. They need sheltered housing and day occupation to fulfill their potentialities, and with contraceptive advice can need less State aid and present fewer problems together than as two single handicapped persons alone.

BIBLIOGRAPHY

Andron, L. & Sturm, M. L. (1963) Is 'I do' in the repertoire of the retarded? *Ment. Retard.*, *11*, 31-4.
Clarke, A. M. & Clarke, A. D. B. (1953) How constant is the IQ? *Lancet*, *2*, 877-80.
Craft, M. (1959) Personality disorder and dullness. *Lancet*, *1*, 856-8.
Craft, A. & Craft, M. (1976) Subnormality in marriage: happiness and the quality of life of married subnormals. *Social Work Today*, *7*, 4, 98-101.
Craft, M. & Craft, A. (1978) *Sex and the Mentally Handicapped*. London: Routledge & Kegan Paul.
Craft, A. & Craft, M. (1979) *Handicapped Married Couples*. London: Routledge & Kegan Paul.
David, H. P., Smith, J. D. & Friedman, E. (1976) Family planning services for persons handicapped by mental retardation. *Am. J. pub. Health*, *66*, 11, 1053-7.
Davie, R., Butler, N. R. & Goldstein, H. (1972) *From Birth to Seven: A Report of the National Child Development Study*. Harlow, Essex: Longman.
Edgerton, R. B. (1967) *The Cloak of Competence*. Berkeley: University of California Press.
Edgerton, R. B. & Dingman, H. F. (1964) Good reasons for bad supervision: 'dating' in a hospital for the mentally retarded. *Psychiat. Q. Suppl.*, *38*, 221-33.
Edmunds, R. H. & Yarrow, A. (1977) Newer fashions in illegitimacy. *Br. med. J.*, *1*, 701-3.
Floor, L., Baxter, D., Rosen, M. & Zisfein, L. (1975) A survey of marriages among previously institutionalized retardates. *Ment. Retard.*, *13*, 33-7.

Garber, H. (1975) The Milwaukee Project: an experiment in the prevention of cultural-familial mental retardation, intervention at birth. In: Bass, M. & Gelof, M. (eds.), *Sexual Rights and Responsibilities of the Mentally Retarded*. Proceedings of Conference of American Association on Mental Deficiency, Region IX, 1972. Revised edition.

Garber, H. & Heber, F. R. (1977) The Milwaukee Project: indications of the effectiveness of early intervention in preventing mental retardation. In: Mittler, P. (ed.), *Research to Practice in Mental Retardation*, vol. I, pp. 119–27. Baltimore: University Park Press.

Gordon, S. (1972) Symposium on sex education. *J. spec. Educn*, 5, 4, 351–81.

Hall, J. E. (1974) Sexual behaviour. In: Wortis, J. (ed.), *Mental Retardation (and Developmental Disabilities): An Annual Review*, vol. VI. New York: Brunner/Mazel.

Harris, A. (1974) What does 'sex education' mean? In: Rodgers, R. (ed.), *Sex Education: Rationale and Reaction*. Cambridge: Cambridge University Press.

Higgins, J. V., Reed, E. W. & Reed, S. C. (1962) Intelligence and family size: a paradox resolved. *Eugen. Q.*, 9, 84–90.

Kempton, W. (1972) *Guidelines for Planning a Training Course on Human Sexuality and the Retarded*. Philadelphia: Planned Parenthood Association of Southeastern Pennsylvania.

Kirman, B. (1975) Some causal factors. In: Kirman, B. & Bicknell, J. (eds.), *Mental Handicap*. Edinburgh: Churchill Livingstone.

LaVeck, G. D. & de la Cruz, F. F. (1973) Contraception for the mentally retarded: current methods and future prospects. In: de la Cruz, F. F. & LaVeck, G. D. (eds.), *Human Sexuality and the Mentally Retarded*. New York: Brunner/Mazel.

Maclean, R. (1979) Sexual problems and family planning needs of the mentally handicapped in residential care. *Br. J. Family Planning*, 4, 4, 13–15.

Mattinson, J. (1975) *Marriage and Mental Handicap*, 2nd ed. London: Institute of Marital Studies, The Tavistock Institute of Human Relations.

*Proposed Guidelines for Sex Education in the Swedish School System* (1974) (Code No. SOU 1974: 59) Stockholm.

Reed, S. C., & Anderson, V. E. (1973) Effects of changing sexuality on the gene pool. In: de la Cruz, F. F. & LaVeck, G. D. (eds.), *Human Sexuality and the Mentally Retarded*. New York: Brunner/Mazel.

Reed, E. W. & Reed, S. C. (1965) *Mental Retardation: A Family Study*. Philadelphia: W. B. Saunders.

Schofield, M. (1968) *The Sexual Behaviour of Young People*. Harmondsworth: Pelican Books.

Shaw, C. H. & Wright, C. H. (1960) The married mental defective: a follow-up study. *Lancet*, 1, 273–4.

Silka, L. & Kiesler, S. (1977) Couples who choose to remain childless. *Family Planning Perspectives*, 9, 1, 16–25.

Tizard, B. & Hodges, J. (1978) The effect of early institutional rearing on the development of eight-year-old children. *J. Child Psychol. Psychiat.*, 19, 99–118.

Tizard, B. & Rees, J. (1976) A comparison of the effects of adoption, restoration to the natural mother, and continued institutionalisation in the cognitive development of four-year-old children. In: Clarke, A. M. & Clarke, A. D. B. (eds.), *Early Experience: Myth and Reality*, pp. 135–52. London: Open Books.

# MINIMUM CONSTITUTIONAL STANDARDS FOR ADEQUATE HABILITATION OF THE MENTALLY RETARDED*

## I. *Adequate Habilitation of Residents*

1. Residents shall have a right to habilitation, including medical treatment, education and care, suited to their needs, regardless of age, degree of retardation or handicapping condition.
2. The institution shall implement the principle of normalization so that each resident may live as normally as possible.
3. No person shall be admitted to the institution unless a prior determination shall have been made that residence in the institution is the least restrictive habilitation setting feasible for that person.
4. No borderline or mildly mentally retarded person shall be a resident of the institution.
5. Residents shall have a right to receive suitable educational services regardless of chronological age, degree of retardation or accompanying disabilities or handicaps. Such educational services shall meet the following minimum standards:

|  |  | Mild | Moderate | Severe/Profound |
|---|---|---|---|---|
| (1) | Class size | 12 | 9 | 6 |
| (2) | Length of school year (in months) | 9–10 | 9–10 | 11–12 |
| (3) | Minimum length of school day (in hours) | 6 | 6 | 6 |

6. Residents shall have a right to receive prompt and adequate medical treatment for any physical ailments and for the prevention of any illness or disability.

## II. *Individualized Habilitation Plans*

1. Prior to his admission to the institution, each resident shall have a comprehensive social, psychological, educational and medical diagnosis and evaluation by appropriate specialists to determine if admission is appropriate.
2. Each resident shall have an individualized habilitation plan formulated by the institution. This plan shall be developed by appropriate Qualified Mental Retardation Professionals and implemented as soon as possible but no later than 14 days after the resident's admission to the institution. Each individualized habilitation plan shall contain:

   a. A statement of the nature of the specific limitations and specific needs of the resident.
   b. A description of intermediate and long-range habilitation goals with a projected time-table for their attainment.
   c. A statement of, and an explanation for, the plan of habilitation for achieving these intermediate and long-range goals.
   d. A statement of the least restrictive setting for habilitation necessary to achieve the habilitation goals of the resident.
   e. A specification of the professionals and other staff members who are responsible for the particular resident's attaining these habilitation goals.
   f. Criteria for release to less restrictive settings for habilitation, including criteria for discharge and a projected date for discharge.

* This appendix is an abridged and modified version of Appendix A in *Wyatt* v. *Stickney* (see Chapter 22, p. 303).

3. As part of his habilitation plan, each resident shall have an individualized post-institutionalization plan. This plan must be developed by a Qualified Mental Retardation Professional and consented to by the nearest relative.

4. In the interests of continuity of care, one Qualified Mental Retardation Professional shall be responsible for supervising the implementation of the habilitation plan.

5. Complete records for each resident shall be maintained and shall be readily available to Qualified Mental Retardation Professionals and to the nearest relative and persons properly authorized by the resident. All information contained in a resident's records shall be considered privileged and confidential. These records shall include: detailed data concerning identification, history, grievances, skills, physical examinations, individual habilitation plan, medication, physical restraints, incidents or accidents, illnesses, treatments, professional and familial visits, et cetera.

### III. Humane Physical and Psychological Environment

1. Residents shall have a right to dignity, privacy and humane care.

2. Residents shall lose none of the rights enjoyed by citizens of the state and of the United States solely by reason of their admission or commitment to the institution, except as expressly determined by an appropriate court.

3. No person shall be presumed mentally incompetent solely by reason of his admission or commitment to the institution.

4. The opportunity for religious worship shall be accorded to each resident who desires such worship.

5. Residents shall have the rights to telephone communication and visitation, except to the extent that a Qualified Mental Retardation Professional responsible for formulation of a particular resident's habilitation plan writes an order imposing special restrictions and explains the reasons for any such restrictions. The written order must be renewed semi-annually if any restrictions are to be continued.

6. Residents shall be entitled to send and receive sealed mail. Moreover, it shall be the duty of the institution to facilitate the exercise of this right by furnishing the necessary materials and assistance.

7. The institution shall provide, under appropriate supervision, suitable opportunities for the resident's inter-action with members of the opposite sex, except where a Qualified Mental Retardation Professional responsible for the formulation of a particular resident's habilitation plan

writes an order to the contrary and explains the reasons therefor.

8. *Medication*
   a. Residents shall have a right to be free from unnecessary or excessive medication. All prescriptions shall be written with a termination date, which shall not exceed 30 days.
   b. Medication shall not be used as punishment, for the convenience of staff, as a substitute for a habilitation programme, or in quantities that interfere with the resident's habilitation programme.
   c. Pharmacy services at the institution shall be directed by a professionally competent pharmacist licensed to practise.

9. Seclusion, defined as the placement of a resident alone in a locked room, shall not be employed. Legitimate 'time out' procedures may be utilized under close and direct professional supervision as a technique in behaviour-shaping programmes.

10. Behaviour modification programmes involving the use of noxious or aversive stimuli shall be reviewed and approved by the institution's Human Rights Committee (an independent multidisciplinary authority) and shall be conducted only with the express and informed consent of the affected resident, if the resident is able to give such consent, and of his guardian or next of kin, after opportunities for consultation with independent specialists and with legal counsel.

11. Electric shock devices shall be considered a research technique for the purpose of these standards and thus subject to the review outlined above.

12. Physical restraint shall be employed only when absolutely necessary to protect the resident from injury to himself or to prevent injury to others.
   a. Orders for restraints by the Qualified Mental Retardation Professionals shall be in writing and shall not be in force for longer than 12 hours.
   b. A resident placed in restraint shall be checked at least every 30 minutes by staff trained in the use of restraints, and a record of such checks shall be kept.
   c. Opportunity for motion and exercise shall be provided for a period of not less than ten minutes during each two hours in which restraint is employed.

13. Corporal punishment shall not be permitted.

14. The institution shall prohibit mistreatment, neglect or abuse in any form of any resident. An appropriate grievance procedure must be implemented to investigate complaints.

15. Residents shall have a right not to be subjected to experimental research and unusual or hazar-

dous procedures without the express and in- formed consent of the resident, if the resident is able to give such consent, and of his guardian or next of kin, after opportunities for consul- tation with independent specialists and with legal counsel. Such proposed research shall first have been reviewed and approved by the insti- tution's Human Rights Committee before such consent shall be sought.

16. Residents shall have a right to regular physical exercise several times a week.

17. Residents shall have a right to be outdoors daily in the absence of contrary medical consi- derations.

18. *Institution maintenance.* No resident shall be required to perform, or promised release for, labour which involves the operation and main- tenance of the institution, or involves the care of other patients. Residents may voluntarily engage in such labour if the labour is compen- sated in accordance with the minimum wage laws.

19. A nourishing, well-balanced diet shall be pro- vided each resident. Specific dietary minima are provided.

20. Each resident shall have an adequate allowance of neat, clean, suitably fitting and seasonable clothing:
    a. Each resident shall have his own clothing, which is properly and inconspicuously marked with his name, and he shall be kept dressed in this clothing.
    b. Clothing, both in amount and type, shall make it possible for residents to go out of doors in inclement weather, to go for trips or visits appropriately dressed, and to make a normal appearance in the community.
    c. Non-ambulatory residents shall be dressed daily in their own clothing, including shoes, unless contra-indicated in written medical orders.

21. Each resident shall have the right to keep and use his own personal possessions, except insofar as such clothes or personal possessions may be determined to be dangerous.

22. a. Each resident shall be assisted in learning normal grooming practices with individual toilet articles, including soap and toothpaste, that are available to each resident.
    b. Teeth shall be brushed daily with an effective dentifrice. Individual brushes shall be pro- perly marked, used and stored.
    c. Each resident shall have a shower or tub bath, at least daily, unless medically contra- indicated.
    d. Residents shall be regularly scheduled for hair cutting and styling, in an individualized manner, by trained personnel.

e. For residents who require such assistance, cutting of toenails and fingernails shall be scheduled at regular intervals.

23. *Physical facilities.* A resident has a right to a humane physical environment.
    a. *Resident unit.* All ambulatory residents shall sleep in single rooms or in multi-resident rooms of no more than six persons. The number of non-ambulatory residents in a multi-resident room shall not exceed ten per- sons. There shall be allocated a minimum of 80 square feet of floor space per resident in a multi-resident room. Screens or curtains shall be provided to ensure privacy. Single rooms shall have a minimum of 100 square feet of floor space.
    b. *Toilets and lavatories.* There shall be one toilet and one lavatory for each six residents. Sufficient sanitary facilities and privacy must be provided.
    c. *Showers.* There shall be one tub or shower for each eight residents. If a central bathing area is provided, each tub or shower shall be divided by curtains to ensure privacy. Showers and tubs shall be equipped with adequate safety accessories.
    d. *Day room.* The minimum day room area shall be 40 square feet per resident. Day rooms shall be attractive and adequately fur- nished with reading lamps, tables, chairs, television, radio and other recreational facili- ties.
    e. *Dining facilities.* The minimum dining room area shall be ten square feet per resident.
    f. *Linen servicing and handling.* Similar detailed provisions are set out for linen and house- keeping services.
    g. *Physical plant.* Adequate heating, air condi- tioning and ventilation systems and equip- ment shall be afforded to maintain tempera- tures. The temperature in the institution shall not exceed 83 degrees Fahrenheit nor fall below 68 degrees Fahrenheit.

### IV. Qualified Staff in Numbers Sufficient to Provide Adequate Habilitation

1. Each Qualified Mental Retardation Professional and each physician shall meet all licensing and certification requirements promulgated by the state for persons engaged in private practice of the same profession elsewhere.

2. *Staffing ratios.* Qualified staff in numbers sufficient to administer adequate habilitation shall be provided. Detailed staffing ratios are set out.

3. Each resident discharged to the community shall have a programme of transitional habili- tation assistance.

4. The institution shall continue to suspend any new admissions of residents until all of the above standards of adequate habilitation have been met.

5. No person shall be admitted to any publicly supported residential institution caring for mentally retarded persons unless such institution meets the above standards.

# PRINCIPAL AUTHOR INDEX

# SUBJECT INDEX